INDEX

Bust of Swift attributed to John Van Nost.
(By courtesy of the National Gallery of Ireland)

The Prose Works *of* Jonathan Swift

INDEX

Compiled by William J. Kunz
Steven Hollander and Susan Staves
under the supervision of
IRVIN EHRENPREIS

ADDENDA, ERRATA, CORRIGENDA
Edited by HERBERT DAVIS and IRVIN EHRENPREIS

Oxford : Basil Blackwell : 1968

13,222

827.5
5977bxz
Index

Printed for Basil Blackwell & Mott Ltd
by Alden & Mowbray Ltd at the Alden Press, Oxford
and bound at Kemp Hall Bindery, Oxford

To the Memory of
Herbert John Davis

this final volume of the work he so
boldly undertook, so imaginatively
sustained, and so selflessly brought
near completion, is dedicated by the
surviving editor and the publisher.

PREFACE

FOR kind assistance in discovering, examining, or transcribing various addenda, we wish to thank Miss E. Halliday, Mr. T. F. Higham (Trinity College, Oxford), Professor Mackie L. Jarrell (Connecticut College), Professor George Mayhew (California Institute of Technology), Mr. Claude Rawson (University of Warwick), Professor A. F. Stocker (University of Virginia), and Mr. David Woolley.

For other improvements in the text or apparatus of the various volumes we are indebted to Mr. T. F. R. G. Braun and Mr. R. H. C. Davis (Merton College, Oxford), Dr. Myles Dillon (Institute of Advanced Studies, Dublin), Professor Maurice Johnson (University of Pennsylvania), Professor Louis A. Landa (Princeton University), Mr. J. C. Maxwell (Balliol College, Oxford), and the late D. Nichol Smith.

We gratefully acknowledge the permission of the following persons and libraries to reproduce parts of books or manuscripts in their collections: the Dean and Chapter of Christ Church Cathedral, Dublin; the Huntington Library, San Marino, California; the Houghton Library, Harvard University; the Hunterian Library, Glasgow; the John Rylands Library, Manchester.

For assistance in preparing the typed copy of the index, we wish to thank Mr. James Gordon (University of Virginia). However irregular or incomplete the index may still appear, we owe a profound debt to the patience, scholarship, and intelligence of Mr. Theodore J. Angus and Mr. Carl P. Daw (University of Virginia), who scrutinized the galleys minutely, making hundreds of corrections and additions.

A most extraordinary acknowledgement is due to the Graduate School of Indiana University for generous grants of money to support the work on the index over a period of several years.

H.D.
I.E.

The CONTENTS

PREFACE   *page* vii

THE INTRODUCTION   xi

ADDENDA

Note to Temple's Letter to Ormond   1

Note on Aristides Quintilianus   2

Advertisement to *A Letter . . . concerning the Sacramental Test*   2

'The Printer to the Reader' in *The Examiners for the Year 1711*   3

Index to *The Examiners for . . . 1711*   4

Notes for *The History of the Four Last Years*   13

Receipt for Parnell's Manuscripts   13

Notes for a 'Proposal for Virtue'   14

Marginalia in Baronius   16

Preface to Sheridan's Sermon   36

Sheridan as Lilly   37

Inscription to Dr. Mead   38

Marginalia in *The Proceedings Touching the . . . Earl of Clarendon*   38

APPENDIXES

A. Letter in *St. James's Evening Post* on Bishop Evans   41

B. Faulkner's Advertisement   42

TEXTUAL NOTES   45

ERRATA AND CORRIGENDA   47

INDEX   59

The INTRODUCTION

THE miscellaneous notes and short pieces collected in this volume raise few questions of authenticity or text, although they range, in period of composition, from the earliest to the last stage of Swift's literary career. The long note on Temple's letter (2 July 1678) to the first Duke of Ormond properly belongs in the first volume of this edition, among Swift's various prefaces to Temple's works. Swift published the note in 1703, when it would have spirited the English readers' defiance of Louis XIV during the opening years of the War of the Spanish Succession.

The note on Aristides Quintilianus appears in a copy of Meibom's *Antiquæ musicæ auctores septem*, 1652, which Swift signed on the title-page, 'J. Swift 1711'. In the sale catalogue of Swift's library, Dublin, 1745, this book (item 223) was starred as having been annotated by Swift: see Harold Williams, *Dean Swift's Library*, Cambridge, 1932. The bookseller who first published the note describes the volume as bearing the spinal decoration typical of the Markree Castle Library, founded in the eighteenth century by the Synge family and dispersed in the twentieth century. (See the textual notes, below.)

Swift's 'Advertisement' to his *Letter . . . concerning the Sacramental Test* as published in the *Miscellanies* of 1711 belongs among the textual notes in the second volume of this edition. Although the 'Advertisement' purports to come from the publisher rather than the author, it was normal for Swift to write such articles himself; and we know that he carefully supervised the preparation of the *Miscellanies*. While the phrasing of the 'Advertisement' is easy to parallel in pieces certainly by Swift, it is unlikely to have come from the hand of Tooke or his agents.

In 'The Printer to the Reader' prefixed to the first collected edition of the *Examiner* (1712) we have a similar article. Morphew would hardly have written such a note, but Swift was in the habit of doing so. The turns of expression (as in the last sentence of the first paragraph) and the opinions (for instance, the sneer at publication by subscription) are quite characteristic of Swift.

The piece belongs among the textual notes in the third volume of this edition.

A more important and amusing composition is the index to the same (1712) edition of the *Examiner*. Again we do not hesitate to make an attribution from essentially internal evidence. To Swift the appeal of a mock-index, offering him fresh opportunities to spear the Whigs, would have been seductive; and the entries seem too clever and elegant for a hired drudge to invent them. One can only credit Swift himself with the following stab at Marlborough:

> The excellent Design of building Fifty new Churches . . . altogether as useful, tho' not so expensive, as building One Palace for One Subject;

or this malevolent cross-reference:

> *Jacobites.* Vide *Whigs*;

or these anomalous topics under *Ministry* (on a subject peculiarly absorbing to Swift):

> The Severity of the late Ministry, and the Lenity of the present, with relation to Libels against them. . . . The latter extremely blameable.

The text belongs in the third volume of this edition, after Swift's contributions to the *Examiner*.

Swift's notes on changes to be made in a draft of his *History of the Four Last Years* were probably written in the spring of 1713. The text, preserved in a holograph now in the Huntington Library, has to do with the seventh volume of this edition (pp. 138–47) and belongs among the appendices to that volume. For a detailed analysis of the manuscript one should consult the essay by G. P. Mayhew, who first published it (see the textual notes, below).

The receipt for Parnell's manuscripts (1723) is written in Swift's usual manner for such notes, and belongs among similar materials in the fifth volume of this edition. We find C. J. Rawson's discussion of its authenticity convincing (see the textual notes, below).

The notes for a *Proposal for Virtue*—a sadly naive scheme for reforming the government of England—seem to date from about 1728, because the reference to the 'late' king places them in the

reign of George II, and the parallels with the *Account of Japan* (above, vol. V, pp. 99–107) suggest a similar time of composition. Having been in touch with the court during his visit to England in 1727, Swift may have imagined he could move the king with a direct appeal for reform; or he may have planned the essay as a number of the *Intelligencer*. The scheme is of course reminiscent of the equally naive *Project for the Advancement of Religion* (above, vol. III, pp. 41–63). The text should be an appendix to vol. XII of this edition.

Swift's pencilled notes in his copy of Baronius make up the most complicated division of this volume, though they would properly be placed among his other marginalia in vol. V. The best indications of their date are the '1729' written by Swift on the flyleaf of Baronius, vol. I, below a summary estimate of the whole work, and the '1728' after a note in vol. VI, p. 505, of Baronius. Many of the notes are no more than rude noises, in which Swift vents his distrust of the historian and his contempt for what he would term the credulity of the Roman Catholics:

spuria haec—Qualis fabula!—mendacissimus nebulo—insigne mendacium—evasio mira—impostura haec—impudentissime—imo de nugis—Quales nugae—hoc est quod expectavi—

Other notes are particularly concerned with style. Lines in the text are then underscored, and in the margin appear such comments as *insulsissima eloquentia—audi male triumphantem eloquentiam—lepide, more suo*; and when Baronius himself calls attention to an *elegans epigramma*, he provokes the scornful comment, *optimus elegantiae arbiter*. In the few more interesting notes Swift seems to be finding some parallel between an event chronicled by Baronius and the ecclesiastical controversies of his own day. Besides questioning all evidence of papal supremacy, he seems occupied with the paradoxes of Erastianism, drawing attention to evidence of imperial authority over the popes; and in two or three remarks on church councils he may be thinking of the great quarrel over the rights of Convocation.

The prefatory letter which Swift wrote for his younger friend Sheridan's sermon on St. Cecilia's Day is dated 25 January 1730–1. Although it has never before appeared in a collection of Swift's works, the evidence for its authenticity produced by

Professor M. L. Jarrell is convincing (see textual notes, below).
The text belongs with Swift's other attacks on the Irish Presbyterians in vol. XII of this edition.

The character of Sheridan as Lilly should have appeared with
Swift's other sketches of him in vol. V above. Presumably, it was
written soon after the certificate Swift quotes, which is dated
22 October 1731.

The inscription to Dr. Mead should probably be grouped with
the marginalia and annotations gathered in the fifth volume of
this edition. Mead's kindness to Swift's protégée, Mary Barber,
may have prompted this gift. (See Swift's *Correspondence*, ed. H.
Williams, vol. V, p. 97, n. 1.) Swift had made a similar present
to George Lyttelton a few months before (ibid., p. 162).

The marginalia in *The Proceedings Touching the . . . Earl of
Clarendon* belong with the other marginalia in vol. V of this
edition. Swift may possibly have read the book during the years
(1715–17) when he was preoccupied with the steps taken against
his own friends, Oxford, Bolingbroke, and Ormond.

The paragraph in the *St. James's Evening Post* was attributed to
Swift by the victim, Bishop Evans, himself, in a letter of 16 September 1721 to Archbishop Wake:

> I verily believe Jonathan Swift is the inditer of the letter, which is
> so full of falsities in fact that I am not much moved when I read
> the prints; only it grieved me that the villain said I had changed my
> principles. I was Rector of a parish soon after I was in priest's
> orders, and bachelor of arts before, or about the time Barrow was
> Bishop of St. Asaph; my father died nine years before I left school
> and my mother, though she had other children, never sent me less
> than thirty pounds for my maintenance in Oxford, besides the
> charges of my degrees, without the assistance of anyone living. . . .
> The letter has many other things in it relating to my conduct here,
> which the whole town, etc., know to be scandalously untrue, and the
> printers would not put them in.[1]

In his edition of Swift's *Correspondence* Sir Harold Williams dismisses the attribution.[2] But inasmuch as Swift detested Evans,
and this sort of hoax was precisely to his taste, we are inclined to
be less peremptory.

[1] See also Swift's *Correspondence*, ed. F. E. Ball (1910–14), III, 86–7 and *n.*; *Correspondence*, ed. H. Williams (1963–65), II, 388–90 and *n.*   [2] II, 390 *n.*

The advertisement of Faulkner's edition of Swift's *Works* belongs with the other appendices relating to that edition in vol. XIII above. Faulkner published a series of such advertisements in the *Dublin Journal* and elsewhere. For some later examples see Swift's *Correspondence*, ed. H. Williams, V, 262–5.

Note to Temple's Letter to Ormond

(1703)

[This is a note by Swift to a letter from Sir William Temple to the first Duke of Ormond, 2 July 1678. It concerns the following sentence: 'And for his Majesty, I have some particular Reasons (which I cannot entertain your Grace with at this Distance) to believe that he is perfectly cured of ever hoping any thing well from *France*, and past the Danger of being cajoled by any future Offers from thence.']

The Secret of the *King* and *Dukes* being so eager and hearty in their Resolutions to break with *France* at this Juncture, was as follows.

    France in order to break the force of the Confederacy, and elude all just Conditions of a general Peace, resolved by any means to enter into separate Measures with *Holland*; to which end it was absolutely necessary to engage the good Offices of the King of *England*, who was look'd upon to be Master of the Peace whenever he pleas'd. The bargain was struck for either 3 or 400 Thousand Pounds. But when all was agreed, Monsieur *Barillon* the *French* Ambassador, told the King; That he had Orders from his Master, before Payment, to add a private Article; by which his Majesty should be engaged, never to keep above Eight Thousand men of standing Troops in his Three Kingdoms. This unexpected Proposal put the King in a Rage, and made him say, ——'*d's fish, does my Brother of* France *think to serve me thus? Are all his Promises to make me absolute Master of my* ——— *come to this? Or, does he think That a Thing to be done with Eight Thousand Men.*

    'Tis possible I may be a little mistaken as to the Sums of Money, and Number of Men; but the main of the *Story* is exactly as I had it from the *Author*.

Note on Aristides Quintilianus

(*c.* 1711)

[Written on the endpaper of a copy of Marcus Meibom, *Antiquæ musicæ auctores septem*, the note refers to the author of *De musica libri III*, which occupies the second volume of Meibom's work.]

TRACTATUM Aristidis Quintiliani ab homine Christiano scriptum fuisse suspicor.

ADVERTISEMENT to *A Letter . . . concerning the Sacramental Test*

(1711)

THE *following Letter is supposed by some judicious Persons to be of the same Author, and if their Conjectures be right, it will be no disadvantage to him to have it here revived, considering the Time when it was Writ, the Persons then at the Helm, and the Designs in Agitation, against which this Paper so boldly appeared. I have been assured that the Suspicion which the supposed Author lay under for writing this Letter, absolutely ruined him with the late M——stry. I have taken leave to omit about a Page which was purely Personal, and of no use to the Subject.*

'THE PRINTER TO THE READER' in *The Examiners for the Year* 1711

(1712)

THE *following Papers, when they were singly Publish'd, having Sold very well, which is the only way I am able to judge of their Goodness, and being likewise mentioned with great Advantage in all Publick Places, where I happened to be*; I mean, by all those Persons, who are in the True Interest of the Church and Kingdom; I have, pursuant to the Advice of my Friends, and, I think, the general Desire of the Publick, Printed them in one small Volume, that so they may be had at a very reasonable Rate : The Author or Authors of them, being above all Regards of doing it by Subscription, tho' I had great Encouragement to pursue that Method. It is conceived, That altho' these Papers were writ for the Publick Service, upon Incidents, as they daily happened; yet in them are treated several Subjects, which may be of general and lasting Use. Neither, perhaps, will Posterity be unwilling to see several Observations made, and Facts related, concerning the late Disposition of Affairs, which they will probably meet no where else, or at least not from any Person so well informed as the Writers of these Papers appear to have been.*

I have prefixed, The Letter to the Examiner; *being a Piece universally allow'd to be written with much Spirit and Judgment, and perfect Knowledge of Affairs: It was Published soon after this Work was undertaken; and the Reader, I hope, will be of Opinion, that the Instructions given in that Letter, were very fully pursu'd.*

I have added a General Index to the Whole, *which, I presume, will be of use to the Reader.*

Index to *The Examiners for ...*
1711
(1712)
A.

A *Ddresses* from all Parts of the Kingdom, shew'd the true
Sense of the Nation, 230. The Addresses against making
any Peace without the entire restitution of *Sp—n*. The Folly,
and Wickedness of it, 237. The true Meaning and Design of
it, *ibid*.

Agrippa. Ancient, and Modern: His Character, 300.

Answer. What some People call *Answering* a Book, or Discourse,
87.

Arbitrary Power. Whether the Tories, or the Whigs and Fanaticks,
are the greatest Friends to it, 244.

Army. Vide Soldiers.

Avarice. The Madness, and unaccountable Effects of it, from
166, to 172. Pernicious, especially in publick Affairs, 167.
Two sorts of *Avarice*: One consistent with Ambition, the other
not, 168.

B.

Bank. The Rising and Falling of its Stocks a mere Amusement, 5,
6, 51. The Usefulness, and Danger of it, 60, 230. Whether the
Directors of the *Bank* ought to be the Directors of the Crown,
ibid. The Cunning and Jargon of Stock-jobbers, 77, 150.

Bender. A Letter from thence, *from 38, to* 42.

Bigamy (Will) His Service to the Church, 138.

Bishops. A Man's disliking the Proceedings of a certain Sett of
Bishops, no Argument of his Aversion to Episcopacy, 130.
No great Credit to the Former, to be cry'd up by those who
are profess'd Enemies to the Latter, *ibid*. A Man may be made
a Bishop, as well as any thing else, by very odd Means, *ibid*.

Britain. The War more prejudicial to *Britain*, in respect of its
Expences, than to *France*, or any of the Allies; and why, 78.

Buckingham (Duke of) His Character, 164.

C.

Church. High-Church, and Low-Church; The Meaning of those Words explained, 43, 44. The true distinction of Persons, with respect to the Church, 44, 45, 71. *He's a good Man, and goes to Church,* 46. High-Churchmen (as they are call'd) not for the Pretender, 69, 157. The Danger of the Church. It was certainly in great Danger, not many Years since; nor was it, even then, any Crime to say so, 88, 89. A man may politically be a Friend to the Church, and yet be a very bad Man, 179, 180. The excellent Design of building Fifty new Churches in *London* and *Westminster,* 258, 259, *&c.* altogether as useful, tho' not so expensive, as building One Palace for One Subject, 260.

Clergy of the Church of *England.* Their Character, and hard Circumstances, *from* 125, *to* 131. They are the greatest Terror to Popery, 52. Their opposing, and confuting it when there was the greatest Danger of it, 125. Charg'd in gross with Qualities utterly inconsistent, 126. The Rage and Malice of a Party against them. *ibid.*

Comprehension, 134.

Convocation. Strangely adjourn'd: And why, 129, 130. The absurdity of such an adjourning Power in the Archbishop, 130. Comparison between the Upper and Lower House, *ibid.* The excellent Character of the present Prolocutor, 131. Great pity that the three Speeches made at presenting Him, were not printed. The last of them very Entertaining, if not Instructive, *ibid.* The pious Designs of the Lower House, still baffled; and by whom, 283, *&c.*

Crassus. A Letter to Him, 169, 170, 171. Twofold; Ancient, and Modern, *ibid. and* 184.

Credit (Publick) Who are the truest Promoters of it; Whigs, or Tories, 12. 51. 146. 151. 154. 219.

Cunning. An Argument of Knavery, not of Wit, 233, 234.

D.

Dartmouth (Earl of) His Character, 165.

Dictionary. A New-fashioned one, *from* 43, *to* 55.

Dissenters. Vide Toleration. Their base compliance with Popery and Arbitrary Power in King *James's* Reign, 125, 226. The Pretender greatly indebted to them, *ibid.* A large Account of

them, *from* 221, *to* 227. A Comparison between Them and the *Jacobites*, *Ibid*. And between them and the Papists, *ibid*. 223. Bubbled by the Whigs, 224. Their Allies or Confederates, 225. Advice to them, 225, 226.

Drinking Damnation, and Confusion, 49. Instance of that execrable Practice, 122.

Dutch. Defended against a surprizing Memorial, said to be presented in their Name, *from* 19. *to* 25. Their Obligations to *Great Britain*, 20. The Whigs and Fanaticks formerly profess'd Enemies to that Republick, 23. Tho' Now They are partial to the *Dutch*, in opposition to the Interest of their own Country, 24.

E.

Ephori, 229.

Examiner. The general Design of the Author, 1, 2, 107. Guesses about the Author, 105, 303. The Difficulty of his Task, *ibid. and* 106, 107, 112, 160, 209, 302. Cross-Examined, *from* 132 *to* 139. Who is not the Author, 161. An Answer to the *Letter to the Examiner*, *from* 172 *to* 178. The Whigs much obliged to him, 210, 211. He is not hir'd, 243, 252. Tempted by the Whigs to come over to their Side, 288.

F.

Faction. Vide *Party*. Who those are that the Whigs call a Faction, 101, 194, 195. The Nature of a Faction, as distinct from those who are Friends to the Constitution, 194.

Faults on both Sides. The plain *English* of that Phrase, 47.

France. The King of *France*'s Letter to the Tories of *Great Britain* answer'd, 9. Who Those are that most promote the *French* Interest, whether Whigs or Tories, 10, 11, 12. The Notion of being in the *French* Interest, according to the Whigs, 51.

French. The Genius and Temper of that People, 198.

Favourites. The Danger of them, 181.

Fulvia, Ancient, and Modern: Her Character, 297, 299.

G.

General for Life. The Danger of such an Officer, 119, 120.

G——n E —— of. A certain Doctor's small Panegyrick upon him examin'd, *from* 32 *to* 38.

Governors, and *Subjects*. The Nature of them, 54.

Gratitude. A Comparison between *Roman* Gratitude, and *British* Ingratitude, *from* 95 to 99.

Guiscard. His Stabbing Mr *Harley*, 197, *&c*. His profligate Character, 198, 201. The Wisdom of a certain Great Man in inviting Him over, and preferring Him, 198. A Comparison between the Affair of *Greg* and *Guiscard*, 199, 209.

H.

Harcourt, Lord-Keeper, his Character, 163.

Harley Mr. The Villainous Design against Him in the Business of *Greg*, 142, 246, 247. His Character, 164. His being Stab'd by *Guiscard*, and his Heroical Behaviour upon that Occasion, *from* 196 *to* 202. An unanimous Concurrence between the *British* Whigs, and *French* Papists against Him; and why, 199, 201.

Heat, and Violence, 48.

Hereditary Right Invested in the *Pretender* by the Whigs, 11. Fundamental to our Constitution, 53, 55. Not inconsistent with Acts of Settlement, 55.

Hope. The successive Hopes of the Whigs, 146.

House of *Hannover*. Who are the best Friends to it, whether Whigs or Tories, 11. 52, 53.

I.

Jacobites. Vide *Whigs*, 244, 245.

Impudence of the Whigs, 173.

Indemnity. Act of Indemnity : The Use and Seasonableness of it, 183, 236, 282.

Interest. Monied and Landed, 12, 22, 75, 219.

Junto, 154, 155, 156. Coalition for a time between the Junto and late Ministry, 183, 282.

K.

King. The true Glory and Greatness of a King or Queen of *England*, 230.

Kirk of *Scotland*, High-Kirk, 190.

L.

Laws, Arts to elude them, 234. Our Laws extremely Defective in many Instances, 235, 236.

Liberty ; a very good Thing. The true Sense of that Word, 47, 48.

Loyalty, and Rebellion, 51, 52.
Lying. A Discourse upon Political Lying, *from* 79 *to* 84.

M.

M——lborough D—— of, not so hardly used, as some People
 represent Him, *from* 92 *to* 99.
Medley ; an Infamous Whig Libel so called. The unexampled
 Impudence and Malice of its Author, in abusing Mr. *Harley*,
 and the Speaker of the House of Commons, 254, 255. The
 excessive Ignorance and Stupidity of That Scribler, 278, 292,
 293. The *Examiner* blames himself for having descended to
 take notice of him, and his Brethren, 304.
Merit, True, and False; the Poetical Genealogy and Description
 of both, 187, 188.
Ministry. Vide *Parliament*. Allegiance paid by the Whigs to the
 late Ministry, 6. The Whigs severe upon the late Ministry,
 even when they think they are pleading in its Defence, 18.
 The Difficulties which the present Ministry encounter'd, 110.
 Scandalously Abus'd and Libel'd by the Whigs, 151, 153, 189,
 232, 253, 254, *&c.* What were to be expected if the late Ministry
 were again in Power, 153, 154, 155, *&c.* The Severity of the
 late Ministry, and the Lenity of the present, with relation to
 Libels against them, 154. The latter extremely blameable, 256.
 Late Ministers unfortunately prais'd for those very Qualities,
 which their Admirers own they chiefly want, 162. Present
 Ministers have their Defects as well as Vertues : An Account
 of both, 163, 164, 165. The late Ministers not obliged to the
 Whigs for their Defence of them, 178. The present Ministry
 of the Queen's own personal voluntary Choice, 189. The
 miserable Condition into which the late Ministry had brought
 the Kingdom, 281, 282.
Moderation. The true Nature of it ; and the Nonsense that has
 been talk'd about it, 48, 49.
Monarchy, Monarchichal, Antimonarchical, 54.
Mountague Sir *James*, his Oratory, 30.

N.

Naturalization General ; The Danger, and Dishonourableness of
 it to this Kingdom, 127, 128, 155.

Nobility. The Necessity of keeping up the Respect due to Birth and Family, 249. University-Education of Noblemen greatly contributes to it, 250.

Non-Resistance, and Passive-Obedience, 54, 205, 206.

O.

Observator, and *Review.* Though Contemptible Wretches in themselves, yet capable of doing much Mischief among the Vulgar, 86.

Oligarchy, 229.

Orators among us; who have attempted to confound both Prerogative and Law in their Sovereign's Presence, 196.

P.

Palatines. The Use of bringing them over, 12. Those who brought them over, Enemies to the Kingdom, 248, 271, 272.

Papists, and Popery. Whether the Whigs or Tories are their openest Enemies, 52, 240, 241.

Parliament. The Zeal of the Whigs for the late Parliament and Ministry, 4, 5, 6, 7, 14, 15, 16, 20, 41, 42, 74, 107. The Necessity there was of changing both, 30 *to* 42, 77, 78, 94, 108, 109, 110, 111, 113 *to* 117, 128, 129, 182, 183, 184, The Difficulties of those Changes, 150. Advice concerning the Elections of Members of Parliament, *from* 56 *to* 62. The present Parliament chosen entirely by the Inclination of the People, without the Influence of the Court, 148, 149, 230. The excellent Character of the present Parliament, *from* 212 *to* 214, and of the present Speaker of the House of Commons, 214. The many great Things done by This Parliament in their First Session, *from* 271 *to* 274.

Party. A Man of no Party, his Character, 45. Party-Aversions and Distinctions in mere Trifles; the Folly of them, 192; especially among the Women, *ibid.* The Genealogy of Party, or Faction, *ibid.*

Passive-Obedience. Vide *Non-Resistance.*

Peace. A Lover, and Disturber of it, 53. The true way to obtain Peace among our selves, 70. A General Peace; who those are that are averse to it, 75, 144, 145. The unreasonable and

impracticable Condition imposed upon the *French* by the late
   M——ry, 144.
People. Their natural Bent and Inclination, 147. Difference
   between That, and a sudden, popular Madness, *from* 147 *to* 152.
   The present Disposition of the People is an Instance of the
   former, not of the latter, *ibid.* The merciful Disposition of
   the *English* Populace, 196.
Persons. Sometimes so connected with Things, that 'tis impossible
   to separate them, 99, 100, 107.
Persecution Two-fold, Positive and Negative, 50, Difference
   between the Church and the Dissenters, with respect to
   Persecution, *ibid.*
Petition of the Party-Writers to the late Ministry, 276.
Petticum Mr. The Counterfeit Correspondence between him and
   Mr. *B—ys* detected, *from* 2 *to* 7, *and from* 13 *to* 19.
Plantations. The shameful Neglect of Religion in our *American*
   Plantations, 262.
Prejudice, and Passion, 112.
Pretender. Whether most opposed by Whigs or Tories, 12, 15,
   25, 52, 53, 244, 245, 266. The great use which the Whigs have
   always made of him, 90, 150.
Pride. The House of Pride ; the Description of it, Built like a
   famous modern Structure, yet unfinished, 302, *it should be* 298.
Prolocutor. Vide *Convocation.*

Q.

Queen. The Behaviour of the Whigs towards Her, 17, 18. 114.
   Her Royal Benefaction to the Church, 127. Her numberless
   Vertues, 127, 143, 182, 262, 280.

R.

Republick. Republican Politicks infinitely dishonourable, and
   mischievous to this Kingdom, 59, 127, 128. The Poorness, and
   Narrowness of Spirit which is joined with them, *ibid.*
Review. *Vide* Observator.
Revolution. The Use the Whigs make of the late Revolution, 50, 51,
   52, 76. The Nature of a *Thorow* Revolution, 126. Revolution-
   Principles, 245. The *Whig*-Maxim concerning Revolutions,
   ibid.

Rochester (Late Earl of) His Character, 163. Behav'd himself in King *James*'s Time, at least as well as the present E—l of G-d-l---n, 178. A little of the late Earl of *Rochester*'s Character 251.

Right Divine. Certainly true: but does not infer indefeasible, or unlienable, 55. Tho' those who in one Sense, affirm the Queen's Right to be indefeasible, are guilty of no Crime, 91. Hereditary. *Vide*, Hereditary Right.

S.

Sacheverel (Dr.) His Interest, and Influence, 16. His eminent Service; and the good Consequences of his Impeachment, 69, 147. The pious Design of those who impeached Him for the Good of the Church, 137. The hopes of the Whigs and Fanaticks from it, 177.

Shrewsbury (Duke of) His Character, 164.

Soldiers. Their proper Province, and the Nature of their Office, *from* 118, *to* 124, 143. Their Zeal for the late Ministry ; and their good Reason for it, 142, 143, 145.

Stanhope (General) Whether his Success in *Spain* proves him to be of the Antimonarchical Party, 29. Whether he got more Glory as a General, or as a Manager, 30.

Stocks. Vide Bank.

St. John (Mr.) His excellent Character, 165. 305.

Sweden (King of) His Character, 38, 39. A Letter concerning his Circumstances at *Bender :* With a Query understood, Whether it may not relate to some-body else? *from* 30 *to* 42.

T.

Tatler. Compared with the Gazetteer, 27, 28. Serious Advice to him, 31. His Modesty and Civility considered at large, *from* 63 *to* 68.

Test-Act. The Design of the Whigs to abolish it; and how that hopeful Project miscarry'd, 135, 136.

Time and Mortality, 131.

Tiranny and Arbitrary Power, 50, 53.

Toleration. Given to the Dissenters when they are out of Power ; and deny'd by them when they are in Power, 50. 190.

Tories. Their Principles with respect to Government, 219, 220. With respect to the Church sufficiently known, *ibid.* The

Original, Progress, and various Application of those fantastical Cant-Words *Whig,* and *Tory* ; and the Sense in which they are both used by the Author, *from* 263 *to* 269.
Treasury. Its Flood-gates, 57.

V.

Verres. His Character, and Impeachment, *from* 101, *to* 104. Twofold : Ancient and Modern, *ibid.* and 138.
Violence. Vide Heat.
Union. A Story of a National Union, 117.
Votes. A Paper of *Whiggish*-Votes, 155, 156.

W.

War. Our prodigious Successes in it; and the little use we have made of them, 144. The Care of the late Ministry to prolong it, 144, 145.
We and They. Us'd in a whimsical Signification, 55.
Whigs. Their Zeal for the Queen, 17. 18. 114, 115. 146. 181. 217. For their Country, 54. 150, 151. For the Protestant Succession, 53. For the Church, 44, 126, *from* 134 *to* 139, 244. For the Universities, 60. 114. For Justice, and the Liberty of the Subject, 114, 156. For the Christian Religion, 136, 155, 217, 218, 224, 228. Their Skill in Arithmetick, 114. Compar'd to Shop-Lifters, 78. The strange Medly which their Party is composed of, 180, 203, 216. Their Impudence, Insolence, and Ingratitude to the Q—— 113, 114, 181, 182. History of the Rise of them in this Reign, 182, 183. The closeness of their Cabals now they are out of Power. Their mischievous and desperate Designs, 185, 186. They are not properly a National Party ; but a little inconsiderable, undone Faction, 216. A Summary Account of them, 240.
Words. The Folly and Danger of popular Words and Phrases, *from* 42, *to* 55.
Giving hard Words. The Folly of that Cant, 46.

FINIS.

Notes for *The History of the Four Last Years*

(1713)

L. 4. P. 21. D. Ormd positively told by th Dutch, that they would not let his Troops pass—&c
—Ibid. D. Ormd could not send th Detachmt; because he had not the Fr Kings orders, & Fr. chicaned because th Cessation could not be Generll—this wise in th Duke.
P. 25. Lisle & doway, here; & satisfd Orders were genrll—
—25. G which th dutch Army might Starve &c
—Say a little more of th Approbation & applaudig th dukes Conduct
29. Abermarle at Denin to secure their Convoy from Marchiennes, too far from their main Army, expose their Conduct there

Receipt for Parnell's Manuscripts

(1723)

[Swift apparently gave this note to the owner of a collection of Thomas Parnell's manuscripts.]

Dec. 5, 1723

Then Received from *Benjamin Everard* Esq; the above Writings of the late Doctor PARNELL, in four stitched Volumes of Manuscript; which I Promise to restore to him on Demand,

JONATHAN SWIFT.

Notes for a 'Proposal for Virtue'

(*c.* 1728)

Proposal for Virtue.
Evry little fellow who has a vote, now corrupted.

An arithmeticall computation, how much spent in Elections of commons, & Sc. Lds, and pensions, ⌜th⌝ and forein Courts; how then can our debts be pd

No fear that Gent^{le.} will not stand and serve without Pensions, that they will let the Kingdom be invaded for want of Fleets and armyes; or bring in Pretd^r &c

An able Council to be got.

How K. will answer his own interest as well as the publick. He is now forced to keep himself bare &c, at least late K— &c was.

perpetuall expedients, stoppings gaps &c, at long run must terminate in something fatal, as it does in private estates.

There may be probably 10000 landed men in Eng^{ld} fit for Parlm^t. This would reduce parl^t to consist of real landed men, & ex viceneto wch is full as necessary for Senates as Juryes. what do the other ⌜do⌝ 9000 do for want of pensions.

It will ease Reputation and profit, requires less time, and no manner of art

In private life Virtue may be difficult by passions infirmityes, temptations, want of power, strong opposition &c. but not in publick administration; there it makes all things easy

Form the Scheam. Suppose a K. of Engld. would resolve to give no pension for Party &c. and call a Parlm^t perfectly free as he could.

What can a K. reasonably ask that a Par^{lt} will [*catchword*: refuse]|| [*verso*:] refuse him, when they are resty, it is by corrupt Ministers

who have designs dangerous to the State and must therefore support themselves by bribing &c

Open fair dealing the best

A contemptuous character of court-art, how different from true politicks; for, comparing the [× . . . . d] talents of two professions that are thought very different. I cannot but think that in the present sense of the word Politician a common sharper or pick-pocket has every quality that can be required in the other, and accordingly I have personally known more than half a dozen who in their time ⌜whe⌝ were esteemed equally to excell in both

Marginalia in Baronius

(*c.* 1728–29)

[Vol. I, *on the fly leaf, in ink, in Swift's hand*:]
                        At vos venite in ignem
                        Annales Baronii Caesaris
                        cacata charta
                Pessimus inter pessimos scriptores,
                falsissimus inter falsissimos,
                Nugacissimus inter nugacissimos,
                Insulsissimus inter insulsissimos,
                Ita post lecturam duodecim
                voluminum irâ et taedio peractam
                censui

                                        Jonath Swift

A.D. 1729

[Vol. I, *Appendix ad Lectorem extra Cath. Eccles. positum.*
'Ne credas, lector hæretice, sed consule opus in mille locis.'
At the foot of the page in the margin, in pencil:]

    Ob insignem tuam charitatem magnam tibi agimus gratiam,
imo et insuper te excusatum habebimus quo minus preces pro
salute nostra frustra impendas

Baronius, Vol. IV	Swift
p. 560: IN NEGOTIORUM FUNCTIONIBUS VIRI DEI CAETERIS PRÆSTANT.	E contrario sentiunt laici clericos minime aptos negotiis secularibus.
p. 600: GREGORIUS SENEX VEXATUS STIMULIS CARNIS FORTITER PUGNAT.	Vere haec ridicula
p. 674: Hieronymus.	crassam aevi sui ignorantiam fatetur Hyeronymus.
p. 701	Quis ferat has nugas? heu nimium fraudum piarum non ad fidem stabiliendam sed suffocandam.
p. 702: EUGENII INFELIX EXITUS.	sed et huic tyranno, ut supra, videre est, humillime et devotissime scripsit sanctorum patrum, insignissimus Ambrosius.
p. 721: Quamquam secundum honorum vocabula, quæ iam Ecclesiæ usus obtinuit, Episcopatus presbyterio major sit . . .	Num igitur hoc novum in Ecclesiâ.
p. 727: At de Ausonio satis.	Optimus sanè Christicola Ausonius.
p. 742: infelix et perditus Zosimus	Zosimus mihi fidelis videtur historicus

Baronius, Vol. V	Swift
p. 1: [Baronius compares his production of a fifth volume with Leah's production of a fifth child in *Genesis* xxx. 17.]	Allusio impia et stolidissima
p. 7: Zosimus. sed quàm mendaciter!	Miror Baronium non laudassee [*sic*] Zosimum, æquè ac se [? fabulatorem]

Baronius, Vol. V	Swift
p. 27: [Baronius tells how a fragment of the true cross put out a fire.]	Miror lignum vetus et aridum incendijs extinguendis inservire.
p. 36: [Baronius relates a miracle involving the corpse of St. Ambrose.]	Miracula nimirùm semper comitantur mortem Sanctorum.
p. 57: DE MONACHIS	Non male describuntur monachi
p. 59: [Baronius suggests that an expression of Claudian, 'Quo, precor, hæc effecta Deo?' refers to the one true God.]	optima conjectura
p. 63: OPUS MANUALE PRAE-SCRIBITUR CLERICIS	optima contentio
p. 120: [Baronius quotes a canon of the Council of Nicæa forbidding a bishop to judge cases 'extra terminos suos'.]	Ergo non Episcopum Romanum
p. 143: [Baronius quotes a story, involving St. John Chrysostom, about the avarice of the Empress Eudoxia.]	sed et hæc Eudoxia quam christianissima et zeli plena describitur?
p. 173: [St. John Chrysostom was accused of stirring up the deans ('Decanos').]	Ergo non adeo recentes decani
p. 196: [Innocent I advises Theophilus to rely upon the next synod and the canons and decrees of the Council of Nicæa.]	Nullum hic signum omnipotentiæ papalis
p. 207: [Baronius infers from appeals made to the Bishop of Rome that his authority was acknowledged.]	Non; sed contrarium—patet ex mille locis, vel a te citatis.

Baronius, Vol. V	Swift
p. 253: Observa & hic, quæso, lector, antiquum sanctorū Patrum pugnandi genus ... primum omnium conciliare sibi consortio fidei sedis Apostolicæ communionem.	Non observo, sed aequè atque alijs Eclesijs, sed gliscere fateor R. Eclesiae paulatim potentiam
p. 262: EPISTOLA INNOCENTII PAPAE AD ARCADIUM IMPERATOREM.	Haec epistola est procul dubio spuria
p. 265: REDARGUITUR IMPOSTURAE COMMENTUM.	Miror miracula a Baronio refutata
p. 272: STILICHONIS MORTE BENE CONSULTUM ECCLESIAE.	imò pessimi hominum si fautores fuerint Christianorum a te laudantur
p. 281: COLLATA DIIS ORNAMENTA SUBLATA.	Miror deorum simulachra et sic ornata, tam diu sub imperatoribus Christianus mansisse.
p. 365: [Discussing the suicidal intentions of the Donatists, Baronius says,] ista sunt quae callidissimi illi in ipsorum Concilio statuêre.	Nimirum seipsos interfecerunt ex calliditate. Strategema subtilissimum.
p. 412: Quam auctoritatem ubique nos misisse manifestum est, ut cunctis regionibus innotescat id quod statuimus omnimodis esse servandum.	Hoc omne spurium aut putide interpolatum, non enim ista ⌜valuit⌝ ætate tantum valuit Episcopus Romanus sed gradatim—gliscebat enormis ista autoritas
p. 423: [Baronius says that after Zosimus at Rome condemned the errors of Pelagius and Caelestius, they were condemned elsewhere.]	ita accidit non virtute damnationis Romanae sed Imperatoris rescripti.
p. 428: [Letter ends:] Dat. IIII. Non. Mart. Honorio XII. & Theodosio VIII.	Vides lector ni fallor, ut irrepsit hic mos Paparum concludendi epistolas nominibus consulum

Baronius, Vol. V   Swift

imperatorum more, in hoc aut priore tomo incepit si bene memini.

p. 447: Augusti utrique miserunt, et eiecerunt Eulalium; et missa auctoritate, revocaverunt Bonifacium, et constituerunt Episcopum Eulalium.

Totum igitur hoc opus, vel te fatente erat penes Imperatoris.

p. 469: Vides igitur accusationes Episcoporum deferri solere ad Romanos Pontifices.

Nil aliud tibi cordi videtur præter potentiam papalam.

p. 501: [An importunate monk excommunicated Theodosius II. The emperor would not eat until the ban was lifted.]

Monachus impudens, et stultus Imperator

p. 529: Scotorum Christianitatem, nempe à tempore Victoris Papae et martyris, qui ... in Scotiam miserit Roma clericos, qui eos docuerint Evangelium.

in Hibernia.
Falluntur, per Scotos enim tunc temporis—semper intelliguntur—populi Hiberniae, si non distinguntur (viz) Scoti in Britannia. erant enim victores hodiernae Scotiae—consule Bedam et alios.

p. 533: [Baronius on England:] in eadem insula (proh dolor!) fæx hæreticorum hodie vi armorum et carnificina sanctorum extorquet?

Gratias nos Angli tibi reddimus Domine Cardinalis.

p. 533: [Concerning St. Germanus, when exposed to a fire:] hospitium sancti viri expavescens flamma transilivit ... et inter globos flammantis incen-

Miraculum Britanicum.

dij incolume tabernaculum . . .
emicuit. Exultat turba mira-
culo. . . .

p. 542: NESTORII EPISTOLA AD CAELESTINUM

Hereticus iste haud satis venera-
bundè ad Papam scribere videtur

p. 559: Certe quidem non sine
consensu Caelestini Papae con-
gregatum fuit Ephesinum Concilium. . . .

Impudentiam hominis! quot
enim concilia vidimus incon-
sulta Episcopo Romano?

p. 590: [Baronius says the reader
has seen ('Vidisti') how the
pope was acknowledged head
of the Catholic Church.]

Video te semper vel falsarium,
vel spuria citantem ex quibus
authoritatem Papae stabilire
frustra conaris

p. 596: [The Council of Ephesus
(431) requests the emperors to
dismiss it.]

Videmus hic et ubique autoritatem Imperatoris in convocandis
et dimittendis Synodis

p. 619: Vides autem omnibus
fuisse perspicuum, ab Apostolica sede accipiendum esse
Evangelium ad conversionem
Gentium. . . .

Video papae satellitem per fas
ac nefas omnia ad Eclesiam
Rom. trahentem.

Baronius, Vol. VI

Swift

p. 63: haud enim passus est Deus
Theodosium diùtius impera-
re. . . .

Imperavit autem annos 42

p. 80: [Baronius quotes a story
of how St. Peter miraculously
corrected a letter written by
Pope Leo.]

Monachorum somnia et delira-
menta

p. 88: non sine auctoritate
Romanorum Pontificum Im-
peratores consuevisse indicare
Synodos.

Hoc millies dudum inculcasti
et millies credo inculcaturus es
sed quo ad me frustra.

p. 95: [At the pseudo-Council of Ephesus the papal legates meet opposition.]

Sed quis agnovit autoritatem horum legatorum vel imò sedis Romanæ

p. 103: [Theodosius summons the pseudo-Council of Ephesus.]

Ubi hic autoritas Rom. sedis?

p. 109: [Letter quoted from Leo to Theodosius, asking that he order a general council to be held ('generalem Synodum iubeatis . . . celebrari').]

Supplicat Imperat. Papa ut concilium generale celebretur.

p. 117: [Pulcheria had Marcian made emperor because no empress had ever reigned alone. But she did not consummate her marriage to him because she had dedicated her virginity to God. Baronius compares her to Mary.]

optima virgo, optimum stratagema

comparatio profanissima

p. 119: Vides . . . morem œcumenici cogendi Concilij, ut id inconsultò et absque auctoritate Romani Pontificis minimè fieret, sed eius arbitrio Imperatores cuncta decernerent. . . . Vides igitur ex his imprimis, lector. . . .

Video stultitiam Imperatorum, et gliscentem Paparum ambitionem.

p. 154: [Baronius lists regulations concerning monks: that they submit to the authority of bishops, that they keep out of ecclesiastical or public business, etc.]

Sed omnia his contraria nunc in Ecles. Rom.

p. 155: [The hand of the dead St. Euphemia miraculously confirms the declaration of faith of the Council of Chalcedon.]

bellissima fidei confirmatio

Baronius, Vol. VI   Swift

p. 177: Non enim *terrore aut violentia* aliquos volumus ad viam trahere veritatis. *Sed recto illud accipias sensu* . . . neminem invitum se cogere ad fidem . . . [Swift's italics].

notetur hoc

Distinctio Jesuitica

p. 180: [St. Leo persuades Attila to turn back.]

Odoratus sum miraculum quoddam futurum

p. 180: [Concerning a vision that Attila is reported to have seen:] non *de duobus* Apostolis . . . sed *de uno* tantum Petro videlicet qui visus sit Attilae, testatur Paulus Diaconus

certè, sufficiebat *unus* Petrus

p. 188: [On Pulcheria:] cùm virginitatem ipsam *ad senectutem* usque servasset . . . [Swift's italics].

non autem usque ad mortem vereor, utpote domi cum viro agens

p. 191: LEO PAPA DUBITAT DE PASCHALI CONTROVERSIA

Hoc videtur incipi futilis ista disputatio de Pascha observanda

Cur non ex infallibilitate suâ poterat discere?

p. 265: [This year the bones of the prophet Elisha were moved from Palestine to Alexandria.]

signata erant ossa, credo

p. 267: [In Constantinople a great fire breaks out when two heretics are consuls.]

Consules haeretici causa incendij

p. 268: [St. Daniel, who had warned the people to repent and avoid the coming evil, says

Num qui praedixit extinguere voluit?

Baronius, Vol. VI	Swift
the fire will stop in seven days; and so it does.]	imò aliter esset Pseudopropheta
PER MALUM DAEMONEM INCENDIUM IMMISSUM	Cur non et hoc praedixit iste Daniel
p. 269: MARCIANUS INCENDIUM SUPERAT	Nebulo iste Sanctus cur non hoc fecit initio incendij?
p. 270: [St. Daniel converts the emperor's master of the horse from Arianism to Catholicism.]	Mirus Arrianos convertendi modus
p. 271: [Baronius prints a letter from a Spanish bishop to the pope, expressing great reverence for him.]	Ideo nimirum et hodie Rex Hispaniae est Catholicissimus
p. 279: [The plague in Rome is linked to the admission of heretics into the city.]	Imo et pestem secum offerunt haeretici.
p. 297: [A Jew, being burned alive, is miraculously rescued and converted.]	Et quid Bodinus diceret de hoc miraculo
p. 312: non esse hominis clericalis professionis, historias suorum temporum scribere. . . .	Quid Burnetus contra hæc?
p. 343: [A legate trying to heal the schism in the church was saved from shipwreck by a miracle. Baronius says the conversion of multitudes, happening soon after, was a greater miracle confirming the earlier.]	Optimus modus miraculum probandi
p. 373: [Baronius quotes from 'rebus gestis omni fide conscriptis sancti Lupi'.]	Ubicunque citat autorem ut maxime fidelem, expectet lector egregia mendacia

Baronius, Vol. VI	Swift
p. 389: [A leading heretic is warned to reflect on a miracle:] puer in aëra à quadam virtute elevatus est, eique praeceptum est, ut in Litania diceretur Trisagion. . . .	Miror omnes hæreticos hoc miraculo non fuisse conversos
p. 415: [Baronius tells of men having their tongues and right hands cut off.]	Tibi Baroni saepius linguam et dextram abscissas optavi
p. 417: qui se hodie Catholicos profitentur haeretici . . .	Sed nos neque linguas neque dextras Papistorum abscindimus
p. 429: SECUNDA ET TERTIA APPARITIO BARNABAE	Necesse est in omnibus hujusce [? farina] fabulis, ut ter appareat
p. 435: [Petrus Fullo, a great foe to Catholicism, dies.]	Cur senex et non vermibus plenus?
p. 437: [Baronius quotes a letter from Pope Felix to the Council of Rome:] Quibus licet ad animarum reparationem nihil deesse videatur: tamen si cui novi aliquid, quod præterire nos potuit, fuerit revelatum. . . .	non autem nunc dierum
p. 441: MUTUS LOQUITUR PRECIBUS S. SEVERINI	Utinam meis precibus tu mutus ex garrulo et mendaci fieres
p. 458: Vides igitur in universa Ecclesia Catholica Romanum Pontificem præsidere solitum arbitrum scripturarum. . . .	Optimus arbiter Scriptorum Pont. Romanus, meorum certè non erit
p. 486: [Baronius quotes a letter from the pope to the emperor, A.D. 494:] Duo quippe sunt,	Autoritas Pontificalis præcedit Imperatoriam

Baronius, Vol. VI   Swift

Imperator Auguste, quibus
principaliter mundus hic regi-
tur, auctoritas sacra Pontificum,
et regalis potestas . . . gravius
est pondus sacerdotum. . . .

p. 489: [The pope, writing to   Optime argumentatur Papa hic
the emperor, defends himself   ⌐ . . . ⌐ ad imperium suum
against the charge of arro-   stabiliendum contra Reges
gance:] Si nos elati sumus, qui
divinum cultum puro atque
illibato cupimus tenore servari;
qui contra Divinitatem quoque
sentiunt, dicant, qualiter non-
cupenter?

p. 502: S. BENEDICTUS EREMUM   Benedictorum   origo,   plena
PETIT   miraculorum

p. 505: Britannia habet sacer-   et eosdem iterum habitura est,
dotes sed nonnullos insipientes   vel potius nunc habet sc. 1728.

p. 515: [Baronius quotes a de-   Nota hæc, et miserum scrip-
cree of Pope Gelasius recom-   toris effugium
mending communion in both
kinds, but he does not interpret
this as applying to laymen.]

p. 517: [Baronius says the   Lupercalia Romae celebrata
Lupercalia was still celebrated   usque ad hoc tempus
in Rome in A.D. 496.]

p. 532: [Both Symmachus and   Duo Papæ creantur
Laurentius are elected to the
papacy.]
[The Arian King Theodoricus   Tacuisses hoc si potuisses.
is asked to decide between the   Judicium Papam elegendæ ad
two popes.]   Regem Arrianum defertur

p. 556: ut Petri vitae merita   optime ratiocinatur Enodius et
transfusa esse in successores   ab eo didicit Baronius. Virtutes

Baronius, Vol. VI	Swift
dicere non dubitarit. . . .	Petri transfunduntur in Successores peto quamdiu hæc durant
p. 606: Vetus et usitatus hic fuit mos haereticorum, ut quò se Catholicos populo exhiberent, Nicaenum Symbolum publice recitarent.	An qui Papam negant negant idem symbolum Nicænum?
p. 607: [A furious controversy rages in 511 over the doctrines of the Council of Chalcedon.]	Eheu, quod genus mortalium in ævo illo qui tot dissentiones suscitarent de ista synodo Chalcedonense!
p. 612: CIRCUIT THEODOSIUS REGIONES, ARMAT OMNES PRO FIDES TUENDA	Certe aut crucem aut helleborum meruit hic malitiosus Theodosius
p. 656: [Baronius calls Anastasius 'vafer et subdolus Imperator hæreticus'.]	Videtur hic Anastasius inter bonos Imperatores numerari debere
p. 657: QUAE PASSI HAERETICI ALEXANDRINI.	Qui latrabant contra Synodum Chalced. in canes versi.
p. 658: hoc nostro sæculo . . . Ecclesiae Catholicae novus Orbis accreverit. . . .	America Papistes apros et ursos experta est
p. 666: Etsi ista roganti, atque curiosè scrutanti judicia Dei . . .	Questio nodosa quam saepe habui in mente, sed responsione non cariturus Baronius. Sed an non tu, Baroni, millies scrutasti dei concilia, et judicia
p. 698: ita ut magno miraculo, rerum versa vice, Æthiopes dealbentur, dum super carbones facies Borealium denigrantur [*sic*].	Pereant tecum Arcadicae tuae facetiae, ineptae illepidae, quibus omnia volumina ad nauseam scatent.

p. 700: [From the instructions of Gabriel, Patriarch of Alexandria, 1593, to his mission to Pope Clement VIII:] eique narrent paupertatis et miserae nostrae ac monachorum nostrorum pupillorum et locorum statum.

Mendici scilicet a mendico missi ad mendicandum argentum, et nihil aliud

p. 707: [The legates accept the decisions of the church councils, especially the Council of Trent.]

Non ego

p. 707: [The legates condemn all heretics and those who reject the teachings of the Roman Catholic Church:] ac damno & reprobo omnes haereses, et auctores earumde, quos et quas reprobat & damnat dicta sancta Catholica & Apost. Rom. Ecclesia

Damnatores damnabit [? deus].

p. 707: [The legates acknowledge the supremacy of the Pope as successor to St. Peter.]

Propter hoc—optimè argentum meruerent miseri monachi

[The long account *De legatione Eccl. Alexandrinæ ad Apostolicam Sedem* ends with the identifications and signatures of the legates. Below, at the end of Vol. VI of Baronius, Swift writes:] Cur non ⌜addidit⌝ quot vestes et quantum auri dedere Papa et Cardinales ad sublevandam pauperiem Eclesiae Æthiopicæ et Schismaticos istos in obedientia erga Pontificem Rom. conservandum

Perdita Anglia Dania Suevia aliqu alijs florentissimis Regionibus, jactet se Papa ob reciperationem Æthiopiam vel potius pretio emptam, vel denique quod verum est, non Æthiopiam sed pauculos tantum mendicantes monachos cum miserrimo Patriarcha

Baronius, Vol. VII	Swift
p. 17: probè scientes, quæ in ea decreta essent, nullarum esse virium, nisi Romani Pontificis consensus accederet. . . .	Nulla decreta licet optima valent sine consensu Papae
p. 42: JUSTINUS DOLO AGIT CONTRA DOLOSUM VITALIANUM	Qui haereticum fraude necat laudatur
Intelligis, lector, quam praestaret hoc saeculo cultus sacrarum reliquiarum	Imò apud ignorantes et fidei corruptores. Videbit lector errores in Ecles. Rom. gradatim gliscentes.
p. 43: [Letter from Justinus to Hormisdas, urging the Pope to clear up a matter of contested doctrine:] HOC ENIM CREDIMUS ESSE CATHOLICUM, QUOD VESTRO RELIGIOSO RESPONSO NOBIS FUERIT INTIMATUM. . . .	Autoritas igitur Papae pendet ab opinione Justiniani
p. 56: . . . Epiphanius moram faceret mittendi ex more legationem ad Romanum Pontificem: exegit ab eo debitum Hormisda Papa, has ad eumdem litteras scribens. . . .	Epiphanius igitur non praestolavit Bullas a Papa
p. 104: Joannes Romanus Pontifex . . . à Theodorico Rege Italiæ ira exæstuante ob Arianos suos in Oriente ecclesiis spoliatos, subite cogitur legationem Constantinopolim ad Iustinum Imperatorem.	Ipse Papa a Rege coactus est ire legatus ad Constantinopl ut Arrianis redderentur Ecclesiae: ubi nunc Papæ autoritas?
p. 122: [A brave man miraculously rescues some saints' relics from a burning basilica.]	Cur non hae reliquiae basilicam ab igne servare poterant?

Baronius, Vol. VII   Swift

p. 123: [St. Ephraim, Patriarch   Cur non et seipsum in ignem
of Antioch, was challenged by   jactavit?
the heretic Stylites to undergo
an ordeal by fire and prove
which of them had the true
faith. When the fire was built,
Stylites refused to descend from
his pillar, and Ephraim threw
his patriarchal stole into the
flames. The fire burned out
after three hours, but the stole
was unharmed.]

p. 145: [Sentence underlined by   Dogma   verissimum,   quod
Swift:] Tantum Principes opin-   probo
ionem veritati præferentes val-
ent, quantum in solitarijs locis
prædones.

p. 145: [Topical gloss marked
by Swift with a pointing hand:]
NULLA FACULTAS IMPERATORIBUS
DE REBUS ECCL. DECERNENDI.

pp. 218–9: [Italicized words   audi male triumphantem elo-
underlined by Swift:] Quid his   quentiam
singulis   recitatis   sententiis,   totus in hoc es, nec ullam
rogo, *firmiùs* dictum, *dilucidiùs* occasionem amittis hae blater-
repetitum,   *instantiùs* inculca-   andi.
tum, *evidentiùs* apertum, atque
gloriosùs   prædicatum   inveniri
potest?

p. 243: [Epiphanius, Patriarch   caveant omnes ne quicquam au-
of Constantinople, suddenly   deant contra Papam. certe enim
died.]   morientur

p. 259: NON EX DIVITIIS SED   Quid valuit igitur donatio
APOSTOLICA AUCTORITATE MA-   Constantina?
JESTAS ROM. ECCL.

Baronius, Vol. VII

Swift

p. 259: [Baronius claims that at a time when the Pope could hardly find money enough to send a mission to Constantinople, the power of the papacy was in no way diminished. Swift underlined the italicized words:] nescio an aliquo *alio tempore magis viguerit* in Ecclesia Romana suprema potestas. . . .

cur igitur coactus ad legationem obeundam Papa, a rege seculari?

p. 262: [Agapetus deposes a heretical bishop without allowing him to see the Pope.]

Laudat Papam qui episcopum inauditum expulit

p. 262: Agapeti Papæ iudicium . . . fuit secundùm supremam Apostolicæ sedis auctoritatem, qua supra omnes canones Pontifex eminet. . . .

Papæ autoritas super omnes canones

p. 271: Rex et Pontifex . . . alter alterum veneratus. . . .

Hic equalis Papa et Imperator—infra, Papa superior futurus

p. 272: DE SUMPTUOSO FUNERE AGAPETI

Hic antequam ultra lecturus sum suspicor miracula super mortem Papae, vel post

p. 273: velum, quod altari superimpositum erat, ultro sublatum est, texitque Papam. . . .

Certe hoc miraculum odoratus sum pessime enim olet.

p. 287: [After capturing Naples, Belisarius was reproached by the Pope for committing unnecessary slaughter, and was forced to do penance ('poenitentiam agere').]

unquamne omittes mendacium quod pro te facit?

p. 316: . . . non tam citò, veluti sub Alarico, tradita Gothis ipsa Urbs fuerit, quando . . . vigebat apud plurimos nobilium superstitio idolorum. Verùm licet purissimi modò Romani, paucis exceptis, essent Christianæ religionis cultores, proculque abhorrerent ab omni cultu deorum: tamen quòd reiecto legitimo sacerdote . . . ob Græcos tale sensit Urbs ipsa flagellum. . . .

Papa rejecto, religio purè culta nil valuit

p. 319: [On the death of Silverius:] audi Anastasium paucis magna narrantem: Sepultus est (inquit) in eodem loco . . . ibique occurrit multitudo malè habentium, et salvantur.

Anastasius hic dignissimus qui a nostro autore saepius citetur

p. 320: Tu es Petrus, et super hanc petram aedificabo Ecclesiam meam

Quia ter negavit Christum Petrus, ideo Christus eum Eclesiæ præfecit

p. 321: [Although Pope Vigilius was elected irregularly, through the help of the empress, he did not support her monophysite position, and consequently he receives the approval of Baronius.]

Si tales Papae legitimi sint, quis illegitimus

p. 321: [Baronius defends the elevation of Vigilius as a providential means of confounding heretics.]

Usque huc nullum verbum emissisti [*sic*] quod non meruit [*sic*] Laqueum

p. 345: [Baronius quotes from St. Gregory the Great.]

Multum debet Baronius huic mendacissimo Gregorio

Baronius, Vol. VII	Swift
p. 349: [Baronius describes the plague in Constantinople, A.D. 544.]	Lucretius pestem Athenis ferè eodem more describit
p. 350: [Baronius credits St. Simeon with ending the plague.]	cur autem saevire permisit pestem Simeon per tres menses?
p. 355: facta est inopia frumenti, vini, et olei, ac pluvia magna, et factus est terræmotus Constantinopoli ... everso die sancti Paschae. ...	Haec omnia acciderunt ob errorem de tempore Paschae
p. 355: de Paschatis die anni huius [*i.e.*, A.D. 545] exortam controversiam, intelligi potest. ...	ingentis momenti controversia
p. 392: [Simeon Salus converts a Jewish glass worker by miraculously causing the cups he produces to break until he makes the sign of the cross.]	Iste Simeon Salus lepidissimus erat Thaumaturgus
p. 392: [Baronius quotes from Leontius, Bishop of Naples and Cyprus.]	Ex praedictis apparet Leontium vel ipsum Gregorium in stultitia et mendaciis vicisse
p. 405: nec ipsarum memor legum Imperatoris, quibus haud semel quidem, sed sæpius quanta esset super omnes totius Orbis Episcopos Romani Pontificis auctoritas declarasset.	Ira cæcus, fatetur autoritatem Papæ pendere a legibus Imperatoris
p. 422: ea adhibita conditione, ut exæquato numero Episcoporum, qui sive ex Italia, sive ex Africa vocarentur, non plures hi essent, quàm qui ab ipso Imp. ex diversis Orientis Ecclesiis Constantinopolim vocarentur.	prudens cautio non observatur in Synodo Tridentina

D

Baronius, Vol. VII	Swift
p. 426: Et usque nunc dispiciebam, utpote falsa, ista quae divulguntur	Si haec epistola vel minimum faceret pro Papae autoritate non esset spuria
p. 459: non esse hoc novum, ut aliqua Synodus, cui nec per Legatos ipse Pontifex interfuerit, sed adversatus fuerit, titulum tamen obtinuerit Oecumenicae. . . .	certe non novum, sed more majorum, cum Papa aequalis erat aliis Episcopis
p. 461: cur ipsi non licuit ex eadem causa, mutato rerum statu, rursum mutare sententiam	et negando et affirmando, et saepe mutando manere infallibilis, nil facilius
p. 462: [Baronius explains the changes of principle of Pope Vigilius in connection with the second Council of Constantinople:] ita pro ratione temporis modò hoc, modò illud adimplens, factus est omnia omnibus, ut omnes lucraretur.	Millies igitur mutando sententiam Papa nunquam fallitur
p. 467: dum duriores coegit Romanam Ecclesiam subire conditiones quam tulerat sub Ethnicis Imperatoribus.	nihil hoc ineptius, non enim erat Ethnicis curae quid Christiani inter se fecerunt [*sic*]
p. 525: Vos qui hujusmodi narrationibus delactamini, attendite	Inter quos ego non sum
MIRACULA CONFIRMANDAE FIDEI CAUSA	sequitur congeries miraculorum
p. 528: DE OBITU S. MEDARDI EPISC.	Miraculum esset si sanctus sine miraculo mortuus esset

p. 536: [Baronius quotes a miracle of a boy stricken by the plague, going to heaven, and returning speaking Greek and Bulgarian.]

Ludus literarius in caelo ubi pueri Graece et Bulgarice loqui docentur

p. 555: Sanctus Gregorius Papa de his agens. . . .

Taedet me hujusce Gregorij omnium mortalium mendacissimi et pessimus poeta, ideoque

p. 561: pauca de venerabili & sapientissimo viro Fortunato . . . [Baronius praises him:] doctus in arte Grammatica, Rhetorica, et Geometria clarissimus extitit. . . .

et pessimus poeta, ideoque saepius a Baronio citatur.

p. 595: licet stylus rudior, veritas tamen ipsa securior atque purior hauritur fonte

certè tu ex veritate ipsa nil hauris nisi falsum

p. 728: *from the Appendix: De Ruthenis ad communionem Sedis Apostolicæ receptis monumentum* [*The Nicene creed accepted, viz.:*] Credo in unum deum Patrem omnipotentem, factorem caeli et terrae, visibilium et invisibilium . . . .

Confessio fidei barbaris digna

Preface to Sheridan's Sermon

(1731)

SIR,

I Return your sermon, and have carefully perused it without making any alterations, only I have set marks in the margin, where a few sentences are less correct in the stile, which although of little consequence from the pulpit, yet should be set right before you send the copy to be printed. As to the doctrines it contains, there is no doubt of your being safe enough upon the article of orthodoxy, and it appears by your quotations, that you have read to very good purpose upon the subject. I am no frequent reader of single flying, occasional sermons, and consequently do not remember to have met with any, where this matter is so fully, and expresly treated.

One thing you are justly conscious of; that you may not probably have taken the properest methods of making your court. You should best know the burden, and how you can bear it. For, I am not perfectly certain, that you will receive thanks from ALL YOUR SUPERIORS (I use that word in it's proper meaning) because I did not observe any one of them in the *church* to countenance either the *performance*, or the *preacher*.

The present language is of another kind. *Our brethren, the dissenters, are not to be disobliged*; *we may serve God without musick*; And, *why should we offend loyal, true* PROTESTANTS, with bringing it into our *churches*, after the practice of *papists*. It is not improbable, that such topicks as these, in all their changes, may be rung in your ears, by whatever *sorry hand* shall be employed to answer you. And, yet perhaps the wind may come from a different corner, than that from whence you are threatened. The arts of gaining *popularity with dissenters* are no ill, or unusual means to make advantage by. The character of *a healing man* will hardly fail of finding it's reward, nor will at all suffer by the deepest wounds, with the most poisoned weapons given to those, who are so unhappy to differ from principles in fashion.

You offer it as one reason for printing your sermon, that some (as I suppose) poor, illiterate, preaching *Sectary* of the *Dissenting way* threatens you with an answer. This I do not altogether comprehend, unless you design to enter into a *course of controversy*,

36

which I take to be worse than any *course of physick*. But this I
suppose ariseth from your putting a greater weight on the wilful,
or malicious clamours of a few hot, ignorant people than I do.
It is true, you are in no danger of provoking *learning, piety*, or
wisdom; but what is a great deal worse, you may provoke *folly,
nonsense, mistaken zeal, malice*, and *interest*.

Therefore, when you thought fit to desire my approbation,
you ought to have distinguished, I do not object against your
sermon; but I may not approve of your printing it. However
I shall not dissuade you, because it may happen, that the sourness
of my temper at present, hath a little tinged my judgment. I am,
Sir, Your most faithful, Humble Servant.   *A.D.*

January, the 25th
1730

Sheridan as Lilly
(1731)

[Swift's character of Dr. Thomas Sheridan as 'Lilly' is introduced
by George Faulkner in a footnote as follows: 'Dr. *Sheridan* was
an eminent School-master, whom the Dean is supposed thus to
describe under the Character of *Lilly*.']

Lilly is a Person very excellent in his Art; perfectly skilled in
the Writings and Languages of ancient *Greece* and *Rome*. He hath
much Invention; often writes humorous Verses that are diverting
enough, but it is defective in Judgment. He is honest, generous,
friendly and good-natured, but without one Grain of Discretion:
And, with all, so heedless, unattentive, shattered and absent, that
you cannot depend a Minute on his Promise or Engagement.
He is somewhat too careless in Expences. How subject he was to
be deceived, appears from the following Certificate under the
Doctor's own Hand, dated *Oct.* 22, 1731.

Dr. Sheridan, *forced to promise and allowed, that he hath been thirty
Times deceived in affirming his Servants and Agents to be honest; does
now, the one and thirtieth Time, positively assert, that his present Agent at*
Quilca, Wooly *by Name, is the most honest, diligent, and skilful Fellow
in* Ireland.

Signed at Dr. *Grattan's* House
Thomas Sheridan.

Inscription to Dr. Mead
(1739)

[Inscription in a copy of Swift's *Works*, Dublin, 1737–41, 6 vols.]
These Six Volumes are presented to the very learned
Richard Mead, M.D. by the supposed Author, who
lyeth under many Obligations to His Humanity and
Friendship.

Deanry House   Jonath: Swift.
Dublin Novbr 7th
1739.

Marginalia in *The Proceedings Touching the . . . Earl of Clarendon*, 1700
(*date uncertain*)

[Sig. A3v of the 'Preface', Swift has a note beside the following
remark: 'We live now (God be thanked) in a Time when we need
not fear Encroachments on our Just Liberties':] a silly tedious
irony [The whole 'Preface'—in which the author sarcastically
praises the wise benevolence of English monarchy and the
honour of the House of Commons—is dismissed as:] a very
foolish Preface J.S.

APPENDIXES

APPENDIX A

Letter in *The St. James's Evening Post*, 8 September 1721,
Dublin, *Aug.* 27

THE 24th instant, being St. Bartholomew's Day, died the Right Reverend John Lord Bishop of Meath of the Gout and Strangury, at the Right Reverend the Bishop of Kilmore's at Kilmore. He was born in Wales, the son of a Farmer there, and educated some time at Oxford, by the Care, Piety and Generosity of Dr. Barrow, Lord Bishop of St. Asaph; from whence he remov'd for London, where he was Curate and Schoolmaster: Afterwards, by his own Ingenuity, and the help of some Friends, he was made Chaplain to the East-India Company, Travell'd as far as the Bay of Bengal, where he married, made a considerable Fortune, and then return'd to England, in the Reign of King William, when he was promoted to the See of Bangor, worth about 5 or 6 Hundred Pounds per Annum; and from thence in the present Reign, translated to the rich See and Diocese of Meath in this Kingdom, which he farm'd out at Two Thousand Three Hundred Pounds per Annum. He was a Man at his first coming over Esteem'd entirely Zealous for the present Government, but he was justly suspected afterwards of favouring some contrary Principles, and has not in the General Opinion of People here, died much lamented.

[In the next number of the newspaper (7–9 Sept.) this letter was reprinted without the concluding phrase ('and has . . . lamented'); but in the number which followed (9–12 Sept.) appeared the statement, 'There are no Letters in Town giving an account of his Lordship's Death', with an apology: 'N.B. The aforesaid Paragraph was taken from a scurrilous letter dated Dublin, August the 27th, sent to the Publisher of this Paper, and seems purposely design'd by many vile Reflections in it, to affront his Lordship, and abuse and deceive the Publick.']

APPENDIX B

Faulkner's Advertisement for His Edition of Swift's *Works*

DUBLIN, Feb. 9, 1733.

The Writings of the Reverend Dr. J.S.D.S.P.D. were published six Years ago in London, in three Volumes, mingled with those of some other Gentlemen his Friends. Neither is it easy to distinguish the Authors of several Pieces contained in them.

But, besides those three Volumes, there are several Treatises relating to Ireland, that were first published in this Kingdom, many of which are not contained in the DRAPIER'S LETTERS.

It hath been long wished, by several Persons of Quality and Distinction, that a new compleat Edition of this Author's Works, should be printed by itself.

But this can no where be done so conveniently as in IRELAND, where Booksellers cannot pretend to any Property in what they publish, either by Law or Custom.

This is therefore to give Notice, that the Undertaker, GEORGE FAULKNER, Printer in Essex-street, proposeth to publish, by Subscription, all the Works that are generally allowed to have been written by the said Dr. S. in four Volumes; two of which shall be put to the Press at 4s. 4d. each, beautifully printed on a fine Paper in OCTAVO, neatly bound in Calves Leather, and lettered on the Back. The said two Volumes shall be deliver'd to the Subscribers by Michaelmas-Term at farthest: Eight Shillings and Eight Pence to be paid at the Time of subscribing, and the Remainder at the Delivery of the Book. And if the Subscriptions are not fill'd up by the first Day of MAY next, the Money shall be returned. Whoever subscribes for six Copies, shall have a Seventh gratis.

The first Volume shall contain the Author's Letters, written under the Name of M. B. DRAPIER, with two additional ones never printed before; and likewise, several Papers relating to IRELAND, acknowledged to be of the same Author.

The second Volume shall contain the Prose Part of the Author's Miscellanies, printed many Years ago in LONDON and DUBLIN; together with several other Treatises since published in small Papers, or in the three Volumes set out and signed JONATHAN SWIFT and ALEXANDER POPE.

The third Volume shall contain the Author's poetical Works, all joined together; with many original Poems, that have hitherto only gone about in Manuscript.

The last Volume shall contain the Travels of Captain LEMUEL GULLIVER, in four Parts, wherein many Alterations made by the LONDON Printers will be set right, and several Omissions inserted. Which Alterations and Omissions were without the Author's Knowledge, and much to his Displeasure, as we have learned from an intimate Friend of the Author's, who, in his own Copy, transcribed in blank Paper the several Paragraphs omitted, and settled the Alterations and Changes according to the original Copy.

In this Edition, the gross Errors committed by the Printers, both here and in LONDON, shall be faithfully corrected; the true Original, in the Author's own Hand having been communicated to us by a Friend in whom the Author much confided, and who had Leave to correct his own printed Copies from the Author's most finished Manuscript, where several Changes were made, not only in the Style, but in other material Circumstances.

N. B. A compleat Edition of the Author's Works can never be printed in ENGLAND; because some of them were published without his Knowledge or Liking, and consequently belong to different Proprietors; and likewise, because as they now stand, they are mingled with those of other Gentlemen h[i]s Friends.

The Author's Effigies, curiously engraven by Mr. VERTUE, shall be prefixed to each Volume. There will also be several other Cuts, proper to the Work.

The whole Work, is to be done on a beautiful Letter and a fine Paper.

TEXTUAL NOTES

NOTE TO TEMPLE'S LETTER TO ORMOND

First published in 1703, in Sir William Temple, *Letters to the King . . . and Other Persons . . . Published by Jonathan Swift, D.D.*, pp. 355–6. See the facsimile of the title-page, above, vol. I, p. 265. In the original the body of the note is italic and the differentiation type is roman. Otherwise we have followed a copy of this edition in the Houghton Library, Harvard University (EC65. T2475. 703l).

NOTE ON ARISTIDES QUINTILIANUS

First published in *Catalogue no. 12* (item *761*) of the Bow Windows Book Shop, Lewes, Sussex. The note appears on the first end-paper of

> *Antiquæ musicæ auctores septem. Graece et Latine*. Marcus Meibomius restituit ac notis explicavit. Amsterdam, L. Elzevir, 1652. 4°, 2 vols. in 1.

The same endpaper is endorsed

> E:S Pr. 4s;6

and was apparently bought at the sale of Swift's library by Edward Synge, Bishop of Elphin, who had been Chancellor of St. Patrick's Cathedral while Swift was Dean. We have followed the transcription in the catalogue of the Bow Windows Book Shop, p. 66, where further descriptive details are supplied.

ADVERTISEMENT TO *A LETTER . . . CONCERNING THE SACRAMENTAL TEST*

First published in *Miscellanies in Prose and Verse*, 1711, p. 314. The present text is taken from a copy of that book in the Houghton Library, Harvard University (16422. 20. 4). It was reprinted without change in the second edition, 1713. (See above, vol. II, p. 275.)

'THE PRINTER TO THE READER' IN *THE EXAMINERS FOR THE YEAR 1711*

First published in 1712, in *The Examiners for the Year 1711*, sigg. A2–2ᵛ. See the facsimile of the title-page, above, vol. III, p. 1. We have followed the copy of this volume in the Houghton Library, Harvard University (11442. 1. 10).

INDEX TO *THE EXAMINERS FOR . . . 1711*

First published in 1712, in *The Examiners for the Year 1711*, sigg. O10–P3ᵛ. See the facsimile of the title-page, above, vol. III, p. 1. We have followed the copy of this volume in the Houghton Library, Harvard University (11442. 1. 10).

NOTES FOR *THE HISTORY OF THE FOUR LAST YEARS*

Huntington Library MS. 14380, first published by G. P. Mayhew in 'Swift's Notes for His *The History of the Four Last Years*, Book IV', *Huntington Library Quarterly*, XXIV (August, 1961), 311–22. We have followed a 'Xerox' reproduction of the manuscript and have ventured to change some of Professor Mayhew's readings.

RECEIPT FOR PARNELL'S MANUSCRIPTS

First published in the preface to *The Posthumous Works of Dr. Thomas Parnell*, Dublin, for Benjamin Gunne, 1758 (also London, for W. Johnston). Reprinted by C. J. Rawson in 'Swift's Certificate to Parnell's "Posthumous Works" ', *Modern Language Review*, LVII (April, 1962), 179–82. We have followed the copy of the 1758 volume in the Houghton Library, Harvard University (15464. 22).

NOTES FOR A 'PROPOSAL FOR VIRTUE'

Hitherto unpublished. We have followed a 'Xerox' reproduction of the manuscript in the Huntington Library (HM 14346). Half-brackets indicate words scratched out. Dots between square brackets indicate illegible words. Swift's abbreviation 'Sc.' means 'Scotch'.

MARGINALIA IN BARONIUS

Hitherto unpublished. Printed from the copy now in the library of Christ Church Cathedral, Dublin:

    Annales ecclesiasticae auctore C. Baronio. Antverpiae MDCXII. 12 vols.
    in folio.

The first volume is in poor condition, with margins badly stained or damaged, and almost two hundred pages destroyed. The rest of the marginalia are mainly to be found in volumes IV, V, VI, and VII—though Swift claimed he read all twelve folios. His comments are written in Latin with a soft pencil; and owing to the condition of some volumes, which have suffered greatly from damp, a number of the entries cannot be deciphered at all. To print the whole of the marginalia together with the necessary references from the text would require much more space than is available in this last volume; and besides it might well prove more tedious than even Baronius himself. We have therefore given only some selections of the more significant comments. For those who may desire the rest, the original volumes remain available in the library of Christ Church Cathedral; and a microfilm is available in the Bodleian Library, Oxford.

PREFACE TO SHERIDAN'S SERMON

First published in Thomas Sheridan, *A Sermon Preached at St. Patrick's Church, O2 St. Cecilia's Day* (Dublin, by S. Powell . . . for the Author, MDCCXXXI), pp. vi–viii. Reprinted, with a detailed presentation of the evidence for attributing the piece to Swift, by M. L. Jarrell in 'A New Swift Attribution: the Preface to Sheridan's Sermon on St. Cecilia's Day', *PMLA*, LXXVIII (1963), 511–15. We have followed Professor Jarrell's text, after collating it with a copy of the original publication.

SHERIDAN AS LILLY

First published by George Faulkner in his edition of Swift's *Works*, vol. VIII (Dublin, 1746), p. 384, as a note to a letter of 14 December 1719 from Swift to Sheridan. We have followed the copy of this volume in the Houghton Library, Harvard University (EC7. Sw551. B746w).

INSCRIPTION TO DR. MEAD

First published in the *Catalogue* of the Hunterian Library, Glasgow, 1930, p. 347. We have followed a 'Xerox' reproduction of the inscription.

MARGINALIA IN *THE PROCEEDINGS*, etc.

First published by Joanna Richardson in the *Times Literary Supplement*, 29 August 1952, p. 565. The notes are in a copy of *The Proceedings Touching the Impeachment of Edward, Late Earl of Clarendon*, 1700, with the signature 'Jon. Swift' on the title-page, which belonged to Charles Wentworth Dilke, 1789–1864. We have followed the transcription given in *TLS*.

APPENDIX A

Printed from the copy of the newspaper in the Bodleian Library, Oxford.

APPENDIX B

This advertisement appeared in the *Dublin Journal*, 10 February 1733 and later. It was also printed at the end of Faulkner's edition of Pope's *The First Satire of the Second Book of Horace, Imitated*, Dublin, 1733, pp. 21–4. In the Bodleian copy of that book, the dateline of the advertisement is March 2. We have followed the text of the original advertisement in the *Dublin Journal*.

ERRATA AND CORRIGENDA

GENERAL NOTE ON ERRATA AND CORRIGENDA

IN references to pages and lines of normal letterpress the lines are numbered exclusive of half-titles, running heads, and footnotes. We use 'f.b.' to show that we are counting from the bottom of the page. Otherwise, we indicate the line by a number after a decimal point or comma. When such indications are not feasible, we describe the reference between square brackets. We also use 'fn.' to mean 'footnote'. The new readings may require a corresponding adjustment of the textual apparatus; but they have usually been incorporated in the reprints of the various volumes, where the apparatus has also been corrected.

ERRATA AND CORRIGENDA

Volume One

Page and line	OLD READING	CORRECTION
xx, f.b. 9	*Miscellanea*	*Miscellanea. The Third Part*
xxxiii, 3	on . . . 1704	upon . . . 1703
xxxv, 7	last	fourth
xxxvii, 10	cleenlyness	cleanlyness
16. 2	Patron's	Patrons
17. 5	*Hand*	*Hands*
21. 24	large	huge
22. 23	written	wrote
30, f.b. 2	always	alway
42. 2	*Moderns*	*Modern*
42. 26	written	writ
45, f.b. 3	in the Town	in Town
61. 14	*retro*	*tetro*
	[But see R. Paulson, *Theme and Structure in Swift's Tale of a Tub,* 1960, pp. ix, 118.]	
106, f.b. 2–1	Garret I am now	*Garrat* I am
107. 1	Whosoever	Whoever
121. 12	Revolution	Revolutions
148. 16	thousands	thousand
149. 25	bestowed on	bestowed
158, f.b. 4	Enemies	Enemy's
159. 25	soft, and the	soft, the
241	[Add, after the title:] Oct. 1, 1706	
246	[Add, after the letter of dedication:] Aug. 6, 1707	

[In the textual notes of the original printing of Volume One, pp. 296–304, a number of corrections should be made. We list these not under the pages of those notes themselves, but rather under the pages of text to which the notes refer. In *English Studies,* XXXVI (April 1955) J. C. Maxwell pointed out one or two errors in the text and suggested a list of further variants from the first edition that should be restored. The following readings have now been incorporated in the text:]

A TALE OF A TUB

Page and line	PRESENT TEXT	VARIANTS
16. 2	Patrons	Patron's 1–5
17. 5	*Hands* 1, 2	*Hand* 3–5
21. 24	huge 1	large 2–5
30, f.b. 2	alway 1–3	always 4, 5
42. 2	*Modern* 1, 2	*Moderns* 3–5
42. 26	writ 1–3	written 4, 5
45, f.b. 3	in Town 1–3	in the Town 4, 5
61. 14	*tetro*	*retro*
106, f.b. 2–1	*Garrat* I am 1	Garret I am now 2–5
107. 1	Whoever 1	Whosoever 2–5
121. 12	Revolutions 1	Revolution 2–5

Volume One
THE BATTLE OF THE BOOKS

Page and line	PRESENT TEXT	VARIANTS
148. 16	thousand 1	thousands 2–5
148. 17	his Enemy 5	this Enemy 1–4
148. 29	Could you not 1–3	Could not you, 4, 5
149. 25	bestowed 1–3	bestowed on 4, 5
158, f.b. 4	Enemy's 1	Enemies 2–5
159. 25	soft, the Leaves	soft, and the Leaves 2–5
161, f.b. 7	t'other 1, 5	the t'other 2–4
164. 16	Champain 5	Champian 1–4
165. 1	would mistake 5	will mistake 1–4

THE MECHANICAL OPERATION OF THE SPIRIT

Page and line	PRESENT TEXT	VARIANTS
175. 6	out 1–3	out of 4, 5
175. 10	those 1	these 2–5
178. 5	a Beam 1–3	an Beam 4, 5
180. 2	him with 1–3	with 4, 5
180. 12	or whether 1–3	whether 4, 5
185, f.b. 1	*Spirit* 1–4	*Spirits* 5
186. 12	or 1–4	and 5
189. 5	*furor* —— 1, 3–5	*furor Uterinus* 2
189, f.b. 13	*Men* 1–5	*Mien* 1711, 1720, H
189, f.b. 6	toward 1	towards 2–5

A DISCOURSE OF THE CONTESTS AND DISSENTIONS IN ATHENS AND ROME

[The following variants should be added, between the two issues, designated *x* and *w*, pointed out by Herman Teerink in *The Library*, 5th ser., IV (December 1949), 201–5:]

Page and line	PRESENT TEXT	VARIANTS
199, f.b. 9	noting	nothing *x*; remarking *w*
202. 24	States	State *x*
203. 13	Dissentions	Dissention *x*
205. 6	Scene of Action	Action *x*
205. 26	briefly	very briefly *w*
210. 18	preserved	served *x*

[Swift's reference to Diodorus on p. 209, l. 6 f.b., '*lib.* 28' should be '*lib.* 18' (chapter 2).]

Volume Two

Page and line	OLD READING	CORRECTION

[Frontispiece: This Briscoe portrait, once thought possibly to be an early portrait of Swift, must now be rejected as unauthentic. As Sir Frederick Falkiner maintained in 1908 (Swift's *Works*, ed. Temple Scott, XII, 3), there is no evidence that Swift was ever painted by anyone other than Charles Jervas and Francis Bindon.]

x, 6–8	[Swift visited Cranford in January 1709.]	
xi, n. 1	p. 153	p. 155

xv, 4	[On the date of Swift's *Sentiments*, probably begun in 1704, see I. Ehrenpreis, *R.E.S.*, III (July 1952), 272.]	
xxiv, 14	*Merlin*	*Merlin* (Luttrell's copy is dated 21 Feb. 1708–9)
47. 127	in Probability	in all Probability
58. 20	Use	Uses
77. 24	refusing	refuse
97. 17	who are	are
163. 8	is an	in an
168. 23	make	makes
169. 7	the	their
257. 4	migrare	migrate
281	[General note on *A Letter . . . concerning the Sacramental Test*:] printed in 1709	published in December, 1708

Volume Three

Page and line	OLD READING	CORRECTION
x, 9	September 30	September 29
x, f.b. 4	Ire-	I re-
xv, fn. 2, l. 1	Dec. 25	Dec. 28
3. 8	altho'	although
108. 9	stlyed	styled
110, f.b. 1	mehtods	methods
117. 17	Pillored	Pilloried
145. 15	at last	at least
	[Similarly, change textual note, p. 276.]	
162, f.b. 1	ate	late
278	[The title near the bottom should read:] SOME REMARKS UPON A PAMPHLET, ETC.	
278, f.b. 8	[The first sentence should read:] First published August 18, 1711.	
279. 1	[The first sentence should read:] First published Sept. 11, 1711.	
279, f.b.3	[Add, as first sentence:] Advertised in *The Post Boy* 2-4 Oct. 1711.	

Volume Four

Page and line	OLD READING	CORRECTION
iii	[Title page: add under title:] *Edited by* Herbert Davis and Louis Landa	
xxviii, f.b. 5	[To 'early as 1704' add this footnote:] George Mayhew notes two entries in Swift's account book for Nov. 1702 to Nov. 1703. If Y fall don't stay to rise [Cf. above, p. 164, l. 7.] Snap short makes look lean [Cf. above, p. 167, l. 5 f.b.] These suggest that Swift was already collecting material in 1703. See *N. & Q.*, Feb. 1961, pp. 49–50.	
9. 24	changes	Changes
17. 6	Princes:	Princes;
20, f.b. 4	Conveniences	Conveniencies
100. 18	higest	highest
101, f.b. 3	want:	want;
112. 27	slackness	slowness
117. 25	surpizing	surprising
118. 8	Persons;	Persons:
122. 20	*Czar of*	*Czar* of
161, f.b. 1	fees	sees

Volume Four

Page and line	OLD READING	CORRECTION
205, f.b. 9	*Maniebrium*	*Manubrium*
206. 9	Adversay	Adversary
277	[After title of *A Dialogue . . . between A and B* add:] from Huntington MS. 14342	
277, f.b. 1	[?a] Planter	Planted
278. 7	Country	County
278. 8	Doll	Dolt
278. 11	strole	shoh [Cf. below, p. 279, l. 21, *shob't*.]
278. 15	Spawleen	Spawlpeen
279. 5	Doll	Dolt
279. 6	Canaught	Conaught
279.7	Soogaun	Sougaun
279. 11	Spanel	Spaned
279	[After last sentence add: See below, p. 302, note on Appendix G.]	
282, f.b. 1	littled	little
285. 1	First printed	First published
287	[In the notes to *Mr. Collins's Discourse* the first sentence should read:] First published Jan. 25, 1712-13.	

[On this volume generally, see Maurice Johnson in *P.Q.*, XXXVII (July 1958).]

The following variants should be added to the list on pp. 285–302.]

A PROPOSAL FOR CORRECTING THE ENGLISH TONGUE

Page and line	PRESENT TEXT	VARIANTS
8. 16	into 12	to 35
11. 9	unharmonious 12	unharmonius 35
19, f.b. 1	Credit 12	Credit, 35

POLITE CONVERSATION

Page and line	PRESENT TEXT	VARIANTS
101. 5	foresee	foretel
102. 18	Reader	Readers
103. 23	Cadencies	Cadences
108. 5	until	till for
109. 4	Reason	Reasons
109. 5	from	who, from
113. 19	every such School	every School
113, f.b. 2	Positively	Positive
115, f.b. 8	Consequences	Consequence
117. 1	confine	compute
118. 15	commanded	commended
120. 7	true	and true
120. 22	the Fountain	the very Fountain
121. 6	poetick Quire	whole Poetick Choir
122. 27	inhumanly	inhumanely

Volume Five

Page and line	OLD READING	CORRECTION
ix, f.b. 8–7	*Works . . . 1702*	*Letters* of Sir William Temple, published in 1700
xi, fn. 1	1598	1598–1600
xii, f.b. 13	*The Letter addressed*	*A Letter*
xiv, f.b. 7	*The Account*	*An Account*
xvi, f.b. 4	edition	editors
xxii, fn. 1	Johnson	Johnston
xxiv. 5	*The Dean of St. Patrick's*	*Dean of St. Patricks*
xxiv, 19–20	*Declaration . . . 1733*	declaration . . . 1734
xxiv, 9	*Tracts on Irish Trade*	tracts on Irish trade
xxxvi, 7	Landsdowne	Lansdowne
6, f.b. 5	his	he
188. 13	festine	festina
191, f.b. 9	Erich	Erick
196. 1	in the evening	at evening
196. 3	John	Jo
196. 4	enclosed	included
196. 7	April 24	April 29
201. 5	imitatorers	imitators
	[The word is written over and corrected, though 'ers' is still left at the end.]	
255	[Title of no. 7:] *REDIVIVUS*	*REDIVIVUS*
279	[Reference to Burnet, vol. IV, p. 489:] Strafford	Stafford
336. 11–12	cates a quack	[?consequence]
336. 21	a tenincue [?]	or feminine

Volume Six

Page and line	OLD READING	CORRECTION
v	[In the table of contents the date of *Some Reasons . . . in a Letter to a Whig-Lord* should be given as 31 May 1712.]	
vii, 7	launched	taken over
viii, f.b. 12	see that	see
xiv, f.b. 1	Feb. 21st	Feb. 22nd
xviii, f.b. 1	Preface	said Preface
101. 11	Ports	Forts
209	[General note on *Some Advice to the Members of the October Club*, first sentence:] printed	published
209	[General note on *Some Remarks on the Barrier Treaty*, first sentence:] printed	published
210	[Note to p. 98, l. 9, present text:] *Genera*	*General*
210	[General note on *A Letter to a Whig Lord*, l. 2:] printed in June, 1712	published May 31, 1712

Volume Seven

Page and line	OLD READING	CORRECTION
ix, 19	Earl of	Earl
27. 6	amd	and
159. 16	with	which
232	[The second note to p. 71, l. 9 (Interest-Interests) should be to l. 13.]	

[The following variants should be added to those listed on pp. 219–46. I use *x* to indicate readings recorded by Percy Fitzgerald in a now vanished manuscript of this book. His readings are recorded in Temple Scott's edition of Swift's *Prose Works*, vol. X, 1902.]

Page and line	PRESENT TEXT	VARIANTS
7, f.b. 2	a great	great F
18. 20	Party	faction *x*
29, f.b. 3	put an end to	complete *x*
72. 1	which Tallies	which F, M.
96–7	[On these pages, *x* consistently reads 'North Britain' for 'Scotland'.]	
114. 12	the Demolition	the Demolishing F; demolishing M

Volume Eight

Page and line	OLD READING	CORRECTION
xv, f.b. 3	printed	published
xxxii, f.b. 8	attainder	impeachment
xxxix, fn. 1	152	150
179. 6	Duty of	Duty to
201	[General note on *The Importance of the Guardian Considered*, first sentence:]	
	31 October	2 November
212	[Note to p. 112, l. 1:]	
	p. 120	*p.* 118

Volume Nine

Page and line	OLD READING	CORRECTION
iii	[Title page: title should read as follows:]	

IRISH TRACTS 1720–1723
edited by Herbert Davis
And SERMONS
edited by Louis Landa

xiii, 14	c onclusion	conclusion
xiii, 15	tend ed	tended
xvii, fn. 1	Forconvenienceall	For convenience all
xix, 28	Thomas Hyde	J. Hyde [Similarly, correct index, below, p. 383.]
xxi, f.b. 8	must have been	was
xxi, f.b. 7	no copy	only one copy
xxi, f.b. 6	me	me (see below, p. 373)
xxv, 9–10	1768 . . . thirteenth . . . octavo	1765 . . . ninth . . . quarto
xxvi, f.b. 15	*Clergyman*	*Gentleman*
26, f.n. †	[This identification, which may not be by Swift, is wrong, and should refer to the Duke of Shrewsbury.]	

Volume Nine

Page and line	OLD READING	CORRECTION
63. 6	lrte	late
69. 8	almos tentirely	almost entirely
99. 9	*Clergyman*	*Gentleman*
214. 20	*Wor ds*	*Words*
214. 21	*S pirit*	*Spirit*
371		

371 [General note on *The Last Speech and Dying Words of Ebenezor Elliston*: The second sentence should be replaced by the following paragraph:]

A copy has been found of the original broadside which Swift must have published at the time of Elliston's execution, May 2, 1722. See *Harvard Library Bulletin*, XIII (Autumn 1959) for a description by Daniel McCue, Jr., of a 'newly discovered' broadsheet of this piece, now in the Houghton Library, Harvard University, bearing the imprint:

DUBLIN: Printed by *John Harding* in *Molesworth's Court* in *Fish-shamble-Street*.

The title contains the date of Elliston's execution, 'this Second Day of MAY, 1722', and the phrase 'Publish'd at his Desire for the Common Good'. Professor McCue's discovery is clearly a copy of the actual sheet which the printer had prepared for sale on the occasion of the execution, and it reveals the following variants from Faulkner's text, printed in 1735 and used as the copytext for the present volume. (The variants noticed here should be added to the textual apparatus.)

Page and line	PRESENT TEXT	VARIANTS
37. 6	Elliston, *who was*	ELLISON, Who is to be 22
39. 21	any Rogue	any 22
40. 23	seen a Tankard worth Fifteen Pounds sold to	seen sold a Tankard worth Fifteen Pounds to 22
40.32	Fifty Pounds	Fifty Pound 22
41. 6	until	till 22
41. 8	Mugs	Muggs 22
41, f.b. 2–1	the Death of a Dog	tho' a Death *contrary* 22

[At the end of the broadsheet of 1722 the following statement was printed, running across the whole page at the foot of the two columns (line endings are indicated here):]

There are likewise to Die Two more one Patrick Mc.Clanen and Stephen Mc.Clanen they say | little or nothing in their Defence, but acknowledge the Facts for which they Die to be true, and die both | Romans.

There were two more to suffer, but are to be Executed in the Country.

Page and line	OLD READING	CORRECTION
376. 8–9	com- | posi or	com- | positor
386		

386 [The entry after 'Tuam, Archbishop of,' in the index should read only, '*see* Vesey, John'. After 'Venus' add:] Vesey, John, Archbishop of Tuam, 270; quoted, 17.

Volume Ten

Page and line	OLD READING	CORRECTION
xii, fn. 2, ll. 4–7	[For the remarks 'I have seen . . . small octavo', substitute the following:] Two copies only are known, one in the Goldsmiths' Library, University of London, and the other in the Rothschild Collection, where there is as well an important, unique copy of a quarto edition which may have been the original trial issue, possibly printed by Patrick Delany, on his own press, from Swift's manuscript, and then sent to Harding, the printer, in this form so as to preserve anonymity. See *The Library*, XIX (June 1938), 108–9. One peculiarity of this printing, the spelling 'DREIPER', might be explained as a misreading of Swift's open 'a' as 'ei'; and the omissions found in the quarto text further suggest that it was an early draft. The folio edition too may be described as a trial state, printed by Harding; and the real first edition (of two thousand copies) would thus be the earliest printed in the small octavo	
xiv, fn. 2	July 1	July 31
xxvii, fn. 2	pp. 204–5	pp. 213–14
10. 15	*somolten*	so molten
207, f.b. 1	Single copies	Copies
207, fn. *	1935	1935 (2nd ed. revised, 1966)
211	[Note to p. 49, l. 16:] I. 6	l. 6
212	[Note to p. 70, l. 1 f.b., present text:] hey will	they will
213	[General note on Letter V, second sentence:] p. 77.	p. 77. The footnotes on pp. 81, 82, 83, 89 were added in 1735.

Volume Eleven

In the original pagination of this volume (xliv, 316) Swift's own prefatory material and his table of contents were counted in roman numerals with the editorial preliminaries. This error was corrected when the volume was reprinted, and the pagination became xxviii, 332. In some reprints the letterpress of p. 283 was substituted for that of p. 215, and *vice versa*.

The first edition of this volume contained an errata slip and, on pp. 285–6, a paragraph in the textual notes suggesting further emendations of the text after it had been set up. In the reprints these errors have been deleted in the textual notes and the emendations have been incorporated in the text. But the corrected apparatus is too long and involved to be reproduced here; so readers who own a copy of the 1941 edition must be directed, regretfully, to pp. 301–22 in the reprints of 1959 and later years.

Volume Twelve

Page and line	OLD READING	CORRECTION
ix, 9	June 15	June 14
ix, fn. 2	1936	1937

Volume Twelve

Page and line	OLD READING	CORRECTION
xxv, fn. 2	[For this sentence substitute the following:]	
	We now know the date was May 27, 1730, the day after the Archbishop received his; see *N. & Q.*, 14 June 1930, p. 416.	
xxxii, f.b. 8	September 4	September 5
xlii, f.b.12	*Presbyterian*	*Presbyterians*
xlii, f.b. 9	to be . . . October 4	on November 5, according to the *Dublin News Letter.*
xliii, f.b. 4	October 6	October 1
xlv, f.b. 8	printed	wrote
51. 4	Span-Fathing	Span-Farthing
59, f.b. 3	not	nor
66, f.b. 5	raising	the raising
123, f.b. 3	sun	sum
156. 2–3	she trary	she hath ever been *offered the Oaths to the Government*: On the con- | trary
160. 23	*Professors*	*Possessors*
175. 20	Thousnad	Thousand
338	[Note to p. 160, l. 23, to be inserted after note to l. 18:]	
	PRESENT TEXT	VARIANTS
	Possessors L, M	*Professors* 35
348	[General note on *Some Few Thoughts concerning the Repeal of the Test*, second sentence:]	
	present text	text

Volume Thirteen

Page and line	OLD READING	CORRECTION
vi	[In list of illustrations, note on frontispiece:]	
	Engraved	Mezzotint
xxviii, 21	John	Jonathan
xxix, fn. 1	of I,	of I.,
xxxiii, 6	1763 . . . *Letter to*	1765 . . . *To*
xxxix, 26	for a	for the
155. 6	*Audeon's*	*Audoen's*
188. 21	What,	What
190, f.b. 2	And,	And
205, fn. 1	p. 137.	p. 137 [in Faulkner's edition.]
205, fn. 2	p. 359	p. 359 [in Faulkner's edition.]

INDEX

NOTE ON THE INDEX

[N.B. Volume XI, *Gulliver's Travels*, was originally (1941) paginated in small Roman numerals to the end of the table of contents. When that volume was reprinted, the style was changed; and Arabic numerals were employed beginning with what had been p. xxix. Because we follow the style of the reprint, any possessor of the 1941 edition of Volume XI will have to subtract sixteen from our references to Arabic numerals, and will also have to treat our pages 1–16 as his pages xxix–xliv.]

Swift's works are entered under their titles; the main entry for each is in boldface. If the first word is an article, we omit it. The date of publication (or, if so indicated, of composition) is supplied in parentheses unless we cannot be sure of it. Next we give the volume and pages of the text (including title-page facsimiles) in boldface.

Swift's relations with other persons are indexed under the names of those persons. He composed special 'characters' of many people, and these we indicate in boldface. His opinions are indexed under the various subjects themselves.

Works not by Swift appear under the author's name or, if that is not known, under the title. Peers are usually entered under their best-known title. Saints are entered under their own names, but places named after them are entered under 'St.' If no country is specified, a place may be presumed to be English. Names of fictitious persons generally appear between inverted commas.

In some long articles, important keywords are printed in boldface. Cross-references to main entries are printed in capitals, but cross-references to other subheadings within the same article are in italics. Within many articles there are not only subheadings under the general, main heading but further divisions of subtopics under these. We print a dash before such subtopics to show that the reference goes back to the preceding subheading and not to the general, main heading.

The miscellaneous information provided by the index will, we hope, make up, to some extent, for the lack of a commentary throughout the separate volumes. No reader will feel more vexed by the errors and inconsistencies than the general editor, who will welcome suggestions for the improvement of the index, addressed to him at the University of Virginia.

I.E.

The volumes in the Library edition of THE PROSE WRITINGS OF JONATHAN SWIFT are numbered as follows:

I. A Tale of a Tub with Other Early Works 1696–1707
II. Bickerstaff Papers and Pamphlets on the Church
III. The Examiner and Other Pieces Written in 1710–11
IV. A Proposal for Correcting the English Tongue. Polite Conversation, Etc.
V. Miscellaneous and Autobiographical Pieces. Fragments and Marginalia
VI. Political Tracts 1711–1713
VII. The History of the Four Last Years of the Queen
VIII. Political Tracts 1713–1719
XI. Irish Tracts 1720–1723 and Sermons
X. The Drapier's Letters and Other Works 1724–1725
XI. Gulliver's Travels 1726
XII. Irish Tracts 1728–1733
XIII. Directions to Servants and Miscellaneous Pieces 1733–1742
XIV. Index. Addenda, Errata, Corrigenda

A

A., Tom: *see* ASHE.

Abbeville, Somme, France: III. 212.

Abbreviations: *see* CONTRACTIONS AND ABBREVIATIONS.

Abercorn, James Hamilton, 6th Earl of, *c.* 1661-1734: and proposal for Bank of Ireland, IX. xix, 311; and *Drapier's Letters*, X. xiii; Privy Councillor and Wood's coins, X. 182.

Abernethy, John, 1680-1740, Irish Dissenting clergyman: *The Nature and Consequences of the Sacramental Test Considered* (1731), XII. xliii.

Abingdon, Montagu Venables-Bertie, 2nd Earl of, *c.* 1673-1743: Macky and JS on, V. 259.

Abjuration Bill, 1702: and Dissenters, II. 125.

'Above board': a gambling term, V. 278.

Abraham, Old Testament patriarch: and free masons, V. 329; and *Polite Conversation*, IV. 167; pun upon name, IV. 239; and Sodom, IX. 238.

Absenteeism, Irish: XII. xxiii; and agriculture, X. 140; and clerical landlords, IX. 58; condemned, IX. ii, 128, 200; XII. xix, xxiii, 6, 9-10, 55, 66-7, 78, 207; and value of gold, XIII. 119-20; history of, XII. 132-3; income of nation wasted, X. 97-8, 128, 140; XII. 20, 66, 71, 76-7, 81, 132, 207; office-holders, IX. 7; recommended ironically, XII. 176; rich absentees, X. 4-5; and Roman Catholicism, XII. 114; ruins country, IX. 200; XII. 80, 136-7; JS condemns, IX. 11, 128; tax on, XII. 116, 126; and wine tax, XII. 125-6; and Wood's coins, X. 22; writings on, XII. xvi.

Absolution: Lord Herbert and JS on, V. 248.

Abstract of the History of England from the Invasion of It by Julius Caesar to William the Conqueror, by JS: **V.** 1-7; analysis, V. ix; erratum, XIV. 53; textual notes, V. 349.

Absurdities, Kingdom of: I. xl.

Académie Française: I. 65; and JS's academy, IV. xiv, 14.

Academies, Italian: I. 65.

Academy, JS's proposed: aims of, IV. 14-21; membership, IV. 14; and Oxford, IV. 14, 16-21; political overtones, IV. xii-xiii; precedents for, IV. 14; previous proposals, IV. xiv; JS's scheme, IV. xi-xvi, 13-16.

Academy of Lagado, described in *Gulliver's Travels*, Book III, and partly modelled on the Royal Society: begging, XI. 179; blind paint mixers, XI. 180; cobwebs for cloth, XI. 180-1; malleability of fire, IX. 180; founded about 1662, XI. 176-7; gunpowder from ice, XI. 180; construction of houses, XI. 180;

improvement of the language, XI. 185–6; medicine, XI. 187–8; improving ministers' memories, XI. 188; physicians, XI. 181; plowing with hogs, XI. 180; political reforms, XI. 188–9, 190–1; reclamation of food from waste, XI. 179–80; naked sheep, XI. 182; sunbeams from cucumbers, XI. 179; word machine, XI. 182–4.

'Academy of Modern Bedlam': I. 105.

'Academy of the Beaux Esprits', imaginary Australian institution: I. 171.

'Acamoth', word taken from Irenaeus' account of the doctrines of Valentinus the Gnostic and meaning 'Wisdom' (Hebrew 'hokhma'): I. 119 and *n*.†, *n*.*.

Acapulco, Mexico: VI. 22.

Accadie, or Acadia: *see* NOVA SCOTIA.

Accomplishment of the First of Mr. Bickerstaff's Predictions (1708), by JS: **II. 151–5**; analysis, II. xii, xiv; authorship, II. xii; composition, II. 153; editions, II. 286; publication, II. xii, 287; textual notes, II. 287; title-page facsimile, II. 151; quotation, II. xi, *n*. 1.

'Account of England by an Indian King': *see* SPECTATOR, No. 50.

Account of the Court and Empire of Japan (*c.* 1728), by JS: **V. 99–107**; editions, V. 351; publication, V. xiv, xv.

Account of the Short Life . . . of Michy Windybank (1721), probably by JS: **IX. 308–10**; background, IX. xvi–xvii, xix–xxi; 'Key', IX. 311; textual notes, IX. 378.

Achaea: and Greece, I. 202.

Achaean League: I. 210.

Acheson, Sir Arthur, 5th Baronet, 1688–1749, of Market Hill, co. Armagh, Ireland: and Carteret, XII. xxviii, 166–8; possibly 'a Person of Quality', XII. 79; JS and Creichton visit him, V. xvii, 120; and JS's *History of the Four Last Years*, VII. xii; JS visits him, XII. xvii, xviii; — visits him (1728–29), VII. xii; — visits him (1730), V. xvi.

Acheson, Lady, *née* Anne Savage, *d.* 1737, wife of Sir Arthur: and JS's *History of the Four Last Years*, VII. xii–xiii; JS orders things for her, V. xviii; — visits her (1728–29), VII. xii.

Achilles: and Ajax, IV. 233; and Homer, I. 242; pun upon name, IV. 232–3.

Act for the Better Securing the Dependence of the Kingdom of Ireland upon the Crown of Great Britain, 1720: *see* DEPENDENCY ACT.

Act for the Preservation of the Inheritance, Rights, and Profits of Lands Belonging to the Church, and Persons Ecclesiastical, 1634: *see* LIMITATION ACT, IRISH.

Act of Explanation, Irish, so-called by JS, but properly A Bill for the Explanation of the Act of Settlement, 1665: and Irish dioceses, IX. 46.

Act of Settlement, Irish, 1660: and Irish dioceses, IX. 46.

'Action', a share in a joint stock company: III. 67.

Actium, Battle of, 31 B.C.: V. xi, 85; XI. 200.

Actors ('players'): conversation, IX. 336-7.

Adam: Josephus on, IV. 46; pride humbled, IX. 273.

Addison, Joseph, 1672-1719, author, statesman, friend of JS: and Bible, IX. 330; borrows Bickerstaff pseudonym, II. 141, n.*; and Richard Blackmore, V. xxxiii, 254; and Lord Blayney, V. xxiv; and Congreve, II. xiv, n.; in conversation, V. 235; and Craggs, XII. 48; *The Freeholder*, V. xxxiii, 251-5; — **JS's marginalia** (written 1727), **V. 251-5**; — — background, V. xxxiii; letter to Halifax, II. xxii, n. 2; on Irish Whigs, IX. 30; Keeper of the Records (in Ireland), X. 58; Oxford esteems him, VIII. xxxv; pun upon name, IV. 275; and Scriblerus Club, XI. xiii, n. 2; and Stella, V. 235; fond of Stella, V. 229; on the sublime, IX. 344; **and JS**, II. xxxi, VIII. 122; — JS introduces him to Blayney, V. xxiv; — not friendly, II. xxxvi, xxxvii; — friendship, II. xxxiii; IX. 29-30; — still on good terms (1717), V. xxxiii; — intimacy in Ireland, III. xx; — and English language, IV. 16 and n.*; — JS recommends him to Oxford, IX. 29; — and *Proposal for Correcting, Improving and Ascertaining the English Tongue*, IV. 287; — and *Whig Examiner*, 28 Sept. 1710, III. xix, 26-7; — JS allegedly

protects him, VII. xxxv; — as JS's 'younger brother', III. 26-7; and *Tatler*, II. xxv-xxvi and n. 1; and authorship of *Tatler*, II. xxviii; — *Tatler* No. 32, II. xxx; contributions to *Tatler*, II. xxxi; Wharton's secretary, V. xxiv, VIII. 121-2, IX. 30; and Wharton's speech, IX. 20.

Address: *see also* 'HUMBLE ADDRESS'.

'Address of the County of Dublin': *see* DRAPIER'S LETTERS.

'Address of the Privy Council of Ireland': *see* DRAPIER'S LETTERS.

Adela or Adeliza (Adelais), Queen of England, *d. c.* 1151, daughter of Godfrey 'Barbatus' of Louvain, 2nd wife of Henry I: marries Henry I (1120), V. 41; receives Matilda (or Maud) the Empress, V. 57.

Adela, or Adelicia, *c.* 1062-1137, daughter of William I, mother of Stephen: V. 41, 263.

Adelais: *see* ADELA.

Adrian IV, *c.* 1100-59, Pope; and Henry II, V. 75, 76.

Advantages Proposed by Repealing the Sacramental Test, Impartially Considered (1732), by JS: **XII. 241-51**; background, XII. xl-xli, 243; editions, XII. xli, xlvii, 345; publication, XII. xli, 241; textual notes, XII. 345-6; title page facsimile, XII. 241.

'Adventure', ship in *Gulliver's Travels*: XI. 80, 83-5.

Advertisement by Dr. Swift, in His Defence Against Joshua, Lord Allen (1730), by JS: **XII. 141**; background, XII. xxiv-xxv; textual notes, XII. 337.

Advertisement Concerning the Theft of Lead from St. Patrick's Roof: see ST. PATRICK'S CATHEDRAL.

Advertisement for the Honour of the Kingdom of Ireland: see FOR THE HONOUR OF THE KINGDOM.

Advertisements: JS censures, II. xxix, 236–7.

Advertisements about Endowments: see WILL OF JS, *and St. Patrick's Hospital.*

Advice Humbly Offer'd to the Members of the October Club (1712), by JS: **VI. 69–80**; background, VI. xii–xiii; composition, VI. xi–xiii; editions, VI. 209; 'Publisher's Preface', probably by JS, **VI. 187–8**; textual notes, VI. 209; title-page facsimile, VI. 69.

Advice to the Free-men of the City of Dublin in the Choice of a Member to Represent them in Parliament (1733), by JS: **XIII. 79–85**; background, XIII. xxiv–xxv; publication, XIII. xxv; textual notes, XIII. 221.

Aeneas: and Virgil, I. 242.

Aeolists, fanatical sect in *Tale of a Tub* (representing Dissenters): I. 95–100, 101, and *passim*; founded by Jack, I. 89.

Aeolus, Greek god of the winds: I. 98; V. 207.

Aesculapius, Greek god of medicine: saves Richard Blackmore, I. 158.

Aesop, *c.* 6th century B.C., traditional author of Greek fables: and Bentley, I. 139; in *Dr. Bentley's Dissertation ... Examin'd*, I. xvii, n.†; frightens Bentley, I. 162; and Grub Street, I. 40.

Aesop and others, *Fables (Aesopi phrygis fabulae*, a schoolbook), allusions and quotations: fly on chariot wheel, by Laurentius Abstemius, II. 115; fox who lost his tail, XII. 60; frog and bull, XII. 133; lion's share, VI. 94; spider and bee, I. 150–1.

Aethiopie, Histoire d': XI. xiv.

Afra: see BEHN, APHRA.

Africans: and the Bible, IV. 33; slave trade, XII. 135, 310.

Agapetus I, St., Pope, *d.* 536: and Anthimus, XIV. 31; funeral, XIV. 31; JS condemns his injustice, XIV. 31.

Agesilaus, *c.* 444–361 B.C., King of Sparta; and Carteret, XII. 161; and Gulliver, XI. 198.

Agis IV, *c.* 262–241 B.C., King of Sparta: and Spartan restoration, I. 210.

Aglionby, Dr. William, *d.* 1705, Envoy Extraordinary to Switzerland, 1702–5: Macky and JS on, V. 261.

Agricola, Gnaeus Julius, A.D. 37–93, Roman general: III. 149; and conquest of Britain, IV. 280.

Agriculture (in Ireland, except as indicated): and absenteeism, X. 140; acreage, IX. 318; bishops improve, IX. 55; and bogs, XII. 87–8; and Carteret, XII. xi; clergy improve, IX. 59; corn famine, XII. 17–20; price of corn, IX. 15; and national debt, XII. 210; encouragement needed, XII. 79, 89; — laws needed, X. 119; England discourages, IX. 15; and imports from England, IX. 48; English and Irish compared, X. 129; farming: *see*

FARMERS; and financial investments, IX. 293; forestry, X. 139; XII. 88; — notes for *Intelligencer*, XII. 306; and grazing, XII. xi–xii, 89, 175–8; — censured, X. 139; XII. 17–9; land mismanaged, IX. 47; limited, XII. 66–7; and manufactures, X. 141; and *Modest Proposal*, XII. 110–1; plowing prohibited, IX. 15; XII. 17–8; and political factions, XII. 22–3; — more valuable than politics, X. 141; — 'whoever could make . . . two blades of grass to grow . . . would deserve better of mankind', XI. 135–6; and populousness, IV. 249; poverty ruins, XIII. 176; prosperity of nation depends on, VII. 69; — 'first cause of a kingdom's thriving', XII. 5–9; scraws, X. 140; and sheep-raising, IX. 15–6; increase of tillage, XIII. xli; turf, X. 139–40; writings on, XII. xvi. *See also* FARMERS; POPULATION.

'Agrippa' in *Examiner*, XIV. 4.

Agrippa, Marcus Vipsanius, *c.* 62–12 B.C., Roman military leader: XI. 201.

Ailesbury, Thomas Bruce, 2nd Earl of, 1656–1741, courtier of James II, imprisoned as a Jacobite, 1690, 1696: and Oxford, VIII. 124.

Aire, Pas de Calais, France: VII. 113.

Airlie, James Ogilvy, 2nd Earl of, *c.* 1615–1703: V. 140, 145, 162.

Airs Moss, a swamp in Ayr, Scotland: V. 147, 157.

Aix-la-Chapelle, i.e., Aachen, Germany: proposed site of peace conference, VII. 37, 39.

Aix-la-Chapelle, Peace of, 1668: and Temple, I. 257, 259, 270.

Ajax: pun upon name, IV. 233; and sheep, XII. 19.

Alaric, *c.* 370–410, Gothic military leader: Rome ('Urbs') given up to him, XIV. 32.

Albemarle, Arnold Joost van Keppel, 1st Earl of, 1670–1718: VII. 146–7, 152; at Denain, XIV. 13; Macky and JS on, V. 259.

Albemarle, Stephen, Earl of: *see* AUMALE.

Albion: legendary name for England, V. 5.

Alcibiades, 450–404 B.C., Athenian general and statesman: III. xix, 26; and Bolingbroke, VIII. 134; fall from power, I. 207–8; symbol for Lord Halifax, I. 207–8.

Alcides: *see* HERCULES, IV. 234.

Alciphron, character in Berkeley's dialogue: freethinker, IX. 115.

Aldershot, Hampshire: home of Charles Viner, XIII. 207.

Aldrovandi, Ulisse, 1522–1605, Italian naturalist: I. 161.

Aldus: *see* MANUTIUS.

Alessandria: *see* ALEXANDRIA.

Alexander VI, 1431–1503, Pope (Borgia): VIII. 77.

Alexander, Bishop of Lincoln, *d.* 1148: V. 56.

Alexander ab Alexandro: IV. 238.

Alexander the Great, 356–323 B.C.: III. 19; V. 83; and Aristotle, IX. 244–5; and Athens, I. 205; and Bucephalus, IV. 238–9; and Diogenes, I. 248; compared to George I, X. 138;

and Greece, I. 208–10; insane, I. 107; Josephus on, IV. 46; pun on name, IV. xxxvii, 236.

Alexandria, province in Northern Italy: VI. 13.

Alexius Mikhailovich, Czar of Muscovy, 1629–1676: V. 155

Algiers, Dey of: V. 93.

Alienation, Court of: and Beaux Esprits, II. 258-9.

All Souls College, Oxford: and Church unity, II. 92.

Allegory: 'to avoid giving offense', I. 173–4; JS would have his allegories understood, III. 58.

Allen, Joshua, 1685–1742, 2nd Viscount: and *Advertisement by Dr. Swift, in His Defence against Joshua, Lord Allen*, XII. xxv; and Drapier, X. xx; and *A Libel on Doctor Delany*, XII. xxv; attacks JS, XII. 141, 145 and n.*, 146; delays JS's freedom of Dublin, XII. xxv–xxvi; 'Traulus', XII. xxvii, xxix, 157–8; and *A Vindication of Lord Carteret*, XII. xxvii; his wife, XII. xxx.

Allies: *see* GRAND ALLIANCE.

Allusiveness in literature: I. 80–1, 133; inaccessible to posterity, II. 32; and Tindal, II. 80–1. *See also* ALLEGORY.

Almanac-makers: censured, II. 141–44, 149–50; praised by Partridge, II. 203–4.

Almanza, Spain, Battle of, 1707: II. 143, III. 149; predicted by Bickerstaff, II. 203, 206; Godolphin ministry blamed, III. 149; and worms, II. 76.

Almelo, Count of: *see* RECHTEREN.

Alnwick Castle, Northumberland: V. 18.

Alsace, or Alsatia, province of France: VI. 38; VII. 113.

Alsatia, a precinct of Whitefriars in London (a resort of criminals): II. 85.

Altranstadt, Treaty of, 1707: VI. 62–3.

Alt Rastadt: *see* ALTRANSTADT.

Ambition: clergy not especially ambitious, II. 10; and creeping, I. 245; and discretion, XII. 38–45; fame as incentive, II. 241; of kings, XI. 53, 171; and poverty, IX. 192; spider's life, I. 244.

'Amboyna', Dutch ship in *Gulliver's Travels*: XI. 217.

Amboyna Massacre, 1624: allusion to, XI. 217.

Ambrose, St., *c.* 340–97: on Eugenius, XIV. 17; miracle, XIV. 18.

America: drought, XII. 176; and Irish beggars, XII. 136; and Irish emigration, XII. 58-60, 66, 67, 76–81; Irish imports from, XII. 127; money in, XII. 58; Penn on, XII. 76; religion neglected in British colonies, XIV. 10; Roman Catholicism in, XIV. 27. *See also* INDIANS, AMERICAN.

Ammianus, Marcellinus, *c.* A.D. 330–*c.* 391, Roman historian: I. 49, *n.*; and Tindal, II. 93.

Amsterdam: and the Assiento, VII. 123; Austria denied a loan, VII. 157.

Anabaptists: I. 88, *n.* 11; III. 144; attack Church of England, II. 3; and freethinkers, IV. 31; Jesuits disguised as, II. 37; and Test Act, II. 119.

Anacreon, ancient Greek poet: death, I. 250.

Anagrams: XI. 191–2, 311.

Analytical Discourse upon Zeal, Histori-Theo-Physi-Logically Considered, imaginary treatise by the author of *Tale of a Tub*: I. xxvii, xl, 86.

Anandall: *see* ANNANDALE.

Anastasius I, Byzantine emperor, *c.* 430–518: JS praises, XIV. 27.

Anastasius Bibliothecarius, *d.* 887, scholar, reputed author of *Liber pontificalis*: JS ridicules, XIV. 32.

Ancestry: nobility an advantage, III. 150–1. *See also* NOBILITY.

Ancients and Moderns controversy: I. xxix and *n.**, 25, 1–165; in France, I. xxix; and Temple, I. 262–3.

Ancus Marcius, legendary King of Rome: I. 212; and 'the sons of a former' king, I. 213.

Anderson, James, *c.* 1680–1739; author of Masonic song, V. 331.

Andromache: and Astyanax, IV. 234; pun upon name, IV. 233–4.

Angers, Maine-et-Loire, France: V. 67.

Angles: and 'England', V. 5.

Anglican Church: *see* CHURCH OF ENGLAND; CHURCH OF IRELAND; CHURCH, EPISCOPAL, IN SCOTLAND.

Anglo-Angli: and *Polite Conversation*, IV. 276–7.

Anglo-Saxon language: V. 5.

Anibal: *see* HANNIBAL.

Animals, fear of: XI. 91.

Anjou, Duke of: *see* PHILIP II, KING OF SPAIN.

Anjou, Earl or Count of: *see* FULK V; GEOFFREY.

Anna Maria, Duchess of Savoy, 1669–1728, wife of Victor Amadeus II, granddaughter of Charles I, grandmother of Louis XV: VIII. 54–5.

Annandale, William Johnston, 2nd Earl, 1st Marquis of, 1664–1721: V. 162.

Annapolis Royal, in Nova Scotia: VII. 115, 132.

Anne, Queen of England, 1665–1714: and JS's academy, IV. 17, 18; accession, I. xxi; Fleetwood's sermon on her accession, VI. 194–5; political changes upon her accession, I. xxi; refuses advice, VIII. 144; and the army, III. 44–5; attacks upon, VIII. 92; — foreseen (1713), VIII. xxxiii; reproves Bolingbroke, VIII. 166–7; makes Bolingbroke only a viscount, VIII. xxxiii; Bothmar provokes her, VII. 144; and Burnet, IV. 62, 67, 74–5, 80, 82, 83; **change of ministry (1710)**, III. xiii–xiv, 49, 198–201, 202–5; VII. 34, 73; VIII. 81–2, 101–3, 107–28, 142, 166–7; — caution in, III. 132–3; — would retain Cowper and Somers, VIII. 103, 'two great officers', 142, 167; — freedom following, VI. 79; — Gallas on, VII. 58; — and Marlborough, III. 19–20; — Mrs. Masham and Oxford solely responsible, VIII. 109; — Oxford's responsibility for, VI. 75; — and reconciliation of parties, VIII. 83; — precedents for, III. 135; — her 'prudence, courage, and firmness', VI. 44; — reasons for, III. xxvi, 3–8, 31–4, 37–40, 94–5; VII. 12; — reasons drama-

tized, VI. 44–5; — her reluctance, VIII. 103; **character**, III. 61–2; VI. 44; VIII. 103, 178; — observer of forms, VIII. 110–1; — impassive, VIII. 110; — opinionated, VIII. 160; — procrastinating, VIII. 137; — reputation of, VI. 93; — 'uncertain timorous nature', VIII. xxiv, 82; 'the latter' and Charles VI, VII. 58; and **Church of England**, III. 16–7, VIII. 112; — 'Queen Anne's bounty' (1704, 'a noble benefaction'), III. 48; — act to build fifty churches in London, III. 157–62; — Convocation, III. 200; — — her letter of 1710, III. 49–50; — and lower clergy, III. 50–1; — loyalty to, I. xxi; — Steele on, VIII. 39; and Cowper, VIII. 142–3; and Creichton, the physician, V. 125–6; **her death**, VII. xxxiii–xxxix; IX. 25; — Austria eager for (1714), VIII. 58; — expected (1712–14), VIII. 173; — expected (1712), VII. 121, 124; — expected (1713), VII. 164; expected by Oxford (1713), VIII. 157; — and Hanoverian succession, V. 104; — Oxford on, VIII. 154; — ends Oxford ministry, VII. xii; — and Parliament, V. 284; — rumored (1712), VII. 152; — rumored (1713), VIII. 154; — and JS, VIII. 131; — and JS's *History of the Four Last Years*, VII. xi; — JS's return to Ireland, IX. xii; — and JS's *Some Free Thoughts*, VIII. xxv, xxviii; — and Treaty of Utrecht, VII. xi; — Whig Junto awaits (1712), VI. 132; — Whig Junto awaits (1714), VIII. 89–90; — and Whig rise to power, VIII. xxviii–xxix; — and Whigs, VIII. 140–1; — Whigs eager for, VIII. 53, 190; — Whigs' 'horrible expectations', VIII. 21; and Dunkirk, VIII. 23; offended by Dutch accusations, VII. 53; Dutch benefit by her reign, VII. 53; insulted by Dutch collusion with Whigs, VII. 110–11; and employments, VIII. 150–51; and Prince Eugene of Savoy, IV. xxxvii, 216; VII. 111; receives Eugene (1712), VII. 24; a 'female man', XI. 243; and First Fruits of the Church of Ireland, III. 48, 52, 74, 170; IX. ix; XII. 186; France acknowledges her (1701), VI. 13; France will not acknowledge her (1702), VI. 94–5; France to acknowledge her (1709), VI. 105; and freethinkers, IV. 31, 33; and throne of France, VIII. 55; expels Gallas from court (1711), VII. 58–9; and George I, VIII. 67, 68, 93–4, 174–5, 176–7; and George II's writ, VII. 175; and Godolphin, I. 268; VIII. 111; — her early disfavour, VIII. 101; — and her dealings with Oxford, VIII. 102; — would remove Godolphin (1707), VIII. 112; and Godolphin ministry, VI. 79; VIII. 24; — they abuse her, III. 201; — they coerce her, VIII. 113; — they oppress her, III. 93–6; guards, VIII. 89–90, 155–6; false musters in guards, III. 170; Guiscard's plot to kill her, III. 110; and Hanoverian succession, II. xvii; VII. xxxvi;

VIII. 164–80; **health** — in 'bad state' (1712), VII. 121; — gout, VIII. 177; — gout (1711), VI. viii; — gout (1712), VII. 31; — illness rumoured (1712), VII. 152; — illness delays Parliament (1712), VII. 31; — reported ill (1713), VII. 164; — illness (1713), VIII. 154; — illness (Dec. 1713), effect on stocks, VIII. xvi; — illness (Dec. 1713), Whigs exploit, VIII. xvi, 90, 183–97; — vigorous (1709), VI. 98; Heinsius, VII. 37–8; and Indian Kings, II. VII. 38; and Indian Kings, II. 265; and Irish Dissenters, II. 133; and Irish Whigs, II. 118; Jacobitism alleged unfairly, VII. xxxiii; and John V of Portugal, V. 125–6; and Joseph I, VII. 58; and Archbishop King, II. 282; Empress of Lilliput partly modelled on, XI. 30–72; cousinship to Louis XIV, VII. 48; VIII. 60; loyalty to, II. 13; **and Marlborough,** V. 85, VII. 22; — would be captain-general for life, VII. 22; VIII. 114–7; — allegedly competing, VII. 29; — her death to be rumoured on his return (1711), VII. 28; — disfavour, III. xvii; — his disloyalty, VII. 29; — dismissal, VII. 30; VIII. 109, 111; — regrets attending dismissal, VIII. 103; — 'her first displeasure', VII. 22; — her grant (1702) fails, III. 94; VI. 130; — and John Hill's regiment (1707), VIII. 112; — allegedly jeopardizes her, VII. 29; — and prerogative, VIII. 116–17; and Lady Masham, VIII. 112; Lady Masham and

Oxford, VIII. 115–16; and ministers, XI. 318; — (1702), III. 94; moderating scheme, VIII. 116; and moderation, IX. 178; and national morals, II. 47–63; as 'Nena, Empress of Japan', V. 99–107; and 'no peace without Spain', VIII. 146–7, 167; 'Norway's Pride', II. 165, 168, 169 and *n.**; finds Nottingham unacceptable, VII. 15, 16; obeisance to, II. 14; **and Oxford,** VIII. 157; — desires his assistance (*c.* 1708), VIII. 116; — compliance hurts him, VIII. 152–3; — his credit at an end (1713), VIII. 159; — on her death, VIII. 154; — and employments, VIII. 142–4; — the end, VIII. 157–8; — esteems him, VII. 73; esteems him early, VIII. 101; — and his impeachment, VIII. 149; — indebtedness to him, VII. 29; — meet secretly (1707), VIII. 102; — meet secretly (1710), VIII. 115–16; — he allegedly rescues her ('prince') VII. 74; — rift, VIII. 154; — he exposes Whigs to her, VII. 20; **and Oxford ministry** — Anne reluctant to be advised, VIII. xxxiii; — her reasons for change (1710), VII. 12; — 'her own free choice', VIII. 48; — they allegedly coerce her, VII. 18; — her share in disintegration, VIII. 160, 161; — ended by her death, VII. xii; — compared with Godolphin's, VI. 71; — and Marlborough's dismissal, VII. 29–30; VIII. 13; — alleged to oppose them (1711), VI. 124; — dislikes restraint, VI. 79; VIII.

146-7; — Steele's views derided, VIII. 22; — treat her well, III. 201; act of general pardon (1708, 'a law'), III. 29; **and Parliament** — amenable to Commons, VII. 2; — her speech (1710), III. 32; — her speech (1711), VII. 17; — Commons' 'dutiful address' (1711) and her reply, VII. 18; — Lords' address (1711), and her reply, VII. 17, 18; — message to Commons (1712), VII. 31; — her speech (1712), VII. 130-4, 151, 152; — — Commons' reply, VII. 134; — — Dutch publish, VII. 136; — — printing, VII. 241; — speech (9 Apr. 1713), VI. 201-3; VIII. 174-5; creation of twelve peers (1712), VII. 20-1; VIII. 15, 23, 148-50; — justification, VI. 132; — 'a resolute necessary step', VI. 124-5; and political parties, VIII. 167-8; and royal prerogative, VI. 123-5; 127, 165, 167-8; VIII. 112; royal prerogative and Ireland, III. 183; and the Pretender, V. 293; VIII. 31, 71-2, 141, 164-79; — her contempt for Pretender, VIII. 178; questions birth of Old Pretender (1688), V. 289; and Prince George's death (1708), VIII. 112-13; and JS's *Project for the Advancement of Religion*, II. xx-xxi; continued prosperity predicted, II. 149; and Protestant succession, II. xvii; VIII. 164-79; 'happy reign' and 'glorious memory' emphasized, VII. xxxiii; and Earl Rivers, VIII. 117; and Duke of Savoy: *see* VICTOR; and Somers, VIII.

142-3; favours Somerset and his Duchess, VII. 13, 14; Somerset misrepresents her, VII. 15, 16; VIII. 147; — respects her, VII, 13; and Duchess of Somerset, VI. 71; VII. 13, 14; VIII. 146, 153; Steele's praise cut short, VIII. 22; Steele vilifies her, VIII. 20; and the succession, V. 292; VII. 26; *see also Hanoverian Succession*; likened to the sun, III. 39; and Sunderland, VIII. 112, 118; — abuses her, III. 80; — his rudeness, VII. 6, 9; **and JS**, VIII. 10; IX. ix; — his character of her, VIII. 110-11; — his criticism, VIII. xxiv, xxxiii, 146-51, 160; — and historiographer's post, VIII. 200; — his 'indulgent royal mistress', VII. 175; — medal, XIII. 156; — under no obligation to her, VII. xxxiv; — political power, IX. ix; — to preach before her, IX. 97; — seeks preferments, VIII. xxxi; — and his *Publick Spirit of the Whigs*, VIII. xxi-xxii, 30; — proclamation against *Publick Spirit of the Whigs*, VIII. 198-9; — JS's seals belonging to, XIII. 154; one of 'three children', II. 21; and Test Act, II. 112; and Tindal, II. 87; and Tories, I. xxi; VIII. 108; Tories alleged to coerce her, VII. 18; favours Tories (1713), VIII. 154-5; and Trarbach, VIII. 59; and Treaty of Utrecht — desires peace, VII. 48; — speech to Parliament (June 1712), VII. 130-4; — her titles disputed, VII. 165; and Walpole, X. 102; and War of the Spanish Succession — peace

preliminaries, VI. viii; **and Whigs,** IV. 282-3; VIII. 19; — abused by, VIII. 56; — abandons them, VIII. 154-5; — permanent aversion from them (1712), VI. 126, 132; — at court, VIII. 67; — and joy at her death, VIII. 183-97; — despises them (1714), VIII. 98; — she fails to discourage (Dec. 1711), VII. 18; — hates them, VIII. 154-5; — her illness pleases, VIII. 154; — allegedly jeopardize her life, (1714), VIII, 89-90; — some loyal to her, VI. 187-8; — attacks on her ministers, VIII. 48; — accused of opposing her, VII. 1; — opposition, IV. 76; — threaten her security, VII. 12; — early sympathies, VIII. 121; and Whitworth, V. 85. *See also* SOME REASONS TO PROVE.

Anne Boleyn, Queen of England, 1507-1536, 2nd wife of Henry VIII: whore, V. 247.

Annesley, Sir Francis, 1585-1660 (1622, Viscount Valentia), statesman: his trial ('certain proceedings'), X. 131.

Annists: XII. 169.

Anonymity, JS's views: Bickerstaff pseudonym, II. 144, 204; XIII. 181; and *Drapier's Letters,* XII. 122; and erroneous conjecture, III. 29-30; and JS's *Proposal for Correcting . . . the English Tongue,* IV. xi-xii; and JS's *Proposal that All the Ladies and Women of Ireland Should Appear Constantly in Irish Manufactures,* XII. 122; affords protection, II. 2; and religious writing, VII. 105; and *Tatler,* II. 173 *n.**; in

vice and virtue, XII. 29-31; wit and learning furthered by, VII. 105-6.

Another Letter to Mr. Harding the Printer: see DRAPIER'S LETTERS.

Anselm, St., 1033-1109, Archbishop of Canterbury: his death, V. 34; restored by Henry I, V. 28; and William II, V. 16-17; his zeal attenuated, V. 34.

Answer of the Right Honourable William Pulteney, Esq., to the Right Honourable Sir Robert Walpole (1730), probably by JS: **V. 111-19;** authorship, V. xv-xvi; editions, V. xvi; textual note, V. 351.

Answer to a Paper, Called a Memorial of the Poor . . . of Ireland (1728), by JS: **XII. 15-25;** authorship, XII. xii, 15; background, XII. xii-xiv; composition, XII. xii, 17, 25; editions, XII. 324; publication, XII. xii, 15; textual notes, XII. 324-5; title page facsimile, XII. 15.

Answer to Bickerstaff (written 1708), possibly by JS: **II. 195-9;** authorship, II. xii; background, II. x-xii; publication, II. xii; reception predicted, II. 197; textual notes, II. 290.

Answer to declaration of inhabitants of the liberty of St. Patrick's: *see* ST. PATRICK'S CATHEDRAL, *liberty.*

Answer to Several Letters from Unknown Persons (written 1729), by JS: **XII. 75-81;** composition, XII. xvi, xvii; manuscript, XII. xvi, 331; publication, XII. xvi-xvii; textual notes, XII. 331.

Answer to Several Letters Sent Me from Unknown Hands (written 1729), by JS: **XII. 85-90;** composition, XII. xvi, xvii, 85; editions, XII. 332; publication, XII. xvi–xvii; textual notes, XII. 332; allusion to ('answer'), XII. 75; possible allusion to, XII. 66.

Answer to the Conduct of the Allies: VI. x, 65.

Answer to the Craftsman (written *c.* 1730), by JS: **XII. 173-8;** authorship, XII. xxxi; background, XII. xxx–xxxi, 311–21; editions, XII. xxxi, 339; and *Modest Proposal*, XII. xxx–xxxi, 173; textual notes, XII. 339.

Answer to the Injured Lady: *see* STORY OF THE INJURED LADY.

Answer to the Occasional Writer, No. II: attack on Bolingbroke and JS, V. xiv.

Answer to the Proposal for the Universal Use of Irish Manufactures: *see* DEFENCE OF ENGLISH COMMODITIES.

'Answerall, Lady,' character in *Polite Conversation*: IV, 129–201, *passim*, 276–7.

Answers to books: JS's views on, I. 4–5.

'Antelope', ship on which Gulliver sails: XI. 20.

Anthems: V. 334.

Anthimus, monophysite Patriarch of Constantinople (deposed in A.D. 536): and Pope Agapetus, XIV. 31.

Antient and Modern Learning: *see* WOTTON, WILLIAM.

Antioch, Turkey: and the Crusades, V. 22.

Antiochus III, 'the Great', 223–187 B.C., Seleucidian ruler: V, 86.

Antipater, *c.* 398–319 B.C., Macedonian general: and Phocion, I. 209–10.

Antiquity, classical: and Christianity, IX. 111; education, IX. 155–6.

Antonius, Marcus, or Mark Antony, *c.* 83–30 B.C., Roman general: at Actium, XI. 201; mean figure, V. xi, 85; profligate, I. 222; the last triumvirate, VI. 80.

Antoninus Pius, A.D. 86–161, Roman emperor: his 'Picts' Wall', which Severus repaired, V. 4.

Antrim, county of Ireland: and Scots, II. 116.

Ants: XI. 127.

Anus: size of, in Irish and English, XII. 220–1.

Anytus, *fl.* 399 B.C., Athenian politician: and Socrates, XII. 24.

Apocrypha: authority, I. 52, *n.**. *See also* BIBLE, QUOTATIONS AND ALLUSIONS, *Apocrypha*.

Apollo: in *Battle of the Books*, aids Temple and Boyle, I. 163; forefather of Sir John Denham, I. 157; Josephus on, IV. 46; and Parnassus, IV. 252; and physicians, IV. 247; and Wotton, I. 162.

Apollonius of Tyana, first century A.D., Greek philosopher: insane, I. 105.

'Aposiopesis': VI. 155.

Appearances (physical, material) *vs.* reality, JS's views: I. xxxvii, 107–10.

Appendix to Dr. Swift's Works, 1767: V. xxxiii.

Appointment of Wynne as Sub-Dean of St. Patrick's: see WYNNE.

Apprenticeship: XI. 62.

Apprenticeships, Irish: over-supply, IX. 203.

Appius, family of: hated by Roman commons, I. 215.

April Fool's Day: IV. 259–60, 267.

Apulia, region of south-eastern Italy: V, 27.

Aquapulco: *see* ACAPULCO.

Aquinas, St. Thomas, *c.* 1227–1274, scholastic philosopher: leads the Moderns, I. 152.

Arabia: and revolutions, I. 174.

Arabians: writing, XI. 57.

Arachne: and Athene, IX. 272–4, 276–7; fable used by JS for Ireland, IX. xv, 18.

Aragon: and Flemings, V. 74.

Aratus of Sicyon, 271–213 B.C., Greek statesman: I. 210.

'Arburman': defined by JS, V. 336.

Arbuthnot, Dr. John, 1667–1735, physician and wit: *Gulliver De-cyphered* attributed to, XI. xxii and *n.* 6; his *History of John Bull,* allusion to 'Squire South', VI. 167; *Memoirs of Martinus Scrib-lerus,* XI. xiii; and *Miscellanies* of JS and Pope, XIII. 204; and Nobel, IV. 260; and Scriblerus Club, XI. xiii; one of 'snarling brood', IV. xxxii, 118; member of 'The Society', XI. xii; intro-duces JS to Princess Caroline, V. xxvii; correspondence with JS, VIII. xxx; and JS's *Gulliver's Travels,* X. xii–xiii, xx–xxi, xxii, *n.* 6.

Arcadius, Byzantine emperor, *c.* 383–408: letter from Innocent I, XIV. 19.

Archer, Richard: acknowledge-ment, XI. 301.

Archimedes, *c.* 287–212 B.C., Greek mathematician: I. 39; IX. 245; and mathematics, I. 249–50; pun upon name, IV. 236.

Architecture: notes on, for *Intelli-gencer,* XII. 306.

Archon, chief magistrate of Athens: I. 205, 211.

Aretino, Pietro, 1492–1557, Italian satirist: his pride, II. 258.

'Argent, Duchess d'', character in *Tale of a Tub*: I. 45–55.

Argia, or Argos: I. 60; riots, I. 199.

Argument to Prove that the Abolishing of Christianity in England May ... Be Attended with Some Inconveniences (written 1708), by JS: **II. 26-39**; background, II. xvii–xix, 191–2; composition, II. xv, 26; editions, II. xv, 277; publication, II. xix–xx; textual notes, II. 277–8; and Whigs, VIII. 122.

Argyle: *see* ARGYLL.

Argyll, Archibald Campbell, 7th Earl of, 1575–1638: Burnet and JS on, V. 266.

Argyll, Archibald Campbell, 1st Marquis of, *c.* 1606–1661: Burnet and JS on, V. 269.

Argyll, Archibald Campbell, 9th Earl of, 1629–1685, royalist: V. 158–60.

Argyll, Archibald Campbell, 2nd Duke of, 1680–1743, general and statesman: and Bolingbroke, VIII. 152; character, V. 261;

Macky and JS, on, V. 261; and Marlborough, VIII. 114–15; and Oxford, VIII. 124; and Oxford ministry, VIII. xxii; and JS's *Publick Spirit of the Whigs*, VIII. xviii–xix, xxi, xxii, xxviii, ('some with great titles') 51; and Tories, VIII. 149; and Whigs, VIII. 166.

Argyll, Archibald Campbell, 3rd Duke of: *see* ILAY.

Arianism: IX. 107; Arians and mission of Pope John I, XIV. 29; philosophical controversy, IX. 160; heresy refuted, IX. 160; JS condemns, IX. 261.

Ariosto, Lodovico, 1474–1533, Italian poet: and advice, I. 241.

Aristides, *c.* 530–468 B.C., Athenian statesman: VIII. 138; fall from power, I. 206–7, 210; impeachment, I. 224; represents Lord Somers in parallel history, I. xx, 14, 206, 210, 224.

Aristides Quintilianus, *c.* 1st century A.D., author of treatise on music: **JS's note on, XIV. 2,** — authenticity, XIV. xi; — textual note, XIV. 43.

Aristophanes: pun upon name, IV. 236; in *Tale of a Tub*, I. xxv; allusions — 'Socrates', in *Clouds*, 218 ff.: I. 33.

Aristotle, 384–322 B.C.: XI. 104, 197–8; and Alexander, IX. 244–5; leads the Ancients, I. 152; fails to 'wound' Bacon, I. 156; and Carteret, XII. 155; **JS's character of, V. 345**; — textual note, V. 359; and Christianity, IX. 113; commentators, XI. 197; his critics, XII. 49; defended, II. 97; and Descartes, I.

146, 156; and his followers, II. 81; IX. 250; on forms of government, II. 15, 84; golden mean, I. 251; on happiness, IX. 246; and Locke, II. 97; deposes Plato, I. 144; pun upon name, IV. 235–6; in sermons, IX. 76; in 'Tables of Fame', II. 241; and tripartite government, II. 83; correct text, IV. 33; unfashionable, II. 97; quotations and allusions — *Dialectica*: I. 51; — — *De interpretatione*: I. 51; — *Metaphysics* XII. 10. 6: VIII. 180; XII. 309. *See also* PROBLEMS OF ARISTOTLE.

Arlington, Henry Bennet, 1st Earl of, *c.* 1620–1685, statesman: Burnet and JS on, V. 268; and Temple, I. 270.

Armada, Spanish: Philip II's disgrace, V. 85.

Armagh, Archbishop of: *see* BOYLE, MICHAEL; MARSH, NARCISSUS; LINDSAY, THOMAS; BOULTER, HUGH.

Armies: British army, — frauds perpetrated, III. 138, 170; — immorality, II. 45, 50–1; — and George I, V. 254; — and change of ministry (1710), III. 44–5; — drink to ruin of Oxford ministry, III. 60; — swearing, IX. 296; — Test Act and officers, II. 123–4; civil authority must rule, III. 43; militia preferred to mercenaries, III. 40–2; XI. 115, 131; raising of, III. 40–2; 'soldier' defined, XI. 246–7; standing army condemned, III. 146, 164; IX. 31–2; XI. 131; — ridiculed, V. 251; and tyranny, V. 20, 180; IX. 33; unnecessary,

XI. 131, 138; naturally desire war, III. 61–3.

Arminians: and religious wars, II. 12.

Armstrong, Sir Thomas, *c.* 1624–1684, royalist: and the Rye House Plot, V. 281.

Arran Island, Firth of Clyde, Scotland: V. 143.

Arran, Charles Butler, 1st Earl of, 1671–1758: Macky and JS on, V. 260.

Art: and nature, I. 248.

Artephius: supposed author of chapbook *Dr. Faustus*, I. 41.

Arthur, King of England: V. 4.

Artibus Perditis: *see* RERUM MEMORABILIUM JAM OLIM DEPERDITARUM.

Artisans, Irish: cheating common, XII. 306; XIII. 89–90; need for employment, XIII. 167; poverty, XIII. 169; riots, III. 169.

Artois, province of France: V. 43.

Arundel, Sussex: pun upon name, IV. 261–2.

Asgill, John, 1659–1738, lawyer, deist: and Burnet, IV. xxv; linked with Burnet, IV. 70; attacks Christianity, II. 36, 72; linked to Molesworth, IV. xxvi-xxviii; 'a most pious lawyer', III. 37; attacked by JS, II. xix, 29.

Ashe, Dillon, or Dilly, *b. c.* 1666, Archdeacon of Clogher, friend of JS: 'Dill' in *Dialogue in the Castilian Language*, IV. 258–9; pun upon name, IV. 264 and *n.**.

Ashe, Richard: and Tom Ashe, IV. 264, *n.**.

Ashe, St. George, *c.* 1658–1718, successively Bishop of Cloyne, of Clogher, and of Derry, JS's tutor and friend: 'bishop', II. xxxv; 'Bp. Cl.' in *Dialogue in the Castilian Language*, IV. 258; friend of Stella, V. 233; and *Tatler*, No. 230, II. xxxiii.

Ashe, Captain Thomas, *b. c.* 1656, Irish friend of JS: IV. 261; 'Tom A.' in *Dialogue in the Castilian Language*, IV. 257–9; dying speech, IV. 263–6.

Ashburnham, John, 1st Earl of, 1687–1737, son-in-law to Ormonde: IV. 284; marries Lady Mary Butler (1710), VI. xvii; and JS's *Letter to a Whig Lord*, VI. xvii–xviii; Tory, VI. xvii; wealth, VI. xviii; and Whigs, VI. xvii.

Ashburnham, Lady Mary, *c.* 1690–1713, wife of John, Lord Ashburnham (later Earl), daughter of Ormonde, favourite of JS: death (1713), VI. xvii; marriage (1710), VI. xvii.

Asia: I. 103; climate discourages commonwealths, II. 17; and Latin language, IV. 8; governed by Pompey, I. 220; prime ministers, V. 117.

Asses: and allegory of JS's *Mechanical Operation of the Spirit*, I. 173–4; and author of *Mechanical Operation*, I. 172–3; and Yahoos, XI. 272–3.

Assiento, i.e., the privilege of supplying Negro slaves to the Spanish colonies in America: Dutch denied, VII. 119–20, 123–4; Dutch would share, VII. 109, 123; VIII. 171; England to have (1711), VII. 43, 48–9, 115,

132; Oxford protects monopoly, VII. 109.

Astell, Mary, 1668–1731, author: *Advertisement* to *Bart'lemy Fair*: *Or, An Enquiry after Wit*, II. xxx–xxxi; *A Serious Proposal to the Ladies*, II. xxix–xxx.

Aston, William: X. 76.

Astraea, starry maiden, Justice in Greek mythology: fled from earth, I. 31, 248; XII. 57.

'Astrologer': mock-etymology, IV. 238.

Astrology: and Bodin, V. 244; ironically censured, II. 141–3, 149–50; discredited, II. 154–5; and lawyers, I. 244; mock-praise, II. 170; praised by Partridge, II. 203; ridiculed, II. 155, 165, 196; 'vindicated' by Partridge, II. 167.

Astronomy: among the Houyhn-hnms, XI. 273; in Laputa, XI. 164–5, 167–71; and the Struld-bruggs, XI. 210.

Asturias, Prince of: *see* LOUIS I OF SPAIN.

Astyanax: pun upon name, IV. 234.

Athanasian Creed: answer to Arians, IX. 160.

Athanasius, *c.* 296–373: and the Trinity, IV. 34.

Atheism: and abolition of Christianity, II. 36–7; and Civil War, IX. 223; and conscience, IX. 166; corrupt, IX. 157; and immorality, IX. 80; and preaching, IX. 77; — neglect of, IX. 214; — ridicule of, IX. 216; and Trinity, IX. 159; unreasonable, IX. 167; vicious, IX. 165; writers denounced, IX. 79. *See also* HERESIES.

Athene, Pallas: as protectress of Ancients, I. 153, 156; and Arachne, IX. xv, 18, 272–4, 276–7; aids Boyle, I. 164; protects Temple, I. 163.

Athenaeum: and *It's Out at Last*, by JS, VI. xx.

Athenian Society: JS's poem on, I. xii; praised by Temple, I. xii.

Athens: I. 193–236; and balance of power, I. 204–5; II. 16; and Cicero, IV. 237; punishment of criminals, II. 236; and Demosthenes, X. 71; compared with England, I. 31; government, I. 204–10; impeachments, I. 205–10; plague at (430 B.C.), XIV. 33; and modern preachers, IX. 112; satire in 'Attick Commonwealth', I. 31.

Athlone, Scotland: hat, IX. 18.

Atholl, John Murray, 1st Marquis of, 1631–1703, royalist: V. 129, 134–5, 158, 159; in 1679, V. 140.

Atreus, in Greek mythology, son of Pelops: Horace alludes to, V. 339; 'Atreus' pseudonym for boor, V. 339.

Atterbury, Francis, 1662–1732, Dean of Carlisle, Bishop of Rochester: VIII. 109; and JS's academy, IV. xi; and Burnet, IV. 60, 289; Burnet and JS on, V. 272; character ('prolocutor'), III. 51; *Dr. Bentley's Dissertation . . . Examin'd* ('Boyle's Examination'), 1698, I. xvii, xxiv; — 'ass' word play and Bentley, I. xxv; — and *Battle of Books*, I. xviii; — 3 editions in a year, I. xvii; — Temple praises, I. xviii; favours new churches, II. 61, *n*.*; and *Examiner*, III. xi, xxvii, 2; VIII.

123–4; and freethinking, IV. 36, 43–4; Macaulay on, I. xvii, *n.*†; and missionaries, IV. 31; declares against Oxford, VIII. 156; prolocutor, III. 51; and Scriblerus Club, XI. xiii, *n.* 2; JS to toast (*c.* 1727), V. 335; and *Tale of a Tub*, I. xxviii; trial of (1722), and *Gulliver's Travels*, XI. xix; — satirized, XI. 190–2.

Atticus, Titus Pomponius, 109–32 B.C., Roman patron of letters: VIII. 142; and Cicero, I. 258; and Somers, I. 14.

Attila the Hun, *d.* A.D. 453: and St. Peter, XIV. 23.

Attilius: *see* REGULUS.

'Atwit, Colonel': character in *Polite Conversation*, IV. 276–7.

Augeas: I. 58.

Augsburg, Bavaria: VI. 38.

Augustan Age: reign of Charles II 'absurdly reckoned', IV. 249.

Augustine, St., of Hippo, 345–430: Austin, IX. 75.

Augustine, St., *d.* 604, 1st Archbishop of Canterbury: converts England, II. 83; converts Ethelbert, V. 4.

Augustus, Gaius Octavius, 63 B.C.–A.D. 14, Roman Emperor: XI. 201; 'boy of eighteen', I. 222; and Carteret, XII. 161–2; and Epicureans, IV. 249; 'the last triumvirate', VI. 80; and Virgil, V. 327.

Augustus I, 1670–1733, King of Poland and Elector of Saxony: V. 85; VI. 17; VIII. 61; and Treaty of Altranstadt (1707), VI. 62–3; and Charles XII, IV. 122; Charles XII pursues into Saxony

(1706), VI. 62; Denmark not to assist him, VI. 62; campaign in Flanders (1708), VI. 63; troops ('Saxons') in Flanders (1711), VI. 30; resignation predicted, II. 148; renounces Polish throne (1707), VI. 62–3; driven from Poland, VI. 17; reclaims Polish throne (1709), VI. 63; resignation of Poland predicted, II. 148; one of the 'princes of the north', VII. 148; acknowledges Stanislaus (1707), VI. 17, 63.

Ault, Norman: IV. xxxiv, *n.* 1.

Aumale, Stephen, Count of (i.e. Earl of Albemarle), *b.* before 1070, *d.* 1121–30, nephew of William I: V. 20–1.

Aumale, William le Gros, Count of, *d.* 1179: V. 54.

Ausberg: *see* AUGSBURG.

Ausonius, Decimus Magnus, *c.* A.D. 310–*c.* 395, Christian poet: JS praises, XIV. 17.

Austin: *see* AUGUSTINE.

Australia, or New Holland: beaux esprits, I. 171; and Gulliver, XI. 148, 283–4. *See also* TERRA AUSTRALIA INCOGNITA.

Austria (Emperor, Empire, Imperialists): barrier, VII. 50; and Barrier Treaty, VI. 88, 105, 113–15; and Catalonia, VIII. 63; 'wretched economy', VI. 51; Emperor: *see* LEOPOLD I; JOSEPH; CHARLES VI; and England — dependence on, VI. 52; — eager for Anne's death (1714), VIII. 58; — disrespect for Anne, VII. 142; — ingratitude to England, VI. 52; — alleged 'understanding' with Godolphin

ministry, III. 205; French threat to (1714), VIII. 60–1; and Grand Alliance: *see* GRAND ALLIANCE; House of Austria: *see* HAPSBURG; suppression of Hungary, VI. 34, 36; impotence, VI. 51–2; and Italy, VIII. 64; — claims in, VII. 164; — interests in, VI. 35; — neutrality desired, VII. 156; — neutrality disregarded, VIII. 63; — threatens to overrun Italy (1714), VIII. 60; plague (1714), VIII. 61; royal house and Somers, I. 15; advantages from Treaty of Ryswick (1697), VI. 11; gains Sardinia (1713), VIII. 54; and Duke of Savoy, VI. 35–6, 52–3; and Spain — misjudges allegiance of Spain, VI. 48; — claim to, denied (1713), VII. 166–7; — English view changes (*c.* 1711), VII. 151; — forces lacking to back claim, VII. 86; — union dangerous, VI. 51–3 and *n*.*; granted Spanish Netherlands (1700), VI. 12; 'Squire South', VI. 167; gains Trarbach, VIII. 59; Turkish war, III. 129; **and Treaty of Utrecht,** VI. 167; — barrier to be formed for (1711), VII. 42; — Dutch stipulations, VII. 152–3; — England's leadership enrages, VII. 124; — to retain Milan, VII. 164; — to retain Naples, VII. 164; — delays peace, VII. 164; — does not sign, VII. 166; — to gain Spanish Netherlands, VII. 155; — may gain certain territories, VII. 133; and War of the Spanish Succession: *see* WAR OF THE SPANISH SUCCESSION.

'Author's Compliment to the Readers &c': title of Section X of *Tale of a Tub* in edition of 1720: I. 285.

Autobiographical Fragment, by JS: *see* FAMILY OF SWIFT.

Avarice: IX. 193; condemned, in Marlborough, III. 80–5; in Wharton, III. 27–9, 180–4.

Aylesford, Heneage Finch, Lord Guernsey, 1st Earl of, *c.* 1649–1719, 2nd son of 1st Earl of Nottingham: compared with his brother, VII. 11; and Sidney's trial, V. 281; Solicitor General, V. 284.

Aylmer, Matthew Aylmer, Lord, *d.* 1720, admiral: Macky and JS on, V. 261.

Ayrly, Earl of: *see* AIRLIE.

B

B., A., the John Doe of counterfeit footmen: XII. 236.

B., A., pseudonym for JS in *An Answer to a Paper, Called A Memorial of the Poor ... of Ireland*: XII. 25.

B., M., pseudonym for JS in *Drapier's Letters*: X, *passim. See also* DRAPIER.

B., W.: prints pirated edition of *Predictions for the Year 1708,* II. 286.

Babel: god of Puritan sects, I. 124.

Babylon: and church hierarchy, II. 90; whore of, Roman Catholic Church, I. 112.

Bacchanal: I. 186–7.

Bacchus: and Parnassus, IV. 252; and Silenus, IV. 247.

Bachet, Claude-Gaspar, 1581–1638, sieur de Meziriac: *Les*

Epistres d'Ovide traduittes en vers françois (1626), IV. 267.

Backgammon: IV. 207.

Bacon, Francis, Baron Verulam, Viscount St. Albans, 1561–1626: 'missed' by Aristotle's arrow, I. 156; compared with Robert Boyle, I. xxxiv; bribery, V. 85; and Clarendon, V. xl; free-thinker, IV. 46; mean figure, V. xi, 85; his merit, XII. 39; on monads, XII. 48; quotations and allusions — (perhaps fictitious) X. 55; — on swearing a judge, X. 162; — *Of Wisdom for a Man's Self*: X. 120.

Bacon, Roger, *c.* 1214–94, philosopher: and free masons, V. 328, 330.

Bailey, Thomas, Dublin agent of William Wood: 'one more', X. 28.

Baillie, Robert, *d.* 1684, patriot, cousin of Burnet: V. 281, 282.

Baker, Sir James: Pope's pseudonym, IV. xxxv–xxxvii.

Baker, Sir Richard, 1568–1645, religious and historical writer: *Chronicle of the Kings of England* and JS's *Abstract*, V. x.

Balaam, prophet in *Numbers* xxii–xxiv: pun upon name, IV. 239.

Balance of Power: *see* CONSTITUTION; INTERNATIONAL RELATIONS.

'Balcan', spirits distilled from black oats: IV. 279, 302.

Baldwin, Henry, London printer or bookseller: publishes JS's *Famous Prediction of Merlin*, II. 288.

Balfour, Colonel, *d.* 1689: V. 173.

Balfour, John, of Kinloch, Covenanter: a murderer of the Archbishop of St. Andrews, V. 135–6.

Ball, Francis Elrington, historical and literary scholar: on authorship of *Account of . . . Japan*, V. xv; on *Answer of . . . Pulteney . . . to . . . Walpole*, V. xv, xvi; on JS's *The Blunders . . . of Quilca*, V. xxix; edition of JS's *Correspondence* corrected, VII. xiii, *n.* 1; on JS's *A Decree for Concluding the Treaty*, V. xxiii–xxiv; on Fountaine and JS, V. xxiii; on JS's *Letter to . . . the Occasional Paper*, V. xiii; JS's letters to Steele, II. xxviii–xxix; authorship of *Tatler*, II. xxxi.

Ballad on the Game of Traffic, poem by JS: I. xxxiv; and *Meditation upon a Broom-stick*, I. xxxiv.

'Balnibarbi', country in *Gulliver's Travels*: XI. 174–92, 203; agriculture, XI. 174–7; map of, XI. 152, 169; no Struldbruggs in, XI. 211.

'Bam', slang for 'bamboozle': IV. 114.

Bamburgh, Northumberland: castle of, V. 21.

Banbury, Oxfordshire: and Gullivers, XI. 9; a centre of Puritanism, I. 184; 'Banbury Saint', inventor of snuffling, I. 184–5.

Band-box: *see* OXFORD, 1ST EARL OF, *band-box*.

'Banditti': II. 242.

Bangor, Wales: JS at inn near, V. 202.

Bank of England: and abolition of Christianity, II. 38–9; attacked, XIV. 4; and coffee houses, VI.

53; and election of 1710, III. 66; election of 1711, VIII. 41; and exchequer bills (1710), VII. 75–6; and Godolphin ministry, III. 226; memorial of 'stock-jobbers' backing Godolphin ministry (1710), VI. 43; and War of the Spanish Succession, III. 134, 224; and Whigs, III. 63, 125.

Bank, projected Irish: advantages, IX. 300; allegory of, IX. 308–10; autopsy, IX. 309; background, IX. xix; birth, IX. 308; controversy, IX. xix; delusion, IX. 294; and *Drapier's Letters*, X. 108; reasons for failure, IX. 306; funeral, IX. 309; ignorance inspires, IX. 294; interest, IX. 299; Lords oppose, IX. 319; objections, IX. 302; papers on controversy, IX. xix, xxi, 281–321; — listed, IX. 320–1; and Parliament, IX. 293; opposed by Parliament, IX. 304; unsupported by Parliament, IX. 294; and poetry, IX. 344; proposal, IX. xix; Protestant support, IX. 302; satires explained, IX. 311; security lacking, IX. 295; security weak, IX. 302; sub scribers, IX. 288–90, 301; — honourable intentions, IX. 317–18; — listed, IX. 304–5, 312–16; — publications concerning, IX. xix–xxi, 281 f.; — ridiculed, IX. 294–5; subscriptions, IX. xx–xxi, 299; — *see also* OFFICIAL LIST; SUBSCRIBERS TO THE BANK; JS's views, IX. xvi–xvii; — contempt, IX. xviii, 22; — motive of objections, IX. 318; — views attacked, IX. 317–18; compared to watch, IX. 303.

Bank of Ireland's Answer, to the Author of the Notes and Queries about Subscribers to the Same (1721), not by JS: IX. 317–18, 378.

Bank Thrown Down (1721 or 1722), poem by JS: publication, IX. xxi.

Bankers: *see* MONEYED MEN.

'Banter': I. 7, 10; II. 176.

Barbados, British West Indies: and Creichton's uncle, V. 125; and Gulliver, XI. 221; servants, XIII. 8.

Barber, John, 1675–1741, printer to the City of London and Lord Mayor of London: and Humphrey French, XIII. xxv; printer of *London Gazette*, IV. xxxiv–xxxv; VI. xxiii; and JS, VIII. 198–9, 205–6; — correspondence interrupted, VIII. xxxii; and JS's *Publick Spirit of the Whigs*, VIII. xxi–xxii; and JS's *Some Free Thoughts*, VIII. xxiv–xxv.

Barber, Jonathan, woollen draper of Dublin: dishonest merchant ('John' an error), XIII. xxviii; and Lord Lieutenant's liveries, XIII. xxviii.

Barber, Mary, *c.* 1690–1757, wife of Jonathan: character, XIII. 73; and Dr. Mead, XIV. xiv; *Poems on Several Occasions* (1734) — background, XIII. xxviii; — subscriptions, XIII. xxviii; **JS's letter on, XIII. 73–5**; — textual notes to letter, XIII. 221; and *Polite Conversation*, IV. xxxiii, 290, 291; JS's will, XIII. 156; and Wagstaff pseudonym, IV. xxix.

Barbican, London: French Prophets in, II. 205.

Barbon, Nicholas, *c.* 1640–1698, economist: 'Barebone', XII. 135.

Barcelona: VI. 38; taken by Allies (1705), VIII. 62.

Barebone, Dr.: *see* BARBON.

Barfleur, Seine-Inférieure, France: V. 40.

Bargains, selling of (coarse question-and-answer game): IV. 108, 117–18.

Barillon, Paul de, d'Amoncourt, French ambassador: and bribe for Charles II, XIV. 1.

Bar-le-duc: *see* PRETENDER.

Barnabas, St., apostle, 1st century A.D.: apparition of, XIV. 25.

'Barn-elms': IV. 284.

Barner, commander of Holstein's troops: VII. 140–1.

Baronio or Baronius, Cesare, 1538–1607, cardinal: *Annales ecclesiastici* (1588–93): **JS's marginalia, XIV. 16–35**; V. x, xxxvii; — analysis, XIV. xiii; — textual notes, XIV. 46; JS's character of Baronius, XIV. 15; deserves hanging, XIV. 25; accused of lying, XIV. 17, 19, 21, 24, 31, 35; style condemned, XIV. 27, 30; JS would have his tongue torn out, XIV. 25; wit condemned, XIV. 17, 22.

Barracks, Dublin: cheat, XIII. 175.

Barrett, John, 1753–1821, Vice-Provost of Trinity College, Dublin: references to *Essay* on JS, I. ix–x; on *Tale of a Tub*, I. ix–x; on *Tripos* attributed to JS, I. ix–x.

Barrier, Dutch: Dutch communication with, VII. 91; and Dunkirk's demolition, VII. 55; and England — English interests served, VI. 88; — and future wars with Dutch, VI. 55; — against England, VI. 28; VII. 91, 114; — England to guarantee (1709), VI. 29; — trade with, VII. 123; fortification, VI. 102; France violates (1701), VI. 12; French invasion before 1709, VI. 107; French revenue from, VI. 89; garrisons, VI. 110, 113–15; — 'Charles III' to subsidize, VI. 89, 114; — self-supporting (*c.* 1701), VI. 89; loss of, VII. 81; and Partition Treaty (1700), VI. 12; revenues from, VI. 102; and Dutch revenue, VI. 110; Dutch revenues opposed, VI. 114; Dutch rule, VI. 89, 101–2; and Spain, VI. 88–9; — to subsidize garrisons, VI. 89; and Spanish Netherlands, VI. 108–9; — border shifted, VI. 115; — government, VI. 114; — subsidies, VI. 102; Tournai, VII. 136, 153–4, 155, 159; towns and revenues, VI. 90; and Treaty of Utrecht, VII. 37, 38, 42, 44–5, 50, 56, 62, 113, 133, 152–5; — France would retain chatellanies under Treaty, VII. 159; — Treaty retards peace (1712), VII. 115, 118; and War of the Spanish Succession, VI. 57; — English expense in War, VI. 61.

Barrier, for Savoy: *see* VICTOR.

Barrier Treaty, between Great Britain and Dutch, concluded at the Hague 29 October 1709: VI. 98–109; and Austria, VI. 88, 105; 'barrier' interpreted, VI. 88–9; Charles VI to guarantee, VI. 94; counter-project, VI.

109–12; — background, VI. 85; — contrasted to final treaty, VI. 109–12; — England's interests neglected, VI. 87-8; — Eugene supports, VI. 113; — Zinzendorf supports, VI. 113; convention to follow ratifications, VI. 105; mutual defence clause, VI. 105; and Dunkirk, VI. 88; Dunkirk omitted, VI. 112; and Dunkirk's demolition (1714), VIII. 59; **and Dutch** — advantages, VI. 91; — and Charles, 'King of Spain', VI. 114; — gives them 'a dominion larger than their own', VI. 87; — to control Flanders, VI. 28; — allegedly bribe Marlborough ('chief advisors'), VI. 87; — government of towns, VI. 89; — troops made available to them, VI. 89, 90; — keeps them in war, VI. 49; **and England** — disadvantageous, VI. 87, 88, 92, 111, 112; VII. 54, 61-2, 90-3, 114; — to guarantee it, VI. 93-4, 103, 107-9; — and Hanoverian Succession, VI. 26-7, *et passim*; — and House of Commons, VII. 79, 94, 116–17, 119; — humiliation, VI. 87, 93, 96; — interest in, VI. 26-7; — would modify (1712), VII. 118–19; — parliamentary resolutions (1712), VII. 79; — popular resentment expected (1711), VII. 116–17; Eugene on: *see* EUGENE; and Grand Alliance, VI. 93-4, 100; Marlborough's refusal to sign ('the other'), VI. 29; — *see also* MARLBOROUGH; and Treaty of Münster (1643), VI. 92, 104, 107; VII. 91-3; Naples omitted, VI. 111, 112; ratification, VI. 106;

and Treaty of Ryswick (1697), VI. 105; secrecy necessary, VII. 54; Sicily omitted, VI. 111, 112; and 'no peace without Spain', VI. 94; and Spanish Netherlands, VII. 61; Spanish Netherlands denied 'King of Spain', VI. 90; other countries to support, VI. 105; superseded by Treaty of Barrier and Succession: *see* BARRIER AND SUCCESSION; JS on, VI. xv–xvi; towns in, VI. 28; VII. 90-1; towns not in, VI. 90, 113; and Townshend: *see* TOWNSHEND; articles of trade, VII. 93; and earlier treaties, VI. 99; and subsequent treaties, VI. 110; VII. 114, 157; and Treaty of Utrecht (1713), VI. 92, 111, 112, 167; VII. 53-4, 111-12, 114, 121, 122; and War of the Spanish Succession, VI. 89; and Zinzendorf, VI. 85, 113-15. *See also* SOME REMARKS ON THE BARRIER TREATY.

Barrier and Succession, Treaty of (1713): VII. 133, 156-8; 'forced' on Dutch, VII. 157, 158; justification, VII. 118–19; Utrecht supports, VII. 157.

Barrow, Isaac, 1614-80, Bishop of St. Asaph: and Bishop Evans, XIV. xiv, 41.

Barry, Mr., Godwin Swift's partner: IV. 282.

Bartholomew Fair: Bickerstaff's prediction for, II. 148, 206; turning girl, III. 147.

Basilovitz, Ivan, or 'John', 1529-84, 1st Russian Czar: and cruelty, II. 22.

Baskett, John, c. 1667-1742, King's printer: VII. 241.

Bassin de Neptune, fountain at Versailles: XI. 120.

'Bastide, Monsieur de la,' pseudonym for de Torcy: III. 210–18.

'Bates, James', surgeon in *Gulliver's Travels*: Gulliver apprenticed to him, XI. 19; 'my good master Bates', XI. 20.

Bath, Somerset: V. 14; Irish absentees in, XII. 71; and *Tatler*, No. 16, II. xxix.

Bath, Earl of: see PULTENEY.

Bath, Henry Frederick Thynne, 6th Marquis of: acknowledgement, VII. 178.

Bath, John Granville, 7th Earl of, 1628–1701, royalist, Lord Lieutenant of Cornwall and Devon: and tenants, IX. 49.

Bath, Order of the: satirized, XI. xix; red ribbon, XI. 39.

Bathgate, West Lothian, Scotland: V. 131.

Bathurst, Allen, 1st Earl, 1684–1775: correspondence with JS, IV. xxxix.

Bathurst, Charles, 1709–1786, London bookseller: and *Polite Conversation*, IV. 97; probably the 'London Bookseller', XIII. 240.

Battle of the Books (written *c.* 1697–8), by JS: **I. 137–65**; analysis, I. xxiv; authorship denied by JS and Thomas Swift, I. 279, *n.**; JS the author, I. 280 and n.†; background, I. xvi–xvii; characters taken from Temple, I. xxix; composition, I. xvii–xviii, 279; editions: see TALE OF A TUB; errata and corrigenda, XIV. 49–50; frontispiece facsimile, an illustration of the battle, facing I. 137; unautho-

rized *Table, or Key*, I. 295; — textual note, I. 304; origin, I. 5–6; publication, I. xviii; sources, I. xxvii–xxix; textual notes, I. 296, 298, facing I. 298; title-page facsimile, I. 137; title-page facsimile (1720), I. 275. *See also* TALE OF A TUB.

'Baudrier, Sieur du': fictitious author of JS's *A New Journey to Paris*, III. 207–18.

Bavaria: VI. 38; Elector of: see MAXIMILIAN; Hapsburgs secure, VII. 89.

Baxter, Richard, 1615–91, Presbyterian divine and author: Burnet and JS on, V. 270.

Bear baiting: XII. 224.

'Bearish, Sir John': character in *Polite Conversation*, IV. 139–40.

Beaumont, Francis, 1584–1616, dramatist: bookseller's copyright, XIII. 206; and English poetry, IV. 273.

Beaumont, Francis, and John Fletcher, 1579–1625: *A King and No King* ('Captain Bessus'), VIII. 54.

Beaumont, Joseph, JS's man of business: V. 196.

Beautiful Young Nymph Going to Bed, poem by JS: composition, XII. xxxiii.

Beauty: 'compleat', IV. 155; wives', IX. 89.

Beaux esprits: censured, II. 257–9; in New Holland, I. 171.

Becket, Thomas, *d.* 1170, Archbishop of Canterbury: V. 78.

'Bedfast, Ephraim', letter-writer in *Tatler*, No. 21: II. 235–7.

Bede, 673–735, historian and scholar: on Scotland, XIV. 20.

Bedford, England: taken by Stephen, V. 52.

Bedford, Hilkiah, 1663–1724: 'non-juring clergyman', VIII. 64–5.

Bedfordshire: pun upon name, IV. 200.

'Bedgers': XII. 306.

Bedlam, Hospital of St. Mary of Bethlehem, London: and conversation, IV. 94; and maxims of state, XII. 131; in *Tale of a Tub*, I. xxvi–xxvii, 111–14; and thieves' celebration, IX. 41; virtuous inmates, XII. 158.

'Beef-Eaters': III. 204.

Beer, E., London bookseller: prints *Mr. Partridge's Answer to Esquire Bickerstaff's Predictions*, II. 201.

Beersheba, city of Palestine: 'from Dan to', IV. 156.

Bees: industry, XI. 127; building methods, XI. 180; life recommended, IX. 336; and free masons, V. 327–8; spider and bee, I. 147–51.

Beggars: children, XIII. 136; **in Dublin,** XIII. xxxviii–xxxix, 137–9; — and badges, IX. 133, 207; — attitude to badges, XIII. 134–5; — refuse badges, XIII. 172; — and bellowers, XIII. 139; — burden, XIII. 133–4; — causes, IX. 206; — not Dubliners, IX. 207; — excluding strangers, XIII. 176; — expelled, IX. 208; — mismanagement, IX. 205; — pride, IX. 208; — and servants, IX. 203–4; — and shopkeepers, XIII. 138; — strangers, XIII. 132; — and

workhouses, XIII. 139, 176; previous employment, XIII. 135; English, XIII. 136; in *Gulliver's Travels* — monstrous in Brobdingnag, XI. 112–13; — none in Lilliput, XI. 63; **Irish** — apprenticeship, IX. 203; — and beadles, XIII. 137; — caused by national hardships, IX. 209; — and clergy, XIII. 137; — economic burden, IX. 201; — and England, XIII. 174; — foolish solutions, XIII. 174; — half of population, XII. 136; — and Holland, XIII. 174; — lack of work, XIII. 176; marriage, XIII. 135, 176; pride, XIII. 134; **JS's views,** XI. 213; XIII. 113, 133, 135; — exportation of, to America, XII. 136; — numerous, XIII. 176; — his personal knowledge, XIII. 134; — treatment of, IX. 205–9; wandering, XIII. 134.

Behmen: *see* BOEHME, JACOB.

Behn, Mrs. Aphra, 1640–89, novelist and dramatist: 'killed' by Pindar, I. 158.

Belasyse, Thomas: *see* FAUCONBERG.

Belcamp, near Dublin, family seat of the Grattans: JS on the walk at, V. 344.

Belfaborac, site of royal palace of Lilliput: XI. 44.

Belfast Lough, Ireland, site of JS's first parish: I. xv.

Belisarius, *c.* 505–65, Byzantine general: captures Naples, XIV. 31; penance imposed on, XIV. 31.

Bell, Sir John, provost of Glasgow: V. 141–2.

Bellarmino, or Bellarmine, Roberto Francesco Romulo, 1542–1621, Italian theologian: I. 41; leads the Moderns, I. 152.

Belphegor, i.e., Baal-peor, in *Numbers* xxi: and pride, IX. 273.

Bench of bishops: 'a certain bench', VI. 125.

Benedict, St., *c.* 480–543: origin of his order, XIV. 26.

Benevolence, duty: ignored in sermons, IX. 173.

Ben-hadad, King of Syria: and Hazael, IX. 349.

Benson, Robert, 1676–1731, Chancellor of the Exchequer: VIII. 126.

Benson, William: *A Letter to Sir Jacob Banks* (1711), III. 100.

Bentivolio: *see* BENTLEY, RICHARD.

Bentley, Richard, 1662–1742, scholar and critic: I. 1–165, *passim*; V. 201; annihilates Ancients, I. 78, *n.**; attacks Ancients, I. 161–2; opposes the Ancients, I. 145–6; in *Battle of the Books*, I. xxiv; attacked in *Battle*, I. xvii; attacked in Boyle's *Phalaris*, I. xvi; 'killed' by Boyle, I. 164–5; 'Bent t'lye', IV. 207; 'Bentivolio', II. xxviii; *Dr. Bentley's Dissertation Examin'd: see* ATTERBURY; attacked by Christ Church wits, I. xvii; disguised as Criticism, I. 155; attacks deists, IV. xvii; his *Dissertation upon the Epistles of Phalaris*, I. 63; — 'Account of a Squabble', I. 22; — attacks Boyle I. xvi–xvii; — JS considers ephemeral I. 5; — parodied in *Tale of a Tub*, I. xxv; and election for fellowships, I.

xxii; edition of Horace satirized, II. xxiv, *n.* 1; 'guardian' of Royal Library, I. 145; 'most deformed of all the Moderns', I. 159–61; and Parliament, I. 277–78; and philology, IV. 231; popular object of attack, I. 132; 'Prince of pedants', I. 277–8; 'rectifier of saddles', I. 116; ridiculed, I. 22; 'attacked' by Scaliger, I. 161; 'star', IV. xxxviii; his style imitated, II. 160 and *n.*†, 161; compared to JS, IV. x; in *Tale of a Tub*, I. xxiv–xxv; — 'ass' word-play, I. xxv; Temple calls him 'pedant', I. xviii.

Bergerac, Savinien de Cyrano de, 1619–55, French author: *Voyage comique*, XI. xv.

Berkeley, Charles Berkeley, 2nd Earl of, 1649–1710, Lord Justice of Ireland: and John Bolton ('to another'), V. 195; and Arthur Bushe ('another person'), V. 195; Macky and JS on, V. 259; and Oxford, VIII. 124; and JS, V. 195; — his chaplain (1699), I. xix, 255; XI. ix; — goes to England with him (1701), I. xix; — *Project for the Advancement of Religion*, II. xx; JS visits, I. xxxiii; JS visits (1708, an error for 1709), II. x.

Berkeley, Elizabeth (*née* Noel), Countess of, 1655–1719, wife of 2nd Earl: likes R. Boyle's *Meditations*, I. xxxiii; dedicatee of JS's *Project for the Advancement of Religion*, II. xx, 43; and JS's *Meditation upon a Broom-Stick*, I. xxxiii–xxxiv.

Berkeley, George, 1685–1753, Bishop of Cloyne: and 'men of

honour', IX. 115; possible allusion to 'philosopher', XI. 87; JS on, XI. xii.

Berkeley, James Berkeley, 3rd Earl of, *c.* 1680–1736: VIII. 119.

Berkeley, William, 4th Lord Berkeley of Stratton, *d.* 1741, statesman: and Irish employments, X. 58.

Berkeley Castle, Gloucestershire: and JS's *Ballad on the Game of Traffic*, I. xxxiv; JS visits (1702), I. xxxiv.

Berkshire: JS visits (1714), VII. xxxvi.

Berlin: VI. 33.

Bernard, Francis, 1627–98, physician: death foretold, II. xi–xii.

Bernier, François, 1620–88, French author, physician, and traveller: death foretold, II. xi–xii; *Suite des Memoires*, I. 178; JS reads his *Grand Mogul* (1697–98), XI. xiv; *Voyages*, XI. xiv.

Berri, Charles, duc de, 1686–1714, third son of the Dauphin, grandson of Louis XIV: VII. 131, 151; compared with his brother, II. 169.

Berwick - upon - Tweed, James Fitz-James, 1st Duke of, 1670–1734, illegitimate son of James II: V. 163.

Besom, or bezom, a coarse broom: I. 240.

Bessborow or Bessborough, co. Kilkenny, Ireland: named after wife of Sir John Ponsonby, IV. 282.

'Bessus, Captain', character in Beaumont and Fletcher's *A King and No King*: VIII. 54.

Bettesworth, Richard, *c.* 1689–

1741, Irish M.P., serjeant-at-law: quarrel with JS, V. 341–3, 359; threatens JS, XIII. xxix.

'Betty': maid in *Polite Conversation*, IV. 146.

Bezom: *see* BESOM.

Béthune, Pas de Calais, France: VII. 113.

Bible: blasphemy in, IV. 45; and Cabalists' misuse of, I. 118, *n.*†; Dissenters' obsession with, I. 122, *n.**, *n.*†; and English clergy, IV. 31; and freethinkers, IV. 30, 31, 37, 48; 'not history', V. 262; interpretation of, satirized, I. 44–55; interpreting, and civil law, IV. 248; standard for language, IV. 14–15; and free masons, V. 324; poets need, IX. 329–30; prophets and free-thinkers, IV. 45; commentators on *Revelation* satirized, I. 51; and other scriptures, IV. 32–3; JS could read at 3, I. ix; correct text, IV. 33; textual note on *Proverbs* i. 20: XII. 324; translations, I. 75 and *n.**; IV. 37–8; understanding, IV. 29, 33–5; and wit, IX. 330.

Quotations and Allusions, Old Testament: 2 *Chronicles* x. 16: IV. 77; *Daniel* ii. 41–3: I. 247; — iii. 5: X. 137–8; — iii. 29: IX. 237; *Deuteronomy* xxxii. 15 ('wexed the fatter'): VI. 43; *Ecclesiastes* i. 18: IX. 148; — v. 12: IX. 192; — vii. 7: IX. 18; — ix. 15: IX. 234; *Exodus* v. 7: IX. 201; — v. 16: IX. 201; — v. 17: XII. 11–12; — xiii. 13 (or xxxiv. 20): IV. 247; — xviii. 21: IX. 156; — xx. 5: VI. 79; — xx. 7: IV. 164; — xx. 16: IX. 180; —

xxiii. 1, 2: IX. 189; — xxxiv. 29, 30 (in Latin): I. 112 and *n.**; *Genesis* ii. 7: III. 34; IX. 264; — ii. 22: IX. 264; — vi. 4: XI. 137; — ix. 7: XIII. 135; — ix. 15: XIII. 295; — xi. 9: IX. 226; — xiii. 18: V. 330; — xviii. 32: IX. 238; — xxv. 29–34: X. 53; — xlix. 5–7: IX. 219; — xlix. 6: IX. 224; — xlix. 6–7: XII. 279; — xlix. 7: IX. 226; *Isaiah* ii. 4: VIII. 54; — v. 20: IV. 77; — lv. 8: IX. 194; — lviii. 1: XII. 244; *Job* vii. 10: I. 21; III. 49; — xxxviii. 11: I. 231; *Jonah* i. 15: I. 231; — iv. 11: IX. 238; *Joshua* vi. 18: X. 12; — ix. 21: IX. 200; — xiv. 26: V. 330; *Judges* xvi. 21: IX. 238; — xx. 1: IV. 156; 1 *Kings* x. 22: IV. 247; — xii. 16: VIII. 67; — xxi. 13: IX. 181; 2 *Kings* viii. 12: IX. 349; — viii. 13: IX. 349; *Leviticus* xxii. 22: V. 179; *Malachi* iv. 1: IX. 176; *Micah* iv. 4: XII. 176; *Proverbs* i. 20–26: XII. 23; — xx. 3: IV. 149; — xxi. 9 and xxv. 24 ('the advice of Solomon'): VI. 44; — xxx. 8–9: IX. 195; *Psalm* xiv. 3: I. 31; — xxvii. 12: IX. 180; — xliv. 12: X. 43; — lvi. 5: IX. 183; — lviii. 4: IX. 215; — lviii. 4–5: IV. 62; X. 22; — lxvii. 6: XIII. 135; — lxix. 9: XII. 160; — ciii. 12: III. 38; cix. 3–5: X. 77; — cxix. 105: I. 183; — cxxiv. 7: XII. 192; — cxliv. 13, 14: IX. 199; 1 *Samuel* xii. 25: II. 95; — xiv. 45: X. xx and *n.* 1; — xvii. 5–6, 9–10: X. 48; **Apocrypha**: *Ecclesiasticus* vii. 6–8; X. 77; 1 *Esdras* iv. 35: III. 12, 13;

1 *Maccabees* xii. 53: I. 21; *Tobit*: I. 244; — v. 16 and xi. 4: I. 53, *n.**; **New Testament**: *Acts* ii. 4: IX. 161; — v. 29: XII. 244; — vi. 13: IX. 182; — viii. 5–24 (Simon Magus): I. 188; — x. 34: IX. 142; — xvii. 28: I. 48; — xx. 9: IX. 210; — xx. 35: IX. 148; — xxiv. 16: I. 42; — xxvi. 25: V. 96; *Colossians* ii. 9: IX. 242; 1 *Corinthians* ii. 1, 4: IX. 214; — iii. 1–2: I. 76; — iii. 10: III. 72; — iii. 19: IX. 241; — v. 6: IX. 187; — vi. 12: II. 17; X. 41; — vii. 7: XII. 276; — vii. 31: V. 121; VIII. 134; — viii. 1: I. 96; — viii. 9–13: III. 55; — ix. 22: II. 54; — ix. 24–5: IX. 244; — xi. 18–19: III. 54; — xi. 29: III. 44; — xii. 21–2, 25, 26: IX. 143; — xiii. 9: IX. 162; — xiii. 12: IX. 165; — xv. 11: IX. 213; — xv. 20: III. 72; — xv. 28: I. 48; — xv. 32: IX. 79; — xv. 51: IX. 162; 2 *Corinthians* i. 12: IX. 150; — iv. 16: I. 129; — xi. 26: III. 110; — xii. 7: I. 188; X. 127; *Ephesians* v. 21: IX. 141; — v. 25: III. 17; — vi. 19: IX. 162; *Galatians* ii. 4, 13: IV. 79; — vi. 10: IX. 232; *Hebrews* xi. 1: IX. 164; — xi. 6: IX. 157, 168; — xi. 17: IX. 163; — xii. 1: I. 224; — xiii. 1: IX. 171; *James* iii. 10: IX. 218; — iii. 15: IX. 247; — iii. 15–17: IX. 241, 247; — iii. 16: IX. 250; *John* i. 1: IX. 161; — ii. 17: XII. 160; — iii. 19: IX. 166; — viii. 44: III. 8; — viii. 58: IX. 161; — x. 30: IX. 161; — xi. 4: I. 229; — xiii. 34: IX. 174; — xviii. 14: X. 41; — xviii. 36: II.

77; — xx. 28; IX. 161; 1 *John*
v. 7: IX. 159; *Jude* 8: II. 29; IV.
82; — 13–16: I. 231; — 22–3:
VIII. 12; *Luke* x. 2: III. 55; —
xi. 25–6: XII. 160; — xi. 26:
III. 16; — xvii. 1: X. 88; —
xxi. 19: I. 3; — xxiv. 46: IX.
166; *Mark* ii. 17: IX. 212; — iv.
7: IX. 216; — ix. 44, 46, 48: I.
66; — xii. 42–4: IX. 197;
Matthew iii. 10: IX. 239; — v.
5: XII. 274; — v. 8: IX. 248;
— v. 15: I. 96; — v. 16: XII.
263; — v. 25–6: X. 84; — v.
39: I. 126; — v. 44: IX. 248,
268; — v. 45: IX. 48; — vi. 3:
V. 90; — vi. 24: IX. 187; —
vi. 34: V. 223; — vii. 4–5: X.
127; — vii. 12: IX. 362; — vii.
14: IX. 196; — vii. 15: IV. 79;
— vii. 23: IX. 353; — x. 16: II.
54; IX. 185; — x. 28: III. 108;
— x. 34: IX. 171; xi. 18–19:
III. 48; — xii. 25: IX. 176; —
xii. 34: III. 195; — xiii. 3–9:
IX. 212; — xiii. 7: IX. 216; —
xiii. 9: IX. 215; — xiii. 11: IX.
162; — xiii. 15: IX. 215; X.
22; — xiii. 25: III. 160, 200–1;
— xiv. 29: IX. 165–6; — xvi.
18: IX. 163; XIV. 32; — xvi.
26: IX. 167; — xvii. 17: V. 142;
— xvii. 20: II. 73; — xvii. 27:
II. 123; XII. 277; — xviii. 20:
IX. 255; — xxi. 12: VI. 43; —
xxi. 13: IX. 225; — xxii. 20–21:
X. 21; — xxii. 39: IX. 232; —
xxiii. 4: X. 43; — xxiii. 24: IX.
167; — xxv. 14–30: IX. 146–7,
149; — xxv. 20: V. 335; — xxv.
35–6: IX. 256; — xxvi. 61: IX.
182; 1 *Peter* iii. 15: IX. 168; —
v. 5: IX. 141, 142; — v. 8: X.

22; *Philippians* — and Tindal, II.
94; — ii. 3: IX. 141; — iv. 11:
IX. 190; *Revelation* vi. 10: X. 24;
— xii. 8: I. 21; — xii. 15–16:
III. 49, 53; *Romans* ii. 22: IV.
66; — ix. 20: I. 231; — x. 14:
IX. 215; — xii. 10: IX. 141; —
xii. 17: IX. 198; — xii. 18: V.
179; — xiii. 1: V. 124; IX. 186,
228; 1 *Thessalonians* iv. 9: IX.
179; 1 *Timothy* iii. 9: IX. 162; —
iii. 16; IX. 162; — v. 8: IV.
251–2; — vi. 20: IX. 242, 244.
'Bickerstaff, Isaac', pseudonym
for JS and others: in *Accomplishment of the First of Mr. Bickerstaff's Predictions*, II. 151–5;
authors usurp name, II. 164; his
autobiography, II. 261–3;
changes character, II. xxvii; in
*Continuation of the Predictions for
. . . the Year 1708*, II. 209–16;
etymology, II. 141, *n.**; in
Harrison's *Tatler*, No. 1, II. 249–
51; — No. 28, II. 260–63; and
'Hiereus' (i.e. JS), II. 262; and
'Hilario' (i.e. Steele), II. 262;
his *Last Will and Testament*,
title-page facsimile, II. 273;
pirated usages of, II. 164; portrait, facing II. 171; in *Predictions for the Year 1708*, II. x–xiv,
xxiv, 139–50, 165, 167, 170,
195–9; predicts his own death,
II. 235–7; reception, II. 172;
Steele's indebtedness, II. xxv–
xxvi, 249–51; VIII. 6; in *Tatler*,
II. 172–87; — No. 21, II. 235–7;
— No. 68, II. 240–2; — No.
258, II. 247; — No. 306, II.
xxxvi; in *Vindication of Isaac
Bickerstaff Esq.*, II. 157–64. *See
also* MR. PARTRIDGE'S ANSWER

TO ESQUIRE BICKERSTAFF'S PRE-DICTIONS.

Bickerstaff's Almanack . . . for 1710: extract, II. 231; mentioned, II. xxiv, *n.* 1; title-page facsimile, II. 229; textual notes, II. 290.

Bickerstaffe's Prediction Confirm'd in the Death of Partridge: II. 269–72, 290.

'Bibulus': 'party-man' in *Discourse of the Contests and Dissentions*, I. 233.

'Biddel, John', ship's captain in *Gulliver's Travels*: XI. 79.

'Bigamy, Will': *see* COWPER.

Big-endians, Lilliputian counterpart of the Jacobites in *Gulliver's Travels*, Book I: XI. 49–50; and Blefuscu, XI. 53; Gulliver accused of complicity, XI. 68–9, 70–1.

Bigod, Hugh, *d.* 1266, justiciar: V. 48.

Billingsgate, fishmarket, London: V. 113; and Jack in *Tale of a Tub*, I. 125.

Bindon, David, *d.* 1760, M.P. for Ennis, Ireland: *Some Reasons Shewing the Necessity . . . for Continuing to Refuse Mr. Wood's Coinage* (1724), X. 215.

Bindon, Francis, *d.* 1765, painter and architect: portrait of JS, facing X. iii; portraits of JS authentic, XIV. 50.

'Bindover', magistrate in *Tatler*, No. 21: II. 235.

Birch, John, 1616–91, Presbyterian colonel, M.P.: on speakership, II. 132.

Birch, Thomas, 1705–66, biographer and historian: MS in British Museum, VII. xxiv; ab-stract of MS of JS's *History of the Four Last Years*, VII. xxiv.

Birchin Lane, London: IV. 207.

Bp. Cl.: *see* ASHE, ST. GEORGE.

Bishops: Apostolic succession and ownership of land, XII. 211; Burnet on, IV. 72–3; and concubines, V. 44; and Glorious Revolution (1688), III. 163; Henry I and investiture, V. 30–1, 34; their power (12th century), V. 55–7; and Puritans, XII. 264–5; satirized, XI. 128, 129; and King Stephen, V. 56–7, 67–8, 71; JS's views — apostolic function, XII. 191; — apostolic institution, XII. 256; — and discretion, XII. 43–4; — and proposed mint in Ireland, XII. 57.

Bishops of the Church of England: bench of bishops, III. 51; and Charles II, II. 9; and lower clergy, III. 74; and clerical clannishness, II. 54; corruption and promotion, XI. 129; episcopacy is best system, II. 5; attacked by freethinkers, II. 37; incomes, II. 30; incomes criticized, IX. 45; and Irish bishoprics, IX. 52; and national morals, II. 48; oppose Bill against Occasional Conformity (1703–4), I. xxi; in Parliament, III. 51, 56, 146; Parliament cannot create, II. 75; and political parties, II. 14; XIV. 4; qualifications, II. 75; seven bishops sent to Tower, VII. 5; Steele praises, VIII. 13–14; ridiculed in *Tale of a Tub*, I. xxvi; and Tindal, II. 99; attacked by Tindal, II. 104–6; Whiggism (1690–1710) of 'a certain bench', III.

xxx, 200; VI. 125, 152–3; VII. 19; Whigs would remove from House of Lords, III. 146.

Bishops of the Church of Ireland: authority limited, V. 87–92; and bills of residence and division, XIII. 205; charity, IX. 55; and national debt, XII. xxxix–xl, 208–12; division of bishoprics, XII. xxxviii. 198–9; Dublin residents, XII. 212; and the economy, IX. 54; and English interest, X. 133; control House of Lords, II. 117, 119 and *n*.†; incomes decreasing, IX. 51; incomes low, IX. 19; — and increase in land values, IX. 46; and inferior clergy, XII. 191–202, 249; compared to lay landlords, IX. 54; and lease-breaking, IX. 53; must be maintained, IX. 51; 'missionaries', XII. 181; nobles as tenants, IX. 55–6; and place-names, IV. 284; their power: *see* SOME ARGUMENTS AGAINST ENLARGING THE POWER OF BISHOPS; Reformation and alienation of church lands, IX. 45; relations with tenants, IX. 53–4, 55–6; and residence regulations, IX. 54; XII. xxxv–xxxix; Sheridan's sermon offends, XIV. 36; tax on, XII. xxxix; and tenants' poverty, IX. 57; and Test Act, XII. 248–9; two types, XII. 181.

Bishops of the Episcopal Church in Scotland: V. 274; and Charles II, II. 86.

'Bitch', a word avoided by *Tatler*: II. 242.

Black Bull, tavern in Fetter Lane, London: and Gulliver, XI. 80.

'Black money': X. 10.

Black Prince: *see* EDWARD.

Black pudding: IV. 36, 115.

Black Swan, public house in Holborn: IV. 259.

Blackall, Offspring, 1654–1716, Bishop of Exeter: *The Rules and Measures of Almsgiving* (1709), IX. 126, *n.* 1.

'Black-Dogs', *c.* 1702–30 counterfeit shillings or other mixed money: X. 33.

Blackheath, a common adjoining Greenwich Park: IV. 283.

Blackmore, Sir Richard, *c.* 1653–1729, physician and poet: V. xxxiii; and Addison, V. xxxiii; Addison and JS on, V. 254; fights for Moderns, I. 158; poetaster, V. 201; frequency of publications, I. 116.

Blackwell, Sir Basil, 1889–, publisher and translator: acknowledgement, V. v; translation of Herodotus, V. v.

Blackwell, Sir Lambert, Envoy Extraordinary to Tuscany (1689–1690, 1697–1705): Macky and JS on, V. 261.

Bladen, Martin, 1680–1746, soldier and politician: translation of Caesar's *Commentaries*, IX. 20.

Blair, castle of, Blair Atholl, Scotland: V. 172, 173.

Blair, Laird of: V. 172, 173.

Blair, Sir Adam, captain: V. 159–60, 167.

Blaney: *see* BLAYNEY.

Blank verse: and rhyme, IX. 335.

Blayney, Cadwallader, 7th Lord, 1693–1733 : introduced by JS to Addison, V. xxiv, 200; insults

JS, V. xxiv, 199–200; JS's petition against: *see* DEAN OF ST. PATRICKS PETITION.

Blefuscu, enemy of Lilliput, modeled on France: and Bigendians, XI. 49–50, 53; Gulliver accused of complicity, XI. 68–71; Gulliver aids, XI. 54; Gulliver aids ambassadors, XI. 54, 69; Gulliver captures their fleet, XI. 51–3; Gulliver visits, XI. 54, 73–4; traditional enmity with Lilliput, XI. 49; preparing to invade Lilliput, XI. 44; war with Lilliput, XI. 49–50, 51–3; map, XI. 18; sues for peace, XI. 54.

Blenheim Palace, Woodstock, Oxfordshire: III. 21, 23; house of pride, XIV. 10; 'one palace for one subject', XIV. 5; 'one palace' and fifty churches, XIV. 5; 'palaces more magnificent', III. 213.

'Bliffmarklub', Luggnaggian word for 'high chamberlain': XI. 206.

Blois, Stephen Henry, Count of, *d.* 1101: V. 41.

Blount, Sir Christopher, *c.* 1565–1601, soldier: VIII. 189.

Blount, Elizabeth, maid of honour to Queen Catherine, mistress of Henry VIII, mother of Duke of Richmond: V. 247.

'Blunder, Tom': character in *Polite Conversation*, IV. 157.

'Blunderbuz, Sir John': character in *Polite Conversation*, IV. 143.

Blunders, Deficiencies, Distresses, and Misfortunes of Quilca (written *c.* 1725), by JS: **V. 219-21**; composition, V. xxix; textual note, V. 357.

Blunt, Sir John, 1st Bart., *d.* 1733: his account of the general mortgage (1707–16), VII. 71–2.

Boccacio, Giovanni, 1313–1375, Italian author: and *Tale of a Tub*, I. xxix; tale of 3 rings, I. xxix.

Boccalini, Traiano, 1556–1613, Italian author: *Advertisements from Parnassus*, mentioned, I. 17.

Bochan, Thomas: *see* BUCHAN.

Bockholdt, Johann: *see* JOHN OF LEYDEN.

Bodin, Jean, 1530–96, French historian and political philosopher: 'Bodinus', XIV. 24; and the Drapier, X. 94; *Les Six livres de la republique* (1576), V. xxxii; — JS's character of, V. 244; — **JS's marginalia, V. 244-7.**

Bodleian Library, Oxford: JS's portrait there, I, frontispiece; a sermon by JS's great-grandfather in, V. 187.

Boehme, Jacob, 1575–1624, German mystic: I. 79.

Bohea tea: IV. 139.

Boileau - Despréaux, Nicolas, 1636–1711, French critic and poet: III. 215; leads the Moderns, I. 152.

Boleyn, Anne: *see* ANNE BOLEYN.

Bolgolam, Skyresh or Skyris, admiral of Lilliput, possibly modelled on Nottingham: XI. 54, 67–72; malice towards Gulliver, XI. 44; opposes Gulliver's freedom, XI. 42.

Bolingbroke, Henry St. John, 1st Viscount, 1678–1751, Secretary of State, 1710–14: III. 72; ambition, VIII. xxxiii, 145; ambitions frustrated, VIII. 151–2;

and Anne's death, VIII. xxviii; Anne reproves him, VIII. 166–7; Bothmar delivers his memorial, VII. 24; and Burnet, IV. 70; and Buys: *see* BUYS; character, III. 80; VIII. 152; — 'an ill dissembler', VIII. 145; — 'skill, credit, and resolution', VI. 44; **JS's character of,** VII. 98; VIII. 134–5; on the Church party, III. ix; and Committee of Secrecy (1715), XI. 67–72; 'the *Craftsman*', IV. 120; and Dartmouth (1711), 'her Majesty's two principal secretaries of state', VII. 47; dismissal (1708), VII. 98; VIII. 113; and Dutch Treaty, VII. 108–9; his education, XII. 47; returns to England (1712), VII. 149; on Eugene of Savoy, IV. 216; meets Eugene (1712), VII. 24; and *Examiner*, III. xxvii; VIII. 123; family, VIII. 134; Faulkner prints writings, XIII. 201; flees to France, VIII. xxxii; XI. 73–4; received at French court (1712), VII. 149; exposes Godolphin ministry, VII. 98; and Guiscard, III. 106, 109, 115–16; VIII. 128; Gulliver partly modelled on, XI. 19–80; allegedly denigrates Hapsburgs, VII. 58; allegedly writing a history, VII. xv; impeachment (1715), VIII. xxxi; XIV. 54; — satirized, XI. 63–73; — and Steele, VIII. xix; alleged Jacobitism, VIII. 48, 87; — satirized, XI. 68–9, 70–1; *A Letter to the Examiner*, III. xi–xii, xxxiii, 221–7; — quoted, III. 94–5; — JS praises, XIV. 3; — JS's reply, III. 85–91; and maids of

honour, IV. 254; and Marlborough, III. xvi–xvii; — meeting possibly alluded to in *Gulliver's Travels*, XI. 67–72; and October Club ('two of the latter'), VII. 100; dines with October Club, VIII. 126; oratory, VIII. 135; letter to Orrery (1744) sold at Sotheby's, VII. xii, *n.* 4; and Oxford contrasted, VIII. 152; — declares against Oxford, VIII. 156; — and Guiscard's attack, VIII. 145; — will 'cut and slash' him in his history, VII. xv; — their irresponsibility, VIII. 86–7; — — *see also* OXFORD MINISTRY; — succeeds Oxford (1714), VIII. 132; quarrel with Oxford, VII. xxxiii, xxxv, xxxvi; VIII. 79; — begins, VIII. 128, 152; — Bolingbroke's ambition ('others'), VIII. 87; — and Guiscard's attempt, VIII. 145–6; — and *Some Free Thoughts*, VIII. xxv–xxvi; — JS attempts to reconcile them, VII. xv, xxxvi, 182; VIII. 158–9; IX. 28; compared with paper knife, IV. 251; decried in Parliament, IV. 85; and the press ('person who advised' Stamp Tax), VII. 103–4; and the Pretender at an opera, VIII. 166–7; and Ridpath's attacks, VIII. 32; alleged Roman Catholicism, XI. 68–9, 70–1; made Secretary of State (1710), VII. 98; resigns as Secretary at War (1708), VII. 98; VIII. 113; abuses Somerset, VII. 14; — will not sit with ('unlucky proceeding'), VI. 72; correspondence with Strafford, VII. 205–

12; **and JS,** VIII. 109; — *Conduct of the Allies*, VI. vii, viii; — dine together, VII. xxxv; — JS dreams about him (1727), V. xxv, 205; — and Faulkner's edition, XIII. xxxv; — close friendship, II. xxxvi; VIII. 134; — knows of *Gulliver's Travels* (1722), XI. xvii; — correspondence used in *History of the Four Last Years*, VII. xv; — advises Orrery to relinquish manuscript of *History*, VII. xvii; — slow in giving JS papers for *History*, VII. x, xi; — discourages publication of *History*, VII. xii, xiv, *n.* 1; — discuss leniency toward Whigs, VI. xii; — and *A Letter to the Writer of the Occasional Paper*, V. xii–xiii, 93–8; XII. x; — loved by JS (1715), VIII. xxxii; — and *Some Free Thoughts*, VIII. xxiv–xxv, xxvii–xxviii; — — 'a certain minister', IX. 25; — and *Thoughts on Various Subjects*, IV. xl; — visits, XII. ix; — visits (1726), XIII. 201; and new *Tatler*, II. xxxv; and Treaty of Utrecht, VII. 148–9; secret negotiations for Treaty criticized (in allegory of royal resentment), XI. 56; made a viscount, VIII. xxxiii, 151–2; and War of the Spanish Succession — Ormonde's restraining orders ('the express'), VII. 126; early ties with Whigs, VIII. 166; and Wycherley, V. 205–6.

Bolton, Charles Paulet, or Powlett, 2nd Duke of, 1661–1722, Whig: Macky and JS on, V. 258; and Gregg, III. xxix, 185–205, 243–58; governor of the Isle of Wight ('governours of islands'), III. 204.

Bolton, John, *c.* 1656–1724: becomes Dean of Derry (1700), V. 195.

Bolton, Theophilus, *d.* 1744, Bishop of Elphin and Archbishop of Cashel: and clerical livings, XII. xxxix; and proclamation against Drapier, X. xx.

Boniface, St., Pope, *d.* 422: and Eulalius, XIV. 20; recalled to papacy, XIV. 20.

Bonn, Germany: and Barrier Treaty, VI. 107, 115.

Bons Mots de Stella, by JS: **V. 237-8**; composition, V. xxvi; textual note, V. 358.

Bonze, Chinese or Japanese Buddhist priest: IV. 32, 33.

'Booby-burrow': IV. 283.

'Borach Mivola', Lilliputian phrase of warning: XI. 24.

Borgia, Cesare, 1478–1507, son of Pope Alexander VI: VIII. 77.

Bothmar, Friedrich Johann von, 1658–1719, Hanoverian general, brother of Johann Caspar: his regiment, VI. 30.

Bothmar, Johann Caspar, Count von, 1656–1732, Hanoverian envoy: Commons' resentment, VII. 119–20; *The Elector of Hanover's Memorial to the Queen of Great Britain* (1711), VIII. 92, 93, 176–7; — delivery to Bolingbroke 'extraordinary', VII. 24; — and George I, VII. 24, 144; — denounces peace proceedings, VII. 24; — publication, VII. 24, 108, 144; — Whig authorship alleged, VII. 24; and Eugene,

VII. 24–5, 26; and Marlborough, VII. 29; misrepresents Oxford ministry, VII. 143; Whigs collude with him, VII. 25, 143, 144.

Bothwell, Lanarkshire, Scotland: V. 142.

Bothwell Bridge, battle of, 1679: V. 131, 137, 139–42; Burnet's alleged misrepresentation, V. xx.

Bothwell, Francis Stewart, 2nd Earl of, 1584–1639: and Captain Francis Stuart, V. 135.

Bothwell, James Hepburn, 4th Earl of, *c.* 1535–78: and Mary, Queen of Scots, V. 86.

Bouchain, near Valenciennes, France: VI. 31, 61; VII. 113, 141; VIII. 57; *Bouchain: In a Dialogue Between the Late Medley and Examiner*, III. xxxii, *n.* 2.

Boucher, or Bourchier, Richard, 1657–1702, a gambler: the Duke of Buckingham's steward, XIII. xx–xxi; example to footmen, XIII. 42.

Boufflers, or Bouffleurs, Louis François, Duc de, 1644–1711, French general: and Burnet, IV. 58.

Boulogne-sur-mer, Pas de Calais, France: III. 210–12, 215, 216.

Boulter, Hugh, 1672–1742, Archbishop of Armagh, Lord Justice of Ireland: on French recruiters in Dublin, XII. xxx; 'primate', X. xxix, 61; on Test Act, XII. xl, xlvi; and Wood's halfpence, X. xxv.

Bourbon family: and balance of power (1714), VIII. 58–9; Parliamentary addresses against, VII. 12; powerful, VII. 131;

Spanish throne and Salic law, VII. 150–1; allegedly averse to Spain (1701), VI. 14; to renounce Spain, VII. 131, 135; deaths and Treaty of Utrecht (1711), VII. 12, 51; union of France and Spain opposed, VII. 42. *See also* WAR OF THE SPANISH SUCCESSION; SPAIN, '*no peace without Spain*'.

Bourchier: *see* BOUCHER.

Bourke, Dr. Francis: acknowledgement, I. vi; on portraits of JS and his friends, I. vi.

Bow Church, (i.e. St. Mary-le-Bow), Cheapside, London: Bow bell, IV. 175.

Bow Windows Book Shop, Lewes, Sussex: XIV. 43.

Bowls, or Bolles, Sir John, M.P. for Lincoln, 1690–1702, leading Tory M.P., reported to have gone mad: I. 111.

Bows, Jerome, *d.* 1616, ambassador to Muscovy in 1583: V. xi, 84.

Bowyer, William, the younger, 1699–1777, of London, called 'the most learned printer of the eighteenth century': and *Directions to Servants*, XIII. x.

Boyer, Abel, 1667–1729, author: *The Political State of Great Britain*, on Guiscard (April 1711), III. 156–7; and *Gulliver's Travels*, XI. xxiii.

Boyle, Charles: *see* ORRERY, 4th Earl of.

Boyle, Henry: *see* CARLETON; SHANNON.

Boyle, Michael, the younger, *c.* 1610–1702, Archbishop of Armagh, Primate of Ireland: Burnet

and JS on, V. 284; and Roman Catholics, XII. 294.

Boyle, Robert, 1627–1691, natural philosopher and chemist: compared with Bacon, I. xxxiv; *Occasional Reflections upon Several Subjects with a Discourse Touching Occasional Meditations* (1665), liked by Countess of Berkeley, I. xxxiii; Burnet and JS on, V. 271; eulogized by Cudworth and Glanvill, I. xxxiv; and JS's *Meditation upon a Broom-Stick*, I. xxxiii-xxxiv; JS parodies, I. 239–40; JS parodies scientific works, I. xxxiv.

Boyle, family of: *see* ORRERY.

Brabant, Belgian province: VI. 90, 109, 113.

Brackdenstown, or Brackenstown, near Swords, Ireland, Lord Molesworth's seat: X. 79, 81, 93.

Bracton, Henry de, *d.* 1268, ecclesiastic and judge: X. 160.

Bradshaw, John, 1602–59, regicide: III. 73; VIII. 4.

Bradshaw and Co., wool merchants, Castle Street, Dublin: imported cloth, XIII. 168.

Brahmans or Brahmins, Chinese: and free masons, V. 328. *See also* HINDUS.

Brauron, Greece, on east coast of Attica: 'a certain Town', orgies, I. 187.

Brazen Head: Walpole's sign, V. 97.

Bread: twelve-penny loaves, XI. 106.

Breasts: in Brobdingnag, XI. 91–2, 112–13, 118–19; of Yahoos, XI. 223.

Brecknock, county of Wales: pun upon, IV. 210.

Bredin, Jerom: X. 76.

Bremen, Germany: one of 'two maritime towns', V. 100.

Brennus, Gallic leader, possibly the one who died in 178 B.C.: and limited monarchy, V. 100.

Brent, Anne: *see* RIDGEWAY.

Brent, Mrs., *d.* 1735, JS's housekeeper: VIII. xxxvii; and Creichton, V. xviii.

Brentford, kings of, characters in Buckingham's *The Rehearsal*: allusions to, VIII. 44; XII. 267.

Bribery: in elections, I. 301–2.

Bridewell Prison, London: V. 94, 116.

Bridgeman, Sir Orlando, 1606–74, Keeper of the Great Seal: his education, XII. 47.

Brisac, i.e., Breisach am Rhein, or Alt Breisach, near Freiburg, Germany: VII. 113; France yields, VII. 132.

Briscoe, C.: acknowledgement, facing II. iii.

Bristol, England: V. 14, 53; X. 67; XI. 20, 221; and Hugh Boulter, X. 61; site of Wood's mint, X. 187, 189; Stephen at, V. 59.

Bristol, John Hervey, 1st Earl of, 1665–1751, 'Lord Hervey' until 1714: and JS's *Modest Defence of Punning*, IV. xxxv, 208, 299.

Britain: 'famous island', I. 116; foolish priests in, XIV. 26.

British Museum, library of: Birch's MSS in, VII. xxiv.

British Visions: II. xxiv, *n.* 1.

Britons: brought to Rome to fight the barbarians, V. 3–4; receive Christianity, V. 4; the

H

Druids their priests, V. 3; heathen, V. 3; painted sky-blue, V. 3; and the Saxons, V. 4.

Brittany, Louis, Duke of, *d.* 1712, great-grandson of Louis XIV, eldest son of the Duke of Burgundy: 'grandson', death, VII. 120.

Britton, or Breton, John le, *d.* 1275, Bishop of Hereford: X. 160.

Brobdingnag (in *Gulliver's Travels*, Part II): XI. 8, 83–149, 293; armies, XI. 115, 138; books, XI. 136–7; described, XI. 111–12; dress, XI. 105; dwarf, XI. 104, 107–9, 116; flies, XI. 109; king—character, XI. 133–5; — educated in philosophy and mathematics, XI. 103; — remarks on England, XI. 129–32; — good sense, XI. 103; — on gunpowder, XI. 134–5; Lilliput contrasted with, XI. 86–7; table manners, XI. 89, 106; map of, XI. 82, 111; royal palace, XI. 112; queen buys Gulliver, XI. 101–3; Wednesday their Sabbath, XI. 98; spelling of name, XI. 8; inhabitants the least corrupted of Yahoos, XI. 292.

Broccoli: JS to buy seeds, V. 334.

Brodrick, Alan, Viscount Midleton, *c.* 1656–1728, Speaker of Irish House of Commons: member of Irish Privy Council, X. 182; his son, X. 99; and JS — sixth *Drapier's Letter*, X. 99–115; — letter Signed by JS, XIII. 181; prosecution of, JS's *Proposal for . . . Irish Manufacture*, IX. xvi; and Irish Test Act, II. xiv–xv.

Brodrick, Thomas, 1654–1730, M.P. for Stockbridge and Guildford, elder brother of Viscount Midleton: 'his collegue', VIII. 12; assaults Lindsay, II. xl; and Wharton, III. 182.

Brome, Alexander, 1620–66, poet: pun on name, IV. 206.

Bromley, Clobery, 1688–1711, son of William: death, III. 120–1.

Bromley, William, 1664–1732, M.P. for University of Oxford, strong high churchman: VII. 22; VIII. 48; attacked, III. 192; 'two of the latter', and October Club, VII. 100; and Oxford, VIII. 156; — *The Congratulatory Speech of William Bromley, Esq.* ('a paper'), III. 147–8, 154–6; son's death, III. 120–1; Speaker of the House of Commons, III. 189; toast to (*c.* 1727), V. 335.

Brompton, John, *fl.* 1436, supposed chronicler: quoted, V. 38, *'comites, barones, et cleri'.*

Brooke, Parson, of Dublin: V. 207.

Broom, Alexander: *see* BROME.

Broom-stick: I. 239–40.

Brotherly Love (written 1717), sermon by JS: **IX. 169-79**; background, IX. 101, 106, 116–19; composition, IX. 133–4; textual notes, IX. 376; title-page facsimile, IX. 169.

Brouders, Alexander, witness to JS's codicil: XIII. 200.

Brown, Mr.: and Creichton, V. 150.

Brown, James: X. 76.

Brown, Thomas, 1663–1704, satirist: and JS, II. x; and Wagstaff, IV. 118.

Browne, Sir John, Bart., *d.* 1762, of the Neale, co. Mayo, Ireland: 'B—', B., X. 28, 37; and *Drapier's Letters*, V. xxxiv; X. xv and *n.* 2; — attacked by JS, X. 28, 37, 210–11; *Essay on Trade in General: and, on That of Ireland in Particular*, V. xxxiv; *Essays on the Trade and Coin of Ireland* (1729), **JS's marginalia**, V. 256–7; — description of volume, V. xxxiv; and home-spun winding sheets, V. 257; *Memorial of the Poor Inhabitants, Tradesmen, and Labourers of . . . Ireland*, XII. 303–5; — authorship, XII. xii–xiii; — background, V. xxxiv; XII. x–xii; — JS's answers, XII. xii, 15–25; — — textual notes, XII. 348; prosecution, IX. 134; *Seasonable Remarks on Trade*, V. xxxiv.

Browne, Peter, *d.* 1735, Bishop of Cork and Ross, classmate of JS, friend of Stella: III. 183; V. 233.

Brownism, i.e., Congregationalism: XII. 244; mentioned, III. 144.

Bruges, Belgium: VII. 142; and British merchants, VI. 85, 91, 116–17.

Brundisium, Italy: Pliny prefers oysters of, IV. 257.

'Brundrecal', Lilliputian Koran or Bible: XI. 49.

Brunet, John: X. 76.

Brunton, Anthony, Dublin merchant: X. 76.

Bruslé de Montpleinchamp, Jean Chrysostôme, 1641–1724: possibly the mocker of M. Biquerstaffe, II. 161.

Brussels: VI. 90, 113.

Brutus, Lucius Junius, Roman consul in 509 B.C., hero of Roman legend: XI. 196; assumed madness, I. 111.

Brutus, Marcus Junius, *c.* 78–42 B.C., Roman statesman: VI. 134; XI. 196. *See also* CICERO.

Bubble, poem by JS: composition, IX. xxv; sent to Ford, IX. xxv.

Bubble, South Sea: *see* SOUTH SEA BUBBLE.

Buccaneers: XI. 222. *See also* PIRATES.

Buchan, or Bochan, Thomas, *d.* 1720, Jacobite general: V. 159.

Buchanan, George, 1506–82, Scottish humanist: leads Moderns' infantry, I. 152.

Bucephalus, horse of Alexander the Great: pun upon name, IV. 238–9.

Buckingham, George Villiers, 1st Duke of, 1592–1628: assassination, III. 106.

Buckingham, George Villiers, 2nd Duke of, 1628–1687, favourite of Charles II: Burnet and JS on, V. 268; letter *To Mr. Clifford, on His Humane-Reason*, source for *Tale of a Tub*, I. 7; *Conference with an Irish Priest* read by JS, I. 7; pun upon name, IV. 274; allusions to *The Rehearsal* — 'two kings of Brentford', III. 199; — 'king of Brentford', VIII. 44; — 'usurping kings', XII. 267.

Buckingham, John Sheffield, 1st Duke of, 1647–1721, statesman, author, friend of Pope: XIV. 4; character, III. 79; Jacobitism, VIII. 165, 166; and JS, VIII. 165; Macky and JS on, V. 257; Whigs hate, III. 72.

Buckley, Samuel, *d.* 1741, London printer and bookseller: arraigned, VII. 98; and Steele's *Crisis*, VIII. xviii, xxi, 33; 'a common writer of news', VII. 98.

'Buddough', a churl: IV. 279, 302.

Budgell, Eustace, 1686–1737, miscellaneous writer: and Pope's *Iliad*, IV. xxxv.

Bulgarian language: miracle of boy speaking, XIV. 35.

Bull, George, 1634–1710, Bishop of St. David's, Anglican theologian: and the Trinity, IV. 34.

'Bumbast-us': *see* PARACELSUS.

'Bumblecasters': on word list of JS, V. 336.

Bunting, Major: V. 170.

Burgess, Daniel, 1643–1713, nonconformist divine: VI. 154.

'Burglum', Lilliputian word apparently meaning 'fire': XI. 55.

Burgundy, Louis, duc de, 1682–1712, grandson of Louis XIV, eldest son of the Dauphin: death ('son'), VII. 120; Bickerstaff's predictions for, II. 147–8, 206; Merlin's predictions for, II. 168–9; renounces Spain, VII. 150.

Burgundy, House of: and English trade, VII. 92.

Burgundy wine: XI. 24.

Burlington, Richard Boyle, 3rd Earl of, and 4th Earl of Cork, 1694–1753: and Irish employments, X. 58.

'Burn everything English but their coal': IX. 17, 337.

Burnet, Gilbert, 1643–1715, Bishop of Salisbury (Sarum), historian and theologian: and Earl of Arran, V. 165; on Charles II, XII. 268; vindicates Clarendon, VII. xxxvi; and clerical clannishness, II. 54 and *n.**; in Creichton's *Memoirs*, V. xix–xx; — Creichton's *Memoirs* not a history of his times, V. 160; and national debt, VI. 10; VII. 68; deprecated, VII. xxxvi; favours Dissenters, V. 276, 277; and Dutch, VII. 68; *Exposition of the Thirty-Nine Articles* ('an author'), III. 18; his father, V. 260; his *History of His Own Time* — on battle of Bothwell Bridge, V. 146; — censured, V. xx, xxxvi, 146, 160; — misrepresents the episcopal clergy, V. 146; — errors in, V. xx; — military matters, V. xix; — priests should not write histories of their own time, XIV. 24; — on rebel army, V. 139; — style, V. 183, 184, 266; — **JS's marginalia, V. 266–94**; — composition and publication of JS's marginalia, V. x, xxxvi, 294 (dated 1739); — **JS's remarks, V. 183-4**; — composition of JS's remarks, V. xxxvi; — provenance of JS's copy, V. xxxvi; *Introduction* to *The Third Part* of *The History of the Reformation of the Church of England*, IV. xxxii, 53–84, 107; on life-leases, IX. 52; Macky and JS on, V. 260; marries Margaret Kennedy (1671), V. 183; on occasional conformity, II. 6; 'absolutely party-mad', V. xxxvii; pastoral letter (October 1704), II. 54; on Presbyterians, XII. 264; on saints, XII. 289; scandal-monger,

V. 267; *Some Letters Containing an Account of Switzerland and Italy* (1686), IV. 60; his son, XII. 77; and Steele, VIII. 36, 38–9, 65; 'the stentor of Sarum', III. 223; *Subjection for Conscience Sake Asserted* (1675) ('the first book'), V. 183; and JS — their acquaintanceship, V. xxxvi–xxxvii; — JS's *Contests and Dissensions* attributed to, V. xxxvi; VIII. 119; — historical writings, IV. ix–xi; — JS attacks *Introduction to . . . History of the Reformation*, IV. xx–xxviii, 53–84; — first meeting, I. xx; — JS 'knows him well', V. 183, 184; and Test Act, II. 97; *Vindication of the Authority, Constitution, and Laws of the Church and State of Scotland*, IV. 60; allusion to *History*, X. 127; wives, V. 183, 287, 294.

Burnet, Margaret, *c.* 1630–*c.* 1685, wife of Gilbert, daughter of John Kennedy, 6th Earl of Cassilis: old when she married, V. 183.

Burnet, Thomas, 1694–1753, pamphleteer and judge, youngest son of Bishop Burnet: *The Life of the Author*, at the end of Gilbert Burnet's *History of His Own Times*, V. 294; 'a rude, violent, party jackanapes', V. 294.

Burnet, William, 1688–1729, son of Gilbert; governor of New York and Massachusetts: 'Viceroyal person', XII. 77.

'Burton, Edmond', Gulliver's father-in-law: XI. 20.

'Burton, Mary', Gulliver's wife: *see* GULLIVER, MARY.

Burton, Samuel, *d.* 1733, alderman, M.P. for Dublin: XIII. xxiv; death, XIII. 79.

Bury Fair: pun on, IV. 264.

Bushe, Arthur, secretary to the Earl of Berkeley: 'another person', V. 195.

Bushell, Brown, *d.* 1651, sea-captain: and Vaughan, X. 161.

Butchers: and physicians, I. 244.

'Butchers halfpence', possibly Rex or Domini groats, equivalent of English halfpence: X. 33.

Butler (in *Directions to Servants*, XIII. 17–27): and bottles, XIII. 21–4, 25–6; breakages, XIII. 26; candles, XIII. 19–20, 23, 27, 213; and playing cards, XIII. 25; china, XIII. 21, 24; company, XIII. 24, 25; serving company, XIII. 18, 25; cutlery, XIII. 21; dish-washing, XIII. 19; drinking glasses, XIII. 17, 21, 26; and family honour, XIII. 23; knives, XIII. 26; perquisites, XIII. 18, 19; pilfering, XIII. 23; and salt, XIII. 21, 23–4; and fellow servants, XIII. 21, 23, 24; and visiting servants, XIII. 23; serving drinks, XIII. 17–19; serving at table, XIII. 17–18; and silver, XIII. 19, 21; table linen, XIII. 19; and tea-making, XIII. 23; vails, XIII. 23.

Butler, Lady Mary: *see* ASHBURNHAM, MARY.

Butler, Samuel, 1612–80, verse satirist: *Hudibras*, II. 85, 93; pun upon name, IV. 274; and Puritans, IX. 121.

Butler, Theophilus: *see* NEWTOWN-BUTLER.

Button, Daniel, critic and coffee-

house manager: and Pope's *Iliad*, IV. xxxv; pun upon name, IV. 209.

'Buxom, Miss': character in *Polite Conversation*, IV. 143.

Buys, Willem, 1661–1749, Dutch statesman: goads Amsterdam (1712), VII. 123; pensioner of Amsterdam, VII. 123; Anne's present to him (£100), VII. 116; and Assiento, VII. 109, 123; and Bolingbroke ('her majesty's minister'), VII. 56–7, 108–9; — conferences, VII. 203–12; — memorandum to Buys, VII. 203–5; and Bothmar, VII. 25, 29; **JS's character of,** VII. 23; Commons' resentment, VII. 119–20; on national debt, VII. 69; his inept diplomacy, VII. 116; arrives in England (1711), VII. 55; leaves England (1712), VII. 115; proposed Anglo-Dutch treaty, VII. 63, 108–9; and Eugene's visit to England (1712), VII. 24–5; visits the Hague (1712), VII. 123; and Heinsius, VII. 163; and good manners, IV. 215; long-winded, VII. 128; and Marlborough, VII. 29; and other ministers, VII. 57; on vote against peace, VII. 19; and peace negotiations (1711–13), VII. 40, 41, 55–7, 61, 128; — authority, VII. 63, 116, 123, 163; — authority misrepresented by him, VII. 23, 56–7; — mocked for lack of authority, VII. 62; and Petkum, VII. 40; powers revoked (1711), VII. 23; and JS, VII. 69; JS misrepresents him, VII. xv; and Treaty of Utrecht, VII. 115–17, 123, 128; VIII. 171;

and Whigs, VII. 23–4, 57, 108, 116, 119.

'Buzzard, Mr.': character in *Polite Conversation*, IV. 141, 163.

'Buzzleers': defined by JS, V. 336.

C

Cabala: and free masons, V. 330.

Cabbalists: and the Bible, I. 118–19.

Cabinet Council: Somerset driven from (Windsor, 1711), VII. 14. *See also* PRIVY COUNCIL.

Cacus, legendary, cattle-stealing monster: and Hercules, I. 91.

Cadiz, Spain: VI. 12, 16, 22.

Cadmus, in Greek mythology, founder of Thebes: Horace alludes to, V. 339; 'Cadmus', pseudonym for boor, V. 340.

Cadogan, William Cadogan, 1st Earl of, 1672–1726, lieutenant-general: III. xiv; V. 265; VII. 141; his mother and JS, III. xiv.

Caelestinus: *see* CELESTINE.

Caelestius, early 5th century A.D., disciple of Pelagius: condemned, XIV. 25.

Caesar, Gaius Julius, 102–44 B.C.: I. 211; III. 19, 42, 44, 100; V. 86, 207; VIII. 180; XI. 195, 196; assassination, III. 106; and Bodin, V. 245; invasion of Britain, V. 3; on druids and free masons, V. 330; and Gracchi, I. 219; on immortality, IX. 245; and Irish absentees, X. 130; and Latin language, IV. 8; Marlborough likened to him, VI. 134; and Pompey, I. 219–22; pun upon name, IV. 237; seal of,

XIII. 154; translation of *Commentaries*, IX. 20.

Caiaphas, high priest (*Matthew* xxvi, *John* xviii): X. 41.

Cain: Josephus on, IV. 45–6; and Roman Catholicism, XII. 295.

Calabria, region of south-eastern Italy: and Hamadryads, IV. 235.

Caledon, co. Tyrone, Northern Ireland: and Creichton, V. 125.

Caledonians, i.e., Scots: V. 4.

'Calentures': XI. 221.

California: XI. 111.

Caligula, 12–41, Roman tyrant: capriciously cruel, II. 22; and danger, X. 170; and fall of Rome, I. 222; cruel tyrant, I. 198.

Calin Deffar Plune, name of former emperor of Lilliput: XI. 68.

Calixtus II, *d.* 1124, Pope: and Henry I, V. 40.

Callidon: *see* CALEDON.

Callières, François de, 1645–1717, French diplomat and author: *Histoire poëtique de la guerre nouvellement declarée entre les anciens et les modernes* (1688), source for *Battle of the Books*, I. xxix, 7–8.

Calves-Head Club: III. 142.

Calvin, John, 1509–64, Swiss theologian and reformer: VIII. 96; and Geneva, IX. 220; and Jack, in *Tale of a Tub*: *see* JACK; and Reformation, I. 84–9; and *Tale of a Tub*, I. 280.

Calvinists and Calvinism: and English exiles, XII. 263–4; Peter Heylyn on, V. 255; and monarchy, II. 101; and religious liberty, XII. 278; and Tindal,

II. 104. *See also* DISSENTERS; HUGUENOTS; PURITANS.

Cambrai, Nord, France: VII. 135.

Cambridge, England: army at, V. 162; Iceni at, V. 263.

Cambridge, Duke of: *see* GEORGE I.

Cambridge University: and 'ciser', IV. 237; George I gives books to, IV. xxxiv, 209; Gulliver at Emmanuel College, X. ix; XI. 19; praised, XII. 51–2; and Prior, III. 209; and puns, IV. 206; and the younger Thomas Sheridan, V. 217; and JS's *Modest Defense Against Punning*, IV. 205; JS's 'vindication', IV. xxxiv. *See also* UNIVERSITIES.

Cambyses II, 'the great', 6th century B.C., King of Persia: 'Eastern King' and Sir William Scroggs, X. 92.

Camden, William, 1551–1623, antiquary and historian: and English language, IV. 231; leads Moderns' infantry, I. 152.

Cameron, Sir Owen, Laird of Lochiel (Logheel): V. 170.

Cameron, Richard, 'the famous covenanter': V. 137, 148.

Campeachy, Bay of, i.e., Gulf of Campeche, in the Gulf of Mexico: XI. 221.

Campeggio, or Campegi, Lorenzo, 1464–1532, Italian cardinal: II. 86.

'Canaught', purchase: IV. 279, 302.

Cannon, Colonel (perhaps Alexander Cannon, commissioned officer of dragoons 1688): V. 173.

Cannons: XI. 134.

Canterbury, England: plot against Henry II in, V. 70–1; St. Andrew's church and JS's ancestors, V. xxiii, 187.

Canterbury, archbishopric of: and Henry I, V. 35; and William II, V. 15; — appoints Anselm, V. 16–17. *See also* ANSELM.

Cant words: *Polite Conversation*, IV. 161, *n.**.

Canting: and conversation, IV. 105; 'ruinous corruption', IV. 8; defined, I. 182–6; and music, I. 182; orators, I. 249–50; imaginary treatise on, I. xl; and warfare, I. 243.

'Canting-brook': IV. 283.

Canute, King of England, Denmark, and Norway, *c.* 995–1035: V. 5–6.

Cape of Good Hope: and Gulliver, XI. 83, 148, 217, 283.

Capel of Tewkesbury, Henry Capel, 1st Lord, 1638–96, Lord Deputy of Ireland: V. 314; and JS, V. 194.

Capel Street, Dublin: Creichton's house, V. xviii.

'Caper, Miss': character in *Polite Conversation*, IV. 146.

Card, Mr., wool merchant, High Street, Dublin: imported cloth, XIII. 168.

Card-players: and conversation, IV. 115–16.

Cardiff Castle, Glamorgan, Wales: V. 33.

Cardonnel, Adam, *d.* 1719, Marlborough's secretary: expulsion from Commons (1712), VII. 67.

Cardross, Henry Erskine, 3rd Lord, 1650–93: V. 137.

Cardross, Mary (*née* Bruce), 2nd wife of 3rd Lord: and John King, V. 137.

Carew, John, *d.* 1660, regicide: III. 127.

Carey, Walter, 1686–1757, M.P. for Dartmouth, chief secretary to Duke of Dorset as Lord Lieutenant of Ireland: XII. xxxv.

Carleton, Henry Boyle, 1st Lord Carleton of, *c.* 1677–1725, Secretary of State: leaves office (1710), VI. 43.

Carlingford, Barnham Swift, Viscount, 1606–35: 'Cavaliero' Swift, V. 187.

Carlisle, Cumberland: V. 177; David I captures it, V. 49–50; and Henry II, V. 66, 75; William II credited with building, V. 27.

Carlisle, Charles Howard, 3rd Earl of 1669–1738: related to Duke of Norfolk, V. 258.

Carmichael, Sir John: V. 146–7.

Carnwath, Lady, error for Harriet (*née* Murray), *b.* 1661, wife of Sir John Dalzell, Bart., mother of 5th Earl of Carnwath: V. 174.

Carnwath, Robert Dalzell, 5th Earl, *c.* 1687–1737: V. 174.

Caroline, Queen of England, 1683–1737, wife of George II: V. 111, 114; Addison and JS on, V. 253; Sheridan's poem on her birthday, V. xxx, 226; and Countess of Suffolk, V. xxviii, 213; JS's bitterness toward, XII. xxxv; JS introduced to her, V. xxvii.

Carr, Charles, *d.* 1739, Bishop of Killaloe: and clerical livings, XII. xxxix.

Carrickfergus, co. Antrim, Ire-

land, seaport: and free masons, V. 329.

'Carrilye, Lady': character in *Polite Conversation*, IV. 146.

'Carrion Row', in Dublin markets: XII. 20.

Carson, a postman: and Oxford's band-box, VI. 196.

Carstairs, William: *see* CARSTARES

Carstares, William, 1649–1715, Presbyterian divine, principal of Edinburgh University: Macky and JS on, V. 262; opposes Occasional Conformity Bill (1711), VII. 97.

Carteret, John, 2nd Lord Carteret and 2nd Earl Granville, 1690–1763, statesman: ironically censured, X. 105–6; character, X. 59–60; **JS's character of,** XII. 153–5; and clergy, XII. 162–6; and deaneries, XII. xxviii; and Delany, XII. xxviii, xxix; and Irish gentry, XII. xi; and Irish House of Commons, XII. xiv; and Irish preferments, XII. xxvii–xxix; and Irish silver, XII. 56; and Duchess of Kendal, X. x, *n.* 1; learned, V. 217; and JS's *Libel on Doctor Delany. And a Certain Great Lord* (Carteret), XII. xxiv–xxv; prorogues Parliament (1725), X. xxv–xxvi; reappointment, XII. xxviii; and recordership of Dublin, XIII. xxiv; and JS's *Seasonable Advice to the Grand Jury*, X. xxii; and Sheridan, V. xxix, 217, 223; Sheridan's sermon on George I's birthday (1725), V. xxix; and Stopford, XII. xxix; **and JS** — correspondence, XII. xxix; —

knows JS to be Drapier, X. xix–xxi; — and *Drapier's Letters*, X. xii–xiii, xvii–xix; — and fourth *Drapier's Letter*, X. 53–4, 56–68, 173; — and seventh *Drapier's Letter*, X. 97, 119, *n.**; — personal friendship, X. xxv, XII. xxv, xxix; — proclamation against JS, XIII. 112; — to travel together to Ireland (1727), V. 207; — JS's vindication of, XII. 153–69; and Tickell, X. xix; favours repeal of Wood's patent, X. xxv; and Wood's coinage, X. xxvii–xxx, 29, 54. *See also* VINDICATION OF HIS EXCELLENCY THE LORD CARTERET.

Carteret, Frances (*née* Worsley), Lady, 1694–1743, wife of Lord Carteret: XII. 154, 155.

Carteret family: XII. 153.

Cartesius: *see* DESCARTES.

Cartago: *see* CARTHAGE.

Carthage: III. 41; V. 36; and balance of power, II. 16; destroyed, I. 218; pun upon name IV. 237–8; and Rome, I. 193–236, *passim*; 'tyranny of the commons', I. 199; and world conquest, I. 202.

Cartwright, Thomas, 1634–89, Bishop of Chester: sodomy, V. 286.

'Cascagians', possibly invented by JS: XI. 57.

Case, Arthur E.: on *Gulliver's Travels*, XI. xxvii, *n.* 1, 301–2.

Case, John, *fl.* 1680–1700, London astrologer and quack: II. 153 and *n.**.

Case of the Laity, with Some Queries: IX. 56; answered by JS, IX. xxii.

Case of the Woolen Manufacturers

... *of Dublin*: XIII. 167–71; analysis, XIII. xxvi–xxvii; authorship, XIII. xxvii; textual notes, XIII. 224. *See also* JS's OBSERVATIONS OCCASIONED BY READING A PAPER ENTITLED THE CASE.

Casimars, or 'French Prophets', fanatical sect: Bickerstaff's predictions for, II. 146, 198; Partridge on, II. 205.

Cassandra: 'prophetess', VI. 189.

Cassel, Nord, France: VI. 102.

Cassilis, John Kennedy, 6th Earl of, *c.* 1604–68: 'a Scotch earl', V. 183.

Cassinus and Peter, a Tragical Elegy, poem by JS: XII. xxxiii.

Cassius Dio, *c.* A.D. 155–*c.* 230, Greek historian: quotation — XLVI. lv. 2: III. 69.

Castile: VI. 37; VIII. 63; and War of Spanish Succession, VII. 85.

Castilian language: *see* DIALOGUE IN THE CASTILIAN LANGUAGE.

Castle Street, Dublin: and George Faulkner, X. 207.

Castle-Fin, co. Donegal, Ireland: V. 129.

Castlemaine, Roger Palmer, 1st Earl of, 1634–1705: husband of Duchess of Cleveland, V. 286.

Castor: and Leda, IV. 235.

Catalonia: VI. 21, 32, 37, 38; and Emperor, VIII. 63; and England, VIII. 62–3; and Philip V, VIII. 62, 63; revolt (1705), VIII. 62; Treaty of Utrecht, and Dutch negotiations (1711), VII. 40; — and Portuguese suspension of arms, VIII. 61; enters War of Spanish Succession (1705–6), VIII. 62; and West Indies, VIII. 63.

Catherine de Medici, 1519–89, Queen of Henry II of France: VIII. 77.

Catholic Church: *see* ROMAN CATHOLICISM.

Catiline, Lucius Sergius, 108–62 B.C., Roman conspirator: III. 82, 84, 148; VIII. 142.

'Cato', JS's pseudonym for Temple: I. xiv.

Cato the younger, Marcus Porcius, of Utica, 95–46 B.C., Roman statesman: VI. 134; XI. 196; freethinker, IV. 43; great figure, V. xi, 84; best Roman, II. 2; and Somers, I. 14; and stoicism, IX. 249; and theatre, IX. 336.

Cattle Act, 1666: XII. 174.

Causes, second: I. 153.

Causes of the Wretched Condition of Ireland, sermon by JS: **IX. 199–209**; background, IX. 107, 127–30, 136; composition, IX. 133–4, 136; textual notes, IX. 376–7.

Cavaliers, supporters of Charles II: V. 176; XII. 267.

Cavan, county of, Ireland: XII. 111; and Sheridan, V. 218; Sheridan's estate in, V: 224.

Caveat emptor: XII. 209.

Cavendish, family of: V. 242.

Celestine (Caelestinus) I, St., Pope, *d.* 432: and Nestorius, XIV. 21.

Celts: *see* BRITONS.

Censors, Roman: and English morality, II. 49.

Censorship: of books weakening church, II. 10–11; and fourth *Drapier's Letter*, XII. 122; evasion of, VIII. 14–15; in Ireland, XII. 57–8; legislation needed, II. 60–1; majority opinion not

voice of God, II. 26–7; would curtail *The Medley*, III. 152–6; and Grand Jury of Middlesex, II. xviii, 191–2; necessity of, VII. 104; personal responsibility, VIII. 15–16, 23; not popish, II. 106–7; postal censorship in America, XII. 60; and freedom of press, VII. 105; and JS's *Proposal for the Universal Use of Irish Manufacture*, XII. 121–3; recommended, XIV. 8; reformation of the stage, II. 55–6; and JS's *Short View of the State of Ireland*, XII. 122; Stamp Tax (1712), helps Whigs, VII. 103–4; censorship of bad style, II. 176; and Tindal, II. 97; and Whitshed, XII. 85 and *n*.*; and Walpole, V. 93, 96, 117–18. *See also* PRESS, *censorship*.

Centaurs: and Ixion, V. 323.

Cercopithecus, lice-eating long-tailed monkey worshipped by Egyptians: I. 46.

Certificate to a Discarded Servant (1739), by JS: **XIII. 166**; textual notes, XIII. 224.

Cervantes, Miguel de, 1547–1616: and true humour, XII. 32; quotations and allusions, I. 124 and *n*.*; — *Don Quixote*, Part II, Prologue, X. 114.

Chalcedon, Council of (A.D. 451): XIV. 22; opponents punished, XIV. 27; JS laments, XIV. 27.

Chaldaic: and Hebrew alphabet, V. 331.

Chaldeans: and free masons, V. 329.

Chamberlayne, Edward, 1616–1703, and his son John, 1666–1723: *The Present State of Great Britain* (*Magnae Britanniae Notitiæ*), VIII. 195.

Chambermaid (in *Directions to Servants*, XIII. 52–6): bed-making, XIII. 52, 55, 56; breakages, XIII. 53, 55; chamberpots, XIII. 53; coachman, XIII. 52; dismissed, XIII. 54; duties, XIII. 52; excuses, XIII. 54, 55; fire, XIII. 54–5; and footman, XIII. 52; gossip, XIII. 53; keys, XIII. 56; lady's clothes, XIII. 55, 56; sweeping, XIII. 55; tea-making, XIII. 56; vails, XIII. 52; washing, XIII. 55; windows, XIII. 55.

Chameleon, or camelion: symbol of Church of England, I. 243.

Chamillart, Michel de, 1652–1721, French statesman: his death predicted, II. 147; prediction ridiculed by Partridge, II. 206.

Chandos, James Brydges, 1st Duke of, 1674–1744: Macky and JS on, V. 260.

Channel, Irish: smugglers, IX. 6.

Channel Row, London: Tatler's apartment in, II. 184, 257.

Change Alley, Royal Exchange, London: XII. 43.

Chapelizod, country residence of Lord Lieutenant of Ireland: gatekeeper, III. 232.

Character and Declaration of the October Club: VI. xii.

Character of Doctor Sheridan (1738), by JS: **V. 216-18**; composition, V. ix; textual note, V. 357.

Character of Mrs. Howard (1727), by JS: **V. 213-15**; analysis, V. xxvi; composition, V. xxvii; textual note, V. 357.

Character of Primate Marsh, by JS: **V. 211-12;** composition, V. xxvi–xxvii; textual note, V. 357.

Character of Richard St——le, Esq; with Some Remarks, by Toby, Abel's Kinsman, etc.: VIII. xiv.

Character of the Present Set of Wits in this Island, imaginary treatise by the author of the *Tale of a Tub*: I. xl.

Charity: V. 87–92; Biblical injunctions, IX. 125; and Corusodes, XII. 42, 43; for deserving, IX. 209; and family, IV. 251–2; and human frailty, XII. 191; motivation, IX. 125, 207; of poor, IX. 197; and poverty, IX. 191; its rewards, IX. 126, 148; and self-knowledge, IX. 361; and shilling, II. 246; Stella's sagacity in bestowing, V. 233; and worldly possessions, IX. 124; and wealth, IX. 194.

Charity schools: IX. 129–30, 136; and swearers' bank, IX. 296; and tenant farmers, IX. 202; over-education, IX. 130; training servants, IX. 204.

Charleroi, Hainaut, Belgium: and Barrier Treaty, VI. 101, 109; and Treaty of Utrecht, VII. 153, 156.

Charles I, King of England, 1600–49: III. 118; V. 84; and alienations, IX. 46; anniversary of death: *see* JANUARY 30; and Bill of Attainder, IX. 222; Burnet and and JS on, V. 266; civil war, VIII. 17; and clergy, II. 102; and conversation, IV. xxxi–xxxii; killed by Cromwell, I. 125 and *n.* ‖; *Eikon Basilike*, V. 268;

and English language, IV. 9; execution, II. 86; V. 156; IX. 222, XI. 49; — murder, II. 10, 20; XII. 290; — 'unnatural murder', XI. 27; and Hampden, X. 20; and Henrietta Maria, V. 86; William Howell and JS on, V. 263; and James II, II. 20; martyrdom, III. 142; IX. 219; XII. 153; — celebrated, VI. 167; XII. 153, 260; and parliamentary acts, V. 268–9; bill against dissolving Parliament (1641), IX. 222; troubles with Parliament, IX. 221; creation of peers, and Tarquinius Priscus, I. 213; and poets, IV. 273; portrait by Van Dyke, XIII. 155; and Presbyterians, XII. 265–6; and Puritans, XII. 257; the rebellion, VI. 9; rebels oppress, IX. 230; regicides, III. 141; and the Revolution, III. 44; and the shilling, II. 244; JS's medal, XIII. 156; JS's view — not entirely blameless, IX. 121; and Thomas Swift, V. 188–9; trial, VIII. 4; and Triennial Act (1641), V. 193–4; weakness, IX. 222.

Charles II, King of England, 1630–1685: V. 120; and Augustan Age, IV. 249; bad prince, V. 283; and Burnet, IV. 62, 68, 83; — compares to Tiberius, V. 283; — and JS on, V. 274, 283; and Church of England, II. 9; and clergy, II. 16, 17; addresses Commons, I. 270–1; and conversation, IV. 105; and Creichton, V. 124, 134–5, 145; and Dalyell, V. 131, 155–6; and Dartmouth, X. 33, 40–1, 56; death and Parliament, V. 284;

and Dissenters, I. 130 and *n*.*; and Dutch War, V. 85; and English language, IV. 10; and France — Temple thinks him cured, XIV. 1; and free-thinking, IV. 109; and Nell Gwyn, V. 273; and James II, V. 283; X. 56, 167; and Leti, X. 110; liberality ('a late monarch'), V. 45; and Meal Tub Plot, I. 42 and *n*. ||; ministers, II. 17; and Duke of Monmouth, V. 139; and passive obedience, III. 145; and popery, V. 277; and rebels (1679), V. 139; reign of 'ease and plenty', VII. 68; and Sheldon, V. 272; and the shilling, II. 245; and the stage, II. 56; intimate with Temple, I. 269; and Tindal, II. 86; one of 'two weak princes', I. 230; 'weak prince', II. 17; and David Williamson, V. 130.

Charles II, King of Spain, 1661–1700: VII. 120; and Dutch wars, VI. 10; and union with France, VII. 44; chooses Philip of Anjou as successor, VI. 11; VII. 150, 151; VIII. 54; — France agrees, VI. 12; and integrity of territories, VI. 11, 17, 48.

'Charles III, King of Spain': *see* CHARLES VI, EMPEROR OF AUSTRIA.

Charles V, Emperor of Austria and King of Spain, 1500–58: V. 85; XI. 234; his African expedition, II. 258; captures Pope Clement VII, V. 86.

Charles VI, Emperor, Archduke of Austria, 1685–1740, second son of Leopold I, brother of Joseph I, styled 'Charles III, King of Spain': III. 205; and Anne, VII. 58; and Barrier Treaty, VI. 94, 105, 111, 114; to guarantee Barrier Treaty, VI. 94; character — mendacity, VII. 25–6; — treachery, VIII. 60; and Dutch Barrier, VI. 89; and projected Dutch treaty, VI. 103, 114; to share control of Flanders with Dutch (1709), VI. 91; dispatches from Gallas, VII. 58; heir, VIII. 61; 'Geryon' (i.e., Spain) and 'Charles III' as king, II. 169–70; and Milan, VI. 112; VIII. 60; and Treaty of Münster, VI. 104; and Naples, VI, 111, 112; and Portocarero, II. 147; alliance with Portugal (1703), VI. 13; and Sicily, VI. 111, 112; and Spain, VI. 45–62; — covets it, VI. 57; VII. 24, 86; — father and brother to cede throne to him (1704), VI. 13, 51, *n*.*; — Spain opposes his accession, VI. 58; — union threatened, VI. 51–3, 167; and Spanish Netherlands, VI. 94, 102–3; — Barrier Treaty deprives him of, VI. 90; — and Dutch Barrier, VI. 102–3, 112, 114; — to yield lands to Dutch, VI. 108–9; — duties, VI. 109; — and Guelder, VI. 107; — deprived of revenue (1709), VI. 110; — can expect no revenue (1712), VI. 89–90; subsidies to, VI. 32, 37; misuses subsidies, VI. 32–3; Treaty of Utrecht and Dutch negotiations (1711), VII. 40; and War of the Spanish Succession — Commons reject his proposal (1712), VII. 25; — would let troops starve, VI. 33; — fails to supply troops, VI. 32.

Charles IX, King of France, 1550–74: St. Bartholomew's Day massacre (1572), Heylyn and JS on, V. 255–6.

Charles XII, King of Sweden, 1682–1718: VI. 17; Bickerstaff's predictions for, II. 148; and Treaty of Altranstadt (1707), VI. 62–3; and Augustus, VI. 62–3; his death (1718), V. 11; England's obligation to him, VI. 62; — obligation not met, VI. 62; in *Examiner*, XIV. 11; on Godolphin's ministry, III. 205; to declare for Emperor Joseph, II. 148; and Poland, V. 85; and Protestants in the Empire, VI. 63; JS invited to his court, V. 11; and Wagstaff, IV. 122; withholds his contingent in War of the Spanish Succession, VI. 62.

Charles the Good, Earl of Flanders, *d. c.* 1130: V. 38, 43, 71.

Charondas, *c.* 6th century B.C., Sicilian lawgiver: and Diodorus, I. 233.

Chatham, Kent: VI. 165; pun upon name, IV. 261.

Chaucer, Geoffrey, *c.* 1340–1400: pun on name, IV. 273.

Chaumont-en-Bassigny, Haute-Marne, France: VII. 114.

Chelsea, in Swift's day a town on the Thames just beyond Westminster: XI. 91.

Cherrytree, Lady: V. 130.

Cheshire, England: and Lord Rivers, IV. 258; and William II, V. 20.

Chester, England: V. 206; JS at (1727), V. xxiv, 201; JS leaves (1727), V. xxv.

Chester, Maud, Countess of, *d.* 1189, wife of Ranulph 'de Gernon', Earl of Chester, and daughter of Robert, Earl of Gloucester: captured by Empress, V. 58.

Chester, Ranulph 'de Gernon', Earl of, *d.* 1153: aids Empress Maud, V. 58–9, 71; Stephen deceives, V. 65–6.

Chesterfield, Philip Dormer Stanhope, 4th Earl of, 1694–1773, statesman: and Faulkner, IX. 100; Macky and JS on, V. 259; and dedication of JS's *Works*, XIII. xliv.

Chetwode, Knightley, 1650–1720, Irish landed gentleman: correspondence with JS, IX. 117; X. xxv.

Children: apprenticeship of charity children as servants, IX. 204–5; corrupted by servants, IX. 204; education, IX. 91–2; XI. 60–3; — evils caused by neglect of, IX. 205; as food, XII. 109–18; JS to avoid, I. xxxvii.

Children's-maid: in *Directions to Servants*, XIII. 63.

Chimney-sweeps: Nottingham disguised as one, VI. 139–41; Tory spies, XII. 222.

Chimney tax: removed under William III, VII. 68.

China: VI. 87; and revolutions, I. 174.

Chinese: XI. 57, 105, 136, 226; and Christ's divinity, IX. 262; and freethinkers, IV. 32, 33; language, I. 66; — purity, IV. 9; and linguistic change, IV. xv; and free masons, V. 328; writing, XI. 57.

Chinuchii, Cardinal de: II. 86.

Cholic: XI. 181.

Cholmondeley, Hugh Cholmondeley, 1st Earl of, *c.* 1662–1725, Treasurer of the Household: Macky and JS on, V. 260; continues in office (*c.* 1711), VIII. 124; still in place (1711), VII. 2.

'Choqued', i.e. 'shocked': VIII. 24.

Christ: divinity, II. 4; IX. 261, 262; and English clergy, II. 54; and freethinking, IV. 31–2, 40, 48; headship of Church, II. 105; and Herod, II. 93; incarnation, IV. 34–5; messiahship, IV. 32; and ancient philosophy, IX. 242; and Plato, IV. 42; second coming, IV. 30; and Socrates, IV. 42; and Test Act II. 102; and Tindal, II. 105; washing of feet, IX. 145; and William Whiston, IV. 36.

Christ Church Cathedral, Dublin: Dean and Chapter, acknowledgment, XIV. vii; Dean, and St. Patrick's Hospital, XIII. 151; and Sheridan, XII. 165; JS's copy of Baronius, XIV. 46.

Christ Church College, Oxford: 'wits' attack Bentley (1698), I. xvii.

Christianity (Christians, etc.): IX. 241–50, 261–3; abolition of, II. 26–39; — advantages, II. 28–31; — consequences, II. 35–9; — disadvantages, II. 31–5; 'absoluta et simplex', I. 49, *n.*; afterlife as central doctrine, IX. 114; attack on, and Trinity, IX. 159; and civilization, IX. 80; classical origins, IX. 111; clergy independent of civil authorities,

II. 76–8; corruption due to heresies, IX. 171; doctrines — vice inspires attacks on, IX, 165; fitted to all times and places, I. 44, *n.*†; hierarchy, II. 77; opposes honour, IX. 115–16; without hypocrisy, IX. 248; impartial, IX. 248; mutual love of early Christians, IX. 171; love supports, IX. 174; Mohammedans similar, I. 173; Nicene creed 'confessio fidei barbaris digna', XIV. 35; orthodoxy made too subtle, IX. 262; 'nominal' and 'real', II. xix, 27–39; and ancient philosophy, IX. 73; ancient philosophy depreciated, IX. 242; Scriptural evidence, IX. 165; JS as apologist, IX. 102; and tale of 3 rings, I. xxix; and Tindal, II. 67–107, 191–2. *See also* CHURCH; CLERGY; FAITH; MYSTERIES; TRINITY.

Chronicles, Latin: and JS's history, V. x.

Chrysostom, St. John, *c.* A.D. 347–407, Greek church father: and Eudoxia, XIV. 18.

Church, John, *d.* 1759, vicar choral of St. Patrick's: XIII. 197.

Church: causes of attendance, IX. 215; — impiety, II. 265; — non-attendance, IX. 211; sleeping in, IX. 210; church and state — emperor's power derived from pope, XIV. 25-6; — kings not judges of church matters, XIV. 30; — pope and emperor equal, XIV. 31; — pope sent on embassy by secular monarch, XIV. 29, 31; — pope subordinate to emperor, XIV.

33; — JS's acceptance of national church, IX. 101–2.

Church, Episcopal, in Scotland: bishops and Charles II, II. 86; Burnet misrepresents, V. xx, 146.

Church of England: and abolition of Christianity, II. 36; act for building of 50 churches in London, III. 157–62, 170, 200; — and Oxford ministry, VII. 3; and Anne, III. 16–17; VIII. 112; — her alleged indifference, VIII. 146–7; — her loyalty to, I. xxi; — Steele on, VIII. 39; and atheism, III. 92; attacks upon, II. 13; bishops: *see* BISHOPS OF THE CHURCH OF ENGLAND; inconsistent charges against, III. 47–8; and civil authorities, II. 77–9, 106, 192; property destroyed in Civil War, IX. 224; comprehension impossible, V. 273; VIII. 84; convocations, III. xv and *n.* 2, 49, 50, 56, 73–4, 158; IV. 70–1; — and Anne's letter, III. 200; — Burnet on, IV. 70–1; discord (1710), III. 50–1; differences with Dissenters 'few and inconsiderable', III. 39; Dissenters and schism, IX. 118–19; doctrinal debates, IX. 107; and education of youth, III. 71; in *Examiner*, XIV. 5; fines of 1661, V. 270; and George I, V. xxxiii, 254; and Godolphin ministry, III. 53–8; — danger to Church, VIII. 40; — ministry 'worries', VI. 42; — *see also* SACHEVERELL; and Henry VIII, V. 250; IX. 220; XII. 181–2; XIII. xxxviii, 123, 126; — he despoils, XII. 181–2; — he oppresses, IV. 72–3; heresies

fought by: *see* HERESIES; 'high' and 'low', III. 163; XI. 48; unknown to Homer, I. 80; and Irish Whigs, II. 118; and James II, III. 46–7; opposes James II, II. 9; and James II's declarations of indulgence, I. 131 and *n.**; lands and Reformation, XIII. 124–5; and life-leases, IX. 52; and Dr. Lloyd, III. 182–3; London parishes, III. 159–60; Martin, in *Tale of a Tub*, I. 65–76, 83–9, 131; missionaries, IV. 30–1; XI. 294; moderation, II. 13; IX. 119; mysteries, IX. 109–10, 163; and obedience to governors, VIII. 37; and Oxford, VIII. 140; and Oxford ministry, III. 199–200; — 'Blackcoats' dine with Oxford, III. 80; — and comprehension, VIII. 86; — neglect it, VIII. 173; — Steele on, VIII. 39; — ministry defends, VII. 3; papacy loses, XIV. 28; and Parliament, II. 78–9; attacked by Partridge, II. x; and passive obedience, II. 15–18; III. 144–5; VIII. 37; most perfect church, I. 85; II. ix–x; and political parties, II. 3–13; — supported by both, II. 14; and Presbyterians, XII. 263–79; and the Pretender, VIII. 38; property and revenue, IV. 64–7; and Protestantism in Europe, VII. 94; and Puritans, IX. 221, 225–6; and Revolution of 1688, II. xvii; and Sacheverell trial: *see* SACHEVERELL; Scotch members, VII. 96–7; — *see also* CHURCH, EPISCOPAL, IN SCOTLAND; sermons and political questions, VIII. 15; subject matter of

sermons, III. 56; 'invention of statesmen and politicians', IV. 43; and Steele, VIII. 35–43; JS defends, II. xvii–xxi, xxxiii; justified in *Tale of a Tub*, I. xvi, 2–3; and Tindal, II. 67–107, 191–2; — he attacks, II. xvii, xviii and *n*. 2; tithes, VIII. 35: and Tories, I. xxi; III. ix; IV. 63; VI. 130; Tory slogan, 'the Church is in danger', III. 16–18; doctrine of the Trinity: *see* TRINITY; unique constitutional status, II. 18; IX. 118, 122; and unity of church, II. 99–101; and universities, III. 37; and Wharton, III. 182–3; and Whig writers, III. 189; and Whigs, III. 89–90, 92, 122–4, 199–200; VIII. 15, 102, 120; — dangerous to it, VI. 78; VIII. 36; — occasional conformity, III. 143–4; — allegedly would restrict sermons, VI. 130; VIII. 35, 37, 40–1; — Whigs threaten (1717), VIII. 88–90; — Whigs undermine, VII. 107; and William III, VIII. 95–6, 148. *See also* CHRISTIANITY; CLERGY; HIGH CHURCH; HIGH CHURCHMEN; IMPROPRIATIONS; LOW CHURCH; MARTIN.

Church-of-England Man: political beliefs, II. 1–25; — on balance of power, II. 16, 23; — on forms of government, II. 14–19; — on monarchy, II. 16–17; — on English monarchy and succession, II. 5, 18–24; — on parties, II. 13–14, 24–5; religious beliefs, II. 4–25; — on clergy, II. 8–10, 12; — on freedom of the press, II. 10–11; — on freethinkers, II. 11; — on

moderation, II. 13; — on rites and ceremonies, II. 5; on schism, II. 11–12; — on temporal power, II. 10; — on toleration, II. 5–8, 12.

Church of Ireland: absenteeism uncommon, IX. 58; and Act of Limitation, IX. 52; Charles I's martyrdom, IX. 219; congregations small, IX. 211; dioceses — and Act of Settlement (1660), IX. 46; — endowed by James I, IX. 46; — united, IX. 46; enemies disowned by 'Whigs', IX. 57; First Fruits: *see* FIRST FRUITS; history of, XII. 183–5; impropriations under Charles I, IX. 46; — reduced, IX. 46; — JS opposes, IX. 47; lands undervalued, IX. 46, 47; Act of Limitation prevents ruin, IX. 51; and mortmain, IX. 52; nation supports, IX. 157; and parliamentary election, XIII. 205; pluralities, IX. 58; properties despoiled, IX. 45; revenues, IX. xxii; and proposed sale of lands, XII. 208–12; and Scots, II. 116; JS as champion, II. xxii; IX. xxii; — sacrifices preferment for, II. xxi; and repeal of Test Act, XII. 246–50; tithes, XII. 76, 78; — tithe of hemp, XIII. xxix–xxx, 97–108; and religious toleration, II. 115; and Wharton, III. 28; VIII. 121. *See also* BISHOPS OF THE CHURCH OF IRELAND; CLERGY; CONVOCATION.

Church of Rome: *see* ROMAN CATHOLICISM.

Church of Scotland: and John Creichton, V. 130–80; allegedly disliked by nobility and gentry,

VII. 96; and public office, VII. 97; synods, V. 179–80; religious test, II. 123; and Whigs, VII. 97; and William III, V. 179–80. *See also* CHURCH, EPISCOPAL, IN SCOTLAND.

Church party: *see* TORIES.

Church, universal: and Tindal, II. 105.

Churches: *see* CHURCH OF ENGLAND, *act to build 50 churches in London.*

Church-goers: impious, II. 265; sleepy, IX. 210–18.

Churchill, Awnsham, *d.* 1728, King's Stationer, M.P.: publishes Temple's letters, I. 255.

Churchill, Charles, Colonel: V. 214.

Churchill, George, 1654–1710, admiral, brother of Marlborough: VIII. 113; Macky and JS on, V. 261.

Churchill, John, *fl.* 1690–1714, London bookseller, partner of his brother Awnsham: IV. 58, 59; publishes Temple's letters, I. 255.

Churchill, W. A.: *Watermarks in Paper in the XVII and XVIII Centuries*, XIII. xii, *n.* 1.

Chypre, Histoire de: XI. xiv.

Cibber, Colley, 1671–1757, actor and dramatist: and *Polite Conversation*, IV. xxxii; and Wagstaff, IV. 123; 'quoted', IV. 121.

Cicero, Marcus Tullius, 106–43 B.C.: III. xix; V. 83; XI. 127; letter to Atticus, I. 258; and Brutus, I. 222; and Carteret, XII. 155; Ciceronian eloquence disliked by JS, IX. xxiv; and Latin, IV. 8; pun upon name, IV. 237; 'free-thinker', IV. 44;

oratory praised, IX. 68–9; pathetic orator, IX. 69; and Somers, I. 14; JS's copy of *De officiis*, V. xxxi; speeches against Verres treated analogically, III. 27–9.

Quotations and allusions: *De amicitia* VII. xxiii: III. 96; *De divinatione* II. lxxii: III. 46 *De natura deorum* III. xl. 94: II. 124; *De officiis*: IV. 267; IX. 112; — I. 23: III. 58; — II. 75: III. 80; — XVII: XIII. 167; *De oratore* ii. 84: III. 91; *Epistulae ad Atticum* II. 8: XII. 299; — IX. 5: III. 132; — XV. 13: III. 110; *Epistulae ad familiares* vii. 6 and 10: I. 106 and n.*; *In Quintum Caecilium* I. 3: III. 24; *In Verrem* II. i. 15: III. 52; *Philippics* I. xii. 29– 30: III. 75: — II. 13: IX. 30; — III. xiii. 32: III. 167 — XII. v. 11: III. 62; *Pro C. Balbo* XVI. 35: VI. 165; *Pro A. Caecina* XXVI. 74: IX. 43; *Pro Cluentio* LIII. 146: III. 136; *Pro Plancio*, XXXIII. 80: III. 19; *Pro Sestio* LXV: III. 106.

Cincinnatus, Lucius Quinctius, 5th century B.C., Roman general: V. 83.

Cinna, Lucius Cornelius, *d.* 84 B.C., Roman statesman: possibly pseudonym for Godolphin, III. 77.

Circle, squaring of: I. 174.

City Cries Instrumental and Vocal: *see* EXAMINATION OF CERTAIN ABUSES, CORRUPTIONS, AND ENORMITIES.

Civil War, 1642–46: allegory of, I. 128–30; Charles I justified, IX.

123; condemned, IX. 122; distinction between Crown's public and private capacities, VIII. 17; destructiveness, IX. 225; and English language, IV. 9; evil effects, IX. 225; lessons of, IX. 225; sermons on, IX. 226–7; and the shilling, II. 244–5; start, IX. 222; 'that unnatural rebellion', VI. 9; and Williamite wars, XII. 132.

Civilization: and Christianity, IX. 80; God's concern, IX. 238.

'Civis': and 'citizen', IV. 252.

'Civitas Dublin', proposed inscription on Irish coins: XII. 105.

'Clapper, Lady': character in *Polite Conversation*, IV. 156.

Clarendon, Edward Hyde, 1st Earl of, 1609–74, Lord Chancellor: VIII. 138, 171; Burne; and JS on, V. 267; on Civil War, IX. 121; his education, XII. 47; on England before Civil War, XII. 264; *History of the Great Rebellion*, II. 12; — style, V. xxxviii; — JS's copy, XIII. 155; — **JS's marginalia, V. 295-32**; — analysis of JS's marginalia, V. x, xxxvii–xlii 'pattern for all ministers', VII. xxxv–xxxvi; defended by his son (1667), III. 152; trial, XIV. 38; wrote 'with the spirit of an historian', V. 267.

Clarendon Press, Oxford: editions of JS's works, I. v; editions of *Tale of a Tub*, I. ix, *n*.†.

Clark, Mary, *fl*. 1677–96, widow of Andrew, London printer: *Ephemerides*, I. 141.

Clarke, Samuel, 1675–1729, meta-

physician: possibly 'Court-Chaplain', IV. 108; *The Scripture Doctrine of the Trinity*, IX. 107.

Class struggle: *see* CONSTITUTION, *balance of power*.

Classes, social: *see* SOCIAL LEVELS AND CLASSES.

Classics, ancient: authors and lobsters, IX. 334; worm-eaten, IX. 333.

'Clatter, Mrs.': character in *Polite Conversation*, IV. 193–4.

Claudian, *fl*. A.D. 395–404, poet: Baronius and JS on, XIV. 18; and monotheism, XIV. 18.

Claudius, Appius, *d*. 449 B.C., decemvir of Rome: 'one of them', I. 198, 215; and Roman senate, I. 218.

Claudius, Tiberius, 10 B.C.–A.D. 54, Roman emperor: V. 3; and conquest of England, IV. 6.

Clavers: *see* DUNDEE, 1ST VISCOUNT.

Clayton, Charlotte (*née* Dyve), Lady Sundon, *d*. 1742, wife of Lord Sundon, favourite of Queen Caroline: V. 214.

Cleanliness: and women, IX. 87; — in Brobdingnag, XI. 118–9.

Cleland, William, captain of dragoons (commissioned captain 1685): V. 159.

Clemens, Joseph: *see* COLOGNE.

Clement VII, *c*. 1480–1534, Pope: V. 86.

Clement XI, 1649–1721, Pope: his death predicted, II. 148, 207.

Clément, Jacques, 1567–1589, assassin of Henry III of France: 'an enthusiastick frier', III. 106–7.

Clements, Henry, *fl.* 1707-19, bookseller: VII. 235.

Clendon, John, *d.* 1719: III. 55, 71; and freethinking, IV. 41.

Cleomenes II, *c.* 260-219 B.C., King of Sparta: and Spartan restoration, I. 210.

Cleopatra, Queen of Egypt, 69-30 B.C.: V. xi, 85.

Clergy: unfit for secular business, XIV. 17.

Clergy of the Church of England: and atheism, IV. 37; — not a subject for sermons, IX. 77-9; authority, and civil power, II. 77-9; — supported by reason, IV. 39-40; baptism by laymen, IV. 34; and Bible (text and translations), IV. 29-35, 37-8; Burnet's contempt for, IV. 68-71, 77-9; Christ (divinity and messiahship), IV. 31-2, 34; clannishness condemned, II. 52-4; and conversation, IV. 109-10; methods of conversion, IV. 41; corruption of, II. 46-7; Corusodes and Eugenio, XII. 41-5; accused of deception, IX. 40; defended, XIV. 5; and belief in the devil, IV. 30, 77-9; discretion and preferment, XII. 38-40; dissension about doctrine, IV. 34-7; — subtleties encourage, IX. 262; Dissenters mistreat, V. 252; religious doubts ('not answerable to God for the doubts that arise in my own breast'), IX. 262; duty of ('defending a post assigned me, and gaining over as many enemies as I can'), IX. 262; education of, IV. 228; IX. 63-4; — fear of pedantry, IX. 65; and education

of children, III. 37, 71; envy and failure, XII. 39; episcopacy, divine institution, IV. 34; hell, IV. 34-5; ignorance among, II. 46; and ignorance of people, IX. 80; immorality of, II. 54-5; IV. 40-1, 68-71, 77-8; and public immorality, IV. 40-1; as justices of peace, II. 55; language and speech, II. 176-7; IX. 65-73; London parishes too large, II. 61; III. 159-60; number of parsons (10,000 in England), I. 25; II. 30; IV. 40; and original sin, IV. 34-5; Oxford ministry backed by, III. 158, 199-200; VII. 3; not persecutors, III. 127; popular under persecution, IX. 262; playwrights ridicule, II. 55, and poets, IX. 330; 'polite assemblies' exclude, IV. 109; poverty of, IV. 65, 78, 228; preaching, IX. 64-79; on predestination, IV. 34; a public expense, II. 30-1; IV. 40; humble social rank, IX. 131; reputation (contempt, dislike, scorn for), II. 35-6; IX. 80, 130, 262; on resurrection, IV. 34; their rights ordained by God, II. 81-7, 92; and the sabbath, IV. 34; and Socrates, IV. 41-2; as theatre-goers, XII. 35-6, 40; Tindal attacks, II. 72-107; — calls them cheats, IV. 45; trinity, and dissension of clergy, II. 38; IV. 35; IX. 77, 107-8, 160, 162, 167-8; on usury, IV. 34; whores tolerated, IV. 40; wives, IV. 226-8. See also BISHOPS OF THE CHURCH OF ENGLAND; CHURCH OF ENGLAND; CONVOCATION; LETTER TO A YOUNG GENTLE-

MAN; MR. COLLINS'S DISCOURSE; PREFACE TO THE BISHOP OF SARUM'S INTRODUCTION; REMARKS UPON A BOOK; THOUGHTS ON RELIGION.

Clergy of the Church of Ireland: and agriculture, IX. 47–8, 59; and *Beggar's Opera*, XII. 35; bishops' power over, XII. xxxv–xxxix; career described, IX. 63–4; career unattractive, IX. 53; charity as duty, V. 87–92; and charity schools, IX. 202–5; and Civil War, IX. 226–7; contempt for, and preaching, IX. 214; decline of, IX. 52–3; dissension among, XII. 193; Dissenters to be resisted, IX. 175–6; bills of division and residence, XIII. 205; duty to warn against temporal evils, IX. 239; education, IX. 63–4, 67; compared with English, XII. 181–2; XIII. 100; House of Lords petitioned, XII. xxxvii; and informers, IX. 183; and Irish cloth, XII. 68–9; and Irish manufactures, IX. 17–18; X. 135 and *n*.*; as justices of the peace, XII. 195; and landlords, XIII. 98–9; learning, IX. 64; and linen industry, XIII. 104; livings, XII. 181–6; — division of, XII. 186, 194–5, 197–202; loyalty to Hanoverian line, XIII. 98; and bill for a modus, XIII. 99, 102; modus unfair to, XIII. 97–108; parishioners' dishonesty, XIII. 100; poverty, V. 90; IX. 58; XII. 194; XIII. 100–1; residence, XII. xxxviii–xxxix, 190–202; respected, II. 119; rights ignored, XIII. 99; self-taxation, XIII. 99, 106; and Test Act—not dependent on, XII. 249; — support it (1708), II. 119-20; — support it (1732), XII. 256; — support it (1733), XIII. 97; tithes, collection difficult, IX. 59; XIII. 98, 100, 103; and Whigs, II. 119; widows, and revenues from swearing, IX. 297; and Wood's coins, IX. 235–6, 239. *See also* CONCERNNG THE UNIVERSAL HATRED . . . AGAINST THE CLERGY; CONSIDERATIONS UPON TWO BILLS; LETTER . . . CONCERNING THE SACRAMENTAL TEST; LETTER TO A YOUNG GENTLEMAN; ON THE BILL FOR THE CLERGY'S RESIDING; SOME REASONS AGAINST THE BILL FOR A MODUS; TITHES OF THE CHURCH OF IRELAND.

Clermont, Council of (1095): V. 21.

Cleveland, Barbara Villiers, Duchess of, *c.* 1641-1709, mistress of Charles II: V. 286.

'Clever': on word list of JS, V. 336.

Clidesdale: *see* CLYDESDALE.

Cliffe, John: mentioned, I. 237.

Clifford, James: acknowledgement, XII. v; and *Maxims Controlled in Ireland*, XII. xxiii; *Swiftiana in Rylands Eng. MS*, V. xxxii, *n.* 1.

Clifford of Chudleigh, Thomas Clifford, 1st Lord, 1630-73, statesman: education, XII. 47; and Stop of the Exchequer (1672), V. 274.

Climate: affects forms of government, II. 17.

'Climenole', in *Gulliver's Travels*,

Laputan word for 'flapper': XI. 159.

Clio, muse of history: I. 156.

Cloaca: IV. 232.

Clodevaus: *see* CLOVIS.

Clodius, Publius Pulcher, *d.* 52 B.C., Roman statesman: pseudonym for Wharton, III. 77, 84; character in *Discourse of the Contests and Dissensions* (probably Sir Edward Seymour), I. 233, 235.

Clogher, Bishop of: *see* RICHARD TENNISON; ST. GEORGE ASHE; JOHN STEARNE.

Clonfert, Ireland, see of: XII. 211.

Clonmel, co. Tipperary, Ireland: Elliston caught, IX. 366.

Clothes: *see* DRESS.

'Cloudy, Mrs.': character in *Polite Conversation*, IV. 166.

Clovis ('Clodevaus'), King of the Salian Franks, *c.* A.D. 466–511: and free masons, V. 327.

'Club': *see* SOCIETY.

'Club, Lady': character in *Polite Conversation*, IV. 168.

'Clumglum', in *Gulliver's Travels*, Lilliputian title comparable to 'marquis': XI. 66.

'Clustril', in *Gulliver's Travels*, Flimnap's informer in Lilliput: XI. 65.

Clutterbuck, Thomas, *c.* 1671–1742, politician: member of Irish Privy Council, X. 205.

Clyde, river in Scotland: V. 142.

Clydesdale, valley of Clyde River, Lanarkshire, Scotland: V. 154.

Cnut: *see* CANUTE.

Coachman (in *Directions to Servants*, XIII. 45–6): allied to groom, XIII. 219; drunkenness, XIII. 45; fellow coachmen, XIII. 46; horses, XIII. 45; wheels, XIII. 46.

Coals, English: not to be burned, IX. 17, 270.

Cobbe, Charles, Archbishop of Dublin, 1687–1765: VII. xvii.

Cobham, Henry Brooke, 11th Lord, 1564–1619, conspirator: and trial of Sir Walter Raleigh, X. 169.

Cockain: *see* COKAYNE.

Cochrane (or Cogheran), Sir John, *d. c.* 1695: helps Argyll, V. 158–60.

Cockburn, Lieutenant-Colonel: V. 129–30.

Cockpit, Whitehall, London: X. 189, 191; attempt to assassinate Oxford, VII. 76–7; Steele's office at, II. xxv.

Codicil to the Will of Dr. Swift: *see* WILL OF JS.

Codrus, legendary last king of Athens: and Solon, I. 204.

Coffee: scarce, II. 76; 'unwholesome', XII. 20.

Coffeehouses: and moneyed men, VI. 53–4; and public opinion, VI. 53–4; and wit, IX. 336. *See also* WHITE'S CHOCOLATE HOUSE.

Cogheran, Sir John: *see* COCHRANE.

Coghill, Marmaduke, *d.* 1739, Irish judge: proclamation against Drapier, X. xx; on Irish House of Lords, X. xxix–xxx; praises JS, XII. xiii–xiv.

Coinage: altered, III. 135. *See also* WOOD'S COINAGE.

Cokayne, Sir Thomas, *c.* 1519–92: his housekeeping, IX. 50.

Coke, Sir Edward, 1552–1634, judge and legal authority: and sixth *Drapier's Letter*, X. 171; and royal prerogative, X. 28, 108; quotation—*The Second Part of the Institutes of the Lawes of England* (1642), X. 9–10.

Colbert, Jean-Baptiste, 1619–83, French statesman, uncle of Torcy: favours peace, VII. 46.

Colbert, Jean-Baptiste, marquis de Torcy: *see* TORCY.

Colbert, Louis-François-Henri: *see* CROISSY, COMTE DE.

Colchester: and oysters, IV. 258.

Colchis, bulls of: and Papal bulls, I. 68.

Coleby, Mr.: robs Irish treasury, X. 28, 37, 66.

Coleortum, near Ashby de la Zouch, Leicestershire: IV. 284.

Coleraine, co. Londonderry, Ireland: living of, and Dunkin, XIII. 189.

Coligny, Gaspard de, 1519–72, French admiral: assassinated, III. 107.

College Green, Dublin: fire, V. xii; and Charles McCarthy, V. 87–92.

Collier, Jeremy, 1650–1726: *Essays upon Several Moral Subjects*, IX. 116 *n.* 1.

Collins, Anthony, 1676–1729, deist: III. 37, 55, 71; and Burnet, IV. xxv; linked with Burnet, IV. 70; *Discourse of Free-Thinking* (1713), IV. x–xi, V. 255; — attacked by JS, IV. xvi–xix, 27–48; *An Essay Concerning the Use of Reason in Propositions* (1707), IX. 111 and *n.*

Cologne, Germany, archbishopric of: VI. 12.

Cologne, electorate of: VI. 113, 115; Hapsburgs secure, VII. 89.

Cologne, Joseph Clemens, Elector of, 1671–1723, brother of Elector of Bavaria: VII. 60; England's ally (1689–97), VI. 14.

Colonies: XI. 322; colonial policy criticized, XI. 294–5.

Colross: *see* CULROSS.

Comets: XI. 164–5, 171, 210.

Comines or Commynes, Philippe de, sieur d'Argenton, *c.* 1447–1511, French historian and statesman: *Mémoires* (1524) — and Creichton, V. 122; — JS's copies, V. xviii, *n.* 2; — JS on, V. xviii, 122; — quoted, X. 171.

Commerce, Treaty of: Parliament to vote on (1713), VIII. 71; defeated (1713), VIII. 21; and Tories, VIII. 22.

Committee of Secrecy, 1715: XI. 67–72.

Common law: V. 6; and Cowper, VII. 10.

Common people: 'my faithful friends' (changed from 'rabble'), X. 88, 213; political wisdom, XIV. 10; and public welfare, IX. 234; 'rabble' ridiculed, I. xl; JS's distrust of, I. xx.

Common-place book: and poetry, IX. 337.

Common Prayer, Book of: and linguistic change, IV. 14–15.

Commons: *see* HOUSE OF COMMONS; DOMINATIO PLEBIS; PARLIAMENT.

Commonwealth, English: failure, IX. 226. *See also* CROMWELL.

Compleat Collection of Genteel and

Ingenious Conversation: *see* POLITE CONVERSATION.

Compleat Jester: I. 38.

Complete Key to the Tale of A Tub, with Some Account of the Authors (1710): on authorship of *Tale*, I. xxx; published by Curll, I. xxx; JS on, I. xxx, 1, 12; and Thomas Swift, I. xxx–xxxii; and Benjamin Tooke, I. xxxi.

Complete Refutation of the False-hoods Alleged Against Erasmus Lewis, by JS: *see* EXAMINER, *JS's contributions*, 2 Feb. 1713.

Complexion: fairness relative, XI. 92, 96.

Compton, Henry, 1632–1713, Bishop of London: V. 289; XII. 270; Burnet and JS on, V. 277.

Compton, Sir Spencer: *see* WILMINGTON.

Communion: and Tindal, II. 93, 191.

Concerning that Universal Hatred, Which Prevails Against the Clergy (1736), by JS: **XIII. 123-6**; background, XIII. xxxvii–xxxviii; textual notes, XIII. 223.

Concordat of Francis I with the Pope, 1516: Burnet on, IV. 71–3.

Condé, Nord, France: VI. 109; VII. 113, 152–3, 161.

Conduct of the Allies (1711), by JS: **VI. 3-65**; analysis, VI. xi, xiv; anonymity, VI. x, xi; JS's 'Appendix', VI. xxvi, 165–9; background, VI. vii–viii; Burnet on, V. 293; charges vindicated, VII. 79; composition, VI. vii–ix, 96; attempts to shorten composition, VI. 85; editions, VI. ix, xi, 96, 205, 207; — Irish, VI. xiii; — postscript to 4th, VI. xi, 65; and *Journal to Stella*, VI. vii–viii; mistakes denied, VI. 96; *Post Boy* on, VI. ix; printer (John Barber), VI. vii, viii, ix (not Morphew); *Protestant Post Boy* on, VI. ix; publication, VI. viii–ix, xxv–xxvi, 205, 207; — 'delay' explained, VI. 53; — promised, III. 203; and *Publick Spirit of the Whigs*, VIII. 52; purpose, VI. xxv; read in Commons, VI. xiv–xv; reception, VI. ix–xi, xii–xv, 65, 92, 95, 96; VII. 79, 'these loud accusations'; and *Remarks on the Barrier Treaty*, VI. xi, xv–xvi; replies, VI. ix–xii; — *see also* FRANCIS HARE (*Allies and Late Ministry Defended*); PROTESTANT POST BOY; REMARKS ON A FALSE . . . LIBEL; REMARKS ON TORIES NEW IDOL; STEELE; and *Some Remarks on the Barrier Treaty*, VI. 49, 85, 92; sources, VI. xi; style, VI. xi; textual notes, VI. 205–9; original title, VI. xxv; title-page facsimile, VI. 3; 'all true', V. 293.

Congé d'élire: II. 91, 105.

Congleton (or Congerton), Cheshire: V. 166, 167.

Congreve, William, 1670–1729, dramatist and friend of JS: bookseller's copyright, XIII. 206; on conversation, IV. xxix; and Halifax, IX. 29; and Oxford, IX. 29; Oxford esteems him, VII. xxxv; pun upon name, IV. 274–5; and Scriblerus Club, XI. xiii, *n.* 2; labelled author of *Squire Bickerstaff Detected*, II. xiv, *n.* 2; **and JS** — JS's poem on: *see* TO MR CONGREVE; —

friendly, II. xxxvi; — allegedly protected by JS, VII. xxxv; — recommended to Oxford by JS, IX. 29; — *Tale of a Tub*, I. 133.

Coningsby, Mrs.: Wharton's conduct with, III. 28-9, 240.

'Conjured spirit': description of JS, I. xi.

Connaught, western province of Ireland: Dublin more miserable, XIII. 134; farmers in, XII. 178; swearing at fairs, IX. 296; and JS's will — no land to be bought there, XIII. 150, 198.

Conolly, William, *d.* 1729, Speaker of the Irish House of Commons and Lord Justice of Ireland: member of Privy Council, X. 182, 205; possibly, 'Somebody', X. 122; and Wood's coinage, X. 7.

Conon, *c.* 444-390 B.C., Athenian general: and Athens, I. 208.

Conon, 1st century A.D., Greek mythographer: and Orpheus, I. 187, *n.*†.

Conscience: IX. 114-15; and church-going, IX. 215; defined IX. 114, 150; and freedom of thought, IX. 263; and honesty, IX. 152; and laws, IX. 157; — depends on God's laws, IX. 114-15; limitations, IX. 150; meaning changed, IX. 151; and religion, IX. 152; self-knowledge, IX. 151; false substitutes, IX. 152; foundation of virtue, IX. 154; guarantees virtue, IX. 158.

Considerations about Maintaining the Poor, by JS: **XIII. 174-7;** authorship, II. xxxiv and *n.* 3; background, XIII. xxxviii-xxxix; textual notes, XIII. 224.

Considerations upon Two Bills . . . Relating to the Clergy of Ireland (1732), by JS: **XII. 189-202;** abstract in *Dublin Journal*, XII. xxxvii-xxxviii; advertisement in *Dublin Journal*, XII. 341-2; background, XII. xxxv-xxxix; composition, XII. xxxv-xxxvi, 202; editions, XII. xxxviii, 341-2; 'a pamphlet', XIII. 205; style, XII. xxxix; textual notes, XII. 341-3; title-page facsimile, XII. 189.

Considerations upon the White Herring and Cod Fisheries, 1749: *see* VERNON.

Constance, Countess of Boulogne, sister of Louis VII: marries Eustace IV, Count of Boulogne, V. 69.

Constantine the Great, *c.* 288-337, Emperor of Rome: I. 55, *n.*†; and Arianism, IX. 261; Christian conversion, IV. 41; 'Donation' and papal authority, XIV. 30.

Constantinople: seat of Roman Empire, IX. 48; 2nd Council of, and Council of Trent, XIV. 33; fire, XIV. 23-4; plague at (A.D. 542 and following), XIV. 33.

Constitution, political: balance of power as principle of English constitution (*i.e.*, among the commons, the lords, and the royal prerogative), I. 195-203, 223-7; III. 121-6; V. 36; VII. 19-21; XI. 138, 171; — and Athens, I. 204-10; — attacked, II. 22-3; — Commons unyielding, VIII. 176; — and history of England, I. 228-36; — and

impeachments, I. 195–236; — and monarchs of England, II. 18–23; — monarch's grants resumed by Commons, VII. 102; — necessity of, VI. 132; — and creation of 12 peers (1711), VI. 132; VIII. 149–50; — and providence, VIII. 138; — and Rome, I. 211–22; — and royal income, VII. 102; — and 'tacking', VII. 102–3; — and taxation, V. 245; changing nature of, II. 84; and church, II. 46–51; — English constitution inseparable from Church of England, II. 18; dispensing power, IX. 32; English constitution oldest extant, II.18; forms of government, I. 195–200, 223–7; II. xvi–xvii; — in Athens, I. 204–10; — and Bodin, V. 244; — Church of England compatible with any form, II. 14; — democracy, V. 246; — expediency varies, II. 17–19; — none ordained by God, II. 14; — none perfect, II. 14–15; — and religious freedom, XII. 278; — republic vs. tyranny, I. 250; — in Rome, I. 211–22; Gothic constitution, III. 41; innovation dangerous, III. 91–2; VIII. 179–80; Irish constitution crazy, XIII. 174; legislative power, II. 74–5; — and clergy, II. 81–2; limited or 'mixed' monarchy as principle of English constitution: III. 13; — and ancient republics ('all well-instituted states'), II. 16; VIII. 37; — and Brennus, V. 100; — clergy defend, IX. 122; — Commons, weakest element, VI. 125; — and Hobbes, VIII.

37; — 'monarch may be too much limited and subject too little', V. 63; — party differences over prerogative, IX. 122; —and sermons of January 30, IX. 122–4; — and war (long war better endured by tyranny than by free country), VI. 60; — Whig doctrine, IX. 122.

majority rule distrusted, VI. 125; XII. 162; military subordinate to civil authority, III. 40–6; R. Nelson's views, II. 21; passive obedience vs. resistance to tyranny, II. 21–2; III. 110–6, 144–5; VIII. 44–5; and Restoration, III. 64–6; and Revolution of 1688, II. xvii; succession — crown and Parliament may exclude next heir, II. 21, 23; V. 279; — hereditary or parliamentary, VI. 129; — legislature (i.e. crown and Parliament) may alter, VI. 27, 92–3; summary of constitution, VI. 165–6; and Tory principle, VI. 42; tripartite nature of English constitution ('when one of the three powers proves too strong for the other two, there is an end of our monarchy'), VI. 132; — and Collins, II. 74–5; tyranny defined, I. 197–203; 223–7; new Whigs inconsistent with constitution, III. 123–4. *See also* GOVERNMENT.

Consultation of Four Physicians upon a Lord That Was Dying, by JS: **IV. 271-2;** analysis, IV. xxxviii; MS provenance, IV. xxxviii; textual note, IV. 302.

Contemporary writers: ignorance

among, censured, II. 173–7; and
Polite Conversation, IV. xxxii;
ridiculed, I. 18–43, 77–82, 90–4,
115–19, 132–5.

Contentment: wealth hinders, IX.
195.

Contests and Dissensions: *see* DIS-
COURSE OF THE CONTESTS AND
DISSENSIONS.

*Continuation of the Predictions for . . .
the Year 1708*: II. 209–16; textual
notes, II. 290; title-page facsimile, II. 209.

Contractions and abbreviations:
attacked, IV. 106, 107, 113–14.

Convention Parliament, 1689: V.
291; opposed to war, VII. 68.

Conversation: XI. 277–8; accomplishments, IX. xxix; degenerate, IV. xxxi–xxxiii; and education, IV. 244; errors of, IV.
87–95; goals for, IV. 92; and
ignorance, IV. 244; and Ireland,
IV. 178–84; and manners, IV.
213, 222; in mixed company,
XII. 40; not to talk much, I.
xxxvii; politics dangerous subject, IX. 187; and pride, IV. 244;
and women, IV. 247; IX. 90;
XII. 307. *See also* DIALOGUE IN
THE HIBERNIAN STYLE; HINTS
TOWARDS AN ESSAY ON CONVER-
SATION; IRISH ELOQUENCE; ON
BARBAROUS DENOMINATIONS IN
IRELAND; POLITE CONVERSA-
TION.

Convocation: III. xv and *n.* 2;
and Anne, III. 49–50, 200;
Atterbury prolocutor, III. 51;
and bishops, III. 50, 74; of 1661,
Burnet and JS on, V. 270; and
new churches, III. 157–8; opposition to meetings of Irish, IX. x;

Irish, and Sacramental Test,
II. 119–20; III. 182; Irish,
suspended, XIII. 103; rights of,
and Baronius, XIV. xiii; sum-
moned (1710), III. 49–51;
attacked by Tindal, II. 103; and
JS's views, XIV. 5; tithe of
hops, III. 131; Whigs dislike,
III. 53, 56.

Conway, Carnarvon, Wales:
Hook's tomb, V. 202; JS at
(1727), V. 202.

Cook (in *Directions to Servants*,
XIII. 27–33): birds, XIII. 28–9;
boiling meat, XIII. 30, 31; relations with butler, XIII. 27, 31–2;
butter, XIII. 32, 33; charwoman,
XIII. 30, 31; children, XIII. 27;
dinner late, XIII. 30, 32; and
dishes, XIII. 28, 30, 32; excuses,
XIII. 33; fellow servants, XIII.
30; fire irons, XIII. 29; and
footmen, XIII, 31, 33; kitchen
fire, XIII. 30; and kitchen staff,
XIII. 29, 37; marketing, XIII.
28, 29, 30; meat as perquisite,
XIII. 28; plucking poultry,
XIII. 216; roasts, XIII. 28, 31, 32,
217; salt, XIII. 32–3; sex, XIII.
27, 215; spits, XIII. 28, 29;
washing hands, XIII. 31.

Cooper, Anthony Ashley: *see*
SHAFTESBURY.

Cooper, Mary, *fl.* 1743–61, widow
of Thomas, London bookseller
sometimes associated with
Dodsley: and JS's *The Story of
the Injured Lady*, IX. x.

Cooper, Thomas, *fl.* 1732–40,
prolific printer and publisher of
pamphlet literature: published
JS's letters to Pope, IX. xii.

Coote, Sir Charles, *c.* 1610–61

(Earl of Mountrath, 1660): and Creichton's father, V. 126–8.

Cope, Robert, *c.* 1679–*c.* 1753, Irish M.P., friend of JS: JS visits (1722), XI. xv.

Copenhagen, Treaty of, 1701: 'our guaranty', VI. 62.

'Coptick': and Steele, VIII. 40.

Copts: and the Bible, IV. 33.

Copy of Dr. Swift's Memorial to the Queen (written 1714), by JS: **VIII.** 200; background, VIII. xxxi; textual note, VIII. 232.

Copy of the Paper with Which Several Persons of the Liberty of St. Patrick's Attended the Rev. Dr. J. Swift, 8 Jan. 1734; V. 341–2; background, V. xxiv; textual note, V. 359.

Copyrights, English: Ireland and England compared, XIII. 206–7; — publishers ('booksellers') have none in Ireland, XIV. 42; possession disputed, XIII. 206.

Corbet, Francis, 1688–1775, treasurer and later Dean of St. Patrick's: rent of vineyard, XIII. 156.

Coriolanus, Gaius Marcus, 5th century B.C., Roman general: V. 86; and Roman balance of power, I. 214.

Cork, city in Ireland: and farmers, XII. 178; and Sheridan, XII. xxviii; Sheridan's sermon at, XII. 163–4; swearing revenues from, IX. 297; JS's freedom, XIII. xxxix, 155; letter from JS, XIII. 190–1; and Wood's coinage, X. 5.

Cork, county of Ireland: agri-

culture in, X. 140; XII. 178; and butter trade, XII. 10.

Cork and Orrery, Emily Charlotte, Countess of, 1828–1912: acknowledgement to, VII. xvii and *n.* 3.

Corn: scarce in Ireland, XII. 17–22, 55; intrinsic value, IX. 51.

Cornbury Park, near Charlbury, Oxfordshire, seat of Lord Cornbury: IV. 283–4.

Coronation oath: V. 194.

Correspondent: see WILLIAM TISDALL.

Corruptio optimi pessimum: I. 3.

Corruption: JS's views on: see DECAY; POLITICS; HUMAN NATURE.

Cortez, Hernan, 1485–1547, Spanish conqueror of Mexico: XI. 293.

Corusodes, discreet clergyman in *Intelligencer* No. 7: XII. 41–4.

Coryton, William, *fl. c.* 1711, London bookseller: III. 175.

Cossing of dogs: XII. 221–2.

Costor: and Irish coinage, X. 29.

Cotton, Charles, 1630–87, poet: pun upon name, IV. 274.

Cotton, Sir John, 1621–1701: and Burnet, IV. 60.

Cottonian Library, London: and Burnet, IV. 60.

Council of 400: I. 204.

Councils of the Catholic Church: and papal supremacy, XIV. 21–2.

'Counterfeit Letter to the Queen', not by JS: XII. xxxv.

'Counterpace': III. 34.

Counter-project: see BARRIER TREATY.

'Countess': dog in *Polite Conversation*, IV. 156.

Country Party: VIII. 84; obsolescence (1712), VI. 78; revived by October Club (1710), VII. 99; share interests with court party (1712), VI. 78; Whigs originate in, VI. 78.

'Couplers, Lady': character in *Polite Conversation*, IV. 196.

Court of Requests, in Westminster Hall: II. 174.

Court party: VIII. 84; share interests with country party (1712), VI. 78; obsolescence, (1712), VI. 78.

Courts and courtiers: XI. 6, 262–3; and selling of 'bargains', IV. 108; and conversation, IV. 108; and discretion, XII. 38–45; extravagant dress and William II, V. 25; and English language, IV. 13; envy within, XII. 39; and free-thinking, IV. 108–9; and Gay, XII. 35; *Hints on Good Manners*, IV. xxxvii; intrigues, XI. 54, 67–74, 175, 204–5, 255; bad manners, IV. 221, 222; maxims for, IV. 252; and misjudgment of others, V. 214; and national morals, II. 47–63; orthography censured, IV. 113; pages, XI. 108, 205; and pedantry, IV. 216; pronunciation of English, IV. 281; and religion, V. 214; and satire, XII. 34; and speech, IV. 10; *Treatise on Good Manners and Good Breeding*, IV. xxxvi–xxxvii.

Courts, bishops': ineffective, IX. 59.

Courtship: XI. 264.

'Covenant-hall': IV. 283.

Covent (or Convent) Garden, Westminster: I. 26; and author of *Answer to Bickerstaff*, II. 197; blessed by goddess of criticism, I. 154–5; and fornication, I. 31; lion in, II. 180.

Coward, Colonel: III. 232.

Coward, William, *c.* 1657–1725, physician, deist: III. 55, 71; anti-Christian, II. 72; and free-thinking, IV. 41; attacked by JS, II. xix, 29.

Cowley, Abraham, 1618–67, poet: leads the Moderns, I. 152; 'killed' by Pindar, I. 158–9; pun upon, IV. 273; JS compares himself to, I. xii; JS admires his poetry, I. xii; JS stops imitating, I. xv; quotation—'Love Undiscovered', ii. 5–6: II. 114.

Cownly, John: JS's tenant, leases for Mrs. Ridgeway, XIII. 154.

Cowper, William, 1st Earl, *c.* 1665–1723, Lord Chancellor: abilities limited, VII. 10; and Anne, VIII. 142–3, 167; Anne attached to 'two great officers', VIII. 103; alleged bigamy, VII. 10; III. 57–8, 78; called 'Will Bigamy', III. 25 and *n.* ‖, 57; XIV. 4; resigns lord chancellorship (1710), VIII. 142–3, 167; Lord Keeper ('guardian'), VII. 10; and Marlborough, VIII. 56, 114; subservient to Whigs, VII. 10; and Viscount Wenman's lunacy, III. 78.

'Coxcomb-hall': IV. 283.

Coxe, William, 1747–1828, historian: *Memoirs of Walpole* (1798), X. x, *n.* 1.

Craftsman: No. 227, XII. 311–21; — JS's answer to, XII. 173–8; — — background, XII. xxx–xxxi; — — textual notes, XII.

6

349; and JS, *A Letter to . . . the
Occasional Paper*, V. xiii–xiv; No.
45 (13 May 1727), V. xiii; turns
news writer, V. xiii; Walpole
attacks, V. 116.

Craggs, James, the elder, 1657–
1721, M.P.: defends Marl-
borough, VII. 22 and *n.**.

Craggs, James, the younger,
1686–1721, Secretary at War,
Secretary of State: VII. 22, *n.**;
and Addison, XII. 48.

Craik, Sir Henry, Bart., 1846–
1927, biographer of JS: and
authorship of *Tatler*, II. xxix.

Crambo: and rhyme, IX. 335.

Cranford, near Hounslow, Lord
Berkeley's seat: JS visits (Jan.
1709, not 1708), II. x; XIV. 50.

Cranmer, Thomas, 1489–1556,
Archbishop of Canterbury: IV.
73; VIII. 16.

Crassus, Marcus Licinius, *d.* 53
B.C., Roman statesman: III. xvii;
pseudonym for Marlborough,
III. 77, 80–5; XIV. 5.

'Cravent': IX. 272.

Crawford, William Lindsay, 18th
Earl of, 1644–98, Presbyterian:
'that poor weak creature', V.
179.

Crawley, Sir Ambrose: *see* CROW-
LEY.

Creation: man and beast compared, IX. 264.

Credit: III. 134–5.

Creech, Thomas, 1659–1700,
translator of the classics: translation of Horace, IV. 100; translation of Lucretius, IV. 37;
— quoted, I. 36, *n.**, 61, *n.*‖;
'killed' by John Ogleby, I. 158.

Creichton, Alexander, *d. c.* 1603,

great-grandfather of Captain
John Creichton: V. 125.

Creichton, Alexander, *b. c.* 1623,
father of Captain John Creichton: V. 125, 126–8.

Creichton, John, *d. c.* 1642,
grandfather of Captain John
Creichton: V. 125.

Creichton, Captain John, *b.* 1648:
and Atholl, V. 134–5; brutali-
ties, V. xxi; made a captain, V.
167; character, V. xx, 121–2;
and Charles II, V. 145; loyalty
to Charles II, V. 124, 134–5; and
Covenanters, V. 130–41; dreams,
V. xxi, 124–5, 144, 152, 154;
family, V. 125–8, 129, 152, 174,
180; and Gulliver, V. xx; and
4th Duke of Hamilton, V. 154,
158, 167–8, 172–77; to be
hanged, V. 172; imprisoned
(1689), V. 171–5; and James II,
V. 153, 159, 164; — oath of
allegiance, V. 168; and John
King, V. 143–4; marriage, V.
xix, 123, 129; bribes Melville,
V. 173–4; **Memoirs**, V. 120–81;
— **'Advertisement'** by JS, **V.
121–2**, xviii, xx; — authorship,
V. xvii–xxi, 120; — editions,
V. xxi; — Faulkner's prefatory
note, V. 120; — income from,
V. 120–2; — MS, V. xviii; —
and Monck Mason, V. xxi; —
publication, V. xviii, 351; — and
Scott, V. xxi; — 'plain un-
affected style', V. 123; — textual
notes, V. 351; — title-page
facsimile, facing V. 120; and
the Laird of Pettencrife, V. 175,
176; and Puritans, V. xxi; religion, V. xx–xxi; reputation, V.
123, 180; and David Steele, V.

157–8; and Francis Stuart, V. 135; and JS, V. xvii–xviii, 120; and Wilson, V. 144–5; wounded, V. 148–9.

Creichton or Crichton, Dr. John, 1688–1726, physician, cousin to Captain Creichton: V. 125–6.

Creon, legendary king of Thebes: I. 31.

Cretensis, Dictys, legendary Greek diarist: IV. 233.

Crew of Stene, Nathaniel Crew, 3rd Lord, 1633–1721, Bishop of Durham: Burnet and JS on, V. 293.

Crichton: *see* CREICHTON.

Crime and punishment: division of booty, IX. 40; canting despised, IX. 41; corruption in childhood, IX. 40; crimes not equal, IX. 247; death, IX. 41; drunkenness, IX. 39–41; unnecessary in England, XI. 252; fences, IX. 40; force of habit, IX. 41; informing, IX. 39; Irish, and servants, IX. 204; in Lilliput, XI. 58–60; pardons, IX. 38; |pickpockets, IX. 41; against public, heinous, IX. 238; — and corrupt judges, XI. 250; stolen goods, IX. 40; transportation ineffective, IX. 38; unrepentant criminals, IX. 38; whores, IX. 39, 40.

Crispin, William, Norman baron who smote Henry I: V. 39.

Critical Essay upon the Art of Canting, Philosophically, and Musically Considered, imaginary treatise: I. xl, 183.

Critics and criticism: I. 116–19; biographical criticism, II. 67–8; classical scholarship, I. 56–64;

IX. 334; criterion of classicism, II. 177; commentators, XI. 197–8; daughter of pride and ignorance, I. 153–4; and eloquence, XII. 33; goddess—disguised as Bentley, I. 155; literary, and morality, II. 56; literary, criterion of time, II. 175–7; and 'low comedy', XII. 33; and 'low humour', XII. 33; maxims of, I. 63–4; and 'musick', XII. 33; and poetry, XII. 33; satirized, I. 25, 56–64; taste, XII. 33; 'taste' of humour, XII. 33; 'True Critick', I. 57–64, 120.

Crockat, Gilbert, *fl.* 1692–1708: *The Scotch Presbyterian Eloquence*, by Jacob Curate (pseudonym for Gilbert Crockat and John Monroe), V. 130; XII. 276 and *n*.†.

Croft, William, 1678–1727, English composer: *Musica Sacra, or Select Anthems* (1724), V. 334.

Crofton, Sir Edward, *c*. 1688–1739, M.P.: member of Privy Council, X. 182.

Croissy, Louis-François-Henri Colbert, comte de, 1677–1747, brother of Torcy: a prisoner at Nottingham (1704), VII. 34.

Crokatt, Gilbert: *see* CROCKAT.

Cromarty (or Cromartie), George Mackenzie, 1st Earl of, 1630–1714, statesman: pun upon name, IV. 260; and JS's *Thoughts on Various Subjects*, IV. xl; thrift, IV. 253.

Cromwell, Oliver, 1599–1658, 'the Protector': III. 44, 73, 146; and balance of power, I. 231; Burnet and JS on, V. 267; and execution of Charles I, I. 125, *n*.

||; and Church of England, II. 9; Clarendon and JS on, V. 312–14, 316, 318, 320; and conversation, IV. 92–3; death, XII. 267; and Countess of Dysart, V. 272; increased England's wealth, VI. 9; genealogy, III. 151; quells Hyde Park mutiny, V. 84; soldiers settled in Ireland, IX. 31; refuses kingship, V. 85; liberty of conscience, IX. 263; and Presbyterian power, XII. 248; sermons, XII. 249; and shilling, II. 245; and Whigs, III. 104; V. 255.

Cromwell, Richard, 1626–1712, Lord Protector: XII. 267.

Cromwell, Thomas: *see* ESSEX.

Crook, Andrew, bookseller and King's Printer in Ireland (Dublin, 1681–1731): IX. 319; and *Humble Address of the Lords*, X. 215.

Cross: relics of the True Cross satirized, I. 74; — fragment puts out fire, XIV. 18.

'Cross I win': VI. 92.

Cross-purposes: children's game, IX. 336.

Crow, Charles, *d.* 1726, Bishop of Cloyne: pun upon name, IV. 260 and *n.**.

Crowley or Crawley, Sir Ambrose, *d. c.* 1714, sheriff of London in 1706: XII. 58.

Crucifix: XI. 216–17.

Crusades: begun, V. 21–2; piety slackens, V. 22–3; successes, V. 22.

Ctesias, *d. c.* 398 B.C., Greek historian and physician: on pygmies, I. 92, *n.**; in *Tale of a Tub*, I. xxv; quotations, I. 61.

Cuckolds: old and young, V. 335.

Cudworth, Ralph, 1617–88, Cambridge Platonist: on Robert Boyle, I. xxxiv.

Cuffe, Henry, 1563–1601, author and politician: VIII. 189.

Culleo ('Leo'), Quintus Terentius, *ff.* 188 B.C., Roman statesman: I. 218.

Culross or Colross, Fifeshire, Scotland: V. 131.

Cumberland, William Augustus, 3rd Duke of, 1721–65: and Gay, XII. 35.

Cumlock: *see* CUMNOCK.

Cumnock, Ayrshire, Scotland: V. 147, 157.

Cunning: VIII. 81; JS's definition, VII. 74, 179.

Cupid: and Diomedes, IV. 233.

'Curcazo': defined by JS, V. 336.

'Curio': character in *Discourse of the Contests and Dissensions* (probably Charles Davenant), I. 233, 235.

Curiosity: JS's views, I. 130.

Curll, Edmund, 1675–1747, bookseller: publishes *A Complete Key to the Tale of a Tub* (1710), I. xxx, ('bookseller') xxxi, xxxii, ('a Prostitute Bookseller') 12; edition of *Letters, Poems and Tales . . . passed between Several Persons of Distinction* (1718), V. xxiii; given copy of *Meditation upon a Broom-Stick*, I. 237; prints pirated edition of *Miscellanies in Prose and Verse*, II. xxxviii; Pope attacks, IV. xxxiv.

Curses: *see* OATHS.

Curtius, Marcus, legendary hero of ancient Rome: madness, I. 111.

Customs: English Commissioners of, and tariff rates, XII. 21; officials, XI. 203.

Cutts, John, Lord Cutts of Gowran, Ireland, 1661–1707, lieutenant-general: Macky and JS on, V. 261.

Cynicism: and wisdom, V. 273.

Cyrus the Great, *c.* 580–529 B.C., Persian emperor: V. 36; and balance of power, I. 197.

D

Daffy, Thomas, *d.* 1680, inventor of Daffy's 'elixir salutis': IV. 264.

Daily Courant: III. xxii; and Erasmus Lewis, VI. 176–7.

Dairy-maid: in *Directions to Servants*, XIII. 63.

Dalhousie, William Ramsey, 3rd Earl of, *d.* 1682, captain of Edinburgh Militia: and Creichton, V. 140, 151.

Dalyell, or Dalzell, or Dalziel, Thomas, *c.* 1599–1685, of Binns, general of forces in Scotland: V. 130–1, 144–7, 151, 153, 155; account of, V. 155–7; character not by Creichton, V. xix; and Charles II, V. 155–6; and James II, V. 157; and Monmouth, V. 139, 142; replaces and rebukes Monmouth, V. 142; and religion, V. 157.

Damme, near Bruges, Belgian port: VI. 101, 109.

Dampier, William, 1652–1715, buccaneer and explorer: *A New Voyage Round the World*, XI. xiv, 5.

Dan, city in Palestine: IV. 156.

Danae: and Jupiter, I. 251.

'Danby': etymology, IV. 234.

Danes: V. 6; invade England, V. 5; and English language, IV. 12.

'Dangle': defined by JS, V. 336.

Daniel Stylites, St., *c.* 409–93: and fire in Constantinople, XIV. 23–4.

Daniel, Samuel, 1562–1619, poet and historian: *Collection of the History of England*, and JS's *Abstract*, V. ix–x; style censured, II. 177.

'Danvers': etymology, IV. 234.

D'Anvers, Caleb, pseudonym for the *Craftsman*: XII. 174.

Darius: and the Banbury Saint, I. 185.

Darling: IV. 282.

Dartmouth, George Legge, Lord, 1648–91, admiral: coining patent compared with Wood's, X. 33, 40–43, 56.

Dartmouth, William Legge, Earl of, 1672–1750, Tory statesman: and Bolingbroke, VIII. 156; Dartmouth 'the principal secretary of state' (1713), VI. 173; VII. 47; character, III. 80; and Dutch treaty, VII. 108; and Duke of Hamilton's death (1712), VI. 198; Jacobitism, VIII. 166; and Erasmus Lewis, VI. xxvii, 173, 178, 200; Lewis his secretary, VI. 200; Macky and JS on, V. 259; and Maculla's project, XII. 94; and Oxford, VIII. 124; and Oxford's quarrel with Bolingbroke, VIII. 156.

Dauphin, Louis, *d.* 1711, eldest son of Louis XIV: death, VII. 120.

K

Dauphiné, France: riot in, predicted, II. 145.

Davenant, Charles, 1656–1714, political economist: Macky and JS on, V. 260; 'those reasoners', I. 200.

Davenant, Henry Molines, diplomat, secretary in Frankfurt 1703–11, envoy extraordinary to Genoa, Modena, and Tuscany, 1714–22: Macky and JS on, V. 261.

Davenant, Mary, daughter of Sir William, wife of JS's uncle Thomas: V. 191.

Davenant, Sir William, 1606–68, poet and dramatist: critic, IX. 332; author of *Gondibert*, I. 156; 'overthrown' by Homer, I. 157; pun upon name, IV. 273; and Thomas Swift, I. 281; grandfather to Thomas Swift, I. xxx; relationship to Swift family, V. 191.

'Davenport': etymology, IV. 234.

Davenport, Sherrington, *d.* 1719, Colonel: XII. 231.

David, King of Israel: compared to Drapier, X. xv; lessons of his life, IX. 246; and *Polite Conversation*, IV. 194; and Wood's coinage, X. 48.

David I, King of Scots, *c.* 1085–1153, brother of Matilda the Empress: V. 75; enormities, V. 52; invades England, V. 49–50, 52; and Henry II, V. 66; and Matilda, V. 49–50; defeated at York, V. 53–4.

'David's sow': drunkenness, IV. 194.

Davies, Godfrey: on *The Story of the Injured Lady*, IX. x, *n.* 1.

Davies, Sir John, 1569–1626, Attorney General for Ireland: *Le Primer report des cases et matters en ley resolves et adjudges en les courts del roy en Ireland* (1615), X. 10.

Davila, Enrico Caterino, 1576–1631, Italian historian: *Historia delle guerre civilli di Francia* cited, III. 107; leads Moderns' infantry, I. 152.

Davis, Mrs., schoolmaster's widow: II. xxix, *n.* 2.

Davis, Charles, *d.* 1755, London bookseller: publishes *Drapier's Letters* (1735), X. 207.

Davis, Herbert John: edition of JS's *Drapier's Letters* (Oxford, 1935), X. xi, *n.* 1; edition of JS's *Prose Writings*, aims and editorial method, I. v–vi; V. xxi–xxii.

Davis's Reports: see DAVIES, JOHN.

Dawson, Richard: X. 76.

'Dealer, Andrew': XII. 54.

Dean of St. Patrick's Petition . . . against the Lord Blaney (written *c.* 1715), by JS: **V. 199–200**; composition, V. xxiv; MS, V. xxiv; textual note, V. 357.

Deane, Richard, 1610–63, admiral and regicide: V. 191.

Deans: XIV. 18.

Death: deathbed conversions, V. 278; *mors omnibus communis*, I. 250; necessary, IX. 263.

Debt, national, of England: King of Brobdingnag horrified, XI. 130–1; and new churches, III. 158; 'we have dieted a healthy body into a consumption', VI. 58; credit deceptive ('dangerous, illegal, and perhaps treasonable'), VI. 56; Dutch example

irrelevant, VII. 69; George I fails to clear, V. 100; Godolphin and navy, III. 136; VII. 72–3; history, VII. 68–73; moneyed interest benefited, III. xxvi, 6–7; VI. 10, 48–9; VII. 68–70; — one part of nation pawned to other, VI. 18; and general mortgage, VII. 70–1; origin, VI. 10–1; Oxford relieves nation, III. 168–70, 198; VII. 3, 75–8; VIII. 126–7; payment of, VI. 54–5; and peace (1715–27), V. 104; and posterity, III. 7; VI. 18–19, 52, 55–6; VIII. 47; — 'a mighty comfort to our grandchildren, when they see a few rags hang up in Westminster-Hall', VI. 55–6; ruin 'infallible', VI. 7; JS will give account, VII. 1; Tories relieve nation, III. xxvi, 120, 167, 198; almost unique, VI. 55; and War of League of Ausgburg, VI. 10; VII. 68; and War of Spanish Succession, III. 7; VI. 5, 7, 10–1, 16, 18–19, 53–9; VII. 3, 22; Whigs benefited, III. xxvi; VI. 154; VII. 69–70; — blamed for, III. 72, 117; and William III, VI. 10–1; VII. 68.

Debt, national, of Ireland: and bishops, XII. xxxix-xl; — their lands to be sold, XII. 207–12; causes of, XII. 123–4; history of, XII. 132–3; indifference toward, XII. 126; payment of, proposal, XII. 207–12; payment of interest, XII. 123–6; value of, XII. 121–2; and wine duty, XII. xxi, 21, 124–6.

Decay of the world, or of human institutions: XI. 137–8, 201–2, 210; conversation, IV. 94; educa-tion, XII. 53; English morals and religion, II. 44–5; Houyhn-hnms take measures to prevent degeneration, XI. 268–9; lan-guage, IV. x–xi; corruption of English language, II. 174–7; moral decay and national de-cline, II. 57; the nobility, XII. 53; the corrupt nobility, XI. 256–7; nobility not decaying, V. 244; religion, II. 265; and social classes, II. 27; Yahoos have degenerated, XI. 272. *See also* CONVERSATION.

Decemviri of Rome: I. 198.

Declaratory Acts: 1719, and Ire-land, X. 35; 1720, JS attacks, X. xviii and *n.* 4.

Decree for Concluding the Treaty Between Dr Swift and Mrs Long, probably by JS; **V. 197-8;** authorship, V. xxiii–xxiv; composition, V. xxiii–xxiv; publication, V. xxiii.

Dedication concerning Dedications: *see* GORDON, THOMAS.

Dedications: V. 11; JS's views, I. 13–16, 30; XIII. 74.

Deering, Mr.: and Robert Grattan, V. 344.

Defence of English Commodities (1720), possibly by JS: IX. 269–77; textual notes, IX. 378; title-page facsimile, IX. 267.

Defoe, Daniel, *c.* 1661–1731: and JS's academy, IV. xiv; *The Con-solidator* ('many others') and JS's *Tale of a Tub*, I. 1; 'fanatick', III. 13; on High Church party, I. xxvi, *n.* ‖; pilloried, II. 113; on regulation of the press, I. xxvi, *n.* ‖; *Review* and JS's *Tale*, I. xxvi, *n.* ‖; *Secret History of the October*

Club, VI. xii; *The Secret History of the White Staff*, VIII. xxx; compared with JS, II. xx; and JS's *Memoirs*, VIII. xxx.

Deism and deists: and abolition of Christianity, II. 36–7; and ancient philosophy, IX. 241–50; and divine revelation, IX. 112; and preaching, IX. 77; ridiculed, IX. 102; 'scribblers', I. 2–3; and Trinity, IX. 108–9; and *Upon the Testimony of Conscience*, IX. 112. *See also* HERESIES.

Delany, Patrick, *c.* 1685–1768, Chancellor of St. Patrick's, Dean of Down, friend of JS: and Carteret, XII. xxviii, xxix, 164–6; fellowship scheme, XIII. 198; and *Letter on Maculla's Project*, XII. xviii; and *A Libel on Doctor Delany. And a Certain Great Lord*, XII. xxiv–xxv; *Observations upon Lord Orrery's Remarks on the Life and Writings of Dr Jonathan Swift*, IX. 98, *n.* 2; **and JS,** IV. xix; — JS's character of, XII. 164–6; — authorship of *The Difficulty of Knowing One's Self*, IX. 104, 105; — and publication of 1st *Drapier's Letter*, XIV. 56; — JS's executor, XIII. 157, 200; — legacy from JS, XIII. 156; — interest in preaching, IX. 99; — and JS's sermons, IX. 98; — JS writes to him concerning Sheridan (10 Nov. 1718), V. xxviii–xxix; — and *Treatise on Good Manners and Good Breeding*, IV. xxxvi; at Trinity College, XII. xxviii; and *A Vindication of His Excellency the Lord Carteret*, XII. xxviii.

De la Warr, John West, 6th Lord,

c. 1663–1723: Macky and JS on, V. 259.

Delgarno, Elizabeth: wife of Captain John Creichton: V. 123, 129.

Delightful Tales: I. 38.

Delilah: pun upon name, IV. 208.

Del Marmol, Ferdinand, baron de, 1832–1913: *Dictionnaire des filigranes classés en groupes alphabétiques et chronologiques*, XIII. xxi, *n.* 1.

Delphi, or Delphos, shrine of Apollo on Mount Parnassus: and Aeolism, I. 101.

Democritus, *c.* 460–370 B.C., Greek philosopher: 'the philosopher' writing on truth, I. 247.

Demosthenes, 384–322 B.C., Athenian orator and patriot: I. 31; XI. 127; fable of, X. 71; great orator, IX. 68–9; on oratory, I. 249; and 'philippizing', I. 224.

Denain, Nord, France: VII. 147, 152.

Denbigh, earls of: motto (*crescit sub pondere virtus*), IX. 272.

Dendermonde, or Termonde, at the confluence of the Dendre and Escaut rivers in Flanders: VI. 90, 101, 109, 113; VII. 114, 122; and Barrier Treaty, VI. 90; and Dutch barrier, VII. 91.

Denham, Sir John, 1615–69, poet: 'killed' by Homer, I. 157 and *n*.*; pun upon name, IV. 274.

Denmark: III. 205; 'these princes', VI. 63; 'princes of the north', VII. 148; compared to England, V. 244; early invasions of England, V. 5; Danish rule of England, V. 6; and Molesworth, II.

99; papacy and church ('Dania'), XIV. 28; troops hired in War of the Spanish Succession, VII. 127. *See also* FREDERICK IV, KING OF; NORTHERN WAR.

Dennis, John, 1657-1734, critic: V. 201; son of Etcætera the Elder, I. 57; and French privateers, IV. 250; praised, I. 249; ridiculed, I. 22; satirized, IV. xl; in *Tale of a Tub*, I. xxiv; and Wagstaff, IV. 118.

Dentists: satirized, XI. 146-7.

Denton, Mr., secretary to Wharton: III. 233.

Dependency Act, 1720: and Ireland, IX. 3-12; Irish opposition, IX. x.

Deptford, on the Thames, west of Greenwich: captain from, XI. 79; pun upon name, IV. 261.

Derby, James Stanley, 10th Earl of, 1664-1736, brother of the 9th Earl: 'scoundrel', V. 258.

Derby, William George Richard Stanley, 9th Earl of, *c.* 1655-1702, brother of 10th Earl: V. 258.

Derbyshire: and Eugenio, XII. 45; and Wagstaff, IV. 116-17.

Derbyshire Knight: *see* LINGER, SIR JOHN.

Dering, Henage, 1665-1750, Dean of Ripon, antiquary: III. 237.

Derry, county of Ireland: V. 126-7.

Derry, deanery of: V. 195; XII. 185.

Derry, diocese of: and Archbishop King, II. 282.

Derry, George, clerk of Dublin:

and Ebenezor Elliston, IX. 367.

Dervishes: and freethinkers, IV. 32, 33.

Desaulnais, Henry: *see* DISNEY.

Descartes, René, 1596-1650: XI. 197; and Aristotle, I. 146; 'killed' by Aristotle, I. 156; insane, I. 105, 107; leads Modern bowmen, I. 152.

Description of a City Shower, poem by JS: praised, II. 172; publication, II. xxvi, xxxiv.

Description of the Kingdom of Absurdities, imaginary treatise by the author of *A Tale of a Tub*: I. xl.

Description of the Morning, poem by JS: background, XII. xxxiv; praised, II. 172; publication, II. xxvi, xxvii.

Desfontaines, Pierre - François Guyot, 1685-1745: translates *Gulliver's Travels* (1727), XI. xxiii and *n.* 1.

Desires: wealth increases, IX. 195.

Despenser, Hugh le, the Elder, 1261-1326, favourite of Edward II: 'the Spencers', III. 93.

Despenser, Hugh le, the Younger, *d.* 1326, favourite of Edward II: 'the Spencers', III. 93.

'Detur dignissimo': and Bentley, I. xxii, *n.**; in dedication of *Tale of a Tub*, I. 14-16.

Devil: father of lies, III. 8; pulls paper with teeth, V. 208. *See also* SATAN.

Devizes, Wiltshire: and Stephen, V. 56.

Devonshire, William Cavendish, 1st Duke of, 1641-1707: ancestry, V. 242.

Devonshire, William Cavendish, 2nd Duke of, 1673–1729 (styled Marquis of Hartington in father's lifetime), Lord Steward, Whig: III. xxix; and Gregg, III. 185–205, 243–58; oratory, III. 79; 'poor understanding', V. 258; removed, III. 204.

Devonshire Man of Wit: IV. 209–10.

De Witt, Johan, 1625–72, Dutch statesman, grand pensionary of Holland: Burnet and JS on, V. 272; letters to Temple, I. 258; William III alleged to have caused his murder, V. 275.

Dialogue between Mad Mullinix and Timothy: see INTELLIGENCER NO. 8.

Dialogue between March and October: VI. xii.

Dialogue between Mr. Freeport, a Merchant, and Tom Handy, a Tradesman, Concerning the Bank, 1721: IX. 321.

Dialogue between the Archbishop of Canterbury and Mr. Higgins: ordered burned, II. 282.

Dialogue in Hibernian Style, by JS: IV. **277-8**; analysis, IV. xxxviii–xxxix; errata, XIV. 52; manuscript, IV. xxxviii, 302; textual notes, IV. 302.

Dialogue in the Castilian Language (1707), by JS: IV. **257-9**; composition, IV. xxix-xxx; MS, IV. xxxvi, 301; textual notes, IV. 301.

Diamonds: XI. 215.

Dice: sharpers and 'Tables of Fame', II. 241–2.

Dickson, R., printer of *Old Dublin Intelligencer*: XII. xxi.

Dictators: Roman, IX. 33.

Dictionaries: XI. 292.

Dictys Cretensis, legendary Greek diarist: IV. 233.

Didymus, *c.* 65 B.C.–A.D. 10, Alexandrian commentator on Homer: XI. 197.

Diemens Land: *see* VAN DIEMEN'S LAND.

Diet of Worms: pun upon name, IV. 264.

Difficulty of Knowing One's Self, sermon probably not by JS: IX. 349–62; authorship, IX. 103–6, 350, *n.*; editions, IX. 103, 104, 379; style, 105–6.

'Digression concerning Criticks', section III of *Tale of a Tub*: I. 56–64.

'Digression concerning . . . Madness', section IX of *Tale of a Tub*: I. 102–14.

'Digression in Praise of Digressions', section VII of *Tale of a Tub*: I. 90–4.

'Digression in the Modern Kind', section V of *Tale of a Tub*: I. 77–82.

'Digression on the nature, usefulness and necessity of Wars and Quarels', 1720, unauthorized addition to *Tale of a Tub*: I. 289–92; textual notes, I. 304.

Digressions, JS on: I. 90–4; allegorized, I. 120–1; tedious in Thomas Herbert, V. 243; weaken Herodotus, V. 243.

Dilke, Charles Wentworth, 1789–1864, antiquarian and critic: VIII. xiv; and JS's copy of *The Proceedings Touching . . . Clarendon*, XIV. 46.

Dill: *see* ASHE, DILLON.

Dillon, Myles: acknowledgement, XIV. vii.

Dimens Land: *see* VAN DIEMEN'S LAND.

'Dimple, Lady': character in *Polite Conversation*, IV. 145.

Dingley, Rebecca, *c.* 1665–1743, intimate friend of JS and Stella: V. 232; moves to Ireland (1701), V. 228; visits Sheridan at Quilca (1725), V. 220; and Stella, V. 227; and JS's library, XIII. xi, *n.* 1; spends summer with JS at Quilca (1725), V. xxix; and JS's will, XIII. 150.

Dioceses, Irish: leases, IX. 56; value of leases, IX. 53–4.

Diodorus Siculus, *fl. c.* 21 B.C., Greek historian: on Moses, IX. 245; quotations and allusions — I: I. 186; I and III: I. 187; I. xv: I. 186; III. lxii: I. 186; IV. iv: I. 186; XI. lxxxvii: I. 225; xv. lviii: I. 199; XVIII. xviii. 1–5 (not XXVIII) and lvi: I. 209; XX. x. 3: I. 199; mistaken allusion, I. 61.

Diogenes, 412–323 B.C., Greek philosopher: insane, I. 105; miseries of poverty, IX. 246; proud, I. 248.

Diomedes, in Greek legend, king of Argos: IV. 233.

Dionysius the Younger, 4th century B.C., tyrant of Syracuse, wrote poems and tragedies: and Plato, IX. 244.

Dionysius Halicarnassus, *d.* 78 B.C., Greek historian and rhetorician: XI. 133; a source for *Discourse of the Contests and Dissensions*, I. 215, 216; and fanaticism, I. 186–7; allusions to *Romanorum Antiquitates*, II. xiv: I. 218; —

IX. lii, liv: I. 215; — x. xxx: I. 215; — x. lv, lix, lx: I. 198.

Dionysus, or Bacchus: worship of, and fanaticism, I. 186–7.

'Dipthong': etymology, IV. 238.

Directions to Servants, by JS: **XIII. 3–65;** analysis, XIII. xii–xiii; anticipated (1711), III. 81–2; background, XIII. xx–xxi; **'Butler',** XIII. 17–27; — composition, XIII. xii–xvii, xxiii; — MS, XIII. ix, xii, xiii–xvi; — MS facsimile, facing XIII. xii; — textual notes, XIII. 211–15; composition, XIII. vii–xxxiii; **'Cook',** XIII. 27–33; — composition, XIII. xvii–xix; — MS, XIII. ix, xii, xvii; — MS facsimile, facing XIII. xvii; — textual notes, XIII. 215–17; editions, XIII, x–xi, xiv–xix, xxi–xxiii, 209; **'Footman',** XIII. 33–45; — background, XIII. xix–xxi; — MS, XIII. ix, xii, xix, xxi; — MS facsimile, facing XIII. xix; MSS, XIII. vii–x, xi, xii, xiii–xvi, xvii, xix, xxi, xlii, 209; — provenance, XIII. xxi–xxiii; publication, XIII. vii–viii, x–xi, xxii; 'Publisher's Preface', by Faulkner, XIII. x and *n.* 2; **'Servants in General',** XIII. 7–15; — composition, XIII. viii–ix; — MS, XIII. viii–ix; style, XIII. xii, xvii–xviii, xix–xx; — Irishisms, XIII. x; textual notes, XIII. 209–20; title-page facsimile of Dublin edition (1745), facing XIII. 3; — London edition, XIII. 3.

Dirty Lane, street in Dublin: IX. 301.

Discourse Concerning the

Fears from the Pretender (1714), by JS: **VIII. 71-2**; composition, VIII. xxii–xxiii; MS, VIII. v, xxii–xxiii, 204; and JS's *Publick Spirit of the Whigs*, VIII. xxiii; and JS's *Some Free Thoughts*, VIII. xxiii, xxvi; textual notes, VIII. 204–5.

Discourse Concerning the Mechanical Operation of the Spirit (written *c.* 1698), by JS: **I. 167-90**; allegory explained, I. 173–4; analysis, I. xxvii–xxviii; authorship, I. 169; — Thomas Swift alleged author, I. 280–1; editions: *see* TALE; errata and corrigenda, XIV. 50; reception, I. xxvii–xxviii; style, I. xxvii; unauthorized *Table, or Key*, I. 292–3; allegedly part of *Tale of a Tub*, I. 280–1; text— revision of scandalous language, 'furor Uterinus', facing I. 298; textual notes, facing I. 298; title-page facsimile, I. 167.

Discourse of the Contests and Dissensions . . . in Athens and Rome (1701), by JS: **I. 193-236**; authorship, V. xxxvi; — denied by Burnet, IV. xxiv; V. xxxvi; VIII. 119; composition, I. xx, 195; VIII. 119; editions, I. 298; errata and corrigenda, XIV. 50; attacked by Charles Leslie, II. xvii; reception, I. xx–xxi; VIII. 119; XI. x; and Somers, V. xxxvi; VIII. 119; style, I. xx; JS recommends bribery in elections, I. 301–2; text — revision to avoid jingle, I. 300; textual notes, I. 298–302; title-page facsimile, I. 193.

Discourse to Prove the An-tiquity of the English Tongue, by JS: **IV. 231-9**; composition, IV. xxxviii; textual notes, IV. 300.

Discretion: XII. 38–45.

Diseases: XI. 253–4, 262.

'Dismal': *see* NOTTINGHAM; HUE AND CRY.

Disney or Desney, or Desaulnais, Colonel Henry, *d.* 1731, French Huguenot, friend of Bolingbroke: and Dunkirk, VII. 142.

Dispensing power: JS's views, IX. 32.

Dispute Adjusted about . . . Repeal of the Corporation and Test Acts: *see* GIBSON, EDMUND.

Dissenters (commonly called 'fanatics' by JS, and normally interchangeable with Nonconformists): and abolition of Christianity, II. 34–5; and church decoration, I. 125, *n.*†; and Church of England — clergy, II. 12–13; V. 252; — foster dislike, IX. 175; — schism, IX. 118; mislead common people, IX. 173; condemned, XIV. 5–6; and Corusodes, XII. 44; emotionalism, IX. 132; their civil and military employments, XII. 249; fanaticism, I. 2; fanaticism defined as 'zeal, with a mixture of enthusiasm', V. 22; and franchise, V. 80; and free press, II. 10; insolence, IX. 175; in Ireland — and bishops, XII. 181; — and Church of Ireland, II. 124–5; — dangerous, II. xxii; — enemies of nation, IX. 172–3; — and Speaker of the House, II. 131–3; — take over, II. 117; — and Test Act, II. 110–

25; XII. xl–xlvii, 243–51, 255–60, 263–79, 299; toleration of, II. 124; and James II, II. 9; V. 285; and Jews, II. 90; and Archbishop King, II. 282; Leslie attacks, I. xxii; and liberty of conscience, II. 101; IX. 151; — limited by 'priest-craft', II. 28; and monarchy, XII. 286, 292; music in church disapproved by, I. 125 and *n.* *; — Sheridan's sermon, XIV. 36–7; — 'whistling', XI. 246; and Bill against Occasional Conformity, I. xxii; disowned by both political parties, II. 2–3; preachers ridiculed, I. 37 and *n.**; preaching, I. 126, *n.**; IX. 132; Presbyterians as political party, III. 126–7; proselytizers, II. 103; identified with Puritans, IX. 121–2, 226; and religious freedom, II. 102; ridicule of their views on doctrine, ritual, church decoration, etc., I. 121–31, and notes; civil rights, IX. 118; agreement with Roman Catholics: *see* ROMAN CATHOLICS; compared to Roman Catholics, V. 280; XII. 286–95; — Dissenters more dangerous, II. 120–2; IV. 77–8; IX. 172–3; XII. xli; all sects would be masters, V. 286; and snuffling, I. 183 and *n.**; JS attacks in *Ode to Sancroft*, I. xiii–xiv; — in *Tale of a Tub*, I. xvi; — 'fanaticism', I. 2; oppose Test Act, II. 110–25; and Tindal, II. 72; toleration of them supported by both political parties, II. 14; against toleration, II. 101; zeal and ignorance, I. 185–6; — as notion and substance, I. 86; —

ridiculed in *Tale of a Tub*, I. xl; — and sexual excitement, I. 129. *See also* ENTHUSIASM; NONCONFORMISTS.

Dissertation upon the Principal Productions of Grub Street: imaginary treatise by the author of *A Tale of a Tub*, I. xl.

'Distaff, Jenny', Isaac Bickerstaff's half-sister in *Tatler*: II. xxviii; and Aristotle, II. 241; letter to Bickerstaff, II. 249–50.

Diversion: imitation of fighting, IV. 247.

Divine authority: and the Trinity, IX. 110.

Divine law: motive of virtue, IX. 154.

Divine right of kings: an 'absurd notion', VII. 150; explained, XIV. 11; in France, VII. 150; and 'no peace without Spain', VI. 45; and Roman Catholicism, IX. 122; Tory doctrine, IX. 122.

Division, Bill of, Ireland, 1732: and clergy, XIII. 205; and Irish House of Commons, XIII. 97.

Dobbs, Richard, *b. c.* 1694, fellow of Trinity College, Dublin: V. 206.

Dobson, wool merchant, High Street, Dublin: imported cloth, XIII. 168.

Dodd, A., *fl.* 1714–1731, London bookseller: III. xxvii, 277.

Dodington, George Bubb, 1st Lord Melcombe, 1691–1762, Whig politician: and Irish employments, X. 58; notebook stolen by JS, V. xxiv–xxv; and Walpole, V. 214.

Dodona, Greece, seat of oracle of

Zeus, centred in oak tree: oaks and free masons, V. 330.

Dodsley, Robert, 1703–1764, printer and publisher: publishes JS (1745), IV. xxxix; printing of JS's sermons, IX. 103, 105.

Dodwell, Henry, 1641–1711, non-juror, scholar: III. 115; 'somebody else', IV. 84.

Dog-kennel: III. 181.

Dogs: cossing of, XII. 221–2; and experimentation, XI. 181; in Wales, V. 205.

Doily, or Doyley, Thomas, *fl.* 1705, linen-draper in the Strand: IV. 267.

Doing Good: A Sermon on the Occasion of Wood's Project (1724), by JS: **IX. 232-40**; analysis, IX. 107, 127–8; background, IX. 127–8, 134–5; X. 109; composition, IX. 127, 133–6; editions, IX. 377; and free press, X. 109; style, IX. 128.

Dolben, Gilbert, 1658–1722, Lord Chief Justice of Ireland: III. 236, 237.

Dolben, John, 1662–1710, M.P., impeacher of Sacheverell: III. 86, 222.

'Dolinc': defined by JS, V. 336.

'Doll': 'as Doll danced', IV. 150.

'Doll, Squire': character in *Dialogue in Hibernian Style*, IV. 278; character in *Irish Eloquence*, IV. 279.

'Dolt, Dick': character in *Polite Conversation*, IV. 149.

Dominatio plebis, i.e., tyranny of the commons: I. 199, 209, 217, 219.

Domitian, A.D. 51–96, Roman emperor: and fall of Rome, I. 222.

Donatists, followers of principles of Donatus, Bishop of Carthage: XIV. 19.

Donegal, county of Ireland: V. 129.

Doneraile, Arthur St. Leger, 2nd Viscount, *d.* 1734: member of Privy Council, X. 205.

Don Quixote: and Pomfret, IV. 250. *See also* CERVANTES.

Dorislaus, Isaac, 1595–1649, Dutch diplomat: Clarendon and JS on, V. 315.

Dorset, Lionel Cranfield Sackville, 7th Earl of (later Duke), 1688–1765, Lord Lieutenant of Ireland: and Lady Allen, XII. xxx; arrival in Dublin, XII. xxxv; arrives in Ireland, XII. xxx; his liveries, XIII. xxviii; appointed Lord Lieutenant, XII. xxix-xxx; pun upon, IV. 274; and JS, XII. xxix-xxx; and pamphlet by JS, XIII. xxv; JS visits, XII. xxxv; and Test Act repeal, XII. xliii.

Dorsetshire: rents in wool, IX. 269.

Douai, Nord, France: VI. 102, 116; VII. 113, 141; and Ormonde's troops, VII. 141; XIV. 13; and War of the Spanish Succession, VIII. 57.

Double-entendre: IV. 109; VII. 8.

Dougatt, Robert, *d.* 1730, nephew of Archbishop King: possibly one of two 'certain Gentlemen', XII. 196.

Douglas, parish, Lanarkshire, Scotland: V. 151.

Douglas, Archibald, *d.* 1667, captain: V. 84.

Douglas, (Honourable) James, *d.*

1692, lieutenant general (3rd Foot Guards) in Scotland: V. 161, 163, 169, 171.

Douglas, Lord William, son of Anne, Duchess of Hamilton, by Lord William Douglas; captain in King's Own Regiment of Scots Horse: V. 175.

Douras, estate in Ireland: called Whigborow, IV. 282, 283.

Dove, Jonathan, almanac maker: *Speculum Anni*, II. 163.

Dover, England: V. 53.

Dover, Henry Jermyn, 1st Lord, 1636–1708, courtier: a 'popish lord', III. 91.

Down, county of Ireland: and *Intelligencer* No. 19, XII. xv; and Scots, II. 116.

Down, deanery of: XII. 185, 201; JS's scheme for, XII. xxxvi–xxxvii.

Downes, Henry, d. 1735, Bishop of Meath, Bishop of Derry: member of Privy Council, X. 182.

Downing, Sir George, c. 1623–84, statesman: XII. 249.

Downs, a roadstead on the coast of Kent: XI. 79, 83, 148, 218, 289; pun upon, IV. 262.

Downton, Thomas, secretary to Sir William Temple: I. 257.

Drake, Sir Francis, c. 1540–96, English privateer and circumnavigator: and convoy of Peruvian silver, II. 243; Spanish bullion, IX. 50

Drama, JS's views on: *see* STAGE.

'Drapier, M.B.', JS's pseudonym in attacks on Wood's coins: London apprenticeship, X. 82, 86; defence of, in sixth *Letter*, X. 100–11, *passim*; education, X. 82, 86; — knows Latin, X. 82; — widely read, X. 124; and Gulliver, X. ix; and *Intelligencer* No. 19, XII. 54, 57; and masons, V. 333; and N.N., X. 170; portrait of JS as Drapier, facing X. 1; proclamation against: *see Letter IV*; pseudonym for JS, X. *passim*; London residence, X, 86; shop in St. Francis Street, Dublin, X. 80, 94; habit of writing, X. 86.

Drapier's Letters (1724), by JS: **X. 1–141**; authorship, X. 89 and *n.**, *n.†*; JS acknowledges authorship, XII. xxvi, 147; — known to be JS, X. xii–xiii, xix–xxi; background, X. ix–xi; and John Browne, V. xxxiv; IX. 135; composition, V. xi; IX. 127 and *n.* 1; X. ix, 207; Dublin edition (1735), V. xxxiv; editions, X. xxvii, 207; XIII. 201; effects, X. ix. xvi–xxxi, 49, 113–14, 205, 211; and Faulkner's preface to *Works*, XIII. 201; and *Gulliver's Travels*, X. ix; XI. 309–10; price, X. 24; printed by Harding, IX. xix; publication, X. xxvii; reception — compared with Inquisition, X. 89–90; JS's triumph, V. xxiv; — and weight of evidence, XII. 85; textual notes, X. 207–14; unpublished letters (i.e. VI and VII), XIV. 42.

Letter I, *To the Shop-keepers*, X. 1–12; analysis, X. xiii; background, X. ix–xi; JS sends a copy to Carteret, X. xiii; composition, X. xi–xii; editions, X. xii, 207–8; price, X. 3; publication, X. xii; XIV. 56; — and *Short View of*

the State of Ireland, XII. x; textual notes, X. 207–9; title-page facsimile, X. 1.

Letter II, *To Mr. Harding*, X. 13–24; background, X. xiv, 187–90, 215; editions, X. 207, 209; embryo, X. xiii–xiv, 153–4, 215; publication, X. xiv; textual notes, X. 209; title-page facsimile, X. 13.

Letter III, *Some Observations upon . . . the Report of the Committee*, X. 25–49; analysis, X. xv–xvi; audience, X. 27; background, X. xiv, 187–8, 191–203; composition, X. xiv; editions, X. 207, 209; — and Browne, V. xxxiv; X. xv and *n.* 2, 48, 203; style, X. xiv–xv; summary, X. 47–8; textual notes, X. 209–11; title-page facsimile, X. 25.

Letter IV, *To the Whole People of Ireland*, X. 51–68; analysis, X. xvii–xix; audience, X. 51 ff.; 'Proclamation Against', X. 53, 69, 81 and *n.**, 97, 101 and *n.**; XII. 147–8, 173; — and censorship, XII. 122; — reasons for, X. xviii–xix; — text, X. 205, 215; textual notes, X. 211–12; title-page facsimile, X. 51.

Letter IVa, *Seasonable Advice to the Grand Jury*, X. 69–71; background, X. xxi–xxii, 73; composition, X. xxi; and fifth *Drapier's Letter*, X. 90–1; editions, X. 207, 212; publication, X. xxi; textual notes, X. 212–13.

Letter IVb, *An Extract of a Book*, X. 73; background, X. xxii–xxiii, 73; and fifth *Drapier's Letter*, X. 90–1; editions, X. 207, 213; textual notes, X. 213.

Letter IVc, *The Presentment of the Grand-Jury*, X. 75–6; analysis, X. xxiii, 75; textual notes, X. 213.

Letter V, *To Viscount Molesworth*, X. 77–94; analysis, X. xxiv–xxv; background, X. xxiii–xxiv; composition, X. 79; 'Directions to the Printer', X. 79–80, 173–4; editions, X. 207, 213; and *Proposal for the Universal Use of Irish Manufacture*, X. 82 and *n.**; 89 and *n.*†; textual notes, X. 213–14; title-page facsimile, X. 77.

Letter VI, *To the Lord Chancellor Midleton*, X. 99–115; 'Advertisement', X. 97–8; analysis, X. xxi; composition, X. xxi, 97, 115; editions, X. 214; publication, X. xxi, 95, 97; signed by JS, XIII. 181; textual notes, X. 214.

Letter VII, *An Humble Address to Both Houses of Parliament*, X. 119–41; 'Advertisement', X. 97–8; analysis, X. xxvi. 97–8; background, X. xxv–xxvi; composition, X. 97, 119, *n.**; editions, X. 214; publication, X. xxvi–xxviii, 95; textual notes, 214.

Letter VIIa, *A Full and True Account of . . . the Execution of William Wood*, X. 145–9; background, X. xvii; composition, X. 145; publication, X. 95; textual note, X. 214.

Appendixes, articles attributed to JS: *Another Letter to Mr Harding the Printer*, X. 155–6, 215; *Dublin News Letter*, 21 Apr. 1724, X. 153–4; *A Letter from a Friend to the Right Honourable*

[Chief Justice Whitshed], X. 157–62; — background, X. xxv; — textual note, X. 215; *A Second Letter from a Friend to the Right Honourable* [Chief Justice Whitshed], X. 163–71; — background, X. xxv; — textual note, X. 215; *Advertisement prefaced to Swift's Works, 1735, Vol. IV*, X. 173–4, 214; *Advertisement* to Letter VI, VII, etc., X. xxi, 97–8, 214.

Addresses Against Wood's Patent: *The Humble Address of the Knights, Citizens and Burgesses* (i.e. Commons), 1723, possibly by JS, X. 177–8; — background, X. x–xi; — textual note, X. 215; *The Humble Address of the Lords*, 1723, possibly by JS, X. 179; — background, X. x–xi; — textual note, X. 215; *Address of the Privy Council of Ireland*, 1724, probably not by JS, X. 181–2; — background, X. x–xi; — textual note, X. 215; *Address of the County of Dublin*, 1724, possibly by JS, X. 183; — background, X. x–xi; — textual note, X. 215.

Reports on Wood's Coinage: *A Copy of the Report Made by Sir Isaac Newton . . . of the Assay*, not by JS, X. 187–8; — background, X. xiv–xvi; — textual note, X. 215; *Post-Boy*, 31 Jul. 1724, X. 189–90; *The Report of the Committee of the . . . Privy-council*, not by JS, X. 191–203; — background, X. xiii–xiv; — textual note, X. 215.

Draw-gloves: children's game, IX. 336.

Dreams: Creichton's, V. 124–5, 144–5, 154–5; Gulliver's XI. 92, 144; interpreting, II. 178–9; JS's, V. 203, 205–6.

Dress (clothes, clothing): beau's, XII. 306; and three brothers in *Tale of a Tub*, I. 44–55, 83–9; clerical, II. 54–5; perhaps a cover for deformities, XI. 260; extravagance introduced by William II, V. 25; Indian king ridicules, II. 266–7; in Ireland, and women's pride, XII. 81; Irish cloth — and the clergy, XII. 68–9; — and landed gentry, XII. 69–70; — and members of House of Commons, XII. 71; — and the nobility, XII. 69–70; and Irish manufactures, XII. 126–7; — notes on, for *Intelligencer*, XII. 306; personal ornaments, XI. 62; philosophy of, I. 46–8; poets' clothes, IX. 339; and soldiers, XII. 49; Stella's modesty in, V. 232; toupees, XII. xxxiii–xxxiv; unnatural, XI. 225–6, 230–1, 234, 236–7, 260, 272; and women's pride, XII. 67, 68, 81; the yeomen's simplicity, XI. 201.

Drewe, John or Robert, *fl.* 1625–26, M.P. for Devizes: X. 85.

Drogheda, co. Louth, Ireland: coinage in, XII. 90; Presbyterian missionary persecuted at, II. 111–12, 282.

Drue: *see* DREWE.

Druids: VIII. 22; and free masons, V. 329–30; no record of their mysteries, V. 3; lived in hollow trees, V. 3.

Drumclog, Lanarkshire, Scotland: V. 136–8.

Drummond, castle of, near Crieff, Perthshire, Scotland: V. 175.

Drummond, Lieutenant General: V. 155.

Drummond, James: *see* PERTH.

Drummond, John: *see* MELFORT, 1st Earl of.

Drummond, John, *c.* 1676–1742, Scottish M.P.: VIII. 171, 'a gentleman'.

Drunkenness: censured, II. 52; criminals, IX. 39, 40; dangers, IX. 186; 'drunk as David's sow', IV. 194.

'Drunlo': Flimnap's informer in Lilliput: XI. 65.

'Drurr', Lilliputian unit of measure, about one-fourteenth of an inch: XI. 48.

Dryden, John, 1631–1700: and JS's academy, IV. xiv; bookseller's copyright, XIII. 206; *The Hind and the Panther*, I. 41; *The Hind* answered in *Tale of a Tub*, I. xxiv; and *The Lovers Quarrel* ('Tommy Potts'), I. 41; pretends to lead the Moderns, I. 152; prefaces, I. 81–2; pun upon name, IV. 274; ridiculed 'now in being', I. 22; **and JS** — parodied in *Tale*, I. 3, 42 and *n*.†; — reasons for JS's dislike, I. xxiv; — relationship, V. 191; — ridiculed in *Tale*, I. xxiv; and Virgil, I. 146; exchanges armour and horses with Virgil, I. 157–8; translation of Virgil, I. 22; dedications of translation, I. 43; quotations — translation of *Aeneid* VI. 194–5: I. 33, *n.**; — *Discourse Concerning Satire*, I. 3; — translation of *Georgics* IV. 793–802: V. 327–8.

Dublin, Ireland: I. v; aldermen, X. 54; beggars: *see* BEGGARS; and *Beggar's Opera*, XII. 32–3; bishop's residence, XII. 212; new buildings, XII. 11, 309; 'Civitas Dublin', XII. 105; representation of clergy (1724), V. 87–92; Common Council, XII. xxiv; criers in, XII. 218–20; crime in, IX. 37, 39; footmen's petition, XII. 235–7; and French recruiters, XII. xxx; Grand Jury of, and *Proposal for the Universal Use of Irish Manufacture*, XII. 121, 122; grand juries, IX. 276; X. 69–76; Grub Street lacking, IX. 341; Grub Street and Lord Mayor, IX. 342; and Archbishop King, II. 282 and *n.* 2; language in, XII. xxxiv, 218–20; and London, X. 130; Lord Mayor, XII. xxiv, xxv, xxix, 29, 54, 100, 116, 141, 145 ff.; M.P. for, XIII. 79–85; — candidates, XIII. xxiv–xxvi; and *Modest Proposal*, XII. 112–3, 116; poets abundant, IX. 340, 344; police, XII. 217; population, XII. 98; recordership, XIII. xxiv, 69–70; improvements in recreations, IX. 344; rich families of, XII. 12; streets dangerous, IX. 208; swearing revenues, IX. 298; **and JS** — made freeman of, XII. xxiv, xxv–xxvii, 141, 145–8; — his freedom of, XIII. 155; — — date, XIV. 57; — influence, IX. xxi–xxii; — reaches (1714), VII. xii; — reaches (Oct. 1727), V. xxv; — receptions, XII. xix and *n.* 2; — writes from (1710), I. xxx; **JS's views** — abuses in, XII. 215–32; — new buildings, XII.

134–5; — needs coins, XII. 98–9; — and landed gentry, XII. 134–5; — his pedestrian ease, V. xxiv; — and women's pride, XII. 135; Tholsel, XII. xxiv; street traffic, V. xxiv; women corrupt, IX. 88; and Wood's execution, X. 145; workhouses, XIII. xxxviii–xxxix, 131; domestic and imported vices of, XII. 29–30. *See also* LINDALINO.

Dublin Castle, seat of the vice-regal court: X. xix; XII. xxviii, 155, 164, 165; JS at (1704 ff.), I. xxxiv.

Dublin College: *see* TRINITY COLLEGE.

Dublin County: *see* DRAPIER'S LETTERS, *Addresses Against Wood's Patent.*

Dublin Intelligence: on John Hoadly, XII. xxvii, *n.* 1; on *Modest Proposal*, XII. xix–xx; on JS's welcome to Dublin, XII. xix and *n.* 2.

Dublin Journal, George Faulkner's newspaper: prints abstract of *Considerations upon Two Bills . . . Relating to the Clergy of Ireland,* XII. xxxvii–xxxviii; — advertisement for *Considerations*, XII. xxxviii, 341–2; advertisement of attack on Walpole, V. xvi–xvii; 'quoted, XII. xxiv and *n.* 2.

Dublin News-Letter: **JS's contributions — 21 Apr. 1724** (on Wood's coins), **X. 153-4;** — — textual note, X. 215; — **4 Jan. 1737** (on relief for Godfrey and Green), **V. 346;** — — textual note, V. 359.

Dublin Philosophical Society, re-

established in 1707: 'the Society', IV. 257.

Dublin, see of: XII. 211.

Duck, Stephen, 1705–56, 'the thresher poet' : IV. 120, *n.*†.

Duck and drake, game of: XII. 162.

Duck Lane, London, centre of second-hand bookshops: IV. 62; XII. 264.

Dudley, Sir Edmund, *c.* 1462–1510, statesman: and blasphemers, II. 30.

Duelling: praised, IV. 214; and religion, IX. 116.

Dugdale, Sir William, 1605–86, antiquary: and Rivers, IV. 258.

Dumblane; *see* DUNBLANE.

Dumfries, Penelope (*née* Swift) Creichton, Lady, wife of 2nd Earl: V. 125.

Dun, Sir Patrick, 1642–1713, Irish physician: and Scotus, IV. 259.

Dunbarton, or Dumbarton, Scotland: V. 142.

Dunbarton, George Douglas, 1st Earl of, *c.* 1635–92, Colonel of 1st Foot: V. 159, 162–3.

Dunblane, or Dumblane, Perthshire, Scotland: V. 157.

'Dunce-hill': IV. 283.

Dundee, John Graham ('Clavers'), 1st Viscount of, 1648–89, Laird of Claverhouse, major general: V. 144, 161, 163–4, 166, 169–71, 172, 173; and pursuit of Argyll (1685), V. 159; Burnet and JS on, V. 290; and suppression of Covenanters, V. 136–41; and James II, V. 163.

Dungannon, co. Tyrone, Northern Ireland: and Alexander

Creichton, V. 125; and John Creichton, V. xix, 129; school, V. 129.

Dunkin, William, *c.* 1709–65, poet, friend of JS: possible reference to 'a young collegian', V. 226; helped by JS, XIII. xliii; JS petitions in his behalf, XIII. 188–9; — background, XIII. xxxviii; — textual notes, XIII. 225; witness to JS's will, XIII. 157; witness to codicil, XIII. 158. *See also* LETTER TO THE PROVOST; LETTER TO THE HONOURABLE THE SOCIETY OF THE GOVERNOUR.

Dunkirk, Nord, France, fortified seaport: and Anne, VIII. 10, 18, 23, 25, 60; and Barrier Treaty, VI. 88, 112; VIII. 59; demolition, IV. 75, 76; V. 113; VI. 88, 112; VII. 43, 48, 55, 114, 132; VIII. 8–12, 17–19, 25, 59–60; — Whigs demand demolition, IV. xx–xxi; England occupies (1712), VI. 189–91; VII. 49, 50–1, 125, 137–8, *et passim*; VIII. 57; John Hill occupies (1712), VI. xxii; VII. 138, 139, 142–3; and Nottingham, 'Dismal', VI. 139–41; and Ormonde, VII. 137–8, *et passim*; 'most important fortress' and Oxford, VII. 74; and privateers, VI. 112; and Steele, VIII. 4–25; JS's letter concerning (1712), VI. xxi–xxii; and Tugghe's memorial, VIII. 4, 8–12, 18, 67; and Treaty of Utrecht, VI. 88; VII. 125, 139–41, 152, *et passim*; and Whigs, IV. xx–xxi; VI. 189–91; VIII. 9, 10, 60, 67, 68.

Dunkirk Still in the Hands of the French, by JS: no text available, VI. xxi.

Dunkirk to be Let: *see* HUE AND CRY AFTER DISMAL.

Dunmore, Charles Murray, 1st Earl of, 1661–1710: V. 162, 163, 164–9.

Duns: *see* SCOTUS.

Dunstable, Bedfordshire: straw trade, IX. 19; larks, XI. 109.

Dunton, John, 1659–1733, London bookseller and author: and Burnet, IV. 70; *Neck or Nothing*, VIII. 32; ridiculed, I. 35; attacks Tories, VIII. 34; a leading Whig writer, VIII. 31–2.

'Dupe': V. 216.

D'Urfey, Thomas, 1653–1723, poet and fashionable playwright: I. 133; ridiculed in *Tale of a Tub* I. xxiv, 22. *See also* ESSAY TOWARDS THE THEORY OF THE INTELLIGIBLE WORLD.

Durham, England: and William II, V. 14.

Durham, Bishop of: *see* CREW.

Dussen: *see* VANDERDUSSEN.

Dutch (or Holland, or States General, or United Provinces): and Treaty of Altranstadt (1707), VI. 62–3; armies, III. 41; — mercenary army, XII. 243, 255; and Assiento, VII. 117, 123; VIII. 170–1; Austria gets Trarbach, VIII. 59; Austria's union with Spain, opposed, VI. 51, *n.**, 53; Austria's Zinzendorf distrusted, VII. 153; barrier for: *see* BARRIER; BARRIER TREATY; and Bickerstaff, II. 150, 207; and Calvinism, II. 101; character of

nation — approved, II. 14–15; — arrogance, VI. 32, 97; — cautious bargainers, VII. 137; — crueller than a heathen, XI. 154–5; — cunning of 'inferior sort', VII. 23; — intractable temper, VII. 118; — parsimony, II. 14; III. 7; — given to 'lower politics', VII. 109; — unstable republic, VII. 69; and Charles 'King of Spain', projected treaty, VI. 103; clergy, II. 98; commonwealth (i.e., republic), II. 14–15; — crazy, VII. 69; — no disgrace, XII. 278; national debt, VII. 68–9; devil in, IV. 30; domestic unrest, VII. 69;

and England — Anne's reign benefits them, VII. 53; — Anne's speech to Parliament (1712), VII. 136; — and Boyer's *Political State*, III. 156–7; — reply to Commons' *Representation* (1712), VII. 98; — meddle in England's domestic affairs (*c.* 1710), VI. 9; — governments different, VII. 69; — and Hanoverian Succession, VI. 26–7, 32, 88, 92–3, 100; — Oxford ministry disliked (1711), VII. 41–2; — misjudge nation, VI. 165; — expect 'revolution' in England (1712), VII. 152; — and English trade: *see* TRADE, ENGLISH; — treaty (1703) disregarded by Dutch, VII. 84; — wars with, I. 270; VI. 9–10; — war with (1665), I. 257, 259; — war with (1672), I. 257; — new wars possible (1711), VI. 55;

and English language, IV. 12; and Eugene, VII. 126, 153; in *Examiner*, XIV. 6; financial experiments, IX. 303; and fisheries, XIII. 111; Flanders and flounders, XII. 228–9; and France — separate peace (in 1678), XIV. 1; — Louis XIV resents rudeness (1709–10), VII. 35; — a threat (1714), VIII. 64; *Gazette*, VI. 165, 173; — memorial against Commons' *Representation*, VII. 98; — Ridpath praised by, VIII. 31; and Godolphin ministry, VII. 23; and Guiscard, VIII. 128; 'illustrissimorum ordinum', VI. 165; interest rates low, VI. 28; and Ireland — and Irish anomalies, XII. 124; — no model for, XII. 79, 124, 131; XIII. 174; and Japan, XI. 215–7; language (i.e., Low Dutch), XI. 216; and Marlborough, VII. 163–4; — bribery, VI. 41–2; Methuen treaties, VI. 24, 25–6; Treaty of Münster: *see* MÜNSTER, TREATY; pirates, XI. 154–5; provinces listed, VI. 99; religion, II. 100–1; — not Christians, XI. 216–17; — Dutch Reformed Church, II. 7; religious freedom, XII. 243, 255, 269; — censured, II. 7–8; and religious wars, II. 12; and Treaty of Ryswick (1697), VI. 11; separate peace: *see* UTRECHT, TREATY OF, *Dutch*; and Spain — antipathy, VI. 115; — would allow Bourbon king, VII. 40; — 'no peace without Spain': *see* SPAIN; — projected treaty, VII. 166–7; and Spanish Netherlands (including Flanders) — Dutch to hold (1709), VI. 90; VII. 61, 91; — garrisons in, VI. 89, 101–2, 109–11; — indebted to Dutch,

VI. 89–90; — Dutch to recover for Spain (1701), VI. 27–8; revenues from, VI. 110; — to share control with Spain (1709), VI. 91; and Tindal, II. 104; **trade** — and Dunkirk, VI. 112; — duties, VI. 28; — in East Indies, VI. 97; — and England: *see* TRADE, ENGLISH; — in Flanders, VI. 101, 109; — monopoly of Flemish trade (1709), VII. 28, 91, 104; — with France, VII. 84; — with France, continued during war, VI. 30; VII. 84; — with France, and duties, on Dutch merchants (1701), VI. 12; — with France, and tariff of 1664: *see* TARIFF OF 1664; — and French privateers, VI. 112; — with Japan, XI. 154–5, 203–4; — and Naples, VI. 111; — and peace negotiations (1711–13), VII. 40–1, 50, 111–12, 133; — and Sicily, VI. 111; — with Spanish empire, VI. 28–9, 47, 92, 104; VII. 92–3, 118–19, 120; — with Spanish Netherlands, duties, VI. 91–2; — war to benefit, VI. 28–9; VII. 89; — during War of Spanish Succession, VI. 32; VII. 84; and Treaty of Utrecht: *see* UTRECHT, TREATY OF; value (ten shillings a head, too dear), V. 275; and War of Spanish Succession: *see* WAR OF THE SPANISH SUCCESSION, *Dutch*; and Whigs, IV. 76; Whigs collude with, III. 205; VI. 23, 42–3, 154, 166; VII. 23, 108, 121, 124; Whigs bribed ('powerful motives'), VI. 87; and Wood's coins, X. 7, 47. *See also* BUYS.

Duties, Christian: brotherly love, IX. 171.

Dutton-Colt, Sir Harry: XII. 231.

Duty: to country, IX. 233; easier for poor, IX. 196.

Duty of Servants at Inns, by JS: **XIII. 163-5**; textual notes, XIII. 224.

Dwarf: in Brobdingnag, XI. 104, 107–9, 116.

Dyet, or Dyott, Richard, a commissioner of stamp duties (1702–1713): counterfeiting, III. 138.

Dying Speech of Tom Ashe (written *c.* 1707–8), by JS: **IV. 263-6**; composition, IV. xxxvi, 263, *n.**; textual notes, IV. 301.

D'Ypres, William: *see* WILLIAM OF YPRES.

Dysart, Countess of: *see* LAUDER-DALE, ELIZABETH MURRAY, DUCHESS OF.

E

E Tow O Koam: Indian King of Rivers, II. 264.

Eachard, John, *c.* 1636-97, vice-chancellor of Cambridge: *The Grounds and Occasions of the Contempt of the Clergy* (1670), IV. 301; IX. 130; replies to answers, I. 4; and Revolution of 1688, IX. 121.

Ears: imaginary treatise on, I. xl.

Earth's revolution: III. 34.

East India Company: and abolition of Christianity, II. 38–9; and coffee houses, VI. 53; and hostilities with Dutch, VI. 97; and election of 1710, III. 66; and Bishop Evans, XIV. 41; and

War of the Spanish Succession, III. 134; and Whigs, VIII. 41.

East Indies: Dutch trade in, VI. 97; Gulliver travels to, XI. 20; silver coins exported, IX. 50.

Easter: JS ridicules controversy over date, XIV. 23, 33.

Echard: *see* EACHARD.

Echlin, Robert, *d.* 1635, Bishop of Down and Connor: III. 237-8.

Eddy, W. A.: and Bickerstaff papers, II. x, *n.* 3.

Edenborough: *see* EDINBURGH.

Edgar, King of England, 934-975: V. 5.

Edgar, King of Scots, *c.* 1074-1107: 'surviving son', V. 18.

Edgar Atheling, *fl.* 1066-*c.* 1125, nephew of Edward the Confessor: V. 6; brother of St. Margaret, queen of Malcolm III of Scotland, V. 29; expelled from Normandy, V. 16.

Edgcumbe, or Edgecomb, Richard, 1st Lord, 1680-1758, statesman: letter to Carteret, X. xxvii-xxviii.

Edinburgh, Scotland: V. 142; castle of, V. 167, 170; and 'cloac', IV. 232; filthy streets, I. 56; poisoned by sewage, IX. 342.

Edmund Ironside, King of England, *c.* 981-1016: V. 6.

Edred, King of the English, *d.* 955: suffers penance from the Abbot of Glastonbury, V. 263.

Education: XI. 60-3; ancient and modern, IX. 155; charity schools, IX. 130, 136, 204-5; curricula, XII. 48-9; — classical, XII. 161; enlarged by classics, IV. 74; and clergy, IX. 80; and conversation, IV. 244; debating, XII. 159; early impressions strongest, II. 59; French tutors, XII. 50, 52; Inns of Court censured, II. 52; and landed gentry, XII. 135; learning by ingestion, XI. 186; Irish schools needed, IX. 202; and liberty of conscience, II. 97; and the military, XII. 49-50; and the nobility, XII. 46-53; philosophy of, XII. 48-9; political history of, XII. 47; and prejudices, II. 32-4; public schools, XII. 48, 51; and religion, II. 34; and social classes, II. 103-4; JS's education, V. 192; moral textbooks, XII. 52; universities censured, II. 51-2; universities praised, XII. 51-2; whipping, XII. 49, 51; and women, XII. 307-8; — neglected, IX. 85; and women's pride, XII. 67. *See also* OF THE EDUCATION OF LADIES; NOBILITY, *education of*.

Edward, *d.* 1093, son of Malcolm III, King of Scotland: V. 18.

Edward, the Confessor, King of England, *c.* 1002-66: V. 6, 60; and English language, IV. 7; and the king's evil, V. 6; his laws re-enacted by Henry I, V. 28; and William I, V. 6.

Edward the Black Prince, 1330-1376, son of Edward III: V. 84.

Edward I, King of England, 1239-1307: and Wood's coinage, X. 9.

Edward III, King of England, 1312-77: and Ireland, IX. 271; and Wood's coinage, X. 10.

Edward IV, King of England, 1442-83: and Symnele (i.e. Lambert Simnel), II. 169.

Edward VI, King of England, 1537–53: and divine right of clergy, II. 82.

Edwards, George: and text of *Gulliver's Travels*, XI. 301.

Edwards, John, 1637–1717, Calvinistic divine: *The Preacher* (1705), IX. 112 and *n*.

Edwin, Sir Humphrey, 1642–1707, Lord Mayor of London: and canting, I. 182–3; attends conventicle, I. 131, *n.*†.

Effeminacy: much complained of in Henry I's time, V. 46.

Effen, Justus van, 1684–1735: on false additions to *Tale of a Tub*, I. xxxii; translation of *Tale* (1721), I. xxxii.

Effernock, near Trim, co. Meath, Ireland: tithes, JS's will, XIII. 152.

Egbert, King of the West Saxons, *d*. 839: V. 4.

Egerton, Sir Thomas (created Lord Ellesmere and Viscount Brackley), *c*. 1540–1617, Lord Keeper and Lord Chancellor: VIII. 184.

Egerton MS. 201; *see* HOLYHEAD JOURNAL, *additional leaf*.

Eglinton, Alexander Montgomery, 8th Earl of, *c*. 1636–1701: his relationship to the Swift family, (i.e., married a granddaughter of Sir Robert Swift), V. 187.

Egypt: drinking of ale, I. 186; exodus from, II. 192; exports bread to Ireland, XII. 19; Egyptians earliest fanatics, I. 186; Egyptians and free masons, V. 327–9; and Moses, IV. 239.

Ehrenpreis, Irvin: acknowledgement, V. v; XII. v; *Swiftiana in Rylands Eng. MS*, V. xxxii; *Swift's History of England*, V. ix, *n*. 1.

Eikon Basilike: *see* GAUDEN, JOHN.

Elagabalus: *see* HELIOGABALUS.

Eleanor of Aquitaine, Queen of England, wife of Henry II, *c*. 1122–1204: V. 67; and Henry II, IV. 7.

Elections: of 1710, III. 64–6, 134; controverted elections, III. 120, 170–1; alleged corruption, III. 37; corruption recommended, I. 301–2; corruption satirized, XI. 128–30; and decayed boroughs, V. 81; management of, III. 10, 12, 72, 138; V. 80–1; VIII. 126, 143, 176; XI. 201–2; — Addison and JS on, V. 252; — and Walpole, V. 103, 105–6, 107; — and Wharton, III. 27–8; under William III, VII. 148. *See also* FRANCHISE.

Elector of Hanover: *see* GEORGE I.

Elector Palatine: *see* JOHANN WILHELM.

Electoral Prince of Hanover: *see* GEORGE II.

Elegy on Mr. Patrige, the Almanack-Maker, who died the 29th of this Instant March, 708, poem by JS: publication, II. xiv.

Elephants: and fleas, IV. 253.

Elisha, Old Testament prophet: and Hazael, IX. 349; bones, XIV. 23.

Elixir, Grand: I. 174.

Elizabeth, I, Queen of England, 1553–1603: VIII. 178, 187–8, 189; her administration exemplary, V. 11, 117; and balance of power, I. 230; and Sir Jerome

Bowes, V. xi; and Burnet, IV. 80; and divine right of clergy, II. 82; Queen Elizabeth's Day celebrated (1711), VII. 28; and Elizabethan writers, II. 177; and English language, IV. 9; and Leicester, V. 117; and free masons, V. 324, 326; and mixed money, X. 10, 55; and money, X. 38; and Perrot, IV. 110; and English poetry, IV. 273; and *Polite Conversation*, IV. 132, 148; restoration of Protestants, IX. 221; and Puritans, XII. 264; her face on shilling, II. 243, 244; silver coinage, IX. 50; and the succession, V. 242; and JS's *Abstract*, V. ix; and Tyrone's Rebellion, X. 38, 40.

Elliot, a soldier: V. 148, 150.

Ellis, Welbore, *c.* 1651–1734, Bishop of Kildare: member of Privy Council, X. 182.

Elliston, Mr.: and Irish coinage, X. 29.

Elliston, Ebenezor: *see* LAST SPEECH AND DYING WORDS OF EBENEZOR ELLISTON; LAST FAREWELL OF EBENEZOR ELLISTON.

'Elogy': characterization of a person, usually favourable, I. 22, 29.

Eloquence: rarity, IX. 213.

Elwood, Daniel: X. 76.

Ely, Bishop of: *see* FRANCIS TURNER (deprived, 1690); SIMON PATRICK (*d.* 1707); JOHN MOORE (*d.* 1714); WILLIAM FLEETWOOD (*d.* 1723).

Elzevir family: and April Fool's joke, IV. 267.

Emigration: *see* IRISH PEOPLE, emigration.

Emmanuel College, Cambridge: Gulliver attends, XI. 19.

Empedocles, *c.* 490–430 B.C., Greek philosopher and statesman: I. 111.

Emperors, Roman: authority over church, XIV. 19, 21.

Employments: *see* OFFICES.

Empson, Sir Richard, *d.* 1510, statesman: and blasphemers, II. 30.

Empson, William: X. 76.

England (Britain, Great Britain): 'Albion', V. 5; compared to Athens, I. 31; and Bickerstaff, II. 144, 149–50; and Bodin, V. 244–7; Buys visits (1711), VII. 55; and Cicero, I. 106; colonies, XI. 294–5; conversion to Christianity, II. 83; V. 4; conversation refined, IV. 101–2, 105; high cost of living, V. 228; crime in, XI. 252; debt: *see* DEBT, NATIONAL; the devil in, IV. 30; and Dutch: *see* DUTCH; economic experiments, IX. 303; XI. 174–8; and France: *see* FRANCE; French in, V. 6; and Grand Alliance: *see* GRAND ALLIANCE; history of, V. 3–78; and Ireland: *see* IRELAND; and Wood's coinage, X. 64–7; linguistic history, IV. 6–7; literary critics, I. 58; maps of, VI. 165; and Northern War: *see* NORTHERN WAR; papacy and 'Anglia', XIV. 28; place names, IV. 280; — Saxon, V. 5; national product, XI. 252; origins of Puritanism, XII. 263–5; revenue, VI. 54; — general excise threatened (1711), VI. 48, 57; — *see also* MALT TAX; LAND TAX;

riots infrequent (1714), VIII. 44;
ancient Roman rule, V. 3–4;
Roman Catholics in, XII. 258;
'modern saints' (i.e., Puritans
and Dissenters), I. 37; the Saxon
heptarchy, V. 4; named by the
Saxons, V. 4, 5; and Scandinavia
— treaties annulled, VII. 148;
personified, as Mr South-British,
II. 247; and state church, XII.
244; and Sweden: *see* CHARLES
XII; SWEDEN; and Test Act,
XII. xlii; trade: *see* TRADE,
ENGLISH; turnpikes, XII. 86–7;
Act of Union: *see* SCOTLAND; and
Treaty of Utrecht: *see* UTRECHT;
and War of the League of Augsburg, VII. 68–9; and War of the
Spanish Succession: *see* WAR OF
THE SPANISH SUCCESSION. *See
also* CONSTITUTION; FRANCE; etc.
English language: antiquity
'proved' by puns, IV. 231–9;
'barbarous', XI. 245; changes in,
IV. 8; contractions, IV. 11, 12;
dialects, IV. 11; etymology, IV.
11–12; fixing of, IV. 8–9; history
of, IV. 6–7, 9–13; inferior to
Continental tongues, IV. 6; in
Ireland, IV. xxxix; necessity of
new words, IV. 15–16; orthography, IV. 11–12; and
preachers, XII. 306; pronunciation, IV. 280–4; JS's plan for
reform: *see* PROPOSAL FOR COR-
RECTING . . . THE ENGLISH
TONGUE.
Englishmen, character of: XI.
127–32; 245–64; love of change,
VI. 153; cold climate does not
produce stupidity, VI. 40; most
degenerate, II. 60; courage, VI.
39; VII. 146; opposed to

hypocrisy, II. 57; Irish absentees
scorned, XII. 310; king's rights
disputed, IX. 220; II. laziness,
266; moral reformation, 59; II.
— not so bad as appeared, III.
158–9; JS said to malign them,
IX. 270; troops disciplined, VI.
39.
'English Tory': *see* STEELE,
Guardian.
Englishman: *see* STEELE, *Englishman.*
Ennodius, Magnus Felix, *c.* 473–
521, Bishop of Pavia: on papacy,
XIV. 26.
Enquiry into the Behaviour of
the Queen's Last Ministry
(written 1715–*c.* 1717), by JS:
VIII. 131-80; composition, VIII.
xxxi–xl; editions, VIII. xxxviii,
215; erratum, XIV. 54; and
History of the Four Last Years, VII.
xii–xiii; VIII. xxxiii, xxxvii,
xxxix; predicts bias of George I
('another discourse'), VII. xxxiii;
manuscript, VII. xii–xiii; VIII.
xxxii, xxxiv, xxxvi–xxxviii, 215–
16; manuscript in Stella's hand,
VIII. xxxi, *n.* 3, xxxiv; and JS's
Memoirs, VIII. xxxiii, xxxvii;
mistakes in, VIII. xxxvi; and
Oxford's trial, VIII. xxxiv; publication, VII. xii and *n.* 6; VIII.
xxxiii–xxxiv, xxxvii–xxxviii, xl,
215; JS's revisions, VIII. xxxviii–
xxxix; style, VIII. xxxviii–xxxix;
textual notes, VIII. 215–31.
Enthusiasm: I. 102–14, 174–90;
worse than atheism, IV. 39; and
established church, XII. 243–4,
255; eternal, II. 34–5; false enthusiasm, I. 243; past and present, I. 241; political enthusiasm

censured, II. 1–2; and politics, II. xv–xvi; in religion, I. xxvii–xxviii, 95–101, 174–90; imaginary treatise on, I. xl; and vision, IV. 252.

Entragues, Catherine-Henriette de Balzac d', 1579–1633, marquise de Verneuil: 'absent female', I. 103.

Envy: and fashion, IX. 200.

Epaminondas, *c.* 430–362 B.C., Theban commander: V. 83; XI. 196; and Somers, I. 14; JS's pun on, IV. xxxviii, 234.

Ephesus, councils of (431 and 449): XIV. 21, 22.

Ephori, Spartan magistrates: I. 198, 210, 223.

Ephraim, *d.* A.D. 545, Patriarch of Antioch: and Stylites, XIV. 30.

Epicureans: corruptors, IV. 249; incorrect, I. 246–7; given to sensuality, IX. 113.

Epicurus, 341–270 B.C., Greek philosopher: XI. 197; corrupted doctrine, I. 247; 'free-thinkers', IV. 42; insane, I. 105; on justice, IX. 247; physics, I. 36; and Stella, V. 231; theory of vision, I. 110.

Epigraphs: classical, IX. 338.

Épine, Francesca Margherita de l', *d.* 1746, Italian singer: Margarita, II. 32.

Epiphanius, *d.* 535, Patriarch of Constantinople: death, XIV. 30; and papal bulls, XIV. 29; and Pope Hormisdas, XIV. 29.

Epiphonemas: IX. 69.

Epping, Essex: Gulliver's estate near, XI. 80.

Epsom, Surrey: Irish absentees in, XII. 71.

Epte, a river of Normandy: V. 38.

Erasmus, Desiderius, 1466–1536: VI. 153; on Christ's divinity, IX. 262; quotation—*Adagia*, X. 68 and *n.*.*

Erastianism: in Baronius, XIV. xiii.

Eric the Forester, 11th century: V. 191.

Erick, Abigail: *see* SWIFT, ABIGAIL.

Erick, or Eyrick, or Herrick, etc., family of Leicestershire: V. 191.

Errata: and Steele, VIII. 16–17.

Esau: sells birthright, like Irish, X. 53.

Esdaile, Mrs. Arundell: acknowledgement to, VII. xxvii, *n.* 1.

Esquire: imaginary, IX. 291–2.

Essay on Modern Education: *see* INTELLIGENCER, No. 9.

Essay on the Fates of Clergymen: *see* INTELLIGENCER, Nos. 5 and 7.

Essay towards the Theory of the Intelligible World, *c.* 1708, attributed to Thomas Durfey: among 'many others', I. 1.

Essex, Algernon Capell, 2nd Earl of, 1670–1710, Constable of the Tower: VIII. 102; his death, VIII. 117; Macky and JS on, V. 259.

Essex, Arthur Capell, 1st Earl of, *c.* 1632–83: his death, V. 281.

Essex, Robert Devereux, 2nd Earl of, 1566–1601: 'Captain General', VIII. 188–9.

Essex, Thomas Cromwell, Earl of, *c.* 1485–1540, statesman: and the English Reformation, IV. 73.

Essex Street, Dublin: and George Faulkner, X. 207.

Established Church: *see* CHURCH

OF ENGLAND; CHURCH OF IRE-
LAND.

Estaple: *see* ÉTAPLES.

Estremadura, province of Portugal: VI. 25.

Étaples, Pas de Calais, France: III.
209.

Etcætera, the Elder and the
Younger: critics, I. 57.

Ethelbert, King of Kent, *c.* 552–
616: Christianized, V. 4.

Ethelred II, the Unready, King of
England, *c.* 968–1016: massacre
of the Danes, V. 5.

Etherege, Sir George, *c.* 1635–
91, poet and dramatist: pun
upon name, IV. 274.

Ethiopia: church, and papacy,
XIV. 28.

Eucharist: *see* COMMUNION.

Euclid: leads the Ancients, I. 152;
clarity, I. 247.

Eudoxia, Empress, wife of Arcadius (married A.D. 395): and
Chrysostom, XIV. 18.

Eugene, Prince of Savoy, 1663–
1736, general: IV. 216–17;
Anne's suspicions of, VII. 122;
visits Anne (1712), IV. xxxvii;
and his armies, VIII. 58; VII.
24; and Barrier Treaty, VI. 85,
90, 91, 113–15; Bolingbroke
meets him (1712), VII. 24; and
Bothmar (1712), VII. 26; character — warmonger, VII. 26, 122,
126, 146; JS's character of, VII.
26; and Charles VI, VII. 25; his
court incensed (1712), VII. 126;
authority of Dutch over him,
VII. 126; VIII. 57–8; Dutch
recognize his inadequacy (1712),
VII. 153; visit to England (1712)
— crowds follow him, VII. 24;

— discouraged by ministry, VII.
111; — purpose, VII. 25–6,
124; — rumoured (1711), VII.
108; — a Whig project, VII.
24–5; French unreadiness for
peace (1711), VII. 57; meets
Marlborough 'in secret' (1712),
VII. 26; and Ormonde, VII. 135,
140; and Oxford — hates
Oxford, VII. 26; — meetings,
VII. 26; — alleged plot against
Oxford, VII. xv, 26–7; — plot
denied by Charles Lucas, VII.
175; and War of the Spanish
Succession — delivers Austrian
proposals (1712), VII. 25; —
would continue war (1712), VII.
146; — chosen as Dutch general,
VII. 122; — eager to fight (1712),
VII. 126; — leads desertion of
Ormonde, VII. 140; — fights
without Ormonde (1712), VII.
147; — and Ormonde's 'restraining orders', VII. 135, 140; — and
Toulon, VI. 35; — would engage Villars (1712), VIII. 57–8;
and Whigs, VII. 111; 'oracle and
idol' of Whigs, VI. 90.

'Eugenio', indiscreet clergyman
in *Intelligencer*, No. 7: XII. 44–5.

Eugenius, Emperor of the West,
d. 394: St. Ambrose on, XIV. 17.

Eugenius III, *d.* 1153, Pope: V.
68.

Eulalius, anti-Pope, early 5th century: displaced by Boniface I,
XIV. 20.

Euripides: quotation from *In-
certa* (ed. Joshua Barnes), *deus
quos vult perdere*, IX. 271.

European Magazine, 1795–96: JS's
marginalia on Burnet, V. xxxvi.

Eusden, Laurence, 1688–1730,

poet: pun upon name, IV. 274.

Eusebius, *c.* 265–339, Bishop of Cæsarea, called the father of Church history: and freethinking, IV. 38.

Eustace II, Count of Boulogne, *d.* 1125: V. 41.

Eustace IV, Count of Boulogne, *d.* 1153, son of Stephen: V. 67–8, 68–9, 72; and Henry of Blois, V. 61; and London, V. 61; urged to raise an army to free Stephen, V. 60.

Eustace, Richard, wool merchant, High Street, Dublin: imported cloth, XIII. 168.

Eustathius of Thessalonica, *d. c.* 1193, Byzantine scholar and author: XI. 197.

Eutyches, 5th century A.D., monophysite heresiarch: early Christian fanatic, I. 188.

Eutychus, a young man of Troas (*Acts* xx. 9–10): falls asleep in church, IX. 210, 214.

Evander, character in *Aeneid*: I. 152; and Virgil, I. 244.

Evans, John, *d.* 1724, Bishop of Meath: autobiographical letter, XIV. xiv; death reported, XIV. 41; and leases, IX. 53; slanderous account of, XIV. 41; — textual note, XIV. 46.

Evelyn, John, 1620–1716, English diarist: and academy, IV. xiv.

Everard, Benjamin: and manuscript of Parnell's poems, XIV. 13.

Evening Post, **JS's contributions:** his part estimated, VI. xxiii; 13 Nov. 1712 (band box), **VI. 196-7;** — background, VI. xxiii–xxiv; 29 Jan. 1713 (Erasmus Lewis), **VI. 200;** — background, VI. xxvi–xxvii.

Ewing, Alexander, *d. c.* 1764, and George, Dublin printers and booksellers: and JS's *History of the Four Last Years*, VII. xviii–xx, xxiii–xxiv.

Examination of Certain Abuses, Corruptions, and Enormities in the City of Dublin (1732), by JS: **XII. 215-32;** background, XII. xxxiv–xxxv; composition, XII. 217; editions, XII. xxxiv–xxxv, 232, 343; publication, XII. xxxiv–xxxv, 215; textual notes, XII. 343–5; alternate title, XII. xxxiv, 343; title-page facsimile, XII. 215.

Examiner (general discussion of the periodical and JS's role): pledges accuracy, III. 68; and Anne, VIII. 14; and Anne's illness (1713), VIII. xvi; authorship, III. xxvii–xxviii; and Burnet, IV. ix–x, 55; *Examiners for the Year 1711* (collected edition, 1712), by JS and others, III. xi, xxvii; — INDEX, by JS, **XIV.** 4–12; — — authorship, XIV. xii; — — textual note, XIV. 45; — **The Printer to the Reader,** by JS, **XIV. 3;** — — authorship, XIV. xi; — — textual note, XIV. 45; — subscription not used, XIV. 3; — title-page facsimile, III. 1; Faulkner's edition of, III. xxvii–xxviii; — preface, possibly by JS, III. 2; and Godolphin ministry, VIII. 15; impartiality, III. 13–14, 36; letters to, III. 131-2; and Marlborough, VIII. 13; No. 2, III. 224; numbering of, III. xxvii–

xxviii; origin, VIII. 123; purpose, III. 31-2; reception, III. 76; XIV. 3; 'not a reformer', III. 82; and Steele, VIII. xii, 8, 10-12, 17, 67; Steele demands it be prosecuted, VIII. 14;

attacks upon JS, III. 59-60, 75-8, 85-9, 116-17, 118-19, 135-6, 171-3; — in *An Answer to the Occasional Writer, No. II,* V. xiv; — and *Conduct of the Allies,* VI. x; — from either extreme, III. 88-90; — by Dr. Hare, III. 87-8; VI. x; — misquotations in attacks, III. 12; — JS's parody of attacks, III. 52-8; — JS reads them, III. 115-16; — and *Tale of a Tub,* VI. x; **JS's role in,** II. xxxv; III. x-xxv; VI. vii; VIII. 123-4; XIV. 3; — impartiality, III. 3-4; JS's attack on Collins announced in, IV. xvi; — quoted in, IV. x; JS defends, VIII. 15; JS's design 'fully executed', III. 171; and JS's *Publick Spirit of the Whigs,* VIII. xviii-xix, *n.*2; and JS on the Revolution of 1688, IX. 123;

No. 2, III. 224; and Tugghe's memorial, VIII. 8; and Whigs, VIII. 14.

Examiner, JS's original contributions [2 Nov. 1710-14 June 1711 (Vol. I, Nos. 14-46 in first edition; 13-45 in reprints and present edition), **III. 1-173**]: 2 Nov. 1710, III. 3-8; 9 Nov. 1710 (on political lying), III. 8-13; 16 Nov. 1710, III. 13-18; 23 Nov. 1710 (bill of ingratitude to Marlborough), III. 19-24; 30 Nov. 1710 (Verres and Wharton)

III. 24-9; — background, III. xvii-xix; — and Cicero, III. xix; — effect on Wharton ('a like occasion'), III. 178; 7 Dec. 1710, III. 29-34; 14 Dec. 1710, III. 35-40; 21 Dec. 1710 (the army), III. 40-6; — background, III. xiv-xv; — JS defends, III. 58-63; 28 Dec. 1710 (Church of England), III. 46-51; — account of, III. xv; — allusion ('a Paper on the Subject'), III. 153; 4 Jan. 1710-11 (*The Examiner Cross-examined*), III. 52-8; — background, III. xviii-xxi; 11 Jan. 1710-11, III. 58-63; 18 Jan. 1710-11 (the Whigs' hopes), III. 63-9; — mentioned, III. 203; 25 Jan. 1710-11, III. 69-75; — comments on, III. xxviii and *n.* 1; 1 Feb. 1710-11 (old and new ministers compared) III. 75-80; — analysis, III. xxi-xxii; 8 Feb. 1710-11 (avarice and Marlborough, Letter to Crassus), III. 80-5; — analysis, III. xvii; — replies, III. xxxii, *n.* 2; — JS defends, III. 95-6; 15 Feb. 1710-11, III. 85-91; 22 Feb. 1710-11, III. 91-6; 1 Mar. 1710-11, III. 96-101; 8 Mar. 1710-11 (political parties), III. 101-5; 15 Mar. 1710-11 (Guiscard's attempt to kill Oxford), III. 106-10; — analysis, III. xxii-xxiii; — mentioned ('a printed account'), VIII. 127-8; — Whig retort, III. 189-90, 245-7; 22 Mar. 1710-11 (passive obedience), III. 110-6; — textual revision, III. xxviii-xxix; — Whig retort, III. 189-90, 247-8; 29 Mar. 1711 (the Examiner and his Whig oppon-

ents), 116–21; — Whig retort, III. 189, 248–9; 5 Apr. 1711 (Whigs and Tories), III. 121–6; 12 Apr. 1711 (Whigs and Dissenters), III. 126–32; — rhetoric, III. xxiv–xxv; 19 Apr. 1711, III. 132–6; 26 Apr. 1711 (circumvention of laws), III. 136–42; — replies, III. xxv; 3 May 1711, III. 142–7; — argument, III. xxiv; 10 May 1711 (Oxford and nobility), III. 147–52; — Whig retort, III. 249–50; 17 May 1711, III. 152–7; 24 May 1711 (London churches), III. 157–62; 31 May 1711 ('Tory' and 'Whig'), III. 162–7; — analysis, III. xxvi; 7 June 1711 (summary), III. 167–72; 14 June 1711 (Examiner victorious), III. 172–3; — authorship, III. xxvii; errata, XIV. 51; textual notes, III. 273–6; **JS's later contributions:** 24 July 1712 (*Remarks on Bishop Fleetwood's Preface*), VI. 159–61; — background, VI. xviii–xx, 192–5; — style, VI. xix; — textual note, VI. 212; 16 Jan. 1712–13 (appendix to *Conduct* and *Remarks*), VI. 165–9; — background, VI. xxvi; — textual notes, VII. 212; 2 Feb. 1712–13 (*A Complete Refutation of the Falsehoods Alleged Against Erasmus Lewis*), VI. 173–8; — background, VI. xxvi, 200; — sources, VI. 173; — style, VI. xxvii; — textual notes, VI. 212.

Excellency of Christianity, sermon by JS: **IX. 241–50;** analysis, IX. 102, 106, 111–14; composition, IX. 133–4; style, IX. 111; textual notes, IX. 377.

Excellent New Song on a Seditious Pamphlet, poem by JS: quoted, IX. xvi.

Exchange Alley, London: III. 10.

Exchequer, Stop of (1672): V. 274.

Excise, Irish: XIII. 83.

Exclusion Bill, 1679: William Howells and JS on, V. 264; Parson's *A Conference about the Next Succession* reprinted to buttress, V. 241; Temple's speech on, I. 270–1.

Executors of JS's will: JS's gifts to, VII. 172; and *History of the Four Last Years,* VII. xvii–xviii; alleged to suppress *History,* VII. 171, 172–3; and Millar, VII. xix; named, XIII. 157, 200; allegedly Whig, VII. 172–3.

Exeter, Devon: V. 50.

Exhortation to the Chapter of St. Patrick's Dublin: see VICARS CHORAL.

Exilles, in Savoy: VII. 114.

'Expect': VIII. 17–18, 93.

Exshaw, John, *d.* 1776, of Cork-Hill, Dublin bookseller and printer: and Faulkner's edition of JS's *Works,* XIV. 42–3; and JS's *History of the Four Last Years,* VII. xviii.

Extract of a Book: see DRAPIER'S LETTERS.

Eumenes, *c.* 361–316 B.C., Greek general and statesman: III. 6.

Eve: and feminine excuses, IV. 250–1.

F

F., Sir A.: *see* FOUNTAINE.

Fable of Midas, by JS: VI. xiv.

'Fade, Mrs.': character in *Polite
Conversation*, IV. 161.

Fagel, Gaspar, 1634–88: Dutch
envoy in London, XII. 269.

Fairbrother, Samuel, *fl.* 1714–34,
Dublin printer, printer to Irish
House of Commons, 1723: and
*Humble Address of the Knights,
Citizens and Burgesses*, X. 215;
and JS, IV. 285.

Fairfax, Ferdinando, 2nd Lord
Fairfax of Cameron, 1584–1648,
Parliamentary general: XII.
265–6.

Fairfax, Thomas, 3rd Lord Fairfax of Cameron, 1612–71, Parliamentary general: V. 86;
Burnet and JS on, V. 267.

Faith: and belief, IX. 261; not
compulsory, IX. 261; defined
by JS, IX. 110; doubts to be
concealed, IX. 262; JS not
answerable for his doubts, IX.
262; free-thinkers and Christians
compared, II. 73; implicit and
explicit, IX. 110–11; personal
conviction, IX. 261; and reason,
IX. 261; want of belief to be
concealed, IX. 261.

Falkiner, Sir Frederick Richard,
1831–1908, Recorder of Dublin:
on portraits of JS, XIV. 50.

Falkland, Lucius Cary, 2nd Viscount, 1610–43: Clarendon on,
V. xxxix–xl; literary style, IX.
65; JS on ('moves grief'), V.
xxxix–xl, 304.

Fall of great men from power,
JS's views: and ambition, VIII.
145; Athenians, I. 206–10;
Henry I loses his son, V. 40–1;
example of Marlborough, VII.
30; vulnerability, I. 242, 245.

False Witness (written 1715),
sermon by JS: **IX. 180-9**;
analysis IX. 106, 116–20; composition, IX. 133–4, 137; textual
note, IX. 376–7.

Fame, JS's views on: I. 106, 118;
allegory of, III. 9–10; Court of
Alienation, II. 258–9; dangerous,
I. 245; and forgetfulness, XII.
191; William Howells a dunce
on, V. 262; ill fame — posterity
ought to know, III. 32; — JS
allegedly would not perpetuate,
III. 59; — and satire, XII. 24–5;
— in 'Tables of Fame', II. 240,
241; — and Tindal's critics, II.
73; and linguistic change, IV.
17–18; and virtue, IV. 244;
vulnerability, I. 242; and Whitshed, XII. 23–5. *See also* History.

Fame, Tables of: *see* Tatler, *Nos.*
67–8, 81.

Familism and Familists (members
of sect called Family of Love):
I. 188; III. 144; XII. 244.

Family: love of, and charity, IV.
251–2.

Family of Swift (*Autobiography,
Autobiographical Fragment*), by
JS, composed *c.* 1738–9 (not *c.*
1728): **V. 187-95**; analysis, V.
xxii; composition, V. xxii; errata, XIV. 53; manuscripts, V.
xxii–xxiii, 352; — facsimile,
facing V. 192; publication, V.
xxii; quoted, I. x; textual notes,
V. 352–6.

**Famous Prediction of Merlin,
the British Wizard** (1709), by
JS: **II. 165-70**; background, II.
xxiv; composition, II. 167; date,
XIV. 51; errata, XIV. 51; publi-

cation, II. 288; style, II. xxiv; textual notes, II. 288–9; title-page facsimile, II. 165.

'Fanatic-hill': IV. 283.

Fanatics and Fanaticism: *see* DIS-SENTERS.

Farmers, Irish: and Bill for a Modus, XIII. 104; evictions of tenants, IX. 201; good tenants, IX. 56; landlords oppress tenants, IX. 201; poverty, IX. 129; XII. 178. *See also* AGRI-CULTURE.

Farnaby, Thomas, *c.* 1575–1647, grammarian: and Wotton, I. xxix–xxx, 8.

Farnham, Surrey, near Moor Park: I. x; IV. 81, 283.

Fashion: and dance instructors, XII. 50; English, scandalous, IX. 17; French tutors, XII. 50, 52; Irish imports, XII. 67–8, 79; in language, II. 173–7; IV. 7–13; and manners, IV. 218; a neces-sary folly, IX. 91; Newton's theory of gravitation, XI. 197–8; and oaths, IV. 110–11; past and present, I. 241; satirized, I. 44–55; and soldiers, XII. 49; toupees, XII. 219 and *n.*†, 235, 236; and William II, V. 25; and women, IX. 87. *See also* DRESS.

'Fashion, Ned': a character in Harrison's *Tatler*, No. 20, II. 186–7.

Fathers of the Church: low opinion of ancient philosophy, IX. 243; arguments not to be imitated, IX. 74.

Fauconberg, Thomas Belasyse, 1st Earl of, 1628–1700: a 'popish lord', III. 91.

Faulkner, George, 1699–1775, Dublin bookseller and printer, publisher of JS's *Works*: *Appeal to the Public*, VII. xvi–xxvi; on Bettesworth, V. 359; and Boling-broke, XIII. 201; and Chester-field, IX. 100; and Archbishop Cobbe, VII. xvii; discharged from censure, XIII. 205; visits England (1741), VII. xvi; visits England (1749), VII. xvii; and Ewings, VII. xxiii–xxiv; and Gay, XIII. 201; facsimile of his hand, facing V. 243; and John Hawkesworth, XIII. 204; Hawkesworth criticizes, I. v; XI. xxvii–xxviii; imprisoned, XIII. 204–6; and W. King, VII. xvi, xxiii; and McAulay's *Some Thoughts on the Tillage*, XIII. 143; and Millar, VII. xvi, xviii; and Orrery, VII. xiv, xvii; at Oxford (1741), VII. xvi; and 2nd Earl of Oxford, XIII. 202; and Pope, XIII. 201; on Dr. Sheridan, XIV. 37;

and JS — prints *Advantages Proposed by Repealing the Sacra-mental Test*, XII. 24; — *Advice to the Freemen*, XIII. xxv; — and *Answer of . . . Pulteney . . . to Walpole*, V. xvi; — conceals authorship of pamphlets, XIII. 206; — *Consultation of Four Physicians*, IV. xxxviii; — corres-pondence, XII. xxxii; — diffi-culties as publisher, XIII. 204; — authorship of *The Difficulty of Knowing One's Self*, IX. 103, 105; — and *Directions to Servants*, XIII. x–xi; — — 'Publisher's Preface', XIII. 5; — publishes *Drapier's Letters* (1725), X. 207; — and *The Examiner*, III. 273;

— friendship, XII. 203–4; — publishes *Gulliver's Travels* (1735), XI. xxv–xxviii, 3, 301; — and JS's copy of Herodotus, V. xxxi and facing p. 243; — *History of the Four Last Years*, VII. xiv–xxi, xxiii–xxvii; — carries letter for him (1737), XIII. 190; — and *A Modest Defence of a Late Poem*, V. 358; — and *Polite Conversation*, IV. 127; — and Pope, XIII. 201; — *Preface to the Bishop of Sarum's Introduction*, IV. 54; — *Presbyterians Plea of Merit*, facing XII. 263; — and Prince of Wales, XIII. 201; — authorized publisher, VII. xvi; — on style, XIII. 184; — *Tatler*, No. 230, II. xxxiii;

edition of JS's Works, Dublin, 1735 and following years: I. v; V. xxxiv; advertisement, XIV. 42–3; — textual note, XIV. 46; arrangement, XIII. 182–3; — Richard Mead's copy, XIV. 38; preparation, I. v; XIII. xxxiii–xxxvii, 202–3; publication, VII. xvi; XIII. 183; subscriptions, XIII. 202; vol. I (1735), 'Publisher's Preface', XIII. 181–3; — title-page facsimile, XIII. 180; vol. I (1763), 'To the Reader', XIII. 201–7; vol. II, 'Advertisement', XIII. 184–5; vol. III, 'Advertisement', XI. 3; — authorship, XIII. 224–5; vol. IV, 'Advertisement', X. 173–4; XIII. 186–7; — authorship, X. 207; — text, X. 207; vol. V (1738), preface to *Examiner*, III. 2.

Faulkner's *Dublin Journal*: *see* DUBLIN JOURNAL.

Fear: chief natural motive, IX. 155.

Faustus: character in chapbook *Dr. Faustus*, I. 41.

Feilding, Robert, *c.* 1651–1712: styled 'Beau Fielding', V. 86; mean figure, V. xi, 86; married daughter of 'Cavaliero' Swift, V. 187.

Feiling, Keith, *b.* 1884, historian: III. ix, *n.* 1.

Felton, John, *c.* 1595–1628, lieutenant: kills Buckingham, III. 106.

Fenestrelle, in Savoy: VII. 114.

Fenocchio: *see* FINOCHIO.

Fenton, Jane (*née* Swift), 1666–1736, JS's sister, wife of Joseph Fenton: V. 191; notifies JS of their mother's death, V. 196.

Fenwick, Sir John, *c.* 1645–97, Jacobite: execution, VIII. 34.

Fergus, legendary first king of Scotland, of Irish origin: and free masons, V. 329.

Ferguson, Colonel, possibly Robert, 'the Plotter', *d.* 1714, or James, his brother, *d.* 1705: V. 173.

Ferguson, Oliver: and *Maxims Controlled in Ireland*, XII. xxiii and *n.* 1.

Fermanagh, county of Ireland: IV. 278.

Fernando Carlo: *see* MANTUA.

Ferne, Mr. or Dr.: IV. 271.

Fernando Carlo: *see* MANTUA.

Fetter Lane, street in London: and Gulliver, XI. 20, 80.

Fetters: and dancing, IX. x–xi.

Feversham, Louis de Duras, 2nd Earl of, 1641–1709, Colonel of the Duke of York's Troop of

Horse Guards, lieutenant-general: V. 162–4.

Few Words upon the Examiner's Scandalous Peace: III. xxv.

Fiddes, Richard, 1671–1725, divine and historian: *Fifty Two Practical Discourses* (1720), IX. 125 and *n*.

Fielding, Robert: *see* FEILDING.

Fife, county of Scotland: V. 131.

Filmer, Sir Robert, *d*. 1653, political writer: censured, II. 15; and the Drapier, X. 94.

Findlater, James Ogilvy, 4th Earl of, and 1st Earl of Seafield, 1663–1730, Scottish statesman: VI. 173, 176.

Finlay, or Finley, Robert, London merchant: and William Wood, X. 28, 37–8.

Finley, a booth-keeper at Bartholomew Fair: II. 206.

Finochio: JS to buy seeds, V. 334.

Fire in Lilliputian palace (allegory of War of Spanish Succession and Treaty of Utrecht): XI. 55–6; and impeachment proceedings, XI. 68–73.

Fire insurance, Irish: English control, XIII. 175.

First fruits and twentieth parts (payments to the Crown), of the Church of Ireland: VIII. 123; and Burnet, IV. 67; and Oxford, VIII. 123; Oxford remits, III. 170; remission, II. 10; III. 74; and residence of clergy, XII. 186; and JS, II. ix, xiv; IX. ix, **JS's commission** (1710), II. xxxiii; — cancelled by Marsh, V. xxvii; — and Ormonde, V. xxvii; JS procures remission, XII. 147;

— JS solicits for, VIII. 121; — Whigs refuse JS, IX. xi; and Wharton, VIII. 121.

First fruits of the Church of England: and Tindal, II. 86.

First Ode of the Second Book of Horace Paraphras'd: and *Address'd to Richard St—le, Esq.*, by JS: quoted, VIII. xv–xvi.

Fishamble Street, Dublin: XII. 221; and John Harding, X. 205; and musical society (performing Handel's *Messiah*), XIII. 196–7.

Fisheries: XIII. 111–13; and Anne, XIII. 111; and Dutch, XIII. 111; Irish, XIII. xxx–xxxiii; Irish, and England, XIII. 111; and Earl of Oxford, XIII. 111.

Fitzgerald, Percy Hetherington, 1834–1925, lawyer, writer, artist: identified, VII. xxv, *n*. 1; letter to John Forster (1857), VII. xxv; collation of JS's *History of the Four Last Years*, VII. xxv–xxvii.

Fitzgerald, Robert, *c*. 1639–98, captain: III. 234–6.

Fitzhamon, Robert, *d*. 1107: V. 25–6.

Flambard, Ranulf, or Ralph, *d*. 1128, Bishop of Durham: imprisoned by Henry I, V. 28; and Robert of Normandy, V. 28–9, 31; an instrument of William II, V. 26.

Flanders: V. 43; and Bickerstaff, II. 144; campaign in (1709), VI. 31; Dutch to control, VI. 28; — to control (1709), VI. 91; — monopolize trade, VI. 28; — oppression, VI. 38; — sovereignty, VI. 90; Earl of: *see*

CHARLES THE GOOD; England's ally (1689–97), VI. 14; and English education, XII. 49; and English trade, VII. 61; and flounders, XII. 228–9; France allegedly governs (1701), VI. 12; France seizes, and Spain, VI. 17; lace from, XII. 79; Marlborough returns from (1711), VII. 28; mercenaries: *see* FLEMISH MERCENARIES; styled 'Mesopotamia', III. 83–5; Spain to administer, VI. 91; trade in, VI. 104; and War of the Spanish Succession, VII. 84, 85; — campaigns in War, VI. 20–1, 87; campaigns of William III, I. 111; wool manufacture, VI. 28. *See also* NETHERLANDS; SPANISH NETHERLANDS

'Flandona Gagnole', Laputan name meaning 'Astronomer's Cave': XI. 167.

Flanflasnic, city in Brobdingnag, in *Gulliver's Travels*: XI. 140.

'Flappers': XI. 159, 160, 161, 165, 166.

Flattery: censured, IV. 221; and humility, IV. 246; self-knowledge weakens, IX. 359; JS's resolve not to be influenced by, I. xxxvii; and vanity, IV. 246; basest vice, IX. 359–60.

Flavian, St., *d.* 449, Patriarch of Constantinople: letter from Leo to him: XIV. 20.

Flax: English modus, XIII. 107.

Fleas: and elephants, IV. 253.

Flèche, Hélie (or Élie) de Beaugency, comte du Maine (or Mans) and de la, *d.* 1110: and William II, V. 23–4.

Fleet Street: and author of *Mechanical Operation of the Spirit*, I. 171.

Fleetwood, William, 1656–1723, Bishop of St. Asaph: *Essay upon Miracles*, VI. 153; praises himself, VI. 153, 155; *Preface* to his sermons, VI. 192–5; — background, VI. xviii–xix; — condemned by Commons, VI. xix, 155; — and *The Spectator, et al.*, VI. xviii–xix, 151; — JS on, 151–5; *Preface* (to a sermon on the Duke of Gloucester's death, 1700), VI. xix–xx, 159–61; — Tory bias, VI. 159; opposes republicanism (*c.* 1700), VI. 161; JS's *Letter of Thanks from My Lord Wharton*, VI. xviii–xix; JS's *Remarks on Bishop Fleetwood's Preface*: *see* EXAMINER, 24 Jul. 1712; JS ridicules, VI. xx; turncoat, VI. 159–61.

Flemish mercenaries: V. 74, 80; and enforcement of censorship, V. 96; and Stephen, V. 70.

Fletcher, Andrew, 1655–1716, Scottish patriot, Fletcher of Saltoun: Macky and JS on, V. 262.

Fletcher, John, 1579–1625, playwright: bookseller's copyright, XIII. 206; and English poetry, IV. 273. *See also* BEAUMONT.

Fleury, André Hercule de, 1653–1743, cardinal, French statesman: lampoon on, V. xv–xvi; — attributed to JS, V. xvi.

Flies: XI. 109.

Flimnap, Lord Treasurer of Lilliput in *Gulliver's Travels*: XI. 54, 68–72, 76; his dexterity, XI. 38–9; governs Emperor, XI. 66; dines with Gulliver, XI. 64; sus-

pects Gulliver of cuckolding him,
XI. 65–6, 68; Walpole the model
for, XI. xix.

Flines, Nord, France: VII. 141.

'Flirtation': defined, V. 336.

Florus, Lucius Annaeus, 2nd century Roman historian: VIII. 37;
quotation, *Epitoma*, I. x. 6: I.
6.

Flounders: and Flanders, XII.
228–9.

'Fluft drin Yalerick Dwuldum
prastrad mirplush', Luggnaggian for, 'My tongue is in the
mouth of my friend': XI. 205.

'Flunec', Blefuscudian name for
a certain wine: XI. 56.

Fly on chariot wheel, fable by
Laurentius Abstemius: allusion
to, II. 115.

Flying Island: *see* LAPUTA.

Flying Post, London newspaper:
and Fleetwood's *Preface*, VI.
xix; knowledge of the world,
VIII. 32; on Oxford ministry,
VIII. 34; — 'impudent reflections' on, VIII. 14; attacks on JS,
VI. xxvi; a leader of Whig press,
VIII. 31, 34; (8 Oct. 1723),
Wood's answer to Irish Parliament, X. 5; and Wood's coinage, X. xvii and *n.* 2.

Foals: XI. 229, 235, 268.

Fo-he: *see* FUH-HI.

Foigny, Gabriel de, *c.* 1630–92:
La Terre australe inconnue (1676),
XI. xv.

Fonseca, Pedro de, 1528–99, Portuguese theologian: and Ford,
IV. xxxvi, 206.

Fontainebleau, Seine-et-Marne,
France: VII. 125.

Fontenelle, Bernard le Bovier de,

1657–1757, French author:
'killed' by Homer, I. 157.

'Fool-brook': IV. 283.

Footman (in *Directions to Servants*,
XIII. 34–45): and candles, XIII.
37; and chambermaid, XIII. 39;
china, XIII. 43; and coaches,
XIII. 38, 41; coffee making,
XIII. 39–40; dishes, XIII. 39,
41; door, XIII. 39; duties, XIII.
33; eavesdropping, XIII. 43;
called by employers, XIII. 37;
scolded by employers, XIII. 139;
errands, XIII. 34, 36, 39, 40;
escort, XIII. 42; fortune, XIII.
42–3; hanging, XIII. 44–5; highwayman, XIII. 44; lanterns,
XIII. 38; livery, XIII. 41;
lobster claws, XIII. 37; manners,
XIII. 33, 35, 42; old age, XIII.
44; petition of footmen, XII.
235–7; privileges, XIII. 33–4;
and fellow servants, XIII. 33,
40, 41; shoe cleaning, XIII. 36,
37, 40; socks, XIII. 41; unemployed, XIII. 43–4; vails,
XIII. 33, 40; waiting at table,
XIII. 34–5, 36, 37, 38, 43. *See
also* HUMBLE PETITION OF THE
FOOTMEN IN . . . DUBLIN.

**For the Honour of the Kingdom
of Ireland** (written 1738), by
JS: **V. 346–7**; textual note, V.
359.

Forbes, Edward (B.A., Trinity
College, Dublin, 1705): expelled
from Trinity College, II. 112;
and Archbishop King, II. 282,
n. 2.

Forbes, George, *d.* **1736**, Lord
Mayor of Dublin: X. 76.

Forbes, George, 1685–1765,
member of Privy Council of

M

Ireland (later 3rd Earl of Granard): X. 205.

Forbes, John: and recordership of Dublin, XIII. xxiv.

Ford, Charles, 1682–1741, intimate friend of JS: and Dependency Act, IX. x; and authorship of *God's Revenge against Punning*, IV. xxxv–xxxvi; and Henry Levi, VI. 174–5, 178; and Erasmus Lewis, VI. 174–5, 178; and *London Gazette*, IV. xxxiv–xxxv; and *Modest Defense of Punning*, IV. 206; and *Mr. Collins's Discourse of Free-Thinking*, IV. xvii; and Motte, XI. xxiv–xxv; possibly, 'Person of Quality', XII. 59; his copy of Savile's history, V. x; **correspondence with JS,** VIII. v, xxiii and *n.* 1, xxiv, xxvii–xxx, xxxiv, xxxvi, xl; XII. xlii; XIII. xi–xii; — *Letters to Ford*, ed. D. Nichol Smith, IX. xi, *n.* 1 — letter to Ford, 8 Dec. 1719 (on Irish politics), IX. xi; — letter to Ford, July 1722, V. xxxii; — letter to Ford, 19 Jan. 1723–24, XI. xvii–xviii; — letter to Ford, 14 Aug. 1725, XI. xi, xviii; — JS's letters to, published 1935, I. v; **and JS** — and *The Bubble*, IX. xxv; — in Dublin (1716), IV. xxxv; — and *Enquiry into the Behaviour of the Queen's Last Ministry*, VIII. xxxvi; — and *Gulliver's Travels*, VIII. xl; XI. xi, xvii–xviii, xxiv–xxvi; — hands similar, XI. xxvi, *n.* 3; — JS's regrets concerning *History of Four Last Years*, VII. xi; — *Letter to a Whig Lord*, VI. xvii; — *A Letter to the October Club*, VI. xi–xii; — and JS's MSS, IV.

xxxiv–xxxv; — and JS's politics, IV. xvi; — and *Some Free Thoughts*, VIII. xxiv, xxvii–xxviii; — attack on Tindal, II. xviii.

Formosa: cannibalism in, XII. 113–14.

Forster, John, *b.c.* 1686, Recorder of Dublin, and Lord Chief Justice of the Common Pleas of Ireland: Solicitor General, III. 239; candidate for Speakership of Irish House of Commons (elected 19 May 1710), II. 130–1, 133.

Forster, John, 1812–76, lawyer, historian, and biographer: collector of JS's works, VII. xxvii; and JS's *Enquiry into the Behaviour of the Queen's Last Ministry*, VIII. xxxvii–xxxviii; and *History of the Four Last Years*, VII. xxv–xxvii; *Life* of JS, I. ix. *n.**; II. x and *n.* 2; and JS's MSS, II. xl, *n.* 1.

Forster, Nicholas, *c.* 1682–1743, Bishop of Killaloe, later of Raphoe, fellow of Trinity College, 1694: bequest to Trinity College, IX. 55.

Forster Collection, in the Victoria and Albert Museum: VIII. xxix; and JS's *History of the Four Last Years*, VII. xxv–xxvi.

Fortitude: in ancient philosophy, IX. 249.

Fort Knocke, or Fort de Knocke, Reninge, near Loo, Belgium: VII. 113.

Fort Louis, Coudekerque-Branche, Nord, France: VII. 113.

Fort St. George, Madras, India: XI. 154.

Fortunatus, Venantius Honorius Clementianus, 6th century Christian poet: Baronius quotes, XIV. 35.

'Forward, Lady', character in *Polite Conversation*: IV. 156.

Fountaine, Sir Andrew, 1676–1753, courtier, collector, virtuoso: and *A Decree for Concluding the Treaty between Dr. Swift and Mrs. Anne Long*, V. xxiii–xxiv; Sir A. F. in *Dialogue in the Castilian Language*, IV. 257–9; puns upon name, IV. 265; and JS, V. xxiii; and JS's *Modest Defence of Punning*, IV. xxxiv; punned with JS, IV. xxix; JS visits, IV. xxix; JS visits (Christmas 1707–8), V. xxiii; possibly, the dedicatee of *Tritical Essay upon the Faculties of the Mind*, I. 246.

Fowl: blinding of, XI. 71.

Fowler, captain of Scottish rebels: V. 147–8.

Fox: fable of fox who lost his tail, I. 88; XII. 60.

Foxe, John, 1516–87: *Book of Martyrs*, 1563, IV. 80.

Foyston, Mary, *d.* 1721, necessary woman to Anne: VIII. 172 and *n.**

Fragment of the History from William Rufus: See REIGN OF WILLIAM THE SECOND.

France and the French: compared with Austria (1714), VIII. 60–1; Bavaria favoured, VII. 60, 148, 153, 155–6; and Bickerstaff, II. 144, 204; — his predictions for, II. 145–8; — predictions ridiculed, II. 207; Blefuscu in *Gulliver's Travels*, XI. 48–56, 67–

78; and Burnet, IV. 61; and Catalonia, VIII. 63; chaos in, predicted, II. 147–8; character — 'esprit', V. 245; — 'serious upon trifles', III. 107; conversation in, IV. 94; — raillery, IV. 91; and crowns of Europe, VIII. 54, 61; diplomacy 'litigious', VII. 164; mode of dress, IV. 247; recompense for Dunkirk (1711), VII. 49, 50–1; and Dutch: *see* DUTCH; and Dutch Barrier: *see* BARRIER, DUTCH;

and England — alliance (1714), VIII. 60; — to acknowledge Anne (1709), VI. 88, 105–6; — and Anne's change of ministry (1710), VII. 35–6; — compared, V. 112; — distrusted in England (1712), VII. 143; — feared by England (1701), I. 235; — and Hanoverian Succession, VI. 26–7; — and mottoes for Marlborough (1711), VII. 28; — in Middle Ages, V. 6–7, 15–16, 19, 38–45, 51, 65–9; — and the Duke of Orleans, VIII. 169–70; — Tories alleged to support, III. 128; — French tutors in England, XII. 50, 52; — early wars, VI. 9–10; — and Whigs, VIII. 9–10;

in *Examiner*, XIV. 6; fiscal experiments in, IX. 303; compared with Gaul, V. 80; and Germany — Protestantism in, VII. 113; — Rhine to be border, VII. 132; government — absolute monarchy, VI. 60; — dauphins, V. 68; — divine right of kings, VII. 150–1; — Salic law, V. 242; VIII. 55; Huguenots: *see* HUGUENOTS; and Ireland — anomalies

of Ireland, XII. 124, 131; — recruiting of soldiers in, XII. xxx–xxxi, 174–5, 311–21; — balance of trade, XII. 125; — wine imported, XII. 9; — wine, proposed tax on, XII. 124–6; — and Wood's coins, X. 8, 19, 47; and Jacobites, satirized in *Gulliver's Travels*, XI. 49–50; literature of, XII. 32; — Ancients and Moderns controversy, I. xxix; — literary critics, I. 58; free masons in, V. 327; Mayors of the Palace supplant Merovingians (721), VI. 44; and Merlin, II. 165, 168–9; money, X. 128; alleged perfidy, VII. 33–4; plague in (1720–22), X. 136–7; failure to establish king in Poland (1696), VIII. 54; poverty (1711), III. 213–14, 217–18; and the Pretender: *see* PRETENDER, OLD; religion in, IV. 79; — clergy, II. 98; — concordat of Francis I, IV. 71–3; — liberty of conscience, IX. 263; and Rome, IV. 8; and Savoy: *see* VICTOR; union with Spain: *see* SPAIN; denied Spanish Netherlands (1709), VI. 103; storm off coast predicted, II. 145; JS allegedly paid by, VI. xv; JS plans visit, XII. ix; and tavern signs, XII. 223; trade—wartime trade with America, VII. 84; — Assiento held for ten years, VII. 132; — wartime trade with Dutch, VII. 84; — with Peru, VI. 22; — Tariff of 1664, VII. 114, 153; — retaliatory tariffs, XII. 125; and Treaty of Utrecht: *see* UTRECHT; and War of Spanish Succession: *see*

WAR; denied West Indies, VI. 47.

Franchise, JS on: and Dissenters, V. 80; and forty shilling freeholders, V. 81.

Francis I, King of France, 1494–1547: and Henry VIII, IV. 72–3; and Leo X, IV. 71, 72.

Frankfort, Germany: Peterborough expected (1711), VII. 58.

Frankland, Sir Thomas, Bart., *c.* 1665–1726, postmaster-general: Macky and JS on, V. 260.

Fraud: *see* HYPOCRISY AND FRAUD.

Fraud Detected (i.e. *Drapier's Letters*): X. 107.

'Fraughauns', bilberries: IV. 278, 302.

Frederick I, King of Prussia, Elector of Brandenburg (as Frederick III), 1657–1713: VII. 113, 133, 137; subsidies, VI. 33; and Treaty of Utrecht, VII. 133; troops hired by Grand Alliance, VII. 137 — may recall troops, VI. 64; and War of the Spanish Succession — a good ally, VII. 133.

Frederick IV, King of Denmark, 1671–1730: one of 'these princes', VI. 63; one of the 'princes of the north', VII. 148; and Treaties of Travendal and Copenhagen, VI. 62.

Frederick Lewis, Prince of Wales, 1707–51, grandson of George I: 'Grandson', VIII. xxvii, 93, 179.

Frederickshall, now Fredrickstad, Norway: V. 11, *n.**.

Freeholders: and management of elections, V. 252.

Freethinkers and freethinking: and abolition of Christianity, II. 36–8; and blasphemy, II. 29; censured, II. 11; and courtiers, IV. 108–9; defended ironically, IV. 38–41; and civil employments, II. 62; most Englishmen are, II. 34; and God, IV. 48; and hell, IV. 48; of history, IV. 41–7; ignorant and vicious, IX. 78; and immortality, IV. 48; and incarnation, IV. 48; Jesuits disguised as, II. 37; and Moses, IV. 48; most men are freethinkers, II. 62; pedants, II. 81; and poets, IX. 329; and preaching, IX. 77; and free press, II. 60–1; rational rights of, IV. 35; reasons (absurd) for, IV. 29–38; worse than Roman Catholics, IV. 77; and Countess of Suffolk, V. 214; rebel against taboos, II. 33; and Tindal, IV. 37, 41, 45; and the Trinity, IV. 48; join Whigs, II. 3; linked with Whigs, IV. xviii, 63, 84.

Freind, John, 1675–1728, physician, politician, and author: VIII. 124; member of 'The Society', XI. xii.

Freinsheim, Johann ('Freinshemius'), 1608–60, German classical scholar: I. 278.

'Frelock', title of Clefren and Marsi, officers who search Gulliver: XI. 33–6.

French, Edmund: X. 76.

French, Humphrey, *d.* 1736, Lord Mayor of Dublin in 1732: administrative ability, XIII. 84; candidate for M.P. for Dublin, XIII. xxv, xxvi, 79; and dishonest merchants, XIII. 85;

made free of Dublin corporations, XIII. xxv; integrity, XIII. 84; JS praises, XIII. xxvi.

French Correspondence Clear as the Sun: *see* IT'S OUT AT LAST.

French language: and good breeding, IV. 217; changes in, IV. 8; mixes with English, IV. 7; — introduced by Edward the Confessor, V. 6; superior to English, IV. xiv, 6; and modern education, XII. 49, 50; and 'pun', IV. 206; and Wagstaff, IV. 118.

French King's Thanks to the Tories of Great Britain: III. 58.

French Prophets: *see* CASIMARS.

'Frescamenti': on word list of JS, V. 336.

Friar and five nuns: V. 335.

Friendly Society, a fire insurance company: I. 67.

Friendship: among the Houyhnhnms, XI. 268; JS's views, advice from friends, I. xxxvii.

Frog and bull, fable of: allusion to, XII. 133.

Frogs: and Gulliver, XI. 121; imported into Ireland, II. xxxiv, *n.* 3; XIII. 175 *n.*

From the Right Hon. Wm. P——y Esq; *To the Right Honourable Sir R——t W——e*: not by JS, V. xvi–xvii.

'Frontless, Dick': character in *Polite Conversation*, IV. 163.

Frowde, Philip, *d.* 1738, poet: and Pope's *Iliad*, IV. xxxv.

Fruah, Laird of: V. 137.

Fruit, JS's taste for: V. 193.

'Fruzz, Lady': character in *Polite Conversation*, IV. 158.

Fulk (or Foulques) V, Count of Anjou, 1095–1143: and Henry I,

V. 38–42; William the Clito marries daughter, V. 41–2.

Full and True Account of the Battel Fought Last Friday: see BATTLE OF THE BOOKS.

Full and True Account of . . . the Execution of William Wood: see DRAPIER'S LETTERS.

Fuller, William, 1670–*c.* 1717, an impostor: and 'James III', the Old Pretender, VIII. 52.

Fulvia, *d.* 40 B.C., wife of Mark Antony: pseudonym for Duchess of Marlborough, III. 77; XIV. 6.

Furnes, Flanders: and Dutch Barrier, VI. 101, 109; VII. 113.

Furnese, Sir Henry, Bart., 1658–1712: and genealogy, III. 151–2 and *n.**.

'Further Digression': title of section X of *Tale of a Tub*, in J. Hawkesworth's edition of 1755.

Further Thoughts on Religion, by JS (really notes for an answer to R. Filmer's *Patriarcha*): **IX. 264**; textual note, IX. 377.

Further Thoughts on Various Subjects: see THOUGHTS ON VARIOUS SUBJECTS (1727 and 1745).

'Fustyes': defined by JS, V. 336.

G

Gabriel, Patriarch of Alexandria: mission to Pope Clement VIII (1593), XIV. 28.

Gad, Tribe of (i.e., gad-abouts): IV. 159.

Gadbury, John, 1627–1704, almanac-maker: and Partridge, II. 163; satirized, II. 142.

'Gadd', i.e., withe: IV. 279, 302.

'Galbet', Lilliputian high admiral: XI. 42, 67.

Galen, Claudius, 2nd century A.D., medical writer: 'fights' for Ancients, I. 156.

Gallas, Johann Wenzel, Count de, 1669–1719, Austrian ambassador in London: maligns Anne and ministry (1711), VII. 58–9; Austrian envoy, VII. 25; JS's character of, VII. 58–9; dispatches to Charles VI, VII. 58; Commons' resentment, VII. 119–20; espionage, VII. 58; expelled from court (1711), VII. 58–9; dismisses Gaultier, VII. 35; — protects him ('foreign ministers'), VII. 34–5; letter intercepted, VII. 25; distrusts Oxford ministry, VII. 58; letters to Zinzendorf (1711), VII. 58–9.

'Gallery, Twelve-Peny': I. 37.

Galligate Bridge road, leading into Glasgow, Scotland: V. 138.

Galloway, a district in south-west of Scotland: and Creichton, V. 147, 177, 178.

Galloway, Lord: see GALWAY.

Galway, Henry de Massue, 1st Earl of, marquis de Ruvigny, 1648–1720, lieutenant-general, Lord Justice in Ireland: III. 234; IV. 281; XII. 159; Bickerstaff's predictions for, II. 198–9; Macky and JS on, V. 261; and Spanish campaign, VI. 37.

Gambling, or gaming: Burnet's style, V. 275; immoral consequences of, II. 46, 50, 51;

and nobility, XI. 131–2; satirized, I. 25; gamblers in 'Tables
of Fame', II. 241–2.
Game Act, Irish: greyhounds, IX.
292.
Games: children's, and poetry,
IX. 334–6; children's, increase
wisdom, IX. 336; on the Greek
model, XI. 269–70.
Gand: *see* GHENT.
Ganges River, in India: XI. 99.
Garter, Order of the: satirized
(blue thread), XI. 39.
Garth, Sir Samuel, 1661–1719,
physician and poet: pun upon
name, IV. 275.
'Garrauns', geldings: IV. 279,
302.
Gassendi, Pierre, 1592–1655,
French philosopher: XI. 197;
leads Modern bowmen, I. 152.
'Gatherall, Dick': character in
Polite Conversation, IV. 179.
Gauden, John, 1605–65, Bishop
of Worcester: *Eikon Basilike*, V.
268.
Gaul: France compared with,
V. 80; and Julius Caesar, I. 220;
V. 245; Gauls and Romans, II.
123.
Gaulstown House, near Duleek,
co. Meath, Ireland, seat of the
Rochfort family: visited by JS,
IX. xxvii.
Gaultier, François, *d.* 1720,
French priest and diplomat:
Croissy recommends him, VII.
34; returns to France (1711), VII.
36, 59; returns to France (1712),
VII. 120; Gallas dismisses him,
VII. 35; and Jersey (1710), VII.
35; visits Nottingham (1704),
VII. 34; and Oxford, VIII. 163;

protected by French ministers
(i.e., Gallas and Tallard), VII.
34, 35; and Torcy, VII. 34, 35,
37; and Treaty of Utrecht, VII.
34–5, 37–8, 41, 59.
Gaveston, Piers, 4th Earl of
Cornwall, *c.* 1284–1312, favourite
of Edward II: III. 93.
Gaven, Thomas: X. 76.
Gay, John, 1685–1732, poet and
dramatist: *Beggar's Opera*, and
Intelligencer, No. 3, XII. 32–7;
— *Opera* defended by JS, XII.
xiv; 'Devonshire Man of Wit',
IV. xxiv; *Fables* (1727), XII. 35;
fall from horse, IV. xxxiv, xxxv,
209–10; Faulkner prints writings,
XIII. 201; *Molly Mogg*, V. 225;
and poetasters, V. 201; pun upon
name, IV. 275; and Scriblerus
Club; XI. xiii; one of 'snarling
brood', IV. xxxii, 118; **and JS**
— correspondence, XII. x, xxix,
xxxiii; — and *Gulliver's Travels*,
XI. xxii; — letter to Gay, Nov.
1730, V. xvi; — *Miscellanies* of
Pope and JS, XIII. 204; — and
Countess of Suffolk, V. xxvii–
xxviii; — JS visits (1727), V.
xxvii; — JS wiser, V. xxv; —
and *To Mr Gay*, XII. xxxiii; and
Walpole, XII. 34–5.
Gazette, Dublin: 14 Oct. 1724, X.
215.
Gazette, Dutch: *see* DUTCH,
Gazette.
Gazette, London: Barber and
Tooke made printers (1711), VI.
xxiii; publishing history, IV.
xxxiv–xxxv; salary of Gazetteer,
VIII. 7; and Wood's coinage,
X. 27.
Gee, Edward, 1657–1730, Dean

of Lincoln: fear of Papists, IV.
250; satirized, IV. xl.

Geel: *see* VAN GHEEL.

Gelasius, Pope, *d*. 496: suppresses
Lupercalia, XIV. 26.

Gelderland: *see* GUELDER.

Geldings: XI. 241, 272–3.

Gemara, a section of the Talmud:
I. 41.

Gemelli: *see* LEIGH.

Gems: *see* STONES, PRECIOUS.

General History of Ears, imaginary
treatise by the author of *Tale of
a Tub*: I. xl, 130; and Bickerstaff,
II. xii, 199.

Genesis: and Isaac, IV. 239. *See
also* BIBLE.

Geneva, Switzerland: Calvinism,
II. 101; XII. 264; and English
Protestants, IX. 220; and re-
publican government, XII. 278.

Genevre, mountain in Savoy:
VII. 114.

Genius, JS's views: and envy,
XII. 39; above money, IV. 20.

Gentleman's Magazine: and *'Squire
Bickerstaff Detected*, II. xiv, *n*. 2.

Geoffrey, *b*. 1134, son of Geoffrey
'Plantagenet' and brother of
Henry II: V. 67; and earldom of
Anjou, V. 74–5.

Geoffrey 'Plantagenet', Count of
Anjou, 1113–1151: V. 65; his
death, V. 66; and Gloucester, V.
63; a grave and cautious prince,
V. 48; father of Henry II, IV. 7;
marries Matilda the Empress,
V. 42; invades Normandy, defeated by Stephen, V. 51; subdues Normandy, V. 59; receives
Stephen's hostages, V. 65; receives pension from Stephen,
V. 51.

Geography: affects forms of
government, II. 17.

George I, King of England,
Elector of Hanover, 1660–1727:
Addison and JS on, V. 251–5;
and Anne, VIII. 67, 68, 174–7;
birthday celebrations (1720), IX.
xv; and Bodin, V. 245; Bothmar misleads him, VII. 144;
Bothmar sanctions his memorial
(1711), VII. 24, 144; and Bremen
('two maritime towns'), V. 100;
burial, V. 265; and Cambridge
University, IV. xxxiv; character,
V. 11, 101; IX. xiii. 28; and the
Church of England, V. xxxiii,
254; VIII. 173–4; — clergy dis-
affected, XIII. 107; clemency, V.
xxxiii, 254; death, V. 101, 102,
215; XII. ix; and *A Dedication concerning Dedications*, IX. xiii; and
Dependency Act, IX. xi; and
Drapier, X. 101–2; — Drapier
loyal to king, X. 62, 69, 86;
to be acknowledged Elector of
Hanover, VII. 113; to remain
Elector (1712), VII. 134; ignorance of English language, customs, etc., V. 101; X. 69–70;
a foreigner, XI. 97; and regent
of France, VIII. 169–70; and
George II, V. 101, 253, 255;
VIII. 178–9; troops hired by
Grand Alliance, VI. 39, 64;
VII. 137; XI. 247; and Hanover
— alleged to send money to, V.
100; — William Howell and
JS on, V. 265; — and Hanoverian favourites ('his hospitality to strangers'), XI. 160–1;
— frequent trips satirized (not to
'leave the island'), V. 100; XI.
172; and House of Commons,

V. 105; and Ireland — approval of Bank, IX. xix; — and Irish Whigs, IX. 56; and Jacobite uprisings of 1715, V. 100, 105, 254; VIII. 218; King of Laputa, partly modelled on, XI. 160–72; patron of learning, XI. 26; Emperor of Lilliput, partly modelled on, XI. xviii, xix; loyalty of people, V. 107; VIII. 218; IX. 186; and Lübeck ('two maritime towns'), V. 100; patron of mathematics, XI. 160–1; his mercenaries in the War of the Spanish Succession, VI. 39, 64; VII. 137; XI. 247; patronizes musicians, XI. 162–3; and Northern War: *see* NORTHERN WAR; and Ormonde ('a general'), V. 252; and Oxford ministry, VII. 24, 143–4; VIII. 140; — they attempt to cultivate him, VIII. 171–2; and the Quadruple Alliance, V. 100; described as 'Regoge, Emperor of Japan', V. 99–107; and Robethon, VII. 143–4; Roman Catholics loyal to, XII. 273; Sheridan's sermon on his birthday (1725), V. xxix, 223; and Sophia Dorothea, V. 265; his statue in Dublin, X. 21; and order of succession, VII. 78; **and JS** — dislike for George, IX. xiii, *n.* 1; — doesn't know him, V. 11; IX. xiii, 26, 28; — submits to him, VII. xxxvi; and Tories, VIII. 94–5; — rejects them, V. 99–101; VIII. 164; — reverses their policies (1714), VII. xxxiii, xxxiv; and universities, V. 286; unwise, V. xxxi; X. xxix; and Treaty of Utrecht, VIII. 170; and Walpole, V. 101;

— 'corrupted ministry', XI. 130; governed by Walpole, XI. 66; **and Whigs,** VIII. 93–4, 109; Whig bias, VI. 132; — foreseen, VII. xxxiii, xxxvi, 143–5; VIII. 132, 157, 173–4, 175; — and civil war, VIII. 218; — in Hanover, V. 99, 100–1; — and prerogative, VIII. 97; — and religion, V. 286;

and Wood's coins: X. ix–xiii, xvii–xviii, xxvii–xxx; addressed by House of Commons of Ireland, X. 177–8; addressed by House of Lords of Ireland, X. 179; — answer to Lords, X. 56, 69–70; addressed by Privy Council of Ireland, X. 181–2; allies of Wood, enemies of king, X. 75; will not force coins on Ireland, X. 11, 153–4; *Gulliver's Travels*, allegory, XI. 309–10; — Flimnap's fall, XI. 39; not involved in dispute, X. 45, 57; opponents of coins, his enemies, X. 65; — loyal to him, X. 76; — will not be punished, X. 43; patent, X. 34–9; — good of nation intended by, X. 34–5, 126; — king allegedly ignorant of, X. 5; no reflections cast on him, X. 101–2.

See also HANOVER, HOUSE OF; HANOVERIAN SUCCESSION.

George II, King of England, 1683–1760, 'Electoral Prince', Duke of Cambridge, Elector of Hanover, son of George I: accession, V. 102; and Compton, V. 103; and Dublin street signs, XII. 232; and George I, V. 101, 253, 255; VIII. 179; 'G.R.: II', XII. xxxv, 232; and Hanmer, V. 103; and Irish Parliament, XII.

xiv; Irish regiments in French army, XII. 174; Emperor's son in Lilliput partly modelled on, XI. xix; and Charles McCarthy, V. 90–92; and Parliament, V. 103–4; and royal prerogative, III. xxviii–xxix; and Pulteney, V. 111, 114, 118, 119; and order of succession, VII. 78; **and JS** — attacked in JS's *Account of . . . Japan*, V. xiv–xv, 101–7; — JS prays for, IX. 240; — preferment in England (1727), V. xiii; — and JS's *Proposal for Virtue*, XIV. xii–xiii; — JS visits him (1726), XIII. 201; Tory leanings ('the heir'), XI. 48; and Walpole, V. 103–7; and Whigs, VIII. 89, 91; possibly wise, V. xxxi; writ for Duke of Cambridge, VIII. 178–9; — and Anne, VII. 175; — Nottingham supports it, VII. 16; — JS on, VIII. 95.

George VI, King of England, 1895–1952: acknowledgement to, VII. vii.

George, Prince of Denmark, 1653–1708, consort of Queen Anne: and George Churchill, VIII. 113; death, II. xxi; III. 95, 165; VIII. 101, 112–13; — increases Whig strength, VI. 43; medal, XIII. 156; Steele his gentleman usher (1706), VIII. 6; hates Whigs, VIII. 112–13, 114.

George, Prince of Hesse Darmstadt, 1654–1705, a commander of the Allied troops in Spain: and Catalonia, VIII. 62; and the Spanish campaign (1705), VI. 21.

George or Joris, David, 1501–56, Dutch Anabaptist: fanatic, I. 188.

George, Richard, *d.* 1728, lieutenant-general: III. 238.

Georgics: *see* VIRGIL.

Geree, John, *d.* 1761, rector of Letcombe Bassett, canon of Hereford, friend of JS: JS visits 'a friend' (1714), VII. xxxvi.

Germain, Lady Elizabeth, *d.* 1769, wife of Sir John, daughter of the Earl of Berkeley: and Lord Lieutenant's liveries, XIII. xxviii.

'German family': *see* HANOVER, HOUSE OF.

German language (High Dutch): Houyhnhnms' language similar to, XI. 234; rough consonants (of 'High Dutch'), IV. 13; Saxon heritage, IV. 7; stability, IV. 9.

Germans and Germany: ancient, government, V. 36; — clergy, no legislative power, II. 82; and British throne, VI. 94; 'dullest nation', I. 242; eagle insignia, XII. 223; and English language, IV. 12; and fanaticism, I. 188; and Hill's Canadian expedition, VI. 23; mint, XII. 9, 11; and proposed mint in Ireland, XII. 57, 90; peasants compared to Irish, IX. 21; Protestantism, V. 12; VI. 63; and Rome, IV. 8; War in Spain and 'rapacious ministry', VI. 21.

Germanus (Germain), St., *c.* 380–448, Bishop of Auxerre: miracle in fire, XIV. 20.

Gertruydenberg (or Geertruidenberg, North Brabant, Netherlands), peace negotiations (1710): VII. 35, 36; articles, VI. 49–50; — and Grand Alliance, VI. 49; Dutch interests served, VI. 50;

— negotiate separately, VII. 40; — reproved for (1711), VII. 57; disadvantages to England, VI. 51; England's impossible demands, VI. 49, 60; failure, VI. 59; VII. 35; France, VII. 41; Preliminary Articles: *see* HAGUE, *peace negotiations*; and Whig interest, VI. 5.

Geryon, in Greek mythology, monster with three bodies: Spain and Merlin, II. 169.

Gesta Romanorum: pun upon, IV. 238.

Geyser: near Holyhead, V. 203.

Ghent, or Gand, Flanders: rumours of Anne's death (1712), VII. 152; and Dutch Barrier, VII. 114; Castle of, and Dutch Barrier, VI. 90, 101, 109, 113; VII. 91, 122; taken by Ormonde (1712), VII. 141–2; and Ormonde's troops ('G'), XIV. 13.

Gherardi, Evaristo, 1663–1700: edits *Le Théâtre italien* (1695–98), XII. 32.

Ghosts: conjured in Glubbdubdrib, XI. 195–202; false relations, I. 242.

Gibb, James, dragoon (in Francis Stuart's—later William Cleland's —company of Royal Scots Dragoons): and Covenanters, V. 145–6.

'Gibeall, Sir Peter': character in *Polite Conversation*, IV. 146.

Gibraltar: to remain British, VII. 43, 45, 48, 115, 119–20, 132; and Walpole, V. 95, 113.

Gibson, Edmund, 1669–1748, Bishop of London: *The Dispute Adjusted about . . . Repeal of the*

Corporation and Test Acts, XII. xlvii.

'Giddy, Mrs.': character in *Polite Conversation*, IV. 195.

Giffard, Martha (*née* Temple), Lady, 1638–1722, sister to Sir William: 'some persons', I. 268; encourages JS's poetry, I. xii; — his letter to (1709), I. xxxvi;— his translation of Virgil, I. xii; opposes publication of Temple's *Memoirs* III, I. xxxvi.

Gifts: Stella's definition of, V. 233.

Gil Blas, hero of novel by Le Sage: his steward, XIII. ix, 51.

Gildon, Charles, 1665–1724, deist and miscellaneous writer: antiChristian, II. 72; and clergy, IV. 37; and freethinking, IV. 41; and Wagstaff, IV. 118.

Gillicranky: *see* KILLIECRANKIE.

Gisors, Eure, France: V. 38.

Glanguenstald, seaport of Luggnagg, *Gulliver's Travels*, Book III: XI. 215.

Glanvill, Joseph, 1636–80, divine, member of Royal Society: on Robert Boyle, I. xxxiv.

Glasgow, Scotland: V. 4; approaches to, V. 138; and Covenanter rebels, V. 138–9, 141–2.

Glassenbury: *see* GLASTONBURY.

'Glimigrim', Lilliputian wine: XI. 56.

'Glonglung', Brobdingnagian unit of distance, about 18 miles: XI. 112.

Gloucester, England: and Empress Matilda, V. 57–8; cathedral, and Wharton, III. 57, 69.

Gloucester, Robert, 1st Earl of, *c.* 1090–1147, illegitimate son of

Henry I: captured and imprisoned, V. 61–2; character, V. 65; his death, V. 65; fights for Empress Matilda, V. 53–65; his devotion to Matilda, V. 65; captures Stephen, V. 55–9; exchanged for Stephen, V. 62.

Gloucester, William, 5th Duke of, 1689–1700, son of Queen Anne: Fleetwood's sermon on his death, VI. xx, 159–61, 194.

Glubbdubdrib, island of sorcerers off Balnibarbi, *Gulliver's Travels*, Book III: XI. 193–202; map, XI. 152.

Glumdalclitch, 'Little Nurse', Gulliver's nurse and instructor in Brobdingnag: XI. 103, 125, 126, 136, 137, 146; acts as his nurse and instructor at court, XI. 102, 104–6, 108, 109, 112–14, 116–19, 121, 122, 124, 139–40; assumes care of Gulliver, XI. 95; and exhibition of Gulliver, XI. 96–100; separation from her distresses him, XI. 141–2.

Glumgluff, Lilliputian unit of length, about one inch: XI. 51.

Gnnayh, bird of prey in Houyhnhnmland: XI. 248.

God: conscience, and love of, IX. 155; hard to tell from devil, I. 99–100, 179–80; government derived from, IX. 238; honour and glory, IX. 263; his judgments searched, XIV. 27; mercy, IX. 262.

Goddard, Jonathan, 1617–75, physician: 'Goddard's Drops', II. 235; IV. 264.

Godfrey, Duke of Lorraine, *c.* 1061–1100, 'Godfrey of Boulogne': crusader, V. 21–2;

chosen king of Jerusalem, V. 22.

Godfrey, Mr., Dublin tradesman: JS recommends case, V. 346.

Godfry, a chemist in Southampton St., London: and JS, V. 334, 336.

Godolphin, Henry, 1648–1733, Dean of St. Paul's: VI. 153.

Godolphin, Sidney, Earl of, 1645–1712, Lord Treasurer: ambition, III. 95, (one of 'a very few') 165; VI. 41; **and Anne**, VIII. 111; — sorry to dismiss him, VIII. 103; — favours him (1702), VI. 41; — and Oxford, VIII. 102, 115–16; — would remove him (1707), VIII. 112; Burnet and JS on, V. 279; fears censure, VII. 22; **JS's character of,** VII. 8–9; High Church (one of 'two or three'), III. 94; corruption ('a certain minister'), VIII. 49; 'cannot be accused of corruption', VII. 76; army debts, VII. 76; and national debt ('a sharper'), III. 34; navy debts, III. 136; VII. 22–3, 72–3; his education, XII. 47; fiscal mismanagement, III. 189; his gambling, III. 80, 96; and James II, VII. 8; — alleged to correspond ('two lords', 1712), VI. 145; VIII. 48; and Junto (1711), VII. 108; lord treasurership — dismissal threatened (1708), VIII. 112–13; — dismissed (1710), II. xxxii; VII. 72–3; VIII. 118; — 'sole management . . . at home', VI. 11; and Marlborough, VIII. 102; — alliance with him, III. 20; ('*One*') VI. 11, 40–1, 59; VII. 9; alliance with Marlborough and moneyed men, VI. 41; 'passion'

for Duchess of Marlborough, VII. 9; — allegedly his mistress, VIII. 111; and Mary of Modena ('Queen at St. Germains'), VII. 8; ministry: *see* GODOLPHIN MINISTRY; 'Mr. Oldfox', III. 25 and *n.**; negligence, VII. 76; humble origins, VII. 8; act of general pardon, VII. 22; poetaster, VII. 9; and Pretender, VIII. 66; — Old Pretender ('which have been tampering'), VIII. 39; and Thomas Proby, III. 181; resigns (1701), VI. 11; and Sacheverell — Godolphin's 'blind pursuit', VI. 74; — his ruin ('a great man'), VI. 74; — trial, VIII. 115; and Scotland — Act of Security, 1703 ('offending ministers'), III. 94–5; VIII. 49; — Act of Union (1707), VIII. 49; and Somers, VIII. 115; and Somerset, VII. 14; JS and his death, VIII. 13; — praises him, I. 268; — turns against him, II. xxxix; praised by Temple, I. 268; Tory ('certain great persons'), III. 164; and Tories — alienates them, VI. 42; — leaves them ('two lords'), VI. 145; — himself a Tory (1701), VI. 11, 42; — one of 'two men' misruling England in 1701, I. 210; — ('certain great persons') III. 164; and Toulon (1707), 'a certain great man', VI. 34; and the Union ('prime minister'), III. 40; called 'Volpone', III. 86, 222; VIII. 115; — by Sacheverell, VII. 9; and Whigs — natural aversion to them, VII. 9; — joins them ('certain great persons'), III. 164; — and principles,

III. 15; — seduce him, VIII. 56; — 'solemn league and covenant', VI. 42; — solicits their support, VI. 42; and War of the Spanish Succession — would continue (1709), VI. 50; — favours (1702), VI. 40; — opposes (1701), VI. 11, 40; — power depends on it, VI. 43; — and subsidies to Portugal, VI. 39.

Godolphin ministry: accounts not passed, III. 149; and Anne, VI. 79; VIII. 24; — abuse her, III. 201; and Austria, III. 205; — deceives them, VI. 21; and Barrier Treaty: *see* BARRIER TREATY; and Bolingbroke, VII. 98; VIII. 113; character opposed to that of Oxford ministry, III. 78–80; XIV. 8; and Church of England: *see* CHURCH OF ENGLAND; SACHEVERELL; alleged corruption, VII. 12, 33, 64–7, 88; and national debt, VII. 70–1; defenders decried, VI. 5–6; 'dog-keepers', VIII. 24; Dutch warned against (1710), VII. 23; and employments, III. 37; and *Examiner*, VIII. 15;

fall (1710), III. 77–8, 202–3; VII. 34, 73; VIII. 101–3, 107–28; — Allies would prevent, VI. 43–4; — false credit sinks, VI. 56; — effect on the economy, III. 4; — Fleetwood on, VI. 154; — Louis XIV allegedly applauds, III. 58–9; — gradual, VII. 4; — moneyed interests would prevent, VI. 43–4; — and public opinion, III. 64–6; — reasons for, III. 37–40, 62–3, 93–6; VII. 4, 12; — reasons for, dramatized, VI. 44; — resort to

coffee houses, VI. 53; — subsequent ingratitude, VI. 131; — and Sacheverell trial, VIII. xxxi; and foreign Protestants, VII. 94; frauds, III. 148–9; and freethinking, IV. 28; and William Gregg, III. 108–9; and Junto, XIV. 7; lotteries, VII. 77; mismanagement, VII. 73; moderating scheme (1708), VIII. 113; negligence, VII. 64, 78, 88; and Oxford, VIII. 113; XIV. 8; — his dismissal (1708), VII. 73; — attempt to prove him a traitor, III. 108–9; — undermines them, VII. 73; and the new Parliament (1711), VII. 17; and pensions, III. 78; and preferments, III. 37–9; and the Pretender, III. 205; parallel to Puritan rebels ('Solemn League and Covenant'), VI. 42; restoration of, IV. 31; and Sacheverell: *see* SACHE-VERELL; and Act of Security (1703), VIII. 114; and Somers, VIII. 114; and Steele, VIII. 67; — defends them, VIII. 13–14; and tallies, VII. 71, 72; Tories, honourable opposition, VI. 130–1; Tories aid common cause, III. 68; VI. 130–1; Tory writers suppressed, III. 188; and Act of Union (1707), VIII. 114; — and Junto, III. 95; and War of the Spanish Succession — ministry permit Allies' defection, VII. 64; — Dutch allegedly persuade them to continue, VI. 57; — funds for, VII. 77; — and mercenaries, VI. 39; — wilful failure to make peace (1709–10), VI. 59, 190–1; VII. 32–3; — would prolong war, III. 119;

— Whigs and the war, VIII. 148–9.

God's Revenge against Punning: *see* POPE.

Godwin, Earl of the West Saxons, *d.* 1053: and Edward the Confessor, V. 6; and *Polite Conversation*, IV. 196.

Goiters: XII. 295.

Gold, Maxwell B.: *Swift's Marriage to Stella*, VII. xiii, *n.* 1, 2.

Golden Fleece: and papal bulls, I. 68, 69.

Golden Mean: *see* ARISTOTLE.

Golden Spy, 1709: 'many others', I. 1.

Goliath: pun upon name, IV. 208; compared to Wood, X. xv, 48.

Goodenough, Richard, *fl.* 1686, Whig conspirator: Burnet and JS on, V. 284.

Good-manners and Good-breeding: *see* TREATISE ON GOOD-MANNERS AND GOOD-BREEDING; HINTS ON GOOD-MANNERS.

Goodman's Holding, property in Dublin: JS's will, XIII. 153.

Goodwin, John, *c.* 1593–1665, democratic Puritan: Burnet and JS on, V. 270.

Goodwin, Timothy, *d.* 1720, London bookseller: publisher of Temple's *Letters to the King*, I. 265.

Gorden, Elizabeth: and Ebenezor Elliston, IX. 366.

Gordon, George Gordon, 1st Duke of, 1649–1716: and Edinburgh Castle, V. 167, 169–70.

Gordon, James: acknowledgment to, XIV. vii.

Gordon, Thomas, *d.* 1750, journalist: *A Dedication concerning*

Dedications, IX. xiii, *n.* 1, 370;
— JS denies authorship, IX.
xiii, 28; — 'Treatise', IX. 28,
370; *The Independent Whig*, IX.
xiii, *n.* 1.

'Gosling, Tom': character in
Polite Conversation, IV. 193–4.

Goths and Gothic institutions:
V. 100; annual parliaments, IX.
32; and balance of power, I. 197;
destroy civilization, IX. 50; con-
quests, II. 83; decline of, VIII.
180; and freedom, X. 86–7;
forms of government, V. 36–7;
and parliamentary history, V.
35–6; and ancient Rome, V. 3;
invade Rome, IV. 8.

Governess: in *Directions to Servants*, XIII. 65.

Government: forms, I. 196–7; V.
36–7; from God, IX. 238; good
government described, IX. 227;
XI. 58–60, 135–6, 270; — and
balance of power, I. xx, 199–
202, 226–7; — and limitation
of property, I. 243; Irish, should
encourage poets, IX. 341;
maxims of state, XII. 131–7;
origins, Adam and Eve, IX. 264;
should serve the people, V. 279;
controlled by property owners,
IV. 245; and state church, XII.
290; JS 'no bigot', II. 2. *See also*
COMMON PEOPLE; CONSTITU-
TION; PARTIES.

Gowrie, John Ruthven, 3rd Earl
of, 1577–1600: conspiracy, JS
on, V. 266.

Gracchi (i.e. Caius Sempronius
Gracchus, *d.* 121 B.C., and his
elder brother, Tiberius, Roman
tribunes): and violent uprisings,
I. 216, 218–19.

Gracchus, Tiberius Sempronius,
c. 163–133 B.C., Roman tribune:
'the elder Gracchus', I. 218;
pseudonym for Sunderland, III.
77.

Graevius, Johann Georg Gräve,
1632–1703, German scholar and
historian, professor at Utrecht:
V. xxxvii.

Grafton, Charles Fitzroy, 2nd
Duke of, 1683–1757, Lord
Lieutenant of Ireland: and Irish
bank scheme, IX. 303–4; suc-
ceeded by Carteret, X. xvii; and
the Drapier, X. 102; government of, XIII. 187; and Irish
bank, IX. xx, 303–4; Macky and
JS on, V. 258; and JS's *Proposal
for the Universal Use of Irish Manufacture*, XII. 122, 147 and *n.*‡; his
security, X. 58 and *n.**; 'almost
a slobber', V. 258; and JS,
prosecution for *A Proposal for
. . . Irish Manufacture*, IX. xvi;
prosecution of Waters, IX. 27;
and Wood, X. 174; and Wood's
coins, X. x, xi, xii, 36 and *n.**;
—— patent, X. 42.

Graham, James (brother to
Richard, Viscount Preston,
made lieutenant-colonel in 1678):
and conversation, IV. 105.

Graham, Robert, *d.* 1679, cornet:
V. 137.

Granard, Arthur Forbes, 1st Earl
of, *c.* 1623–95: V. 154.

Granard, Arthur Forbes, 2nd
Earl of, *c.* 1656–1734: V. 154;
and William III, 165–6.

Grand Alliance, Treaty of (1701),
'Confederacy' of England, Uni-
ted Provinces, Austria, etc., in the
War of the Spanish Succession:

and earlier Anglo-Dutch treaties, VI. 17; articles, VI. 24; — 'the whole strength of the nation', VI. 18; eighth article, VII. 51; — JS's translation, VI. xi, 47; — and projected union of Austria and Spain, VI. 51 and *n.**, 52; and Barrier Treaty (1709), VI. 93–4, 100–1; Bickerstaff's predictions for, II. 146; — ridiculed by Partridge, II. 205–7; dissension, VII. 119, 123, 128–9, 135–7; — harmful to Dutch, VII. 112, 145–6, 149, 151–2, 154, 155; — allegedly promoted by France, VII. 41–2; — England denies, VII. 56; — resolved, VII. 153, 160–1; Dutch insult Wishart (1710), VI. 32; and Dutch Barrier, VI. 89; and treaty at Gertruydenburg (1710), VI. 49; Hanoverian Succession, VI. 88; VII. xxxvi; interests unequal, VI. 8–19; VII. 88; final meeting (1713), VII. 162–3; purposes, VII. 81–2; quotas, III. 198; VI. 21, 29–30; VII. 82; — Austria fails to meet, VI. 33, 34; VII. 25–6, 86; — Dutch fail to meet, VI. 30, *et passim*; VII. 57, 59, *et passim*; and 'no peace without Spain': *see* SPAIN; and Spanish Netherlands, VI. 27–8. *See also* UTRECHT, TREATY OF; WAR OF SPANISH SUCCESSION.

Grand Jury: *see* DUBLIN; MIDDLESEX.

Grant, Francis, London merchant: *The British Fishery Recommended to Parliament* (1734), XIII. xxxi; *A Letter to a Member of Parliament, Concerning the Free British Fisheries*, XIII. xxxi; letter from JS, XIII. xxx–xxxiii, 111–13. *See also* JS's LETTER TO FRANCIS GRANT.

Grant, Sir Francis of Cullen, Bart., *c.* 1660–1726, father of Francis Grant: XIII. xxxiii.

Grant, Robert, later in Royal Scottish Dragoons ('a gallant Highland gentleman'): V. 131–3.

Grants, Royal: inquiry into, proposed (1711), VII. 100–2.

'Grands Titres, Madame de': character in *Tale of a Tub*, I. 45–55.

Granville, Grace, Countess, *c.* 1667–1744, mother of Lord Carteret: and JS's seal, XIII. 153.

Granville family: XII. 153.

Grapeshot: XI. 134.

Gratitude and ingratitude, JS's views: ingratitude a crime, XI. 60; ingratitude of kings, XI. 54.

Grattan, James, M.D., 1673–1747, son of Patrick: and Sheridan's certificate, XIV. 37; JS's bequest, XIII. 154; JS's will, XIII. 155.

Grattan, John, *d.* 1754, prebendary of Clonmethan: and seventh *Drapier's Letter*, X. xxvii, xxviii; JS's executor, XIII. 157, 200; and JS's will, XIII. 155.

Grattan, Robert, *c.* 1678–*c.* 1741, prebendary of St. Audoen's: his walk at Belcamp, V. 344; JS's executor, XIII. 157, 200; and JS's will, XIII. 155.

Gravesend, boundary port of London: pun upon, IV. 261.

Gravitation or 'attraction', law of:

XI. 171; will not last, XI. 197–8.

Grazing: XII. 89; censured, XII. 8; and corn famine, XII. 17–19; ironical proposal for, XII. 175–8; JS attacks, XII. xi, xii. *See also* AGRICULTURE.

Great and Small Figures, by JS: *see* MEAN AND GREAT FIGURES.

Great Britain: *see* ENGLAND.

Greece and Greeks, ancient: no national debt, VI. 55; and education of gentlemen, XII. 46; expansion of, IV. 9; fanaticism in, I. 186; **government**—balance of power, I. 195–200, 204–10; II. 16; — and climate, II. 17; — constitutional reform, III. 65; — impeachments, I. 223–7; — republicanism, VIII. 37; XII. 45, 278; — revolutions, II. 23; — secrecy in, VIII. 77; heroes' names punned upon, IV. 232–7; history, VIII. 37; XI. 198–201; learning, cradle of, I. 90; literature, II. 76; — ancients and moderns, I. 79–80, 142–52, 156–9; — satire, I. 31; nobility, I. 204–10; III. 150; oratory, IX. 68–9, 213; patriotism, XI. 196; philosophy, I. 104–5; — inferior to Christianity, IX. 111–12, 241–50; religion, IV. 41–6; — and Cicero, IV. 44; — praised, III. 146; wars—victory trophies, I. 143; and women's conversation, IX. 91.

Greek language: and Sir Arthur Acheson, XII. 167; and Carteret, XII. 154; and linguistic change, IV. xv, 16; and Christ, IV. 42; and English contractions, IV. 113; lacks contractions, II. 175;

derived from English, IV. xxxviii, 231–9; and Eugenio, XII. 44; miracle of boy speaking, XIV. 35; and modern curricula, XII. 48, 49; language of New Testament, I. 54, *n.*†; and 'pun', IV. 205–6; purity, IV. 9; and Thomas Sheridan, XII. 162–3.

Green, Anthony, Dublin tradesman: JS recommends case, V. 346.

Greene, Miss Lucy and sister: biographical data, VII. xxv, *n.* 3, xxvii, *n.* 1; and manuscript of JS's *History of the Four Last Years*, VII. xxv–xxvii, xxvii, xxvii, *n.* 1.

Greenknock: *see* GREENOCK.

Greenland: XI. 112.

Greenock, Renfrewshire, Scotland: V. 160.

Greenshields, Rev. James: imprisoned (15 Sept. 1709) for using English Prayer Book in Edinburgh, III. 96, 100–1.

Greenwich, England: XI. 79; pun upon, IV. 261.

Gregg, William, *d.* 1708, clerk in Oxford's (i.e., Harley's) office, executed for treason: III. xxiii–xxiv, xxix–xxx, 60 and *n.**, 190, 191–4, 196–7, 246–54; compared with Guiscard's attempt, III. 108, 116, 148, 197, 246–53; and Harley, III. 190, 198; *A Letter to the Seven Lords*, III. 243–58; and Whigs, III. 146, 148–9.

Gregory the Great, St., *c.* 540–604, Pope: source for Baronius, XIV. 32; and Britain, V. 4; and Leontius, XIV. 33; accused of lying, XIV. 32; — stupid liar,

XIV. 33; — worst liar and worst poet, XIV. 35.

Gregory Nazianzus, 4th century Church Father: Burnet agrees with, on synods, V. 276; JS on, XIV. 17.

Gresham College, 1660–1710, meeting place of the Royal Society: XI. 110; blessed by goddess of criticism, I. 154–5; and author of *Mechanical Operation of the Spirit*, I. 172; satirized, I. 38; author's thanks to, in *Tale of a Tub*, I. 115.

Greyhounds: and squires, IX. 292–3.

Griffin, Edward, 1st Lord Griffin of Braybrooke, *d.* 1710: V. 260.

Griffin, James, 2d Lord, 1667–1715: 'drunken companion', V. 260.

'Grildrig', Gulliver's Brobdingnagian sobriquet meaning 'mannikin': XI. 95, 132.

Grimston, William Luckyn, 1st Viscount, *c.* 1683–1756: *The Lawyer's Fortune; or, Love in a Hollow Tree* (1705), IV. xxx, 144; IX. 20.

Gronovius, Johannes Fredericus, 1611–71, classical scholar: V. xxxvii.

Groom (in *Directions to Servants*, XIII. 46–51): drunkenness, XIII. 48, 49, 50; and fodder, XIII. 48, 49; horse shoes, XIII. 49–50; horses at inns, XIII. 163; inns, XIII. 47–50; and inn servants, XIII. 163; journeys, XIII. 46, 49; livery, XIII. 50; master's horses for hire, XIII. 51; ostler, XIII. 47; overspending, XIII. 46–7; and fellow servants, XIII.

48, 49, 50; stable-boy, XIII. 47; vails, XIII. 49.

Grub-street, London, collective name for literary hacks: I. 38; Dublin lacks, IX. 341; facilities, IX. 342; imaginary treatise on, I. xl; pirate *Predictions for the Year 1708*, II. 197; drain for wit, IX. 341.

Grultrud, Brobdingnagian town crier: XI. 97.

Grynæus, Simon, 1493–1541, Swiss reformer and scholar: *Novus Orbis*, XI. xiv.

Guagninus, Alexander, 1538–1614, Italian traveller and writer: *Sarmatiæ Europeæ descriptio* (1578), I. 178; III. 40.

Guardian: see STEELE.

Guards: false musters in, III. 170.

Guelder, or Guelderland (i.e. Gelderland), Dutch province: and Barrier Treaty, VI. 99, 107, 113, 115; and Gulliver, XI. 217.

Guelfs and Ghibellines: III. 162.

Gué Nicaise (near Les Andelys, Eure, France), battle of, 1119: V. 39.

Gueses: see GUEUX.

Gueux, 'beggars': I. 88 and *n.*†.

Guicciardini, Francesco, 1483–1540, Florentine historian: leads Moderns' infantry, I. 152.

Guildford, Francis North, 2nd Lord, 1673–1729: 'mighty silly fellow', V. 260.

Guildhall, London: author's thanks to, in *Tale of a Tub*, I. 115.

Guillim, John, 1565–1621: *A Display of Heraldrie* (1610), V. 190.

Guinea: and Gulliver, XI. 217.

Guiscard, Antoine de, 1658–1711, abbé de la Bourlie, French spy:

III. 115–16; JS's character of, VIII. 127–8; compared with Gregg affair, III. 108, 116, 148, 197–8, 246–53; and the law, III. 138–9; attempt on Oxford (i.e., Harley), III. 106–10, 157 ('one accident'), 168, 194, 195, 246–54; VII. 76–7, 99; VIII. 126–7; — parliamentary addresses, III. 192; — and Whigs, III. 146, 148–9; JS's character of, VIII. 127–8; and Whigs, III. 108–10.

Guiscard, Louis, comte de, 1651–1720, governor of Namur, brother of Antoine: VIII. 127.

Guise, François de Lorraine, duc de, 1519–63, assassinated: III. 107.

Gulliver, Lemuel: accidents, painful, XI. 90, 116–8, 121–4; attacks on — by Blefescudians, XI. 52; — by boy, XI. 90; — by dog, XI. 117; — by dwarf, XI. 107–8, 116; — by flies, XI. 109; — by frog, XI. 121; — by kite, XI. 117; — by Lilliputians, XI. 22, 31; — by monkey, XI. 121–3; — by rats, XI. 93; — by savages, XI. 284; — by wasps, XI. 109–10; — by Yahoos, XI. 224, 265–7; visit to Blefuscu, XI. 54, 73–8; to be blinded, XI. 71–3; — easy punishment, XI. 73; boats —in Blefuscu, XI. 75–8; — in Brobdingnag, XI. 120–1; — in Houyhnhnmland, XI. 281–2; body odour, XI. 119; bravery and cowardice, XI. 90–1, 109–10, 123–4; at Cambridge University (Emmanuel College), X. ix; XI. 19; makes chairs, XI. 125–6, 276; his children, XI. 80, 149, 289–90; — dreams of them,

XI. 92; clothing — in Brobdingnag, XI. 95, 105; — among Houyhnhnms, XI. 236–7, 276; — in Laputa, XI. 162; — in Lilliput, XI. 33, 63–4; makes comb, XI. 125, 146; complexion, XI. 92; confined (caught, captured, imprisoned)—by Brobdingnagians, XI. 86–8, 97, 99, 139; — by Lilliputians, XI. 21–2, 27–8; — by mutineers, XI. 222; departures — from Blefuscu, XI. 75–80; — from Brobdingnag, XI. 140–3; — from Houyhnhnms, XI. 280–2; — from Laputa, XI. 174; — from Luggnagg, XI. 215; and disease, XI. 112–13, 186–8, 253–4; and Dutch, XI. 155, 203–5, 216–17; and dwarf at court of Brobdingnag, XI. 107–9, 116; eating and drinking — in Brobdingnag, XI. 89–90, 105–6, 123; — on desert island, XI. 156; — among Houyhnhnms, XI. 230–3, 276; — in Laputa, XI. 161; — in Lilliput, XI. 23–4, 30, 32–3, 44–5, 56, 64, 71; education, XI. 19; England — praised and defended ('beloved country'), XI. 79, 106–7, 127–9, 294–5; — reproached, XI. 245–7, 251–9; exhibited, 96–100; fire in palace of Lilliput, XI. 55–6; freed from confinement, XI. 44–5, 101–2; on great men, XI. 196; called 'Grildrig', XI. 95; on *Gulliver's Travels*, XI, 5–8, 291–2; gunpowder, XI. 133–4; hat, XI. 41–2; on history, XI. 198–200; human nature and Gulliver's nature — in Brobdingnag, XI, 103–4; — 'lover of mankind'

XI. 230; — and Yahoos, XI. 229–30, 235–43, 259–64, 272–3, 278–9, 289; on immortality, XI. 207–14; impeachment, XI. 67–73; languages, XI. 31, 154–5; on law, XI. 248–50, 315–18; — his own lawsuits, XI. 130, 248; lodgings — in Brobdingnag, XI. 97, 99, 105, 113–14, 139–40; — among Houyhnhnms, XI. 276; — in Lilliput, XI. 27–8, 31–2; on luxury, XI. 251–3; maids of honour, XI. 118–19; his marriage, XI. 20; knows mathematics, XI. 163, 166, 173; on medicine, XI. 253–4; military conduct — Blefuscu's navy, 51–3; — in Brobdingnag, XI. 115, 131, 138; — cavalry exercise, XI. 40–1; — gunpowder, XI. 133–4; — scimitar, XI. 36–7; — on warfare, XI. 245–7; motive in writing, XI. 5–8, 291–3; and music, XI. 126–7, 162–3, 173; and mutiny, XI. 222; nakedness (or genitals exposed), XI. 42, 119, 236–7, 265–6; made a nardac, XI. 53; on nobility, XI. 257–8; oaths — in Lilliput, XI. 33, 42–3; — in Luggnagg, XI. 205–6; on old age, XI. 211–14; on patriotism, XI. 106–7, 127, 133, 196, 201, 258–9; on philosophical systems, XI. 197–8; and pirates (or buccaneers), XI. 154–5, 221–2; on plots, XI. 191–2; portrait, facing XI. iii, 1; on pride, XI. 296; his property, XI. 80, 144; called 'Quinbus Flestrin', XI. 34, 68; reading, XI. 20, 136–7, 234–5; on sailors, XI. 243–4; searched, XI. 33–6; shipwrecked, XI. 20–1; sorrel nag's

affection, XI. 281, 283; speech (attempts at conversation, learning to talk)—in Brobdingnag, XI. 89, 100, 103; — return from Brobdingnag, XI. 147; — among Houyhnhnms, XI. 226–7, 232, 234–7; — in Laputa, XI. 157–8, 160–1; — in Lilliput, XI. 31, 33; plays spinet, XI. 126–7; and JS — and Creichton, V. xx; — pseudonym for JS, V. xiv; — JS's freedom of Dublin, XII. xxvi; letter to Sympson, XI. 5–8; transportation to capital of Lilliput, XI. 26–7; truthfulness, XI. 8, 9, 146–7, 238–40, 258, 287, 291–2; on tyrants, XI. 196; urine and fæces — in Brobdingnag, XI. 93–4, 124; — in Laputa, XI. 179–81; — in Lilliput, XI. 25, 29, (fire in palace) 55–6, 70; vanity and modesty, XI. 107–8, 123–4, 147–8; — Houyhnhnms reduce his vanity, XI. 258; no war, XI. 134–5, 247, 293; his watch, XI. 35, 37; and wife, XI. 20, 80, 149; — dreams of, XI. 92; — pregnant, XI. 221; — repels her, XI. 289–90; — tolerates her, XI. 295–6; and women — breasts, XI. 91–2, 112–13, 119; — Brobdingnag, queen, XI. 101–2; — complexions, XI. 91–2, 119; — in Laputa, XI. 165–6; — in Lilliput, treasurer's wife, XI. 65–6, 68; — maids of honour, XI. 118–19: *see also* GLUMDALCLITCH.

Gulliver, Mary (*née* Burton), Lemuel's wife: XI. 20, 80, 149, 154, 206, 218, 221, 289, 295.

Gulliver's Travels (1726), by JS: **XI. 1-296**; analysis, XI. ix, xi,

xii, xv–xvi; and Arbuthnot, XI. xx–xxi; authorship, XI. 7; background, XI. xx–xxi; and Abel Boyer, XI. xxiii; composition, XI. x, xii–xiv, xvi–xxi, 3, 5–10; and *Drapier's Letters*, X. ix; editions, XI. xxii–xxviii, 301–2; — Faulkner, Dublin, 1735, XI. xxv–xxviii, 301; — Motte, London, 1726, XI. ii, xxiii, xxiv–xxv, xxvi, 5–8, 297, 299; — serialized (1726), XI. xxiii; errata, XIV. 56; frontispieces, facing XI. iii, 1; illustrations — Gulliver's portrait, facing XI. iii, 1; — loadstone in Laputa, XI. 169; — word machine in Laputa, XI. 183; inconsistencies in, XI. xiii–xix; intent, XI. 5–8, 292–3; Johnson on, XI. xi; *A Letter from Capt. Gulliver to His Cousin Sympson*, XI. xxvii. 5–8; maps — Lilliput, XI. 18; — Brobdingnag, XI. 82; — Laputa, XI. 152; — — Balnibarbi, XI. 169; — Houyhnhnms' Land, XI. 220; and *Memoirs of Martinus Scriblerus*, XI. xiii–xiv, xviii; and *A Modest Inquiry into the Reasons of the Joy Expressed upon the Spreading of a Report of Her Majesty's Death* (partly by JS), VIII. xvi, *n.* 4; Nora Mohler on, XI. xx; nautical jargon parodied, XI. 84; Marjorie Nicolson on, XI. xx; Orrery on (1752), XI. xv; Émile Pons on, XI. xixii;– publication, XI. xviii, xxi–xxii, xxiv; *The Publisher to the Reader*, XI. 9–10; reception, XI. xxii–xxiv; XII. ix; 'sea-language', XI. 9–10, 84; — criticized, XI.

7; sources, XI. xiii–xvi, xviii, xx; William Stratford on, XI. xxiii; style, XI. xi–xii, xxi, xxiv, 94; — 'plain and simple', XI. 9, 291; and *The Substance of What Was Said by the Dean*, XII. xxvi; JS's hopes for, XI. xviii; *Tale of a Tub* compared to, XI. ix–xi; text — errors in 1st edition, XIV. 43; textual notes, XI. 301–22; XIV. 56; title-page facsimiles, XI. 1, 297, 299; translations, XI. xxii–xxiii.

Gunpowder: Gulliver offers to King of Brobdingnag, XI. 134–5.

Guns: XI. 134.

Guthkelch, A. C., and David Nichol Smith, edition of *Tale of a Tub*, 1920: acknowledged, I. ix and *n.*†; on JS's reading, I. xxiii, *n.*†

Guy of Warwick, legendary hero: pun upon name, IV. 233.

Gwithers or Guither, Charles, *b. c.* 1660, physician, fellow of Trinity College, Dublin, and a member of Dublin Philosophical Society: and frogs, XIII. 175, *n.*

Gwyn, Eleanor ('Nell'), 1650–87, actress and mistress of Charles II: V. 273.

Gyllenborg, Karl Gyllenborg, Count de, 1679–1746, Swedish ambassador, friend of JS: JS dedicates a book to him, V. ix–x, 11–12.

Gypsies: IV. 103–4.

H

H., Dr.: *see* HOWARD.

H., T.: *Mechanical Operation of the Spirit* dedicated to, I. 171.

Hackston, or Haxton, David, Laird of Hackston, *d.* 1680: captured, V. 148, 150; assassination of Archbishop Sharp, V. 135–6.

Hæmorrhoids: V. 71.

Hague, Holland: and William Harrison, II. xxxvi; peace negotiations (1709), which produced the Preliminary Articles for Gertruydenberg (1710), VII. 32–6; — Dutch, VII. 40, 50; — England's demands impossible, VI. 6, 49, 50–1, 59; — and France, VI. 60; VII. 32–4, 41; — and Godolphin ministry, VII. 33; — Marlborough, VII. 22; — 'a mock treaty', VI. 6; — Preliminary Articles, VI. 49–50; and Temple, I. 270; theatre, IX. 344.

Hakluyt, Richard, *c.* 1552–1616, author: *Principal Navigations, Voyages and Discoveries* (1598–1600) — JS's copy, XI. xiv.

Hale, Hal, or Halle, Brabant, Belgium: and Dutch Barrier, VI. 90, 101, 109, 113.

Hale, Sir Bernard, 1677–1729, Lord Chief Baron of the Exchequer of Ireland: member of Privy Council, X. 205.

Halifax, Charles Montagu, Earl of, 1661–1715, Whig statesman, member of Junto: letter from Addison, II. xxii, *n.* 2; still in office as Auditor of the Exchequer (1711), III. 204; and Congreve, IX. 29; his education, XII. 47; Gregg and seven lords, III. 195, 204, 243–58; Macky and JS on, V. 258; impeached (among 'Whig ministers'), I. xx; and Oxford's

alleged treason, III. xxix; Partition treaties, I. xx; represented by Pericles and Alcibiades, I. 207–10, 224; pun upon name, IV. 274; and JS, II. xxi; III. xii; IV. xxiv; VIII. 119. 120; — on dangers of uniting Church, II. xiv.

Halley, or Hally, Edmund, 1656–1742, astronomer: and Bickerstaff, II. 149.

Halliday, Miss E.: acknowledgment, XIV. vii.

Hamadryads: pun upon, IV. 235.

Hambden, John: *see* HAMPDEN.

Hamilton, Lanarkshire, Scotland: V. 137–8, 140, 154.

Hamilton Moor, Lanarkshire, Scotland: V. 139, 140.

Hamilton of Preston: 'loyal house', V. 137.

Hamilton, Mr.: and William Wood, X. 29.

Hamilton, Elizabeth (*née* Gerard), Duchess of, *d.* 1744, wife of 4th Duke, daughter of Lord Gerard: VI. xxv, 199.

Hamilton, James Douglas, 4th Duke of, 1658–1712, styled Earl of Arran until 1698: and Creichton, V. 158; death, VI. xxiv–xxv, 197–9; duel with Mohun (1712), V. 294; VI. 197–9; Macky and JS on, V. 261; sent to the Tower, V. 165.

Hamilton, John, colonel of the Foot Guards (served 1689–1715): and the Duke's death, VI. 197–9.

Hamilton, Sir Robert, Bart., 1650–1701, Covenanter: V. 136, 154.

Hamilton, Sir Thomas (mistakenly named William by Creichton),

d. 1672, of Preston: V. 136, 154.

Hamilton, William Douglas, Duke of, 1634–94: V. 159, 167–8; and Creichton, V. 154, 172–7; and William III, V. 165.

Hamilton, Sir William, of Preston: *see* THOMAS HAMILTON.

Hampden, John, 1594–1643, statesman: and the Drapier, X. 20.

Handel, George Frideric, 1685–1750, composer: first performance of *The Messiah* and JS ('licence to . . . assist'): XIII. 196–7.

Hands, Dr., physician: pun upon name, IV. 258.

Hangovers: XI. 252.

Hanmer, Sir Thomas, 4th Baronet, 1677–1746, Speaker of the House of Commons, Tory: and George II, V. 103; identified, VII. xi, *n.* 1; and Prior, III. 211; called 'Ramneh', V. 103; pens Commons' *Representation* to Anne (1712), VI. xvi; VII. 79–94; elected Speaker (1714), VIII. 52 and *n.**; and JS — and *History of the Four Last Years*, VII. xi, and *n.* 2; — and prosecution of *A Proposal for . . . Irish Manufacture*, IX. xvi.

Hannibal, 247–182 B.C., Carthaginian general: and Antiochus, V. 86; and Gulliver, XI. 195; pun on name, IV. 237.

Hanover, Germany: XII. ix; George I's visits to ('Tedsu'), V. 100; — king forbidden to leave island, XI. 172.

Hanover Club: IV. xviii, 28; VIII. xv.

Hanover, House of: disparaged

as 'German family', VII. xxxiii; — as 'Hanover family', VII. xxxvi; and Dublin street cries, XII. 228; and Irish bishops, XII. 181; and Irish Whigs, II. 118; and Scotland, VIII. 49. *See also* GEORGE I.

Hanover Square, London: and *Dialogue in the Castilian Language*, IV. xxx–xxxi, 172.

Hanoverian Succession (or Protestant Succession): may be altered, III. 18; VI. 27, 65; VIII. 51, 52; and Anne, VIII. 93–4, 163–80; Anne, and doctrine of 'resistance', VIII. 44–5; attacks upon (1714), VIII. 64; and the Barrier Treaty, VI. xvi, 26–7, 87, 88, 99–100, 104–6; VII. 90, 93; VIII. 52–3; Burnet's views attacked, IV. 75; and Dutch, VI. 26–7, 88, 92–3, 100; VIII. 52–3; and employments, III. 34; Bishop Fleetwood on, VI. xviii–xix, 194; French acknowledgement, VI. 26–7; VII. 48, 130; and guarantees of foreign powers, VI. 92–4; VII. xxxvi; heir in residence, VIII. 95; Archbishop King entirely supports, II. 282; and 'moderation', IX. 178; Oxford secures, VII. xxxiii, xxxvi; and Oxford ministry, V. 265; VIII. xxvi–xxvii, 40, 163–80; — allegedly oppose, VII. 144; VIII. 47–8; — and 'resistance', VIII. 44–5; no pamphlets against, VIII. 168–9; and party controversy, VIII. 90–2; both parties support, II. 13–14; and 'popish plot', IV. 61; and popish pretenders, VIII. 54–5; precedence established

(1712), VII. 78; security summarized, VIII. 92–3; and Sophia, VIII. 71; support of, VIII. 65–6; JS accepts, II. xvii; VII. xxxvi; IX. 30; JS on, VIII. xxvi–xxvii; and Tories, VIII. 48, 92; — limited support, VIII. xvii; — support it, VIII. xxvii; and Treaty of Utrecht, VII. 43, 50, 114; VIII. 169–71; and Wagstaff, IV. 121; and Whigs, IV. xxi; VI. 93. *See also* GEORGE I; PRETENDER: PROTESTANT SUCCESSION; SUCCESSION TO BRITISH THRONE.

Hanseatic League: and Treaty of Münster (1643), VI. 104.

Happiness: and charity, IX. 148; wealth opposed to, IX. 194, 195.

Hapsburgs: and union of Austria and Spain, VI. 51–3; Bolingbroke allegedly denigrates, VII. 58; deaths, VII. 12; Spain — allegedly favours (1701), VI. 14; VII. 86; — claim to, denied (1713), VII. 166–7; effect of deaths on Treaty of Utrecht, VII. 51; benefit from War of the Spanish Succession, VII. 89.

Harcourt, Simon Harcourt, 1st Viscount, 1661–1727, Lord Chancellor: III. 72; VI. 187; VIII. 101, 114; and Bolingbroke, VIII. 152; his education, XII. 47; Lord Keeper, III. 78; and Oxford, VIII. 124, 156, 157; and Oxford ministry, VIII. 144; to be made a peer (1711), III. 149–50; made a peer, VIII. 128; praised, 'present Lord Chancellor', VIII. 45; and Sacheverell's trial, VIII. 45; Steele on 'present Lord Chancellor', VIII.

45; Lord Keeper and JS, II. xxxvi; VII. 17; early ties with Whigs, VIII. 166.

Hardicanute: *see* HARTHACNUT.

Harding, John, *d.* 1725, Dublin printer: and *Another Letter to Mr. Harding the Printer*, X. 155–6; death, X. 123; and *The Declaration of the Grand Jury . . . of the Liberty of St. Patrick's*, X. xvi; and *Directions to the Printer*, X. 79–80, 173–4; and *Drapier's Letters*, X. xii and *n.* 2, 92, 113; XIII. 201; — No. 1: X. 1, 3; XIV. 56; — No. 2: X. 13–24; — No. 3: X. 25; — No. 4: X. 51, 53; — No. 5: X. xxiv, 77–80; *see also* DUBLIN NEWS-LETTER; and Irish House of Commons, IX. xxi; imprisoned with wife, X. 79; and *Letter to Mr. Harding*, X. xiv and *n.* 2; and *A Letter to the King at Arms*, IX. 293; and free masons, V. 323–33; Proclamation against Drapier, X. xix–xxii, xxvi, 71, 101, *n.**; JS defends, XII. 85; prints JS's letters, XIII. 186; works for JS, IX. xix; taken into custody, IX. xxi; *Weekly News-Letter*, X. xii, xiii, xiv, and *n.* 2; — 1 August, 1724, X. 13–24.

Harding, John, *fl.* 1678–1713, London bookseller: and JS's *Meditation upon a Broom-Stick*, I. 237.

Harding, Sarah, *fl.* 1725–28, Dublin printer, widow of John Harding: prints *An Answer to a Paper Called a Memorial of the Poor of Ireland*, XII. xii; prints *The Intelligencer*, facing XII. 29; prints *Modest Proposal*, facing

XII. 109; and *Short View of the State of Ireland*, XII. x, 3, 122.

Hare, Francis, 1671–1740, Marl-borough's chaplain: *The Allies and the Late Ministry Defended against France and the Present Friends of France*, VI. x–xi; *Barrier Treaty Vindicated*, VI. xvi; *The Charge of God to Joshua*, III. xxxii–xxxiii; — Mrs. Manley's attack, III. 263–72; sermon before Commons (1708), III. xxxiii; on *The Examiner*, VI. x; *Letters Addressed to a Tory-Member on the Management of the War*, III. xxxiii, 63, 87–8; *The Negotiations for a Treaty of Peace, in 1709*, III. 87–8; and JS, III. xxxii–xxxiv; JS's reply to him, VI. 95–7.

Harley, Sir Edward, 1624–1700, governor of Dunkirk, Oxford's father: letter from Thomas Swift, V. 190.

Harley, Robert: *see* OXFORD, ROBERT, 1st Earl of.

Harley, Thomas, *d.* 1738, cousin to Robert; M.P. and a secretary of the Treasury: VIII. 171; visits The Hague (1712), VII. 119–20; at Hanover (1712, 1714), VIII. 171, 174, 175; visits Hanover (1712), VII. 143; — reasons for, VII. 144–5; 'Tom', II. 174.

Haro, Sir Charles: *see* TYRAWLEY.

Harold II, King of England, *c.* 1022–1066: V. 6–7.

Harrington, James, 1611–77, political philosopher: *Common-wealth of Oceana*, I. 231; III. 115; 'rotation', allusion to *Oceana* (1656) and *Rota* (1660), I. 24.

Harris, W.: *History of Dublin*, XIII. xxxix, *n.* 1.

Harrison, Mary, or Molly, daugh-ter of Martha Whiteway, after-wards Mrs. Deane Swift: JS's bequest to, XIII. 153; gives her a book (1736), V. xxxv.

Harrison, William, 1685–1713, poet, friend of JS: death, VI. xxiii; JS's protégé, II. xxxvi; VI. xxiii; JS and continuation of *Tatler*, II. xxxv, xxxvi; 'young fellow', II. 262.

'Harry', i.e., Bolingbroke: V. xiv.

Harry the Great: *see* HENRY IV, of France.

Harte, Walter, 1707–74, author: and JS's sermons, IX. 100.

Harthacnut (or Hardicanute), King of England and Denmark, *c.* 1018–42: V. 6.

Hartmann, Cyril Hughes: *Games and Gamesters of the Restoration*, XIII. xx, *n.* 1.

Hartstonge, John, 1654–1717, Bishop of Ossory (1693) and Derry (1714): one of 'two bishops', VIII. 122.

Harvard College Library: Orrery Papers, VII. xiv, *n.* 5.

Harvey (or Hervey), Daniel, made lieutenant-general of dragoons in 1707: III. 231.

Harvey, William, 1578–1657, physician: leads dragoons of Moderns, I. 152; 'wounded Aga', I. 156.

Harwich, Essex: III. 45.

Hastings, William, 1st Lord Hastings, *c.* 1430–83: Louis XI's pension, V. 246.

Haukyns or Hawkyns, John, *fl.* 1530, London bookseller: and

Merlin, the British Wizard, II. xxiv and *n.* 2; prints translations of Merlin, II. 165, 167.

Hawkesworth, John, *c.* 1715–73, editor and biographer of JS: and Faulkner's edition of *Gulliver's Travels*, I. v; XI. xxviii; Faulkner's text criticized, I. v; life of Swift, I. ix. *n.*†; edition of *Miscellanies* of JS and Pope, XIII. 204; publishes *Preface* to JS's *History of the Four Last Years*, VII. 1, *n.**; and authorship of *Tatler*, Nos. 74 and 81, II. xxxii.

Haxton: *see* HACKSTON.

Hayes, Dr. Richard, librarian of the National Library, Dublin: XII. xxv, *n.* 2.

Hayward, John 1905–65: acknowledgements, I. vi; XII. v; Nonesuch edition of JS's selected works, I. v.

Hazael, anointed King of Syria by Elisha: and Elisha, IX. 349.

'Hazard, Will': character in *Tatler*, No. 230, II. 174–5.

Health: XI. 253–4, 269–70; disease and poverty, IX. 193; disease and riches, IX. 193; illness affects behaviour, IX. 361; poverty improves, IX. 192.

Heath, Edw. and Jo.: V. xxxiii.

Heawood, E.: *Watermarks*, XIII. xii, *n.* 1.

Hebrew language: derived from English language, IV. xxxviii, 231–9; alphabet and free masons, V. 325–6, 331.

Hector: and Andromache, IV. 233; and Astyanax, IV. 234; in tables of fame, II. 239.

Hedges, Sir Charles, *d.* 1714,

Secretary of State: and Marlborough's secret service money, VII. 67.

Heinsius, Antonie, 1641–1720, Grand Pensionary of Holland: and Anne, VII. 38; — message to her (1711), VII. 39–40; and Barrier Treaty, VI. 99, 106–9; and Buys ('his master's mind'), VII. 56; 'the menacing pensionary', VI. 167; and Hague peace negotiations (1709), VII. 32–3; and Petkum, VII. 40, 41; and Strafford (Raby, Ambassador), VII. 38; and Treaty of Utrecht, VII. 39; VIII. 171; — informed of French negotiations (1711), VII. 38; — delays peace (1712–13), VII. 163; — eager for peace, VII. 41; — and separate peace (1711), VII. 40; — preliminaries, VII. 52; — secrecy, VII. 38, 40.

'Hekinah Degul', Lilliputian phrase expressing wonder: XI. 22, 24.

Helen: character in chapbook *Dr. Faustus*, I. 41.

Helicon, mountain of Boeotia, sanctuary of the muses: I. 61; and *n.*‖; and Wotton, I. 162.

Heliogabalus, or Elagabalus, *c.* 204–22, Roman emperor: XI. 198.

Hell: allegorized as 'fire', I. 52 and *n.*‖; back room of alehouse, IX. 41; and English clergy, IV. 34; escape from, I. 33; and freethinkers, IV. 35, 39, 48; tailor's, I. 46.

Helsham, Dr. Richard, *c.* 1683–1738, JS's physician: executor of JS's will, XIII. 200.

Hen that laid a golden egg: II.
30; XII. 12.

Henley, Anthony, *d.* 1711, Whig
writer and M.P.: his dying
farmer, IV. 244.

Hennecy, Colonel, French officer:
recruits in Ireland for French
Army, XII. xxx.

Henrietta Maria, Queen of England, 1609–69, wife of Charles I,
daughter of Henry IV of France:
Burnet and JS on, V. 267;
Charles I gives her a diamond
buckle, V. 86.

Henry I, King of England, 1086–
1135: marries Adela of Louvain,
V. 41; and Anselm, V. 30–1,
34–5; surnamed 'Beauclerc', V.
27; **JS's character of,** V. 46–7;
and English constitution, II. 84;
death, V. 46, 48; and Fulk V,
V. 42; grievances against, V. 60;
and investiture of bishops, V.
30–1, 34; defeats Louis VI, V.
38–9; Louis VI encourages
rebellions, V. 41; marries Edith,
or Matilda, V. 29, 35; —
allegedly disinherits her, V. 48;
routs Count of Mortain, V. 30;
credited with originating Parliament, V. 35–6, 37; his popularity, V. 27; and Robert, Duke
of Normandy, V. 27–35; and
Roger, Bishop of Salisbury, V.
56; introduces scutage, V. 35,
routs Earl of Shrewsbury, V. 30;
and the succession, V. 41–2;
at Tenchebrai (1106), V. 31–3;
and Theobald of Blois, his
nephew, V. 38; quells Welsh
rebellion, V. 34–5; his son,
William, V. 39–41; seizes
treasure of William II, V. 27.

Henry II, King of England, 1133–
1187, first Plantagenet king: and
Pope Adrian IV, V. 75, 76;
dispossesses his brother of Anjou,
V, 74–5; becomes Duke of
Aquitaine and Earl of Poitou, V.
66–7; and Becket, V. 78; birth,
V. 42, 44; character, V. 77–8;
and the Church, V. 77–8; conspiracy against, V. 70–1; William
D'Ypres banished by, V. 74;
journeys to England (1149), V.
66; marries Eleanor of Aquitaine, V. 67; and English language, IV. 7; proclamation
banishing foreigners, V. 74; goes
to France (*c.* 1146), V. 65;
crowns 'Henry III', V. 68; and
Ireland, V. 75–7; rescues crown
lands, V. 74; dispossesses
Malcolm IV of his English
holdings, V. 75; besieges Malmesbury, V. 68; and mercenaries,
V. 74; popular esteem, V. 73;
final agreement with Stephen,
V. 68–70; and the succession, V.
47; and William, son of Robert
of Normandy ('infant son'), V.
44.

Henry III, King of England,
1207–72: Parsons and JS on, V.
241.

Henry IV, King of England, 1367–
1413: and Wood's coinage, X. 10.

Henry VII, King of England,
1457–1509: V. 250; legacy, IX.
49; and translation of Merlin, II.
165, 167; compared to Vespasian, IX. 49–50.

Henry VIII, King of England,
1491–1547: despoils Church, IX.
220; XII. 181; XIII. 123;
cruelty, II. 22; and divine right

of clergy, II. 81–2, 85; 'successor' to Henry VII, I. 230; and Irish dependency, X. 62, 84; and More, V. 248; XIII. 123; compared (unfavourably) with Nero, V. 249; and nobles, I. 230; and Norfolk, V. 249; and papal power, XIII. 123; and Perrot, IV. 110; and precedence of royal princes, VII. 78; persecutes Protestants, IV. 72; and the Reformation, II. 30–1; IV. 73; ('the Emperor his father') XI. 49; and Roman Catholicism, IV. 65, 67, 72; XIII. 123; 'sacrilegious tyrant', XII. 181–2; JS's detestation of, V. xxxiii, 247–51; XIII. xxxviii, 123, 126.

Henry III, King of France, 1551–89: III. 106.

Henry IV, Henry of Navarre, King of France, 1553–1610: III. 106; V. 84; 'great prince', I. 103 and *n*.*, *n*.†; Voltaire's epic on, V. 109.

Henry V, Emperor, 1081–1125: V. 34; his death, V. 41.

Henry of Blois, *d.* 1171, brother of Stephen, Bishop of Winchester: V. 48, 72; and Eustace IV, V. 61; and Matilda, V. 60–3; and Stephen, V. 57, 61–4.

Henry Frederick, Prince of Wales, 1594–1612: Burnet on his death, V. 266.

Henry of Lancaster, 3rd Earl of Lancaster, *c.* 1281–1345, grandson of Henry III: and Leicester hospital, IX. 49.

Henry of Scotland, Earl of Huntingdon and Northumberland, *c.* 1114–52, son of David I: V. 50, 52, 54, 55.

Henry, the 'Young King', 1155–83, son of Henry II: crowned ('succeeding reign', 1170), V. 68.

Herbert, Edward, 1st Lord Herbert of Cherbury, 1583–1648, author and diplomat: *The Life and Raigne of King Henry the Eighth* (1649), V. xxxii-xxxiii; — JS's marginalia, V. 247-51.

Herbert, Sir Thomas, 1st Bart., 1606–82, traveller and author: a coxcomb, V. 243; *A Relation of some Yeares Travaile*, V. xxxii; XI. xiv; —JS on, V. 243.

Hercules: and stolen oxen of Cacus, I. 91; divine ancestry, I. 57; and Hydra, IV. 235; pun upon name, IV. 234; seal of, XIII. 154; worshipped, I. 57.

Hereditary Right of the Crown of England Asserted, possibly by Hilkiah Bedford: VIII. 64–5.

Hereford, England: and Robert of Gloucester, V. 53.

Herefordshire: and William II, V. 20.

Heresies (atheists, deists, Socinians, Unitarians): III. 55–6, 92; atheism, III. 92; cause of calamities, IX. 171; and schemes of comprehension, III. 71; Deism's 'noble schemes', III. 49; Deists oppose Church, VI. 78; first Christian Dissenters, IX. 171; — fanatics before A.D. 500, I. 187–8; Socinians oppose Church, VI. 78; and Whigs, III. 122, 124. *See also* ATHEISM; SOCINIANISM; etc.

Hermes: and the Banbury Saint, I. 184.

Hermit: and noise, IX. xi.

Hermitage wine: III. 217.

Herod the Great, King of Judea, *d. c.* 4 B.C.: and Christ, II. 93.

Herodotus, *c.* 480–*c.* 425 B.C.: leads the Ancients' infantry, I. 152; and English historians, V. xxxvii; on horns, I. 244; on Scythians, I. 60; **JS on** (1720), **V. 243**; JS's copy of, V. xxxi; in *Tale of a Tub*, I. xxv; quotations and allusions: I. 59: I. 205; I. 32: I. 91; II. 77: I. 186 and *n.**; III. 85–6: I. 185; IV: I. 60; IV. 2: I. 93; IV. 7 and 31: I. 94; IV. 129: I. 60; IV. 191: I. 60; VIII. 123–4: I. 14.

Herring, Thomas, 1693–1757, Archbishop of Canterbury: opposes *Beggar's Opera*, XII. 36 and *n.**.

Herring fishery, letter by JS on: *see* LETTER TO FRANCIS GRANT ESQ. ON THE HERRING FISHERY.

Herrings: XII. 218–19.

Hertford, Earl of: *see* SOMERSET.

Hervey, John Hervey, Lord, 1696–1743: and *Polite Conversation*, IV. xxxii.

Hervey, John, 1st Earl of Bristol: *see* BRISTOL.

Hesse Darmstadt: *see* GEORGE, PRINCE OF.

Hesse Kassel, in central Germany: VII. 113.

Hesse Kassel, Charles, Landgrave of, 1654–1730: VII. 113.

Hewson, John: *see* PARTRIDGE.

Heylyn, Peter, 1600–1662, ecclesiastical writer: *Aerius Redivivus, or the History of the Presbyterians* (1670), **JS's opinion** (1728), **V. 255-6**; — background, V. xxxiii–xxxiv.

'Hhnm Yahoo', Houyhnhnm phrase, possibly meaning 'the folly of a servant': XI. 275.

'Hhuun', Houyhnhnm for 'hurry', 'go on': XI. 227, 229.

'Hibernian patriot', epithet for JS: V. xxiv.

Hibernian Patriot (i.e., *Drapier's Letters*): X. 207.

Hickeringill, Edmund, 1631–1708, pamphleteer: IV. 62.

Hickes, George, 1642–1715, Dean of Worcester, non-juror: III. 115; a learned, pious man, V. 278; *Preliminary Discourse to Spinoza Revis'd*, II. xvii and *n*. 4; *Queries Relating to the Birth and Birthright of a Certain Person* (i.e., the Pretender), VIII. 64 (attributed to him); possibly, 'a third', IV. 84; and Tillotson, IV. 47; and Matthew Tindal, II. 69, 71, 107; attacks Tindal, II. xviii and *n*. 2.

'Hiereus' (from Greek for 'priest'): pseudonym for JS, II. 262.

Higgins, Francis, 1669–1728, Archdeacon of Cashel, 'the Irish Sacheverell': dialogue with Thomas Tenison, II. 282; linked to JS, IV. xxvii.

High Church Politics: or the Abuse of the 30th January consider'd (1710): XI. 121, 123.

High Churchmen: and abolition of Christianity, II. 31; attack clergy, II. 8; control English Commons, II. xvi; party violence in 1703-4, II. 1-4; and free press, II. 10-11; and non-resistance, II. xvi–xvii, 16; and Stillingfleet, II. 79; support Test

Act, II. 131; and Tindal, II. 99, 103; unfashionable, II. 62.

High Dutch: *see* GERMAN.

Higham, T. F.: acknowledgement, XIV. 7.

Highgate, Middlesex, northern suburb of London: and *Polite Conversation*, IV. 154.

High-heels, political party in Lilliput, *Gulliver's Travels*, Book I, modelled on the Tories: XI. 48.

'Hilario': pseudonym for Steele, II. 262.

Hilary, St., *d.* 368: and freethinking, IV. 38.

Hill, G. Birkbeck: edition of Johnson's *Lives of the English Poets*, corrected, VII. ix, *n.* 2.

Hill, John, *d.* 1735, colonel and major general, brother of Lady Masham: VIII. 112; Canadian expedition (1711), III. 198; VI. 23; governor of Dunkirk, VI. xxii, 139–41, 190; VIII. 59; takes Dunkirk (1712), VII. 139–43; and Mrs. Masham ('the Governor'), VI. 190; West Indies (i.e. Canadian) expedition, III. 198.

Hill, Richard, 1655–1727, diplomat: Macky and JS on, V. 261.

Hill, Samuel, 1648–1716, Archdeacon of Wells: attacks Tindal, II. xviii, *n.* 2.

Hills, Henry, the younger, *d.* 1713, London printer: prints *Merlin, the British Wizard*, II. 288.

Hind and the Panther: *see* DRYDEN, JOHN.

Hinde, wool merchant of Castle Street, Dublin: imported cloth, XIII. 168.

Hindus: and freethinkers, IV. 32, 33.

Hints on Good-manners, by JS: **IV. 221-2**; analysis, IV. xxxvii; composition, IV. xxxvi; publication, IV. xxxvi, 299; textual notes, IV. 299.

Hints towards an Essay on Conversation, by JS: **IV. 87-95**; background, IV. xxxi–xxxii; textual notes, IV. 290.

'Hippo' for 'hypochondriac': IV. 114.

Hippocrates, 5th to 4th century B.C.: leads the Ancients, I. 152; quotations and allusions — *Aphorisms* XXXII. 6: IV. 252; — *De aere, aquis, et locis* 35, 36: I. 175–6; — *De genitura* III: I. 129.

'Hipps', for 'hypochondriacks': IV. 114.

Historiographer royal: JS's ambition, V. x; **JS's memorial** (1714), **VIII. 200**; — background, VIII. xxxi; — textual note, VIII. 232.

Histoire d'Æthiopie: JS reads, XI. xiv.

Histoire de Chypre: JS reads, XI. xiv.

History, JS's views on: III. 117; V. ix–x; Bible not history, V. 262; and Burnet, IV. ix; Clarendon writes with the spirit of an historian, V. 267; historians as foot soldiers, I. 152; Herodotus among those who deserve highest praise, V. 243; and historians, I. 242; historians' lies, XI. 195–202; and inventions, I. 242; value of letters, I. 258; and linguistic change, IV. 17–19;

'mercenaries', I. 152; use of parallel history, I. xx; and the present, I. 24; present and future, I. 243; priests should not write histories of their own time, XIV. 24; often romances, V. 262; 'times of ignorance', I. 242; historians as 'ushers' to the tables of fame, II. 240; value, I. 243; and writers, I. 242, 243; and his political writing, V. x.

History of England, by JS: *see* ABSTRACT.

History of Martin, unauthorized addition to *Tale of a Tub*, 1720: I. 286–91; textual note, I. 304.

History of Poetry (1726), by JS: **IV. 273-5**; publication, IV. xxxvi; textual notes, IV. 302.

History of the Four Last Years of the Queen (written 1712–13), by JS: **VII. xxix-167**; JS foresees acceptance of, VII. xxxv; accuracy stressed, VII. xxxvi, 1; *Advertisement*, VII. 171–7; audience intended for, VII. 2; authorship, VII. ix–x, xxii, xxiv, xxviii; background, VII. xi–xii; and Bolingbroke, VII. x–xii, xiv, *n*. 1, xxxiii; 'chief cause' of JS's writing it, VII. xi; characters in, VIII. 141; — approach to, VII. 5, 12; — censured by Charles Lucas, VII. 174–5; and Clarendon's *History of the Rebellion*, V. xxxix–xl; composition, IV. xvi–xvii; V. xxxv–xxxvi; VII. x–xiii, xv, xxxi, xxxii, xxxvi, 1, *n*.*, 171, 182; IX. xiv–xv, 26; — revisions slight, VII. xv, xxvi–xxvii, xxxiii, xxxvi; — 'written at Windsor', VII. xxii, xxiv, xxv, xxxi, xxxiii; Craik on, VII. ix–x,

xxiv–xxv; Ewings' edition, VII. xviii–xx; Faulkner edition (volume IX of *Works*), VII. xix–xx; Millar edition, VII. xvii–xx, xxvii, xxviii, 171–7; 'spurious' editions advertised, VII. xvii; and JS's *Enquiry into the Behaviour of the Queen's Last Ministry*, VIII. xxxiii, xxxvii; errata, XIV. 54; and executors of JS's will, VII. xvii; and Faulkner, VII. xiv, xvi–xxi, xxiii–xxvii, 1, *n*.*; XIII. xxxiv; 'gentleman' who had a MS, VII. xix; — non-existent, VII. xxi; and Godolphin's memory, VIII. 13; and Misses Greene, VII. xxv–xxvii; JS hints at, VIII. 101, 172; historical value, V. x; impartiality, VII. xxxiv–xxxv, 1; Samuel Johnson on, VII. ix and *n*. 2; and Archbishop King, VII. x, xvi; Erasmus Lewis on, VII. ix and *n*. 2, xi, xiv–xv, xvii; and Charles Lucas, VII. xx–xxi; — his *Advertisement* to Millar's edition, VII. 171–7; and John Lyon, VII. xvii; Macaulay on, VII. ix;

manuscripts — Birch makes abstract, VII. xxiv–xxv; — handed to Archbishop Cobbe, VII. xvii; — compared, VII. xxiii, xxv, xxvi; — facsimiles, VII, frontispiece and facing 76; — Faulkner, VII. xvii–xviii, xx, xxiii–xxiv; — Fitzgerald, VII. xxv–xxvii; — Kendrick copies one, VII. xviii and *n*. 1; — 'locked up' in W. King's study, VII. xvi; — for Millar's edition, VII. xix, xx, xxi, xxvii, xxviii; — Orrery, VII. xii, xvi, xvii, xxiii, xxv; — JS leaves 'original

with the ministers' (1713), VII. xxxiii; — Martha Whiteway, VII. xviii, xx, xxiii, xxv; — Windsor manuscript, VII. xxi–xxviii, 1, *n*.*, 50, *n*.*, 76, 219–46; and JS's *Memoirs*, VIII. xxxvii, xxxix; mistakes found in, VII. xv; Nichols on, VII. ix and *n*. 1; **notes by JS for Book Four, XIV. 13;** — composition, XIV. xii; — textual note, XIV. 45; and Orrery, VII. ix and *n*. 2, xiii, xiv, xvi; 2nd Earl of Oxford, VII. xiv. *n*. 1; and Oxford ministry, VIII. ix; and A. Pope, VII. xii; **Preface** by JS, **VII. xxxiii-xxxvi;** — composition, VII. 1, *n*.*; — and Orrery, VII. xiii, xxiii; publication, VII. xii–xxviii, 171–7, 182; XIII. xli; — 'attempts to suppress it', VII. 171; — delayed, VIII. ix, 141, 148; — rumoured by *Examiner* (Jan. 1714), VIII. xix–xx; hinted at in *Publick Spirit of the Whigs*, VIII. xix–xx, 56–7; purpose, VII. xi, xxxiv, xxxv; and *Some Considerations upon . . . the Death of the Queen*, VIII. xxix; Temple Scott on, VII. ix–x; sources, VII. x, xi, xv, 176, 181–218; Stanhope on, VII. ix; style, VII. xxii; textual notes, VII. 219–46; title inaccurate, VII. 1, *n*.*; title-page facsimiles, VII. xxix, xxxi; Tory bias, VII. xii, 172, 173, 174, 176; account of Treaty of Utrecht praised, VII. xv; Whigs to attack, VII. xxxvi.

History of the Last Session: *see* HISTORY OF THE FOUR LAST YEARS.

History of the Second Solomon

(written *c*. 1729), by JS: **V. 222-6;** background, V. xxx; textual note, V. 357.

Hitch, Charles, *d*. 1764, London bookseller: and *Directions to Servants*, XIII. x.

'Hlunnh', Houyhnhnm for 'oats': XI. 232.

'Hnea Yahoo', Houyhnhnm for 'the Yahoo's-evil', *i.e.*, 'disease': XI. 262.

'Hnhloayn', Houyhnhnm for 'exhortation': XI. 280.

'Hnuy illa nyha maiah Yahoo', Houyhnhnm for 'Take care of thy self, gentle Yahoo': XI. 283.

Hoadly, Benjamin, 1676–1761, Bishop of Bangor, and successively of Hereford, Salisbury, and Winchester: attacks deists, IV. xvii; Harcourt compared to, VIII. 45.

Hoadly, John, 1678–1746, Archbishop successively of Dublin and Armagh, brother of Benjamin: made freeman of Dublin, XII. xxvii; and repeal of Test Act, XII. xlvi.

Hoare, Sir Richard, 1648–1718, Lord Mayor of London in 1713: VI. 199; letter from Queen, VIII. xvi.

Hobbes, Thomas, 1588–1679: VIII. 37; anti-Christian, II. 72; censured, II. 15–18; and the Drapier, X. 94; on executive and legislative powers, II. xvi; 'free-thinker', IV. 47; leads Modern bowmen, I. 152; *Leviathan*, I. 24 — frontispiece, I. 181; state of nature, IV. 115–16; and Plato, I. 146; Stella on, V. 231;

compared with Tindal, II. xviii, *n.* 2, 88.

Quotations and allusions to *Leviathan*; — on reason and religion, IX. 80; — I. vi: VIII. 139; — I. x: XII. 156; — II. xxix: XII. 161, 278; — conclusion (present age the oldest), I. 147.

Hobby horses: school of, I. 25 and *n.**.

Hochstädt, Germany, on the Danube, between Ulm and Donauwörth: battle of, VI. 31.

Hock-Norton, or 'Hogsnorton' (now Hook Norton, near Chipping Norton, Oxfordshire): IV. 190.

Hoeuft, Gedeon, Dutch plenipotentiary, canon of the chapter of the Church of St. Peter at Utrecht: VI. 99, 106–9.

Hoffman, Francis: *More Secret Transactions*, III. xxx; *Secret Transactions*, III. xxix, 192–3.

Hoffmann, Johann Philipp von, *d.* 1724, Austrian minister in London: and Eugene's visit to England (1712), IV. xxxvii, 216–17; VII. 108, 111.

Hogarth, William, 1697–1764, artist: and copyrights, XIII. 206; and JS's mock-proposal for a history of corruption, V. 346–7.

Hogs: XI. 180.

Hogsnorton: *see* HOCK-NORTON.

Holborn, borough of, London: IV. 62; and Nobel, IV. 259.

Holinshed, Raphael, *d. c.* 1580, historian: *Chronicles*, and JS's history, V. x.

Holland and Hollanders: *see* DUTCH.

Holles, John: *see* NEWCASTLE, 1ST DUKE OF.

Holmes, Sir Charles, librarian at Windsor Castle: buys manuscript of JS's *History of the Four Last Years*, VII. xxiii.

Holstein, north German state: and Petkum, VII. 40.

Holt, Sir John, 1642–1710, Lord Chief Justice: on legal interpretation, X. 109–10.

Holy Ghost: IX. 209, 257, 362; and Tindal, II. 91; and the Trinity, IX. 159–61, 168.

Holyhead, Anglesey, Wales, port for Ireland: XII. ix, xi; geyser, V. 203; JS at (1727), V. xxiv–xxv; JS's burial, XIII. 199.

Holyhead Journal (1727), by JS: **V. 201-8**; analysis, V. xxv; composition, V. xxiv–xxv; errata, XIV. 53; **additional leaf** (Egerton MS. 201), **V. 335-6**; textual notes, V. 357.

Holy water: 'universal pickle', I. 67–8.

Home (or Hume), James Home, 5th Earl of, *d.* 1687: and Covenanters, V. 140; and Creichton, V. 151.

Home (or Hume), Charles Home, 6th Earl of, *d.* 1706: and Creichton, V. 175.

Homer: fights for Ancients, I. 152, 156–7; not blind, XI. 197; and Carteret, XII. 155; commentators, XI. 197; and Greek, IV. 9; *Iliad* in a nutshell, II. 90; and linguistic change, IV. xv, 16; and literary fame, I. 242; ironically praised, I. 79–80, 81; and Rome, I. 211; similes imitated, I. 163–4 and *n.**; correct text, IV.

33; and *Tobit*, I. 244; and
Trojans, IV. 232. Allusions to
Iliad i. 70: I. 153; — ii. 212–64:
I. 160; — iii. 234–6: I. 158.

Hompesch, Reinier Vincent,
Baron of, 1660–1733, Dutch
general: VII. 142, 152.

'Homunceletino', JS's Italian
coinage meaning 'mannikin': XI.
95.

Honesty: and conscience, IX. 152.

Honeywood, Philip, *d.* 1752,
general: III. xiv.

Honour: cant, IX. 116; capri-
cious, IX. 153; not founded on
virtue, IX. 116; opposed to
Christianity, IX. 115–16; personal obligation, IX. 154; substituted for conscience, IX. 153;
vice conquers, IX. 153; and
virtue, IX. 152.

*Honour and Prerogative of the
Queen's Majesty . . . Defended
Against the Unexampled Insolence
. . . of the Guardian*: VIII. xi, xii,
('another pamphleteer') 8, 10,
('another adversary') 12.

Hooker, Richard, *c.* 1554–1600,
theologian: style praised, II.
177.

Hook's tomb, at Conway, Carnarvon, Wales: V. 202.

Hooper, George, 1640–1727,
Bishop of Bath and Wells: JS to
toast (*c.* 1727), V. 335.

Hope, Thomas: *An Essay upon
English Bubbles*, IX. xix.

Hopewell, a ship in *Gulliver's
Travels*: XI. 153.

Hopkins, Edward, *d.* 1716,
English M.P., Secretary to Duke
of Grafton: and Irish employments, X. 58 and *n.**.

Hoppe, H. R.: acknowledgement,
XI. 301.

Hops, tithe of: III. 131.

Horace: edited by Bentley, II.
xxiv, *n.* 1; coarseness, V. 338–40;
preferred over Juvenal, XII. 33;
perpetuated the memory of his
imitators, V. 201; and Roman
manners, II. 28; JS wiser, V.
xxv; imitated by Temple, I. 262;
on women, V. 338–40.

Quotations and allusions: *Ars
Poetica* (i.e., *Epistles* II. iii), 2–4:
I. 69; —5: I. 247; — 60–2:
IV. 16; — 139; III. 52; — 179–
88: V. 339–40; — 309–10: IX.
331; — 343: I. 77 and 237; —
388: IV. 100; *Epistles* I. ii. 58
(not Juvenal): I. 249; — I. ii.
62: I. 250; — I. vi. 1: VIII.
133 ('admire at nothing'); — I.
vii. 96–8: I. 279; — I. x. 24: I.
248; — I. xiv. 43: I. 8; — I. xix.
19: I. 232; — II. ii. 44: III. 162;
— II. ii. 102: IX. 339; — III. iii.
150: II. 79; *Epodes* XVII. 56:
III. 85; *Odes* I. ii. 23–4: III. 8; —
I. v. 5: II. 177; — I. xviii. 10–
11: I. 180; — II. i. 6: I. 232; —
II. i. 7: VIII. 142; — II. xiii. 31–
2: III. 90; — III. v. 15–18, 26–8:
X. 168; — III. vi. 1–3: III.
157; — III. vi. 5: II. 57; — III.
xi. 35: facing XI. iii and 1; —
III. xxiv. 21: III. 147; — III.
xxiv. 25–9: II. 46; — III. xxv.
7–8: I. 26 and *n.**; — III. xxx. 1:
IV. 16 and facing X. 1; *Satires*
I. i. 31: I. 34; — I. iii. 107: I.
104; — I. iv. 44: IX. 338; — I.
iv. 85: XII. 24; — II. i. 1–3: III.
35; — II. i. 20: XI. 293; — II. i.
41–2: III. 152; — II. i. 45:

III. 172; — II. iii. 71: I. 128; — II. iii. 141: I. 31 and *n.**; — II. vi. 77–8: III. 101.

Horace, Part of the Seventh Epistle of the First Book Imitated, poem, by JS: I. 278–9.

Horatii and Curiatii, legendary Roman and Latin heroes in reign of Tullus Hostilius: III. 98.

'Horatio', a character in Harrison's *Tatler*, No. 20: II. 187.

Hormisdas, St., Pope, *d.* 523: XIV. 29.

Horn, Andrew, *d.* 1328, chamberlain of London: *Mirror of Justices*, X. 9.

Hornbeak, Katherine: and JS's *A Letter to a Young Lady*, IX. xxvii, *n.* 1.

Horses: V. 133–4; XI. 240–1, 272–3; coachman and, XIII. 45–6; groom and, XIII. 46–51; at inns, XIII. 163–5; throw shoes, V. 202. *See also* HOUYHN-HNMS.

Hort, Josiah, *c.* 1674–1751, Bishop of Kilmore and Ardagh, later Archbishop of Tuam: and Bishop Evans, XIV. 41; *A New Proposal for the Better Regulation and Improvement of Quadrille*, printed by Faulkner, XIII. 205; and Sheridan, V. 224.

Hosiers: XI. 20.

Hospitals, Irish: patients, IX. 202–3; Dr. Steevens', XIII. 150, 198; — Stella's legacy, V. 235–6; Swift's, XIII. xlii–xliii, 149–52, 192–3, 203. *See also* ST. PATRICK'S HOSPITAL.

Hostreham (*i.e.* Wareham, Dorset): Henry II lands, V. 73.

Hottentots: and Ireland, XIII. 112.

Houghton Library, Harvard University: acknowledgement, XIV. vii.

House of Commons, English: accomplishments (1710–11), III. 167–72; accounts not passed (1711), III. 170; Anne's speech to (1711), VII. 17–18; — speech (1712), VII. 130–4; reject Austrian proposals (1712), VII. 25; and balance of power (with king and peers), I. 195–203, 223–36; VIII. 119; — advantage of peers, VI. 124–6; expel Cardonell (1712), VII. 67; character, perseverance of, VII. 102; and *Conduct of the Allies*, VI. xiii–xiv; conflict with Charles I, IX. 222; — refuse taxes, IX. 221; Committee of Secrecy: *see* OXFORD, EARL OF, *impeachment*; corruption, VI. 125; XI. 129–30; — reform proposed by JS, XIV. 14–15; resent Dutch envoys (1711–12), VII. 119–20; elections — annual elections recommended, IX. 32; — satirized, XI. 128–30; — corruption recommended, I. 301–2; — *see also* ELECTIONS; FRANCHISE; and *Extract of a Book*, X. xxiii; and Ned Fashion, II. 186; Fleetwood's *Preface* condemned (1712), VI. xix; attack Godolphin ministry (1712), VII. 64, 78, 98; and royal grants, VI. xvii, 134–5; VII. 100–1; devotion to Hanoverian family (1712), VII. 78; — and precedence, VII. 78; impeachment of Whig ministers (1700–1), I. xx; IV. xxiv; — condemned, I. 228–36; — 'proceedings', V. 11; incompetence

in, II. 129–30; encourage learning (1710), III. 37; subordination to Lords, VI. 125–7; VII. 20; and Marlborough, VII. 22; — censure him (1712), VII. 65–7; and corrupt ministries, VI. 125; congratulatory speech to Oxford, III. 154–5; — esteem him, VII. 76; place bill fails (1711), VII. 95–6; praised (1712), VII. 67; Puritans influence, IX. 221; *Representation* (1711), III. 171; — (1712), VII. 79–94; address against 'Peace without Spain' defeated (1711) VII. 18; Speaker: *see* SPEAKER; no spiritual powers, XII. 244–5; Stamp Tax (1712), VII. 103–4; and tariffs, XII. 125; and Tindal, II. xviii, 87; Townshend censured, (1712), VII. 79; treaties reviewed (1712), VII. 80–94; oppose Treaty of Commerce, VII. xi; inquiry into non-existent treaty (1712), VII. 64; unpopular (1701), I. 235; Walpole's bribery of, V. 105, 106; expel Walpole (1712), VII. 65; and William III — Dutch guards, V. 85; — his grants to be resumed (1712), VI. xvii, 134–5; VII. 100–1; and War of the Spanish Succession — desire peace, VII. 2; — Ormonde's 'restraining orders' (1712), VII. 129; — vote funds (1712), VII. 25. *See also* PARLIAMENT; ST. STEPHEN'S CHAPEL.

House of Commons, Irish: tax on absentees, XII. xxi, 126; Bill of Division, XIII. 97; and bishops, XIII. 205; — their lands to be taxed, XII. xxxix, 207–12; and Carteret, XII. xiv; and clergy's residence, XII. 189–202; and Irish cloth, XII. 71; and *Considerations upon Two Bills . . . Relating to the Clergy of Ireland*, XII. xxxvi–xxxix; and national debt, XII. 126; and tithe of hemp, XIII. 97–103; *Humble Address*, 1723 (Wood's halfpence): *see* DRAPIER'S LETTERS; and *Humble Petition of the Footmen in . . . Dublin*, XII. xxxiii, 235–7; *A Letter to a Member of Parliament in Ireland. Upon the Chusing a New Speaker There*: *see* LETTER TO A MEMBER OF PARLIAMENT IN IRELAND; Molesworth's pamphlet, IX. 58–9; and political party lines, II. xxii; Speaker of, II. xxxii–xxxiii, 129–35; — and John Forster, II. 130–1, 133; JS attacks, IX. xv; and Test Act (1733), XIII. 97; — repeal, II. 131–5; XII. xlvi, 244–50; and toleration of Dissenters, II. 124; most members Whigs, II. 118; tax on wine, XII. xxi–xxii, 20, 124–6; and Wood's coinage, X. 5, 20, 21, 24; — *see also* HUMBLE ADDRESS OF THE KNIGHTS, CITIZENS AND BURGESSES.

House of Lords, English: address (10 Apr. 1713), VI. 181–3; — *see also* HUMBLE ADDRESS OF THE RIGHT HONOURABLE THE LORDS; address (11 Mar. 1714), VIII. 198–9; — background, VIII. xxi–xxii; — textual note, VIII. 232; and Bill against Occasional Conformity (1703–4), I. xxi; and balance of power (with king and commons), I. 195–203, 230–6; bishops in ('a certain bench'), VI. 125; — Whigs would remove,

III. 146; and Hugh Boulter, X. 61; bribery ('certain methods'), VI. 125–6; precedence over Commons, VI. 125–7; VII. 20; and Hanover family (1712), VII. 78; *Humble Address* of 10 Apr. 1713: see HUMBLE ADDRESS OF THE RIGHT HONOURABLE THE LORDS; impeachment of five lords (1700–01), I. xx, 222–5, 234–6; IV. xxiv; VIII. 119; Irish appeals to, X. 128, 131; creation of 12 peers, VII. 19–21; VIII. 148–50; — 'a resolute, necessary step', VI. 124–5; Scottish peers in ('certain lords'), VI. 72–3; VIII. 50–1; — abused in JS's *Publick Spirit of the Whigs*, VIII. xviii–xix, xxi–xxii, facing xxii, 30, 50–1, 198; and *Polite Conversation*, IV. 113; and royal prerogative, VI. 131, 136; private interests represented, VI. 126; and JS's *Publick Spirit of the Whigs*, VIII. xxi–xxii; — address against, VIII. 198–9; JS charged with sedition (1713), VIII. 198–9; Tory majority (1712), VII. 13, 17, 31; — and Oxford ministry, VIII. 82; — assured by creation of peers (1712), VII. 20; and vote of 'no peace without Spain' (1711), VI. 43, ('unexpected turn') 73; VII. 17, 18–19, 42; VIII. 146–7; — a Whig stratagem, VI. 75–6, 123–4; Whiggism of (1690–1711), VI. 125–6; VII. xxii, 13, 19–20; — and Godolphin ministry, VI. 125; and William III — grants not to be examined (1711), VI. 134–5; VII. 101. *See also* PARLIAMENT.

House of Lords, Irish: and absenteeism, X. 130–1; address against Wood: see DRAPIER'S LETTERS; and bank scheme, IX. 319; and bishops in, II. 117; — JS attacks, XII. xxxv–xxxix, 186, 191–202, 207–12; — and unfilled bishoprics, VIII. 140; and clergy's residence, XII. 190–202; order Faulkner's arrest, XII. xxxviii; and King George's wisdom, X. xxix–xxx; *Humble Address* of (concerning Wood's halfpence): see DRAPIER'S LETTERS; and JS's *A Libel on Doctor Delany*, XII. xxv; membership, II. 119 and *n*.†; JS's contempt, IX. x; and repeal of Test Act, XII. xlvi; and JS's *On Wisdom's Defeat in a Learned Debate*, X. xxix–xxx; and Wood's coins: see HUMBLE ADDRESS OF THE LORDS.

Housemaid (in *Directions to Servants*, XIII. 60–2): brass polishing, XII. 61; and candles, XIII. 61; and chamberpots, XIII. 60–2; and footman, XIII, 62; and hearths, XIII. 61, 62; and pets, XIII. 62; water disposal, XIII. 62.

Housekeeper: in *Directions to Servants*, XIII. 65.

House steward: in *Directions to Servants*, XIII. 51.

Houyhnhnms, in *Gulliver's Travels*, Part IV: arts (sciences, crafts), XI. 273–4; conversation, XI. 277–8; attitude towards death, XI. 274–5; their dwellings, XI. 228, 231; system of education, XI. 269–70; Gulliver's master, XI. 5, 234; — rids him of deceit, XI. 292; — sees Gulliver naked,

XI. 236–7; — in Parliament, XI. 271–3; island described, XI. 223; — map, XI. 220; their language, XI. 226–7, 234; their ignorance of lying, XI. 235, 240; marriage and eugenics, XI. 268-9; meaning and etymology of 'Houyhnhnm', XI. 235; medicines, XI. 273; a sorrel nag bears Gulliver affection, XI. 281, 283; parliamentary government, XI. 270, 271-3, 279-80; 'the perfection of nature', XI. 235; without pride, XI. 296; truly rational creatures, XI. 225–80; social stratification among, XI. 256; table manners, XI. 231; their virtues, XI. 268, 289, 293-4; writing unknown to them, XI. 234-5; plan to exterminate the Yahoos, XI. 271-3.

How, Thomas, *d.* 1733, mayor of Dublin in 1733: X. 76; XIII. xxvi.

Howard, Colonel, Puritan officer: XII. 249.

Howard, Henrietta: *see* SUFFOLK, COUNTESS OF.

Howard, Ralph, 1638–1710, Professor of Physic, Trinity College, Dublin: Dr. H. in *Dialogue in the Castilian Language*, IV. 257-9; pun upon name, IV. 264; punned with JS, IV. xxix.

Howard, Robert, 1683–1740, Bishop of Elphin, son of Ralph Howard: and clerical livings, XII. xxxix.

Howe, John Grubham (Jack How), 1657–1722, Tory politician: I. 111; possible model for Clodius in *Discourse of the Contests and Dissensions*, I. 233, 235.

Howell, William, *c.* 1638–83, Whig historian: *Medulla Historiae Anglicanae*, V. xxxv; — **JS's marginalia** (1734–6), **V. 262-5.**

Howth, Ireland: XII. 219.

Hudibrastic verses: I. x, xiv.

Hudson's Bay: XII. 76; Britain secures, VII. 43, 49, 114, 132; and War of the Spanish Succession (1689-97), VI. 11.

Hue and Cry After Dismal (1712), by JS: **VI. 139-41**; authorship, VI. xxi; background, VI. xxii; editions, VI. xxi, 210-11; facsimile of original broadside, VI. ii; textual notes, VI. 210-11.

Hugh the Great, *d.* 1102, brother of Philip I, King of France: V. 21.

Huguenots, or Hugonots: I. 88 and *n.**; III. 162; and Charles II, IV. 109; and Dutch manufactures, VI. 28; and religious wars, II. 12; St. Bartholomew's Day massacre (1572) — Heylyn and JS on, V. 255-6; and Tindal, II. 104; and Tories, IV. 63; and Treaty of Utrecht, VII. 115, 165.

Human nature: I. 77–82, 83, 106, 107–10; and advice, I. 241; avarice and ambition, III. 80–5; avarice is natural, XI. 260–1; mocked in Brobdingnag, XI. 107, 132; broom-stick analogy, I. 239–40; conscience not dependable, V. 26; IX. 114–16, 150-8; contemplation, IX. 359; 'contemptible', XI. 137, 147; corruption more natural than perfection, VIII. 180; cynical, IX. 116; degeneration, IX. 264;

XI. 137; — treatise on, I. xl; depraved, II. 10; IX. 113, 155, 359; evil more natural than good, III. 136–7; ('violence in an ill cause') VI. 78; ('the degenerate nature of man') XI. 60, 259; factions are natural, II. 1–2; fanaticism and enthusiasm, I. 102–14, 174; followers and leaders, I. 232–3; causes of hatred, VIII. 169; inconsistency, I. 244; IV. 245; inequality and Providence, IX. 147; 'It is the mistake of wise . . . men that they expect . . . reason and virtue from human nature', V. 79; in life and literature, II. 187; lust, III. 80, 85; miserable, IX. 190; moral reformation, II. 44–5, 47–8, 50, 57, 59; moralism and the golden age, XI. 137; motivation, IX. 155; the passions triumph, VIII. 87; the past and present, I. 241; 'the incompatibility of power', VIII. 153; prejudices, I. 242; pride, IV. 245; IX. 145–6; XI. 296; prudence, II. 60; men only capable of reason, VIII. 46–7; — 'God has given the bulk of mankind a capacity to understand reason', VIII. 77; reformation sometimes impossible, XII. 24–5; revenge, I. 243; seeks rewards, IX. 244; self-interest, IX. 125; mind a *tabula rasa*, I. 250; talents from God, IX. 146; talents for service, IX. 146; uncleanliness, XI. 263; uselessness of vice, XI. 243–4; a mixture of virtue and vice in all men, V. 25; and war, XI. 134–5, 247–8; wisdom not invulnerable to

malice, V. xvii, 116. *See also* YAHOOS.

Humble Address of the Knights, Citizens and Burgesses: see DRAPIER'S LETTERS.

Humble Address of the Lords [*sc.* of Ireland]: *see* DRAPIER'S LETTERS.

Humble Address of the Right Honourable the Lords . . . in Parliament Assembled [i.e., the English House of Lords, voted 10 Apr. 1713], by JS: **VI. 181-3**; composition, VI. xxvii–xxviii; manuscript facsimile, facing VI. xxviii–1; textual notes, VI. 212–13; title-page facsimile, VI. 181; **vote for** — facsimile of JS's draft, facing **VI. 183.**

Humble Address of the Right Honourable the Lords . . . in Parliament Assembled (i.e., the English House of Lords, 11 Mar. 1714): *see* HOUSE OF LORDS, ENGLISH, *address.*

Humble Address to Both Houses of Parliament: *see* DRAPIER'S LETTERS.

Humble Petition of the Doctor, and the Gentlemen of Ireland (1707), by JS: **IV. 261-2**; composition, IV. xxix–xxx; editions, IV. 301; manuscript, IV. xxxvi, 301; textual notes, IV. 301.

Humble Petition of the Footmen in . . . Dublin (1733), by JS: **XII. 235-7**; analysis, XII. xxxiii–xxxiv; composition, XII. 235, 237; textual notes, XII. 345.

Humble Representation of the Clergy of the City of Dublin, To . . . William [King] Lord Archbishop (1724), by JS: **V.**

87-92; analysis, V. xi–xii; textual note, V. 350.

Hume, Earl of: *see* HOME.

Hume or Humes, Thomas, *fl.* 1715–28, Dublin printer: and Swearers Bank, IX. 298; and JS, IX. xix.

Humility: false, and repentance, IX. 353–4; self-knowledge increases, IX. 359.

Humour: JS's view, I. 10; XII. 32–7.

Hungary: VI. 34; Austria suppresses, VI. 36; troops, VII. 58–9; alleged fear of war (1711), VII. 59.

Huningue, or Gross-Huningen ('Hunningen'), Haut-Rhin, France, near Bâle: fortress to be demolished, VII. 113.

Hunsdon, William Ferdinand Carey, 8th Lord, 1684–1765: 'beggarly Dutchman', VIII. 172.

Hunter, Robert, *d.* 1734, governor of New York: II. xxv.

Hunterian Library, Glasgow: acknowledgement, XIV. vii.

Huntington Library: acknowledgement, XIV. vii.

'Hurgo', a great lord in Lilliput: XI. 23, 25.

Hutchins, Henry: on *Gulliver's Travels*, XI. 319.

Hutcheson, Hartley, prosecutor of hawkers: censured, XII. 156.

Huxelles: *see* UXELLES.

Huy, or Hoei, between Liége and Namur, Belgium: and Barrier Treaty, VI. 107, 115.

Hybris, i.e., pride: personified, I. 57.

Hyde, Anne, Duchess of York, 1637–71, first wife of James II,

mother of Queen Anne: VIII. 96; son dies in infancy, V. 264.

Hyde, J., *d. c.* 1728, Dublin bookseller: XI. 301; recommended by JS ('Thomas' an error), IX. xix; works wrongly ascribed to JS, IX. xix, xxiv–xxvi.

Hyde, Thomas: error for HYDE, J.

Hyde Park, London: X. 130; Cromwell quells mutiny in, V. 84; and *Polite Conversation*, IV. 146.

Hyde Park Corner, London: boundary point for fashionable Westminster, I. 26.

Hydra: I. 58; pun upon, IV. 235.

Hyperbolus: I. 31.

Hypocrisy and fraud: Christianity opposes, IX. 248; 'a greater crime than theft', XI. 58; even kings and angels deceived by, V. xvii, 116–17; preferable to open vice, II. 57; pretence becomes reality, II. 57; and professed principles, II. 2–4; and religion, IX. 157.

I

Iceland, or Ysland: compared to Ireland, XII. 10.

Iceni, British tribe in Norfolk: V. 263.

'Ickpling Gloffthrobb Squutserumm', etc.: Luggnaggian for, 'May your cælestial Majesty outlive the sun, eleven moons and an half', XI. 205.

Idleness: destroys virtue, IX. 196.

Idols: Christian emperors tolerate, XIV. 19; object of worship,

I. 179; Roman Catholic, I. 54; tailors, I. 46.

Ignorance: father and husband of Criticism, I. 153; mother of devotion, IX. 80, 294; mother of superstition, IX. 80.

Ilay, Archibald Campbell, Earl of (later 3rd Duke of Argyll), 1682–1761, brother of John, 2nd Duke of Argyll: 'some with great titles', VIII. 51; and Whigs, VIII. 166.

'Iliac passion': V. 71.

Iliad: in a nutshell, I. 90. *See also* HOMER.

Imagination: XI. 163–4.

Immorality: *see* MORALITY.

Immortality: V. 262; ancient belief, IX. 156; goddess, I. 20–1; heathen ridicule, IX. 245; Struldbruggs, XI. 207–14.

Impeachment proceedings, JS's views: I. 192–236; and liberty, VIII. 119; and Wharton, III. 175.

Impedimenta literarum: I. 10.

Imperium in imperio (i.e., church as independent power within state): II. 74, 76, 79; XII. 36.

Importance of the Guardian Considered (1713), by JS: **VIII 3-25**; analysis, VIII. xiii–xiv; background, IV. xx–xxi; VIII. x–xiii, 4; composition, IV. xx; date, XIV. 54; publication, VIII. xiii, 201; style, VIII. xiii–xiv; textual notes, VIII. 201; title-page facsimile, VIII. 3.

Impropriations: William II began, V. 15. *See also* HENRY VIII.

Inchiquin, William O'Brien, 3rd Earl of, *c.* 1666–1719: III. 239–40.

'Incog', for 'incognito': IV. 114.

Incurables, and JS's hospital: *see* ST. PATRICK'S HOSPITAL.

In Defence of the Art of Punning, ballad: IV. xxxv.

Indemnity, acts of: XI. 255.

Independents: attack Church of England, II. 3; Jesuits disguised as, II. 37; and Presbyterians, XII. 265, 266, 267; JS's contempt for, I. xxii. *See also* DISSENTERS.

Index expurgatorius: II. 176; JS proposes, IV. xi.

India: asses in, I. xxv, 60; Irish exports from, X. 138–9; XII. 126–7; and revolutions, I. 174; serpents, I. 61; silks from, XII. 9, 79; — in England, X. 138–9.

Indian kings: *see* SPECTATOR, No. 50.

Indiana University: acknowledgment, XIV. vii.

Indians, American: barter system, XII. 58; and English, I. 179; and settlers, XII. 60, 176.

Indies, Spanish: treasures of, XII. 223.

Individualism, JS's views: inadequacy, IX. 146.

Indulgence, Declarations of, 1687, 1688: I. 131 and *n.**.

Infallible Scheme to Pay the Publick Debt: *see* MATTHEW PILKINGTON.

Informers: IX. 32–3; XI. 58, 190–2; condemned, II. 57; IX. 117; despicable, IX. 180; harm society, IX. 236; and innocence, IX. 185; innocent people seduced, IX. 183; misrepresentations, IX. 182; professional spies, IX. 183; vicious motives,

IX. 184; in William II's employ, V. 15.

'Ingenuous': definition, III. 191–2.

Ingoldsby, Richard, *d.* 1712, general, Lord Justice of Ireland: III. 235, 240.

Injured Lady: *see* STORY OF THE INJURED LADY.

Innocent I, St., Pope, *d.* 417: letter to Arcadius, XIV. 19; and Theophilus, XIV. 18.

Innocent II, Pope, *d.* 1143: V. 86; and Stephen, V. 50.

Innovators and innovations, JS's views: I. 102–114; XI. 176–8; and abolition of Christianity, II. 35–9; and conversation, IV. 105–6; and dreams, II. 178–9; daughter of ignorance, I. 242; in language, IV. xv, 9–13; — censured, II. 174–7; oral style, XII. 93; past and present, I. 241; satirized, I. 102–14. *See also* ACADEMY OF LAGADO.

Inns of Court: censured, II. 52; and injustice, I. 31; and Irish economy, XII. 9.

Inquisition: V. 118; XI. 288; and the Drapier, X. 90; and Gee, IV. 250; in Portugal, burns *Predictions for the Year 1708*, II. 160.

Insane, JS's hospital for: *see* ST. PATRICK'S HOSPITAL.

Insects: compared with man, XI. 107, 134, 180.

Inspiration: poetic, and clothing, IX. 339; religious: *see* ENTHUSIASM.

Intelligencer (1728): Sheridan's and JS's contribution, No. 15 (reprint of *Short View of the State of Ireland*, with an introduction by Sheridan), XII. 325; — analysis, XII. xiv; — authorship, XII. xiv.

JS's contributions: XII. 29–61; authorship, XII. xiv–xv, 325; background, XII. xiv; editions, XII. xiv–xv; errata, XIV. 57; manuscript, XII. 348–9; notes for, XII. 306; publication, XII. xiv–xv; and JS's *Discourse, to Prove the Antiquity of the English Tongue*, IV. xxxviii; and JS's *Maxims Controlled in Ireland*, XII. xxiii, *n.* 1; textual notes, XII. 325–9.

JS's contributions, individual numbers: No. 1, XII. 29–31; — analysis, XII. xv; — authorship, XII. xiv–xvi, 325; — editions, XII. 325; — textual notes, XII. 325; — title-page facsimile, facing XII. 29; **No. 3** (on *The Beggar's Opera*), XII. 32–7; — analysis, XII. xiv; — composition, XII. 32; — editions, XII. xiv, 325; — textual notes, XII. 325–6; **No. 5** (combined with No. 7, as *An Essay on the Fates of Clergymen*), XII. 38–45; — editions, XII. xiv, 325; — textual notes, XII. 326–7; — title, XII. 325, 326; **No. 7** (combined with No. 5, as *An Essay on the Fates of Clergymen*), XII. 38–45; — editions, XII. xiv, 325; — textual notes, XII. 327; — title, XII. 325, 326; **No. 8** (*i.e., Mad Mullinix and Timothy*, verses by JS), analysis, XII. xxviii–xxix; **No. 9** (*i.e., An Essay on Modern Education*), XII. 46–53; — editions, XII. xiv,

325, 327; — textual notes, XII. 325, 327–8; — title, XII. 325; **No. 19**, XII. 54–61; — analysis, XII. xiv–xv; — and *An Answer to Several Letters from Unknown Persons*, XII. xvi–xvii; — composition, XII. 54, 61; — editions, XII. xv, 325; — textual notes, XII. 328–9. *See also* SHERIDAN, DR. THOMAS.

International relations, JS's views: and agriculture, XII. 5; balance of power, I. 197; and national morality, II. 57–8; past and present, I. 241; and patriotism, II. 63.

Invention: and memory, I. 84; and youth, IV. 243. *See also* MEMORY.

Ipres: *see* YPRES.

Ireland: absenteeism: see ABSENTEEISM; and Agricola, IV. 280; agriculture: *see* AGRICULTURE; anomalies, economic and political, XII. 5–12, 79, 124–6, 129–37, 309–10; Attorney-General, X. xxii and *n*. 1; bank: *see* BANK, IRISH; bread prices, XII. 19; cabins, V. 206; censorship of press, XII. 122; — printers prosecuted, XII. 57; church: *see* CHURCH OF IRELAND; clergy: *see* CLERGY OF THE CHURCH OF IRELAND; climate, XII. 310; cost of living — high, XII. 11, 132–3, 309; — low, V. 228; craftsmen: *see* ARTISANS, IRISH; debt: *see* DEBT, NATIONAL, IRISH; Declaratory Act (1720) attacked, X. xviii and *n*. 4; **economic decay**, IX. 4, 7; XII. xix, 10–11; XIII. 90; — causes, IX. 199–209; X. 128–32; — caused by England,

XII. 131; — not Ireland's fault, XII. 7; — and productivity, IX. 199; — remedies, IX. 199–209; X. 134–41; XII. 68; and England: see IRELAND AND ENGLAND; excise, XIII. 83; famine and hunger, XII. 10, 78, 122; — and scarcity of corn, XII. xii, xix, 17–22, 55, 303–5; financial condition — bank harmful, IX. 302; — bank needed, IX. 300; — bankers condemned, XII. 11; — and devaluation of guinea, XII. 66–7; — interest rates low, XII. 11, 133–4, 309, 310; — — ten percent (in 1701), V. 228; forests, XII. 6, 8, 10, 88; government, subservient to England, IX. 5; and Henry II, V. 76; House of Commons: *see* HOUSE OF COMMONS, IRISH; House of Lords: *see* HOUSE OF LORDS, IRISH; houses and building, XII. 10, 11, 118; and *Intelligencer* — purpose, XII. xiv–xv; **imported luxuries condemned**, IX. 200–1; X. 135, 138–9; XI. 251–3; XII. 7, 9, 66–8, 71, 81, 121, 123, 126–7; — cloth, IX. 201; X. 135; XII. 126–7; — coffee, XII. 127; — lace, XII. 126; — and Parliament, X. 135–9; XII. 127; — tax opposed, XII. 136; — tea, XII. 126–7; — wine excepted, XII. 124–6; — women, XII. 80, 126–7; 'Irish interest' (*i.e.*, persons, institutions, and forces placing Ireland's welfare before England's) — some Englishmen support, IX. 12; — and M.P. for Dublin, XIII. 80; James II, II. 105; justice, X. 30–1, 35, 39; **land** —

acreage, IX. 290, 318; — bogs, XII. 87-8; — grants of William III ('conquered lands'), I. 218-19; — high cost of, XII. 11, 134, 210, 309-10; — ownership, IX. 290; — ownership and the law, X. 134; — value rises, IX. 47; — *see also* rents; liberty, X. 31, 35, 39; — and bank scheme, IX. 302; — nation denied common rights, XII. 124; manufactures: *see* MANUFACTURES, IRISH; and masons, V. 329; meat prices, XII. 19-20; mining, XII. 7; misery — intolerable, IX. xi; — and self-interest, IX. 157;

money — copper money lacking, XII. 93, 96, 98; — Dartmouth's patent, X. 33, 40-3; XII. 94, 99; — and gentry, XII. 100; — history of coinage, X. 40-2; — leather, XII. 176-7; — Maculla's project, XII. xvii-xviii, 93-105; — mint proposed, XII. 7, 9, 11, 57, 90, 98-105; — Moore's patent, XII. 94, 99; — silver money lacking, XII. 54-61, 71, 76, 93-4, 98; — *see also* WOOD'S COINS;

mottoes, IX. 335-6; Navigation Act, XII. 8, 66, 132; public offices — and absenteeism, IX. 7; — corruption of office-holders, XIII. 84; — reversions, X. 58-9; — *see also* IRELAND AND ENGLAND, '*English interest*'; peerage, IV. 284; people: *see* IRISH PEOPLE; place-names, IV. 280-4; politics, IX. xi; — divisive, IX. 176; — ignorance of, X. 58; — parties, II. 117-19; III. 177; X. 132-4; XII. 22-3; — parties and public offices, XII.

xxvii-xxix, 153-69; port facilities, XII. 6, 8; poverty, IX. 4, 7; XII. xix, 10; XIII. 90; — and bishops, IX. 57; Presbyterian clergy, V. 272; alleged prosperity ridiculed, XII. 10; and Puritans, XII. 257-8; — Civil War, IX. 225; — Commonwealth, IX. 11; — Rebellion, V. 257; X. 40; Rebellion of 1641, V. 125-6; XII. 132; recruiting by French, XII. 173-8, 311-21; rents, XII. 59, 66, 67; — high, X. 128; XII. 76-9, 118, 207; XIII. 176; — history of, XII. 133; — rising, XII. 6, 10-11; — paid in wool, IX. 269; roads neglected, XII. 86-7; and Scotland: *see* SCOTLAND; shipbuilding, XII. 6, 8, 10; and Stella, V. 235-6;

and JS — championed by him, II. xxii; IX. ix; — motive as champion, 'perfect hatred of tyranny and oppression', XIII. 112; — his concern with Ireland (1707-13), IX. ix; — exile for him, IX. ix; — and his freedom of Dublin, XII. xxvi-xxvii; — hostility to him, IX. 117; — politics, IX. 117; — and William III, I. xxi; JS's views — 'absolutely undone', XII. xviii-xix; — 'folly established as a law', XIII. 174; — 'a most obscure disagreeable country', V. 11; — (on remedies) 'a dose to the dead', XII. xxxv;

and *Tale of a Tub*, I. xvi; taxes, XII. 309; — high, XII. 21; — on wine, XII. 124-6; Tories: *see* TORIES, IRISH; tourists lacking, XII. 6, 9; trade: *see* TRADE, IRISH; unemployment, XII. 135-

6; weavers: *see* WEAVERS; and Wharton: *see* WHARTON; Whigs: *see* WHIGS, *in Ireland*; and William III: *see* WILLIAM III; wool, act for burial in (1734), XIII. xxix; wool trade: *see* WOOLLEN TRADE, IRISH.

Ireland, poem by JS: quoted, XII. xi.

Ireland and England: and anomalies of Ireland, XII. 131; and church revenues, XIII. 81; civilizing influence of England, IX. 274; during Commonwealth, IX. 11; conquest, IX. 4–5; cost to England, IX. 19; cost of living compared, V. 228; XII. 125–6; **dependence** of Ireland on England, IX. 8–9; X. 84–94; — colonialism condemned, IX. 128; — doctrine criticized, IX. 8–9; — doctrine denied, IX. 128; X. xviii, 62; — Dependency Act (1720), IX. x; X. xviii, *n.* 4, 62; — dependence of England on Ireland, X. 128–32; — recommended ironically, XII. 175–8; Dissenters — among English settlers ('fanatical'), IX. 30; — Presbyterians, XII. 248; 'English interest' (*i.e.*, persons, institutions, and tendencies subordinating Irish welfare to English profit and power), XIII. 81; — no cause for complaint, IX. 275; — limited, IX. 11; — and M.P. for Dublin, XIII. 80; — opposed to Irish, XIII. 81; — and public offices, IX. 6; X. 132; XII. xli–xliii, 6, 9, 76–7, 248; — Irish submission to, IX. 5; and Whigs, XII. 153–69; government of Ireland, III.

177–8; — distrusted, XIII. xxv; — compared with Romans in Britain, V. 3; 'impositions' of Ireland ridiculed, IX. 18; language — and Hebrew alphabet, V. 331; and English language, IV. xxxix, 278–9, 280–4; loyalty to England, II. 114; IX. 7; English misconceptions, X. 103–4; bill for modus, XIII. 101–5; obligations to England, IX. 6; **oppression** by England, II. 113–14; V. 242; IX. xv, 6; X. 55; XII. xi–xii, xli, 6, 8–12, 117; XIII. 81; — allegory, IX. 3–12; — Ireland denied common rights, IX. 199–200; — deserved, IX. 18; — and politics in Ireland, X. 30–1, 35, 39; politics compared, XIII. 82–3; and Roman Catholics, X. 126; and Test Act, II. 113–17; XII. 263–9; trade balance — burn everything English but their coal, IX. 17; — prohibit English goods, IX. 16–19; — *see also* TRADE, IRISH, *balance*; wealth compared, XII. 86.

Irenæus, 2nd century A.D., Church Father: on 'bythus and sigé', I. 119 and *n.*†; on Marcosian heretics, I. xxxix, 18, *n.*, 119, *n.*†.

Ireton, Henry, 1611–51, Parliamentary general and regicide: III. 73; XII. 265.

Irish Eloquence, by JS: **IV. 278–9**; analysis, IV. xxxviii–xxxix; glossary, IV. 302; manuscript, IV. xxxviii, 278, 302; textual notes, IV. 302.

Irish people: size of anus, XII. 220–1; barbarous (in Middle Ages), V. 75–6; beggars — ex-

portation, XII. 136, 176; — treatment of, IX. 205–9; XIII. 131–40, 172–3; cheating and corruption, XIII. 112; — cottagers, XII. 306; — farmers, XII. 306; — merchants and shop-keepers, XII. 69–70, 306; — due to oppression, XII. 306; — servants, IX. 203–4; children, XII. xxi, 109–18; — burden to poor people, IX. 201; — education, IX. 202–5; clothing, XII. 10–11, 118; corruption: *see* FOR THE HONOUR OF THE KINGDOM OF IRELAND; divisions and dissensions, X. 132–5; XII. 116; — concord urged, X. 132–4; — Dissenters cause, IX. 172–3; — informers cause, IX. 183; — and political parties, IX. 176; — Wood's coins 'the great uniter', X. 61; emigration condemned, IX. 129; XII. 18, 22, 58–61, 66–7, 75–81, 176, 315; — and Roman Catholics, XII. 291–2; tenant farmers — 'live worse than English beggars', XII. 11; illiteracy, IX. 202; industry, XII. 77; landlords oppressive, IX. 21, 54, 58, 201; XII. 81, 116–18, 133; — and *Modest Proposal*, XII. 112; language (Celtic) — barbarous, should be abolished, XII. xvii, 89; laziness, IX. 201, 203, 206–7, 209; XIII. xxxiii, 176; loyalty to King George, IX. 234: luxury, IX. 201; manners, IV. xxxvii, 221; — civilizing needed, XII. 88–9; — 'to be civilized by rewards', XII. 88; — in Middle Ages, V. 75–6; early marriages, XIII. 176; patriotism (public spirit or benevolence) — inspired by opposition to Wood's coins, X. 113; — lacking, IX. 172–9, 233–5; X. 3, 22–3, 53; XII. 75; XIII. 112; population, IX. 290; XII. 99; — declining, IX. 201; XII. 89; — overpopulation, XII. 109, 135–6, 174–5, 310; — overpopulation and foreign armies, XII. 174–5; — Roman Catholic birthrate, XII. 112, 114; poverty, X. 139; XII. xii, xxi, 67, 99, 306; — half are beggars, XII. 136; — 'two thirds are beggars', XII. 99; — and *Modest Proposal*, XII. 109–18; pride, IX. 200–1; purity (ironical), I. 178; Roman Catholics not dangerous, IX. 172; X. 104; — less dangerous than Dissenters, II. 120–4; XII. xli, 258–9, 272–3; — lion at one's feet and cat at one's throat, II. 122; compared to Scots, IX. 3–12; X. 131; XII. 306; servants—vicious, IX. 203–4; slaves, IX. x; — not English slaves, X. 61–3; speech (English), XII. xxxiv, 218–20; — brogue, IV. 280–4; swearers, IX. 295; and JS — he avoids Irish acquaintance, V. 204; — his contempt for them, IX. xv; — accused of inciting their discontent, IX. 271; JS on them — they have 'less sense, and more evil nature' than any part of Europe, IX. 307; — 'a most profligate and abandoned people', V. 11; — viciousness denied, XII. 88–9; wits and heroes, IX. 274–5.

Irish Rebellion, 1641: V. 125, 126, 257; XII. 132; — and prosperity, X. 40.

'Ironside, Nestor': *see* STEELE, *Guardian*.

Irony: in Gay's *Beggar's Opera*, XII. 36; in *Tale of a Tub*, I. 4.

Iroquois Indians: correspondence with, I. 172.

Irvin, Dr., physician to the Horse-guards, brother of Gerard: V. 151-3.

Irvin, Sir Gerard, Bart., *d.* 1689, lieutenant-colonel: and Creichton, V. 129, 152, 154; and Creichton's father, V. 126-7.

Isaac, son of Abraham: pun upon name, IV. 239.

Isaac, *d.* 1740, French dancing master: II. 186 and *n*.*; IV. 104; possibly misspelled as 'Le Sac', XII. 50.

Isaacs, J. H.: *see* SCOTT, TEMPLE.

Israelites: garments of, I. 44, *n*.†.

Islay, Earl of: *see* ILAY.

Isle of Man: mint, XII. 9, 11.

Isle of Wight: XI. 193.

Italian language: XI. 157; superior to English, IV. xiv, 6; and Englishwomen, IV. 13; stability, IV. 9.

Italy and Italians: Austrian neutrality, VII. 156; and Bickerstaff, II. 144; cruelty, VII. 26; and English language, IV. 12; in fable of lion and virgins, II. 182; and Gee, IV. 250; on Godolphin ministry, III. 258; and Goths, V. 36-7; invaded by Emperor Henry V, V. 34; and Irish anomalies, XII. 310; liberty, III. 103; literature in, XII. 32; — and low humour, XII. 33; music censured, XII. 36-7; — singers, II. 32; neutrality in, VII. 156; — disregarded (1714),

VIII. 63; and the Old Pretender, VIII. 64; pun upon name, IV. 207; compared with ancient Rome, V. 80; ancient Rome gives vote to, I. 218; silence, III. 107; silks from, XII. 79; tyrants in, III. 41, 146; and War of the Spanish Succession, VI. 29, 33-4; VII. 89; — campaigns, VII. 88; — proposed diversion in (1711), VI. 35; — *see also* EUGENE; Treaty of Utrecht, VII. 43.

It's Out at Last: or, French Correspondence Clear as the Sun (1712), probably by JS: **VI. 189-91**; authorship, VI. xx-xxi; publication, VI. xx, 213; textual notes, VI. 213.

Ittersum, Ernst Hendrick van, 1669-1733, Dutch diplomat: VI. 99, 106-9.

Ivan: *see* BASILOWITZ.

Ixion, Greek mythological criminal, bound on a wheel: I. 247; and Juno, V. 323.

J

Jack, one of three brothers in *Tale of a Tub*, representing Calvinism: I. 44-55, 65-76, 83-9, 100-2, 120-31; 'singular adventures', I. 121-31; expelled by brother, I. 76; revealed to be John Calvin, I. 84; destroys his coat, I. 86-8; portrait of, facing I. 44, 84; foreshadowed in JS's *Ode to Sancroft*, I. xii-xiv. *See also* HISTORY OF MARTIN.

Jack and Jill nursery rhyme: IV. 156.

Jackson, John, *d.* 1751, vicar of Santry: V. xxxi; JS gives him a

book, V. xxxi, *n.* 5; JS's will, XIII. 155.

Jacobites: allegedly few, VI. 27; VIII. 33, 168; in Dublin, XII. 220–32; and Carteret, XII. 153–69; and France, satirized in *Gulliver's Travels*, XI. 49–50; historical parallel to, V. 31–2; in Ireland, XII. 272–5; 'Jacks', II. 174; alleged plots, XI. 311; 'a ruined party', II. 20; and Stillingfleet, II. 79; JS denies charge, IX. 27; XII. 145–6; and Whigs, IV. 121; Whigs against church, IX. 56; Whigs identified with, XIV. 7, 12.

James I, King of England, 1566–1625: accedes to the throne of England (1603), V. 125; and Church, XIII. 123; and Church of Ireland, XII. 183–4; courtiers, V. 266; and English language, IV. 9; and Irish bishoprics, IX. 46; possibly 'King', X. 155–6; and free masons, V. 326; and mixed money, X. 55; and peace, X. 40; and English poetry, IV. 273; and *Polite Conversation*, IV. 171; and Order of the Thistle ('Monarch'), I. 29; and the Union, VIII. 48–9.

James II, King of England, 1633–1701 (created Duke of York in 1644; reigned as King, 1685–8; called 'Pretender' after accession of William III, February 1689): V. 120; 'the abdicated king', VII. 8; — JS's term impugned, VII. 176; abdication, II. 20, 21–3; XI. 49; and Airlie, V. 162; prosecutes seven bishops, VII. 5; Burnet and JS on, V. 284–91; and Sir Owen Cameron,

V. 158–9; and Church of England, II. 9; and clergy, II. 16, 94; and constitutional monarchy, IX. 122; and Creichton, V. 153; and Dalyell, V. 157; Declarations of Indulgence (1687, 1688), I. 131 and *n.**; and Dissenters, II. 115; III. 144; V. 285; and Exclusion Bill (1679–80), V. 241, 264; — proposed (1679), V. 279; flees (1688), V. 163; alliance with France, V. 288; eager to break with France (in 1678), XIV. 1; Godolphin's loyalty, VII. 8; Godolphin and 'Pretender', VIII. 39, 66; and Granard, V. 165, 166; made few grants, VII. 102; and Irish money, IX. 300; as James VII of Scotland, V. 136; and Knox, X. 41, 56; and Marlborough, V. 162; and Middlesex Grand Jury, X. 167; and mixed money, X. 7; and money, X. 39; and 'newmen', XII. 47; nobles desert him (1688), V. 162–3; oaths of allegiance to, V. 165–6, 167, 168; one of 'two weak princes', I. 230; and 'Popish plot', IV. 61; plot to restore him, VIII. 39; possibly, 'a late reign', I. 234; resistance to him justified, IX. 230; hopes to return, III. 204; and Roman Catholicism, II. 105; III. 200, 204; XII. 257, 268–71; Roman Catholicism imposed, IX. 229; seduced to Roman Catholicism, IX. 224; joined by Scottish Jacobites at St. Germains, V. 177; symbolized by Tarquin, I. 213; and Tindal, II. 70, 104; and Tories, IV. 63; V. 255; and Whigs, III.

127; VIII. 10; pardons Whigs (1692), III. 146; and William III, V. 85; and William III's invasion, V. 161.

James Edward, 'James III', son of James II: *see* PRETENDER, OLD.

January 30th, anniversary of the death of Charles I: abolition proposed, IX. 121; — opposed by JS, IX. 121–2; change in JS's attitude, IX. 122; sermon preached by JS, IX. 219–31.

Japan: *An Account of the Court and Empire of Japan*, by JS, V. 99–107; and Dutch, XI. 154–5, 203–4, 215–17; and Gulliver, XI. 79, 111, 193, 215–17; trade with 'Luggnagg', XI. 215; map, XI. 152; mercy of Japanese, XI. 155; no Struldbruggs in, XI. 211; and Wood's coinage, X. 56.

Japan, Account of: *see* AN ACCOUNT OF THE COURT AND EMPIRE OF JAPAN.

Jarrell, Mackie L.: acknowledgement, XIV. vii; on *Polite Conversation*, IV. xxxiii, *n.* 1; on JS's preface to Sheridan's sermon, XIV. xiii, xiv, 46.

Jason, legendary leader of Argonauts: I. 69; and free masons, V. 330.

Jauguis: *see* YOGIS.

Jeffrey, Francis, Lord, 1773–1850, literary critic: VI. xviii.

Jeffreys of Wem, George Jeffreys, 1st Lord, 1648–89, Lord Chief Justice: V. 290.

Jehuda Hannasi: *see* JUDAH HANASI.

Jenkins, Sir Leoline, 1623–85, diplomat: and Temple, I. 269.

Jennings, the horse-courser, a coiner: III. 237.

Jermyn, Henry, 1st Lord Dover: *see* DOVER.

Jeroboam, King of Israel: and priests, IX. 226.

Jerome (Hieronymus), St., 347–*c.* 419, Church Father: and free-thinking, IV. 38; JS on, XIV. 17.

Jersey, Edward Villiers, 1st Earl of, *c.* 1656–1711: death, VII. 16; and Gaultier (1710), VII. 35; Prior his secretary, III. 209; and Prior's trip to France, III. 211; intended for Lord Privy Seal, VII. 16.

Jerusalem: captured, XII. 116; Crusaders conquer it, V. 22–3; and the Crusades, V. 21; destruction threatened, IX. 182; Duke of Normandy, reported to be king of, V. 27; becomes a school for war, V. 23.

Jerusalem Misna: *see* MISHNA.

Jervas, Charles, *c.* 1675–1739, portrait-painter and translator of *Don Quixote*: and Stella, V. 237; his portraits of JS, I, frontispiece; III, frontispiece; portraits of JS authentic, XIV. 50.

Jesuits: III. 88, 97; and crier of flounders, XII. 229; disguised as free-thinkers, II. 37; motto for, IV. 249; and Satan, IV. 79; and Whigs, III. 143–4.

Jethro, father-in-law of Moses (*Exodus* iv. 3, 4, 18): advice to Moses, IX. 156.

Jewels: *see* PRECIOUS STONES.

Jewish religion: and tale of three rings, I. xxix.

Jews: III. 102, 130; beggars, II.

90; and Christ, IV. 32; Dutch, and swearing revenues, IX. 298; and English language, IV. 239; exodus from Egypt, II. 192; factions among, XII. 116; and freethinkers, IV. 30, 31, 33; compared to Greeks, IX. 73; not heathens before the coming of Christ, V. 3; and the Inquisition, X. 90; and Josephus, IV. 45–6; and Jupiter, IV. 235; and free masons, V. 324–31; and Old Testament prophets, IV. 45; and Parliament, II. 74; and St. Paul, II. 54; IV. 31; in St. Paul's Cathedral, IV. 31; pun upon, IV. 207; read backwards, I. 186; and religious freedom, II. 89; Simeon Salus converts a Jew, XIV. 33; and tale of three rings, I. xxix; Tindal on, II. 192; toleration of, II. 7; and religious toleration, II. 115; and Turks, IV. 39. *See also* ISRAELITES.

Jezebel, wife of Ahab in Old Testament: and false witness, IX. 181.

Job: and *Polite Conversation*, IV. 196.

Jockeys: XI. 224–5.

Johann Wilhelm, Elector Palatine, 1658–1716: to keep his title, VII. 133–4; troops supplied to Grand Alliance, VII. 137.

John I, St., Pope (in office 523–6): mission to Constantinople, XIV. 29.

John 'Lackland', King of England, 1166–1216: cruelty, II. 22; and Innocent III, V. 86; possessions, IX. 49.

John II, King of France, 1319–64: and the Black Prince, V. 84.

John V, King of Portugal, 1689–1750, son of Pedro II: and Bickerstaff, II. 160; and Spain, II. 169–70; his venereal disease, V. 126. *See also* PORTUGAL.

John, or Jack, of Leyden (i.e., Jan Beukels), 1509–36, Dutch Anabaptist: I. 88 and *n.*‖; fanatic, I. 188; insane, I. 107.

Johnson, Betty: maid in *Polite Conversation*, IV. 134–5.

Johnson, Edward, Stella's father: V. 227.

Johnson, Esther, or Hester, 1681–1728, JS's beloved friend 'Stella': and Addison, V. 235; — his appreciation, V. 229; and St. George Ashe, V. 233; *Bon Mots de Stella*, V. 237–8; — praised, V. 229; — publication, V. xxvi; and Peter Brown, V. 233; kills burglar, V. 229–30; JS's character of her, V. xxv–xxvi, 227–36; charity, V. 233; conversation, V. 230, 233–5; death (28 Jan. 1728), V. xxv, 227; and Mrs. Dingley, V. 227; estate, V. 228; family, V. 227; 'a little too fat', V. 227; finances, V. 228, 231–3; funeral, V. xxvi; and gifts, V. 233; health, V. 228, 231, 232; — JS distressed by (1727), V. 204, 207; her hospitality, V. 232, 233; illness (1727), V. xiii; XII. ix; — last illness, V. xxv; moves to Ireland (1701), V. 228; love for Ireland, V. 235–6; and Charles Jervas, V. 237; and Thomas Lindsay, V. 233; and William Lloyd, V. 233; her memory, V. 228, 231; and JS's *Miscellanies in Prose and Verse*, II. xxxviii; Ormonde

esteems her, V. 230; and Tobias Pullein, V. 233; at Quilca (1725), V. xxix, 219–21; her recipe for improving stale beer, V. 203; her servants love her, V. 229; and Thomas Sheridan, V. 237; — advises him on expenses, V. xxix, 222; bequest to Dr. Steevens' Hospital, V. 236; **and JS** — correspondence, V. 208, XII. xxxiv; — and *Enquiry into the Behaviour of the Queen's Last Ministry*, VIII. 215–16; — he unable to attend her funeral, V. 229; — *Holyhead Journal* written to her, V. xxv, 201–8; —— *see also* JOURNAL TO STELLA; — his poems to, V. xxvi; — at Quilca (1725), V. xxix; — and his views on language, II. xxxiii; and Sir William Temple ('a person'), V. 228; and follies of other women, V. 230; knows few other women, V. 235. *See also* ON THE DEATH OF MRS. JOHNSON.

Johnson, Maurice: acknowledgement, XIV. vii; on text of JS's works, XIV. 52.

Johnson, Samuel ('Julian'), 1649–1703, Whig clergyman and pamphleteer: IV. 62.

Johnson, Samuel, 1709–84: on Grimston's *Love in a Hollow Tree*, IV. xxx; and *Merlin, the British Wizard*, II. xxiv, *n.* 2; on JS's *History of the Four Last Years*, VII. ix, xx; on *Tale of a Tub*, I. xxii–xxiii.

'Johnson, Tom': character in *Polite Conversation*, IV. 135.

Johnston family of Scotland: V. 125.

Johnston, Archibald, *c.* 1610–63, styled Lord Warriston; Lord Advocate of Scotland, uncle to Burnet: Burnet and JS on, V. 269, 271.

Johnston, Denis: *In Search of Swift*, censured, V. xxii and *n.* 1.

Johnstoun, or Johnston, James, *c.* 1642–1737, Secretary of State in Scotland under William III; Lord Clerk Register of Scotland, 1704–6: 'treacherous knave', V. 262.

Jonah: and Nineveh, IX. 238.

Jones, master of a packet-boat at Holyhead: V. 205.

Jones, John: X. 76.

Jones, John, *c.* 1664–1715, Dublin schoolmaster: author of *Tripos of Terrae Filius*, at Trinity College, Dublin, 1688 (attributed to JS), I. x.

Jones, Richard Foster: *Ancients and Moderns* (1936), I. xxix, *n.**.

Jones, Thomas: copy of *Gulliver's Travels*, XI. 301.

Jones, Sir William, 1631–82, Attorney-General and M.P.: and Whitshed's dissolving of the grand jury, X. 171; and Temple, I. 271.

Jonson, Ben, *c.* 1573–1637, dramatist and poet: and English poetry, IV. 273; misquotation, *On the Townes Honest Man*, ll. 33–4: XII. 38; *Volpone*, III. 71.

Joris, David: *see* DAVID GEORGE.

Joseph I, Emperor, 1678–1711, Archduke of Austria, King of the Romans, son of Leopold I: and Anne, VII. 58; Charles XII of Sweden to declare for, II. 148; death, VI. 35–6, 51; and

Duke of Savoy, VI. 35–6; and Silesian Protestants ('the footing'), VI. 63; to cede Spain to his brother (1704), VI. 51, *n.**; Spanish campaign of 'the Archduke' (1704), VI. 21; renounces Spanish throne ('his brother'), VI. 167; and War of the Spanish Succession — little regard for allies, VI. 34–5; — fails to fulfil quotas, VI. 33; — reasons for war, VII. 81. *See also* AUSTRIA.

Josephus, Flavius, 37–*c.* 100, Jewish historian: 'free-thinker', IV. 45–6.

Joshua, successor to Moses: and oak trees (*Joshua* xxiv. 26), V. 330.

Journal, poem by JS: on Rochforts, IX. xxvii, xxix.

Journal of a Dublin Lady, poem by JS: and scandalmongers, IX. xxx.

Journal to Stella, by JS: and *Conduct of the Allies*, VI. vii–viii, xiv–xv; on *History of the Four Last Years*, VII. x, xi; compared with *Holyhead Journal*, V. xxv; Williams' edition, IV. v.

Journalier (i.e. changeable or moody): VIII. 65.

Journals of the House of Commons of the Kingdom of Ireland: allusion to, II. xxxii, *n.* 3.

Judah Hanasi, or Jehuda Hannasi, *c.* A.D. 135–201, redactor of the Mishna: I. 41.

Judgment: and age, IV. 243, 244.

Judgment, Day of: I. 243; and the Drapier, X. 81.

Judges: biased, IX. 185; duties, X. 90–2, 157–71; ridiculed in *Tale of a Tub*, I. xxvi, 32 and

n.*, ('the Bench') 34; satirized in *Gulliver's Travels*, XI. 248–50, 317–18. *See also* JUSTICE; LAW.

Juno: and Ixion, I. 247; V. 323.

'Juno', meaning money: I. 32 and *n.**.

Junto or Junta, a group of Whig leaders (Halifax, Orford, Somers, Sunderland, and Wharton): and Anne — await her death (1712), VI. 132; — oppose her, VI. 128, 131–2; atheism ('leaders'), III. 47; caprice, III. 225; VI. 129–30; characters, III. 77; defined, VII. 13 and *n.**; Dissenters their 'adherents and followers', VII. 21; errors in judgment ('a new set'), VI. 75; and *Examiner*, III. xi; and Godolphin ministry, XIV. 7; in *Gulliver's Travels*, XI. 54; new heads (1711), VII. 108; evade laws, III. 139–42; leadership ('half a dozen'), VI. 127, 128, 129, 131; motives, VI. 134; — allegedly would replace monarch, III. 72, 73; will repeal their Occasional Conformity Bill, VII. 21; attempt to ruin Oxford ministry, VI. 77, 128, 131; — misrepresent ministry, VI. 127; oppose peace, VII. 108; plans of, III. 71–3; and the press, III. 136, 221; rise of 'a set of men' (1706 ff.), VI. 43; Somerset 'caressed and flattered by', VII. 13; and Spanish campaign, III. 53; Act of Union and Godolphin ministry, III. 95; Whigs controlled by, VII. 21. *See also* WHIGS, *leaders*.

Jupiter (or Jove): convokes the gods, I. 152–3; and Ixion, V. 323; and oaks, V. 303; Jupiter

Pluvius, god of rain, I. 36 and *n.**; pun upon name, IV. 235; and Wotton, I. 162.

Justice: Astraea has fled, I. 31, 248; XII. 57; Epicurus defines, IX. 247; in Ireland, X. 30-1, 35, 39; and law, XI. 248-50; religious justice, II. 101-2; three wise judges in hell, XII. 57. *See also* JUDGES; LAW.

Justin I, Byzantine emperor, *d.* 527: kills Vitalian, XIV. 29.

Justin Martyr, 2nd century A.D., Christian apologist: Christ and reason, IV. 42; on the Deity, IX. 245.

Juvenal: and Horace, compared, XII. 33; quotations and allusions — I. 49-50: II. 58; — I. 50: VI. 3; — II. 24: III. 142; — IV. 1: VI. 159; — X. 70-1: IV. 76: — XIV. 321: II. 264.

K

'Kabob': on word list of JS, V. 336.

Kaye, F. B., ed., *The Fable of the Bees*, 1924: IX. 116, *n.*

Kearney, John, 1741-1813, Provost of Trinity College, Bishop of Ossory: copy of *Gulliver's Travels*, XI. 301.

Keble, Samuel, *fl.* 1674-c. 1715, London bookseller: and *Representation* of the House of Commons (1711), VII. 235.

Kehl, Fort of, in Baden: VII. 113, 132.

Kemp, Corporal: and William III, V. 163.

Kendal, Ermengarde Melusina, Countess von der Schulenburg, Duchess of, 1667-1743, mistress of George I: her pension, X. 44; and Walpole, XI. xix; supports Walpole in 1721 ('the King's cushions'), XI. 39; and Wood's coins, X. x and *n.* 1.

Kendrick, Roger, verger of St. Patrick's Cathedral, amanuensis for JS: and *History of the Four Last Years*, VII. xviii and *n.* 1; and codicil to JS's will, XIII. 158, 198.

Kent, county of: V. 60, 61; and Sir George Rooke, X. 109.

Kent, Godwin, Earl of, *d.* 1053: daughter marries Edward the Confessor, V. 6; and *Polite Conversation*, IV. 196.

Kent, Henry Grey, 1st Duke of, 1671-1740, Whig, Lord Chamberlain: Macky and JS on, V. 259; gives up his office, VIII. 117-18; probably in error for the Duke of Shrewsbury, IX. 26, *n.*†; 'very short of —', III. 79.

Keppel, Arnold Joost van: *see* ALBEMARLE.

Kerr, Andrew, *d. c.* 1680, a soldier: V. 150.

Key, to *Account of . . . Michy Windybank*, possibly by JS: IX. 311.

Keynes (Kaynes, Cahaines, etc.), William de, *fl.* 1100-41, a knight serving Empress Matilda: seizes Stephen (1141), V. 59.

Kidd, William, *d.* 1701, pirate: V. 265.

Kildare, Bishop of: *see* ELLIS, WELBORE.

Kilkenny School: JS attends, V. 192.

Killaloe, Bishop of: *see* LINDSAY, THOMAS.

Killigrew, Henry, colonel, made lieutenant-colonel of Dragoons in 1710: VI. xxii, 139–40; and Wharton, IV. 249.

Killiecrankie (Perthshire, Scotland), battle of, 1689: V. 173, 175.

Kilmainham, co. Meath, Ireland, near Dublin: X. 183; robbery, IX. 366.

Kilmarnock, near Irvine, Ayrshire, Scotland: V. 145.

Kilmore, co. Armagh, Northern Ireland: and Bishop Evans, XIV. 38.

Kilmore, Bishop of: *see* HORT.

Kilpatrick, Dunbartonshire, Scotland: V. 159.

Kilroot, prebend in the cathedral of Down and Connor; parish of Kilroot in co. Antrim, Ireland: JS appointed, I. xv; — his first living (1695–6), V. 194; — his prejudices against Dissenters confirmed, I. xvi; — resigns, January, 1698, I. xviii; *Tale of a Tub*, probably begun, I. xvi.

Kilsythe: *see* LIVINGSTONE.

Kinard: *see* CALEDON.

King, James, *c.* 1699–1759, vicar of St. Bride's, Dublin; prebendary of Tipper in St. Patrick's Cathedral: and Lord Newtown's legacy, XIII. 158; and JS's will, XIII. 156; — executor, XIII. 200; — witness, XIII. 197.

King, John, *d.* 1679, Covenanter; chaplain to Lady Cardross: V. 132–3, 136–7; captured, V. 136, 143–4.

King, Peter, Lord King of Ockham, 1669–1734, Lord Chancellor: VIII. 40.

King, Thomas, *d.* 1709, nephew of Archbishop King: possibly, one of two 'certain gentlemen', XII. 196.

King, William, 1650–1720, Archbishop of Dublin: badges for the poor, XIII. 172; beloved, II. 282; character, X. 71; — gullible, V. xii; — JS's character of, II. 282; charity, IX. 55; and Drogheda affair, II. 282; and George I, X. xxix–xxx; and Irish manufacture, IX. 18; 'late Archbishop', XII. xxxix, 165; and *Letter to the Archbishop of Dublin, Concerning the Weavers*, XII. 65–71; and Charles McCarthy, V. xii, 87–92; praised, IX. 18; — overpraised, IX. 274; and primacy, V. xii; and *Proclamation against Drapier*, X. xix–xx, 71; and residence of the clergy, XII. 201 and *n.**; *State of the Protestants of Ireland under the Late King James's Government* (1691), II. 282; **and JS**, II. ix; — and JS's academy project, IV. xiii; — cordial terms, 1724, V. xii; — correspondence, II. xxi (1708), xxxii, *n.* 2, xxxiii; IV. xxvi–xxvii; — — JS's letters to (1708), II. xiv–xv; — — letter to JS (1711), III. xxxiv–xxxv; — — letter to JS (1712), VI. xxi–xxii; — and *Drapier's Letters*, V. xii; X. xi–xii, xix–xxi, xxv, xxix–xxx, 71; — and *History of the Four Last Years*, VII. x; — *Humble Representation of the Clergy to*: *see* HUMBLE REPRESENTATION; — and *Letter from a Member of the House of Commons in Ireland . . . Concerning the Sacramental Test,*

II. xxiii; — and *Proposal for the Universal Use of Irish Manufacture*, XII. 121; — and primacy, V. xii; — relations strained, IX. 117; — messenger for Trueman and Layfield, XII. 75; — opposition to Wood's coins, V. xii; X. xi–xii, xix–xxi, xxv, xxix–xxx, 71; visitation of 1712, V. 89.

King, William, 1663–1712, student (i.e., fellow) of Christ Church: on *Tale of a Tub* (among 'Treatises'), I. 1; *Some Remarks on the Tale of a Tub* (1704), on authorship of *Tale*, I. xxviii; JS on, I. 5.

King, William, 1685–1763, Principal of St. Mary Hall, Oxford, and friend of JS: at Bath (1741), VII. xvi; and Faulkner, VII. xvi–xvii; Jacobite, VII. xiv; and JS's *Directions to Servants*, XIII. viii, xxi; and JS's *Enquiry into the Behaviour of the Queen's Last Ministry*, VIII. xxxviii, 216; and JS's *History of the Four Last Years*, VII. xiii–xvi; and JS's hospital, VII. xxiii; and *Polite Conversation*, VII. xiii and *n.* 1.

Kings: addresses no sign of popularity, V. 107; choice of advisers, IX. 225; and balance of power (with nobles and commons), I. 195–203, 226–7, 230–1, 235–6; II. 14–19; V. 36–8; XI. 138; beggarly kind, XI. 247; belligerent, V. 288; and exorbitancies of church, V. 17–18; no judgment in church affairs, XIV. 30; cruelty, XI. 205; — and mercy, XI. 69, 70, 72–3; — mercy on a coin, XI. 216; — George I not merciful, V. 254;

— Stephen not cruel enough, V. 51; kings dine alone, V. 206; duties, IX. 144, 229–30; badly educated, IX. 142–3, 229; good king exemplified, XI. 135–6; Henry VIII, 'a dog, a true king', V. 247; ingratitude, XI. 54; subject to law, X. 55; 'seldom get their meat hot', XI. 109; ministers deceive, V. 116–17; X. 5; subject to all the misfortunes of other men save casualty, V. 24; obeisance, XI. 204–5; oppression and allegiance, V. 252; IX. 228–31; republic may be better, XII. 278; William II uniquely trustworthy, V. 25; untrustworthy, XI. 77; — Stephen, V. 51; like war, V. 288; XI. 245–6; 'word of a king' ridiculed, V. 295, 300–1, 308. *See also* MONARCHY; DIVINE RIGHT.

King's Bench, court of: and Sparta, I. 223.

King's evil, i.e., scrofula: and Edward the Confessor, V. 6.

King's Head Tavern: XII. 160.

King's Library, British Museum, London: acknowledgement, facing II. 171. *See also* ROYAL LIBRARY.

Kingstown, now Dun Laoghaire, port of Dublin: manuscript of JS's *History of the Four Last Years*, VII. xxv.

Kirk: *see* CHURCH OF SCOTLAND.

Kirkubry: *see* KIRKCUDBRIGHT.

Kirkcudbright, port at the mouth of the river Dee, south Scotland: and John King, V. 137.

Kirkwood, Episcopal clergyman of Galloway: V. 178.

Kirleus, Mrs. Mary: London quack, II. 153 and *n.**.

Kit-Cat Club: IV. xviii, 28; alleged atheism, VI. 151; and Anne Long, V. 197–8; 'profaneness and immorality', VI. 152; and JS's *Conduct of the Allies*, VI. ix. *See also* LETTER OF THANKS.

Kitchen: as cook's dressing room, XIII. 31; servants' rendezvous, XIII. 11.

Knocke, Fort of, in Reninge, near Loo, Flanders: and Barrier Treaty, VI. 101, 109.

Knockgray (near Carsphairn, Kirkcudbrightshire, Scotland), Laird of: V. 137.

Knox, John, *c.* 1513–72, Scottish reformer: 'knocking Jack', I. 89 and *n.* 11.

Knox, John: patent to coin money, X. 41, 197, 199, *n.* 2; — contrasted with Wood's, X. 30, 33, 37, 42–3, 56.

Koran, or Alcoran: and Christ's divinity, IX. 262; and freethinkers, IV. 32.

L

L., L.: *see* PEMBROKE.

Labia latrantia (barking mouths): IX. 270.

La Bruyère, Jean de, 1645–96, French moralist: *Caractères* (1688), I. 17; invents words, IV. 8.

Lacedæmon: *see* SPARTA.

Lacus lucrinus: *see* LUCRINUS.

Ladder: political ambition, I. 34–8; political pamphlets, I. 37 and *n.*†.

Ladies Library: *see* STEELE.

Lady's Dressing-Room, poem by JS: defended, V. 337–40.

Laelius, Gaius, *b.c.* 186 B.C., Roman statesman and general, friend of Scipio Aemilianus: XII. 161–2.

Lagado, metropolis of Balnibarbi, in *Gulliver's Travels*, Part III, possibly modelled on London: XI. 162; academy: *see* ACADEMY OF LAGADO; description, XI. 174–5; map, XI. 169.

Lamachus, *d.* 414 B.C., Athenian general: and Alcibiades, I. 207.

Lambert, Sir Multon, or Malton, *d.* 1758, gentleman usher of the black rod, Ireland: and Faulkner's release, XIII. 205.

Lambert, Ralph, *c.* 1666–1732, chaplain to Earl of Wharton, Bishop of Dromore (1717), Bishop of Meath (1727): 'the Lieutenant's chaplain', VIII. 121; 'one of them', II. 284; and Wharton, II. xxi; and JS, II. xxiii, xxiv.

Lambeth Palace (in Lambeth, on the right bank of the Thames, across from Westminster), residence of Archbishop of Canterbury: IV. 81.

Lambin, Denys, 1516–72, French scholar: I. 44, *n.*†.

Lanark ('Lanerick'), in central Lanarkshire, Scotland: Covenanters and Creichton, V. 137, 144, 151, 153.

Lancaster, House of: VI. 9.

Lancaster, Earl of: *see* HENRY.

Lancastershire, England: dialect, IV. 187.

Land: English, low rents, IX. 49;

values, and depreciation of money, IX. 47. *See also* IRELAND, *land*.

Land, Henry, sexton of St. Patrick's: JS's houses, XIII. 153; codicil to JS's will, XIII. 199.

Land steward: in *Directions to Servants*, XIII. 51.

Land tax: VI. 48, 54, 56, 57; enacted (1711), VII. 18; must continue (1711), VI. 54–5; and national income, VI. 18.

Landa, Louis: acknowledgement, XIV. vii; introduction to JS's sermons, IX. 97–137; — editor, XIV. 51, 54; introduction to volume IV, IV. ix–xxviii.

Landau, in the Palatinate, Germany: France to give up, VI. 38; VII. 113, 132.

Landed interests: and bishops' lands, XII. 210; Dublin houses, XII. 135; and education, IV. 227, 228; XII. 46–53, 135; and French, V. 6; and George I, VIII. 173, 218; determine government, IV. 245; in Ireland, and copper coins, XII. 100; — and Irish cloth, XII. 69–70; basis of law, X. 134; London homes, XII. 134; opposed to moneyed men, VII. 70; IX. 32; — opposed to 'men at ease', VI. 59; — ruined by them, III. 68; VI. 53; 'most to be depended upon', VIII. 48; lose power, III. 5; and Qualification Bill (1710), III. 169–70; JS's views attacked, VI. xi; — and his *Conduct of the Allies*, VI. ix; and Tories, VI. 126; — mostly Tory, III. 66; and War of the Spanish Success-

ion, VI. 10; — bear burden of, VI. 56, 59; — 'destroying' them, VI. 59; — funds for, VI. 56; — desire peace, VI. 126–7; and Whigs, III. 12, 124–5; — decay, VI. 42; — oppose, VI. 78; — alleged opposition, VI. 5; and William III, VII. 69;

Landed Property Qualification Bill: *see* QUALIFICATION BILL.

Landlords, Irish: lay and clerical, IX. 54; — dishonest, IX. 59; oppressive, IX. 129, 201; XII. 81, 116–18, 133; exorbitant rents, IX. 21; XIII. 176; tenants oppressed, IX. 21, 201; XII. 11; — and *Modest Proposal*, XII. 112.

Landrecies, Nord, France: and Ormonde, VII. 140.

Land's End, Cornwall: V. 81.

Lanerick: *see* LANARK.

Lanfranc, *c.* 1005–89, Archbishop of Canterbury: V. 14–15, 241; and William II, V. 13, 14–15.

'Langden', anagram of 'England': XI. 191.

'Langro Dehul san', Lilliputian orator's phrase: XI. 23.

Langston, Francis, *d.* 1723, English general: III. 232.

Language: IV. xl; affectation ruins, IX. 68; Chinese resists resolution into alphabet, XI. 226; in Dublin, XII. xxxiv, 218–20; reasons for change, IV. 7–9; English corrupted, II. 174–7; esoteric language, legal jargon, XI. 250; fixation, IV. 9; flux, XI. 213; 'Gothick' monosyllables, II. 175; Irish, XII. 89; Irishisms, IV. xxxix, 278–84, 302; London, 'a sort of jabber', XI. 8; new fangledness, XI. 7;

obscure words, IX. 65; philo-sophical or universal language satirized, XI. 185–6; proposals for correction, IV. x–xvi, 5–21; — proposals attacked, IV. xii, xiii–xiv; — previous proposals, IV. xiv; purity, IV. xi; sailors and merchants multilingual, XI. 55; scholars neglect, IX. 65; style and propriety, II. xxxiii–xxxiv; IX. 65–8; universal, XI. 185–6; vocabulary related to wants and passions, XI. 242, 244. *See also* CONVERSATION; PRO-POSAL FOR CORRECTING, IM-PROVING AND ASCERTAINING THE ENGLISH TONGUE.

Langueveny: *see* LLANGEFNI.

Lansdowne, William Petty, 1st Marquis of: *see* SHELBURNE.

'Lap', old Laputan word meaning 'high', or 'the dancing of the sunbeams on the sea': XI. 162.

Lapland: and Ireland, XIII. 112; compared to Ireland, XII. 10; Laplanders, I. 100; — and Irish, XII. 116.

Laputa, the flying island in *Gulliver's Travels*, Part III, sometimes representing England, sometimes the court of George I: XI. 203, 293; astronomical attainments, XI. 170–1; peculiar customs, XI. 159, 161, 162, 163; description, XI. 156–7, 167–80; rescues Gulliver, XI. 156–7; methods of enforcing the king's authority, XI. 171–2; Lindalino rebels, XI. 309–10; means of locomotion, XI. 167–70; map, XI. 152, 169; preoccupation with mathematics and music, XI. 160, 161, 163–4, 166, 173,

176; description of the people, XI. 159–60; — disputatious and uneasy, XI. 164–5; characteristics of women, XI. 165–6.

Laracor, vicarage of, near Trim, co. Meath, Ireland: JS presented to (1700), V. 195; — threatens flight to (1708), II. xxi; — his will, and the poor, XIII. 153; — his will, and vicars of, XIII. 152.

Larks: as food, XI. 24, 106.

La Rochefoucauld, François, duc de, 1613–80: *Maximes*, admired by JS, I. xxxv; — and JS's *Thoughts*, I. xxxv.

Last Farewell of Ebenezor Elliston to This Transitory World (1722), by JS: **IX. 365–7**; publication, IX. xxi; textual notes, IX. 371, 379.

Last Speech and Dying Words of Ebenezor Elliston (1722), by JS: **IX. 35–41**; background, IX. xxi; publication, XIV. 55; reception, IX. xxi, 37, *n.*; textual notes, IX. 371; XIV. 55.

Last Speech and Dying Words of the Bank of Ireland (1721), probably by JS: **IX. 306–7**; authorship, IX. xxi; background, IX. xvi–xvii, xix–xxi; textual note, IX. 378.

Last Will and Testament of Isaac Bickerstaff, Esq.: title-page fac-simile, II. 273.

Last Will and Testament of Jona-than Swift: *see* WILL OF JS.

Lati: *see* LETI.

Latimer, Hugh, *c.* 1485–1555, Protestant martyr: oaths, IX. 271.

Latin language: and Sir Arthur Acheson, XII. 167; and Bicker-

staff, II. 150; language of early
Britain, V. 5; and Carteret, XII.
154; and the Drapier, X. ix, 82;
and English language, IV. xiv–
xv, xxxviii; — contractions, IV.
113; — lacks contractions, II.
175; — derived from English,
IV. 231–9; and Eugenio, XII.
44; and freethinkers, IV. 37; and
linguistic change, IV. 8, 14, 15,
18; and modern curricula, XII.
48, 49; never pure in England,
IV. 6–7; and physicians, IV.
271–2; skipped by readers, I. 82;
JS comments in, V. 243; XIV.
15–35; language of Vulgate, I.
54 and n.†

Latino-Angli (JS's language
game): and *Polite Conversation,*
IV. 276–7.

Laud, William, 1573–1645, Archbishop of Canterbury: Burnet
and JS on, V. 267–8; his merit,
XII. 39.

Lauderdale, Elizabeth (*née*
Murray), *suo jure* Countess of
Dysart, and Duchess of, *c.*
1628–98: and Cromwell, V. 272.

Lauderdale, John Maitland, Duke
of, 1616–82: Burnet and JS on,
V. 276.

Laundress: in *Directions to Servants,*
XIII. 64.

Laurcalco, a character in *Don
Quixote* (I. xviii), giant lord of
the Silver Bridge: I. 124.

Laurelmen: XII. 169.

Law and justice: abuses, I. 3; and
weak arguing, V. 279; and
balance of power, I. 195–236;
interpreting, and the Bible, IV.
248; and Church of England,
II. 78–9; circumvention of, III.

136–42; and clergy, II. 76–8;
common law and Edward the
Confessor, V. 6; too complex,
IV. 246; complexities absurd,
XI. 136; and conscience, IX.
157; defined (will of majority
of those who own land), X.
134; delays, V. 82; divine law
and civil law, II. 106; divine
law and laws of nature compared, II. 77; and divine right of
clergy, II. 81–3, 85–7, 92; XII.
57; in England and Ireland,
compared, X. 30–1, 35, 39, 104–
5; and envy, XII. 39; frauds
plausibly defended, V. 111–12;
human and divine, II. 75; in
Ireland, XII. 124; and Irish
dependency, X. 86–94; — and
Irish independence, XII. 6,
8, 9; — English, forced on
Ireland, IX. 6; a rare judge who
advises against confessing, V.
278; judges corrupted, II. 55;
— incompetent, XI. 249–50,
317–8; — and Test Act, XII.
245; packed juries, V. 280;
and landed gentry, X. 134;
lawyers, I. 244; — they consti-
tute 'a confederacy of injustice',
XI. 248–51; — they misdirect
government, II. 23; lawfulness
should be rewarded, XI. 59; and
legal interpretations, X. 109–10;
limits operation of conscience,
IX. 263; lords ill-equipped to
judge, XI. 128, 129; and maxims
of state, XII. 131; national and
divine law, XII. 244; and
nobility, XI. 128, 129; often
powerless, II. 75–6; use of precedents attacked, X. 39–40; precedents perpetuate injustice, XI.

249, 317; determined by property owners, IV. 245; and reason, IV. 213; and religion, II. 74–5; and satire, XII. 33; satirized, XI. 249–50, 261, 315–18; — 'the Bar', I. 34; — 'Inns of Court', I. 31; — 'Talents', I. 111–12; slow processes of, XI. 250; summarized, XI. 130; and tyranny, I. 250; compared with Yahoo squabbles, XI. 261. *See also* JUDGES; JUSTICE.

Laws for the Dean's Servants (1733), by JS: **XIII. 161-2**; textual notes, XIII. 224.

Laws of the Twelve Tables (Roman legal code, *c.* 450 B.C.): I. 215.

'Layfield, Patrick', pseudonym for a writer of *Letter from Some Farmers . . . Removing to the British Plantations* (1729): one of the 'gentleman', XII. 75–81; JS answers, XII. 85–90.

Leach, Dryden, London printer, JS's cousin: prints Harrison's *Tatler*, II. xxxv.

Leadenhall, market in the City of London: I. 73.

League: *see* LIGUE.

Leah (*Genesis* xxix–xxx): and Baronius, XIV. 17.

Learned Comment Upon Dr. Hare's Excellent Sermon Preach'd Before the D[uke] of Marlborough, on the Surrender of Bouchain, partly by JS: III. 263–72; authorship, III. xxxiii–xxxiv; date, XIV. 51; textual note, III. 279.

Learning: abuses in, I. 1–2 and *passim*; and poetry, IX. 331–4; summaries valuable, IX. 334. *See also* EDUCATION; PEDANTRY.

Le Blanc, Vincent, 1554–1640: *Les Voyages fameux*, XI. xiv–xv.

Lechmere, Nicholas, Lord Lechmere of Evesham, 1675–1732, Whig lawyer and statesman: III. 71; and political sermons, VIII. 40.

Le Clerc, Jean, 1657–1736, Swiss theologian: and Bickerstaff, II. 160–1.

Lectures upon a Dissection of Human Nature, imaginary treatise by the author of *A Tale of a Tub*: I. xl.

Leczinski: *see* STANISLAUS.

Leda: pun upon name, IV. 235.

Lee, Jemmy: *see* LEIGH.

Lee, Nathaniel, *c.* 1653–92, poet: pun upon name, IV. 274.

Leeds, Thomas Osborne, Duke of, 1632–1712, statesman: his education, XII. 47.

Leeson, Joseph, *d.* 1741, brewer in Dublin, speculator in houses: XII. 135 and *n.**, 310.

Leeward Islands, West Indies: XI. 221.

LeFanu, Thomas Philip, *b.* 1858: *Catalogue of Dean Swift's Library in 1715*, V. xxxi, *n.* 1.

LeFanu, William: acknowledgement, XII. v, xxxvi, *n.* 1.

Leibniz, Gottfried Wilhelm von, 1646–1716, German philosopher: and Bickerstaff, II. 160.

Leicester, England: V. 14; X. 47; JS visits (*c.* 1688), I. x.

Leicester Fields, London: Sir A. Fountaine's house there, V. xxiii; and Newton, IV. 122; scene of anecdote, I. 28.

Leicester House, London, seat of George II's court as Prince of

Wales: Countess of Suffolk the favourite, V. 213; JS visits, V. xxvii.

Leicester, Robert Dudley, Earl of, *c.* 1532–88: favourite of Elizabeth, V. 117.

Leigh, Jemmy, Westmeath landlord: 'Gemelli', IV. 257.

Leighton, Robert, 1611–84, Archbishop of Glasgow: and Act of Supremacy in Scotland, V. 274; killed by Burnet's bringing him to London, V. 282.

Lelius: *see* LAELIUS.

'Lelop - Aw', i.e., Walpole, minister of 'Japan': V. 103.

Le Mans, Sarthe, France: Hélias de la Flèche besieges (1099), V. 23–4.

Lent: and birth-rate, XII. 112.

Leo the Great, St., Pope, *d.* 461: and Attila, XIV. 23; and Easter controversy, XIV. 23; miraculous letter, XIV. 21.

Leo X, 1475–1520, Pope: and Francis I, IV. 71, 72.

Leo, Terentius: *see* CULLEO.

Leontius, A.D. *c.* 485–*c.* 543, theologian: and Gregory the Great, XIV. 33; stupid liar, XIV. 33.

Leopold I, Emperor, 1640–1705, father of Joseph: suppresses Hungary (1704–5), VI. 34; misjudges Spanish allegiance, VI. 48; — (1704), VI. 21; and Spanish throne, VI. 13; — to cede Spain to son Charles (1704), VI. 13, 51, *n.**; in War of the Spanish Succession, VI. 33.

Lepidus, Marcus Aemilius, *d.* 13 B.C., Roman triumvir: V. 85; 'the last triumvirate', VI. 80.

'Lero, lero, lilibulero' (refrain of song 'Lilliburlero'): V. 289.

Le Sac, Mr., a dancing master (possibly in error for 'Isaac'): XII. 50.

Leslie, Charles, 1650–1722, journalist, non-juror: III. 115; VIII. 91; *The Case of the Regale and the Pontificat* (1700), II. 74; *The Case Stated between the Church of Rome and the Church of England* (1713), IV. 79; pamphlets against Dissenters, I. xxii; *A Letter from a Gentleman in Scotland to His Friend in England, against the Sacramental Test* (1708), condemned by Commons ('a paper'), 1710, III. 55; — reply to, II. xl, *n.* 1; denounce religious moderation, II. 13; praised, II. 87; *Proposal for an Union with the Gallican Church*, IV. 79, 84; and *The Rehearsall*, periodical (1704–9), III. xii, 13–14; censured by JS, II. xvii; JS's contempt for, I. xxii; JS criticizes, IV. 79–80; attacks Tindal, II. xviii, *n.* 2.

Leslie, David: *see* NEWARK.

Leslie, John, 1571–1671, Bishop of Clogher: his son, IV. 79.

Lesmahagow, Lanarkshire, Scotland: V. 154, 157.

L'Estrange, Sir Roger, 1616–1704, Tory journalist: Burnet and JS on, V. 279; frequency of publication, I. 116; Moderns led by, I. 152; parodied in *Tale of a Tub*, I. xxiv, 3, 42 and *n.*†.

Letcombe Bassett, Berkshire: JS at (1714), VII. xii, 181.

Leti, or Lati, Gregorio, 1630–1701, writer and traveller: X. 110.

Letter from a Friend to the Right Honourable Chief Justice Whitshed: see DRAPIER'S LETTERS.

Letter from a Gentleman in Scotland to his Friend in England against the Sacramental Test, reply to, not by JS: II. xl, *n.* 1.

Letter from a Lady in Town to Her Friend in the Country, concerning the Bank, probably by JS (1721): IX. **299-305**; background, IX. xvi–xvii, xix–xxi; textual notes, IX. 378.

Letter from a Lay-Patron to a Gentleman, Designing for Holy Orders, by JS: see LETTER TO A YOUNG GENTLEMAN.

Letter from a Member of the House of Commons in Ireland . . . Concerning the Sacramental Test (published in December, 1708) by JS, **II. 109-25**; **Advertisement** (1711), by JS, **XIV. 2**; — authorship, XIV. xi; — and text, II. xxxix, 284; — textual note, XIV. 45; analysis, II. xxi–xxiv, xxxix; IX. ix; XII. xl; background, II. ix, xiv–xv, xvi, xxi; date, XIV. 51; editions, II. xv, xxiii, xxxix, 281; Godolphin ministry turned against JS, XIV. 2; publication, II. xix–xx, xxi; VIII. 121, 122; XII. xl; style, II. xxii, xxiii; textual notes, II. 281-4; title-page facsimile, II. 109; attack on Whigs, XIV. 2.

Letter from Dr. Swift to Mr. Pope, by JS (10 January 1721): **IX. 23-34**; background, IX. xii–xv, xvi; editions, IX. xii, 370; textual notes, IX. 370-1.

Letter from Some Farmers . . .

Removing to the British Plantations: JS answers, XII. 75-81; JS orders printing of, XII. 75.

Letter from the Grand Mistress of the Female Free-Masons (1724), attributed to JS: V. 323-33; note on attribution and text, V. 358.

Letter from the Pretender, to a Whig-Lord (1712), by JS: **VI. 145-6**; background, VI. xxii; textual notes, VI. 211.

Letter of Advice to a Young Poet, not by JS: IX. 325-45; authorship, xxiv–xxvii; textual notes, IX. 378; title-page facsimile, IX. 325.

Letter of Thanks from My Lord Wharton to the Lord Bishop of S. Asaph, in the Name of the Kit-Cat Club (1712), by JS: **VI. 147-55**; background, VI. xviii; editions, VI. 212; publication, VI. xix; style, VI. xviii–xix; textual notes, VI. 212; title-page facsimile, VI. 147, 149.

Letter on Maculla's Project about Halfpence and a New One Proposed (written 1729), by JS: **XII. 93-105**; analysis, XII. xviii; authorship, XII. xvi; background, XII. xviii; composition, XII. xvi, xvii–xviii, 93, 97, *n.**; MS, XII. xvi, xviii, 332; textual notes, XII. 332-4.

Letter to a Friend: see MECHANICAL OPERATION OF THE SPIRIT.

Letter to a Member of Parliament Concerning the Free British Fisheries: see LETTER TO FRANCIS GRANT ESQ; ON THE HERRING FISHERY.

Letter to a Member of Parliament in Ireland, upon the

Chusing a New Speaker There (dated 1708 but written in 1710), by JS: **II. 129-35**; background, II. ix, xxxii–xxxiii; composition, II. xxxii, 129, 285; textual notes, II. 285–6.

Letter to a Member of Parliament Touching the Late Intended Bank: IX. 321.

Letter to a Young Clergyman: see LETTER TO A YOUNG GENTLE-MAN.

Letter to a Young Gentleman, Lately Enter'd into Holy Orders (1720), by JS: **IX. 61-81**; analysis, IX. xxii–xxiv, 131; and classical morality, IX. 111; style, IX. xxiv; and JS's views on sermons, IX. 99; and *Tatler*, No. 230, II. xxxiii–xxxiv; textual notes, IX. 372–3; and theological controversy, IX. 108; title-page facsimiles, IX. xxiii, 61.

Letter to a Young Lady, on Her Marriage (written in 1723), by JS: **IX. 83-94**; addressee, IX. xxvii; analysis, IX. xxvii, xxix–xxx; composition, IX. xxvii, xxx, 85; editions, IX. xxvii, 373; MS, IX. xxvii; MS facsimiles, IX. xxviii, 83; textual notes, IX. 373–5.

Letter to Francis Grant Esq; on the Herring Fishery (written in 1734), by JS: **XIII. 111-3**; background, XIII. xxx–xxxiii; textual notes, XIII. 222. *See also* GRANT.

Letter to Henry Maxwell, Esq; Plainly Shewing the Great Danger that the Kingdom has Escaped, and the Great Inconveniences, that must of Necessity Have Happen'd, if a Bank Had Been Establish'd in the Kingdom: IX. 321.

Letter to Isaac Bickerstaff, Esq; Occasion'd by the Letter to the Examiner: III. xi–xii.

Letter to Lord Chancellor Midleton: see DRAPIER'S LETTERS.

Letter to Mr. Harding the Printer: see DRAPIER'S LETTERS.

Letter to the Archbishop of Dublin, Concerning the Weavers (written in 1729), by JS: **XII. 65-71**; composition, XII. xvi, xvii; erratum, XIV. 57; MS, XII. xvi, 329; publication, XII. xvi–xvii; textual notes, XII. 329–30.

Letter to the Gentlemen of the Landed Interest in Ireland, Relating to a Bank: IX. 320.

Letter to the Honourable the Society of the Governor ... for the New Plantation in Ulster (1739), by JS, on behalf of William Dunkin: **XIII. 189**; background, XIII. xliii; textual note, XIII. 225.

Letter to the King at Arms. From a Reputed Esquire, One of the Subscribers to the Bank (1721), by JS: **IX. 291-3**; background, IX. xvi–xvii, xix–xxi; textual note, IX. 378.

Letter to the Lord Chancellor Midleton: see DRAPIER'S LETTERS.

Letter to the October Club: see SOME ADVICE.

Letter to the Printer, of *Some Thoughts on the Tillage of Ireland* (1737), by JS: **XIII. 143**; analysis, XIII. xl–xli; textual notes, XIII. 223.

Letter to the Reverend Mr. Dean

Swift, Occasion'd by a Satire Said to be Written by Him (1719): IX. xiii, *n.* 2.

Letter to the Right Honourable the Lord Viscount Molesworth: *see* DRAPIER'S LETTERS.

Letter to the Right Worshipful the Mayor . . . of the City of Corke (1737), by JS: **XIII. 190-1**; background, XIII. xxxix; effect, XIII. 190, *n.* 2; textual notes, XIII. 225.

Letter to the Seven Lords of the Committee, Appointed to Examine Gregg: III. xxx. 243–58; textual note, III. 279.

Letter to the Shop-keepers: *see* DRAPIER'S LETTERS.

Letter to the Whole People of Ireland: *see* DRAPIER'S LETTERS.

Letter to the Writer of the Occasional Paper (1727), by JS: **V. 93-8**; and Bolingbroke, V. xii–xiv; composition, V. x, xii–xiii; textual note, V. 350.

Letters, Poems, and Tales . . . Passed between Several Persons of Distinction (1718), by JS and others: published by Edmund Curll, V. xxiii, 356.

Letters to the King . . . and Other Persons: *see* TEMPLE.

Letters Written by Sir W. Temple . . . and Other Ministers of State: *see* TEMPLE.

Levant, the eastern Mediterranean: XI. 19, 153.

Levi, Henry: *see* LEWIS.

Levinge, Sir Richard, 1656–1724, Irish statesman and judge: III. 239; *A Relation of Several Facts* (about Wharton), possibly by Levinge, III. 232–40.

Levingstone, Sir Thomas: *see* TEVIOT.

Lewis, Erasmus, 1670–1754, statesman, friend of JS: Anne's letter to the Emperor, III. 191; and *Daily Courant*, VI. 176–7; Dartmouth's secretary, VI. 173, 200; and Charles Ford, VI. 174–5; *Refutation of Falsehoods Against*, by JS: *see* EXAMINER, *JS's contributions*, 2 Feb. 1713; and JS — Lewis called '*mon ami prudent*', VII. xv; — and Barrier Treaty, VI. xiv; — correspondence, VII. 181, 182; — — Jan. 1715, VIII. xxxi; — — (1717), VIII. xxxv; — and publication of *Gulliver's Travels* (1726), XI. xxi–xxii; — *History of the Four Last Years*, VII. xi, xiv–xvii; — urges JS's return to London (1713), VIII. x; JS to toast (*c.* 1727), V. 335.

Lewis, or Levi, Henry, a Hamburg merchant: and Erasmus Lewis, VI. 174–8; mistaken for Erasmus Lewis, VI. xxvi–xxvii, 200.

Lexington, Robert Sutton, 2nd Lord, 1662–1723, diplomat: and commercial treaty with Spain, VII. 155; Macky and JS on, V. 259; in Madrid, VII. 166.

Leyden, Holland: John of: *see* JOHN; University, and Gulliver, XI. 19, 217.

'Lhnuwnh', Houyhnhnm for 'retire to his first mother' (*i.e.*, die): XI. 274–5.

A Libel on D[octor] D[elany]. And a Certain Great Lord [*i.e.*, Carteret], poem by JS: analysis, XII. xxiv–xxvii; and Hutcheson, XII. 156.

Libertas et natale solum, Whitshed's motto: X. xxii–xxiii, 101; XII. 8 and *n.**.

Liberty: defined, X. 134–5; a history of, III. 102–3; and law, IX. 32.

Liberty of conscience: and abolition of Christianity, II. 28; and action, II. 102; defined, IX. 263; and Irish Whigs, II. 118; and schools, II. 97; and Tindal, II. 101; Tindal on, II. 191–2.

Library of JS: II. 280; V. v, xxi, *n.* 1, xxxi, *n.* 1; sale, XIII. xi, *n.* 1.

Libya: asses, I. 60.

Lice: in Brobdingnag, XI. 113; Scottish proverb, XII. 195; and tailors, I. 46.

Liège, Belgium: Louis XIV seizes, VI. 12; and Barrier Treaty, VI. 107, 115; bishopric, secured by Hapsburgs, VII. 89; proposed site of peace conference, VII. 37, 39, 54.

Lier (Lierre), near Antwerp, Belgium: and Barrier Treaty, VI. 90, 101, 109, 113.

Lier, Frederick van Reede, Baron of, 1630–1715, Dutch diplomat: VI. 98, 106–9.

Life, on earth: difficulties intentional, IX. 196; despicable, IX. 263; trial, IX. 196.

Life and Adventures of a Shilling: see *Tatler,* No. 247.

Ligue, La (French Roman Catholic political movement directed by Henri de Guise and his brother, *c.* 1575–*c.* 1595): and April Fool's joke, IV. 267.

Lille (or Lisle), Nord, France: and Dutch Barrier, VI. 90, 102, 109,

116, 117; VII. 113; French demand, VII. 152; and Marlborough, VI. 31; and Ormonde VII. 141; XIV. 13.

Lillie, Charles, perfumer, of Beaufort Buildings in the Strand; one of the publishers of the collected *Tatlers:* and Morphew, II. 249–51.

Lillieroot, Nils Eosander, comte de, 1636–1705, Swedish diplomat: VI. 62.

Lilliput, in *Gulliver's Travels,* Part I: XI. 19–80, 293; false accusers punished, XI. 58; acquitted persons recompensed, XI. 58; animals, XI. 57; army, XI. 40, 42; begging unknown, XI. 63; Big-endians, XI. 49–50; war with Blefuscu, XI. 49–50; — would subjugate Blefuscu, XI. 69; Brobdingnag contrasted with, XI. 86–7; burial customs, XI. 57–8; courage, XI. 24, 26; crown, given to Lady Suffolk, V. xxvii; description of, XI. 29; diversions at court, XI. 38–41; employments go to the morally upright, XI. 59;

Emperor — allegorical significance discussed, XI. xviii–xix; — description of, XI. 30–1; — economy, XI. 45; — an equestrian, XI. 30; — governed by Flimnap, XI. 66; — former emperor, XI. 68; — dines with Gulliver, XI. 64; — Gulliver loses his favour, XI. 66; — forbidden to climb on Gulliver, XI. 27; — hears of Gulliver's landing, XI. 26; — orders search of Gulliver, XI. 34–7; — sends for Gulliver, XI. 26–7; —

patronizes learning, XI. 26;
— views military exercises, XI.
40–1; — ministers perform for,
XI. 38–9; — his name, XI. 43;
— and political parties, XI. 48;
— politics, XI. 48; Emperor's
son, politics, XI. 48;
  Empress — vows revenge on
Gulliver, XI. 56; — views military exercises, XI. 40; — and
palace fire, XI. 55–6; fraud
detested, XI. 58; ingenuity, XI.
24–7, 44–5, 63–4; ingratitude a
capital crime, XI. 60; inhabitants age more quickly, XI. 61,
62; law-abiding citizens rewarded, XI. 59; map, XI. 18;
mathematics, XI. 26; royal palace, XI. 46–7, politics, XI. 48;
proportions, XI. 57; religious
conformity and public offices,
XI. 60; religious controversies,
XI. 49–50; keen sight, XI. 57;
and JS's freedom of Dublin, XII.
xxvi; tailoring, XI. 63–4; writing, XI. 57.

Lilly: *see* LILY.

Lily, William, *c.* 1466–1522,
grammarian: and Wagstaff, IV.
113.

Lima, Peru: VI. 22.

'Limber, Charles': character in
Polite Conversation, IV. 167.

Limitation Act, Irish, 1634, for
the preservation of the inheritance, rights and profits of lands
belonging to the church, and
persons ecclesiastical: and
Church of Ireland, IX. 52; encourages importing of English
bishops, IX. 52; still needed,
IX. 57; repeal — advantages, IX.
56; — bishops favour, IX. 51; —

and clerical recruitment, IX. 53;
— end of ecclesiastical benefi-
cence, IX. 55; — effect on
Trinity College, IX. 55.

Lincoln, England: IV. 160; V.
58, 59; surrendered to Stephen,
V. 66; JS visits, 1710, II. xxxii,
n. 2.

Lincoln College, Oxford: II. xviii,
n. 2.

Lincolnshire: and Eugenio, XII.
45.

Lindalino, second city of Balnibarbi, *Gulliver's Travels*, Part III,
probably modelled on Dublin:
interpreted as Ireland, XI. xix;
rebellion of, XI. 309–10.

Lindsay, Robert, *d.* 1743, Justice
of the Common Pleas of Ireland:
'eminent lawyer', X. 114;
'eminent person', X. 48; JS's
executor, XIII. 157, 200; and
JS's will, XIII. 153.

Lindsay, Thomas, *d.* 1724, Bishop
of Killaloe (1696–1713); of
Raphoe (1713–14); Archbishop
of Armagh and Primate of
Ireland (1714–24): one of 'two
bishops', VIII. 122; and Brodrick, II. 117; charity, IX. 55;
death, V. xii; in *Letter from a
Member of the House of Commons in
Ireland . . . Concerning the Sacramental Test*, II. 110, 117; and
Stella, V. 233; possibly, error
for 'Killala', II. xl, *n.* 1; lost
letter from JS, II. xxxviii,
xxxix–xl.

Lindsay, William Lindsay, 2nd
Earl of: *see* CRAWFORD, 18th
Earl.

Lindsey, Dr.: V. 152–3.

Lindsey, Robert Bertie, 4th Earl

and 1st Marquis of, 1660–1723:
Macky and JS on, V. 259.

Linen industry, Irish: improvements, IX. 47; manufacture,
XIII. 97–108; merchants
knaves, XIII. 176; and poets,
IX. 341; and Spain, XIII. 113;
trade, and Spain, XIII. 176;
replaces wool, IX. 8.

'Linger, Sir John', the Derbyshire knight in *Polite Conversation*: IV. xxxii, 116–17, 129–201,
276–7.

Lingua franca, a trader's language: XI. 31.

Linlithgow, George Livingstone,
3rd Earl of, *d.* 1698: V. 129, 140,
145, 151, 159, 163, 164.

Linschoten, Jan Huyghen van,
1563–1611: *Voyages into ye Easte
and West Indies*, XI. xiv.

Lion: fable of the sick, II. 72; and
virgins, dream of, II. 179–83.

Lipsius, Justus, 1547–1606,
Flemish classical scholar: and
pedantry, IV. 216.

Lisle: *see* LILLE.

Lismahego: *see* LESMAHAGOW.

Literary career: JS views, I. 115–
18, 132–5; JS's views on his
own, XII. 22–3; — Drapier's
success, XII. 85.

Literary style: *see* STYLE, LITER-
ARY.

Literature: I. 115–18; ancient and
modern, I. 77–82, 141–65; and
anonymity, VII. 105–6; and
good breeding, IV. 217; cen-
sored, in Ireland, XII. 57–8; and
education, IV. 228; and eloquence, XII. 33; and experience,
II. 187; Horace's advice, IV.
100; of Houyhnhnms, XI. 273–4;

humour and wit, XII. 32–3;
letters, I. 258; French origin of
memoirs, I. 269; modern books
censured, I. 33–43; II. 173–7; —
immorality of modern literature, II. 55–6; and 'musick', XII.
33; poetry as an art, IX. 327–45;
poets and historians, I. 242,
243; posthumous publications,
II. 163–4; preachers need, IX.
63–4, 74; — not light literature,
IX. 67; publishing, IV. 249;
satire, XII. 33–4; textbooks and
morality, XII. 52; too many
books written, IV. 246; tran-
sience of literary achievement,
III. 32; XI. 292; — and linguistic change, IV. 14–15;
universal application, I. 174;
and women, IV. 226–7; IX. 90–
2.

Lithmahegow: *see* LESMAHAGOW.

Little Britain, London: XII.
264.

Littleton, Sir Thomas, *c.* 1647–
1710, Speaker of the House of
Commons in England: and
Speaker of the House, II. 132.

Liturgical music: Dissenters hate,
I. 125; 'whistling', XI. 246.

Liverpool, England: XI. 80.

Livingston, James, Lord Kilsythe and Viscount, 1616–61:
and Creichton, V. 166–75.

Livingston, Thomas: *see* TEVIOT.

Livy (Titus Livius), 59 B.C.–A.D.
17, Roman historian: III. 26;
leads the Ancients' infantry, I.
152; correct text, IV. 33; quotations — III. lv: I. 218; — IV.
i–vi: I. 217; — v. xlvii, 1–5:
IV. 247; — VI. xlii: I. 216; —
'obscurest causes', XXVII. ix. 1:

VIII. 172; — XXVIII. l–lx: I. 218; — *Periochae* lviii: I. 218.

Llandegai, near Bangor, Caernarvonshire, Wales: JS visits tomb of John Williams, V. 202.

Llangefni ('Langueveny'), Anglesey, Wales: JS stops at, V. 202.

Lloyd, Edward, author and publisher: and *Memoirs of the Chevalier de St George* (1712), IV. xxvi.

Lloyd, Owen, *c.* 1664–1743, Dean of Connor: and Wharton, III. 182–4; wife, III. 182–3.

Lloyd, William, *d.* 1716, Bishop of Killala: I. 237; possibly confused with 'Killaloe', II. xl. *n.* 1; friend of Stella, V. 233.

Lob's Pound (*i.e.,* prison): IV. 137.

Locke, John, 1632–1704: constitutional monarchy and *Two Treatises of Government* (1690), IX. 123; — and Steele, VIII. 43; 'dangerous author', X. 86; *Essay concerning Human Understanding*, II. 97; 'idea', II. 80; on innate ideas, II. 97; morality based on religion, IX. 115; *Reasonableness of Christianity* ('other works') disapproved, II. 97; scepticism, IX. 110; style, II. 80; 'tabula rasa', I. 250; and Tindal, II. xviii, *n.* 2, 80, 85, 97.

Locket's, eating house in Charing Cross, London: I. 45.

Lockhart, Lady, wife of Captain Mair: V. 176–7.

Lombard, James, wool merchant, High Street, Dublin: importation of cloth, XIII. xxvii, 168.

Lombard Street, London: and Bickerstaff, II. 204; goldsmith's death predicted, II. 145.

Lomellino, or Lomellina, district of Piedmont, in northern Italy, south of Mortara: Duke of Savoy to have, VI. 13.

London, England: XI. xxi, 19, 97; and esoteric allusions, VII. 2; VIII. 5; and avarice, I. 31; and *Beggar's Opera*, XII. 32; act to build 50 churches in, III. xxv, 157–62, 170, 200; VII. 3; large congregations, II. 61 and *n.**; and conversation, IV. 116–17; and Cromarty, IV. 253; Danes attack it (9th century), V. 5; Dissenters in, XII. xlii; drapers in, XII. 70; and the Drapier, X. ix; and Dublin, 30; election of 1710, III. 66; and English gentry, XII. 134; the great fire (1666), and building, III. 159; and Gulliver's apprenticeship, X. ix; XI. 19; observed by Indian king, II. 264–7; influence on Britain, II. 50, 59; and Lagado, in *Gulliver's Travels*, XI. 174; Leicester Fields — Fountaine's house, V. xxiii; — mountebank, I. 28; literary capital, VII. 2; and Lorbrulgrud, in *Gulliver's Travels*, XI. 99, 112–15; and Matilda the Empress, V. 60–1; parishes, III, 159–60; speech, IV. 11, 281; XI. 7; XII. xxxiv; and St. Albans, XI. 97; affection for Stephen, V. 59, 60; JS arrives in (1703), I. xxi; JS leaves (1727), V. xxiv; three brothers in, I. 45–55.

London Bridge: XI. 91, 99.

London Journal: and Wood's coinage, X. 27.

Londonderry, Ireland: besieged (1689), XII. 270; and William III, V. 264.

Long, Anne, *d.* 1711, friend of JS: death, V. xxiii; VI. xxiii–xxiv; — JS's account, VI. 196; — **JS's memorandum, V. 198;** — textual note, V. 356; papers, V. xxiv; Wharton's lines on, V. 197, *n.**. *See also* DECREE FOR CONCLUDING THE TREATY.

Long, Sir James, Bart., 1682–1729, brother of Anne Long: and sister's death, V. xxiii; VI. xxiii–xxiv, 196.

Long Acre, London: II. 141, *n.**.

Longheads: *see* MACROCEPHALI.

Longinus, Dionysius Cassius, *c.* A.D. 210–273, Greek philosopher: on the Deity, IX. 245.

Longitude: V. 206; Parliamentary award offered for determination of, XI. 210.

Longleat manuscripts: VII. vii, 178.

Lorbrulgrud, 'pride of the universe', capital of Brobdingnag, *Gulliver's Travels*, Part II: described, XI. 111–15; — map, XI. 82; Gulliver taken there and exhibited, XI. 99; militia, XI. 138.

Lord Lieutenant of Ireland: cost of government, IX. 19, 369.

Lord Mayor of London, in *Tale of a Tub*: I. xxv–xxvi, 131 and *n.†*; Lord Mayor of Dublin and *Modest Proposal*, XII. 116.

Lords: *see* HOUSE OF LORDS; NOBILITY.

Lorraine: to be French (1700), VI. 11.

Lorraine, Henri II, duc de Guise

and de, 1614–64: and Roman Catholics of Ireland, XII. 294.

Lorraine, Leopold Joseph, duc de, 1679–1729; interposes for Dutch, VII. 42; and the Pretender, VII. 158; VIII. 67–8.

Lorraine, Paul, *d.* 1719, ordinary of Newgate: and Gregg, III. xxix, 192–3, 196–7; and dying 'Speeches', I. 35.

Lorretto, Chapel of: I. 74 and *n.**.

Lothian, Robert Kerr, 1st Marquis of, 1636–1703, statesman: V. 179.

Lot's wife: IV. 179.

Lotteries: Godolphin's and Oxford's contrasted, VII. 77.

Loughall, co. Armagh, Ireland: JS visits, 1722, XI. xv.

Louis I, King of Spain, 1707–24: Bickerstaff's predictions for ('Prince of Asturias'), II. 145, 215.

Louis VI, 'the Fat', 'the Gross', King of France, *c.* 1081–1137, son of Philip I: V. 21; and Fulk V, V. 42; defeated by Henry I, V. 38–9; marriage of Matilda the Empress and Geoffrey Plantagenet, V. 42; encourages Norman rebellions, V. 41; and William, son of Robert of Normandy, V. 43.

Louis VII, 'the Young', King of France, *c.* 1120–80: and Eleanor of Aquitaine, V. 66–7; and Pope Eugenius III, V. 68; and Henry II, V. 67; and Stephen, V. 69.

Louis XI, King of France, 1423–83: VIII. 77.

Louis XIV, King of France, 1638–1715, 'the most Christian King': III. 215; Anne's cousin,

VII. 48; VIII. 60; castellanies,
VII. 159–60; Charles II refuses
bribe (1678), XIV. 1; death,
expected (1711), VI. 58; — predicted, II. 147, 199; — prediction attacked by Partridge, II.
206; desires Dunkirk, VIII. 10;
will not negotiate with Dutch
(1711), VII. 36; — resents rudeness (1710), VII. 35–6; claim to
English throne, VIII. 54–5; and
The Examiner, III. 58; allegedly
governs Flanders directly (1701),
VI. 12; on Godolphin ministry,
III. 205, 258; goodness and
greatness, IV. 249; past gran-
deur, VI. 61; 'a mighty king', I.
104 and *n*.*; as Orodes, III. 85;
and Oxford ministry, VIII. 58–9;
and pensions, IV. 20; and
people's welfare, III. 213–14,
217; control over Philip V,
slight, VI. 58; — their interests
differ, VIII. 59; and 'Popish
plot', IV. 61; power, VIII. 53;
and Matthew Prior, III. 209–18;
and Duchess of Savoy, VIII. 54;
and Scotland ('great man'), IX.
8; and Spain — might rule it,
VI. 15; — renunciation, VII. 44,
50, 149, 155, 165; — he usurps it,
VII. 81; and Steele, VIII. 9–10;
and Tindal, II. 88; **and Treaty
of Utrecht** — 'bound up' by it,
VII. xxxvi; — would deal
separately with England (1711),
VII. 36; — speech offering
peace (1712), VII. 137; — his
titles disputed, VII. 165; assists
Turks against Austria, III. 129;
peace negotiations (1709–10) in
War of the Spanish Succession,
VII. 22, 32–3; — hopes from,

III. 224; — tyranny an advantage, III. 267; early wars, VI.
61; wealth, III. 213–14; and
Whigs, VIII. 9–10.

Louis XV, King of France, 1710–
74, great-grandson of Louis
XIV: VII. 131; Bickerstaff's predictions for, II. 148, 213; great-
great-grandson of Charles I,
VIII. 54; Dauphin (1711), VIII.
54; death expected (1712), VII.
151; Ireland's 'truest and best
ally', XII. 174; and regent (*i.e.*,
Duke of Orleans), VIII. 169;
and union of France and Spain,
('a child of two years'), VII. 121;
VIII. 169.

Louis de France, the Dauphin ('le
Grand Dauphin'), 1661–1711,
son of Louis XIV: Bickerstaff's
predictions for, II. 146, 169,
204–5, 206; renounces Spain,
VII. 150.

Louse: in Scotch proverb, XII.
195.

Love: brotherly, IX. 171–9; —
taught by God, IX. 179; legacy
of Christ, IX. 171; of neighbour,
IX. 232; passionate love is
irrational, I. 244; — and marriage, I. 244–5; IX. 85–6, 89, 94.

Lovers Quarrel, ballad, story of
Rosamond, called 'Tommy
Potts': I. 41.

Low Church party: Leslie attacks,
I. xxii; and Oxford ministry,
VIII. 166; violent in 1703–4, I.
xxi.

Low Churchmen: and abolition
of Christianity, II. 31; attack
clergy and universities, II. 8;
challenged in *Letter from a
Member of the House of Commons in*

Ireland . . . Concerning the Sacramental Test, II. xxii; JS denies his sympathies toward, II. xiv; support Test Act, II. 131.

Low Countries: *see* DUTCH.

Low Dutch: *see* DUTCH, *language*.

Low heels, political party in *Gulliver's Travels*, Part I, modelled on the Whigs, XI. 48.

Loyalty Defined, poem attributed to Lord Hervey, IV. 120.

'Lubber, Dick', character in *Polite Conversation*: IV. 162.

Lübeck, Germany: V. 100, one of 'two maritime towns'.

Lucan (Marcus Annæus Lucanus), A.D. 39–65, Roman poet: fights for Ancients, I. 158; quotations and allusions — 1. 23: I. 2; — 1. 181–2: III. 4; — IV. 455–6: III. 46; — V. 264–7: VI. 3; — VI. 191–2: X. 105.

Lucas, Charles, 1713–71, physician, 'the Wilkes of Ireland': VII. xx and *n.* 2; esteemed by Johnson, VII. xx; prosecuted (1749), VII. xx, *n.* 2, xxi; on JS's conduct, VII. 172; and JS's *History of the Four Last Years*, VII. xx–xxi, xxviii; — *Advertisement*, VII. 171–7.

Lucas, Robert, Lord, governor of the Tower, turned out by Queen Anne: Macky and JS on, V. 259.

Lucas, Theophilus, *Memoirs of the Lives, Intrigues and Comical Adventures of the Most Famous Gamesters and Celebrated Sharpers* (1714): XIII. xx, *n.* 1.

Lucretius: Creech's translation, IV. 37; insane, I. 105; on the plague at Athens (430 B.C.),

XIV. 33; and religion, IX. 329; JS's copy of, V. xxxi and *n.* 5; 'system of atheism', IV. 37.
Quotations and allusions — 1. 62–79: II. 70; — 1. 141–2: I. 77; — 1. 934: I. 89; — II. 80–224: I. 36; — II. 292: I. 105; — II. 1042–3: I. 193; — III. 938: I. 133; — III. 1057: IV. 19; — IV. 3–5: I. xxxix; — IV. 526–7: I. 36 and *n.**; — IV. 1048: I. 103; — IV. 1055: I. 103; — IV. 1065: I. 103; — V. 94–5: III. 126; — V. 107: I. 95; — V. 107–8: I. 229; — VI. 786–7: I. 61; — VI. 1138–1286: XIV. 33. *See also* CREECH.

Lucrinus, Lacus (Lake Lucrine), Campania, Italy: oysters, IV. 257.

Ludlow, Shropshire: V. 53; — castle, and Stephen, V. 55.

Ludlow, Edmund, *c.* 1617–93, Parliamentary general, regicide: III. 44; *Memoirs*, V. 121; XII. 270; — on Charles II, XII. 265; — Whigs reprint, III. 143.

Luggnagg, island of the Struldbruggs in *Gulliver's Travels*, Part III: XI. 193, 203–17; begging forbidden in, XI. 213; trade with Japan, XI. 215; map, XI. 152.

'Luhimuh', Houyhnhnm name for a sort of wild rat: XI. 266.

Lull (Lully, Lullius), Raimon (Raymundus), *c.* 1235–1315, Catalan mystical philosopher: and free masons, V. 328.

'Lumos Kelmin pesso desmar lon Emposo', Lilliputian for 'swear a peace with him and his kingdom': XI. 33.

Lunatics, JS's hospital for: *see* ST. PATRICK'S HOSPITAL.

Lupercalia: Gelasius suppresses, XIV. 26.

Lupus, St., *c.* 383–479, Bishop of Troyes: Baronius quotes, XIV. 24.

Lustrog, religious prophet of Lilliput, *Gulliver's Travels*, Part I: XI. 49.

Lusus naturæ: XI. 104.

Luther, Martin, 1483–1546: and Calvin's doctrines, VIII. 96; and the Drapier, X. 132; and the English Reformation, IV. 73; and fanaticism, I. 188; model for Martin, in *Tale of a Tub*, I. 7, 84, 280.

Luxembourg: VII. 153, 156.

Lycurgus, 7th–6th centuries B.C., semi-legendary Spartan legislator: V. 36; and balance of power, I. 200.

Lycurgus, *d.* 324 B.C., Athenian orator: II. 94.

'Lyhannh', Houyhnhnms' name for a certain swallow-like bird: XI. 273.

Lyndon, Charles: X. 76.

Lyndsay, Mr., a poet: V. 202.

Lynham, John: robber, IX. 366.

Lyon, John, 1702–90, prebendary of St. Patrick's, manager of JS's affairs in his last years: VII. xxi, *n.* 1; Mrs. Dingley's executor, XIII. xi, *n.* 1; and JS — JS's copy of Burnet's *History of His Own Times*, V. xxxvi; — and *History of the Four Last Years*, VII. xvii–xviii, xx–xxi; — his library, XIII. xi, *n.* 1; — lists manuscripts 'found in the Dean's study', VII. xxi; — and a manuscript, II. xl, *n.* 1; — on JS's sermons, IX. 98; — on *Tale of a Tub*, I. ix; — witness to codicil to will, XIII. 158.

Lys (Lis, or Leie), river of northern France and Belgium, joining the Escaut at Ghent: VII. 142.

Lysander, *d.* 395 B.C., Spartan admiral and diplomat: VIII. 77; and Alcibiades, I. 208; and Athens, I. 198.

Lyttelton, George, 1st Lord, 1709–73: JS presents his *Works* to, XIV. xiv.

M

Macarell (or Macarel), John, Registrar of Barracks: candidate (successful) for M.P. for Dublin, XIII. xxv, 79; made free of Dublin corporations, XIII. xxv; 'honest Gentleman' and placeman, XIII. 84.

Macartney: *see* MACCARTNEY.

McAulay (or M'Aullay, etc.), Alexander, judge of the Consistorial Court of Ireland: and *A Letter to the Printer* [of *Some Thoughts on the Tillage of Ireland*], XIII. 141–3; *Some Reasons against the . . . Modus*, XIII. xxx; JS's opinion of, XIII. xl; JS's will, XIII. 153, 155; — executor, XIII. 157; *Some Thoughts on the Tillage of Ireland* (1737), XIII. xl–xli.

Macaulay, Thomas Babington, 1st Lord, 1800–59: on *History of the Four Last Years*, VII. ix; marginalia in *Dr. Bentley's Dissertations . . . Examin'd*, I. xvii, *n.*†.

McCarthy (or M'Carthy), Charles,

resident of College Green, Dublin: V. 87–92; ruined by fire, V. xii.

Maccartney (or Macartney), George, *c.* 1660–1730, general: III. xiv; Queen Anne's guard ('two or three'), VIII. 155–6; duel with Duke of Hamilton, V. 261; — Hamilton's death, VI. 197–9; — allegedly murders Hamilton, VII. 155.

McClanen, Patrick: condemned to die, XIV. 55.

McClanen, Stephen: condemned to die, XIV. 55.

Macclesfield, Thomas Parker, Earl of, *c.* 1666–1732, Lord Chief Justice, Whig: and Hilkiah Bedford ('Non-juring Clergyman'), VIII. 64–5; and *Conduct of the Allies*, VI. ix, 92; and *Hereditary Right of the Crown of England Asserted*, VIII. 64–5; William Howell and JS on, V. 265; and Sacheverell, VIII. 40; prosecutes Tory supporters (1712), VII. 19; Whiggish hopes (in January 1712), VI. 73; and Wood's coins, X. 29.

MacCormack, a robber: IX. 366.

McCoy, major general: V. 166, 170–1, 173.

McCue, Daniel: on JS's *Last Speech . . . of Ebenezor Elliston*, XIV. 55.

McDonnel family of Scotland: V. 160–1.

McDonnel, Laird of Cappagh near Inverlochie, Scotland: V. 160–1, 170.

Macedonia: III. 41.

MacFadden, Elizabeth: *see* SHERIDAN.

MacFadden, Mrs., Dr. Thomas Sheridan's mother-in-law: V. 217.

Machiavelli, Niccolo di Bernardo, 1469–1577: III. 19, 41, 64–5, 146.

Machines, oratorical: in *Tale of a Tub*, I. 4, 34–9.

McKabe, a soldier: V. 150.

'Mackay, Andrew': father of Andromache, IV. 233–4.

McKenzie, wool merchant, Essex Bridge, Dublin: imports cloth, XIII. 168.

McKenzie, Captain: V. 161.

MacKenzie, Sir George, 1636–91, king's advocate, author: Burnet and JS on, V. 278.

Mackintosh family of Scotland: V. 160–1.

Macky, John, *d.* 1726, author, government agent or spy: *Memoirs of the Secret Services of John Macky, Esq.* (1733), V. xxxiv–xxxv; — **JS's annotations to, V.** 257–62; and Princess Sophia, V. xxxv.

Macleod, Neil, Laird of Assynt, Sutherlandshire, betrayer of Montrose: Howell and JS on ('this false Scot'), V. 263.

Macrocephali ('longheads'): I. 175–6.

Maculla, James: visits JS, XII. xviii. *See also* JS's LETTER ON MACULLA'S PROJECT.

Mad Mullinix and Timothy: *see* INTELLIGENCER No. 8.

Madagascar: XI. 222, 283.

Madagascar, Straits of: XI. 83.

'Maddors', wooden cups: IV. 279, 302.

Madman of Cordova (*Don*

Quixote, Part II, Prologue): X. 114.

Madness, JS's views: I. 102–14; enlarges virtues, XII. 158; and enthusiasm, I. 172–90; hospital for, XIII. 149–52; and maxims of state, XII. 131; and oppression, IX. 18; sometimes a virtue, IX. 18, 271; and visions, IV. 252.

Madox, Thomas, 1666–1727, legal antiquary, historiographer royal: William Howell and JS on, V. 265.

Madrid: VII. 125; and the Inquisition, X. 90.

Magdalen College, Oxford: V. 286; and James II, XII. 270–1; 'one of the universities', II. 9; and William III, II. 9.

Magliabecchi, Antonio, 1633–1714, Italian bibliographer: and Bickerstaff, II. 161.

Magna Carta (1215): III. 114; and balance of power, I. 231; and the Bill for a Modus, XIII. 102; binds even Parliament, V. 279.

Mahomet: *see* MOHAMMED.

'Maiden-head': IV. 233.

Maidenhead, Berkshire: V. 163.

'Maids', in *Directions to Servants*: XIII. 52–63.

Maids of Honour: IV. 108; in Brobdingnag, XI. 119; ridiculed, IV. 254.

Maintenon, Françoise d'Aubigné, marquise de, 1635–1719, second wife of Louis XIV: III. 214, 215, 216, 217.

Mainwaring (or Maynwaring), Arthur, 1668–1712, Auditor of the Imprest, Whig politician and journalist: *The British Academy*,

attacks JS, IV. xiv; *The Medley*, attacks JS, IV. xiii; and Steele, VIII. 6, 7.

Mair, Captain: V. 176.

Majority vote: true meaning, VII. 17.

Malcolm III (Canmore), King of Scotland, *c.* 1031–93: fights William II, V. 16; killed, V. 18; his daughter Matilda (or Edith) marries Henry I, V. 29.

Malcolm IV ('The Maiden'), King of Scotland, *c.* 1141–65: and Henry II, V. 75.

Maldonada (seaport of Balnibarbi; *Gulliver's Travels*, Part III): XI. 203, 204; 'about as large as Portsmouth', XI. 193; map, XI. 169.

Malmesbury, Wiltshire: and King Stephen, V. 68.

Malone, Anthony, 1700–76, Chancellor of the Exchequer of Ireland: and JS's freedom of Cork, XIII. 190, *n.* 1.

Malt Tax: VI. 18, 48, 54, 55, 56, 57.

Malta, Knights of: and free masons, V. 329.

Mamre, Abraham's dwelling place (*Genesis* xiii. 18): oaks and Abraham, V. 330.

Man, Jenny, proprietress of coffee house: VIII. 66.

Manaboleth: and free masons, V. 326, 331.

Mandeville, Bernard, *c.* 1670–1733, author: compared with JS, II. xix; IX. 116.

Manilius, Marcus, Roman poet, contemporary of Augustus: and Solomon, IV. 45.

Mankind, JS's views on: *see* HUMAN NATURE.

Manley, Francis: V. xxxv; acknowledgement, V. v.

Manley, Mary de la Rivière, 1663–1724, writer, daughter of Sir Roger Manley: and the *Examiner*, III. xxvii–xxix; *A Learned Comment Upon Dr. Hare's Excellent Sermon, etc.*, III. xxxiii–xxxiv, 261–72; *A Modest Enquiry into the Reasons of the Joy . . . upon the Spreading of a Report of Her Majesty's Death* (partly by JS), VIII. 183–97; — bibliography, VIII. 232; — composition, VIII. xvi–xvii; — publication, VIII. xvi–xvii, 232.

Manners: art of making people easy, IV. 213, 221; bad manners and vanity, IV. 244–5; in a 'censorious world', I. 243, 245; in church, IX. 210–18; of clergymen, II. 52–5; in conversation, IV. 88–93, 104–18, 244; corruption of, II. 45–7, 51–2; keeping one's distance, IV. 247; in everyday life, IX. 145; carried to extremes, II. 184–7; and genius, I. 242; good manners expounded, IV. 213–18, 221–2; of Houyhnhnms, XI. 267–9, 274–5; ill company, like a dog, I. 245; in Ireland, IV. xxxvii, 221; party politics undermine, IX. 79; of servants, XIII. 7–65, 161–5; sleeping in company, IX. 217; and soldiers, XII. 49; and theatre-going, IX. 343; of a wife, IX. 85–94. *See also* HINTS ON GOOD MANNERS; TREATISE ON GOOD MANNERS.

Mans: *see* LE MANS.

Mansell, Thomas, Lord Mansell of Margram, *c.* 1668–1723, privy councillor, Tory: VIII. 166; Macky and JS on, V. 260.

Mantua, Duchy of: VI. 38; Hapsburgs secure, VII. 89.

Mantua, Ferdinand Carlo Gonzaga, last Duke of, 1652–1708: Bickerstaff foresees peace mission, II. 148; and Savoy, VI. 13.

Manufacture, Irish: XII. 10; and agriculture, X. 141; and clergy, IX. 17–18, 68–9; cloth, XII. 69–71; crippled by England, XII. xi, 6–7, 116, 309; — linen, XII. 116–17; and gentry, XII. 69–70; and House of Commons, XII. 71, 138–9; linen, XII. 76; and nobility, XII. 69–70; poetry, IX. 337; price and quality control, X. 135; XII. 69–70; and pride, XII. xix, xxi–xxii; and shopkeepers, IX. 17; woollens, XII. 65; women ruin, XII. 7–9, 121–7; and women's fashions, IX. 17; XII. 67–8. *See also* SHOPKEEPERS, IRISH; TRADE, IRISH.

Manuscripts of JS, collections: IV. xxxviii; and booksellers, XIII. 182; word games, IV. xxxiii, xxxvi.

Manutius, Aldus, *c.* 1450–1515, scholar and printer: and April Fool's joke, IV. 267.

Maple, Frederick: and Humphrey French, XIII. xxvi.

Maple, William, Dublin chemist: 'person' assays Wood's coinage for Irish House of Commons, X. 31–2.

Mar, Charles Erskine, 5th Earl of, 1650–89, colonel: V. 140, 151, 159.

Mar, John Erskine, 6th Earl of,

1675–1732: Macky and JS on, V. 262.

Marais, Monsieur de, silk merchant at Boulogne, III. 210–11.

Marathon: and Miltiades, I. 206.

Marble Hill, Twickenham, residence of Countess of Suffolk: JS visits, V. xxvii.

Marc-Antonio: *see* RAIMONDI.

March Club: formation, VII. 100 ('a new one'); VIII. 126.

Marchiennes, Nord, France: convoy from, XIV. 13.

Marcianus, *c.* 391–457, Emperor of the East: and fire in Constantinople, XIV. 24.

Marcosian heretics: I. 18, *n.*

Marcus: *see* MINUCIUS.

Margaret, St., Queen of Malcolm III of Scotland, *d.* 1093: V. 18; sister of Edgar Atheling, V. 29.

Margarita: *see* ÉPINE.

Marginalia by JS: V. xxx–xl, 241–320; XIV. 2, 15–35, 38.

Maria Theresa, Queen of France, wife of Louis XIV, 1638–83: VII. 150.

Mariana, Juan de, 1537–1624, Spanish historian: leads Moderns' infantry, I. 152.

'Maritime powers': applied contemptuously to England, VI. 22; VIII. 62; *see also* ENGLAND; DUTCH.

Marius: *see* VICTORINUS.

Marius, Gaius, *c.* 155–86 B.C., Roman general: V. 84; VI. 80; and Gracchi, I. 219.

Market Hill, co. Armagh, Ireland, seat of Sir Arthur Acheson: 'his Estate', XII. 166–7; JS visits (1728), VIII. xxxvi; — (1728–9), VII. xii–xiii; — (1729, sum-

mer), V. xviii; XII. xvii, xviii, xix; — (1730, summer), V. xviii; — and Creichton's visit, V. xvii, 120; — and Sheridan, V. xxx, 225.

Markree Castle, Ireland: Synge family library, XIV. xi.

Marlborough, John Churchill, Duke of, 1650–1722, general and statesman: ambition, VI. 134; ambition to be captain-general for life, III. xvii, 42, 45, 72; VI. 44–5, 145 ('that commission'); VII. 7; VIII. 13, 56, 114–15; — controverted, VII. 22; ambition to be king, VI. 45, 97; VII. 7, 28, 175; VIII. 114; and Anne: *see* ANNE; Anne's grant (1702) fails, III. 94; VI. 130; and Argyll, VIII. 114–15; augmentation of troops in 1702, VI. 29; 'large presents' from Austria, VI. 34; avarice, III. 21–4, 80–5, 95, 165 ('a very few'); VI. 41–2; and Barrier Treaty, VI. 85; — refuses to sign, VI. 29 ('the other'); and Bolingbroke, III. xvi–xvii; — possibly alluded to in *Gulliver's Travels*, XI. 67–72; and Bothmar, VII. 29; alleged bribery, VI. 87 ('chief advisers'); Burnet and JS on, V. 288; and Buys, VII. 29; likened to Caesar, III. xvi, 19, 42, 44; VI. 134; character, III. xvii; **JS's character of**, VII. 7–8; — avarice, VI. 41–2, 189–91; VII. 7–8, 29, 79; — cowardice, unjustly charged, VII. xv; 'high church', III. 94 ('two or three'); censured by Commons (1712), VII. 65–7; — foresees censure, VII. 22; alleged corruption, VI. 34; — precedents

claimed (1712), VII. 65; and Cowper ('a person'), VIII. 56, 114; 'Crassus', III. 77, 80–5; — likened to Crassus, III. 77, 83–5; — styled 'Crassus', III. 95–6; XIV. 5; cruelty, VI. 190; — delights in war, VII. 7; dismissal (1711), VI. 133; VII. 27; — and JS's *Conduct of the Allies*, VI. ix; — losses attending, VII. 30; — news of it spreads, VII. 28; — and opposition to Oxford ministry, VI. 126; — reasons for, summarized, VIII. 109–10; — still in place (1711), VII. 2; created duke (1702), III. 21; and Dutch — tells them Anne is dying (1713), VII. 164; — co-operates with them, VI. 38; his education, VII. 7; XII. 47, 49; meets Eugene 'in secret' (1712), VII. 26; military effect of his fame, III. 19–20; VII. 27; returns from Flanders (1711), VII. 28; — strategy in Flanders (1709), VI. 31; Fleetwood praises, VI. 195; likened to French Mayors of the Palace, VI. 44–5; 'the General', II. 29; and Godolphin ('one'), VI. 11, 40–1, 59; VII. 9; — their alliance, III. 20; — and Godolphin ministry, would prevent their fall, III. 43; grant opposed by Tories, III. 94; VI. 130; grants made to, III. 21–4; indifference to popularity, VII. 28; alleged ingratitude to, III. 19–24; and James II — alleged correspondence (1712), VI. 145 ('two lords'); — intrigue against James (1688), V. 162; Knight of the Garter, III. 21; legal action

begun against (1712), VII. 67; Macky and JS on, V. 257; and Merlin, II. 165, 168, 169; military career, successes, VIII. 109; — prefers battle to negotiation, VI. 190; — military talent, III. 87; VII. 7; navy neglected by, VI. 23; and Northumberland, VIII. 102; and Bill against Occasional Conformity (1711), VII. 21–2; and Oxford, III. xvi–xvii; — Oxford ministry might conciliate him, VII. 29; — would ruin them, VI. 126, 133; VII. 29; opposes peace, VI. 133; — and peace negotiations (1709) — encumbers Strafford (Raby), VII. 38–9; — rejects French proposals, VI. 59; VII. 22; perquisites, VI. 41–2, 61; probably meant by 'Polyperchon', I. 209; and Pretender, VIII. 66; — and the Old Pretender, VIII. 39 ('which have been tampering'); instead of providence, III. 158–9; and battle of Ramillies—alleged peace offer following, VI. 43; return (1711), designed to cause rebellion, VII. 28; — flags in Westminster Hall, VI. 55–6; — 'mock parade', VII. 28–9; 'sea not his element', VI. 23; secret service money, alleged misuse, VI. 133; alleged to lose self-control, VII. 29–30; and Steele, VIII. 67; Steele defends, VIII. 13–14; 2½ per cent of subsidies, VI. 41; 'one subject' and his palace, XIV. 5, 10; **and JS** — campaign to discredit Marlborough, III. xvi–xviii; — denies attack upon, III. 60 ('particular persons'); — cowardice,

VII. 7, 27, 29; and Tories, III. 164 ('certain great persons'); — Tory (1702), VI. 42; — alienates them, VI. 42; — Tory bias subverted, VII. 7; — leaves them, III. xii–xiii, 15, 135, 164; VI. 145 ('two lords'); and translation of Caesar's *Commentaries*, IX. 20; and Treaty of Utrecht — allegedly undermines (1713), VII. 29, 163–4; — not to be informed (1711), VII. 38, 39; vengefulness, VII. 164; **and War of the Spanish Succession,** III. 263–72; — would continue war, VI. 50; — in Flanders, III. 83–5 ('Mesopotamia'); — encourages inequality of quotas, VII. 79; — gains from, III. 19–24, 215; — and perquisites, VI. 42; — self-aggrandizement, VI. 20, 43; VII. 29, 65–6; VIII. 56; — success, VII. 27; — asks for additional troops (1702), VI. 29; — refuses to engage Villars (1711), VIII. 57, 58; wealth, VII. 29, 67; VIII. 53; XI. 131; — supports his power, VII. 30; **and Whigs** — heads cabals (1712), VII. 29; — disaffection (1710), III. xvii; — joins them, III. 164 ('certain great persons'); — 'our hero', VI. 153; — and Junto (1711), VII. 108; — and his true principle ('two great men'), III. 15; — they seduce him, VIII. 56; — his selfishness in joining, VII. 29; — 'solemn league and covenant', VI. 42; — solicits support, VI. 42; his 'winter foraging', VI. 41.

Marlborough, Sarah Churchill (*née* Jennings), Duchess of, 1660–1744, favourite of Queen Anne: III. 72; **and Anne** — dismissal, VIII. 167; — queen favours her (1702), VI. 41; — loss of favour, VIII. 110–11; — friendship declines, VIII. 101; — 'imprisons' Anne, VIII. 116; — Anne an 'indulgent mistress', VII. 8; — and Prince George's death (1708), VIII. 112; — money, III. 24; atheism, VII. 8; 'a brawling woman', III. 26, 38; VI. 44; disgrace, V. 85; 'Fulvia', III. 77; XIV. 6; and Godolphin — allegedly his mistress, VIII. 111; — alliance, VIII. 102; — Godolphin's 'passion for', VII. 9; and William Grimston, IV. xxx; haughty, III. 133–4; 'a haughty, imperious wife', III. 26, 38; insolence, III. 136; Johnson's anecdote, IV. xxx; and Marlborough's indebtedness to, VII. 8; and Oxford, VIII. xxxv; — Oxford's meetings with Anne, VIII. 115; and Pretender — 'Lady' alleged to correspond with him, VI. 145; her resignation, V. 85; and rudeness of son-in-law (of 'Lady'), VII. 9; **JS's character of,** VII. 8; and Tories — 'Lady' leaves them, VI. 145.

Marly-le-Roi, Seine et Oise, France: and Louis XIV, II. 147, 199.

Maroc, Voyage de: XI. xiv.

Marprelate tracts: XII. 264.

Marr, Earl of: *see* MAR.

Marr, Episcopal clergyman in Whitehaven: V. 177–8.

Marriage: child-eating an en-

couragement, XII. 115; clergy-men's hasty, V. 217; and com-panionship, IX. 86; many evils, IV. 252; goals of, IV. 226; none in heaven, I. xxxv, 244; among Houyhnhnms, XI. 268–9; Irish marriages improvident, IX. 201; XII. 310; in Lilliput, XI. 60; and love, IV. 247; and *Modest Pro-posal*, XII. 115; modesty a virtue, IX. 86; and morality, IV. 227; ends raptures, IX. 89; and reason, IX. 263; and Struld-bruggs, XI. 212; unhappy, I. 245; wife's proper conduct, IX. xxvii–xxx, 85–95; 'the load of a wife', XI. 212; not with a young woman, I. xxxvii.

Mars: and *Polite Conversation*, IV. 165; pun upon, IV. 234.

Mars (the planet): moons of, XI. 170–1.

Marseilles, France: plague in (1720–2), X. 136–7; XIII. 113.

Marsh, Narcissus, 1638–1713, Archbishop of Armagh and Primate of Ireland: V. xxvii; charity, IX. 55; death (1713), V. xxvi; made Primate (1703), V. xxvi; **JS's character of, V. 211–12;** — analysis, V. xxvi-xxvii; — textual note, V. 357; and JS — certificate required (1964), V. xxvii.

Marten, John, *fl.* 1706–11, sur-geon: IV. 58–9; VIII. 9.

Martial, *c.* A.D. 40–104, Roman satirist: and oysters, IV. 257.

Martin, character in *Tale of a Tub* representing Church of England: I. 44–131, *passim*; alters his coat, I. 83–8; expelled by brother, I. 76; revealed to be Martin Luther,

I. 84, *n.**; portrait of, facing I. 44 and 85. *See also* HISTORY OF MARTIN.

Martyrdom of King Charles I, sermon by JS (1765): **IX. 219–31;** analysis, IX. 101, 106; back-ground, IX. 116, 120–4, 134; composition, IX. 133, 134; date, IX. 120; editions, IX. 377; style, IX. 120–1; textual note, IX. 377.

Marvell, Andrew, 1621–78, poet and M.P.: compared with Tin-dal, II. xviii, *n.* 2; *The Rehearsall Transpros'd* (2 pts., 1672, 1673), V. 273; — answer to Parker, I. 5; — echoed by JS, VIII. xvii, *n.* 1; — JS admires, I. 5.

Mary, Blessed Virgin ('Deipara'): images, I. 54, *n.†*; milk, I. 74 and *n.†*; pictures, I. 52, *n.**; and Pulcheria, XIV. 22.

Mary I, Queen of England, 1516–58: and Church, XIII. 123; money, IX. 50; persecution of Protestants, IX. 220; 'sister', IV. 80.

Mary II, Queen of England, 1662–94, daughter of James II: VIII. 95; one of 'three children', II. 21; and Sancroft, II. xvii; William Howell and JS on, V. 264.

Mary of Modena, Queen of England, 1658–1718, wife of James II: flees (1688), V. 289; Godolphin's 'passion for', VII. 8; and William III, VII. 8.

Mary, Queen of Scots, 1542–87: and Bothwell, V. 86; and Bur-net, IV. 62, 80; and Roman Catholicism, IV. 66.

Mary, Countess of Namur, daugh-ter of Philip II of France: V. 243.

Masham, Abigail (*née* Hill), Lady Masham, *d.* 1734, lady in waiting and confidant to Queen Anne: III. 72; VIII. 102; and Anne, VIII. 112, 168 ('a Lady'); and John Hill, VI. 190 ('the governor'); and Louis XIV, VI. 190; and change of ministry, VIII. 109; and Nobel, IV. 260; and Oxford, VIII. xxxiii, 115–16, 153, 156, 157; Duchess of Somerset replaces her (1711), VI. 71 ('an opportunity'); and JS, VIII. 109, 110; — informs him, VIII. 149 ('a most excellent lady'); **JS's character of**, VIII. 153; Whig charges against, III. 37–8.

Masham, Samuel, Lord Masham of Otes, *c.* 1679–1758, husband of Lady Masham: VIII. 166.

Mason, William Monck, 1775–1859, Irish historian: on Creichton's *Memoirs*, V. xxi; *The History and Antiquities of . . . [St. Patrick's Cathedral]*, 1820, V. xxi, *n.* 2; — on JS's sermons, IX. 98, *n.* 3; quoted, XII. xlvi.

Masons, free: and JS, V. 323–33, 358.

Masqueraders: their conversations, IV. 116; unmasking, not fair, I. 109.

'Match, Lady': character in *Polite Conversation*, IV. 164, 168.

Mathematics: and King of Brobdingnag, XI. 103; in Lilliput, XI. 26, 45; and politics, XI. 164; practical applications, XI. 136.

Mather, Samuel, 1674–1733, clergyman of Witney, Oxfordshire: possibly author of sermon of 29 May 1705, II. 101.

Matilda, or Maud, Queen of England, 1080–1118, wife of Henry I, daughter of Malcolm III of Scotland: her character and descent, V. 29; dies, V. 41; Henry marries her with consent of general assembly, V. 35.

Matilda of Boulogne, *c.* 1103–1152, consort of Stephen, King of England, daughter of Eustace III of Boulogne: V. 60, 61, 62.

Matilda (or Maud), The Empress, 1102–67, daughter of Henry I, cousin to Stephen, consort (married 1114) of Emperor Henry V, later of Geoffrey Plantagenet, son of the Count of Anjou (married 1128): V. 40, 50, 51, 55, 57, 75; character, V. 60, 63–4; and David I, V. 49–50; and her father's death, V. 48; marries Geoffrey, V. 48; Henry I allegedly disinherits her, V. 48; bears Henry II, V. 44; marries Emperor Henry V, V. 34, 35 (*bis*), 48; alienates Henry of Blois, V. 61; — Henry of Blois approves her queen, V. 60; — renounced by Henry of Blois, V. 62–3; flees London, V. 61; deprived of the throne, V. 48; oath of fealty to, V. 48, 49; escapes from Oxford, V. 64; plays dead, V. 62; Robert, her illegitimate brother, rebels, V. 52–3; Robert, Earl of Gloucester's devotion to her, V. 65; and Roger, Bishop of Salisbury, V. 57; and Stephen, V. 71, 72; — his accession, V. 48; — defeats and captures Stephen, V. 55–9; — Stephen besieges her in Oxford, V. 63–4; succession

settled in her, V. 41–2; wearies of war, V. 65; and William, son of Robert of Normandy, V. 44.

Matilda, d. 1120, illegitimate daughter of Henry I: V. 40.

Matilda, daughter of Geoffrey, wife of Prince William (Henry I's son): V. 42.

Matveof, A. A., ambassador of Peter the Great: III. 138 ('the ambassador').

Mauberge, Nord, France: VI. 101, 109; VII. 113, 152.

Maude, daughter of Henry I: *see* MATILDA THE EMPRESS.

Maurice (or Morrice, etc.), Theodore, *c.* 1670–1731, Archdeacon of Tuam: urges Captain John Creichton's nephew to give him money (1726): V. 126.

Maximilian II, Maria Emanuel, Elector of Bavaria, 1662–1726, Spanish Governor of the Southern Netherlands: ambition, VIII. 61; electoral status, VII. 156, 164; prediction of his death, VII. 205–6; England's ally (1689—97), VI. 14; England's enemy (1701–13), VI. 16; France favours, VII. 148, 153, 155–6; and **Treaty of Utrecht**, VII. 160; — not to attend, VII. 60; — to retain Charleroi, VII. 153, 155–6; — and retention of Dutch towns, VII. 153; — England agrees to French demands for, VII. 155–6; — and Franco-Dutch negotiations, VII. 152; — to retain Luxembourg, VII. 153, 155–6; — — opposed by Austria, VII. 164; — Ménager's quibbling, VII. 160; — to retain Namur,

VII. 153, 155–6; — to gain Sardinia, VII. 156.

Maxims Controlled in Ireland (written *c.* 1728), by JS: **XII. 131-7**; allusions to, XII. 124; authorship, XII. xxiii and *n.* 1; composition, XII. xxiii; draft, XII. 309–10; — manuscript facsimile, facing XII. 131; textual notes, XII. 309–10, 336, 348–9.

Maxims Examin'd, by JS: *see* MAXIMS CONTROLLED IN IRELAND, *draft*.

Maxwell family of Scotland: V. 125.

Maxwell, Henry, *d.* 1730, M.P. for Donegal: and Bank of Ireland, IX. xx, 302, 303; *Mr. Maxwell's Second Letter to Mr. Rowley. Wherein the Objections against the Bank are Answered* (1721), IX. 320; *Reasons Offered for Erecting a Bank in Ireland* (1721), IX. 320; and *Subscribers to the Bank*, IX. xx.

Maxwell, J.C.: acknowledgement, XIV. vii; on the text of *A Tale of a Tub*, XIV. 49.

May, Humphrey, *d.* 1722, Clerk of the Crown for Ulster: and Wharton, III. 232.

Mayhew, George P.: acknowledgement, V. v; XIV. vii; on JS's *History of the Four Last Years*, XIV. xii, 45; 'A Missing Leaf from Swift's *Holyhead Journal*', V. 358; on *Polite Conversation*, IV. xxx; XIV. 51; on JS's will, XIII. 225.

Maynard, Sir John, 1602–90, judge: Burnet and JS on, V. 278.

Maynwaring, Arthur: *see* MAINWARING.

Mayo, Thomas F.: *Epicurus in England (1650–1725)*, 1934, IX. 113, *n.* 1.

Mead, Richard, 1673–1754, physician: IV. 271; **JS's inscription to** (1739), **XIV. 38**; — occasion, XIV. xiv; — textual note, XIV. 46; copy of JS's *Works*, XIV. 38.

Meal Tub Plot (1679): I. 42 and *n.*‖.

Mean and Great Figures: see OF MEAN AND GREAT FIGURES.

Meath, Ireland, diocese: most valuable in Ireland, IX. 46; tithes, XII. 211.

Meath, Bishop of: *see* HENRY DOWNES.

Meath, Chambre Brabazon, 5th Earl of, *c.* 1645–1715: III. 234.

Mechanical Operation of the Spirit: *see* DISCOURSE CONCERNING THE MECHANICAL OPERATION OF THE SPIRIT.

Medardus, St., *c.* 470–*c.* 560, Bishop of Vermandois: death and miracles, XIV. 34.

Medea: Horace alludes to, V. 339.

Media: and Cyrus, I. 197.

Medical analogies (i.e., the human body and its ills as metaphor for the state): the body politic, I. 195; — and 'Body Natural', I. 246–7; XI. 187–8; from Cicero (*Pro Sestio* 65), III. 106; cure for Irish disease, XII. 124; and English domination of Ireland, XII. 8; dogs and Ireland, XII. 263; gout and Irish trade, XII. 79; hospitals and absentees, XII. 12; the plague and Irish lack of silver, XII. 55; political parties and half-people, III. 101–2; XI.

189; 'political surgeon', I. 103; XII. 157–8; religion and the human body, II. 62, 66–9; — remedies temporarily painful, III. 67; — roaring may be therapeutic, III. 77; — zeal as 'a great ferment in the blood', V. 22.

Medicine: in Academy of Lagado, XI. 181, 187–9; consultation of four physicians, IV. 271–2; in Lilliput: *see* LILLIPUT, *medicine*; madman (coprophiliac) as doctor, I. 112–13; mock-recipe for a, I. 78–9; political frauds compared with, V. 111–12; religion and physicians, I. 244; satirized, IV. 271–2; XI. 253–4, 262; — Warwick Lane (i.e., Royal College of Physicians) ridiculed, I. 113, 115; swearing prescriptions (by Irish physicians), IX. 297; 'the unskilfulness of a surgeon', V. 44; women's illnesses, XII. 68; the universal medicine, XI. 210.

Meditation upon a Broomstick (written *c.* 1703, published 1710), by JS: **I. 237–40**; background, I. xxxiii–xxxiv; parody of Boyle, I. 239; composition (*c.* 1703), I. xxxiii–xxxiv, 239; editions, I. xxxiii, 302; style, I. xxxii, xxxiv; textual notes, I. 302; title-page facsimile, I. 237.

Mediterranean Sea: and Pompey, I. 220; and War of the Spanish Succession, VII. 83.

Medley, Whig newspaper: III. xvi–xvii, xviii, xxiii–xxiv, xxix, 202; condemned, XIV. 8; allegedly libellous, III. 152–6; and Oxford ministry, III. 188–9; slander, III. 188–9. *See also* A LETTER TO THE SEVEN LORDS.

'Megalopolis', fictitious Greek city: I. 97.

Meibom, Marcus: *Antiquae musicae auctores septem*, XIV. 2; — JS's copy, XIV. xi, 43.

Melampus, seer in Greek mythology: early fanatic, I. 186.

Melancholy: and enthusiasm, I. 175; and ghosts, I. 242; hard work the cure for, XI. 263-4; and madness, I. 102-14; marriage and spleen, IV. 252; school of spleen, I. 25.

Melcombe, Lord: *see* DODINGTON.

Melfort, John Drummond, 1st Earl of, 1650-1715, lieutenant-general, Secretary of State for Scotland: V. 160; — and Erasmus Lewis, VI. xxvi-xxvii, 174, 175, 177, 200.

Melons: JS to buy seeds, V. 334.

Melville, George Melville, 1st Earl of, 1636-1707, Secretary of State for Scotland: and battle of Bothwell Bridge (1679), V. 140-1; and Creichton, V. 173-4.

Melville, Sir James, 1535-1617, of Hallhill, autobiographer: V. 266.

Memoirs, vogue of: VIII. 108.

Memoirs of Sir W. Temple: *see* TEMPLE.

Memoirs of Capt. John Creichton (partly by JS): *see* CREICHTON, JOHN, *Memoirs*.

Memoirs of Martinus Scriblerus: *see* SCRIBLERUS CLUB.

Memoirs of the Chevalier de St. George: *see* EDWARD LLOYD.

Memoirs of the Life of That Most Noble Thomas Late Marquess of Wharton: III. xviii-xix.

Memoirs, Relating to That Change Which Happened in the Year 1710 (written 1714), by JS: **VIII. 107-28**; analysis, VIII. xxxi; background, VIII. xxx; composition, VIII. xxx-xxxi, xxxvii; and *Enquiry into the Behaviour of the Queen's Last Ministry*, VIII. xxxiii, xxxvii; and *History of the Four Last Years*, VII. xii; VIII. xxxvii, xxxix; manuscript, VII. xii-xiii; VIII. 210-11; publication, VII. xii and *n*. 6; VIII. xxxvii, 210; — delayed, VIII. 141; style, VIII. xxxi; textual notes, VIII. 210-14.

Memoranda from Forster MS.: *see* MEMORANDUM OF THINGS TO BE DONE.

Memorandum of Things to Be Done in the City (written 1727), by JS: **V. 334-5**; textual note, V. 358.

Memorandum on Mr. Grattan's Walk at Belcamp (written *c.* 1733-34), by JS: **V. 344**; textual note, V. 359.

Memorial of the Poor Inhabitants, Tradesmen, and Labourers of ... Ireland: *see* JOHN BROWNE.

Memory: and invention, I. 84; and observation, IV. 251.

Ménage, Gilles, 1613-92, French scholar: allusion to, II. 252.

Ménager, Nicolas le Baillif, Count of St. Jean Ménager, 1658-1714, French merchant, peace envoy: character 'of a merchant', VII. 159; favours Dutch, VII. 143; visits England (1711), VII. 46; Polignac disparages him, VII. 159; quarrel with Rechteren, VII. 154, 158-9; and Treaty of

Utrecht, VII. 47, 48, 49–51, 60; — misrepresents France's position (1711), VII. 46–7; — delays peace (1713), VII. 164, 165; — signs preliminaries (1711), VII. 195, 197; — quibbles, VII. 159.

'Mendez, Pedro de' (Portuguese ship's captain in *Gulliver's Travels*, part IV): XI. 286–9, 321–2.

Menin, Belgium, on the Lys, near Courtrai: VI. 101, 109, 116; VII. 113.

Mercenary troops: XI. 247; historians as mercenaries, I. 152. *See also* WAR OF THE SPANISH SUCCESSION.

Merchants, Irish: ignorant, X. 136; XII. 174; and duty on wine, XII. 125; and Wood's coins, X. 15–16. *See also* TRADE, IRISH.

Mercurius Rusticus: V. 188.

Mercury: and Alcibiades, I. 207; and Jupiter, I. 153; winged cap, IV. 252.

Meredyth, Thomas, *d.* 1719, lieutenant-general, forced to sell out in 1710: III. xiv; 'an accident', III. 45; 'two or three', VIII. 155–6.

'Merit': genealogy, III. 98–9.

Merlin: and free masons, V. 328, 330. *See also* FAMOUS PREDICTION.

Mesnager, N.: *see* MÉNAGER.

Mesopotamia (i.e. Flanders): III. 83–5.

Metaphysics, JS's views on abstractions, XI. 136.

Methuen, Sir Paul, 1672–1757, diplomat: II. 160, *n.**; character, V. 261; Macky and JS on, V. 261.

Methuen Treaties (Portuguese

Alliance, 1703): articles, VI. 24–6, 37, 39; — against union of Austria and Spain, VI. 51, *n.**; Austria ignores, VI. 37; decried, VI. 26; 'folly and contradiction', VI. 25; Portugal defects, VII. 85; equality of quotas in, VII. 85; ratified, VI. 37.

Mews, Peter, 1619–1706, Bishop of Winchester: V. 288.

Mexico: X. 103; and Cortez, XI. 293.

'Mezeriac': *see* BACHET.

Microcosm: man as a, I. 47, 246.

Microscope: XI. 113.

Middlesex County, England: Grand Jury, and Drapier, X. 73; — and James II (as Duke of York), X. 167; — and Tindal, II. xviii, 191–2.

Middleton, Charles Middleton, 2nd Earl of, *c.* 1650–1719, statesman, Jacobite: V. 165; VI. 145; and Erasmus Lewis, VI. 174, 177; Macky and JS on, V. 262; and JS, III. xx, *n.* 3.

Midleton, Alan Brodrick, Viscount, 1660–1728, Irish statesman and Speaker of the Irish House of Commons: and Carteret, X. x, *n.* 1; and George I, X. xxix; figure in *Letter from a Member of the House of Commons in Ireland . . . Concerning the Sacramental Test*, II. 110, 112, 130; and proclamation against Drapier, X. 205; and *Drapier's Letters*, X. xxiv; — and sixth *Drapier's Letter*, X. xxi, xxiii; his son, X. x, *n.* 1; retires as Speaker of Irish House of Commons, II. xxxii, 130.

Milan, duchy of: VI. 12, 13, 16, 38, 57, 112; VII. 89, 133; and Treaty of Utrecht — Austria to retain, VII. 164; — Austria retains 'arbitrarily', VIII. 60.

Mildendo (capital of Lilliput, *Gulliver's Travels*, Part I): described, XI. 46-7.

Militia: in Brobdingnag, XI. 115, 138; Irish — and Swearing Act, IX. 297.

Millar, Andrew, 1707-68, London bookseller: and JS's *History of the Four Last Years*, 'Advertisement', VII. 171-7. *See also* FAULKNER; HISTORY OF THE FOUR LAST YEARS, *editions*.

Milles, Thomas, 1671-1740, Bishop of Waterford: 'another', II. ix; character in *Dialogue in the Castilian Language*, IV. 258-9.

Mills, Dr.: *see* MILLES.

Miltiades, late 6th and early 5th centuries B.C., Athenian general: III. 61; and Athens, I. 205; fall from power, I. 206; impeachment, I. 224; pseudonym for Lord Orford, I. 205-6, 224.

Milton, John, 1608-74: and bookseller's copyright, XIII. 206; Burnet and JS on, V. 270; divorce tracts, II. 91; — *Doctrine and Discipline of Divorce*, II. 67; pretends to lead the Moderns, I. 152; on Nimrod, IX. 264; pun upon name, IV. 274; *Paradise Lost*, III. 682-9: V. 116; — to be rhymed, IX. 335; — analogy with Whigs, III. 8-9; — allusion to III. 654-735: V. xvii, 116.

Mindelheim, Germany, principality of: III. 21-2, 23; Leopold makes Marlborough a prince of, VI. 34.

Minellius (Jan Minelli, Dutch scholar, *c.* 1625-83): and Wotton, I. xxix-xxx, 8.

Minerva: and *On Wisdom's Defeat in a Learned Debate*, X. xxx.

Minions: III. 93.

'Minister': Steele's use of word, VIII. 24-5.

Ministerial responsibility, JS's views on: V. xvii, 116-17; XI. 318; Athens and Rome, I. 193-227, *passim*; England, I. 228-236; Junto avoids, III. 140; and moral reformation, II. 61-3; Oxford's refusals to defend himself, VIII. 160-1; and passive obedience, III. 114; and 'the prince can do no wrong', VIII. 23; and royal prerogative, VII. 20; Steele's distortion, VIII. 17, 23; and Treaty of Utrecht, VI. 127; 'cautious writers' blame ministers, VII. 24.

Ministers of state: II. 14; XI. 262-3; arbitrary power, IX. 32-3; and Burnet, IV. 62, 74-5, 83, 84; characterized, XI. 255-6; and employments, XI. 190; and John Gay, XII. 35; language, IV. 14; personal economy, IV. 246; preferment of dunces, IV. 245; and the Pretender, IV. 75; and public morals, II. 46-53, *passim*; and satire, XII. 34; and war, XI. 245-6; poetic ability, IX. 327; should be virtuous, II. 48-9; VIII. 80; XIV. 14-15; Yahoo equivalent, XI. 262-3.

Minorca: IV. 209; to be British, VII. 115, 132.

Mint, Royal, Tower Hill, London;

and assay of Wood's coinage, X. 187; dishonesty in, XII. 97; and Newton, IV. 122.

Minucius Felix, Marcus, 3rd-century Christian apologist: 'free-thinker', IV. 46.

Miracles: and Holy Ghost, IX. 161; against reason, IX. 165; Roman Catholic, I. 65–76; — ridiculed, XIV. 18, 21, 24, 25, 30, 33–5; — — 'smells bad', XIV. 31.

Mirandola, Italy: VI. 38.

Mirror of Justices: see ANDREW HORNE.

'Misanthropus': pun upon, IV. 238.

Miscellanea: see TEMPLE, SIR WILLIAM.

Miscellaneous Works, Comical and Diverting: *by T. R. D. J. S. D. O. P. I. I.* (1720), by JS: I. 275–95; title-page facsimile, I. 275; textual note, I. 304.

Miscellanies in Verse and Prose (1711), by JS: analysis, II. xxxvii–xl; contents, I. xxxiii–xxxiv; editions, II. xxxviii, 275; preparation, XIV. xi; publication, I. xxxii–xxxiii; II. xxxvii–xxxviii; XIV. 41; 'The Publisher to the Reader', by JS, **IV. 268-70**; — authorship, IV. 302; — textual notes, IV. 302; reception, II. xxxviii; textual note, II. 275.

Miscellanies of JS and Pope (1727–32, 4 vols.): composition (1732), XII. x; copy annotated by JS, I. v; editions, XIII. 204; publication (1726, an error), XIII. 184, 202; XIV. 43; and *Letter from a Member of the House of Commons in Ireland . . . Concerning the Sacramental Test*, II. 110; *Volume I* — JS's copy, II. xiv and *n.* 3; — additions to *Thoughts*, I. xxxv; *Volume II* (1727), II. 110; *The Last Volume* (i.e., III, 1727), contents, V. xxvi; *Volume III* (i.e., IV, 1732), and *An Infallible Scheme to Pay the Publick Debt*, XII. xxxii; — and *Intelligencer*, XII. xiv.

'Mischief': Whig and Tory meanings, III. 196.

Mishna, of Babylon and Jerusalem: I. 41.

'Misosarum, Gregory', pseudonym for JS in *A Preface to the Bishop of Sarum's Introduction*: IV. 53, 55, 288.

'Misoxulos', pseudonym for author of *Another Letter to Mr. Harding the Printer*: X. 156.

Missionaries: Christian and Heathen, IV. 31.

Mist, Nathaniel, *d.* 1737, journalist (imprisoned 1721): *Weekly Journal* prints part of *Short View of the State of Ireland*: XII. 122.

Mr. Collins's Discourse of Free-Thinking, Put into Plain English, by Way of Abstract, for the Use of the Poor (1713), by JS: **IV. 25-48**; analysis, IV. x, xi, xvi, xix–xx; authorship, IV. xvii; background, IV. ix–xi, xvi–xvii, xix; style, IV. xviii, xix; textual notes, IV. 287; title-page facsimile, IV. 25.

'Mob', word censured by JS: II. 175–7; IV. 113.

Modena, Duchy of: VI. 38.

Modena, Mary of: see MARY OF MODENA.

Moderation: definition, IX. 178; — 'new' meaning, IX. 178; — word misused, IX. 175; ecclesiastical, defined by JS, IX. 119; — opposed by JS, IX. 119; political implications, II. 13.

'Modern Paradox': I. 147 and *n*. *.

Moderns: *see* ANCIENTS AND MODERNS.

Modest Defence of a Late Poem . . . Call'd 'The Lady's Dressing-Room' (1732), probably by JS: **V. 337-40**; textual note, V. 358.

Modest Defence of Punning (written 1716), by JS: **IV. 205-10**; analysis, IV. xxxiv, xxxv–xxxvi; composition, IV. xxxiii–xxxiv, 205; errata, XIV. 52; manuscript, IV. xxxiii–xxxiv, 299; — provenance, IV. xxxiv–xxxv; textual notes, IV. 299.

Modest Defence of the Proceedings of the Rabble in all Ages, imaginary treatise by the author of *Tale of a Tub*: I. xl.

Modest Enquiry into the Reasons of the Joy . . . upon the Spreading of a Report of Her Majesty's Death (partly by JS): *see* MANLEY, MRS. MARY DE LA RIVIÈRE.

Modest Proposal (1729), by JS: **XII. 109-18**; allusion to, XII. 173; analysis, XII. xix–xxi; and *Answer to the Craftsman*, XII. xxx–xxxi; background, XII. xix, xx; composition, XII. xix, 109; editions, XII. xix, xx, 335; and *Maxims Controlled in Ireland*, XII. xxiii; reception, XII. xx; style, XII. xix, xx; textual notes, XII. 335-6; title-page facsimile, facing XII. 109.

Modesty: and genius, VII. 105; and good manners, IV. 221; parable concerning, I. 28; recommended in wives, IX. 86.

Modus (i.e., for tithe of hemp and flax): bill for, probable effect, XIII. 104; JS's views, XIII. xxx. *See also* SOME REASONS AGAINST THE BILL FOR SETTLING THE TYTH.

Mogul, Great: in Whitechapel, I. 126.

Mohammed, *c.* 570–632, founder of Mohammedan religion: III. 92; great figures, V. xi, 84; and Jews, IV. 39; rides ass to heaven, I. 172–3.

Mohammedans: and Christ's divinity, IX. 262; fanatics, I. 188; and Parliament, II. 74; and tale of three rings, I. xxix; and Tindal, II. 88; toleration of, II. 7.

Mohler, Nora M.: on *Gulliver's Travels*, XI. xx.

Mohocks: account of, VII. 26–7; Eugene allegedly would use them, VII. 26; Whigs allegedly instigate, VII. 27.

Mohun, Charles Mohun, 4th Lord, 1677–1712, notorious rake: death, VI. xxiv–xxv, 197-9; VII. 155; duel with Hamilton, V. 294; VI. 197-9; Macky and JS on, V. 259; a Whig tool, VI. 199.

Moleau: *see* MOLO.

Molesworth, Robert, Viscount Molesworth of Swords, Lord Molesworth of Philipstown, 1656–1725, Privy Councillor of Ireland: VIII. 37; *Account of Denmark*, II. 99; and Burnet, IV. xxv; — linked with Burnet,

IV. 70; 'dangerous author', X. 86–7; and the Drapier, X. 93–4; and fifth *Drapier's Letter*, X. xxiv–xxv, 77–94; *The Encouragement of Agriculture*, IX. xxii; — JS's opinion, IX. 58–9; and *Proposal for the Universal Use of Irish Manufacture*, X. 83 and *n.**; residence in Ireland, X. 93; JS attacks, IV. xxv–xxviii, 70, 289.

Moliere: *L'Avare*, quoted, I. xvii, *n.* †.

Moll, Herman, *d.* 1732, Dutch-born cartographer: XI. 284.

Molo (or Moleau), Franceso, resident of Poland at the Hague: VII. 118, 143.

Moloch: mentioned, I. 20.

Molucca Islands, Indonesia: XI. 83.

Molyneux, John: 'Brother-in-law' of William Wood, X. 145, 148 and *n.**

Molyneux, Sir Thomas, Bart., 1661–1733, professor of medicine: Dr. Molnx in *Dialogue in the Castilian Language*, IV. 257–9; punned with JS, IV. xxix.

Molyneux, William, 1656–98, philosopher: *The Case of Ireland's Being Bound by Acts of Parliament in England* (1698): X. xviii; Drapier invokes, X. 62, 86 ('dangerous author').

Momus, god of criticism: ancestor of critics, I. 57; patron of Moderns, I. 153–4; aids Wotton, I. 163.

Monarchy, JS's views: IX. 101; absolute monarchy not supported in *Genesis*, IX. 264; king assures balance of 'nobility and people', I. 195–203; V. 36–7; VII. 20–1; and Bodin, V. 244, 245, 246; incompatible with Calvinism, II. 101; and coining of money, X. 37–41, 54–5 and *passim*; dispensing power opposed, IX. 32; English monarchy and succession, II. 18–23; and hatred, VIII. 168–9; historical arguments for, II. 16–17; limitations of, X. 28; royal pensions, IV. 20; 'the prince can do no wrong', VIII. 23; princes uneducated, VIII. 138; and public morality, II. 47–63, *passim*; royal assent, X. 134; and state church, XII. 249–50; uninterrupted succession essential to hereditary right, V. 47. *See also* DIVINE RIGHT; KINGS.

Monasteries: degeneration, XIII. 124; endowments, XIII. 124; and papacy, XIII. 124; and parishes, XIII. 124.

Money: and avarice, XI. 251–2; 'black money', X. 10; copper not legal tender, X. xiii; depreciation, V. 81; XIII. xxxvii, xl, 101; — and land values, IX. 47–8; — and increase in silver supplies, IX. 50; devaluation of the English guinea, XII. 56–7; and education, XII. 46–53; and genius, IV. 20; gold supply increasing, IX. 50; 'great divider', X. 61; hoarding of, II. 244; no intrinsic value, IX. 51; Irish counterfeits, XIII. xl; Irish depreciation and T. C. D. stipends, IX. 55; Irish lack of copper money, X. 43 and *passim*; XII. 93, 96, 98; — and nobility and gentry, XII. 100; mint in Ire-

land, X, *passim*; XII. 7, 9, 11, 57, 90, 98–105; Irish silver scarcity, XII. xxiii, 54–61, 76, 93, 94, 98; — quick remedy for, XII. 71; Irish money unstable, IX. 300; X. 33–4, 39, 187–8; Roman devaluation, IX. 48; Saxon value, IX. 48–9; value of Irish coins, X, *passim*; XII. 94; — and Maculla, XII. xviii; — alternative to Maculla's project, XII. xviii; opposed to agriculture, III. 5, 6–7; — as basis of prosperity, 'physick, instead of food', VI. 58; — 'artificial wealth of funds and stocks', VI. 16; precious metals in, V. 246; and royal prerogative, X. 28, 34, 37–9, 54–6; — the Drapier defended, X. 104–11, *passim*; social stratification the result of, XI. 251–3; — Wood's coinage, IV. xxxi, xxxviii. *See also* WILLIAM WOOD.

Moneyed Interest: 'artificial wealth', VI. 16; and national debt, VII. 69–70; generated by national debt, VI. 10; Godolphin ministry encourages, III. 165; Hare's views, VI. x–xi; and landed interests, VII. 70; — against landed interests, IX. 32; jargon, III. 7; and the Marlborough-Godolphin alliance, 'solemn league and covenant', VI. 42; 'men at ease', VI. 59; attempts to embarrass Oxford ministry through weakening credit, III. 5, 67–8, 70; national pawnbrokers, VI. 18; exercise of power, III. 124–5; gain power, III. 5; 'plundering the public' (1690–1700), VI. 16; and

qualification bill, III. 169–70; allegedly spread rumours to affect stock prices, III. 67; stocks and national wealth, III. 6; 'usurers', VI. 56, 59; and War of the Spanish Succession, III. 134; — bear no burden, VI. 59; — and peace negotiations (1709–10), VI. 50; — profits, VI. 41, 42–3, 48–9, 56; — would continue war, VI. 53–4, 57; and Whigs, VI. 42; VII. 69–70; and William III, VII. 69–70.

Monkeys: cat's paw and monkey, I. 247; Gulliver and monkey, XI. 121–4.

Monks: ancient and modern compared, XIV. 22.

Monmouth, Charles, Earl of, 1658–1735: error for Molesworth, IV. xxv, 289.

Monmouth, James Scott, 1st Duke, 1649–85, illegitimate son of Charles II: V. 139, 156, 160, 167; and Argyll, V. 158; battle of Bothwell Bridge (1679), V. 139–42; rebellion to restore Puritanism, V. 254; rebuked by Dalyell, V. 142. *See also* FITZROY, JAMES.

Monsieur, Monsieur: III. 209.

Monsoon: XI. 84.

Mont Genèvre, in Savoy: VII. 114.

Montagu, Charles: *see* HALIFAX.

Montagu, Ralph Montagu, 1st Duke of, 1638–1709: Macky and JS on, V. 258.

Montaigne: allusions, *De l'Inconstance de nos actions*, XII. 246.

Monteleon, Marquis de, Spanish ambassador: VII. 166.

Montferrat, Duchy of, in northern Italy: VI. 13.

Montreuil, Pas de Calais, France: III. 212.

Montrose, James Graham, 1st Marquis of, 1612–50: and Lord Airlie, V. 162; Burnet on, V. 267; and Charles I, V. 310, 315; betrayed by Macleod of Assynt, V. 263.

Montrose, James Graham, 3rd Marquis of, 1657–84, colonel: V. 140.

Montrose, James Graham, 1st Duke of, 1682–1742: V. 262.

Moon: and Irish imports, XII. 67; and lost things, I. 241.

Moor, A., London bookseller: and *Considerations upon Two Bills . . . Relating to the Clergy of Ireland*, XII. 189; publishes *Drapier's Letters* (1730), X. 207.

Moor, Henry: *see* MORE.

Moor, John, apothecary: VIII. 9.

Moor, Roger: *see* MOORE.

Moor Park (Sir William Temple's estate near Farnham, Surrey): Temple retires to (*c.*1689), I. x; JS takes up residence (*c.*1689), I. x; JS returns to (1691), I. x–xii; JS's pleasant life there (1691–2), I. xii; JS at (1689–99), V. 193–4; JS leaves (1699), I. xix.

Moore, Arthur, *c.* 1666–1730, Lord Commissioner of Trade and Plantations, M.P. for Grimsby: and Prior, III. 211.

Moore, John, 1646–1714, Bishop of Ely: III. 184.

Moore (or Moor), Colonel Roger, *fl.* 1644, politician: and Maculla's project, XII. 94; patent for coinage, X. 30, 41.

Moorfields, London, site of Bed-

lam: IV. 62; author's thanks to, in *Tale of a Tub*, I. 115.

Moralists: XI. 137.

Morality: and anonymity, XII. 29–31; and discretion, XII. 38–45; JS attacks double standard, II. xx; and dreams, II. 178–9; faith strengthens, IX. 164; and free press, II. 97; immorality denies Christ, II. 4; and literature, II. 56; low morals rewarded, II. 62–3; and peers, I. 243; and philosophy, IX. 73; and ancient philosophy, IX. 246; and political faction, IX. 79; and prejudice, I. 243; present state, II. 44–7; — plan for improving, II. 47–63; as a qualification for office, II. 47–51; XI. 59; XIV. 14–15; reformation of, XII. 24–5; and religion, IX. 79; religion essential to, IX. 152; and satire, I. 31–2; XII. 35; moral justifications of satire, XII. 34; and school texts, XII. 52; and self-interest, IX. 152; usefulness, I. 244; and wisdom, I. 243.

More, Henry, 1614–87, Platonic writer and theologian: on Hell, IV. 34–5; *Observations upon Anthroposophia Theomagica* (1650), I. 79 and *n.* †.

More, John: *see* MOORE.

More, Sir Thomas, 1478–1535: V. 84; XI. 196; *Apology* (1533), IV. 71; executed, V. 248; great figure, V. xi, 84; and Henry VIII, XIII. 123; *Utopia*, XI. 8; 'the only man of true virtue that ever England produced', V. 247.

Morgan, Pierpont, Library (New York): manuscript of *Family of*

Swift, by JS, V. xxii; *Modest Defence of Punning*, IV. 299; Orrery correspondence, V. xxii; — manuscript of JS's letter to Orrery (1737), VII. xiii, *n.* 1.

Morice, Davy: V. 202.

Morley, George, 1597–1684, Bishop of Winchester: Burnet and JS on, V. 282–3.

Morocco: and revolutions, I. 174. *See also* MAROC.

Morphew, John, *fl.* 1706–20, London bookseller: III. 207, 261; VI. 3, 69, 83; VII. 235; and Bickerstaff, II. 249, 250, 251; and JS's *Mr. Collins's Discourse of Free-Thinking*, IV. 25; and the *Examiner*, III. xxvii; — *Examiners for . . . 1712*, XIV. xi; and Parker, VI. ix; publishes *Predictions for the Year 1708*, II. 139, 197, 286; publishes *A Preface to the Bishop of Sarum's Introduction*, IV. 53, 55; publishes *Letter from a Member of the House of Commons in Ireland . . . Concerning the Sacramental Test*, by JS, II. 109; and JS, VIII. 198–9.

Morrice, Archdeacon: *see* MAURICE.

Morshead, Sir Owen, librarian of Windsor Castle: acknowledgement to, VII. vii.

Mortain, Stephen, Count of: *see* STEPHEN, KING OF ENGLAND.

Mortgage, general: VII. 76; and national debt, VII. 71–2.

Mortimer, family of: VIII. 135.

Mortmain, Statute of: II. 89; IV. 66, 67; 'dead hand', IX. 52.

Moses: and Bank directors, IX. 300; and the Drapier, X. 90; and free-thinkers, IV. 48; horns, I. 112; Josephus on, IV. 46; and Manilius, IV. 45; and ancient philosophy, IX. 245; pun upon name, IV. 239; wise statesman, IX. 156.

Mostyn, Flintshire: and coal trade, IX. 19.

Motte, Benjamin, *d.* 1738, London bookseller and printer: XI. 297, 299; publishes *Gulliver's Travels* (1726), XI. xxi–xxvi, 297, 299; and *Polite Conversation*, IV. 97.

Mountjoy, William Stewart, 2nd Viscount, *d.* 1728: member of Irish Privy Council, X. 182.

'Mount-loggerhead': IV. 283.

'Mount-rebel': IV. 283.

'Mount-regicide': IV. 283.

Mount Sinai: Josephus on, IV. 46.

'Moving discourse': IX. 70.

'Muckworm, Sir Peter': character in *Polite Conversation*, IV. 195.

Muggletonians: III. 144; XII. 244; and free-thinkers, IV. 31.

Müller, Johann ('Regiomontanus'), 1436–76, mathematician and astronomer: leads Moderns' engineers, I. 152.

'Munodi, Lord' (ex-governor of Lagado, in *Gulliver's Travels*, Part III; possibly modelled on Lord Oxford): XI. 174–8.

Münster, Treaty of (1643): and Barrier Treaty, VI. 92, 104, 107; VII. 61, 91–2, 92–3; England does not observe, VII. 92–3; and Hanseatic League, VI. 104; Spain does not observe, VII. 92–3.

Murray, Captain: V. 169, 171.

Murray, Lieutenant: V. 169, 171.

Muscovy (i.e., Russia): Bicker-staff praised in, II. 160.

Muses: no longer invoked, IX. 338.

Musgrave, Sir Christopher, *c.* 1632–1704, statesman: and Bedlam, I. 111.

Music, JS's views: and canting, I. 182; Italian music censured, XII. 36–7; liturgical, XI. 246 ('whistling'); — Dissenters' aversion, I. 125; XIV. 36–7; music of the spheres, XI. 162.

Mutual Subjection, sermon by JS: IX. 141-9; analysis, IX. 106–7, 124-6; composition, IX. 133-4, 137; textual note, IX. 375-6; title-page facsimile, IX. 139.

Myrmidons: and political repre-sentation, I. 235.

Mysteries, Christian: defended, IX. 162-3; disbelief unprofit-able, IX. 167; exercise in faith, IX. 163; and priests, IX. 163; and vice, IX. 166; will of God, IX. 162. *See also* TRINITY.

N

N.N.: signature of author of *A Letter from a Friend to the Right Honourable Chief Justice Whitshed*, X. 162; signature of author of *A Second Letter from a Friend to the Right Honourable Chief Justice Whitshed*, X. 171; and *Drapier's Letters*, X. xxv.

Naboth (1 *Kings* xxi): and false witnesses, IX. 181.

Naboth's Vineyard (Swift's rented garden, about three acres of land, south of the deanery): JS's lease on field, XIII. 156.

Nagasaki, Japan: XI. 216–17 ('Nangasac').

Naggin: XIII. 214; jill, XIII. xv, 22.

Namur, Belgium: VI. 28, 101, 109; VII. 153, 156.

Nangasac (i.e., Nagasaki), Japan: XI. 216–17.

'Nanunculus' (JS's Latin coinage, meaning 'mannikin'): XI. 95.

Naples, Italy: Belisarius captures, XIV. 31.

Naples, Kingdom of: VI. 57, 111; Austria attacks (1707), VI. 34-5; to be French (1700), VI. 11; Hapsburgs regain, III. 224; VII. 89; and Treaty of Utrecht — Austria to retain, VII. 133, 164.

'Nardac' (highest Lilliputian title, comparable to 'duke'): XI. 53, 55, 66, 76.

Naseby, Battle of (1645): III. 118.

Nassau van Wordenberg, Cor-nelis, Count van, 1675–1712: sent to Ormonde's camp, VII. 141-2.

Nations: causes of their pros-perity, XII. 5-7; — contrasted with Ireland, XII. 7-12.

Naturalization of foreign Protes-tants: III. 48, 71; VII. 94; bill against, III. 169; Tories oppose, VI. 130.

Nature: nothing in vain, I. 247-8. *See also* HUMAN NATURE.

Naunton, Sir Robert, 1563–1635, statesman: style censured, II. 177.

Navarre and Flemings: V. 74.

Navigation Act of 1661: Ireland's exemption (1663) ended, X. 35; and Ireland, XII. 8, 66, 132.

Navy, British: Charles I, IX. 225; debt on, III. 32, 34, 136, 170, 198; VII. 3, 22, 72–3, 76, 77, 83; and fines for swearing, IX. 295; French trade maintained against, VII. 84; Oxford provides for, VII. 3; payments to, VII. 72; and War of League of Augsburg (1689–97), VI. 11; and War of the Spanish Succession — ignored during, VI. 22, 38; — losses to French privateers, VI. 60; — and Methuen Treaties, VI. 25–6; — and Portugal, VI. 25; — quotas, VI. 31; VII. 82; — exceeds prescribed war quota, VII. 83; — war strategies, VII. 83; — weakened by war, VII. 83–4; — war-time trade, VII. 84.

'Ne exeas regno': origin of writ, V. 15.

Nebuchadnezzar: and Epicureans, I. 247.

Neighbour: duty to, IX. 232.

Neile: *see* NESLES.

Nelson, Robert, 1665–1715, religious writer and non-juror, author of *Fasts and Feasts of the Church of England* (1704): II. 21 and *n.* *; and Berkeley, II. xx; JS praises, II. xvii.

'Nena' (i.e., Queen Anne), Empress of Japan: V. 99.

Nepos, Cornelius, 1st century B.C., Roman historian: *Miltiades* 4, 7: I. 206.

Neptune: pun upon, IV. 235; threat to winds, III. 149.

Neptune, Bassin de, fountain at Versailles: XI. 120.

Nero (Lucius Domitius Ahenobarbus), A.D. 37–68, Roman emperor: and conquest of Britain, V. 3; capriciously cruel, II. 22; death, V. 85; Henry VIII compared unfavourably with, V. 249; and fall of Rome, I. 222; and Tindal, II. 100; cruel tyrant, I. 198.

Nerva (Marcus Cocceius), A.D. 32–98, Roman emperor: V. xxxix; — his reign ('a time') compared with Charles I's, V. 296.

Nesles, Pas de Calais, France: III. 212.

Nestorius, *d.c.* 451, Patriarch of Constantinople, founder of Nestorian heresy: and Celestine I, XIV. 21.

Netherlands: *see* DUTCH; FLANDERS; SPANISH NETHERLANDS.

Netherlands, Spanish: *see* SPANISH NETHERLANDS.

Neumarché, Maine-et-Loire, France, castle of: V. 67.

Neuster, Adam, *d.* 1576, German Socinian, theologian: fanatic founder of 'Family of Love', I. 188.

'Neverout, Thomas': character in JS's *Polite Conversation*, IV. 116, 129–201, *passim*, 276–7.

Nevis, British colony in the West Indies: III. 169.

Newark, Nottinghamshire: Gulliver lives near, XI. 9.

Newark, David Leslie, 1st Lord, *d.* 1682, military commander: and battle of Bothwell Bridge (1679), V. 140–1.

New Brissac (Neuf Brisach), in Alsace: VII. 113.

Newcastle, Northumberland: V. 21; captured by David I, V.

49–50; fires in, IV. 258; Henry II seizes, V. 75.

Newcastle, John Holles, Duke of, 1662–1711, Lord Privy Seal, Whig: cheats daughter, V. 258; death, VII. 16; Macky and JS on, V. 258; his wealth, V. 258; and Whigs, VIII. 166.

Newcastle, Thomas Pelham-Holles, Duke of, 1693–1768: and Boulter, XII. xl, xlvi.

Newcomb, Thomas, *fl.* 1614–67, printer: VII. 241.

New England: and William Wood, X. 44.

New Forest: V. 23, 24.

Newfoundland: fisheries, XIII. 111; and French fisheries, VII. 49; Treaty of Utrecht restores to England, VII. 43, 49, 114, 132.

Newgate Gaol, London: V. 94, 116; XII. 127; Gregg, III. 148, 189, 249; Guiscard, III. xxii, 109, 116; and papa pardons, I. 70, 75; prisoners stripped, I. 88; writers in, II. 67.

Newgate Street, London: and Gulliver's father-in-law, XI. 20.

New Guinea: and Gulliver, XI. 217.

New Holland (i.e., Australia): XI. 148, 284. *See also* AUSTRALIA.

New Journey to Paris: Together with Some Secret Transactions Between the Fr[enc]h K[in]g, and an Eng-[lish] Gentleman, by JS (1711): **III. 207-18;** background, III. xxxi; date, XIV. 51; JS's purpose, III. xxxii; reception, III. xxxi; textual notes, III. 279; title-page facsimile, III. 207.

Newmarket, Suffolk: Godolphin at (1710), VII. 14; Pembroke at, V. xi, 85; Somerset at (1710), VII. 14.

New Proposal for the Better Regulation and Improvement of Quadrille, attributed to JS: *see* HORT.

New Testament: Greek text, I. 54 and *n.*†; and Manilius, IV. 45; will in *Tale of a Tub,* I. 44, *n.*‖. *See also* BIBLE.

Newton, Sir Isaac, 1642–1727: I. 10; III. 215; and Bentley, IV. xxxviii, 231; assays coins, X. 29; on Irish coinage, IV. xxxi; Master of the Mint, IV. 122; and mathematics, IV. xxxviii, 231; 'obscure mechanick', IV. 123; error in distance of sun, XI. 162; and Wagstaff, IV. 122-3; and Wood's coins, X. xiv and *n.* 3, xv–xvi; — assay of coins, X. 16–17, 31, 187–8, 189–90, 215.

Newtown-Butler, Theophilus, 1st Lord, *c.* 1669–1724: X. 58; legacy to Anne Ridgeway, XIII. 157.

New York: emigration to, XII. 76.

Niagara Falls: XI. 141.

Nice, Alpes-Maritimes, France: infidels driven from, V. 22.

'Nice, Mrs.': character in *Polite Conversation,* IV. 157.

Nicene Creed: XIV. 27; 'confessio fidei barbaris digna', XIV. 35.

Nicetas Acominatus, *d. c.* 1216, Byzantine historian: 'Greek writer', IV. 72.

'Nicholas, John' (ship's captain in *Gulliver's Travels*): XI. 80, 83–5.

Nichols, John, 1745–1826, printer

and author: and JS's *Mr. Collins's Discourse of Free-thinking*, IV. xvii; on JS's *History of the Four Last Years*, VII. ix and *n.* 1; and JS's *Letter to a Whig Lord* (1712), VI. xvii; revises Sheridan's edition of JS (1801), II. xxxii; — and *Miscellaneous Pieces in Prose and Verse . . . not Inserted in Mr. Sheridan's Edition of the Dean's Works*, 1789, XIII. xxvii; and Deane Swift, XI. xxvi, *n.* 3; reprints false additions to *Tale of a Tub*, I. xxxii; and authorship of *Tatler*, II. xxxi–xxxii; edits *Tatler* (1786), II. xxviii and *n.* 4; and authorship of *Tatler*, No. 32, II. xxx; edition of JS's *Works* (1801), Macaulay's copy, VII. ix; — note on *History of the Four Last Years*, VII. ix, *n.* 1.

Nichols, John, d. 1767, Surgeon-General of Ireland, JS's surgeon: JS's will, XIII. 154.

Nicias, *d.* 414 B.C., Athenian soldier and statesman: and Alcibiades, I. 207.

Nicolson, Marjorie: on *Gulliver's Travels*, XI. xx.

Nicolson, William, 1655–1727, Bishop of Derry: and the Drapier, X. xxx–xxxi.

Niddisdale, Earl of: *see* NITHS-DALE.

Niepe, forest in Belgium: VI. 102.

Nieuhof (Nieuwhof), Johan, 1618–72: *Legatio batavica ad magnum Tartariae chamum Sungteium, modernum Sinae imperatorem* — copy owned by JS, XI. xiv.

Nieuport: *see* NIEUWPOORT.

Nieuwpoort, West Flanders, Bel-

gium: VI. 28, 91, 101, 109; VII. 90–1, 114, 122, 153.

Nigel, Bishop of Ely, *d.* 1169: V. 56.

Nijmegen (or Nimeguen), Gelderland province, Netherlands: French troops approach (1701), VI. 13; Peace of (1678), 'the peace concluded 1679', I. 267; — and Sir William Temple, V. 193; — and Temple's *Memoirs*, I. 269.

Nile River: XI. 99; hidden source, I. 248.

'Nimble, Dick': character in *Polite Conversation*, IV. 191.

Nimeguen: *see* NIJMEGEN.

Nimrod (*Genesis* x. 8–10): Milton on, IX. 264; and proposed mint in Ireland, XII. 57.

Nineveh: compared to Ireland, IX. 238.

Ninus, mythological founder of Nineveh: I. 202.

Nithsdale, Robert Maxwell, 1st Earl of, *b. after* 1586, *d.* 1646: family, V. 129.

'Nnuhnoh' (an animal in Houyhn-hnmland, about the size of a rabbit and covered with a fine down): XI. 276.

Noailles, Louis Antoine, Duke of, 1651–1729, Archbishop of Paris, Cardinal: death predicted, II. 145, 155, 161, 196, 218.

Nobel, Richard, *d.* 1713: JS's April Fool's joke, IV. 259–60.

Nobility, JS's views on: corrupt, XI. 256–7; not in decline, V. 244; education, III. 150–1; IV. 227, 228; XII. 46–53; gambling, XI. 131–2; genealogy satirized, XI.

198–9; and their inferiors, XI. 200; insolence, II. 257–8; in Ireland, and copper coins, XII. 100; and Irish cloth, XII. 69–70; and judicature, XI. 128, 129; and the law, XI. 128, 129; lose political offices, XII. 47–8; praised, III. 150–2; their speech, IV. 10; and spleen, XI. 263–4; and White's Chocolate House, XII. 50; young, education of, XI. 61–2, 128, 129; — *Gulliver's Travels* to entertain, XI. 9. *See also* ANCESTRY; CONSTITUTION, *Balance of Power*.

'Nomptoc': anagram of Compton, V. 103.

Nonconformists and Dissenters: character, mean and illiterate, VII. 96; and Church of England, differences insignificant, III. 39; paucity of churches encourages, III. 160; and Godolphin ministry, III. 54; increase and naturalization of foreign Protestants, VII. 94; and James II, III. 144; and bill against occasional conformity (1711–12), VI. 76; VII. 21; and ordination of priests, III. 55–6; and Oxford ministry, VI. 127, 129; their preaching ought to be outlawed, XI. 131; Quakers, VII. 106–7; and Whigs, III. 126–32, 143, 145–6; VI. 76, 78; — encouraged by Whigs, VII. 107; and William III, III. 5–6. *See also* PURITANS; DISSENTERS.

Nonesuch Press, edition of JS's selected works: I. v.

Non-jurors: III. xxiv, 68, 104, 115; VIII. xxvi, 91, 173; bishops, III. 163; and Robert Nelson, II.

xvii, 21 and *n*.*; and political parties, II. 3; restraints upon, III. 127; and Tories, III. 189.

Non-Resistance, doctrine of: II. xvi–xvii; folly, II. 16, 19. *See also* PASSIVE OBEDIENCE.

Norfolk, Thomas Howard, Duke of, 1683–1732: and the Earl of Carlisle, V. 258.

Normandy: Geoffrey Plantagenet invades, V. 51; Henry I conquers, V. 40; and Robert, Duke of Normandy, V. 13; William Rufus in, III. 288; V. 15, 19.

Normans: invade England (1066), V. 6–7; Norman Conquest and modern age, I. 211–12.

Normanton, Charles Agar, 1st Earl of, 1736–1809, Archbishop of Dublin: sale of library, XIII. xi.

'North, A.', pseudonym for JS in *Intelligencer* No. 19: XII. 61.

North America: XI. 193; Cortez, XI. 293; and England, VI. 117; fortune-tellers, I. 186; fanciful map of, XI. 82; and *Modest Proposal*, XII. xxi; and peace (1711), VII. 49; religion in colonies, III. 161; and Treaty of Utrecht, VII. 43.

Northampton, England: Stephen's court, V. 66; and Wood's coins, X. 104.

Northern War (begun 1699): VII. 148; England potentially involved, VI. 62–3; — Treaty of Copenhagen (1701), VI. 62 ('our guaranty'); and France (1711), III. 209–10; and War of the Spanish Succession, VI. 62–4.

North Pole: IV. 284.

Northumberland, George Fitzroy (formerly Palmer), 1st Duke of,

1665–1716, lieutenant-general, privy councillor, illegitimate son of Charles II by Barbara Villiers: VIII. 102, 117; Macky and JS on, V. 258.

Northumberland, Henry of Scotland, Earl of Huntington and of, *c*. 1114–52, son of David I: 'eldest son', V. 50, 52, 54, 55.

Northumberland, Robert de Mowbray, Earl of, *fl.* 1081–95: confined for life, V. 21; defeats Scottish Army, V. 18; defeated by William II, V. 20–1.

Norway: Queen Anne as 'Norway's pride' (i.e., wife of Prince George of Denmark), II. 165, 168, 169 and *n.**; and Danes, V. 5.

Norwich, England: V. 14, 50.

'Notable, Miss': character in JS's *Polite Conversation*, IV. 115, 116, 129–201, *passim*, 276–7.

Nottingham, England: French prisoners at, VII. 34; Gaultier at (1704), VII. 34.

Nottingham, Daniel Finch, 2nd Earl of, later 6th Earl of Winchelsea, 1647–1730, Secretary of State, nicknamed 'Dismal': Queen Anne finds him unacceptable, VII. 15, 16; avarice, VII. 15; Burnet and JS on, V. 288; compared with his brother (1st Lord Guernsey), VII. 11; censured, V. 245; **JS's character of,** VII. 11–12, 15; pretends loyalty to the Church, VII. 11, 16, 21; opposes seizure of Dunkirk, VI. 140; and Dutch, VI. 139; would invite Electoral Prince (George II) to reside in England, VII. 16; and his father,

VII. 11; Macky and JS on, V. 258; and JS's *Hue and Cry after Dismal*, VI. xxii, 139–41; *Observations on the State of the Nation* (1713), VIII. 34; proposes bill against Occasional Conformity, VII. 16, 18; — moves it, VII. 21; — 'so profound a politician', VI. 127; refuses minor offices, VII. 16; deserts Oxford ministry (1710–11), VII. 16; — they distrust him, VII. 15; — would ruin them (1711), VII. 100–1; desires of preferment ignored (1711–14), VII. 16; possible model for Skyresh Bolgolam (*q.v.*) in *Gulliver's Travels*, XI. 42–80; son in Commons (1711), VII. 101; and vote of 'no peace without Spain', VII. 17, 18; VIII. 146; 'Squash', his servant, VI. 139–41; and Steele's *Crisis*, VIII. 32, 34; would lead Tories, VII. 11–12; — his Tory principles, VII. 11; and Robert Walpole, VII. 18; **and Whigs** — joins them (1711), III. 38; VII. 11, 16, 29, 108; — their bargain, VII. 16; — divides the party, VII. 21; — they despise him, VI. 129 ('example of apostacy'); — '2' and Pretender, VI. 145; — apparently hates them, VII. 15; — they hope to get strength, VII. 15, 29; they praise 'that person', III. 38; — their 'great proselyte', III. 53; — turncoat, VI. 141; opposes accession of William of Orange, VII. 11; — takes post under him, VII. 11.

Nottingham, Heneage Finch, 1st Earl of, 1621–82, father of Daniel Finch, 2nd Earl: VII. 11.

Nottingham, Henry Fitzroy, Earl: *see* RICHMOND.

Nottinghamshire: Gulliver's home, XI. 9.

Novara, Italy: VI. 13.

Nova Scotia: VII. 115, 132.

Novaya Zemlya (Nova Zembla), Russian island: I. 153.

Numa Pompilius, legendary successor to Romulus as King of Rome: I. 212.

Numerology: ridiculed in *Tale of a Tub*, I. 4, 34–5.

Nunneries: and virginity, II. 180.

'Nurse', in *Directions to Servants* (*q.v.*): XIII. 64.

Nutt, John, publisher and printer: publishes *Contests and Dissensions*, I. 193; publishes *Tale of a Tub*, I. xxxix.

Nuttall, Joseph: grand juryman of Dublin (1724), X. 76.

O

Oak trees: and free masons, V. 329–30.

Oates, Titus, 1649–1705, chief witness in Popish Plot, perjurer: IV. 62; Burnet and JS on, V. 278.

Oaths (curses, swearing): and faith, IX. 157; in *Tale*, I. 10, 25. *See also* PROFANITY.

Oatlands: IV. 283.

Obedience, political: people's duty, IX. 186; of subjects, IX. 230. *See also* PASSIVE OBEDIENCE.

Objections against the General Bank in Ireland, 1721: IX. 321.

O. Brazile, an imaginary island: I. 78 and *n.* †.

Obscenity, JS's views on: Mrs. Johnson denounces, V. 234–5; in *Tale of a Tub*, I. 10; — ridiculed, I. 92–3.

Observations Occasioned by Reading a Paper, Entitled, The Case of the Woollen Manufacturers of Dublin (written *c.* December, 1733), by JS: **XIII. 89–92**; background, XIII. xxvi–xxviii; composition, XIII. xxvii; publication, XIII. xxvii; textual notes, XIII. 221.

Observator: attacked, III. xxiii–xxv, 189, 202; XIV. 9; and the church, III. 189; and Archbishop King, II. 282; an illiterate scribbler, III. 13; on the Test Act, II. 113; Whigs' best paper, III. 154. *See also* JOHN TUTCHIN.

Occasional Conformity, Bill against (1703–4): I. xxi; II. xi, xvi; III. 39; and Dissenters, I. xxii; — their contempt for conformity, III. 123–4; — warned not to abuse occasional conformity (1711), III. 131; enacted, VII. 18; lost in House of Lords, I. xxi; and Nonconformists, VI. 76; Nottingham proposes it, VII. 16, 18, 21; a Dissenter complains to Oxford, VII. 21; 'a speedy passage', VII. 21; JS undecided, I. xxi; — views, II. xvi; — writes against, I. xxi; and Test Act, II. 103; — Test Act not persecution, II. 122; and Tindal, II. 94; and Wharton, III. xviii; Whigs promise to repeal (1711–12), VII. 21; a Whig stratagem, VI. 76, 127; VII. 16, 21–2; 'swallowed' by

Whig lords, VII. 18; and worms, II. 76.

Occasional Paper, Letter to: *see* LETTER TO THE WRITER OF THE OCCASIONAL PAPER.

Occasional Writer, letters, by Bolingbroke: V. xii.

Oceana: *see* JAMES HARINGTON.

October, ale brewed in October: II. 185; VI. xii.

October Club: VIII. 83, 84; character, VI. xii, 71; *The Character and Declaration of*, VI. xii; formation, VI. xii, 187–8; VII. 99; VIII. 143; enemies of Godolphin ministry, VII. 99; and High Church, VII. 99; lack information, VI. 74, 80; Jacobites, VI. xii; and liberty of conscience, II. 5–8; membership, VI. 187; humoured by ministry, VIII. 125–6; and Oxford—indebtedness to him, VI. 75 ('one great person'); — no cause to dislike him, VI. 79–80; and Oxford ministry, VI. 71–80; VII. 99–100; *Secret History*, VI. xii; and JS—he complains about it, VI. xii; — allegedly dines with, VI. 187; — refuses to dine with them (1711), VI. xii; — his *Letter to*: *see* SOME ADVICE HUMBLY OFFER'D; urges strong action against Whigs, VI. 73.

'Oddity': on word list of JS, V. 336.

Ode Occasioned by Sir William Temple's Late Illness, by JS: composition, I. xv.

Ode to Dr. William Sancroft, by JS: composition, I. xiii.

Ode to the Athenian Society, by JS: publication, I. xii; mentioned, XI. x, *n.* 1.

Ode to the King on His Irish Expedition (written *c.* 1691), by JS: I. xi.

Odo, *d.* 1097, Bishop of Bayeux and Earl of Kent: conspiracy to depose William II, V. 13–14.

Of Mean and Great Figures Made by Several Persons, by JS: **V. 83-6**; analysis, V. x–xi; textual notes, V. 350.

Of Public Absurdities: see PUBLIC ABSURDITYES.

Of the Education of Ladies (written *c.* 1728), by JS: **IV. 225-8**; analysis, IV. xxxvii–xxxviii; **Hints, XII. 307-8**; — composition, XII. xxiii–xxiv; — textual notes, XII. 348; textual notes, IV. 300.

Offices, public: conscience necessary, IX. 157; and free-thinkers, II. 62; Ireland and England compared, XIII. 82–3; Irish, XIII. 80; — controlled by England, IX. 11; placemen corrupt, XIII. 80–1; property qualifications for, III. 119, 169–70; V. 80–1, 104; methods of selecting, XI. 39, 59, 190. *See also* PREFERMENT.

Official List of Subscribers to the Bank (1721): IX. 312–16, 378.

Ogilby ('Ogleby'), John, 1600–76, translator of the classics: 'kills' Thomas Creech, I. 158.

'Ogle, Sir John': character in *Polite Conversation*, IV. 156.

Ogleby: *see* OGILBY, JOHN.

Old age: XI. 207–14; and comets, IV. 247; and memory, V. 122, 123; JS's resolutions, I. xxxvii; talkativeness, V. 123; and wisdom, IV. 243, 244; and youth, IV. 243, 246, 251.

Old Dublin Intelligence: on taxes and tithes, XII. xxi.

Old English: V. 5.

Old Jewry, street in London: XI. 20.

Old Jury (i.e. Old Jewry): XI. 20.

'Oldcastle', pseudonym: V. xvii.

Oldham, John, 1653–83, poet, satirist: 'killed' by Pindar, I. 158; pun upon name, IV. 274.

Oldmixon, John, 1673–1742, historian: criticizes JS's *Proposal for Correcting, Improving and Ascertaining the English Tongue*, IV. xii–xv.

Old Testament: prophets and 'free thinkers', IV. 45. *See also* BIBLE.

Omphale, legendary queen of Lydia: and Hercules, IV. 234.

On Barbarous Denominations in Ireland, by JS: **IV. 280-4**, 302; analysis, IV. xxxviii–xxxix; erratum, XIV. 52; textual note, IV. 302.

On Good-Manners: *see* TREATISE ON GOOD-MANNERS.

On Mr. P[ultene]y Being Put Out of the Council, poem by JS: composition, XII. xxxiii.

On Poetry: *A Rapsody*, poem by JS: composition and publication, XII. xlvii.

On the Bill for the Clergy's Residing on Their Livings (written *c.* January 1732), by JS: **XII. 181-6**; background, XII. xxxv–xxxvi; composition, XII. xxxvi; manuscript, XII. xxxvi, 339–40, 341; textual notes, XII. 339–41.

On the Death of Mrs. Johnson [Stella], by JS (1728): **V. 227-**36; composition, V. xxv–xxvi, 228, 229, 233; XII. x; publication, V. 358.

On the Irish Bishops, poem by JS: XII. xxxix.

On Wisdom's Defeat in a Learned Debate, poem believed by JS: X. xxx.

O'Neill, Sir Phelim, *c.* 1604–83, Irish politician: XII. 287.

Opera: Italian opera censured, XII. 36–7; ridiculed, IX. 27; and soldiers, XII. 49; JS's views, II. xxv; and *Tatler* No. 4, II. xxvii.

'Opiniâtre': I. xxxvii.

Oppression: makes a wise man mad, IX. 18; and wisdom, IX. 271.

Orange: and Jacobitism, XII. 225; and William III, XII. 225.

Oratory: V. 22, 112; and Henry I, V. 47; lost art, IX. 213; periods, XI. 23; simplicity essential, IX. 68; and stirring of emotions, IX. 69; suited to audience, IX. 69.

Orchies, Nord, France, near Lille: VII. 141.

Order, social: Christian love, IX. 171; English constitution and social classes, I. 230; individual contributions essential, IX. 142; inequalities inevitable, IX. 126; good manners and social classes, IV. 213; princes need subjects, IX. 144; requires mutual subjection, IX. 144; rulers and subjects, IX. 142–3; scandalmongers condemned, IX. xxx, 93; servants and masters, XIII. 7–15.

Orford, Edward Russell, 1st Earl of, 1652–1727, Lord High Admiral, member of Whig Junto,

impeached (1700–1): represented by Miltiades and Themistocles, I. xx, 205–7, 210, 224; Partition treaties and 'Whig Ministers', I. xx.

Orford, Robert Walpole, 1st Earl of (2nd creation): *see* WALPOLE.

'Orgueil, Countess d'', character in *A Tale of a Tub*: I. 45–55.

Origen, Adamantius, *c.* 185–253, Church father: defence of Christ, IV. 42; 'free-thinker', IV. 46.

Orkney Islands: and Irish fisheries, XIII. 113.

Orkney, Elizabeth (*née* Villiers), Countess of, *c.* 1657–1733, mistress of William III: Howell and JS on, V. 264; JS and her picture, XIII. 155; and William III, V. 285.

Orkney, George Hamilton, 1st Earl of, 1666–1737, general, 5th son of 3rd Duke of Hamilton: Macky and JS on, V. 261.

Orléans, Le Père Pierre-Joseph d', *fl.* 1688–1734, Jesuit writer: XII. 132.

Orléans, Philippe, duc d', 1674–1723, regent of France: VII. 131; VIII. 169–70.

Ormonde, Elizabeth Butler (*née* Preston), Marchioness (later, Duchess) of, 1615–84, wife of 1st Duke: V. 190.

Ormonde, James Butler, 1st Duke of, 1610–88, statesman, soldier, courtier: and Godwin Swift, V. 190; Temple's letter to, XIV. 1.

Ormonde, James Butler, 2nd Duke of, 1665–1745, Lord Lieutenant of Ireland, general: III. 72, 231, 232; V. 289; Addison and JS on, V. 252 ('a general'); and Albemarle, VII. 147; XIV. 13; and Anne's death, VIII. 90; and Anne's guards, VIII. 156; attainder (20 Aug. 1715), VIII. xxxii (error for 'impeachment'), 132; Burnet and JS on, V. 294; character, VII. 126, 134–5; — beloved by his soldiers, VII. 141; **JS's character of**, VIII. 132–3; and Dunkirk, VII. 137–8; Dutch oppose his troops, XIV. 13; and First Fruits, V. xxvii; and George I, V. 252 ('a general'); in *History of Four Last Years*, XIV. 13; impeachment (1715), VIII. xxxi–xxxii; XIV. 54; — flies to France, VIII. xxxii; — and Steele, VIII. xix; Jacobitism, VIII. 166; — alleged, VIII. 47–8; and Battle of Landen (1693), VIII. 133; Lord Lieutenant of Ireland (1710), V. xxvii; Macky and JS on, V. 257; and Humphrey May, III. 232; and Lord Oxford, VIII. 124, 155–6, 157; praised, XII. 47, 287; and Benjamin Pratt, III. 183; Stella esteemed by, V. 230; **and JS** — conversation (1713), VI. xvii; — correspondence with JS, IV. xxxv; — — intercepted (1715), VIII. xxxii; — dear to JS, VIII. xxxii; — JS defends his flight, V. 252; — and Ireland, IX. ix; and Battle of Vigo Bay (1702), VIII. 133; — possible allusion to, in *Gulliver's Travels* (fleet taken), XI. 51–3; **and War of Spanish Succession** — size of army, VII. 127; — takes Bruges, VII. 141–2; — orders to Cadogan (1712), VII. 141; — Captain-General (1712), VII. 27,

122; — discretionary power in Belgium (1712), VII. 142; — and Dutch — their letters to him (1712), VII. 126–7; — — refuse him passage, VII. 141; XIV. 13; — fears for his person (1712), VII. 141; — captures Ghent, VII. 141–2; XIV. 13; — stays in Ghent (1712), VII. 142; — 'restraining orders', VII. 122, 125–7, 135–9; — — allies desert, VII. 127, 140; VIII. 57; — — 'express' received from Bolingbroke, VII. 126; — — Eugene's message (1712), VII. 140; — — 'those facts', VIII. 133; — — justified, VIII. 57–8; — — mercenaries desert, VII. 135–9; — — Villars signals him, VII. 126; — letter from Villars, VII. 152; and Wharton, III. 183–4, 232; and Whigs, III. xxviii, *n.* 1.

Ormonde, Mary (*née* Somerset), Duchess of, *d.* 1733, daughter of Duke of Beaufort, 2nd wife of 2nd Duke of Ormond: and JS. letter (24 April 1714), VIII. xxiii.

Oroway, Richard: and Ebenezor Elliston, IX. 366.

Orpheus: castrates himself, I. 187; early fanatic, I. 186.

Orrery family: Orrery papers, in Harvard College Library, VII. xiv, *n.* 5; — and Faulkner's publishing rights, VII. xvi, xvii.

Orrery, Charles Boyle, 4th Earl of (1674–1731): aided by Apollo, I. 163; and Richard Bentley, II. 160, *n.*†; attacks Bentley, I. xvi; pretended author of *Dr. Bentley's Dissertation . . . Examin'd* (1698, 'Boyle's Examination'), by Francis Atterbury (*q.v.*) and others,

I. xvii, xviii, xxiv–xxv; — 'Remarks', I. 5; *Epistles of Phalaris* (1695), I. xvi; — edits *Phalaris*, I. 145, *n.**; 'one', I. 162; praised, I. 139; JS admires, I. 5; attacks Wotton and Bentley, I. 163–5.

Orrery, John Boyle, 5th Earl of, 1707–62, friend and biographer of JS: and Mary Barber, IV. xxxiii; XIII. 73; — letter from JS on Mary Barber's *Poems*: see BARBER, MARY; character, XIII. 73; correspondence, in Morgan Library, V. xxii; — and manuscript of *The Family of Swift*, by JS, V. xxii; and *Dialogue in the Castilian Language*, IV. xxx; on *Gulliver's Travels*, XI. xv; and William King, VII. xiii, xiv; and JS's *Letter to Pope*, IX. xii; manuscript of *Polite Conversation*, IV. xxxiii; *Remarks on . . . Swift* (1762), MS. notes, IX. xvii, *n.* 1; — Macaulay's copy, VII. ix; returns to England (1737), VII. xiii; on JS's sermons, IX. 97–98 and *n.* 1, 103–5, 107; — authorship of *The Difficulty of Knowing One's Self*, IX. 103–5; — sermon on the Trinity, IX. 107; **and JS** — JS bids him 'farewell for ever' (1737), VII. xiii; — and *Enquiry into the Behaviour of the Queen's Last Ministry*, VIII. xxxviii. 216; — and *History of the Four Last Years* — consults Bolingbroke, VII. xvii; — — consults Erasmus Lewis, VII. xvii; — — gives manuscript to Faulkner, VII. xvii; — — delivers manuscript to W. King, VII. xiii, xxiii; — — retains manuscript, VII. xvi, xxv;

— — discourages publication (1738), VII. xiv; — — JS asks him to see W. King about, VII. xiv; — — JS's executors instruct him, VII. xvii, xx; — and *Polite Conversation*, IV. 290; — and JS's will, XIII. 155; and Whigs, VIII. 166.

Orrery, Margaret (*née* Hamilton), Countess of, 2nd wife of 5th Earl: gift to JS, XIII. 155.

Orrery Papers: *see* ORRERY FAMILY.

Orthodoxy, Christian: made too subtle, IX. 262.

Orthography: and conversation, IV. 104; phonetic spelling attacked, IV. 113.

Osborne, Francis, 1593–1659, writer: style censured, II. 177.

Osborne, Thomas: *see* LEEDS.

Osiris: and fanaticism, I. 186–7.

Ossory, Bishop of: *see* TENISON, EDWARD.

Ossuna, Duke of: *see* OSUNA.

Ostend, Belgium: Britain not to demand, VII. 122; and Dunkirk squadron, II. 214; and Dutch Barrier, III. 224; VI. 28, 90, 91, 113, 116, 117; VII. 61.

Ostend Company: V. 95.

Ostracism: and class struggle, I. 206, 225.

Osuna, Téllez Girón y Benavides (Francisco Maria de Paula), 6th Duke of, 1678–1716: VII. 166.

Otanes: Persian judge, whose father (Sysamnes) was flayed by Cambyses, X. 92.

Otho I, 912–73, Holy Roman Emperor: R. Parsons and JS on, V. 241.

'Otomy' (i.e., anatomy, or skeleton): IV. 161.

Ottoman Empire: *see* TURKS.

Otway, Thomas, 1652–85, poet: pun upon name, IV. 274.

'Outed' (Laputan word for 'wing'): XI. 162.

Ovid: and April Fool's joke, IV. 267; Athene and Arachne, IX. 18, 272–4. Quotations and allusions: *Ars Amatoria* ii. 147: VI. 3; *Epistulae ex Ponto* II. ix. 47–8: II. 184; *Metamorphoses* vi. 5–145: IX. 18, 272–4; — vi. 136: I. 244; — viii. 203–5: III. 13; — xii. 56–61: III. 8; — xiii. 353: III. 40; — xv. 158–61: II. 260; *Tristia* i. 9. 5: I. 251.

Oxford, England: V. 56; and Empress Matilda, V. 61, 63–4; Stephen besieges, V. 63–4.

Oxford, Henrietta (*née* Cavendish Holles), Countess of, wife of 2nd Earl: JS's snuffbox, XIII. 153.

Oxford, Robert Harley, 1st Earl of, 1661–1724, Lord Treasurer: III. 72; and Swift's Academy, IV. 14, 16–21, *passim*; Addison esteemed by him, VII. xxxv; and Anne: *see* ANNE; and the army, III. xiv; attacked by journalists, VII. 74; VIII. 32, 136; — by Tories, VIII. 140, 156; attempts on his life: *see* band-box; *Guiscard*; and Atterbury, II. 61, *n**; band-box(1712), VI. xxiv, 196–7; — and Whigs, VI. 199; and Bolingbroke: *see* BOLINGBROKE; OXFORD MINISTRY; and Hugh Boulter, X. 61; and Bromley, *The Congratulatory Speech of Wil-*

liam Bromley, Esq., III. 147–8, 154–6 ('a paper'); and Burnet, IV. 70; Chancellor of the Exchequer, VII. 76; VIII. 103, 118; character, VIII. 152; — his 'cunning' qualified, VII. 74; — 'deaf to all advice', VI. 74; — decisiveness, VII. 73; — faults alleged, VII. 19; — 'the greatest, the wisest, and the most uncorrupt minister, I ever conversed with', III. xxiii; X. 102; — indifference to denigration, VII. 74; — memory, VII. 75; — sincerity, VI. 78; — 'skill, credit, and resolution', VI. 44; **JS's character of**, III. 79–80; VII. 73–5, 178–80; VIII. 135–8; — draft, VII. 178–80; — manuscript, VII. vii, 178; and Church of England — act for building fifty new churches in London (1711), III. 170; VII. 3; — First Fruits remitted, III. 74; and Church of Ireland — First Fruits, III. 74, 170; VIII. 123; a commissioner of public accounts (1710), VII. 73; and Commons — they esteem him, VI. 134, 135; VII. 76; — March Club ('a new one'), VII. 100; and Congreve, VII. xxxv; IX. 29; and dancing, XII. 50; and national debt, V. 113; VII. 3, 73–7; VIII. 126–7; — his project ridiculed, VII. 77; and navy debt, VII. 3, 76, 77; weekly dinners, VIII. 124; dismissal (1708), VII. 98; VIII. 101, 113; dismissal (1714), VIII. 132; — inevitability of, VIII. 157; and John Drummond, VIII. 171 ('a gentleman'); and Dublin

street cries, XII. 226–31; his education, XII. 47; withholds employments, VIII. 137 *et passim*; encourages men of letters, VIII. 7, 135–6; and Eugene — he hates Oxford, VII. 26; — meetings, VII. 26; — alleged plot against Oxford, VII. xv, 26–7; — — denied by Charles Lucas, VII. 175; — — JS's evidence, VII. 27; in the *Examiner*, XIV. oo; and exchequer bills, VII. 75–6; family, VIII. 135; and fisheries, XIII. 111; Gaultier, VIII. 163; — Gaultier directed to, VII. 35; possibly 'gentleman', II. 132; and George I, VIII. 157; — forbidden the court (1717), VIII. xxxv; and resumption of grants (1711), VI. 134; great figure, V. xi, 84; 'greatest minister I ever knew', IV. 217; and Gregg, III. xxix, 108–9, 190, 191, 193, 194, 195–8, 246–54; **Guiscard's attack**, III. xxii–xxiii; VIII. 126–7, 145; — attempt, III. 106, 115–16, 194–5, 197–8, 246–54, *passim*; VII. 76–7; — and the law, III. 138–9; — Oxford's composure following, III. 109; — parliamentary addresses, III. 120, 198; — strategic, VII. 99; — JS's *Examiner* on, III. 106–10; and Hanoverian succession — secured by him, VII. xxxiii; — his selflessness, VII. xxxvi; health, sickness (1711), VI. 72; impeachment(1715), VIII. xxxi, 149; XIV. 54; — acquitted by Lords (1717), VIII. xxxiv; — Committee of Secrecy, VIII. 163; — imprisoned, VIII. xxxii; —

Steele's arguments, VIII. xix;
and Irish politics, IX. ix; alleged
Lord Treasurer — restores
credit, VII. 76; — allegedly
would resign (1713), VIII. 154;
— — (1714), VIII. 156; — 'public thrift', VII. 19; Macky and
JS on, V. 260; and Marlborough,
III. xvi–xvii; and Mrs. Masham,
VIII. 110, 113–14, 115, 153, 156,
157; moderation, criticized for,
VIII. 124–6; Munodi possibly
modelled on, XI. 174–8; and
Ormonde, VIII. 155–7; decried
in Parliament, VIII. 85; subject
of *Part of the Seventh Epistle of
the First Booke of Horace Imitated*,
by JS, I. 278; credited with
peace, VII. 74, 75; and vote
against peace (1711), VII. 19; to
be made a peer (1711), III. 147–
52; and creation of twelve peers,
VII. 19–20; VIII. 149–50; portrait by Zincke, XIII. 154; his
power ambiguous, VI. 79;
praised, X. 102 and *n.**; and
preferment, IV. 246; Presbyterianism, denied, VIII. 67; and
the Pretender, VIII. 163–80;
procrastination, VI. 74; VII. 19,
75; VIII. xxvii, xxxiii, 140; —
and Anne, VIII. 137, 151, 157;
— infects the court, VIII. 110;
— extenuations, VI. 79–80;
'reputed to be chief minister',
VIII. 47; hoards responsibility,
VI. 74 ('strongest shoulders');
VIII. 81, 87–8, 140; and Ridpath's attacks, VIII. 31–2; and
Roman Catholics, XII. 286; and
Scriblerus Club, XI. xiii, *n.* 2;
Secretary of State, VII. 73; —
dismissed (1708), VIII. 101, 113;

secretiveness, VI. 74 ('great
abilities'); VII. 74; VIII. 77,
78–9, 80–1, 85–6, 87 ('some'),
88, 137; — reciprocated, VIII.
81; introduces Act of Settlement
(1701), VII. xxxiii; Somerset
seeks him out, VII. 14; and
South Sea Company, VII. 76;
as speaker, VIII. 136; Speaker
of the House, VII. xxxiii; —
not eloquent but persuasive, V.
260; — three times (February
1701, December 1701, June
1702), III. 79; VII. 73; VIII.
136; and Steele: *see* STEELE;
Sunderland will not forgive,
VII. 9.

   and JS: VIII. 109; — and JS's
academy project, IV. xi–xv, 5–6,
20–21; — Addison recom-
mended, IX. 29; — approached
by JS, II. xxxiii; — and band-
box ('a gentleman'), VI. 196–7;
— and the Barrier Treaty, VI.
xiv; — refuses to be his chaplain, VII. xxxv; — and *Conduct
of the Allies*, VI. viii; — Congreve recommended, IX. 29;
— correspondence (1717), VIII.
xxxv; — dedication of *Proposal*,
IV. 3, 5; — defends Oxford,
VIII. xxix, xxx; — dine together
often, VII. xxxv; — Saturday
dinners, VIII. 124; — esteem for
Oxford, III. xxiii; — First Fruits,
V. xxvii; IX. ix; — friendship
very close, II. xxxvi; — — intimacy, VIII. xxxv; — — exagger-
ated by JS's enemies, VIII. 108;
— and Historiographer's post,
VIII. 110; — and *History of Four
Last Years*—JS uses his correspondence, VII. xxxiv; — —

slow in giving JS papers, VII. x, xi; — first meeting (1710), VIII. 122–3; — early meetings, III. x; — JS writes pamphlets for, II. xxii; IV. xvi; — JS's personal loyalty, VI. xvi–xvii; — their politics similar, II. xv; — and JS's preferment, VIII. xxxi; — and *Proposal for Correcting . . . the English Tongue*, IV. xii–xv, 285; — JS restrains criticism, VIII. xxvii–xxviii; — offers to attend Oxford in retirement (1717), VIII. xxxv; — Rowe recommended, IX. 29; — his scholarship humbles JS, IX. 28; — secretiveness of 'a great minister', VIII. 78–9; — Steele recommended, IX. 29; — JS urged to return to London (1713), VIII. x; — Thomas Swift's letters to Sir Edward Harley, V. 190;

and Tories, VIII. 140; — loses their support, VIII. 150–8; — loses support of other ministers, VIII. 157–8, 161–2; and Toulon, VI. 97; in the Tower (1715–17) VIII. 164; trial, V. 84; VIII. 163–4; — and *Enquiry into the Behaviour of the Queen's Last Ministry*, VIII. xxxiv; Walpole contrasted with, V. 113; and War of the Spanish Succession—stops unwarranted subsidies, VI. 39; — opposes war, VII. 26; and Whigs—they would ruin him ('Z'), VI. 145–6; — — failure ('parade to the tower') (1712), VI. 135; — alleged to sympathize with them, VII. 100; — early ties between, VIII. 166; — they would undermine him, VI. 78–9; VII. 100; on White's

Chocolate House, XII. 50. *See also* OXFORD MINISTRY.

Oxford, Edward Harley, 2nd Earl of, 1689–1741, son of Lord Treasurer: and Faulkner, XIII. 202; — Faulkner's edition of JS, XI. xxv; XIII. xxxv; — visits (1741), VII. xvi; marries Lady Holles, V. 258; and William Stratford, XI. xxiii; **and JS**— JS's bequest, XIII. 154; — *History of the Four Last Years*— Oxford criticizes, VII. xv; — — discourages publication, VII. xiv; — — reads it, VII. xiv, *n.* 1; — letter to Oxford (16 Feb. 1732/3), XI. xxv.

Oxford, Henrietta (*née* Cavendish), Countess of, 1694–1755, wife of 2nd Earl, daughter of 1st Duke of Newcastle: cheated by father, V. 258; JS's snuffbox, XIII. 153.

Oxford ministry: accomplishments, VI. 75; and Anne: *see* ANNE; Army officers drink ruin of (1710), III. 44–5, 60; and Asiento, VII. 109; attacks upon foreseen (1713), VII. xxxiii; and Barrier Treaty, VII. 90–94; Buys misrepresents his authority, VII. 23; and Catalonia, VIII. 61–3; character of, III. 78–80; — likened to Brutus and Cato, VI. 134; — not of 'sublime abstracted Roman virtue', VI. 133; inconsistent charges against, VIII. 86; and Church of England—'Black-coats' dine with Oxford, III. 80; — and comprehension, VIII. 86; — ministry defends it, VII. 3; — funds to build churches, VII. 3; — neg-

lect it, VIII. 173-4; — clergy support ministry, VII. 3; lack 'communication and concert', VIII. 85-6; and Treaty of Commerce, VIII. 21; Commons support (1712), VI. 126; corruption alleged, VII. 51; and national debt, III. 6-8, 168-9, 170, 189; difficulties anticipated (1710), III. 33-4; weekly dinners, VIII. 124; disinterested, III. 78-80; VI. 64, 78; VIII. 85, 144, 179-80; — denied by Steele, VIII. 15; and Dunkirk, VI. 89-91; VII. 74 ('fortress'); and Dutch—Anne's indignation declared (1711), VII. 110-11; — Dutch distrusted, VII. 38; — claim ministry lacks support (1711), VII. 41-2; and management of elections, III. 66; VIII. 126, 149; Eugene's visit discouraged (1712), VII. 111; and *Examiner*, VIII. 123-4; fall, VIII. 140-1; — anticipated (1713), VIII. 21; — their own responsibility for, VIII. 82; — results unexpected (1712), VI. 80; — unnecessary, VIII. 177-8; and *Flying-Post*, VIII. 14; formation, VII. 35; and France—alleged correspondence, VI. 189-91; — allegedly Francophile, VIII. 22, 23-4, 39, 169-70; — French hope for peace, VII. 34, 35, 36; friendships within (1711), VII. 144; Gallas distrusts, VII. 58; and George I — they fail to cultivate him, VIII. 140; — attempt to cultivate him, VIII. 171-2; — George turned against (1712), VII. 144; compared with Godolphin's ministry, XIV. 8; willing

to examine royal grants, VII. 101; and Guiscard's attack, III. 108; and Hanoverian Succession, VIII. xxvi-xxvii, 90-1; — allegedly Jacobite, VII. xxxiii, 144; VIII. 18, 31, 39-40, 47-8, 163-80; — — 'private insinuations', VI. 76; and Lords, VIII. 82; and Lords' vote against peace (1711), VI. 123-4, VII. 110-11; lotteries, VII. 77; will not rely on 'management', VII. 16-17; and Marlborough—might conciliate him, VII. 29; — his dismissal, VI. 133; — — controverted, VII. 27-8; — — reasons for, VII. 28-9; — — regrettable, VII. 28, 29; — his return (1711), VII. 28-9; — would ruin them, VI. 133; described as moderates, III. xiii, 66; VI. 130, 187-8; VII. 99; VIII. xxvii, 124-5, 166; — various explanations of moderation, VIII. 83-5; — tolerate Whig press, III. 70-1; and Nottingham—apprehensive of him, VII. 15; — he turns against them, VII. 16; and the October Club, VI. xii, xiii, 71-80; VII. 99-100; VIII. 83, 84, 125-6; and Nonconformists, VI. 127, 129; — *see also* DISSENTERS; and Parliament—alleged fear to face them without a peace (1712), VII. 154, 158; patriotism, VII. xxxvi; creation of twelve peers (1712), VII. 20; — controverted, VII. 20-1; — decried by Lucas, VII. 175; — justification, VI. 124-5, 132; — 'motives', VII. 20; alleged popery, VIII. 31; rise to power, false credit sinks,

VI. 56; — and the economy, III. 4; — God's punishment, VI. 195; praised, III. 198-9; converts from Presbytery, VIII. 67; and the press—Whig pamphlets tolerated, VII. 104, 105; and the Pretender, III. 69; VIII. xxv-xxvi, 86, 140-1, 163-80; and the Protestant Succession, V. 265; refinements, VIII. 138-9; alleged republicanism, VIII. 86; Robinson made Lord Privy Seal, VII. 3; Somerset declares 'open war against' them, VI. 72; VII. 15; and Steele: *see* STEELE; support, VIII. 82; — failing (1714), VIII. 85;

and JS—*Conduct of the Allies*, VI. ix; — their defender, VI. vii, viii; VIII. xxxix; — and the *Examiner*, III. 31, 78; — few gifts, VII. xxxiv-xxxv; — intimacy, III. xxv; VII. x, xxxiii-xxxiv, xxxv; VIII. xxvi-xxvii, 90-91, 107, 124, 165-6; — — limited, VIII. 110; — *History of the Four Last Years* a vindication of them, VII. xi; — no money paid him, VII. xxxiv-xxxv; — his pamphlets ('active pens'), VII. 104; — JS denies tie (1711), III. 194, 202; — and *Publick Spirit of the Whigs*—reward for discovery of author, VIII. xxi-xxii, 30; — would have JS return to London (1713), VII. 181;

and Tories: *see* TORIES; **and Treaty of Utrecht**—disinterested, VII. xxxvi; — and ministerial responsibility, VI. 127; — secret negotiations criticized, XI. 56; their 'wisdom and courage', VII.

166; — Whig resistance, VII. 98; *see also* UTRECHT, TREATY OF, *England*; Walpole's ministry contrasted with, V. 113; and War of the Spanish Succession—they desire peace, III. 6-8; alleged weakness, VII. 144; **and Whigs**, VII. 1, 4; — acknowledge ministers' abilities, VIII. 82; — attempts to ruin ministry, VI. 130, 134-5; VII. 18-19, 100-2; — hatred, VI. 76-80; — Junto misrepresents ministers, VI. 127; — leniency of ministry, VI. 73, 74, 75-6, 77, 80, 126, 130; — and Whig Jacobites, VIII. 39; — Whig attacks upon, arbitrary, III. 58-9; — — Anne insulted by, III. 59-60; — Whig libels tolerated, III. 152-7; — and Whig writers, III. 30-1; — — indulgent, III. 188, 189; — *see also* SOME REASONS TO PROVE; and Whimsicals, VIII. 82-3.

Oxford regiment: VIII. 102, 117.

Oxford University: Carteret at, XII. 153-4; and 'ciser', IV. 237; college rents in kind, IX. 51; and Corusodes, XII. 41; decree of 1683, III. 144; and Eugenio, XII. 44; Great Tom, XII. 41; education of Horatio, II. 187; praised, XII. 51-2; and Steele's *Crisis*, VIII. 38; JS takes M.A., I. xii; and Tindal, II. 101; legacy from Charles Viner, XIII. 207. *See also* UNIVERSITIES.

Oysters: IV. 257-8; shells, powdered, V. 203.

Ozell, John, d. 1743, translator: and *Polite Conversation*, IV. xxxii.

P

P., A., pseudonym for JS in *Proposal for an Act of Parliament, to Pay Off the Debt of the Nation*: XII. 205.

Packington's Pound: tune of, IX. xvi.

Pages, at court: XI. 108.

Painter's coffee-house, Dublin: and free masons, V. 331.

Painters Wives Island, an imaginary island: I. 78, *n*.†.

Painting, Dutch: and English poetry, IX. 335-6.

Pais de Waas: *see* WAAS.

Palatinate: Elector Palatine: *see* JOHANN WILHELM; immigrants, III. 169; — Commons' resolution against (1711), III. 149; — money for, XIII. 175; — naturalization suspect, VII. 95; troops in Flanders (1711), VI. 30; — in Spain, VI. 37.

Palestine: crusades, V. 21-2; and Henry IV of France, I. 103.

Pall Mall ('Pellmell'), London: III. 22, 23; pun upon, IV. 150.

'Palmer, Parson': character in *Polite Conversation*, IV. 184.

Palmerston, Henry Temple, 1st Viscount, *c.* 1673-1757, nephew of Sir W. Temple: and Irish public offices, X. 58.

Palsgrave, John, *d.* 1554, chaplain to Henry VIII: II. xxiv, *n.* 2.

Pamphleteering: *see* PRESS.

Pamphylian Sea: and Alexander, IV. 46.

Panciroli (Pancirollus), Guido, 1523-99, Italian lawyer, author of *Rerum memorabilium jam olim deperditarum*, I. 98 and *n*.*.

Pandora's Box: and philosophers, I. 248.

Panegyric: difficult art, IX. 339; few materials for, I. 30.

Panegyric upon the World, imaginary treatise by the author of *Tale of a Tub*: I. xl.

Panegyrical Essay upon the Number Three, imaginary treatise by the author of *Tale of a Tub*: I. xl.

'Pannell, Abraham' (Gulliver's first commander): XI. 19.

Paper Left by William Gregg, etc.: III. xxix.

Papers Concerning the Bank Controversy: IX. 320-1.

Papists: *see* ROMAN CATHOLICISM.

Paracelsus (Theophrastus Bombastus von Hohenheim), 1493-1541, Swiss alchemist and physician: 'Bumbastus', 'Christophorus', 'Theophrastus', I. 96 and *n*.*; fights with chemicals, I. 152; and excrement, I. 104, *n*.†; and Fountaine, IV. 258; insane, I. 105; fights for Moderns, I. 156; and Molyneux, IV. 257; 'quack', IV. 271.

Parents and children: among Houyhnhnms, XI. 268-70; Irish children, IX. 207; in Lilliput, XI. 60-63; miser's heir, II. 244; poor people, IX. 192; and education, XII. 46-53. *See also* IRISH PEOPLE, *children*.

Paris: fire predicted, II. 146-7; — denied by Partridge, II. 205; and Gee, IV. 250; and gold lace, I. 51; JS plans visit, XII. ix.

'Paris' (pseudonym for a judge), I. 32 and *n*.*.

Parker, a Lancashire gentleman: V. 150.

Parker, George, 1651–1743, almanac-maker: *Ephemeris* (1707), II.
xi; attacks Partridge, II. xi–xii.

Parker, Thomas: *see* MACCLES-
FIELD, EARL OF.

Parker's Penny Post: *Gulliver's
Travels* serialized in (1726), XI.
xxiii.

Parkgate, English port, on the
Dee estuary near Chester: and
JS, V. 206.

Parliament, English (British): and
abolition of Christianity, II. 35,
36, 105; and Queen Anne —
address to her (13 Mar. 1710–11)
III. 120; — Anne's speech (1712),
VII. 130–4; and authors, II. 76;
and Bank of England (1709–10),
VII. 76; and bishops, II. 75; and
Burnet, IV. 62, 67, 68, 74–5, 83;
and Charles I, II. 244; and
Church of England, II. 5, 78–9,
106; and clergy, II. 76–8, 97; —
legislative power of clergy, II.
81–3, 85–6, 92; Convention
Parliament (1689), II. 21; Copyright Acts, XIII. 206; corruption — reform proposed by JS,
XIV. 14–5; and courts of law, II.
55; and Cromwell, I. 231; and
Dissenters, II. 28; and education, IV. 228; three estates, XII.
244; in the *Examiner*, XIV. 9;
and Henry VIII, V. 244; —
a tyrant over them, V. 249;
history of, V. 35–8, 47, 72–3;
and Inns of Court, II. 52; and
Irish cattle trade, XII. 174;
compared with Irish Parliament,
X. 30–1; caused Irish rebellion,
IX. 223; and Irish Test Act,
II. 113; — Parliament mistrusted,
II. 113–14; legislative power, II.

74–5; and literary censorship, II.
26–7; Lords abolished, IX. 223;
lotteries, III. 134–5; — *see also*
LOTTERIES; majority in, Addison
and JS on, V. 252; and moral
reformation, II. 59–61; mortgage
extended (1702), VII. 70; packing of, V. 284; place bills, XIII.
83; powers, II. 74–6; V. 277;
— no spiritual powers, II. 75;
praise for 1710 Parliament, XIV.
9; privilege of Parliament, V.
82; prorogation, I. 18; Puritan
parliaments nullified, V. 268–9;
Qualification Bill (1710), III. 119;
ridiculed, I. 32; compared with
Roman senate, XI. 195–6;
Rump Parliament, XII. 267–8;
sessions, 1710 (dissolution), VII.
14; — 1711, VII. 17–18; — 1712,
VII. 31, 34, 64–107; — 1713,
prorogued, VII. 158, 160, 161,
162; suits of clothes occupy, I.
47; visited by brothers in *Tale
of a Tub*, I. 45; author's thanks,
in *Tale of a Tub*, I. 115; power of
taxation, V. 245; English taxes,
IX. 220; and Tindal's *Rights of
the Christian Church*, II. 75–6; —
Whigs support, III. 37, 54, 142;
Tory majority (1710–13), VIII.
143; and Wagstaff, IV. 122; and
War of the Spanish Succession
— peace preliminaries (1711),
VII. 57; — 'no peace without
Spain', VII. 12, 15; Whig opposition in (1710), VII. 4. *See also*
HOUSE OF COMMONS; HOUSE OF
LORDS.

Parliament, Irish: loyal address
(1707), IX. 7; and *Advantages
Proposed by Repealing the Sacramental Test, Impartially Consi-*

dered, XII. xli; annual elections recommended, IX. 32; and bank scheme, IX. xix, xxi, 293, 304; — forbidden, IX. 319; and charity laws, IX. 136; 'the Club', XIII. xxxviii; corrupt, XIII. 82, 83; corruption since Revolution, IX. 79–80; Dissenters in, II. 118; seventh *Drapier's Letter* addressed to, X. xxvii, 119–41; and England — loyalty, IX. 10; — remedy for oppression, IX. 11–12; — JS's advice, IX. 11–12; compared with English Parliament, X. 31; and George I, X. 34; and George II, XII. xiv; and Irish concord, X. 134; 'Irish interest', XIII. 81; and Irish manufacture, IX. 16; — members urged to use, XII. 127; members mad (1715), IX. 117; not minding pamphlets, XII. 309; and Pembroke, IV. 257; *Presbyterians Plea of Merit*, XII. xlii; prorogued (1725), X. xxv–xxvi; XII. xxx; act against swearing, IX. 295; and repeal of Test Act, XII. xliii–xlvii, 283–95; and tithes, XIII. 95–108; and Wood's coins, X. ix–xi, xiii, xxviii–xxix, 27, 29–31, and *passim. See also* JS's HUMBLE ADDRESS TO BOTH HOUSES OF PARLIAMENT.

Parnassus, mountain in Greece, mythological seat of Apollo and the muses: IV. 252; origin of battle between ancients and moderns, I. 142, 145.

Parnell, Thomas, 1679–1718, poet: manuscript of poems — **JS's receipt for** (1723), **XIV. 13**; — authenticity, XIV. xii; — —

textual note, XIV. 45; *Posthumous Works*, XIV. 45; and Scriblerus Club, XI. xiii.

Parodies by JS: I. xxxiv; of Bentley, I. xxv, 56–64, 77–82; of Robert Boyle, I. xxxiv, 237–40; of Dryden, I. 3, 42; of L'Estrange, I. 3, 42.

Parody as a literary device: in *Tritical Essay*, I. xxxv; in *Tale of a Tub*, I. 3.

Paros, Ægean island: and Miltiades, I. 206.

Parry, Benjamin, *c.* 1673–1736, M.P. for Dungarvon, member of Privy Council of Ireland: X. 205.

Parsons, Robert, 1546–1610, Jesuit controversialist: *A Conference About the Next Succession to the Crowne of Ingland* (1594) — JS's copy, V. xxxi; — **JS's marginalia** (written *c.* 1705), **V. 241-3**; style praised, II. 177.

'Partage' (i.e., portion): VII. 164.

Parties, political: I. 195–236; III. 101–5; in almanacs, II. 143; Anne disables 'sting of faction', VII. 20; and balance of power, I. 195–203, 223–27; — Athens, I. 204–10; — England, I. 228–36; — Rome, I. 211–222; and Carteret, XII. 155–69; and abolition of Christianity, II. 31; and Church of England, II. 8–9; and cossing of dogs, XII. 221–22; 'cure' proposed, XI. 189; court and courtly parties, 'suspended for better times and worse princes', VI. 78; and degeneracy of taste, III. 35; differences not important, II. 13–14, 266; VI. 123–36; foster dissension, VI. 55;

VII. 4; — drive friends apart, II. xxxvii and *n.* 2; IX. 176; — and political extremists, II. 24–5; III. xii; satirized in *Gulliver's Travels*, XI. 48–50, 189; 'high' and 'low', II. 14; in Ireland, II. 118–19; IX. 176–7; — and Irish House of Commons, II. xxii; — Irish political issues, X. 132–34; journalists and majority power, VIII. 14; management of, and secrecy, VIII. 77–9; Marlborough's alliance with faction a symptom of his ruin, VII. 30; absurd maxims produced by, VII. 107; moderation recommended, II. 1–2; and morality, II. 58; parties necessary, II. 2; no more than two possible, VIII. 180; past and present, I. 241; and *Presbyterians Plea of Merit*, XII. xlv; and religious sects, II. 2–13; serpentine, VIII. 89; and slander, II. 4; and Tindal, II. 70; and independent thinking, I. 228–36; V. 253; Wharton exemplifies their nature, VII. 10; 'High-Flying Whigs', II. xxxii–xxxiii; Whigs and Tories, VIII. 120; — disagree about means, III. 13; — divisions meaningless, II. 13–14, 266; III. xxvi; VI. 123–36; —not divided in principles, III. 15; — principles no longer involved, VI. 123, 127, 128, 131; VII. 3–4; VIII. 71; — terms should be dropped, III. xii–xiii; VI. 5, 123; VII. 3; violent in 1703–4, I. xxi; *see also* HIGH CHURCH; LOW CHURCH; TORIES; WHIGS.

Partition Treaty, the first (1698):

and impeachment of Whig ministers, I. xx.

Partition Treaty, the second (1699): and legacy of Charles II of Spain, VI. 48; 'clogs' peace, VI. 11; and France, VI. 11; — France ignores, VI. 14; — violates, VI. 12; impeachments following, VIII. 119; —allegory, I. 206–9; 'infamous', VIII. 54; and Philip V, VI. 11; and division of Spain, VI. 48; — Spain rejects, VI. 11; and Spanish throne, VIII. 54; revives war, VI. 61.

Partridge (Patrige, etc.), John (*alias* John Hewson), 1644–1715, almanac-maker: II. xxviii; almanac, *Merlinus Liberatus* (1704), II. xii; — (1706), II. xii; — (1708) — frontispiece facsimile, II. 137; —— praised ironically, II. 167; — (1709) — attacked by JS, II. 157–64; — extract, II. 225, 290; —— reception, II. 162; in *Answer to Bickerstaff*, II. 196–8; censured and mocked, II. 139–50; death described, II. 151–5, 163–4; — predicted, II. xii, 145, 196; — prediction attacked by him, II. 204; — 'proved', II. 162–4; reiterated in Bickerstaff's *Vindication*, II. xxiv; existence denied, II. 250; grandmother's medicines, II. 155; papers concerning, I. v-vi; George Parker attacks, II. xi–xii; *Mr. Partridge's Answer to Esquire Bickerstaff's . . . Predictions*, II. 201–7, 290; — background, II. x–xii; — publication, II. xii; — textual notes, II. 290; — title-page facsimile,

II. 201; portrait, II. 137; quotations — almanac (1699), II. xi; — (1700), II. xi–xii; — (1706), II. x–xi; JS attacks, II. x–xiv.

Paschal II (Ranieri), Pope, *c.* 1050–1118: captured by Emperor Henry V, V. 34; urges King Henry I to subdue Robert, V. 33–4; and investiture of bishops, V. 30–1, 34.

Pasquin, legendary 15th century Roman: his statue in Rome, II. 261.

Passions: and preaching, IX. 68–70; and Puritans, I. 188–90; and reason, I. 107–10; IX. 263; XI. 267–8; ridiculous, IX. 89; uncontrollable, IX. 351.

Passive obedience: II. 16; III. 110–16; and clergy, II. 101; III. 6, 72; and Tories, III. 125, 144–5.

Patents: V. 293; for coining money, X. 30, 37–42, 196–9; — Wood's patent, X. 30–43 and *passim*.

Paterculus, Caius Velleius, 1st century A.D., Roman historian: quotation — II. iii. 4: X. 163.

Patience: under oppression, IX. 228–30; self-knowledge teaches, IX. 360; and suffering, V. 208.

'Patlego': on word list of JS, V. 336.

Patricians versus plebeians: I. 195–236. *See also* CONSTITUTION, *Balance of power.*

Patrick, Simon, 1626–1707, Bishop of Chichester and of Ely: Burnet and JS on, V. 271, 273.

Patriotism: all men may have, IX. 234; ancient and modern, IX. 155–6; decay of, IX. 156; XI. 201–2; in Ireland: *see* IRISH

PEOPLE, *patriotism*; neglected, IX. 233; defence against traitors, IX. 237; honest witness, IX. 188.

Patronage: Britain, government and literature, XII. 34–5; Greek clients and patrons, I. 212; Ireland, government and poetry, IX. 341.

Paul, St.: allegories, IX. 262; and free-thinkers, IV. 31; and the laity, II. 54; and ancient philosophy, IX. 242; on reformation, XII. 276; ridiculed, II. 92; corresponds with Seneca, IV. 44–5; style obscure, IX. 66. *See also* BIBLE, *New Testament.*

Paulet: *see* BOLTON.

Paulson, R.: on text of *Tale of a Tub*, XIV. 49.

Paulus Diaconus, 8th century historian: on Attila, XIV. 23.

Paulus Macedonicus, Lucius Æmilius, *c.* 229–160 B.C., Roman general: and commissions for life, III. 42.

Pausanius, *fl. c.* A.D. 150–200, Greek geographer: quotations and allusions — II. 31. 5 : I. 134; — II. 38 : I. 60; — VIII. 36. 6 : I. 97; — X. 18. 4: IV. 247; in *Tale of a Tub*, I. xxv.

Pawnshops: and Swearing Act, IX. 297.

Peace: legacy of Christ, IX. 171, 248.

Pearce, Sir Edward Lovet, *c.* 1699–1733, architect: XII. 306; gives JS a book, V. xxxi.

Pearson, J., and Co., London: manuscript of JS's *History of the Four Last Years*, VII. xxiii.

Pearson, Nathaniel: on Dublin grand jury, X. 76.

Pearson, Philip: on Dublin grand jury, X. 76.

Peasants: French, compared to Irish, IX. 21; Irish, compared to German and Polish, IX. 21.

Pedantry: I. xvi; definition, IV. 90, 215; and manners, IV. 215–16; in preachers, IX. 65–8; attacked in *Tale of a Tub*, I. xxiii–xxiv, 10, 56–64; Wotton an 'unmannerly pedant', I. xviii.

Pederasty, school: I. 25.

Peerage: *see* HOUSE OF LORDS; NOBILITY.

'Pegasus': pun upon, IV. 210.

Pelagius, *d. c.* A.D. 420, founder of heresy denying original sin: condemned, XIV. 19.

'Peloponnese': pun upon, IV. 237.

Peloponnesian War (late 5th century B.C., between Athens and Sparta and their respective allies): and Pericles, I. 207.

Pembroke, Thomas Herbert, 8th Earl of, *c.* 1656–1733, Lord Lieutenant of Ireland: III. 181; IV. xxix; Lord High Admiral, II. xxi; and Tom Ashe, IV. 263, 265; L. L. in *Dialogue in the Castilian Language*, by JS, IV. 257–9; and Dodington, X. 58; and *Dying Speech of Tom Ashe*, by JS, IV. xxxvi, 263–6; mean figure, V. xi, 85; picture of birds, XIII. 155; and anti-Irish propaganda, II. 111–12; JS accompanies to England (1707), II. ix; JS attends (1708), II. xv; JS puns with, I. xxxiv.

Pendergrass, Thomas: *see* PRENDERGAST.

Penelope's web: I. 250.

Penmaenmawr, Carnarvonshire, Wales: JS writes verse for inn at (1727), V. 201–2.

Penmany (*i.e.*, Penmynydd), Anglesey, Wales: Owen Tudor's tomb, V. 202.

Penn, William, 1644–1718, Quaker: on America, XII. 76; Burnet and JS on, V. 285; — 'spoke very agreeably and with much spirit', V. 285; and freethinkers, IV. 31; pamphlet dedicated to him, XII. 76; JS familiar with, XII. 76.

Penny London Post: *Gulliver's Travels* serialized in (1726), XI. xxiii and *n.* 5.

'Pennyless, Patrick': XII. 54.

Pensionary: *see* HEINSIUS.

Pensions: IV. 20; and corruption, XI. 129–30; and Godolphin ministry, III. 78; of Irish absentees, X. 128; XII. 9.

People, common: easily corrupted, VI. 80; 'dextrous at pulling down', I. 219; 'my faithful friends', X. 88; most are freethinkers, II. 34; on good government, IX. 227; recognize hyperbole, II. 13; imaginary treatise on, I. xl; and liberty in England and Ireland, X. 30–1, 35, 39; loyalty to king, IX. 186; and 'moderation', IX. 178; necessary to commonwealth, IX. 143; and obscure words, IX. 65; the body politic, I. 195–203, 204–210; politics not their concern, IX. 173, 177, 179, 186; and *Predictions for the Year 1708,* II. 196; 'rabble', X. 213; reasonable, VIII. 77; riches of a nation, VII. 94–5; IX. 15, 129; XII. 6, 22,

89–90, 109–18, 135–6, 309; enemies of science, XI. 185; agree with JS, IX. 30; taste in humour, XII. 33.

People, Irish: *see* IRISH PEOPLE.

'Peplom Selan' (an uninterpreted Lilliputian phrase): XI. 25.

Pepys, Samuel, 1633–1703: *Diary*, V. xi and *n*. 2.

Perceval (or Percival), John, *d*. 1718, of Knightsbrook, Irish M.P., JS's friend and neighbour at Laracor: V. 196.

Pericles, *c*. 500–429 B.C., Athenian statesman: fall from power, I. 207, 210; impeachment, I. 224; pseudonym for Lord Halifax, I. xx, 207, 210, 224.

Peripatetics: defined by JS, V. 345.

Perle (or Parel), fort of Kalloo, in northeast Flanders: and Dutch Barrier, VI. 101, 109.

Perpetual motion: XI. 210.

Perpetuities (i.e., leases in perpetuity): pernicious practice, IX. 51.

Perrault, Charles, 1628–1703, French author and critic: descended from Momus, I. 57; 'killed' by Homer, I. 157.

Perron, Jacques Davy, Cardinal, 1556–1618: oratory, XII. 159.

Perrott, Sir John, *c*. 1527–92, Lord Deputy of Ireland: his oath, IV. 110.

Persecution: of Christians, promotes unity, IX. 171; religious, pointless, IX. 261.

Perseus, mythological hero: divinity, I. 57.

Perseus, King of Macedonia, *b*. *c*. 212 B.C.: mean figure, V. 85.

Persia and Persians: V. 83; XI. 105; and Athens, I. 206–7, 224; and free-thinkers, IV. 32, 33; Persian paintings, XIII. 155; and revolutions, I. 174; Turks' war against, II. 38.

Perth, James Drummond, 4th Earl of, 1648–1716, Jacobite courtier at St. Germains: and Erasmus Lewis, VI. xxvi–xxvii, 174, 175, 177, 200.

Peru: VI. 22, 23; and revolutions, I. 174; silver from, in shilling, II. 243.

Petalism: and class struggle, I. 225.

'Peter', personification of Roman Catholic church in *Tale of a Tub*: I. 44–55, 65–76, 83–7, 127–8, 131; expels his brothers, I. 76; oaths, I. 10; picture, facing I. 44, 76; becomes projector, I. 65–70; on transubstantiation, I. 7. *See also* HISTORY OF MARTIN.

Peter, St.: and Attila, XIV. 23; denied Christ, XIV. 32; founding of church ridiculed, XIV. 26–7; like Jupiter, IV. 235; and Archbishop King, IX. 274.

Peter I, 'The Great', Czar of Russia, 1672–1725: V. 85; and Charles XII, IV. 122; 'great prince', III. 138; 'these princes', VI. 63; 'princes of the north', VII. 148.

Peter II, King of Portugal, 1648–1706, father of John V: and treaties of 1703, VI. 25–6, 37.

Peter the Cruel (*i.e.*, Pedro of Castille), 1334–69, King of Castille and Leon: II. 22.

Peter the Fuller (Petrus Fullo), *d*. 488, monophysite Patriarch of Antioch: death, XIV. 25.

Peter the Hermit, *d.* 1115, French preacher: and the Crusades, V. 22.

Peter pence: V. 76.

Peterborough, Charles Mordaunt, Earl of Monmouth and 3rd Earl of, *c.* 1658–1735, soldier and diplomat: V. 288; and Austrian espionage (1711), VII. 58; expected in Frankfurt (1711), VII. 58; and Erasmus Lewis, VI. 175, 178, 200; Macky and JS on, V. 259; 'Monmouth' error for 'Molesworth', IV. xxv, 289; and Lord Oxford, VIII. 124; his steward, XIII. ix, 51; and JS, I. xx; III. x; — letter of May 1714, VIII. xxii; and Tories, VIII. 149; sent to Vienna (1711), VI. 35; and Whigs, VIII. 166.

Peters (or Peter), Hugh, 1598–1660, Puritan: VIII. 41.

'Petites Morales': II. 184.

Petition to the House of Lords, against the Lord Blaney: see DEAN OF ST. PATRICK'S PETITION.

Petkum, Edzard Adolf, Dutch diplomatic agent: in *Examiner*, XIV. 10; and peace negotiations (1711), VII. 40–41.

Petronius, Gaius, *d.* A.D. 66: VIII. 135; characteristics of poet, IX. 332–3; — and free thought, IX. 329; quotations — I ('Haec vulnera'): X. 170; — 118: IX. 332–3.

Pettencrife (or Pittencrieff, Dunfermline, Fifeshire), Laird of: V. 175–6.

Petty, Sir William ('Captain John Graunt'), 1623–87, economist: *Natural and Political Observations*

... *Upon the Bills of Mortality*, III. 159.

Peyton, Sir Robert, Whig politician and judge: XII. 230 and *n.**.

Pezron, Paul, 1639–1706, French philologist: IV. 231.

Phaedrus, Gaius Julius, 1st century A.D., Roman fabulist: quotations — II, *Epilogue*, l. 3: IX. 274; — IV. 10. 1: I. 248.

Phaeton, son of Helios, in Greek mythology: XI. 148.

Phalaris, Epistles of: I. 164; proved forgery by Bentley, I. xvi–xvii; frightens Bentley, I. 162; edition of 1695, ostensibly by Charles Boyle, later 4th Earl of Orrery, I. xvi, 145, *n.**; — preface attacks Bentley, I. xvi; discredited, I. 139; praised by Temple, I. xvii.

Phidias, early fifth century B.C., Athenian artist: and Alexander, X. 138.

Philalethes, Eugenius: see VAUGHAN, THOMAS.

Philip I, King of France, 1052–1108: William II buys him off, V. 15–16, 19.

Philip II, King of Macedonia, *c.* 382–336 B.C.: VIII. 77; and Greece, I. 208.

Philip II, King of Spain, 1527–98: V. 85; VIII. 77; and Bodin, V. 247; cruelty, II. 22.

Philip V, King of Spain, 1683–1746, Duke of Anjou, grandson of Louis XIV: III. 209–10; and Austria, VII. 166–7; and Catalonia, VIII. 62, 63; Charles II of Spain chooses him as successor, VI. 11; VII. 150, 151; VIII. 54;

death predicted, II. 145; Dutch acknowledge as King of Spain (Feb. 1700), VI. 11, 14; —(1701), VI. 17; Dutch treaty projected, VII. 166–7; England acknowledges as King of Spain (17 April 1701), VI. 11, 14; differences with England settled (1713), VII. 166; renounces French throne (1712), VII. 125, 129, 130–1, 135, 149–50, 151, 155, 165; Grand Alliance does not acknowledge, VII. 166; Irish recruits, XII. 174; and Louis XIV, II. 88; VII. 81; — influence of Louis slight, VI. 58; — interests differ (1714), VI. 58; VIII. 169–70; — Louis asked to drive him from Spain (1709–10), VI. 50, 58, 190–1; VII. 32; and Merlin, II. 170; and Partition Treaty (1700), VI. 11; pretends to Portugal, VI. 13; power, VIII. 53; and Spanish throne, VII. 81; VIII. 169; — Dutch approval, VI. 53; — and Grand Alliance, VI. 47; — Louis XIV's control, VI. 15; — Spaniards support him, VI. 48; and Treaty of Utrecht, VII. 40, 60; — not represented, VII. 166; — to cede Sicily, VII. 133; and troops for Spanish Netherlands, VI. 89.

Philippeville ('Philippe'), Namur, Belgium: fort, and Dutch Barrier, VI. 101, 109.

Philips, Ambrose, 1674–1749, poet: 'party mad', II. xxxvi; JS's letter to (1708), II. xv.

Philips, John, 1676–1709, poet: *The Splendid Shilling* (1701), II. 246.

Philistines: and *Polite Conversa-*

tion, IV. 136; pun upon name, IV. 208.

Philology: satirized, I. 57–63; XI. 161–2.

'Philomath, T. N.': pseudonym for JS, in *Famous Prediction of Merlin, the British Wizard*, II. 165–170.

Philopoemen, *c.* 250–183 B.C., Greek general: I. 210.

Philosopher's stone: I. 174; and Steele, VIII. 21–2.

Philosophers and philosophy: ancient — Christianity superior, IX. 111–14, 243–4; — — doctrines, IX. 73; — — God in ancient philosophy, IX. 245; — — lessens Christian influence, IX. 243; — — morality, IX. 73; — and free thinking, IV. 41–5; — inadequacy of ancient philosophy, IX. 241; — and modern philosophy, I. 156; — and poetry, IX. 332; — Providence ignored, IX. 245; — and revelation, IX. 73–4; — — sole lack of ancient philosophy, IX. 74; — and sermons, IX. 73; — JS recommends, IX. 74; — JS's respect for, IX. 111; — and virtue, IX. 249; clichés ridiculed, I. 246–51; *lusus naturae*, XI. 104; natural, and perpetual motion, XI. 210; — and reason, XI. 267–8; the new philosophy, VIII. 21; speculative — systems ridiculed, I. 33–4, 102–7; XI. 197–8.

Philpott, Mary, *d.* 1627, JS's great-grandmother: character, V. 187–8; portrait, V. 188.

Phipps, Sir Constantine, 1656–1723, Lord Chancellor of Ire-

land: and Delany, XII. 164–5; and Irish justice, X. 158; and Molesworth, IV. xxvi–xxvii.

Phipps, John, *d.* 1759, vicar choral of St. Patrick's: XIII. 197.

'Phizz': IV. 113.

Phocion, *c.* 400–318 B.C., Athenian general and statesman (pseudonym for Earl of Portland): fall from power, I. 209, 210; impeachment, I. 224; and Miltiades, I. 205; as Portland, I. xx, 205, 209, 210, 224.

Phoenicians: and free masons, V. 329; 'Phoenician tongue', I. 34.

Phoenix: and plan for Irish clergy, XII. 202.

Photius, patriarch of Constantinople, *c.* 820–*c.* 895, lexicographer and theologian: *Bibliotheca*, I. 60; quotations and allusions — ed. Bekker (1824), p. 46: I. 92; — p. 47: I. 61; — pp. 48–9: I. 60; — p. 140a: I. 187.

Physic: *see* MEDICINE.

Physicians: *see* MEDICINE.

Physicians, Royal College of: *see* WARWICK LANE.

Pickering, Danby, *d.* 1781, barrister: *The Statutes at Large* (1763), IX. 134.

Pickering, Gilbert, 1st Bart., 1613–68, Parliamentarian: William Howell and JS on, V. 264.

'Pickle, Thomas': and *Modest Defence of Punning*, IV. 209.

Picts: invade Britain, IV. 6–7; 'the Picts Wall', V. 4.

Pictures: and poetry, IX. 335.

Piedmont, region of northwest Italy, with Turin at the centre: VII. 114; goiters, XII. 295.

'Pile': game of cross and pile, VI. 92.

Pilkington, Laetitia, 1712–50, author, adventuress, and friend of JS: and *Gulliver's Travels*, XI. xxv; *Memoirs* (3 vols., 1748–54), IX. 98, *n.* 2; and JS's sermons, IX. 98; Wood's coins, IX. 127, *n.* 1.

Pilkington, Matthew, *c.* 1701–74, poet, clergyman, friend of JS: and *Gulliver's Travels*, XI. xxv–xxvi, XII. xxxii; *An Infallible Scheme to Pay the Publick Debt* by him, XII. xxxi–xxxii; — not by JS, V. 337; — and *Gulliver's Travels*, XII. xxxii; serves as messenger for JS, XII. xxxiv–xxxv.

Pindar, *c.* 520–*c.* 440 B.C.: leads the Ancients, I. 152; and Carteret, XII. 161; 'slays' Oldham, Mrs. Behn, and Cowley, I. 158–9.

Pinkethman (or Pinkeman), William, *d.* 1725, actor: booth at Bartholomew Fair, II. 206.

Piozzi, Hester Lynch Thrale, 1741–1821: papers, and JS's *Maxims Controlled in Ireland*, XII. xxiii.

Piper, Charles, Count, 1647–1716, minister of Charles XII of Sweden: VI. 63.

Pirates: XI. 154–5, 222, 294.

Pisistratus ('Pysistratus'), *d.* 527 B.C., Athenian tyrant: and Solon, I. 205.

'Pistorides', i.e. the son of a miller: pseudonym for Sir Richard Tighe, XII. xxvii, xxix, 155, 156–7, 160.

Place Bill (1712): *see* HOUSE OF COMMONS, ENGLISH.

Placentia, Newfoundland: to be British, VII. 114, 132.

Plagiarism: discouraged, IX. 333; of inventions, XI. 184–5; JS disavows, I. 6–8.

Plague: VIII. 61; at Marseilles, XIII. 113, 176.

Planetary Worlds: I. 174.

Plantagenet: surname introduced, V. 42.

Plantagenet, Geoffrey: *see* GEOF-FREY.

Plate (Plata) River in Argentina: and peace (1711), VII. 49, 115.

Plato: VIII. 43; XI. 268; leads the Ancients, I. 152; and Aris-totle, V. 345; and Carteret, XII. 155, 161; and Diogenes, I. 248; and Dionysius the younger, IX. 244; 'free-thinker', IV. 42; defines happiness, IX. 246; and Hobbes, I. 146; ridicules the Moderns, I. 147; morality, IX. 73; — highest heathen, IX. 248; termed naive, I. 251; 'Platonicks', I. 189–90; Platonism blamed, IV. 95; and poetry, IX. 332; Scotus and Aristotle depose, I. 144; and Stella, V. 231; correct text, IV. 33; *Works* — JS's copy, XIII. 155.

Allusions and quotations: *Apology* 26–7: II. 12; *Republic*: III. 115; — I. 347d: I. 225; VI. 79; — v. 477–80: XI. 268; *Symposium* 189–92: III. 101.

Plautus, Titus Maccus, *c.* 251–184 B.C., Roman playwright: and Roman conversation, IV. 92; quotations — *Amphitryon* 410–11: VI. 173, motto; — *Amphitryon* 438: II. 249, motto.

'Plenipo': IV. 113–14.

Pliny the Elder, *c.* A.D. 23–79, Roman naturalist: and oysters, IV. 257; quotations and allu-sions — *Natural History* VII. 21, 85; I. 90; — VIII. 51 (77): I. 30 ('Plutarch' an error).

Pliny the Younger, A.D. 62–113, Roman letter-writer: quotation — *Epistles* II. 1: I. 267.

Plots: 'a plot-discovering age', IX. 33; all begin with talk, V. 280; Gulliver on, XI. 190–2; in Ireland, IX. 180–9.

'Plump. Mrs.': character in *Polite Conversation*, IV. 196.

'Plump, Tom': character in *Polite Conversation*, IV. 196.

Plutarch, *c.* A.D. 46–*c.* 120: III. 19; character of a man revealed in trifles, III. 120; V. xix, 124; 'free-thinker', IV. 42–3; and Greek language, IV. 9; and linguistic change, IV. 16; on Pompey and Caesar, I. 219; JS on, V. xix; a source of JS's historical arguments, I. 216; quotations and allusions — erroneous, I. 30; — *Alcibiades* 18–20, 23–7, 33, 35–9: I. 207–8; — *Alexander* XIV. 2: I. 248; — *Aristides* 6–8: I. 206–7; — *Caesar*: X. 130; — *Caesar* 13: I. 219; — *Demosthenes*: X. 71; — *Nicias* 15–30: I. 207–8; — *Pericles* 8–9, 14, 23: I. 207; — *Phocion* 17, 26–7, 32–5: I. 209; — *Pompey* 22, 25, 30: I. 220; — *Septem sapientium convivium* 5: I. 182; — *Solon* XXI. 1 ('de mortuis'): XII. 24, 227; — *Themistocles* 1, 10–15, 22–4, 31: I. 207; — *Themistocles* 2: I. 62; — *Titus Quinctius Flaminius*

XVII. 7: I. 30; — *Vitae*: I. 186.

Pocammock, Laird of: V. 134.

'Pocock, Captain' (ill-fated ship's captain in *Gulliver's Travels*): XI. 221.

Poddishaw, Laird of: V. 133–4.

Poems on Several Occasions: *see* BARBER, MARY.

Poet Laureate, Irish, proposed: IX. 345.

Poetry: necessary accomplishment, IX. 327; bank compared to, IX. 344; benefit to society, IX. 327; composition, IX. 327–45; dress, IX. 338–9; England encourages, IX. 345; among the Houyhnhnms, XI. 278; — they 'excel all other mortals', XI. 273–4; Irish, and learning, IX. 332; learning unnecessary, IX. 332–3; lucrative, IX. 327; and philosophy, IX. 332; — Plato's influence, IX. 332; publication, IX. 341–2; ridiculed, I. 25 and *n*.*; subjects, IX. 339; 'sum of all learning' (Sidney), IX. 332; JS's views, XIII. 74; virtue ignored, IX. 329. *See also JS's* HISTORY OF POETRY.

Poets: Bible reading, IX. 329–30; character — waspish, IX. 340; and classical education, IX. 333–4; classified, IX. 345; corporation proposed, IX. 344–5; number in Dublin, IX. 344; employment, IX. 340, 345; and English language, IV. 13; first steps, IX. 339; — low writing, IX. 340; and free thinkers, IX. 329; and immortality, I. 242; Irish — low writing, IX. 340; — reverence lost, IX. 332;

learning of gentlemen poets, IX. 333; and monosyllables, IV. 11; and plagiarism, IX. 333; priesthood, IX. 330–1; prose composition, IX. 337–8; qualifications, IX. 338; reading, IX. 337; religion, IX. 328; and shoemakers, IX. 336.

Poining's Act: *see* POYNING'S ACT.

Poland: Bickerstaff's predictions for, II. 148; compared to England, V. 244; and Louis XIV (1696), VIII. 54; peasants compared to Ireland's, IX. 21; 'these princes', VI. 63; 'princes of the north', VII. 148. *See also* NORTHERN WAR.

Polignac, Melchior de, 1661–1741, French diplomat, made a cardinal in 1713: character, VII. 159; Louis XIV trusts, VII. 62; belittles Ménager, VII. 159; and Molo, VII. 143; and Robinson, VII. 143; and Treaty of Utrecht, VII. 60.

Polite Conversation (1738), by JS: **IV. 97–201**; analysis, IV. xxxii; background, IV. v, xxviii–xxxi, xxxiii, 100–1, 124; XII. xxxiii; date, XIV. 51; editions, IV. xxix, 290–1; errata, XIV. 51; and W. King, VII. xiii and *n*. 1; manuscript, VII. xiii and *n*. 1, xxx, xxxiii, 302; **notes by JS for, IV. 276–7**; — composition, IV. xxx; — textual note, IV. 302; and Orrery, VII. xiii and *n*. 1; printing, XIII. xli; publication, IV. xxviii, 97, 127, 290–1; sources, IV. xxxii–xxxiii; style, IV. xxviii; — 'Introduction', IV. xxxii; and *Tatler* No.

31, II. xxix; — No. 11, IV. xxix; textual notes, IV. 290–9; XIV. 52; title-page facsimiles, IV. 97, 127; and *Tritical Essay*, I. xxxv; 'Wagstaff' as pseudonym, IV. xxix.

Politics (political theory, politicians, etc.; for the political career of JS, *see* SWIFT): and balance of power, I. 195–203; and Charles I's execution, IX. 101; and *Mr. Collins's Discourse of Freethinking*, IV. xvi, xvii–xviii; common sense best guide, VIII. 77, 138–9; corruption general, XI. 129–31, 187–8, 255–6; corruption — causes, IX. 79; extremists deplored, II. xv–xvi; genius ('great parts') a fault, IV. 251; good government needs none, IV. 246–7; 251; Irish — breeds informers, IX. 180; — compared with English, X. 31; — issues reviewed, X. 132–4; and Academy of Lagado, XI. 187–92; and lying, III. 8–13; and morality, XI. 59, 187; not mysterious, VIII. 77–8; XI. 59, 135–6; two parties normal, VIII. 180; common people not concerned in, IX. 173, 177, 179, 186; 'a plot-discovering age', IX. 33; and *Polite Conversation*, IV. 120; 'politician' defined, XIV. 15; politicians—never take advice, IX. 28; — less valuable than farmers, X. 141; XI. 135–6; reputation of power, VIII. 160; principles unsteady, IX. 33; public and private interests, XII. 248; refiners — 'too common', III. 208; — and mathematics, XI. 164; — invariably wrong, VIII.

126; and religion, XI. 60; — religion not invented by politicians, II. 34; and satire, XII. 33, 34; secrecy an error, VIII. 80–81, 137; self-interest as the key, VIII. 177, 179; senseless, IX. 27; shameful, XII. x; trifles influence, VIII. 171–2; undesirable, XII. 22–3. *See also* CONSTITUTION; PARTIES; SENTIMENTS OF A CHURCH-OF-ENGLAND MAN; SWIFT, JONATHAN, *Politics*.

Pollard, Margaret: acknowledgement, V. v.

Pollock, Sir Robert Pollock, Bart., *d.* 1735, Laird of: V. 172.

Pollux: and Leda, IV. 235.

Polybius, *c.* 202—*c.* 120 B.C., Greek historian: on balance of power, V. 36; and tripartite ('mixed') government, I. 200; II. 83; quotations and allusions — II. 41–71: I. 210; — v: I. 217; — vi: I. 210, 217; — vi. iii. 5–8: I. 200; V. 36; — vi. ix, lvii: I. 217; — vi. x: I. 217; — vi. x. 6–14: I. 200; — vi. li. 1–2: I. 200; — vi. li. 5–6: I. 216; — vi. li. 6: I. 199; — viii. i: I. 210; — x. xxi: I. 210; — xi. ix: I. — 210.

Polyperchon, 4th century B.C., Macedonian soldier (probably a pseudonym for Marlborough): and Phocion, I. 209.

Polyphemus: and Ulysses: *see* ULYSSES.

Pomfret, John, 1667–1702, poet: *Poems* (1702), IV. xxxix–xl, 249–50.

Pompey, 'The Great' (Gnaeus Pompeius), 106–48 B.C., Roman general, triumvir: V. 85; VI.

134; XI. 195; and Caesar, I. 219–222; and Gracchi, I. 219.

Pons, Émile: on *Battle of the Books*, I. xxix, *n.*‖; on *Gulliver's Travels*, XI. xi–xii; on *Tale of a Tub*, I. xvi, *n.*†; — parallels with *Meditation upon a Broomstick*, I. xxxiv, *n.*‖.

Ponsonby, Sir John, *c.* 1609–1678: names Bessborough after wife, IV. 282.

Poor Law, Irish: and beggars, IX. 207.

Poor Man's Contentment, sermon by JS (published 1762): **IX. 190-8**; analysis, IX. 106–7, 124, 126–7; composition, IX. 133–4; style, IX. 126; textual notes, IX. 376–7. *See also* SERMONS.

Poor people: *see* BEGGARS; POVERTY.

Poor Robin's Almanack, by William Winstanley and others: II. 163; and London fire, IV. 207.

Pope, head of the Roman Catholic Church: authority — and other bishops, XIV. 34; — deference of bishops to popes, XIV. 20; — above canons, XIV. 31; — denied, XIV. 8, 18, 21, 22; — — councils independent of Pope, XIV. 21; — — closing of letters as evidence, XIV. 19–20; — — Pope sent on mission by secular monarch, XIV. 29, 31; — Donation of Constantine, XIV. 30; — equal to emperor's, XIV. 31; — and emperors' stupidity, XIV. 22; — subordinate to emperor's, XIV. 22, 29; — forgeries support, XIV. 21; — kings' prerogative usurped, XIV. 26; — and Nicene Creed,

XIV. 27; and bishops, II. 94; bulls, XIV. 29; — satirized, I. 69 and *n.**, *n.*†; would promote new crusades, V. 23; dress, I. 71, *n.*†, *n.*‖; effigy burned, VII. 28; enemies sure to die, XIV. 30; and England, II. 83; XIII. 123; would rule England but for Reformation, V. 17–18; adored from fear, II. 90; feet kissed, I. 71 and *n.**; powerless in France, II. 116; infallibility ridiculed, XIV. 34; — satirized, I. 74; and miracles, XIV. 31; as Peter in *Tale of a Tub*, I. 65–76; schism in papacy ended by Theodoric, XIV. 26; Tindal on, II. 192; titles, I. 71 and *n.**.

Pope, Alexander, 1688–1744, poet, friend of JS: and fame of dunces, V. 201; and Faulkner — *Works* printed by Faulkner, XIII. 201; *God's Revenge against Punning*, IV. xxxiv–xxxvi and *n.* 1; translation of *Iliad*, IV. xxxv; *Miscellanies* : *see* MISCELLANIES OF POPE AND SWIFT; signature on copy of Puckle's *The Club* (1713), V. xxxii, *n.* 2; pun upon name, IV. 275; and Scriblerus Club, XI. xiii; and *Memoirs of Martinus Scriblerus*, XI. xiii and *n.* 3; one of 'snarling brood', IV. xxxii, 118;

and JS: correspondence, IV. xxviii; VIII. xxxii, xxxvi; XII. xiii, xiv, xv, xix, xxiv, xxx; — letter to Pope (1721): *see* LETTER FROM DR. SWIFT; — letter to Pope (1 May 1733), XI. xxv and *n.* 3; — letter to Pope (8 Jul. 1733) quoted, V. xxiv; — JS's letter not received (1721), IX.

370; — manuscripts, VII. xiii and *n.* 1; in JS's dreams (1727), V. xxv, 205–6; letters to Pope on *Gulliver's Travels* (29 Sept. 1725), XI. xviii, *n.* 3; — (26 Nov. 1725), XI. xi; — (27 Nov. 1726), XI. xxiv and *n.* 3; letter from Pope about *Gulliver's Travels* (1726), XI. xxii; JS tells him of *History of the Four Last Years*, VII. xii; and JS's sermons, IX. 100; additions to *Thoughts*, I. xxxv; JS visits, XII. ix; — (1726, 1727), XIII. 201; — (1727), VII. xii; visits JS in Letcombe Bassett, Berkshire (1714), IX. 25; in JS's will, XIII. 154.

Popery: *see* ROMAN CATHOLICISM.

Pope's Head Tavern: XII. 160.

Popham, Sir John, *c.* 1531–1607, Lord Chief Justice: and trial of Sir Walter Raleigh, X. 169.

Popish VIII. plot: 39.

Population: Houyhnhnms control population growth, XI. 268; 'people are the riches of a nation': *see* PEOPLE, COMMON; — and naturalization of foreign protestants, VII. 94–5; — not correct, XII. xxiii; — not in Ireland, XII. 66–7, 135–6, 309, 310; possessions limited, I. 243. *See also* IRISH PEOPLE, *emigration*; PEOPLE, COMMON.

Pork: 'all Pork', I. 30.

Pornography: *see* OBSCENITY.

Porsenna, Lars, late 6th century B.C., Etruscan prince: Temple compared to, I. 6.

'Porter', in *Directions to Servants*: XIII. 52.

Porter, Sir Charles, *d.* 1696, Lord Chancellor of Ireland: Burnet and JS on, V. 284.

Portland, Hans Willem Bentinck, 1st Earl of, 1649–1709: and Boufflers, IV. 58; impeached (1701), I. xx; and Partition treaties ('Whig ministers'), I. xx; 'Phocion' in JS's *Contests and Dissensions*, I. xx, 205, 209, 210, 224; Prior his secretary, III. 209; and JS, V. 193–4; and Triennial Act (1693–4), V. 193–4.

Portland, William Henry Bentinck, 2nd Earl of, later Duke, 1682–1726: 'a dunce', V. 258.

Portland Papers: VII. 178.

Port Mahon, in Minorca: to be British, V. 113; VII. 43, 48, 119–20, 132; — remains British, V. 95.

Portocarero, Luis Manuel Fernandez de, 1635–1709, Cardinal Archbishop of Toledo: prediction of his death, II. 147; — attacked by Partridge, II. 205.

Portolongone ('Port-longue'), Elba, Italy: Austria demands, VII. 164.

Portsmouth, England: V. 29, 57; XI. 193, 221; brewers' fraud, III. 82, 138.

Portugal: character — cowardly and undisciplined, VI. 39; and England—England to defend against Spain (1714), VIII. 62; — Methuen Treaties: *see* METHUEN TREATIES; food ample (1711), VI. 39; and Gee, IV. 250; enters Grand Alliance, VI. 13; Gulliver rescued by Portuguese ship, XI. 285–9; kings of, VI. 25; Bickerstaff's *Predictions* burned, II. 160; Spain — Portugal part of,

II. 169–70; Spain threatens, VIII. 61; and Treaty of Utrecht, VI. 166; VII. 113, 133; — agrees to general peace, VII. 165; — late in accepting, VIII. 61–2; — signs (1713), VII. 166;

and War of the Spanish Succession, VII. 85; and Austria, VI. 24–6; campaigns, VI. 21; VII. 87; Dutch abandon campaign, VII. 85; duties on soldiers' clothes, VI. 39; England saves, VI. 87; English money exported to, III. 7; English subsidies, VI. 37, 39; interests in, VI. 13, 25; quotas unfulfilled, VI. 37–9: VII. 85; fails to supply troops, VI. 38–9. *See also* JOHN V; PETER II.

Portuguese Alliance: *see* METHUEN TREATIES.

Post-Boy (Dublin newspaper): on Wood's coins (31 Jul. 1724), X. xiv, *n.* 2; extract, X. 189–90, 215.

Post Boy (London newspaper): and Fleetwood's 'Preface', VI. 151; Lady Giffard's attack on JS, I. xxxvi ('advertisement'); and Anne Long, V. xxiii; and Steele, VIII. 67;

JS's contributions, 2 Aug. 1711 (Barber and Tooke appointed printers of *Gazette*), VI. xxiii; **27 Dec. 1711** (Anne Long's death), **VI.** xxiii–xxiv, **196; 13 Nov. 1712** (band-box plot), **VI.** xxiii–xxiv, **196-7; 18, 20 Nov. 1712** (Duke of Hamilton), **VI.** xxiii–xxv, **197-9; 3 Jan. 1713** (proclamation against Maccartney, possibly by JS), **VI.** xxiii–xxv, **199; 29 Jan. 1713** (Erasmus Lewis, possibly by JS), **VI.**

xxvi–xxvii, **200; 17 Feb. 1713** (William Harrison's death), **VI. xxiii;**

on JS's *Conduct of the Allies*, VI. ix; JS parodies, VI. xix–xx; JS's part estimated, VI. xxiii; and Wharton, III. xxi.

Post-Man (London newspaper): quoted (17 Apr. 1724), X. 153.

Posterior: riddle on ('certain person'), IX. 281–84.

'Posterity, Prince': in *Tale of a Tub*, I. 18–23; and *Battle of the Books*, I. 280; and Bookseller, I. 13.

Post Office: intercepts JS's mail, VII. xiv.

'Poticary': apothecary, IV. 191.

Potter, John, *c.* 1674–1747, Archbishop of Canterbury: attacks Tindal, II. xviii, *n.* 2, 69.

Poulett, John Poulett, 1st Earl, *c.* 1668–1743, Lord Steward of the Household: VIII. xxxvi, 118, 124; Macky and JS on, V. 259; and Oxford's quarrel with Bolingbroke, VIII. 156.

Poverty: advantages, IX. 197; behaviour of poor man, IX. 126; blessings, IX. 192; causes, IX. 191; — self-induced, IX. 206; deserved, IX. 191; farmers, IX. 129; honest and dishonest, IX. 191; in Ireland, XII. xiii–xv, xxiii, 10–11, 109–10; — causes, IX. 199–209; XIII. 176; miserable state, IX. 246; and public evil, IX. 235; and salvation, IX. 126, 197–8; not unjust, IX. 126–7; and wealth, IX. 190. *See also* BEGGARS.

Powell, Stephen, *fl.* 1697–1724, Dublin printer: prints Whig pamphlets, XII. xxxii.

Power: from God, IX. 228; follows property, IX. 220; political — and Providence, IX. 147; — and talent, dangerous without religion, IX. 156.

Powerscourt, parish about eight miles south of Dublin, prebend of St. Patrick's Cathedral (Stagonil), held by John Towers: JS at, XIII. vii.

Powis (or Powys), Sir Thomas, 1649–1719, Solicitor General and Attorney General under James II: Burnet and JS on, V. 284.

Powlett: *see* POULETT.

Poynings' Act (1494): and Irish law, IX. 270; and Irish liberty, X. 39; and Wood's coins, X. 112.

Poynings, Sir Edward, 1459–1521, Lord Deputy of Ireland (1494–95): X. 39.

'Pozz': IV. 113.

'Pozz, Lord': character in *Polite Conversation*, IV. 137–8.

Pragel Pass, in northern Italian Vaudois: 'valley of Pragela', VII. 114.

Praise: 'pension paid by the World', I. 28.

Prasini and Veneti, Roman factions: III. 162; their ribbons, II. 32.

Pratt, Benjamin, *c.* 1669–1721, Provost of Trinity College, Dublin, later Dean of Down: character, III. 183–4; bequest to T.C.D., IX. 55; and Wharton, III. 183–4.

Pratt, John, *b. c.* 1670, Deputy Vice-Treasurer of Ireland, younger brother of Benjamin

Pratt: *A Relation of Several Facts* (about Wharton), possibly by Pratt, III. 232–40.

Prayer for Stella (written 1727), by JS: **IX. 256-7**; textual note, IX. 377.

Prayers for a Sick Person [*i.e.*, Stella] **During Her Illness** (written 1727), by JS: **IX. 253-5**; textual note, IX. 377.

Preachers, Puritan: and passions, IX. 68; ridiculed, I. 34, 98–101, 121–8, 176–90. *See also* DISSENTERS; CANTING.

Preaching: IX. 64; absent parishioners need, IX. 212; aims, IX. 101, 216; — faith and reason, IX. 214; — persuade men to do their duty, IX. 70; — show men their duty, IX. 70; atheists ridicule, IX. 216; in blank verse, IX. 338; canting and rhetoric, I. 241; — and war, I. 243; and commonplace books, IX. 75–6; and Corusodes, XII. 43–4; defended by JS, IX. 130; delivery, IX. 213; and Eugenio, XII. 45; use of Greek and Latin, IX. 75; inattention and worldliness, IX. 215, 216; ineffectual, IV. 246; IX. 210; note on, for *Intelligencer*, XII. 306; misbehaviour of congregations, IX. 212; neglect — and decay of religion, IX. 214–15; — sleeping worst, IX. 215; objections, IX. 213; obscurity condemned, IX. 65–8; passions excited, II. 33; pathos ineffectual, IX. 69; and pedantry, IX. 67; quotations, IX. 75; rational arguments needed, IX. 70, 132; simplicity needed, IX. 77, 102, 131–2; and sin, IX. 215; slang

and bad company, IX. 68; and sleeping, I. 34; IX. 210–18; subjects — atheism, IX. 77; — benevolence, IX. 73; — deism, IX. 77; — definition of duties, IX. 70; — freedom to choose them, V. 88; — mysteries not to be explained, IX. 77; — the stage, IX. 343; JS's interest in, IX. 99; not neglected by JS, IX. 98; vicious men threatened, IX. 215; vocabulary, II. 177; the wicked ignore, IX. 210, 211; wit, IX. 72–3. *See also* CANTING; SERMONS.

Precedents, legal: X. 40; XI. 249, 317.

Predictions for the Year 1708 (1708), by JS: **II. 139–50**; analysis, II. xii; — by author of *Answer to Bickerstaff*, II. 195–9; attacked by *Mr. Partridge's Answer to Esquire Bickerstaff's . . . Predictions for the Year 1708*, II. 201–7; authorship, II. 197; background, II. ix–xii; composition, II. x; editions, II. 197, 286; — pirated editions, II. xii; imitations, sequels, etc., II. xi–xiv, xxiv and *n.* 1, 209–16, 229–31, 262, 269–73, 290; allusion in *Letter concerning Sacramental Test* (1709), II. 284; publication, II. x, 153; reception, II. xii, 195–6, 211, 262; — in Europe, II. 160; textual notes, II. 286–7; *Some Reflections upon Mr. Bickerstaff's Predictions: see* ANSWER TO BICKERSTAFF; title-page facsimile, II. 139; — pirated edition, II. xiii.

Predictions for the Year 1712: II. xxiv, *n.* 1.

'Preface' to Mrs. Barber's *Poems*, by JS: *see* BARBER, MARY.

'Preface of the Author,' section of *Battle of the Books*: I. 140.

Preface to the Bishop of Sarum's Introduction (1713), by JS: **IV. 53–84**; composition, IV. xx, 54; editions, IV. xxiv–xxviii, 288; and Molesworth, IV. xxiv–xxviii; publication, IV. xxi, 53, 54, 288; textual notes, IV. 288–90; title-page facsimiles, IV. 53, 54.

Prefaces, dedications, and introductions: satire on, I. 13–16, 81–2; JS's views, II. 43–4; IV. 58–9. *See also* STYLE.

'Prefatory Letter' to Mrs. Barber's *Poems: see* BARBER, MARY.

Preferment: Carteret's practice, XII. 162–9; English practices satirized, XI. 128–9, 254–5, 262–3; by kings and ministers, IV. 246; and morality, II. 47–59; and party politics, II. 24–5, 62.

Prejudices: real and unreal, I. 1; and religion, II. 11; and virtues, I. 243.

Prendergast, Sir Thomas, 1st Bart., *c.* 1660–1709, soldier and Jacobite: William Howell and JS on, V. 264; and plot to assassinate William III (1696), V. 264.

Prerogative, royal: III. 59; VIII. 40–1; army commissions, III. xiv–xv; and balance of power, III. 125; Charles I, IX. 220; and clergy, III. 47–8; coinage, III. 135; X. 17–18, 28, 37–8, 54–6, 196; — lawful metals only, X. 9–10, 108; likened to crown jewels, VIII. 17; lawfulness of debate concerning, III. 108–9;

and Drapier, X. 104–11; and George I, VIII. 174; — JS's change of mind, III. xxviii–xxix, 275, 276; Irish charged with disputing, X. xvii–xviii, 61, 85; — legally exercised in Ireland, X. 198–9; and law, X. 134; limits, III. xxviii–xxix and *n.* 1; — tyranny opposed, III. 113–14; and Marlborough, VII. 30; ministerial appointments, III. 135; VII. 3; VIII. 164; and 'moderation', IX. 178; peers, created by Queen Anne, VII. 20; VIII. 15, 23, 147–51; and public welfare, X. 34; punishment of state criminals, III. xv; and recruitment of soldiers, XII. 312–13; Tories champion, II. 14; III. 105, 125, 167; universities loyal, V. 286; making war and peace, VIII. 23; X. 54; and war — emergency powers, X. 33; weak (in 1711), III. 138, 141, 276; Whigs against, III. 123, 142–6, 172; VII. 20; Whigs increase, III. 164; not concerned in Wood's coinage, X. 85, 106. *See also* CONSTITUTION.

Presbyterians: III. 104; Burnet and JS on their ministers, V. 269; and Charles I, XII. 265–7; and John Creichton, V. 130–80; Dissenters identified with, III. 126–7; Heylyn and JS on, V. 255–6; and Independents, XII. 265, 266, 267; in Ireland, V. 271, 272; — Church of Ireland outnumbered, XII. 248, 249, 256; — dangerous, II. 131; — not oppressed, II. 111; — and Parliament, II. 117–19; — and Protestant unity, XII. 275–7; —

Scottish settlers in Ulster, V. 271; ('encroachments') IX. 10; XII. 78; — and repeal of Test Act, II. 119; XII. 246–60, 263–79; and James II, XII. 268–71; Jesuits disguised as, II. 37; and Archbishop King, II. 282; Leslie attacks, I. xxii; and morality, XII. 246; and Occasional Conformity Bill (1703–4), I. xxii; and Pretender, XII. 271–2; Puritan origins, XII. 263–5; and the Restoration, XII. 267–8; and Roman Catholics, XII. 272; JS's history of, XII. xliv–xlv, 263–6; unity, III. 97; — disunity, III. 129; and Whigs, III. xiii–xiv, 92, 122; and William III, XII. 271. *See also* DISSENTERS; NONCONFORMISTS; PRESBYTERIANS PLEA OF MERIT; PURITANS.

Presbyterians Plea of Merit . . . Impartially Examined (1733), by JS: XII. 263–79; allusions to, XII. 284, 293; background, XII. xl–xlv, 284; and Clarendon's *History of the Rebellion*, V. xxxix; composition, XII. xlii; editions, XII. 347; reply to, XII. xliv–xlv; textual notes, XII. 347; title-page facsimile, facing XII. 263.

Present Miserable State of Ireland, not by JS: authorship, XII. xv–xvi; publication, XII. xv.

Presentment of the Grand-Jury of the County of the City of Dublin: see DRAPIER'S LETTERS.

Presentment of the Grand Jury for the County of Middlesex, of the Author, Printer and Publisher of a Book Intitled, The Rights of the Christian Church Asserted, etc.: II. xvii–xviii, 191–2, 290.

Press (journalists, newspapers, pamphlets): censorship recommended, II. 60–1; III. 99–100; VII. 103–4; XI. 131; — Defoe's recommendation, I. xxvi, *n.*‖; freedom of the press, VII. 105–6; — abused by Walpole ministry, V. 94–7; — and anonymity, VII. 105–6; — Ireland and England compared, X. 107–11; — preserved by Tories, III. 35, 70–1, 188–9; — abused by Whigs, III. 70, 99–100, 153–6, 188; VII. 104–5; — 'Whiggish principle', V. 96; Hanover family spared, VIII. 168–9; immorality, II. 60–1; III. 99–100, 135–6, 153–4; journalists as camp-followers, I. 152; libel laws evaded, III. 153–6; VIII. 14–15; ministerial writers privileged over opposition, III. 99–100, 135–6; VIII. 14; overloaded, I. 27–8; religion undermined, II. 36–7, 60–1; VII. 103–4; Stamp Tax (1712) ineffectual, VII. 103–4, 105; — JS curtailed by, VI. xx; and Test Act, II. 111–13; titles misleading, VIII. 5; titles multiplied, I. 43; triviality, I. 38–43; Whig writers — paid well, VIII. 31; — subsidized, VIII. 31–4; — tolerated, III. 135–6.

Preston: *see* HAMILTON OF PRESTON.

Preston, Battle of (1715): X. 62.

Pretender (i.e. James II): *see* JAMES II.

Pretender (i.e., 'Old Pretender', or Prince of Wales and Chevalier de St. George, son of James II), 1688–1766: abjured, II. 13; and Anne, V. 293; VIII. 71–2, 163–

80; — her contempt for him, V. 293; VIII. 178; — questions his birth (1688), V. 289; court at Bar-le-Duc, VIII. 48; and Barrier Treaty, VI. 27; birth, III. 164; V. 289; VI. 129; VIII. 52, 91; — Burnet on, V. 183; — Burnet and JS on, V. 292; — and the common people, III. 146–7; — allegedly dies (1688), V. 287; — warming pan, V. 287; and Bolingbroke, VIII. 48; and Burnet, IV. xxiii. 61, 68, 74–5, 80–1; V. 183, 292; character, VIII. 91; — allegedly stupid, VIII. 33, 91; one of 'three children', II. 21; and Church of England, VIII. 38; conversion, VIII. 65, 91; not dangerous, IV. 78; V. 293; and Drapier, X. 62, 69, 107, 170; and *Drapier's Letters*, X. xxiv, xxv; and Dunkirk, VIII. xi, 60; and the *Examiner*, III. 73, 88;

and France, IV. 75; VIII. 91; — acknowledged by French, VI. 12–13, 16–17; — England wishes him expelled, VII. 114, 120, 130, 158; — France to expel him (1709), VI. 27, 106; — expelled (1713), VII. 158, 165, 175–6; — historical parallel to, V. 31–2; — parallel to 'Charles III' and Grand Alliance, VI. 14; — and candidates for his successor, VIII. 54;

and Godolphin ministry, III. 205; reportedly handsome (1714), VIII. 33; and Ireland — abhorred by Irish, X. 35, 76, 132–3; — invasion rumours, XII. 114, 163–4, 259–60, 271–2; — and Irish recruits for French

army, XII. xxxi, 312–20; — Irish support ridiculed, XII. 217–32; — Irish Tories detest, II. xxii, 118; — Irish 'old Whigs' abhor, XII. 156; to go to Italy (1714), VIII. 64; and Archbishop King, II. 282; and Erasmus Lewis: see LEWIS; and Duke of Lorraine, VIII. 67–8; motto for Marlborough's return (1711), VII. 28; *Memoirs of the Chevalier de St. George*, IV. xxvi; and Nonconformists, III. 46–7; and Oxford ministry, III. 69; VI. 76; VIII. xviii, xxv, 18, 47–8, 83, 86, 155, 163–80; and Oxford — conspiracy alleged, VIII. 9; historical parallel to, V. 31–2; and Parliament, IV. 61; VI. 93; and party politics (1714), VIII. xxiii, 71; and *Proposal for the Universal Use of Irish Manufacture*, X. 137; and rebellion of 1715, V. 104–5; renunciation of, VI. 129; and Roman Catholics in England, VIII. 91; court at St. Germains, VIII. 48; and Saxon language, IV. xiii; and Scotland, VIII. 50; and succession to the British throne, II. 20; lacks support, VI. 27; VIII. 41, 65–6, 90–2, 165–6, 168, 190–2; and JS, IX. 27; XII. 146; XIII. 185; and the Tories, III. 131; V. 104–5; — charged with supporting him, II. xxi, 62; III. 115, 132, 142–3; VII. 28; — no correspondence, VI. 145; and Treaty of Utrecht, VIII. 169–71; and Whigs, III. 17; VIII. 10, 52; — would bring him in, III. 146–7; VIII. 39; — and Dissenters, III. 46–7; — journalists'

theme, VIII. 31; — their obsession with him, III. 94; VIII. 10, 65–6. *See also* LETTER FROM THE PRETENDER.

Priam, King of Troy: IV. 233.

'Prichard, William' (Gulliver's captain): XI. 20.

Pride: I. 141–2, 180; all men self-important, II. 2; IV. 243; among the *beaux esprits*, II. 257–9; of beggars, IX. 208; and boastfulness, IV. 245; and conversation, IV. 244; and flattery, IV. 246; Gulliver's impatience with, XI. 296; and long words, IX. 66; and manners, IV. 213–14, 218; and Irish manufactures, XII. 9; philosophers' sin, I. 248; and preferment, II. 50; a primary motivation, IX. 125; as self-love — charity satisfies, IX. 126, 148; — and fortune, I. 245; — and joy at funerals, I. 245; — and morality, IV. 243; — and patriotism, XII. 248; — and stoicism, I. 244; and social subordination, IX. 145; unnatural, XI. 296; in women, XII. 67–8; — Dublin, XII. 135; — and Irish manufactures, XII. xix, xxi–xxii, 126–7.

Prideaux, Humphrey, 1648–1724, orientalist: William Howell and JS on, V. 265.

Priestcraft: unfashionable, II. 62; and Tindal, II. 72.

Priests: *see* CLERGY.

'Prim, Widow': character in *Polite Conversation*, IV. 158–9.

Primate of the Church of Ireland: *see* ARMAGH, ARCHBISHOP OF.

Prime minister: 'the ablest dog in the pack', XI. 263; Asiatic institution, V. xvii, 106, 117; character,

XI. 255-6, 318; term coming into use, VII. xxxv. *See also* MINISTERIAL RESPONSIBILITY.

Principles of Deism Truly Represented and Set in a Clear Light, in Two Dialogues between a Sceptick and a Deist (1708): 'a late Discourse', I. 1.

Prior, Matthew, 1664-1721, poet, diplomat, and friend of JS: and Boileau, III. 215; and Bolingbroke's quarrel with Oxford, VIII. 158; character, VII. 44; VIII. 158; — wit and humour, VII. 160; Commissioner of Trade, III. 209; correspondence surrendered (1714), VIII. xxxi; Dutch intrigue revealed to 'British minister', VII. 42; and *Examiner*, III. xxvii; VIII. 123-4; — authorship denied, III. 76-7; — 'Mr. * * *', III. 102; mission in France (1711), III. xxxi-xxxii; — secret journey, VII. 44, 46; visits France (1712), VII. 149, 153; and Gee, IV. 250; and Hanmer, III. 211; health, III. 217; and Jersey, III. 211; — his secretary, III. 209; and Louis XIV, III. 209-18; Macky and JS on, V. 260; and Arthur Moore, III. 211; at Paris (1697), III. 209, 211; — (1713), VII. 160; and peace preliminaries (1711), VII. 44; — fictitious account, III. 207-18; poet, III. 209; Portland's secretary, III. 209; pun upon name, IV. 274; and Treaty of Ryswick, III. 209; fellow of St. John's, Cambridge, III. 209; member of 'The Society', XI. xii; and JS —

academy project, IV. xi; — *Conduct of the Allies*, VI. viii; — on House of Lords (1711), VII. 17; — and *A New Journey to Paris*, III. xxxi-xxxii; letter to *Tatler*, II. 247; and Treaty of Utrecht — Franco-Dutch correspondence (1711), 'British minister', VII. 42; — Minister Plenipotentiary, VII. 160; — mission to France (1711), III. xxxi-xxxii; 207-18; VII. 44, 46; at Versailles (1711), III. 213-16; VII. 44; and Whigs ('one who is . . . innocent'), III. 77.

Prior, Thomas, *c.* 1682-1751, philanthropist: lists absentees, XII. 126.

Privateers: English, VI. 22; French, VI. 60; — and Dunkirk, VI. 112.

Privilege of Parliament: V. 82.

Privy Council, English: V. 115-16; and John Browne, X. 28-9, 37; XII. xiii; author's thanks, in *Tale of a Tub*, I. 115; and Wood's coins, X. 25-49, 57, 125, 155-6, 189-203.

Privy Council, Irish: *Address*, 1724 (on Wood's coins): *see* DRAPIER'S LETTERS; and clergy's residence, XII. 189-202; compared with English, X. 31; and fourth *Drapier's Letter*, X. 53, 173; and George I, X. 34; and *A Libel on D[octor] D[elany]. And a Certain Great Lord*, by JS, XII. xxv; list of members (1724), X. 182, 205; and mixed money, X. 10; and Wood's coins, X. 20, 21, 24.

Problemes of Aristotle ('*Aristotle's Problems*'), not by JS: II. 241.

Proby, Thomas, 1665–1729, Surgeon-General of Ireland: and Wharton, III. 181–2.

Proceedings Touching the Impeachment of Edward, Late Earl of Clarendon (1700): **JS's marginalia, XIV. 38**; — date, XIV. xiv.

Profanity: IV. 109–112; censured, II. 55; used by Ned Fashion, II. 187; and Wharton, IV. 249.

Progne (or Procne), in Greek mythology, sister of Philomela: Horace alludes to, V. 339; 'Progne' as name for a coarse woman, V. 340.

Project for the Advancement of Religion, and the Reformation of Manners (1709), by JS: **II. 41-63**; background, II. xx–xxi; composition, II. xv, 43; errata, XIV. 51; and JS's *Proposal for Virtue*, XIV. xiii; publication, II. xv, xix–xx, xxvi, xxvii–xxviii, 278; and Steele, II. xxvii–xxviii; style, II. xxviii; textual notes, II. 278–9; title-page facsimile, II. 41; and Whigs, VIII. 122.

'Project, for the Universal Benefit of Mankind' (1720): unauthorized addition to *Tale of a Tub*, I. 293–4; textual note, I. 304.

Projectors, Grand Academy of: *see* ACADEMY OF LAGADO.

Property: and law, IV. 245; a trust, IX. 146. *See also* LAND.

Proposal for an Act of Parliament, to Pay Off the Debt of the Nation (1732), by JS: **XII. 205-12**; analysis, XII. xxxix–xl; composition, XII. 207; textual notes, XII. 343; title-page facsimile, XII. 205.

Proposal for Correcting, Improving, and Ascertaining the English Tongue (1712), by JS: **IV. 3-21, 285**; analysis, IV. xii, xiv–xvi; background, IV. ix–xiv; composition, IV. xi, 5, 21; errata, XIV. 51; and *Letter to a Young Gentleman*, IX. xxiv; manuscript, IV. xi, 285; preface to Faulkner's edition, probably by JS, IV. 285; publication, IV. xi, 285; reception, IV. xii, xiii–xiv, xv; signed by JS, XIII. 181; and *Tatler* No. 230, II. xxxiii–xxxiv; textual notes, IV. 285–7; XIV. 52; title-page facsimile, IV. 3.

Proposal for Giving Badges to the Beggars in All the Parishes of Dublin (1737), by JS: **XIII. 129-40**; background, XIII. xxxviii–xxxix; composition, XIII. xxxviii; style, XIII. xxxix; textual notes, XIII. 223; title-page facsimile, Cooper edition, XIII. 129; — Faulkner edition, facing XIII. 129.

Proposal for the Universal Use of Irish Manufacture (1720), by JS: **IX. 13-22**; allusion to, XII. 121; background, IX. xv–xvii; composition, IX. xv; XII. 121; and *Drapier's Letters*, X. 3 and *n.**; — fifth *Letter*, X. 82 and *n.**, 89 and *n.†*; and free press, X. 109 and *n.**; publication, IX. xv, 369; reception, IX. xv, xvi, 26; XII. 121; style, IX. xv; textual notes, IX. 369–70; title-page facsimile, IX. 13; Whitshed prosecutes, IX. xii, xvi, 26–7; X. 137 and *n.**.

Proposal for Virtue, by JS: notes

for (*c.* 1728), **XIV. 14-15;** — composition, XIV. xii–xiv; — textual note, XIV. 46.

Proposal Humbly Offered to the P[arliamen]t for . . . Preventing the Further Growth of Popery (not by JS): authorship, XII. xxxii; and *Tatler*, XII. xxxii.

Proposal that All the Ladies and Women of Ireland Should Appear Constantly in Irish Manufactures (written 1729), by JS: **XII. 121-7;** background, XII. xix–xxii; composition, XII. 121; textual notes, XII. 336.

Prostitutes: and Catiline, IV. 247; and clergy, IV. 40; and criminals, IX. 38–41; and disease, XI. 253; in Dublin, XII. 230; ill-treated, I. 243; licenses, II. 55.

Protestant Post Boy: denounces JS's *Conduct of the Allies*, VI. ix, x.

Protestant Succession: *see* HANO-VERIAN SUCCESSION; SUCCES-SION TO THE BRITISH THRONE.

Protestantism: in Germany, V. 12; VI. 63; VII. 133; inner re-servations, X. 45–6; union of, and Corusodes, XII. 44; union of — against Papists, II. 120; — impossible, XII. 275-7; 'Protes-tants' (i.e., Dissenters), mostly Whigs, IV. 74. *See also* DIS-SENTERS; HUGUENOTS; NON-CONFORMISTS.

Proverbs: Latin quotations, I. 247–251; 'plagiarism' of wit, IV. 102.

Providence: death no evil, IX. 263; and marriage, IX. 263; and natural evils, IV. 245; ancient philosophers distrust, IX. 245;

and predestination, I. 123–4 (cf. I. 298).

Prussia: and Barrier Treaty, VI. 105; troops — payment for, VI. 33; — may be recalled, VI. 64; and Treaty of Utrecht, VI. 167; — signs (1713), VII. 166; and War of the Spanish Succession, VI. 13; — Austrian offers to, VII. 136-7. *See also* FREDERICK III.

Psalmanaazar, George, *c.* 1679–1763, impostor: XII. 113–14.

Psalms: Sternhold's versification, IV. 273.

Ptolemy, 2nd century A.D., Greek astronomer and geographer: V. 206; his astronomy, III. 34.

Public Absurdities in England, by JS: **V. 79-82;** analysis, V. x–xi; manuscript, V. 349; tex-tual notes, V. 349–50.

Public Accounts, Commissioners of: Oxford one, VII. 73; Report to Commons (1712), VII. 64-7.

Public opinion: against genius, I. 242; and great men, I. 245; and orators, I. 250; Restoration effected by, III. 64-6.

Public Record Office (London): acknowledgement to, VII. vii; materials for *History of the Four Last Years*, VII. xv, 183.

Public spirit: *see* IRISH PEOPLE, *patriotism*; PATRIOTISM.

Publication (literary), JS's atti-tude: I. xix.

Publick Spirit of the Whigs: Set Forth in Their Generous Encouragement of the Author of the Crisis (1714), by JS: **VIII. 29-68;** advertised, VIII. xvii; 'Advertisement', VIII. 30;

analysis, VIII. xviii–xix; background, IV. xxv–xxvii; VIII. xv–xviii; composition, VIII. xvii–xviii, xx; — 'disgustful task', VIII. xvii, 66–7; and *Conduct of the Allies*, VIII. 52; and *Discourse Concerning the Fears from the Pretender*, VIII. xxiii; errors, VIII. 48 and *n.**; — acknowledged, VIII. xviii–xix; and *History of the Four Last Years*, VIII. xix–xx, 56–7; and House of Lords, VIII. xxi–xxii; — address against, VIII. 198–9; — resolution against, VIII. xxi; and Oxford ministry, VIII. xxii; proclamation against, VII. xxxiv; VIII. xviii–xix, xxi–xxii, 30, 198–9; — facsimile, facing VIII. xxii; publication, VIII. xvii, xix, xxii, 29–30, 201; Queen knows authorship, VII. xxxiv; reception, IV. xxvii; VIII. xix–xxii; sources, VIII. xix; style, VIII. xviii–xix; textual notes, VIII. 201–4; title-page facsimile, VIII. 29.

Publicola, Lucius Gellius, *d. c.* 31 B.C., Roman admiral: XI. 201.

Publishers: Irish and English compared, XIII. 206–7.

'Puckaun', a he-goat: IV. 279, 302.

Puckle, James, *c.* 1667–1724, author: *The Club*, V. xxxii, *n.* 2.

'Puddledock, Countess of': character in *Polite Conversation*, IV. 149.

Pue's Occurrences (Dublin newspaper): IV. 282.

Pullein, Tobias, 1648–1713, successively Bishop of Cloyne and Dromore: friend of Stella, V. 233.

'Pulpit' (i.e., Puritan preachers): I. 34, 37; Caledonian, I. 35; Puritan tracts, I. 37 and *n.**.

Pulteney, Sir William (later Earl of Bath), 1684–1764, statesman: *Answer . . . to . . . Walpole*: see ANSWER OF THE RIGHT HONOURABLE WILLIAM PULTENEY; and George II, V. 118, 119; and Henry Levi, VI. 175–6; and Erasmus Lewis, VI. 175–6; praised, VI. 176; JS to toast (*c.* 1727), V. 335; and JS's 'On Mr. P——y Being Put Out of the Council', XII. xxxiii; and Walpole, V. xv–xvi, 111–19.

'Pun': mock-etymology, IV. 205–6.

Punch: and Burnet, IV. 58; and Popish plots, XII. 222–6.

Punctuality: IV. 217–18.

Punic Wars: and balance of power, I. 216; and Carthage, I. 199, 218.

Puns by JS: IV. xxxiii–xxxvi; V. 335; on baking, IV. 260; 'Castilian' (*i.e.*, in Dublin Castle), IV. 257–9; on dying, IV. 263–6; etymological, IV. xxxviii, 231–9; and his interest in language, IV. xl; Latin as English, IV. 271–2, 276–7; medical, IV. 260, 271–2; nautical, IV. 261–2; and Lord Pembroke, I. xxxiv; IV. 261–2; on poets' names, IV. 273–5; and *Polite Conversation*, IV. xxix–xxx, 276–7; against William Wood, X. 145–7.

'Puppy-ford': IV. 283.

Purchas, Samuel, *c.* 1575–1626, author: *Hakluytes Posthumus, or Purchas His Pilgrimes* (1625), in JS's library, XI. xiv.

'Purefoy, Robert' (Gulliver's surgeon on voyage to Houyhnhnmland): XI. 221.

Purgatory: flame-coloured satin, I. 52, *n.**; large continent, I. 66, *n.**.

Puritan rebellion (1642) and Civil War: and arbitrary power, III. 145–6; execution of Charles I (1649), III. 127, 141, 145, 189, 196, 200; IX. 219–31; XII. 290; — unnatural XI. 27; Clarendon and JS on, V. 295–320; disunity caused, III. 122; allegory of ears, I. 128–30; effects, II. 17; fanatics responsible, III. 200; and attacks on Harley, III. 117–18; and military power, III. 44; parliaments nullified, V. 268–9; regicide, III. 141; and schism, II. 11; success as justification, III. 118; — Whigs defend, III. 123, 142–3, 189.

Puritans and Puritanism: army establishes, III. 44; and balance of power, I. 230; and Samuel Butler, IX. 121; compared to Charles I, IX. 121; and Church of England — destroy Church, IX. 226; — united against Church, II. 3; would convert England, IX. 220; corrupting, IX. 225; and John Creichton, V. xxi; and divination, V. 125; and episcopacy, XII. 264–5; Geneva origins, XII. 263–4; government vacillating, IX. 223; history of Puritans, I. 128–31; XII. 263–70; madness during regime, II. 65; found Nonconformity, IX. 221; opposition necessary, IX. 227–8; their pamphlets, XII. 264; not persecuted, III. 127;

become Presbyterians, XII. 265; republican principles 'corrupting the nobility', VII. 21; and Roman Catholics, IX. 221; — compared, XII. 257–8; — identified, I. 127–8; 'Round-heads', I. 176; III. 162; called 'saints', I. 37 and *passim*; and religious wars, II. 12; and Whigs — ancestors of Whigs, VII. 5; — zealots, VIII. 42; forms of worship, II. 11; — extempore prayer, VI. 154; — ridiculed (doctrine, ritual, church decoration, etc.), I. 121–131, and notes. *See also* DISSENTERS; JACK; PRESBYTERIANS.

Purity, spiritual: needed for vision of God, IX. 248.

Putland, John, 1710–1773, Irish surgeon: copy of Macky's *Memoirs*, V. xxxv.

Pygmalion: pun upon name, IV. 236.

Pyrenees, Treaty of the (1659): I. 259; VII. 150.

Pyrrhus, King of Epirus, *c.* 318–272 B.C.: and genius, IX. 339.

Pythagoras, 6th century B.C., Greek philosopher: and fables, I. 40; metempsy chosis, II. 261.

Q

Quadrille, card game: IV. 115–16.

Quadrille, New Proposal: see HORT.

Quadruple Alliance (1718): 'alliances' and Hanover, V. 100.

Quakers: III. 144; affirmation for oath ('absurd heresy'), VII. 107; and Collins, IV. 28; employed in commerce and trade, VII. 106;

fanatics, I. 189; and Irish employments, XII. xliii; Jesuits disguised as, II. 37; and revelation, XII. 245; and swearing revenues, IX. 298; and the Test Act, III. 55; and tithes, II. 102; XII. 78; women preachers, I. 99 and *n.**.

Qualification Bill (Landed Property Qualification Bill: 'An Act for Securing the Freedom of Parliaments', 9 Ann. c. 5): praised, III. 119, 169–70.

Quare, Daniel, 1648–1724, clockmaker: IV. 198; JS's watch, XIII. 153.

'Queasy, Lady': character in *Polite Conversation*, IV. 161.

Quebec: Hill's expedition (1711), III. 198; VI. 23.

Queensberry, William Douglas, 1st Duke of, 1637–95: and Creighton, V. 145, 173–4, 176–7.

Queries Relating to the Birth and Birthright of a Certain Person [*i.e.*, the Pretender], attributed to George Hickes: VIII. 64.

Queries Relating to the Sacramental Test (1732), by JS: **XII. 255–60**; background, XII. xl–xlii; composition, XII. 255; editions, XII. xlvii, 346; textual notes, XII. 346.

Queries Wrote by Dr. J. Swift: see QUERIES RELATING TO THE SACRAMENTAL TEST.

Quesnoy (Le Quesnoy, Pas-de-Calais, France): siege contemplated, VII. 126.

Questions and commands: children's game, IX. 336.

Quilca, co. Cavan, Ireland (home of Thomas Sheridan): finances,

V. 224; and composition of *Gulliver's Travels*, XI. xviii, xxi; housekeeping difficulties, V. 219–21; Wooly the agent, XIV. 37. *See also* SHERIDAN, THOMAS, *Quilca*.

'Quinbus Flestrin' (Lilliputian phrase meaning 'great man-mountain', i.e., Gulliver): XI. 34, 68.

Quintana, Ricardo, *The Mind and Art of Jonathan Swift*: on JS's *Tale of a Tub*, I. xxviii, *n.†*.

'Quiet': defined, V. 336.

Quotations: preachers', IX. 75-6.

R

Rabble: *see* COMMON PEOPLE.

Rabelais, François, *c.* 1494–*c.* 1553, French satirist: III. 38; V. 254; XI. xv; allusion — V, xxix: XII. 112 and *n.**; and true humour, XII. 32.

Raby, 3rd Baron: *see* STRAFFORD, Thomas Wentworth, 3rd Earl.

Racan, Honorat de Bueil, seigneur de, 1589–1670, French poet: and Ménage, II. 252.

Raillery: *see* WIT.

Raimond IV, comte de Toulouse, 1042–1105, crusader: V. 22.

Raimondi, Marcantonio, *c.* 1475–*c.* 1534, engraver: and April Fool's joke, IV. 267.

Raleigh, Sir Walter, *c.* 1552–1618, statesman and writer: and jealousy, VIII. 138; his trial, X. 169.

'Ralph': defined by JS, V. 336.

Ralph, Bishop of Durham: *see* FLAMBARD, Ranulf.

Ramble, by JS (written *c.* 1691),

poem to a young lady in Ireland: I. xi.

Ramillies, Belgium: Battle of (1706), VI. 31; — discourages French, VI. 60; — peace refused, III. 270; VI. 43.

Ramus, Petrus (Pierre de la Ramée), 1515–72, French humanist: XI. 197; and Corusodes, XII. 41–2.

Ranelagh, Richard Jones, 1st Earl of, 1641–1712: Macky and JS on, V. 259.

'Ranfu-lo' (Lilliputian word for breeches): XI. 34.

Raphoe, Ireland: deanery of, XII. 185.

Raps, counterfeit copper coins: X. 4, 32, 33, 47, 146; XII. 101, 103.

Ratcliff, Captain: and punch, XII. 225.

Rathfarnham, Ireland, near Dublin: Sheridan's house at, V. 216, 223–4.

Ratisbon (or Regensburg), city in Bavaria: IV. 264.

'Rattle, Ned': character in *Polite Conversation*, IV. 166–7.

Ravillac (or Ravaillac), François, 1578–1610: assassin of Henry IV of France, I. 103; III. 106.

Rawson, C. J.: acknowledgement, XIV. vii; on JS's receipt for Parnell's manuscripts, XIV. xii.

Ray, John, 1627–1705, naturalist: *A Collection of English Proverbs*, IV. xxxiii.

Razors: 'with Wits as with Razors', I. 29.

Read, Sir William, *d*. 1715, oculist in ordinary to Queen Anne: his newspaper advertisements, VIII. 9.

Readers, audience, etc.: I. 40, 115–17; bad taste common, I. 132–3; III. 35; VII. 104; object to coarseness, V. 340; politics and taste, III. 35; XII. 32–3; reading like listening, IV. 253; satire ineffectual, I. 29–32; XI. 5–8; women, XII. 307, 308.

Reading, England: V. 163; abbey church, V. 46; Henry I buried there, V. 46.

Reason: 'Reason alone is sufficient to govern a rational creature', XI. 259, 315; another man's, IX. 261; and the constitution of England, II. 74–5; reason corrupted is worse than brutishness, XI. 248, 259; and deism, IX. 109; in Europe, a pretence, XI. 247, 248; God's gift, IX. 154; among the Houyhnhnms, XI. 225–6, 237–44, 259–64; 267–80; and law, II. 74–5; IV. 213; and good manners, IV. 213–14, 217, 218, 221; most men would be governed by, VIII. 77; and miracles, IX. 166; much, not to be expected, V. 78; and mysteries, IX. 164; narrow range of reason, IX. 109; and party politics, II. 2–4; limited by passions, IX. 263; passions threaten, I. 107–10; rationalism and the Trinity, IX. 109; and religion agree, II. 70, 73; sermons require, IX. 132; things above reason, IX. 164; and truth, IX. 166; and virtue, IX. 154; and wrong opinions, IX. 78.

Reasons against Lowering the

Gold and Silver Coin (1736), by JS: **XIII.** 117-120; background, XIII. xxxvi–xxxvii; textual note, XIII. 223.

Reasons Concerning the Immediate Demolishing of Dunkirk: *Being a Serious Enquiry into the State and Condition of that Affair, etc.*: VIII. xi.

Reasons for the Repeal of the Sacramental Test (not by JS): quoted, XII. 291, 292.

Reasons Humbly Offered to the Parliament of Ireland, for Repealing the Sacramental Test, in Favour of the Catholicks (composed 1733), by JS: **XII. 283-95;** background, XII. xl–xlvi; composition, XII. xlii, xlv–xlvi, 283, 295; textual notes, XII. 347-8; title-page facsimile, XII. 283.

Reasons Why We Should Not Lower the Coins: *see* REASONS AGAINST LOWERING.

Rebellion, Irish (1641): English parliament blamed, IX. 223; civil war started, IX. 222.

Rechteren, Adolf Henrik, Count of, Baron of Almelo, 1658–1731, Dutch diplomat: quarrel with Ménager, VII. 154, 158–9.

Red Sea: Josephus on, IV. 46.

Redheads: XI. 266, 267.

Redriff: *see* ROTHERHITHE.

Reede, Baron of: *see* LIER.

Reflection: and faults, IX. 359; and guilt, IX. 357; and leisure, IX. 356–7; neglected, IX. 355; painful, IX. 356; and self-knowledge, IX. 355.

Reformation, Protestant: allegory of, I. 65–76, 83–9, 95–101, 120–31; disgraced by irreverence to clergy, II. 9; corruption, XIII. 125; in England, I. 83–9, 95–101, 120–31, 188–90; and enthusiasm, I. 172–90; and Henry VIII, IV. 73; XII. 181–2; XIII. 123–6; — persecuted Protestants, IV. 72; lands of the church alienated, IX. 45; XIII. 124–5; and religious polemics, I. xxvii; a schism, XI. 49–50.

Regal library: *see* ROYAL LIBRARY.

Regency Act (1706): secret committee, VIII. 97.

Regiomontanus: *see* MÜLLER, JOHANN.

'Regoge' (i.e., George I), Emperor of Japan: V. 99–107.

Regulus, Marcus Atilius, *d. c.* 250 B.C., Roman general and statesman: V. 83; X. 168.

Rehearsal, play: *see* BUCKINGHAM; Tory periodical: *see* LESLIE, CHARLES.

Reigate, Surrey: pun on name, IV. 284.

Reign of Henry I, by JS: **V. 27-47.**

Reign of Henry II, by JS: **V. 73-8.**

Reign of Stephen, by JS: **V. 47-73.**

Reign of William II, by JS: **V. 13-27;** composition, V. ix–x; characters in, V. 24.

Reign of William II, Henry I, etc. (written *c.* 1700), by JS: **V. 11-78;** composition, V. ix–x, 11–12; dedicatory letter, V. 11–12; textual note, V. 349.

Reimond: *see* RAIMOND.

Relation of Several Facts, Exactly as They Were Transmitted to Me

From Ireland: III. xx, 231–40.

Relativity of size and sense: XI. 86–7, 92, 147–9; hearing, XI. 126; sight, XI. 92, 96, 119; — Lilliputians' keen sight, XI. 57; smell, XI. 118–19.

'Reldresal' (principal secretary for private affairs in Lilliput): XI. 39, 65, 73; Gulliver defended by, XI. 70, 71; history of Lilliput, XI. 48–50.

Relics, holy: JS ridicules, XIV. 23.

Religion: above reason, IX. 166; absence causes vice, IX. 157; Christian union, IV. 76, 79; and civil government, II. 106; common sense, IX. 108; congregations too large, II. 61; and conscience, IX. 152; basis of conscience, IX. 154; 'left to every man's conscience', XI. 49–50; contempt for, IX. 211; controversies condemned, IX. 107–8; corruptions attacked in *Tale of a Tub*, I. xvi; — *see also* CHRISTIANITY; veneration of the Cross, XI. 246; decay of — and neglect of preaching, IX. 214; decayed, II. 265; degeneration, I. 242; like love, by dissembling grows real, II. 57; will not tolerate duelling, IX. 116; enthusiasm and fanaticism, I. 174–190; eradicated, I. 243; against extremists, II. xvii; and free press, II. 60–61; freedom of, beneficial, II. 102; — limited, II. 87–90, 96; and hate, I. 241; XII. xlvii; — destroyed by hatred, IX. 174; heathen scriptures, IV. 32–3; honour weakens, IX. 154; and hypocrisy, II. 57; IX. 157; — attacked in *Mechanical Operation*, I. xxvii, 175–90; and ignorance, IX. 80; often eschewed for the sake of immorality, II. 38, 70; V. 26; and Irish Test Act, II. xiv–xv; Judgement Day, I. 243; and love, I. 241; like love ('by much dissembling, at last grows real'), II. 57; and marriage, IV. 227; requires miracles, I. 242; and morality, II. xx–xxi; essential to morality, IX. 152; liturgical music, I. 125 and *n*.*; — ('whistling'), XI. 246; to awe people, IX. 156; and physicians, I. 244; and poets, IX. 328–9; political parties undermine, IX. 177; present state, II. 44–7; — plan for improving, II. 47–63; revelation, IV. xix; — essential, IX. 74; salvation: *see* SALVATION; and satire, XII. 33, 35; and self-love, IV. 243; state church, XII. xli, 78–9, 290, 331; — corruption in, XII. 244; — and liberty of conscience, XII. 243, 244; — need for, XII. 243–5; and Tindal, II. 67–107; transubstantiation, I. 72–4; XI. 246; liturgical vestments, XI. 246; religious wars are ridiculous, XI. 49–50, 246; and wisdom, IV. 247; impedes wit, IX. 329. *See also* CHRISTIANITY; CHURCH OF ENGLAND; FAITH; TEST ACT, IRISH and ENGLISH; THOUGHTS ON RELIGION.

'Relplum Scalcath' (Brobdingnagian for 'freak of nature'): XI. 104.

Remarks on a False, Scandalous, and Seditious Libel: VI. x.

Remarks on Mr. Maxwell's and Mr. Rowley's Letters. Setting Forth the Advantages of a Bank and Lumbards in Ireland (1721): IX. 320.

Remarks on the Tories New Idol: VI. x.

Remarks upon a Book, Intitled, The Rights of the Christian Church Asserted (written *c.* 1708), by JS: **II. 65-107**; background, II. xvii–xviii; composition, II. xviii, 67, 280; errata, XIV. 51; textual notes, II. 280–1; title-page facsimile, II. 65.

Remarks upon Remarks: or the Barrier Treaty . . . Vindicated (1711): VI. xv.

'Remora': delays, VIII. 82.

'Rep': reputation, IV. 113.

Repentance: cheating in, IX. 352–3; defined, IX. 352; trust betrayed, IX. 353; uncertainty, IX. 352.

Report from the Committee of Secrecy (1715): 'state pamphlet', VIII. 163.

Report of the Committee of the . . . Privy Council: see DRAPIER'S LETTERS.

Representation (i.e., *Humble Representation* of the House of Commons, on the State of the Nation, 1712), partly by JS: **VII. 80-94**; authorship, VI. xvi; VII. 79–80; debate on, delayed, VII. 94; Dutch reply, VII. 98; and Hanmer, VI. xvi; VII. 79–80; publication, VII. 98, 235; JS praises, VII. 80, 97–8.

Republics: condemned, XIV. 10; praised, XII. 278.

Requests, Court of (hall off Westminster Hall, for walking and waiting): and Irish appeals to English House of Lords, X. 131.

Rerum memorabilium jam olim deperditarum libri II, by G. Panciroli: '*De Artibus Perditis*', I. 98 and *n.**.

Residence, Bill of (Ireland, 1732): and clergy, XIII. 205.

Resolutions, pious: IX. 353.

Resolutions of the House of Lords in Relation to . . . the Bank: IX. 319, 378; background, IX. xxi.

Resolutions When I Come to Be Old: see WHEN I COME TO BE OLD.

Resolutions Without Doors upon Resolutions Within Doors: VI. xiv.

Respublica Literaria: II. 105.

Restoration of Charles II (1660): and Charles I's execution, IX. 219–20; Commonwealth's failure, IX. 226; and education, XII. 47; and free-thinking, IV. 109; and language, IV. 10, 11; people's will, III. 64–6; and poets, IV. 274; and Presbyterians, V. 140–1; XII. 267–8; and religious sects, II. 3; and Church of Scotland, V. 140–1. *See also* CIVIL WAR; COMMONWEALTH; PURITANS.

Resurrection: new faculties given, IX. 165.

'Rétablir': ambiguous, VII. 55.

Revelation, Christian: IV. xix; essential, IX. 74; and ancient philosophy, IX. 242, 243.

Revenue, Commissioners, in Ireland: absenteeism, X. 128; and Wood's coins, X. x, 44–6.

Revenue, English: fines for swearing, IX. 295.

Revenue, Irish: fines for swearing, IX. 295.

Review (periodical written by
Defoe, 1704–13): attacked, III.
13–18; and the Church, III. 189;
condemned, XIV. 9; libellous,
III. 202; by an illiterate scribbler,
III. 13; and Whigs, III. 189.

Revolution of 1642: *see* PURITAN
REBELLION.

Revolution of 1688: V. 99, 289;
and almanac-makers, II. 163;
and astrology, II. 149; and
Church of England, II. 9;
Church principles, IX. 123; Civil
War contrasted, IX. 123–4, 230;
and clergy, II. 16; confusion
following, V. 168; JS's contem-
poraries not responsible for,
VIII. 168; and contractions in
speech, IV. 106; and national
debt, VII. 68–9; and the Devil,
IV. 30; in *Examiner*, XIV. 10;
would to God the Exclusion
Bill had passed, V. 264; consequence on Ireland, XII. 132;
justified, IX. 122–4; and Nonconformists, III. 46–7; oppression the cause, IX. 229; and
philology, IV. 231; and poets,
IV. 274–5; and political parties, II. 14; and Presbyterians,
XII. xliv–xlv; effect on religion,
IX. 224; 'I would have been for
a regency', V. 291; restores
republican spirit, VII. 5; and
Roman Catholics, II. 71; 'the
ruin of the kingdom', III. 47;
and JS's sermons, IX. 102;
settlement, II. 20–3; JS accepts
settlement, II. xvii; and terms

'Whig' and 'Tory', III. 163; and
Tories (1714), VIII. 92; partisan
support of Tories, IX. 121; and
Whigs, IV. 283; and Whig
principles, VIII. 120; and Whig
writers, III. 189; and William
III, XI. 245.

Revolutions: JS's views on, IX.
31; like girl at Bartholomew
Fair, III. 147.

Rewards and punishments, eternal: and human nature, IX. 244;
and virtue, IX. 156.

Reynard the Fox: I. 41 and *n*.†.

Rhætia: Switzerland, home of
Paracelsus, I. 152.

Rheinfels, fort on the west bank
of the Rhine near St. Goar and
south of Koblenz: 'Rhinfelt',
VII. 113.

Rhine river: VII. 132.

Rhinfelt: *see* RHEINFELS.

Rhuddlan, Flintshire, Wales: Ridland, V. 201.

Rhyme: and poetry, IX. 335.

Rice, J. A.: annotated copy of
Tale of a Tub, I. xxxii, *n.**.

Richard III, King of England:
cruelty, II. 22.

Richards, Captain, son of Solomon: zealous Presbyterian, XII.
270.

Richards, Solomon (*sic*: correction of 'Jacob'), *d.* 1691, Colonel,
made governor of town of Wexford, Ireland, in 1658: and
James II, XII. 270.

Richardson, Joanna: on JS's copy
of *The Proceedings Touching the
Impeachment of . . . Clarendon*,
XIV. 46.

Riches: and corruption, IX. 194;
disadvantages, IX. 193–6; and

disease, IX. 193, 196; dishonesty, IX. 194; and happiness, IX. 194; preferred to poverty, IX. 190; and Providence, IX. 147.

Richmond, Charles Lennox, 1st Duke, 1672–1723, illegitimate son of Charles II by Louise de Kérouaille, Duchess of Portsmouth: Macky and JS on, V. 258.

Richmond, Frances (*née* Stuart or Stewart), Duchess of, 1647–1702; Burnet and JS on 'Mrs. Steward', V. 271.

Richmond, Henry Fitzroy, Duke of, *c.* 1519–36, illegitimate son of Henry VIII: V. 247.

Richmond Lodge, residence of George II as Prince of Wales: JS visits, V. xxvii; XIII. 201.

Riddle, on the Posteriors, poem by JS: IX. xvii, *n.* 1.

Ridge, Thomas, *d.* 1730, M.P. for Poole: 'the brewers at Portsmouth', III. 138.

Ridgeway, Anne, JS's housekeeper (daughter of Mrs. Brent, wife of Anthony Ridgeway): and *Directions to Servants*, XIII. vii; Lord Newtown's legacy, XIII. 157; JS's bequest, XIII. 154; codicil to JS's will, XIII. 198; — witness to codicil of JS's will (1737), XIII. 200.

Ridgeway, Anthony, cabinet maker of Dublin: married to Anne Brent, XIII. 158.

Ridicule: *see* SATIRE.

Ridland, Flintshire, Wales: V. 201.

Ridpath, George, *d.* 1726, Scottish editor of Whig *Flying-Post*: Dutch *Gazette* praises, VIII. 31;

impudence, VIII. 14; compared to Steele, VIII. 31–2, 54; leading Whig writer, VIII. 21, 31, 193.

Right of Precedence Between Physicians and Civilians Enquir'd into (1720): not by JS, IX. xxv–xxvi.

Rights of the Christian Church Asserted: *see* TINDAL.

Ringsend, port of Dublin: swearing revenues, IX. 297.

Rivers, Richard Savage, 4th Earl, *c.* 1654–1712, Constable of the Tower: appointed Constable of the Tower, VIII. 102, 117; and Hanover, VII. 144; VIII. 171; Macky and JS on, V. 258; and Marlborough, III. xvii; VIII. 102, 117; and Oxford, VIII. 124; pun on name, IV. 258; and JS, II. xxxvi; III. xvii; and Tories, VIII. 149; and Whigs, VIII. 166.

Rivière and Son: bind manuscript of JS's *History*, VII. xxii–xxiii.

Robert, Duke of Normandy, *c.* 1052–1134, son of William I: V. 38; blinded, V. 33; character, V. 13, 45; and the Crusades, V. 22, 27–9, 33–4, 241; death, V. 45; duchy pawned (1096; to William II, *not* to Philip I), V. 23; invades England, V. 29–30; grievances, V. 19; and Henry I, V. 27–30, 31–3, 35, 46; imprisoned at Cardiff Castle (1107), V. 33; misses William I's funeral, V. 13; and William II, V. 14, 16, 19–20.

Roberts, James, *c.* 1671–1754, London printer and publisher: publishes *A Letter to the Reverend Mr. Dean Swift*, IX. xiii, *n.* 2.

Robethon, Jean, *d.* 1722, Huguenot, advisor to Elector of Hanover (later George I): turns Elector against Tories, VII. 143–4; VIII. 172 and *n.*‡.

Robins, Thomas: on Dublin grand jury, X. 76.

Robinson, John, 1650–1723, Bishop of Bristol, Lord Privy Seal, envoy to Sweden: character, VII. 159; and Dutch Treaty, VII. 108; goes to Holland (1711), VII. 111; fears for life (1712), VII. 136; plenipotentiary, VII. 12–13, 63, 117; made Lord Privy Seal, VII. 3 and *n.**, 16; and Polignac (1712), VII. 143; at Utrecht, VII. 13, 117, 127–8, 136, 137, 153, 157, 165; — ambassadorial rank, VII. 162, 165; — authority, VII. 128; — French quarrel with Dutch, VII. 158, 159, 163; — signing delayed, VII. 163.

'Robinson, William' (ship's captain in *Gulliver's Travels*, Part III): XI. 153–4.

Rochester, England: V. 14.

Rochester, Bishop of: *see* ATTERBURY.

Rochester, John Wilmot, 2nd Earl of, 1647–80, poet and courtier: VI. 153; pun upon name, IV. 274.

Rochester, Laurence Hyde, Earl of, 1642–1711, Lord President, Tory: III. 72; character, III. 78–9; death, VII. 16; — JS's obituary, III. 152; in *Examiner*, XIV. 11; and James II, III. 91; one of 'two men' misruling England in 1701, I. 210; and Somerset, VII. 13; Temple praises, I. 268.

Rochford (or Rochfort), William Nassau de Zuylestein, 2nd Earl of, 1681–1710: regiment, III. 231.

Rochfort, Deborah (*née* Staunton), wife of John: 'Young lady', recipient of JS's *Letter*, IX. xxvii, 83–95.

Rochfort, George, *c.* 1682–1730 (son of Robert Rochfort), M.P. for West Meath, Ireland: marriage, IX. xxvii.

Rochfort, John, *c.* 1692–*c.* 1770 (son of Robert Rochfort), M.P. for Ballyshannon, Ireland: character, IX. 89; marries Deborah Staunton, IX. xxvii, 85; witness to JS's will, XIII. 157.

Rock Savage (or Clifton), Cheshire: IV. 258.

Rodenhuysen, Belgian fort, near Mendonk, between Ghent and Sas van Gand: and Barrier Treaty, VI. 101, 109.

Roermond: *see* RUREMOND.

'Roger': defined by JS, V. 336.

Roger, Bishop of Salisbury, *d.* 1139; account of, V. 56–7.

Rolt, Mr. (probably husband of Swift's cousin Patty): money for, V. 334.

'Roman': pun upon, IV. 238.

Roman Catholicism (Roman Catholics, 'popery', 'papists', etc.): Apostles ridiculed, II. 92; — and St. Paul, II. 92; avarice V. 22; bishops — Tindal on, II. 192; bribery and corruption, V. 34; papal bulls satirized, I. 68 and *n.*†, 69; and Burnet, IV. 61–9, 74–5, 78–9, 80–84; celibacy satirized, I. 71 and *n.*‖; 75 and *n.*‖; ceremonies satirized, I.

67 and *n.*†; and abolition of
Christianity, II. 37; civil power
of the Church, I. 76 and *n.**;
communion, I. 75 and *n.*†;
confession satirized, I. 66; converted to Protestants, II. 120;
corruption, XIII. 125; and Corusodes, XII. 44; agree with
Dissenters, I. 127, *n.**; Dissenters more dangerous, XII.
xli; joined by Dissenters, II. 9;
— compared to, XII. 284-95;
— similarities, I. 127-8; and
England — (12th century), V.
17-18; — not dangerous in
England, IV. 77-8; — Ireland
and England compared, XII.
258; — less dangerous in Ireland than England, X. 126; —
political parties disown, II. 2-4;
— Reformation, IV. 73; —
allegedly would divide England
into sects, III. 143; errors grow,
XIV. 29; foreign allegiance, II.
115-16; and freethinkers, IV.
31; and Gee, IV. 250; Holy
Water satirized, I. 67 and *n.*‖,
*n.**, 68 and *n.**; ignorance, IX.
80; improvements, IV. 76; in-
dulgences satirized, I. 67 and
*n.**; and insurrection, XII.
286-9; and Ireland — bank
scheme, advantage over Protestants, IX. 302; — high birth
rate, XII. 112, 114; — not
dangerous, II. xxii, 111, 116,
120; XII. 258-9, 273; — flee
Ireland, XII. 291-2; — Middle
Ages, V. 75-6; — powerless
in, IX. 172; — and rebellion,
IX. 223; — recruits in France
and Spain, XII. 174; — and Test
Act, XII. 283-95; Jesuits

allegedly encourage schisms, III.
97-8; and King John, V. 86; and
religious justice, II. 101-2; use
of Latin and Greek, IX. 75;
mottoes on Marlborough's
return (1711), VII. 28; miracles,
VIII. 34; and monarchy, XII.
286, 292; 'most absurd system',
XII. 272-3; and mysteries, I.
72-4; IX. 163; — the Trinity
and Tindal, II. 91; orgies, I.
186-7; penitents, I, 75 and *n.**;
Peter pence, V. 76; pope: *see*
POPE; 'Popish times', II. 10; and
the Presbyterians, V. 271; and
the Pretender, VIII. 91; X.
132-3; — no danger of a popish
successor, VI. 93; VIII. 34;
priests, registration of, II. 120;
Protestants shut out, I. 76 and
n.†; and Puritans, II. 11; —
compared, XII. 257; and ancient Rome, II. 93; saints, VIII.
21; — intercession of, V. 25;
superstition, V. 22, 25-6; super-
stitious and enslaving, I. 74 and
*n.**; in *Tale of a Tub*, contrasted
with Church of England, I. xvi,
('superstition') 2; allegory of
Tale of a Tub, I. 280; and tavern
signs, XII. 222-6; author's dis-
guise in *Reasons Humbly Offered
. . . for Repealing the Sacramental
Test*, XII. xlv-xlvi; and Tindal,
II. 67-107; 191-2; — Tindal
argues for, II. 93, 94, 105; —
Tindal, a papist, II. 90, 106; and
toleration, II. 7, 115; and
Tories, IV. 63, 75-6; Tories
charged with encouraging, VII.
28; transubstantiation satirized,
I. 72 and *n.*‖, *n.**, 73-4; XI.
246; unfashionable, II. 62;

usurpations of (12th cent.), V.
17–18; and Wagstaff, IV. 121;
weakness unifies, III. 97; and
Whig pamphlets, VIII. 31; loyal
Whigs, XII. 286; — allegedly
encourage, III. 143–4; whoring
licenses, IX. 247; and William
III, II. 118; IV. 100; and Wood's
coins, X. xxiv, xxv, 53–4, 61.
See also JACOBITES; PETER; POPE;
POPISH PLOT.

Romances: French — and exalted
passions, IX. 86; — and women,
XII. 308; histories often are
romances, V. 262; Spanish, VIII.
163; writing them is therapeutic,
V. 262.

'Romantick': VI. 9; (pun on
'Roman') VIII. 21.

'Rome' : pun upon, IV. 207.

Rome (ancient Rome and
Romans): VI. 87, 133, 134; VIII.
174; and Americans, compared,
XII. 60; and authors, II. 76;
barbarians invade, II. 123; IV.
6, 14; V. 3–4; IX. 48; and Julius
Caesar, X. 130; the Caesars, V.
68; censors' function, II. 49;
and the early Christian Church,
II. 93, 95; and Cicero, IV. 237;
and 'civis', IV. 252; conquest of
England, V. 3–4; conversation,
IV. 92; cradle of learning, I. 90;
no war debt, VI. 55; decay of,
IV. 8; Dutch compared with,
VI. 87; education, XII. 46; and
Epicureans, IV. 249; government, I. 211–222; II. 84; V. 36;
— and balance of power, II. 16;
— constitutional reform, III. 65;
— dictators' function, IX. 33; —
republicanism, VIII. 37; —
secrecy in, VIII. 77; — senate —

compared with British Parliament, XI. 195–6; — — and
Regulus, X. 168; heir to Greece,
IV. 9; and Hannibal, IV. 237;
history, VIII. 37; and Horace,
II. 28; ingratitude to generals,
III. 19; VI. 133; liberty encouraged learning, II. 17–18;
military policies — armies, III.
40–1, 42; — generals, III. 19,
22–4; — injustice, XI. 200–1;
plebeians' encroachments, III.
150; Popes control, I. 55 and
n.†; population encouraged, VII.
95; ancient priests, II. 100; and
JS's *Presbyterians Plea of Merit*,
XII. xlv; and punning, IV. 205;
rhetoric, VIII. 44; expel Tarquin
the Proud, I. 213; II. 23;
temples, III. 159; causes of
wealth, IX. 48; impoverishment
of West, IX. 48.

Romney, Henry Sidney, Earl of,
1641–1704, courtier, friend of
Sir William Temple: Burnet and
JS on, V. 288; Macky and JS
on, V. 258; 'an old vitious
illiterate rake', V. 195; and JS's
preferment, V. 195.

Romulus, mythical founder of
Rome: and Julius Caesar, I. 211;
and Latin, IV. 8.

Ronquillo, Don Pedro, Spanish
ambassador to court of James
II: V. 289.

Rooke, Sir George, 1650–1709,
admiral: trial, X. 109–10.

Rooke, George, linen draper of
Dublin: shrewd Quaker, XII.
xliii, 299 and *n.**.

Rooke, Heyman, 1653–1725,
major-general: III. 238.

Roper, Abel, 1665–1726, Tory

journalist who started *The Post Boy*: 'humble slave', VI. xxiii; compared with Steele, VIII. 9; and JS, VI. xxiii, xxvi.

Rosamund (i.e. Rosamond Clifford, *d. c.* 1176), mistress of Henry II: V. 77.

Roscommon, Wentworth Dillon, 4th Earl of, *c.* 1637–85, poet: and JS's academy project, IV. xiv.

Rose Tavern, Russell Street, London: I. 49.

Rosicrucians: I. 118, 119.

Ross, Earl of (probably in error for William Ross, 12th Lord Ross of Hawkhead, *q.v.*): V. 151.

Ross of Hawkhead, William Ross, 12th Lord, *c.* 1656–1738, Scottish soldier and statesman: and Creichton, V. 151, 159.

Rotherhithe (Redriff), suburb of London, on south bank of Thames: XI. 218; Gulliver arrives there (1702), XI. 80; — (1706), XI. 148; — (1710), XI. 218; — (1715), XI. 289; Gulliver's garden, XI. 295; Gulliver's house, X. ix; XI. 9.

Rothes, John Leslie, 1st Duke of, *c.* 1630–81: Duke of Monmouth visits, V. 142.

Rothschild, Victor, Lord: acknowledgements to, I. vi, xix, *n.**; V. v, xxxi, xxxiii; VIII. v; *The Rothschild Library*, V. v; *Some Unpublished Marginalia of Jonathan Swift*, V. xxxii, *n.* 4; JS's manuscripts, VIII. xxiii, *n.* 1; XIII. xi.

Rotterdam, Holland: Jews to farm swearing revenues, IX. 298; would continue war (1713), VII. 164.

Rouen, France: and Duke Robert, V. 32.

Rouillé, Pierre, seigneur de Marbeuf, 1657–1712, French diplomat: and peace negotiations (1709), VII. 33.

'Roundhead-bawn': IV. 283.

Roundheads: I. 176; III. 162.

Rowe, Nicholas, 1674–1718, poet and dramatist: and authorship of *Squire Bickerstaff Detected*, II. xiv; and JS, II. xxxvi; — recommended to Oxford, II. xxxvi; IX. 29; letter to *Tatler*, II. 247.

Rowlands: *see* VERSTEGEN.

Rowley, Hercules, *c.* 1679–1742, M.P. for Londonderry: *An Answer to a Book, Intitled, Reasons Offered for Erecting a Bank in Ireland* (1721), IX. 320; *An Answer to Mr. Maxwell's Second Letter to Mr. Rowley Concerning the Bank* (1721), IX. 320; and Irish bank, IX. xx, 303.

Roxburghe (or Roxborough), John Ker, 1st Duke of, *c.* 1680–1741: and Nottingham, VII. 16.

Royal Exchange, London ('Change Alley'): XII. 7, 43.

Royal Library: *see* WINDSOR CASTLE.

Royal Library, or St. James's Library, in St. James's Palace: site of battle of books, I. xxxix, 137, 139, 145, 152, 153, 155.

Royal Society of London for Improving Natural Knowledge (founded in 1660; given royal charter in 1662): recommends academy, IV. xiv; Academy of Lagado partly modelled on, XI. 176–92; Bickerstaff's intellectual heirs, II. xxviii; Gulliver

donates giant wasp stingers, XI. 110; *Philosophical Transactions* and *Gulliver's Travels*, XI. xx; ridiculed — 'certain projects . . . one', I. 24; — 'Academy', I. 25.

Rufus, Geoffrey, Bishop of Durham, *d.* 1141: V. 54.

Rumford: 'ride to Rumford', IV. 186.

Rumney, Earl of: *see* ROMNEY.

Rumours, evil: spread by ill-wishers, IX. 237.

Rump Parliament: III. 146.

'Run', a gambling term: V. 275.

Runic alphabet: and Hebrew alphabet, V. 331.

Ruremond (Roermond), Limburg, Netherlands: and Dutch Barrier, VI. 115.

Russia (Muscovy, Muscovites): ambassador molested (1709), III. 138; and Bickerstaff, II. 160; defeat Charles XII, V. 85; Czar's cruelty, III. 205; and Dalyell ('Dalziell'), V. 130–1; guarantees to 'princes of the north', VII. 148; war possible (1711), VII. 59; — 'these princes', VI. 63. *See also* ALEXIUS; NORTHERN WAR; PETER I.

Ruthenians: and papacy, XIV. 35.

Rutherford, Samuel, 1600–1661, Scottish divine: 'half fool, half mad', V. 267.

Ryan, M. J.: acknowledgement to, VII. xxvii, *n.* 1.

Rye-gate: pun on 'Reigate', IV. 284.

Rylands Library, Manchester, England: acknowledgement,

XIV. vii; letter by W. King in, VII. xiv, 4; JS's manuscripts, XII. 306–10.

Rymer, Thomas, 1641–1713, critic and historian: praised, I. 249; ridiculed, I. xxiv, 22, 57.

Ryswick, Treaty or Peace of (1697): I. 133, n.*; and Barrier Treaty, VI. 105; Treaty of Commerce follows, VI. 117; England not benefited, VI. 11; France ignores, VI. 12; good enough, VI. 61; William Howell and JS on, V. 264; and Somers, VII. 6; succession neglected, VI. 94–5, 105; and Sweden, VI. 62; and Tariff of 1664, VI. 12; compared with Treaty of Utrecht, VII. 6.

S

Sa Ga Yean Qua Rash Tow, an Indian King in *Spectator*, No. 50: his observations on England, II. 264–7.

Sabbath: in Brobdingnag, XI. 98, 106.

Sacheverell, Henry, *c.* 1674–1724, Tory clergyman (impeachment and trial, 1710): and the Devil, IV. 30; in *Examiner*, XIV. 11; calls Godolphin 'Volpone', VII. 9; Hare compared to, III. 271–2; and missionaries, IV. 31; and passive obedience, IV. 35; Somers opposes impeachment, VII. 6; Tories oppose impeachment, VI. 130;

trial, IV. 45, 70; — aftermath, VIII. 84; — and Church of England, VI. 126; — election following, VIII. 142–3; — and

Godolphin, VIII. 115; — Godolphin's 'blind pursuit', VI. 74; — Godolphin ministry ruined, III. 64; — and change of ministry, VIII. xxxi; — 'one of their members', VII. 3; — parties muster, VIII. 149; — and peace (1713), VI. 126–7; — and popular opinion, VII. 34; — Steele denies Church's danger, VIII. 39; — JS's knowledge of, VIII. xxxi; — and *Tatler*, VIII. 6; — Tories defend him, VII. 3; — Tories' slogan, VIII. 164; — unnecessary, III. 70–1; — 'unpopular quarrel' weakens Whigs, VI. 126.

Sacramental Test: *see* TEST ACT; A LETTER FROM A MEMBER OF THE HOUSE OF COMMONS.

Sacraments: and repentance, IX. 353.

Sacrilege: and tithes, IX. 60.

Saffold, Thomas, *d.* 1691, quack doctor: motto from handbill, VI. 173.

Saggard (*i.e.*, Saggart), co. Dublin, Ireland: property for St. Patrick's Hospital, XIII. 203.

Sailors: XI. 243–4; Irish — bastards and swearing revenues, IX. 297.

St. Andrews, Archbishop of: *see* SHARP, JAMES.

St. Andrew's church: *see* CANTERBURY.

St. Asaph, Bishop of: *see* FLEETWOOD, WILLIAM.

St. Bartholomew's Day massacre (1572): Heylyn and JS on, V. 255–6.

St. Christopher (or St. Kitts), Leeward Islands: Britain secures, VII. 48, 114, 131–2; recompensed for French attacks, III. 169.

St. Donas, fort near Sluis in the Netherlands: and Dutch Barrier, VI. 101, 109.

St. Dunstan-in-the-East, church in London: II. 180.

St. Francis Street, Dublin: site of Drapier's shop, X. ix, 80, 94.

St. George, Sir Oliver, Bart., *d.* 1695, M.P. for Galway: and Irish bank schemes, IX. 311.

St. George's Channel, between Wales and Ireland: and Wood's coins, X. 31, 106.

St. George's Chapel: *see* WINDSOR.

St. Germains (court of James II at St. Germain-en-Laye, near Paris): Scottish Jacobites at, V. 177. *See also* PRETENDER, Old.

St. James's Evening Post, London newspaper: JS's possible contribution (8 Sept. 1721, supposed death of Bishop Evans), XIV. 41; — authorship, XIV. xiv.

St. James's Library: *see* ROYAL LIBRARY.

St. James's Palace, London: and conversation, IV. 117; Ned Fashion visits, II. 186.

St. James's Park, London: and *Polite Conversation*, IV. xxxii, 130–31, 148.

St. James's Street, London: and Simon Wagstaff, IV. 101.

St. Jean, Hostelerie de, in Paris: III. 210.

St. John: *see* BOLINGBROKE.

St. John of Jerusalem, knights of: and masons, V. 329.

St. Malo, seaport, Ille-et-Vilaine, France: and Dunkirk, VI. 191.

St. Mary Axe, off Leadenhall

Street in the City of London: church of, and lion, II. 182.

St. Mary's Abbey, Dublin: sugar house burns, V. 346.

St. Patrick's Cathedral, Dublin: clock for, V. 334; and Delany, XII. 166; lead stolen — **JS's advertisement** (1739), **XIII. 194**; liberty of, X. 114; XIII. xxix; — paper presented by residents to JS (1734), V. xxiv, 341-2; — — **JS's answer, V. 342-3,** 359; and JS — accounts kept by him, XIII. xliii; — his dream, V. xxv; vicars choral and public concerts, XIII. 196.

St. Patrick's coin, 1678 Dublin halfpence and farthings: X. 33.

St. Patrick's Hospital, Dublin, founded by JS: charter, XIII. 151-2; endowment, XIII. 203; Faulkner offers £200 for a manuscript by JS, VII. xvii; governors — and the Ewings, VII. xix; Dr. King's subscription schemes, VII. xxiii; regulations, XIII. 150-52; site, XIII. xxxvi; and JS — **advertisements** (1738-9), **XIII. 192-3**; — — background, XIII. xlii; — — textual note, XIII. 225; — his bequest, XIII. 150; — his copyrights, VII. xviii-xix; — his *History of the Four Last Years,* VII. xvii-xix; — investments, XIII. 193; — trustees, XIII. 151-2; — his will, XII. xxi.

St. Paul's Cathedral, London: XI. 114; churchyard, I. 171; and freethinkers, IV. 31; and Indian King, II. 264-5; 'Pole's', IV. 158.

St. Stephen's Chapel (*i.e.,* House of Commons): 'Chappel', III. 223; and Steele, VIII. 12; and Whitshed, X. 159. *See also* HOUSE OF COMMONS.

St. Stephen's Green, Dublin: and Wood's effigy, X. 148.

St. Venant, Pas de Calais, France: and Dutch Barrier, VII. 113.

Saints: *for separate saints, see under names, as* JEROME, PAUL, etc.; and free-thinkers, IV. 46.

'Saints' (*i.e.* Puritans): ridiculed, I. 37, 176, 189, and *passim.*

Salamis: and Themistocles, I. 207.

Salic law (excluding females from succession to French throne): VII. 150-1.

Salisbury, England: bishopric, II. 86; cathedral, XI. 114; in Glorious Revolution, V. 162; pun upon name, IV. 262; site of Stonehenge, I. 124.

Sallust (Gaius Sallustius Crispus), Roman historian, 86–34 B.C.: *Catiline* 5 (quoted): III. 82; — 24. 4: IV. 247.

Salmanaazor: *see* PSALMANAZAR.

Salt: appetite for, XI. 232.

Salus populi: see GOVERNMENT.

Salvation: easier for poor, IX. 197; and social class, IX. 142; and wealth, IX. 190.

Samson and Delilah: compared to Irish people, IX. 238.

Sanchar: *see* SANQUHAR.

Sancroft, William, 1617–93, Archbishop of Canterbury: and Burnet, IV. 59–60; Burnet and JS on, V. 277, 285, 291; JS's poem on, I. xiii; sent to Tower, XII. 270; JS praises, II. xvii.

Sanders (possibly Robert Saunders, Dublin lawyer): and Swandlingbar, IV. 282.

Sanderson, Captain: and Creichton, V. 152.

Sanderson, Robert, 1660–1741, historian, co-editor of *Foedera*: government by consent, IX. 19.

Sandwich, Kent: name, IV. 284.

Sandwich, Edward Montagu, 3rd Earl of, 1670–1729: Macky and JS on, V. 259.

Sanquhar (Sanchar), Dumfriesshire, Scotland: V. 137.

Sanson, Nicolas, 1600–67, French mapmaker: his *Atlas*, XI. 100.

Sappho: and false virgin, II. 181.

Saracens: and the Crusades, V. 21.

Sardinia, kingdom of: Austria gains (1713), VIII. 54; VII. 133, 156.

Sarmatia: *see* SCYTHIA; GUAGNINUS.

Sas van Ghent, Zeeland, Netherlands: and Dutch Barrier, VI. 104, 108, 109; VII. 92.

Sastras ('Shaster'), Hindu law books: IV. 32.

Satan: I. 100, 179. *See also* DEVIL.

Satire: I. 29–30; aims, XII. 33–4; definition, I. 140; difficulty, IV. 243; easy, IX. 339; in England, I. 31–2; evildoers punished, III. 141; and John Gay, XII. 35; none in JS's *History of the Four Last Years*, VII. 1; and ill fame, XII. 24–5; ineffectual, I. 29–32; XI. 5–8; of lawyers, I. 31, 244; and 'low humour', XII. 33; and parallel history, III. 26, 29; and point of view, III. 117, 118–19; 'revenge on the world', I. 243; ridicule called an easy art, IX. 217; satirists as scavengers, IX. 342; subjects for, XII. 33;

none in *Tale of a Tub*, I. 29–32. *See also* JS, *Literary career*.

Saturninus, Lucius Appuleius, *d. c.* 99 B.C., Roman demagogue: and Marius, I. 219.

Saul, King of Israel: and the Drapier, X. xv, 48.

Saunders, Anderson, *d.* 1719, M.P. for Toghmor: and Wharton, III. 237.

Savage, Philip, *d.* 1717, chancellor of the Exchequer of Ireland: and Wharton, III. 234, 140.

Savages: and Gulliver, XI. 230, 284, 285.

Savile, Sir Henry, 1549–1622, scholar: *Rerum anglicarum scriptores post Bedam* (1596), V. x.

Savoy, region of south-eastern France, on the Italian frontier: chimney-sweepers, VI. 140.

Savoy, Duke of: *see* VICTOR AMADEUS II.

Savoy, Duchess of: *see* ANNA MARIA.

Saxon language: and 'Abraham', IV. 239.

Saxons: V. 35; Germanic background, II. 82, 83; invade Britain, IV. 7; V. 4; converted to Christianity, II. 83; V. 4; place names, V. 5.

Saxony: Charles XII invades (1706), VI. 62; one of the 'princes of the north', VII. 148; one of 'these princes', VI. 63.

Scaliger, Julius Caesar, the elder, 1484–1558, Italian scholar: berates Bentley, I. 161; *De subtilitate*, I. 130 and *n.*†; and pedantry, IV. 216.

Scandalum magnatum: I. 32; XII. 46.

Scandinavia: *see* DENMARK; GOTHS; NORTHERN WAR; SWEDEN.

Scarborough, Mrs., wife of Charles: and Erasmus Lewis, VI. 173.

Scarborough, Charles, Clerk of the Board of Green Cloth: and Erasmus Lewis, VI. 173.

Scarborough, Henrietta Marie, daughter of Charles, Maid of Honour: and Erasmus Lewis, VI. 173–4.

Scarborough, Richard Lumley, Earl of, *c.* 1650–1721, general: Burnet and JS on, V. 288; opposes peace 'without Spain', VII. 17; and JS's *Letter to a Whig Lord*, VI. xvii.

Scarron, Paul, 1610–60, French author: verses on destruction made by time, V. 335.

Schelde, river in Flanders: and trade with Flanders, VI. 28, 51, 104; VII. 92, 142.

Schemes from Ireland, for the Benefit of the Body Natural, Ecclesiastical, and Politick (London, 1732): XII. xxxii.

'Schoits, John Emmanuel', imaginary mountebank: IX. 285.

Schomberg, Frederick Herman von Schönberg, 1st Duke of, 1615–90, general: on France, VI. 40; and writing on military matters, V. xix, 267.

Schütz, Augustus, *d.* 1757, Keeper of the Privy Purse, Master of the Robes: and Mrs. Howard, V. 214.

Scipio Africanus Major, Publius Cornelius, *c.* 236–*c.* 183 B.C., Roman general and statesman: and Carteret, XII. 161–2; and envy, VIII. 138; great figure, V. 83; impeached, I. 218; and Marlborough, III. 42; and Rochester, III. 152; and government of Rome, II. 84.

Scipio Africanus Minor (Publius Cornelius Scipio Aemilianus), *c.* 185–129 B.C.: and Polybius, I. 217.

Scipio Asiaticus, Lucius Cornelius, *d. c.* 184 B.C., Roman soldier and statesman: 'his brother', I. 218.

'Scotch lord': possibly John Ramsay, Earl of Holderness, V. 85.

Scotch Presbyterian Eloquence: see CROCKAT, GILBERT.

Scotland and Scots: and pun on 'Andromache', IV. 233–4; and apparitions, III. 10; Caledonians, V. 4; and Calvinism, II. 101; character — 'beggarly nation', V. 184; — parsimonious, II. 116; 'poor, fierce northern people', VIII. 49; climate, XII. 46; Covenanters and John Creichton, V. 130–80, *passim*; and Cromarty, IV. 253; description, IX. 3–4; early inhabitants, XIV. 20; education, XII. 46; and England — hatred of, IX. 4; — invasion of 1708, II. 76; — invasion of twelfth century, V. 16; — wars, VI. 9–10; lacks episcopacy, II. 116; Episcopal Church: *see* BISHOPS OF THE EPISCOPAL CHURCH; CHURCH, EPISCOPAL IN SCOTLAND; and Ireland — compared, IX. ix–xi; XII. 78, 306; — absentees, X. 131; — Irish anomalies, XII. 310; — colonists dislike Church

of Ireland, II. 116; — emigration to Ireland, XII. 184, 185, 306; — 'encroachments', IX. 10; — England's treatment compared, IX. 3–12; — Irish preferments and 'another seminary', XII. 250; — well-treated in Ulster, V. 271; — Wood's coins, X. 127; — worse in Ireland, XII. 306; Johnstons and Maxwells, V. 125; and Louis XIV, IX. 8; and masons, V. 329; personified as William North-Britain, II. 247; — ridicule of 'North Britain' and 'North British' as terms, II. 247; parliamentary representation (1714), VIII. 50; Parliaments (Estates) in 1689, V. 169; peerage, IV. 284; — numerous, VIII. 50; Picts, V. 4; Presbyterian Church ridiculed — satire 'beyond the Tweed', I. 29; — 'Sylva Caledonia', I. 35; — *see also* PRESBYTERIANS; and the Pretender, VIII. 50, 170; and Puritan rebellion, V. 268; IX. 4; rebellion (1715), V. 100, 104–5; religion, IX. 4; — dangerous, II. 131; and the Revolution of 1688, V. 264; Roman invasion, V. 4; salt trade, VI. 117; Scotch Patronage Bill, VII. 97; and Act of Security (1703), VIII. 49; speech — pun on 'Abraham', IV. 239; — conversation, IV. 95; — pronunciation of English, IV. 281; and Act of Supremacy, V. 274; in Sweden, II. 134–5; taxes, VIII. 50–1; tithes in, XII. 78; Act of Union, IX. x; VIII. 50; — allegory of, IX. x, 7–8; — dissolution proposed (1713), VIII. 50; — England not bene-

fited, VIII. 49; — and Godolphin ministry, III. 95; — and Junto, III. 95; — and freedom of the press, II. 26; — Scottish overtures rejected, VIII. 49; — and Act of Security (1703), VIII. 114; — Steele on, VIII. 48–52; — and JS, IX. x, xi; — terms, VIII. 50–1. *See also* MALCOLM III; DAVID I.

Scotland Yard, London: author's thanks, in *Tale of a Tub* (possibly alluding to Wells's Coffeehouse), I. 115; 'North-Briton Yard', II. 247.

Scott, Temple (pseudonym for J. H. Isaacs, 1864–1939), editor of JS's *Prose Works* (1897–1908): I. v; on JS's *History of the Four Last Years*, VII. ix–x, xxvii; and JS's *Mr. Collins's Discourse of Free-Thinking*, IV. xvii; on JS and beggars, IX. 136.

Scott, Sir Walter, 1771–1832, poet and novelist, editor of JS's *Works* (1814; 2nd ed., 1824): II. xix, *n.* 1; on *An Argument against Abolishing Christianity*, II. xix; on Creichton's *Memoirs*, V. xxi; reprints false additions to *Tale of a Tub*, I. xxxii.

Scotus, Joannes Duns, *c.* 1265–*c.* 1308, Scholastic philosopher: I. 41; XI. 197; and Aristotle, II. 81; leads the Moderns, I. 152; deposes Plato, I. 144; pun upon name, IV. 259.

Scriblerus Club (Arbuthnot, Gay, Lord Oxford, Parnell, Pope, JS, meeting in 1714): *Memoirs of Scriblerus* — authorship, XI. xiii; — and Gulliver's Travels, XI. xiii-xiv, xviii.

Scripture: *see* BIBLE.

Scrofula: *see* KING'S EVIL.

Scroggs, Sir William, *c.* 1623–83, Lord Chief Justice: compared to Whitshed, X. 91–2, 167.

Scrope (or Scroope), John, *c.* 1662–1752, Secretary to the Treasury: report on Wood's coins, X. 187–8.

Scutage ('reasonable aid for marrying the King's daughter'): introduced by Henry I, V. 35.

'Scuttle, Lady': character in *Polite Conversation*, IV. 156.

Scythia (or Sarmatia) and Scythians: our ancestors, I. 178; III. 40; and asses, I. 60–61; ate no corn, XII. 19; and grazing, XII. 8; and Hippocrates, I. 175; and Irish diet, XII. 19, 178; long-heads, I. 175–6; mares, I. 93; pens, I. 94; and Tartars (*i.e.*, England and Scots), III. 40.

Seal, Dr. (probably Harvey Seale), Register to Archbishop King: XII. 121.

Seasonable Advice to the Grand-Jury: *see* DRAPIER'S LETTERS.

Second Letter from a Friend to the Right Honourable Chief Justice Whitshed: *see* DRAPIER'S LETTERS.

Second Whigg-Letter, from William Prynne to Nestor Ironside Esq.: VIII. xii.

Secret History of the October Club: *see* DEFOE.

Secretaries of State: correspondence used in *History of the Four Last Years*, VII. xxxiv. *See also* BOLINGBROKE.

Security, Act of (1703): VIII. 49; and Godolphin ('offending minister'), III. 94–5; and Act of Union, VIII. 114.

Sedley ('Sidley'), Sir Charles, *c.* 1639–1701, wit and dramatist: anecdote, X. 88.

Selden, John, 1584–1654, lawyer and scholar: compared with Tindal, II. xviii, *n.* 2.

Self-control: passions uncontrollable, IX. 351.

Self-interest: and morality, IX. 152.

Self-knowledge: charity increased by, IX. 360–2; evil and self-deceit, IX. 354; reasons for ignorance, IX. 355; lack of, IX. 351; painful, IX. 357; prejudice hinders, IX. 357; self-criticism difficult, IX. 350.

Self-love: *see* PRIDE.

Semiramis, Queen of Babylon: and masons, V. 324.

Sendivogius, Michael, *d.* 1636 or 1646, alchemist: I. 79.

Seneca, Lucius Annaeus, *c.* 4 B.C.–A.D. 65, Roman moralist and playwright: *Epistles*, IX. 112; 'free-thinker', IV. 44–5; quotations, VIII. 189; — *De beneficiis* i. i. 4: III. 24.

Sentiments of a Church-of-England Man, by JS (published 1711, dated 1708, possibly written 1704): **II. 1-25**; analysis, II. xv–xvii; composition, II. xv, 1; date, XIV. 51; editions, II. xv, 275; and Heylin, V. xxxiv, 256; publication, II. xix–xx; and Revolution of 1688, IX. 123; and sermon on *Martyrdom of Charles I*, IX. 120; textual notes, II. 275–6; and Whigs, VIII. 122.

Septennial Act (1716): 'modern

invention', VIII. 176; ridiculed, V. 277.

Sequels (or second parts): I. 116.

Sermons: aimed at humble audience, IX. 168; composition, IX. 71–72; in JS's *Letter to a Young Gentleman*, IX. 99; occasional sermons, XIV. 36; pathos condemned, IX. 70; should not be read, IX. 71–2; simplicity recommended, IX. 65–6. *See also* PREACHING.

Sermons, by JS: analysis, IX. 100–1, 106; arrangement, I. v–vi; authenticity, IX. 97; composition, IX. 133–7; date, IX. 100; destroyed by him, IX. 99; his opinion of them, IX. 97–100; political position, IX. 101; publication, IX. 99–100; religious doctrines, IX. 101; style, IX. 100–3; for separate sermons see under titles: BROTHERLY LOVE; CAUSES OF THE WRETCHED CONDITION OF IRELAND; DOING GOOD; EXCELLENCY OF CHRISTIANITY; FALSE WITNESS; MARTYRDOM OF KING CHARLES I; MUTUAL SUBJECTION; POOR MAN'S CONTENTMENT; SLEEPING IN CHURCH; TESTIMONY OF CONSCIENCE; TRINITY.

Servant, Certificate: *see* CERTIFICATE.

'Servant' discarded by JS: *see* CERTIFICATE TO A DISCARDED SERVANT.

Servants: accusations, XIII. 13; breakages, XIII. 10; candles, XIII. 14–15; candlesticks, XIII. 14; cheating, III. 81–2; doors, XIII. 9, 13–14; drunkenness, XIII. 11, 23; duties to master, IX. 144; and master's guests, XIII. 12; duty at inns: *see* DUTY OF SERVANTS AT INNS; called by master, XIII. 10, 12; errands, XIII. 13; furniture, XIII. 10; staying at home, XIII. 11; and inns, XIII. 163–5; Irish — and crimes, IX. 204; — and English families, IX. 204; — vicious, IX. 203–4; knives, XIII. 10; leaving, XIII. 9, 13; lying, XIII. 12; malingering, XIII. 11; master's duties, IX. 144; messages, XIII. 8; and pets, XIII. 14; petticoats, XIII. 11; scolding, XIII. 7, 12; specialization, XIII. 9; stealing, XIII. 9; JS's — absence, XIII. 161; — drunkenness, XIII. 161, 162; — fines, XIII. 161–2; — not be influenced by, I. xxxvii; — laws for, XIII. 161–2; — lies, XIII. 161; — wages, XIII. 161; — waiting at table, XIII. 162; tale-bearing, XIII. 11, 15; and tools, XIII. 14; unanimity, XIII. 11; vails: *see* VAILS: viciousness, IX. 203; their visitors, XIII. 11, 14.

'Servants in general': rules, XIII. 7–15.

'Servants', laws for JS's: *see* LAWS FOR THE DEAN'S SERVANTS.

Servius Tullius, semi-legendary king of Rome, 6th century B.C.: chosen Protector of Rome, I. 213.

Settlement, Act of (1701): VI. 194; and Barrier Treaty, VI. 99–100; George I to remain in England, XI. 172; repeal possible, VI. 27, 65, 92–3; VIII. 51, 52; Oxford introduced, VII. xxxiii; JS praises, VII. xxxvi.

'Seven lords' (who examined Gregg): *see* BOLTON; DEVONSHIRE; HALIFAX; SOMERS; SOMERSET; TOWNSHEND; WHARTON.

Seven Wise Masters: and Plato, I. 146.

Severinus, St., *d.* 507: makes dumb man speak, XIV. 25.

Severus, Septimius, 146–211, Roman emperor: and Picts' Wall, V. 4.

Sewell, George, *d.* 1726, journalist: and Burnet, IV. xxii and *n.* 3.

Sexual relations: XI. 266–7, 289; perverse, XI. 264; during pregnancy, XI. 263.

Seymour, Sir Edward, 1633–1708, Bart., Speaker of the House of Commons: and Bedlam, I. 111; possible model for Clodius in JS's *Discourse of the Contests and Dissensions*, I. 233, 235.

Shadwell, Thomas, *c.* 1642–92, playwright: pun upon name, IV. 274.

Shaftesbury, Anthony Ashley Cooper, 1st Earl of, 1621–83, statesman: Clarendon on, V. xxxix; education, XII. 47; JS on, V. xxxix, 303.

Shaftesbury, Anthony Ashley Cooper, 3rd Earl of, 1671–1713, essayist and moralist: *Characteristics* (1711), IX. 114–15 and *n.* 1; *Letter on Enthusiasm*, not read by JS, I. 3; and authorship of *Tale of a Tub*, 'another book', I. 3.

Shakespeare Head edition of JS's works: *see* DAVIS, HERBERT.

Shakespeare, William: bookseller's copyright, XIII. 206; his learning, IX. 332; and English poetry, IV. 273; quotation from *Hamlet* III. ii. 282: II. 242.

Shannon, Henry Boyle, Earl of, *c.* 1686–1764, Whig politician, Irish Privy Councillor, Chancellor of the Exchequer of Ireland: and Drapier, X. 205; Macky and JS on, V. 260; and Wood's coins, X. 182.

Sharp, James, 1613–79, Archbishop of St. Andrews: Burnet and JS on, V. 266, 268, 269, 271, 273, 278; murdered, V. 135–6; murderer's punishment, V. 148.

Sharp, John, 1645–1714, Archbishop of York: and Compton, XII. 270; and Dr. Lloyd, III. 183; and JS's *Project*, II. xx; condemns *Tale of a Tub* ('weightiest men'), I. 3; and religious allegory of *Tale of a Tub*, I. xiv, xxix; and 'Tables of Fame', II. 241–2.

Shaster: *see* SASTRAS.

Shelburne, William Petty, 2nd Earl of, afterwards 1st Marquis of Lansdowne, 1737–1805, statesman: and Swift's copy of Burnet's *History*, V. xxxvi.

Sheldon, Gilbert, 1598–1677, Archbishop of Canterbury: Burnet and JS on, V. 272; and Charles II, V. 272.

Sheridan, Elizabeth (*née* MacFadden), wife of Dr. Thomas Sheridan: character, V. 222–3.

Sheridan, Dr. Thomas, 1687–1738, priest and schoolmaster, friend of Swift, father of Thomas Sheridan (1719–1788), grand-

father of R. B. Sheridan: *The Blunder of all Blunders*, reply to JS's *The Wonder of all the Wonders*, IX. xvii, *n.* 1; and Carteret, V. xxix, 223; XII. xxviii, 162–4, 166; and school in Cavan, V. 218; certificate concerning his servants, XIV. 37; chaplain to Lord Lieutenant (1725), V. xxix; character — credulous dupe, V. xxx, 216; — indiscretion and improvidence, V. 217, 222–6; — pride, V. 224, 226; — great teacher, V. xxx, 216; **JS's character of**, V. 216–18, 222–6; **JS's character of, as 'Lilly'** (1731), **XIV. 37;** — date, XIV. xiv; — textual note, XIV. 46; — *see also* CHARACTER OF DOCTOR SHERIDAN; HISTORY OF SECOND SOLOMON; his *Contes à rire*, IV. xxxix, xl; death (10 Oct. 1738), V. xxx, 216; family, V. 217, 222–3; at James Grattan's house, XIV. 37; and Bishop Hort, V. 224; contributions to *Intelligencer*, V. xxx; XII. xiv; — no. 6, XII. xv; — introduction to no. 15, XII. xv; alleged Jacobitism, V. 223, 226; marriage, V. 217; monument proposed, V. 218; poem on Queen Caroline, V. xxx, 226; preferments—living of Dunboyne, co. Meath, V. 217–18; — living of Rincurran, co. Cork, V. 217; preferment blocked by principles, XIV. 36; puns, V. 238; home at Quilca, V. 219–21; XI. xviii, xxi; — dilapidated, V. xxix, 219–21; house at Rathfarnham, V. 216, 223–4; sermon on birthday of George I (1725), V. xxix, 223; XII. xxviii, 163–4; — and Tighe, XII. xxviii; *A Sermon Preached at St. Patrick's Church* (1731) — **JS's preface, XIV. 36-7;** — — authenticity, XIV. xiii–xiv; — — textual note, XIV. 46; and Stella, V. 237; — her advice, V. 222; — her illness (1727), V. xiii;

and JS, V. xxviii–xxx; — JS's poem on 'Ballyspellin', V. 225; — correspondence, VIII. xxxvi–xxxvii; XII. ix, x; — and *Drapier's Letters*, X. xxvi, xxviii; — JS's manuscripts, VII. xii; — poem on funeral for JS's muse (1718), V. 222; — JS visits Quilca (1725), V. xxix, 219–21; XI. xviii; — JS's sermons, IX. 98–9; — tour together (1728), V. xxix; — JS's *Vindication of Lord Carteret*, XII. xxviii; — word games, IV. xxxviii, xl; and Tories, V. xxx, 226.

Sheridan, Thomas, 1719–88, actor and author, son of Dr. Sheridan, father of R. B. Sheridan, biographer of JS and editor of his works: on *The Difficulty of Knowing One's Self*, IX. 104–5; education, V. 217 and *n.**; *Life of Swift* (1784), I. xxxiii; on JS's *Meditation upon a Broomstick*, I. xxxiii–xxxiv; edition of JS's *Works*, revised (1801), II. xxxii.

Sherlock, William, *c.* 1641–1707, Dean of St. Paul's: *The Doctrine of the Blessed Trinity Stated and Defended* (1719), IX. 109–10 and *n.*; *Sermons Preach'd upon Several Occasions* (1700), IX. 109–10 and *n.*

Shiell, William, *d. c.* 1753,

Registrar of St. Patrick's Cathedral: XIII. 196.

Shilling: Queen Elizabeth's — superstition of, II. 244; *Tatler* concerning: *see* TATLER, no. 249.

Shoemakers: and poets, IX. 336.

Shopkeepers, Irish: cheats, XII. 306; lack common sense, IX. xv, 17; dishonesty, IX. 17; and Irish manufacture, IX. 17; too political, IX. 173–4; poverty, IX. 201; JS's judgement, XIII. 89; and poets, IX. 341. *See also* TRADE, IRISH.

'Shop-lifters': III. 91.

Short Character of His Ex[cellency] T[homas] E[arl] of W[harton] L[ord] L[ieutenant] of I[reland] (1710), by JS: **III. 175-84, 231-40;** analysis, III. xix–xxi; background, III. xviii–xx; and Carteret, X. xviii; publication, III. xix–xx, 277; textual notes, III. 277–8.

Short Defence of the People of Ireland, Occasion'd by the View of a Letter from Mr. Wood . . . (1724): X. 67.

Short Remarks on Bishop Burnet's History, by JS: *see* BURNET, GILBERT, *History*, *JS's remarks*.

Short View of the State of Ireland (1728), by JS: **XII. 3-12;** authorship, XII. x–xi; background, XII. xi–xiii; composition, XII. 5; and Drapier, XII. x; and *Intelligencer*, XII. xv, 325; publication, XII. x, 3, 122, 323, 325; reception, XII. 122; JS praises, XII. 66; textual notes, XII. 323; title-page facsimile, XII. 3.

Shots (Lanarkshire, Scotland), Kirk of: V. 140.

Shovell, Sir Clowdisley, 1650–1707, admiral: II. 143; his death predicted, II. 203, 206.

Shower, John, 1657–1715, Presbyterian minister in London: 'one of them', VII. 21.

Shrewsbury, England: V. 14; and Stephen, V. 53; and Welsh, V. 20; and William II, V. 14.

Shrewsbury, Charles Talbot, Duke of, 1660–1718, statesman: and Bolingbroke, VIII. 152; Burnet and JS on, V. 288; character, III. 79; V. 257; VIII. 156; — able minister, VII. 160; — insincere, IX. 26; at French court (1713), VII. 157; and Gaultier, VII. 35; on George I, VIII. 173; and royal Guards, VIII. 157; Lord Chamberlain, III. 79; VIII. 102, 117–18; Lord Lieutenant of Ireland, VIII. 156; Macky and JS on, V. 257; and Oxford, VIII. 124; JS and historiographer's post, 'an employment', IX. 26; and Torcy, VII. 160, 164–5; and Tories, VIII. 149; at Utrecht, VII. 160–2; — agrees to general peace, VII. 165; and Wharton, VIII. 118; and Whigs, III. xxviii, *n.* 1; VIII. 166.

Shrewsbury, Robert de Bellême, Earl of, *c.* 1052–*c.* 1113: and Henry I, V. 30–3.

Shrewsbury-cake: and poetic style, IX. 338.

Shropshire, England: XI. 143; and William Wood, X. 29.

'Shuttle, Dick': character in *Polite Conversation*, IV. 195.

Siam: and missionaries, IV. 31; religion of, IV. 31-3.

Sibyls: I. 99.

Sican, John, Dublin merchant, friend of JS: X. 76.

Sicily: and Athens, I. 207-8; and Austria, VI. 57; and balance of power, I. 202; and Barrier Treaty, VI. 111; commonwealth, I. 196; disposition uncertain (1712), VII. 133; to be French (1700), VI. 11; Ireland signified by, III. 27-9; Rome invades, I. 198; Duke of Savoy gains it (1713), VII. 155; VIII. 54.

Sidley, Sir Charles: *see* SEDLEY.

Sidney, Mr.: *see* ROMNEY.

Sidney, Algernon, 1622-83, political philosopher: 'dangerous author', X. 86; *Discourse Concerning Government* (1698), III. 143.

Sidney, Sir Philip, 1554-86: *Defence of Poesie* (1595), IX. 327; — quotations, *ad initium*, IX. 332; — *ad finem*, IX. 335; — *ad finem* (last paragraph), IX. 340; on Irish poetry, IX. 332; pun upon name, IV. 273.

Silenus: and drunkards, IV. 247.

Silesia: Protestants' 'footing', VI. 63.

Silverius (or Sylverius), St., Pope (in office 536-7): death and miracles, XIV. 32.

Simeon Salus, St., *d. c.* 589: converts Jew, XIV. 33; a charming magician, XIV. 33.

Simeon Stylites the younger, *c.* 517-*c.* 592: and plague in Constantinople (A.D. 542), XIV. 33.

Simmons, George: and JS's *Modest Defence of Punning,* IV. 209.

Simnel (or Symnele), Lambert, *fl.* 1487-1525, impersonator of Earl of Warwick: and Merlin, II. 165, 168, 169.

Simon Magus, sorcerer in *Acts* VIII. 5-24: fanatic, I. 188.

Simpson, Ralph, *fl.* 1680-1704, London bookseller: publishes Temple's *Letters*, I. 255.

Sin: attractive, IX. 354-5; desire makes attractive, IX. 358; conscious purpose, IX. 354; customary, IX. 361; false contrition, IX. 352; false knowledge encourages, IX. 361; persistence in, IX. 354; preaching vain, IX. 215. *See also* VICE.

Singleton, Henry, *c.* 1682-1759, Prime-Sergeant and later Chief Justice of the Common Pleas in Ireland: executor of JS's will, XIII. 157, 200; and JS's *History of Four Last Years*, VII. xvii; — and Millar, VII. xx-xxi.

'Singular, Lady': character in *Polite Conversation*, IV. 194.

Sinzendorf: *see* ZINZENDORF.

Sirloin: etymology, IV. 171.

Six-penny-worth of Wit: I. 38.

Skelton, Lady Barbara, *d.* 1741, wife of Charles Skelton and daughter of Earl of Sussex: and Erasmus Lewis, VI. 173-4.

Skelton, Charles, *fl.* 1714, son-in-law of Earl of Sussex, lieutenant-general in French service: and Erasmus Lewis, VI. xxvi-xxvii, 173-8, 200.

Skinner, Stephen, 1623-67, lexicographer: IV. 231.

Skotia: Greek land of darkness, alluding to Scotland, I. 97.

'Slamecksan' (name of Lilliputian

Low-heel party; i.e., the Whigs): XI. 48.

'Slardral' (Brobdingnagian gentleman usher): XI. 101.

Slave trade: see ASSIENTO.

Slavery: slave trade proposed for Ireland, XII. 135–6.

Slaves: tend to be tyrants, IX. 21.

Sleep: poor people's, IX. 192.

Sleeping in Church, sermon by JS: IX. 210-18; analysis, IX. 99, 107, 130–2; composition, IX. 133–4; textual notes, IX. 376–7.

Sleeping pills: V. 151.

'Slumskudask' (Luggnaggian word for 'gratuity'): XI. 213.

Sluys canal, Zeeland, Netherlands: 'Sluice' and Barrier Treaty, VI. 101.

Smalridge, George, 1663–1719, Dean of Christ Church and Bishop of Bristol: and freethinking, IV. 43–4; and missionaries, IV. 31.

Smallpox: VIII. 80; XI. 201.

'Smart, Lady': character in *Polite Conversation*, IV. 129–201, *passim*, 276–7.

'Smart, Lord': character in *Polite Conversation*, IV. xxxii, 129–201, *passim*.

Smedley, Jonathan, *b.* 1671, *d.* 1729 or later, Dean of Clogher: enemy of Swift, VIII. xiv.

Sminia, Hessel van, Dutch plenipotentiary, Secretary of the Chamber of Accounts of the Province of Frizeland, Netherlands: and Barrier Treaty, VI. 99, 106–9.

Smith, David Nichol, 1875–1962, Merton Professor of English Literature (Oxford University):

acknowledgement, I. vi; V. v; XIV. vii; on Bickerstaff, II. xxiv, *n.* 1; edition of JS's *Letters to Ford*, II. xviii and *n.* 1; IX. xi, *n.* 1; edition of *Tale of a Tub*: see GUTHKELCH.

Smith, E., London bookseller, *fl.* 1686–1715: and JS's *Short Character* of Wharton, III. 277.

Smith, John, corncutter: VIII. 9.

Smith, John, 1655–1723, Whig politician, Speaker of the House of Commons, Chancellor of the Exchequer: Macky and JS on, V. 260.

Smithfield, London: Protestant martyrs burned ('fires'), IV. 62, 63, 65, 68, 80, 83.

Smock Alley, Dublin: and whoring licences, IX. 297.

Smyrna Coffee-House, Pall Mall, London: Dutton-Colt and Davenport at, XII. 231.

'Snilpall' (Lilliputian title of honour, granted for law-abiding behaviour and meaning 'Legal'): XI. 59.

Snow, John, Bailiff of Stockbridge, Hants.: and Steele, VIII. 3–25.

Snuffling: I. 183–85.

Social levels and classes: XI. 200; educational differences, II. 103–4; equal before God, IX. 142; God's will, IX. 126, 143; and good manners, IV. 213; hierarchy approved, IX. 124; among the Houyhnhnms, XI. 256; masters and servants, IX. 124; mutual assistance, IX. 143; mutual subjection defined, IX. 142; — no cause for complaint, IX. 147; obedience, IX. 143; —

prevents chaos, IX. 143; and
presumptuousness, XI. 124; and
religious freedom, II. 102; rich
and poor, IX. 142-8, 190-8;
XI. 251; subordination, IX.
141-9; — Christ's example, IX.
145; — and envy, IX. 146; —
guests and hosts, IX. 145; —
rich and poor, IX. 190-91; —
rulers subject to laws, IX. 144;
— subjects and ruler, IX. 144.
See also ORDER, SOCIAL.

'Society, The' (or, 'The Club'),
club formed by Bolingbroke,
including JS, Prior, Arbuthnot,
Ormonde, Orrery, and others:
XI. xii–xiii.

'Society de propagando', fictitious publisher of *Miscellaneous
Works, Comical and Diverting*
(1720): I. 275.

Society for Propagating the
Gospel in Foreign Parts: IV.
30-31.

Society, Royal: *see* ROYAL SOCIETY.

Socinians (Socinus, Socinianism;
doctrines of Faustus Socinus,
1539-1604, Italian religious
reformer): and abolition of
Christianity, II. 36-7; anti-
Christian, II. 72; and Charles II,
IV. 249; and clergy, IV. 37; and
Collins, IV. 28; and free-think-
ing, IV. 37; Roman Catholics
oppose, XII. 286; Scots oppose,
V. 311; vain, IX. 261; and
Whigs, III. 92; IV. 63; and
Whiston, IV. 31, 34, 36. *See also*
HERESIES.

Socrates: in Aristophanes' *Clouds*,
I. 33; and Aristotle, I. 247; and
astrology, II. 142, 144; and
Carteret, XII. 161-2; 'a Chris-

tian', IV. 42; Diogenes calls
him mad, IX. 250; great figure
in dying, V. 83; and Epaminondas, IV. 234; and fame, XII. 24;
'free-thinker', IV. 41-2; and
Grub Street, I. 40; last words,
IX. 245; morality, IX. 73; and
Oxford ('wise and honest man'),
VI. 79; and later philosophers,
II. 80; 'prince of philosophers',
XI. 268; as poet, IX. 332; and
public service, I. 225; his religion, II. 12; his head on JS's
seal, XIII. 200; no sect, IX. 249;
and Somers, I. 14; virtues
celebrated, XI. 196, 268; wisest
man, I. 247.

Sodom: compared with Ireland,
IX. 238.

Soho, London: pun upon name,
IV. 207.

Soldier: definition of, XI. 246-7;
act forbidding service to a
foreign prince (12 Anne 2, c. 11),
XII. 174.

Solomon, King of Israel: 'free-
thinker', IV. 45; and gold, IV.
247; and Gregorio Leti (or Lati),
X. 110; temple, and free masons,
V. 324.

Solomon, Second: *see* HISTORY OF
THE SECOND SOLOMON.

Solon, *c.* 640 B.C.–*c.* 558 B.C.,
Athenian lawmaker: Athenian
law, I. 209-10; and Athens, I.
202; and the Council of Four
Hundred, I. 204-5; philosophy
inadequate, IX. 113, 246.

*Some Advice Humbly Offer'd to the
Members of the October Club*: *see*
ADVICE HUMBLY OFFER'D.

**Some Arguments against En-
larging the Power of Bishops,**

in Letting of Leases, With Remarks on Some Queries Lately Published (1723), by JS: **IX. 43-60**; background, IX. xxii; textual notes, IX. 371-2; title-page facsimile, IX. 43.

Some Considerations Humbly Offered . . . in the Choice of a Recorder (1733), by JS: **XIII. 69-70**; background, XIII. xxiv; textual notes, XIII. 221.

Some Considerations upon the Consequences Hoped and Feared from the Death of the Queen (1714), by JS: **VIII. 101-4**; background, VIII. xxviii–xxix; composition, VIII. xxix–xxx; and *History of the Four Last Years*, VIII. xxix; manuscript, VIII. xxix, xxx, 210; — facsimile, facing VIII. 101; textual notes, VIII. 210.

Some Farther Account of the Original Disputes . . . about Farthings and Halfpence (1724): 'a pamphlet', X. 64-6.

Some Few Thoughts Concerning the Repeal of the Test (composed 1733) by JS: **XII. 299**; background, XII. xl–xliv; composition, XII. xlii; textual notes, XII. 348.

Some Free Thoughts upon the Present State of Affairs (composed 1714), by JS: **VIII. 75-98**; and Bolingbroke, VIII. xxvii–xxviii; composition, VIII. xxiii–xxv, xxvii, xl; — 'Discourse', IX. 25; and *Discourse Concerning the Fears from the Pretender*, VIII. xxiii, xxvi; Charles Ford on, VIII. xxiv; manuscript, VIII. xxiv–xxv, xxvi–xxviii, 205; —

facsimiles, facing VIII. xxiv, xxv; preface, VIII. xxviii; publication, VIII. xxiv–xxv, xxviii, xl, 205-6; textual notes, VIII. 205-9; title-page facsimile, VIII. 75.

Some Further Reasons Against the Bill for Settling the Tyth (1734), by JS: **XIII. 105-8**; textual notes, XIII. 222.

Some Observations upon a Paper, Call'd the Report of the Committee: see DRAPIER'S LETTERS, No. 3.

Some Queries Humbly Offered (1732), by JS: **XIII. 205**.

Some Reasons Against the Bill for Settling the Tyth of Hemp, Flax, &c. by a Modus (1734), by JS: **XIII. 95-108**; 'Advertisement', XIII. 95; background, XIII. xxix–xxx, 95; textual notes, XIII. 222; title-page facsimile, facing XIII. 94.

Some Reasons to Prove, That No Person Is Obliged by His Principles, as a Whig, to Oppose Her Majesty or Her Present Ministry. In a Letter to a Whig-Lord (1712), by JS: **VI. 121-36**; analysis, VI. xvi–xviii; date, XIV. 53; publication, VI. xvi; style, VI. xviii; recipient of 'Letter', VI. xvii–xviii; textual notes, VI. 210; title-page facsimile, VI. 121.

Some Remarks on the Barrier Treaty (1712), by JS: **VI. 83-117**; 'Appendix', VI. 165-9; — background of 'Appendix', VI. xxvi; background of *Some Remarks*, VI. xi, xiv–xvi; — 'some discourses', VII. 78-9; composition, VI. xiv–xv; and *Conduct of*

the Allies, VI. xv, 49, 85, 92; erratum, XIV. 51; projected ('Discourse'), VI. 49; reception, VI. xv–xvi; — 'accusations', VII. 79; textual notes, VI. 209–10; title-page facsimile, VI. 83.

Some Remarks on the Letters Between L[ord] T[ownshe]nd and Mr Secretary B[olingbrok]e: VI. xv–xvi and *n*. 1.

Some Remarks upon a Pamphlet, Entitl'd, A Letter to the Seven Lords of the Committee, Appointed to Examine Gregg (1711), by JS: **III. 185-205**; background, III. xxix–xxxi; date, XIV. 51; publication, III. xxx, 278; textual notes, III. 278; title-page facsimile, III. 185.

Some Thoughts on Free-Thinking (composed about 1712), by JS: **IV. 49-50**; composition and publication, IV. xx, 287-8; textual notes, IV. 287-8.

Somers, John, *d*. 1681, attorney, of Clifton, Severn Stoke, Worcestershire, father of Lord Chancellor: a 'noted rogue', V. 258.

Somers (or Sommers), John, Lord, 1651–1716, Lord Chancellor, member of Whig Junto: Anne attached to ('two great officers'), VIII. 103, 142-3; and Aristides, I. 14; as 'Aristides' in *Contests and Dissensions*, I. xx, 206, 210, 224; defends seven bishops (1688), VII. 5; — 'late reign', I. 15; on Whig bishops, VI. 152-3; Burnet and JS on, V. 279; and Cato, I. 14; character — adultery ('gallantry'), III. 79; — deist ('conversed with Toland'), III. 79; — formality, VIII. 119; — frank manner, VIII. 137; — republican, VII. 5; **JS's character of** (1704), I. 15; — (*c*. 1712), VII. 5-6; and Cicero, I. 14; constitution of England, X. 109; and sixth *Drapier's Letter*, X. 171; his education, XII. 47; and Epaminondas, I. 14; humble family, V. 258; VII. 5; — 'from the dregs', III. 78; — 'new-men', XII. 47; 'extraordinary genius', VII. 7; 'sublimest genius', I. 14; and Godolphin, VIII. 114; Gregg and Harley, III. xxix; Gregg and the seven lords, III. 187-205, 245-58; impeachment (1701), I. xix–xx; greatest lawyer JS has known (1724), X. 109; Lord President (1708), II. xxi; VIII. 113, 121; — among 'chief leaders', VI. 43; — *'presided'* in coach-box, III. 25; Macky and JS on, V. 258; and Marlborough, VIII. 114; and second Partition Treaty (1699 — 'advisers'), VIII. 54; and Pretender ('which . . . have been . . . tampering'), VIII. 39; contrasted with Rochester, III. 78-9; Sacheverell's prosecution opposed (1710), VII. 6; VIII. xxxi, 115; and Socrates, I. 14;

and JS — and Addison, IX. 30; — on dangers of opposing Church, II. xiv; — *Contests and Dissensions* attributed to, V. xxxvi; VIII. 119; — he deserts Somers (1710), III. xii; — intimacy, VII. 5-6; VIII. 119-20; — first meeting (*c*. 1702), I. xx; IV. xxiv; — *Tale of a Tub*

dedicated to him, I. xxii, 13–16, 280; II. xxxvii; — and Wharton, VIII. 121;

on Union, VIII. 49 and *n.**; opposes Treaty of Utrecht, VII. 6; and Archbishop Tenison, XII. 40; leads Whigs, VII. 5–7.

Somerset, Algernon Seymour, 7th Duke of, 1684–1750, styled Earl of Hertford in father's lifetime: and Oxford regiment, VIII. 102, 117.

Somerset, Charles Seymour, 6th Duke of, 1662–1748, Whig politician, Master of the Horse: ambitious for the crown, VII. 13; and Anne, VII. 13; VIII. 147, *n.**; 161; — he misrepresents her (Dec. 1711), VI. 72, 124; VII. 15, 17; Bolingbroke refuses to sit in Council with him ('husband', 'unlucky proceeding'), VI. 72; VII. 14; character — obsequious, VI. 72; — no judgment, V. 257; **JS's character of,** VII. 13–15; and the Church, VII. 21; and Godolphin, VII. 14; Gregg and Harley, III. xxix; Gregg and the seven lords, III. 187–205, 245–58; Macky and JS on, V. 257; Master of the Horse, VII. 2, 13; — fears dismissal (1712), 'husband', VI. 72; — — 'very good courtier', VI. 124; — remains in office (*c.* 1711), III. 204; VIII. 124; — 'certain lord' not dismissed, VIII. 161; and Oxford, VI. 124; VII. 14–15; and Oxford ministry — he declares open war, VI. 72; VII. 15; against dismissal of Parliament (1710), VII. 14; — 'some',

VIII. 142; against peace 'without Spain', VII. 15; shallow politics, III. 79; and Rochester, VII. 13; contrasted with Shrewsbury, III. 79; smells bad, III. 79; and Whigs — their contempt for him, VII. 13–14; — leads Junto (1711), VII. 108; — supports them (1711), VII. 29; — unsteady (1710–11), 'one of your neighbours', VI. 124; and William III, VII. 13; wife 'neither lov'd nor esteem'd him', VI. 72.

Somerset, Elizabeth Seymour (*née* Percy), Duchess of, 1667–1722, Mistress of the Robes, favourite of Queen Anne, Whig: and Queen Anne — Anne's affection ('good nature'), VI. 71; — her ascendancy over Anne, VIII. 146, 167–8; — Anne favours, VII. 13, 14; 'neither lov'd nor esteem'd' husband, VI. 72; replaces Duchess of Marlborough (1711), 'an opportunity', VI. 71; and Lady Masham, 'another object', VIII. 153.

Somerset, Henry Fitzroy, Duke: *see* RICHMOND.

Somerset, Robert Ker (or Carr), Viscount Rochester, Earl of, *c.* 1587–1645: and death of Prince Henry, V. 266.

'Soogaun', plaited straw: IV. 279, 302.

Sophia, Electress of Hanover, 1630–1714, granddaughter of James I, niece of Charles I: and Barrier Treaty, VI. 99–100; death, VIII. 93; and order of Hanoverian succession, VII. 78; and John Macky, V. xxxv;

residence in England, suggested, VIII. 71; 'presumptive successor', VI. 93.

Sophia Dorothea (daughter of George William, Duke of Lüneburg-Celle), 1666–1726, wife of George I: William Howell and JS on, V. 265.

Sorcerers: *see* GLUBBDUBDRIB.

'Sourdis, Marquis de', in *A New Journey to Paris*: III. 217.

South, Robert, 1634–1716, prebendary of Westminster and rector of Islip, witty preacher and writer: and contradictory doctrines, IV. 35; supports widow of JS's uncle, V. 191; on the Trinity, IV. 34.

'South, Squire' (i.e., Austria), character in John Arbuthnot's *History of John Bull*: VI. 167.

South America: and England, VI. 117.

South Sea Bubble (1720): and bad taste, IX. 27; in *Gulliver's Travels*, XI. xix, 177–8; bill to prevent repetition, IX. 294; and interest rates, IX. 303; and Irish Bank project, IX. xvi, 294, 306; landowners' interest disregarded, IX. 32; and money shortage, IX. 300.

South Sea Company: act for (1711), III. 170, 198; and debt, VII. 72; opposition, VII. 77; purpose, VII. 76; and Swearers Bank, IX. 296; JS misrepresents, VII. xv.

Southampton, Thomas Wriothesley, 4th Earl, 1608–67: praised, XII. 47.

Southerne, Thomas, 1660–1746, playwright: pun upon name, IV. 274.

Southwell, Edward, 1671–1730, Irish Secretary of State: letters from Coghill, X. xxii, *n.* 1, xxx, *n.* 1; XII. xiii; and Irish employments, X. 58; on assays of Wood's coins, X. 187–8, 195.

Southwell, Sir Robert, 1635–1702, Irish Secretary of State: fails to employ JS, I. xi.

'Sowins', thin porridge: IV. 279, 302.

Spain (Spaniards, Spanish Empire): and Austria — English aid a hindrance to Charles, VI. 14; — Hapsburgs reportedly favoured by (1701), VI. 14; VII. 86; — union opposed, VI. 51–3; and Bickerstaff, II. 144, 204; 'Catholicissimus' title of king, XIV. 24; character decayed, V. 80; court of 'Charles III', VI. 37; clergy, II. 98; and Dutch — antipathy, VI. 14, 115; — and Dutch Barrier, VI. 88–9, 113–15; and England — allies (1689–97), VI. 14; — Cromwell's wars, VI. 9; — enemies (1701–13), VI. 16; and English language, IV. 12; and English trade: *see* TRADE; **and France, union of crowns,** VI. 15; VII. 37, 40, 42, 44, 112–13, 115, 120, 129, 148; — and balance of power, VII. 121, 151; — Dutch threatened, VI. 12; — France favours, VII. 150; — French princes renounce Spanish throne, VII. 121, 150, 165; — alleged aversion for French (1701), VI. 14; — Grand Alliance prohibits, VI. 47; — guarantees against, VI. 58; VII. 50, 131, 151–2, 165; — Louis XIV could not attack Philip V (1709–10),

VI. 50, 190–1; VII. 32; — Orleans opposes, VIII. 169–70; —— and Partition Treaty (1700), VI. 11, 14; — Philip V renounces French throne, VII. 121, 125, 131, 135, 149–50, 165; — would subordinate Spain, VII. 121, 131, 151; — cause of war, VII. 130; — war promotes, VI. 14, 17; — Whigs foresee (1714), VIII. 59; and Edward Gee, IV. 250; and the Goths, V. 36–7; humour in literature, XII. 32, 33; and Ireland — Irish cloth, XII. 70; — and Irish linen, XIII. 113, 176; — Irish manufactures, X. 136; — recruiting, XII. xxxi, 174; mercenary soldiers (12th century), V. 74; and Moors, V. 21; and Treaty of Münster: *see* MÜNSTER;

'**no peace without Spain**', i.e., the principle that no peace be made with France while Spain, etc., remains in Bourbon hands — alternative policies, VI. 58; — Queen Anne's policies, VI. 16, 124; VII. 12, 15, 17, 18, 31; — Article 37 of Preliminaries of 1709, VII. 32–3; — policy attacked, VI. 6, 21, 45–64; VII. 12, 51; — and Austria (or the Emperor), VII. 24, 51; — and Barrier Treaty (1709), VI. 94, 111, 112; — coffee-house motto, VI. 53–4; — Commons reject policy (1711), VII. 18; — and Dutch, VII. 41–2, 108; VIII. 170–1; — Dutch abandon policy (1711), VI. 53, 57; VII. 40, 109, 110, 153–5; — foolish principle, XIV. 9–10; — and Godolphin ministry, VI. 112; VII. 12; —

and Grand Alliance (1701), VI. 45–8, 51 and *n.**, 52; VII. 12, 51; — and Emperor Joseph's death (1711), VI. 51–3; — Lords' vote on (1711), VI. 43, 71, 123–4; VII. 17, 18; — motto for Marlborough's return (1711), VII. 28; — and moneyed interests, VI. 53–4; — and Oxford ministry, VI. 76; VII. 58; VIII. 147–8; — Parliament divided (1711), VII. 15; — Parliamentary addresses, III. 140; VII. 12; — and peace preliminaries (1711), VII. 112; — and the press, III. xxv; — and selfish interests, VI. 45; — Somerset advocates, VII. 15; — and war party, VI. 76; a Whig stratagem, VI. 76, 123–4; VII. 18–19, 108;

and *Polite Conversation*, IV. 154; and Portugal: *see* PORTUGAL; and Rome, IV. 8; and Spanish Netherlands, VI. 89; — duties, VI. 117; — to regain (1701), VI. 27–8; succession — historical parallel, V. 42–3; and tavern signs, XII. 223; trade, VII. 37, 120; — with Ireland, X. 136; XII. 70; XIII. 113, 176; and Tyrone's Rebellion, X. 10; and Treaty of Utrecht — Portuguese interests, VII. 133; — may yield territories, VII. 133; and War of Spanish Succession — campaigns in (1704–5), VI. 21; and West Indies, VII. 12, 31, 43, 48, 77, 84, 132; — French control threatened, VI. 14; war debt, VI. 55; and Wood's coinage, X. 19. *See also* CATALONIA; WAR OF THE SPANISH SUCCESSION.

Spaniels: XI. 117.

Spanish language: English inferior, IV. xiv, 6; stability, IV. 9.

Spanish Netherlands (i.e. modern Belgium, except Luxembourg and Liége): and Barrier Treaty, VI. 90, 100–1, 115; VII. 61; granted to Charles VI of Austria (1700), VI. 12; and Dutch — antipathy, VI. 115; — debt to (1712), VI. 89–90; — garrisons, VI. 101; — Dutch oppressions, VI. 38; — Dutch to possess (1709), VI. 38; VII. 61, 91; — revenues, VI. 102; France excluded from (1709), VI. 103; France seizes (1701), VI. 12, 16; Spain to regain (1701), VI. 27–8; and Treaty of Utrecht, VII. 113. *See also* FLANDERS; NETHERLANDS.

'Sparkish, Lord': character in *Polite Conversation*, IV. 129–201, *passim*, 276.

Sparta: XI. 198; and Athens, I. 195–236, *passim*; Athens displaced by, I. 208; diarchy and balance of power, I. 196–7, 200; II. 16; political constitution, V. 36; attempts to restore, I. 210.

Speaker of the House of Commons: 1701–5: Robert Harley (1661–1724); 1705–8: John Smith (1655–1723); 1708–10: Richard Onslow (1654–1717); 1710–13: William Bromley (1664–1732); 1714–15: Sir Thomas Hanmer, Bart. (1677–1746).

Speciali gratia, JS's degree: V. 192.

Spectacles: Gulliver's, XI, 36, 52–3; JS to buy, V. 334.

Spectator: and Fleetwood's 'Preface', VI. xviii, 151, 159, 160; and Steele, VIII. 7, 16, 18; — on the clergy, VIII. 36; and JS's academy project, IV. 16; JS's contributions, II. xxxii, xxxvi–xxxvii, 141, *n*.*, 173, *n*.*; — no. 50 (Indian Kings), **II. 264-7**; — — authorship, II. xxxii, xxxvii, 173, *n*.*; — — textual note, II. 290; — **no. 575** (happiness and misery), **II. 268**; — — textual note, II. 290; on 'true sublime', IX. 344; Wharton to employ Steele, VI. 153.

Speech of John Ketch Esq. (on Fleetwood's 'Preface'): borrows from *Tale of a Tub*, VI. xix.

Spelling, school: I. 25; — correct: *see* ORTHOGRAPHY.

'Spendal, Mrs.': character in *Polite Conversation*, IV. 148–9.

'Spendall, Sir John': character in *Polite Conversation*, IV. 193.

Spenser, Edmund, 1552–99: and English language, IV. 7; and English poetry, IV. 273; ministry of wit, IX. 330.

Spheres, music of the: XI. 162.

Spider and the Bee: JS's fable in *Battle of the Books*, I. 147–51.

Spiders: XI. 180, 181; suspense, a spider's life, I. 244.

Spinoza, Baruch (or Benedict), 1632–77, philosopher: anti-Christian, II. 72; compared with Tindal, II. xviii, *n*. 2.

Spirit, JS's views: I. 95–101, 171–90.

'Splacknuck' (Brobdingnagian animal about the size of a man): XI. 96, 97, 103.

Spleen (i.e., melancholy, hypochondria, vapours): cured by hard work, XI. 263–4; and ghosts, I. 242; and matrimony,

IV. 252; noble blood, XI. 257; school, I. 25; 'Splendida bilis', I. 31; Tindal's design, II. 87; vapours, I. 102–14.

Splendid Shilling: see JOHN PHILIPS.

'Sprang' (monetary unit in imaginary Japan): V. 105, 106.

Sprat, Thomas, 1635–1713, Bishop of Rochester and Dean of Westminster: Burnet and JS on, V. 279.

'Spruce, Mr.': character in *Polite Conversation*, IV. 141.

'Sprug' (Lilliputian gold coin about the size of a spangle): XI. 65, 78, 79.

'Squash', Nottingham's servant: see NOTTINGHAM.

'*Squire Bickerstaff Detected*, anonymous sequel to *Predictions for the Year* 1708: II. 217–23; authorship, II. xiv; background, II. x–xiv; textual notes, II. 290.

Squire, Thomas, c. 1678–1739, rector of Coleraine, Ireland: death, XIII. 189.

Squires, Irish: qualifications, IX. 292.

Staff-Hall: imaginary seat of Staff family, II. 231.

Stafford, William Howard, 1st Viscount, 1612–80: trial, V. 279.

Staffordshire: and Bickerstaff, II. 249, 253.

Staffs, family of: and Simon Wagstaff, IV. xxix.

Stage, JS's views on: clergy at performance, XII. 35–6; Dublin, and poetry, IX. 343; — school for poets, IX. 336–7, 343; folly ridiculed, III. 81; humour, XII. 32–7; and public welfare, IX. 343; pulpit supported by, IX.

343; reformation needed, II. 55–6; ridiculed, I. 36–7.

'Stage itinerant' (*i.e.*, hack writers): I. 34–6; explanation, I. 38.

Stair, John Dalrymple, 2nd Earl of, 1673–1747, field marshal, ambassador to France, Whig: VIII. 169.

Stamford, Thomas Grey, 2nd Earl of, 1653–1720: Macky and JS on, V. 259.

Stamp tax: see PRESS.

Standard, War of the: V. 53–4.

'Stang' (a rood of land): XI. 29.

Stanhope, Alexander, d. 1707, Envoy Extraordinary to the United Provinces (1700–6), father of 1st Earl: Macky on, V. 261.

Stanhope, James Stanhope, 1st Earl, 1673–1721, general, statesman, Whig: surrenders at Brihuega, 'a general', III. 53; in *Examiner*, XIV. 11; his gambling, IV. 208, 299; Harcourt compared to, VIII. 45; and *London Gazette*, IV. xxxiv–xxxv; Macky and JS on ('the son'), V. 261; and Sacheverell's trial, VIII. 40; commercial treaty with Spain, VI. 51.

Stanhope, Philip Henry, 5th Earl, 1805–75, historian: VII. ix.

Stanislaus Leczinski, 1677–1766, set up as King of Poland by Charles XII: acknowledged (1707) by Augustus, Elector of Saxony, rival King of Poland, VI. 17, 62–3; accession predicted, II. 148; and Treaty of Altranstadt (1707), VI. 62–3; England's tentative guarantee, VI. 63.

Stanley, Sir John, Bart., 1663–1744, Commissioner of Customs of Ireland: on taxation, XII. 125.

Stannard, Eaton, *c.* 1685–1755, Recorder of Dublin: XIII. 190, *n.* 1; and recordership of Dublin, XIII. xxiv, 69–70; and JS — executor of will, XIII. 157, 200; — freedom of Cork, XIII. xxxix, 190; — legacy, XIII. 153.

Star Chamber: court unjust, IX. 221

States General: *see* DUTCH.

Stationers' Register: I. xx.

Staunton, Deborah: *see* ROCHFORT.

Staunton, Thomas, *d.* 1732, Irish lawyer (LL.D., *honoris causa*, Trinity College, Dublin, 1728), M.P. for Galway, Master in Chancery, legal adviser to JS: father of Deborah Rochfort, IX. 85.

Staunton, Mrs. Thomas: mother of 'young lady', IX. 85.

Stearne (or Sterne), Enoch, cousin to John Stearne, Clerk to Irish House of Lords (honorary LL.D., 1726): IX. 319.

Stearne, John, 1660–1745, Dean of St. Patrick's, Bishop of Clogher, friend of JS: friend of Stella, V. 233; JS writes to, II. xiv–xv.

Steele, David, captain of Scottish rebels: and Creichton, V. 154–5, 157–8.

Steele, Sir Richard, 1672–1729, author, politician, friend of JS: and Addison, VIII. xv, 5; and alchemy, VIII. 16, 19, 21–2; on Queen Anne, VIII. 22; arrest for debt (1712), VIII. 14; and Bickerstaff, II. 250–51; — borrows pseudonym, II. 141, *n.**; and bishops, VIII. 13–14; and Bolingbroke's impeachment, VIII. xix; and Burnet, IV. 288; — copies him, VIII. 36, 65; and censorship, VIII. 15–16; JS's character of, VIII. 5–6; — as Hilario, II. 262; and Church of England, VIII. 35–43; — denies attacks upon, VIII. 36; and Church of Ireland, VIII. 37; and Anthony Collins, IV. xviii; Commissioner of the Stamp Office (1710–13), VIII. 6; — resignation, VIII. xxi, 11, 21; Commons expel (1714), VIII. xxi; *The Crisis . . . with Some Seasonable Remarks on the Danger of a Popish Successor*, VIII. xv–xvii; — acts of Parliament in, VIII. 48; — advertised, VIII. 32, 51; — authenticity of records, VIII. 34–5; — Commons condemn, VIII. xx–xxi; — composition and publication, VIII. xv–xvi, 32–3; — 'Preface', VIII. 43–5; — profits from, VIII. 33, 38; — prosecution urged, VIII. 51–2; — sedition, VIII. 40, 41; — subscription, VIII. xv, 32–3; — JS's reply, VIII. xvii–xx, 29–68; — title, VIII. 51–2; — title-page, VIII. 34–5; debts, VIII. 14, 21, 22; — bailiffs threaten him, VIII. 12, 14; dog-keeper anecdote, VIII. 23–5; 'expects' demolition of Dunkirk, VIII. 17–18, 93; Dunton's style superior, VIII. 32–34; and Dutch, VIII. 62; *The Englishman*, IV. 57 and *n.**, 63, 69; — attacked, IV. xxi; — invective, IV. 77; — for 22

Oct. 1713, VIII. xv; — *The Englishman, Being the Close of the Paper So Call'd* (i.e., *The Englishman* for 15 Feb. 1714), VIII. xx-xxi, 7, 32, 37, 67; and *The Examiner*, VIII. xii, 67; — in *Examiner* (as *Tatler*), XIV. 11; — demands prosecution, VIII. 14; falsehoods, VIII. 62, 67; and Fleetwood, VI. 159; VIII. 36, 38–9; *Flying-Post* defends (1714), IV. xxvii; — superior to Steele, VIII. 32, 34; Gazetteer (1707), VIII. 6, 7; gentleman usher to Prince George (1706), VIII. 6; — resignation, VIII. 11; a 'gentleman born', VIII. 60, 68; on government, VIII. 43–4; grammatical errors, VIII. 32, 36, 46; and *The Guardian* (1713), IV. 57–8; VIII. xi, xii, 3–25; — *Examiner* attacks, VIII. 17–18; — JS attacks, IV. xxi; — letter from 'English Tory' (7 Aug. 1713, on Dunkirk), VIII. x, xiii, 7–12; and Hanmer, VIII. 52 and *n*.*; on Hanoverian Succession, VIII. 52–5, 66; on Harcourt, VIII. 45; character as Hilario, II. 262; humour, VIII. 6; *The Importance of Dunkirk Consider'd*: *in Defence of the Guardian of August the 7th*, etc. (1713) — attacked by JS, IV. xx–xxi, xxv; VIII. xii–xiv, 4–25; — erratum, VIII. 16–17; ingratitude, VIII. 6–7, 9, 11, 16–17, 18; 'journalier', VIII. 65; publisher of *Ladies Library* (1714), II. xxxi; on liberty, VIII. 46; M.P. for Stockbridge (1713), VIII. xii, 8–9, 11–13, 18; military career, VIII. 16, 19; *Mr. Steele's Apology*

for Himself and His Writings, II. xxviii and *n*. 2; VIII. xvii and *n*. 2; Molesworth and JS, IV. xxv–xxvii; name spelled *St——*, VIII. 15 and *n*.*; and Ormonde, VIII. xix; and Oxford, VIII. xix, 6–7, 11; IX. 29; and Oxford ministry, VIII. 11, 15, 20, 23, 36; on the passions, VIII. 46–7; playwright, VIII. 5; and *Post-Boy*, VIII. 67; *Pretender's Declaration*, XII. 320; prosecution urged, VIII. 58; Protestant fears ridiculed, IV. 63; VIII. 193; linked to Puritans, VIII. 4, 16, 17, 45; compared to Ridpath, VIII. 54; sedition, VIII. 68; and *The Spectator* (1711–12), II. xxxvi; VIII. 7, 36; style, VIII. 6, 41, 44, 46, 53, 55, 65; — cadence without meaning, VIII. 22, 36; — 'civility', VIII. 39; — hackneyed, VIII. 16, 36, 52; — imitative, VIII. 5, 20;

and JS — 'Brother-Scribler', VIII. xiii, 4, 13; — fight in pamphlets (1713–14), IV. xxiv, xxv; VIII. x, xii–xxii; — friendship, II. xxv–xxvi, xxviii, xxxiii, xxxiv; — friendship dies, II. xxxvi–xxxvii; — ingratitude to JS, VIII. 16; — JS's *Miscellanies* (1711), II. xix–xx; — Molesworth, IV. xxv–xxvii; — recommended to Oxford, IX. 29; — JS attacks in *Preface to Bishop of Sarum's Introduction*, IV. xxi; — on JS's *Project for the Advancement of Religion* (1709), II. xx, xxvii–xxviii; — in JS's *Proposal for Correcting, Improving and Ascertaining the English Tongue*, IV. 287; — allegedly protected by JS,

VII. xxxv; IX. 29–30; — and *Tatler*, II. xxviii, xxxi; — — no. 32, II. xxx; — —Harrison's continuation, II. xxxv;

The Tatler, II. xxv–xxxv; VIII. 6–7, 36; — authorship, II. xxv–xxxii; VIII. 6–7; — 'Bicker-staff', VIII. 6; — quotations, no. 1: II. xxvii; — — no. 4: II. xxvii; — — no. 5: II. xxviii; — — no. 7: II. xxviii; — — preface to vol. IV: II. xxvi; treachery, VIII. 21; treason, VIII. 51–2; XII. 320; on the Union, VIII. 48–52; and Virgil, VIII. 43–4; and Whigs, VIII. 7, 16, 31.

Steevens (Stevens, Stephens, etc.), Richard, M.D., *c.* 1654–1710, physician, founder of Steevens' Hospital, Dublin: his hospital, XIII. 150, 198; — Stella's bequest to, V. 236.

Steffenswaert (*i.e.*, Stevensweert), Limburg, Netherlands: and Dutch Barrier, VI. 115.

'Stella': *see* JOHNSON, ESTHER.

Stella, Journal to: *see* JOURNAL TO STELLA.

Stella's Birthday. March 13. 1726–7, poem by JS: quoted, V. xxvi.

'Stentor of the Chappel': probably Robert Walpole, III. 223.

'Stentor of Sarum': Bishop Burnet, III. 223.

Stephen, St.: martyrdom, IX. 182.

Stephen, King of England, *c.* 1099–1154, son of Stephen of Blois, grandson of William I: accession, V. 48; in battle, V. 59; and the bishops, V. 56–7, 71; castles permitted, V. 49, 50, 55, 72; JS's character of, V. 71–2;

and Earl of Chester, V. 65–6, 71; cowardice, V. 64; and David I of Scotland, V. 49–50, 53–4; death, V. 71; and Pope Eugenius III, V. 68; and Geoffrey Plantagenet, V. 51; and Earl of Gloucester, V. 55–9, 62, 65; haemorrhoids, V. 71; and Henry I, V. 41; and Henry II, V. 66, 68–70; and Henry of Blois, Bishop of Winchester, V. 57, 61; and Innocent II, V. 50; and Louis VII, V. 69; and Matilda (Maude) the Empress, V. 41, 48–66, 71, 72; too merciful, V. 51; Count of Mortain, V. 30–3; nobility resist, V. 50–1, 53; oath of fealty to, V. 48; takes Oxford, V. 64; religion, V. 72; invades Scotland, V. 52; son (Eustace), V. 67–8, 69; and succession, V. 67–8; usurper, V. 71.

Stephen Henry: *see* BLOIS.

Stephens: *see* STEEVENS; STEVENS.

Stepney, George, 1663–1707, diplomat and poet: pun upon name, IV. 274; Macky and JS on, V. 260.

Sterling, Scotland; *see* STIRLING.

Sterne: *see also* STEARNE.

Sterne, Richard, *c.* 1596–1683, Archbishop of York: Burnet and JS on, V. 282.

Sternhold, Thomas, *d.* 1549, versifier of *Psalms*: IV. 273.

Stevens (or Stephens), Captain John, *d.* 1726, translator: and *Polite Conversation*, IV. xxxii; and Wagstaff, IV. 118.

'Steward', in JS's *Directions to Servants*: XIII. 51; *see also* 'HOUSE STEWARD'; 'LAND STEWARD'.

Steward, Mrs.: *see* RICHMOND, DUCHESS OF.

Stewart, Francis: *see* STUART.

Stewart (or Stuart), Sir Robert, *d. c.* 1670, Irish royalist leader: and Creichton's father, V. 125–9.

Stewart, Sir William: *see* MOUNTJOY.

'Stiles, John', bookseller (probably a pseudonym): prints pirated edition of *Predictions for the Year 1708,* II. 286.

Stilicho, Flavius, *c.* A.D. 359–408, Roman general: Baronius praises, XIV. 19.

Stillingfleet, Edward, 1635–1699, Bishop of Worcester: on fanaticism, I. 127, *n.**; and Tindal, II. 79 and *n.**.

Stirling (or Sterling), Scotland: Creichton at, V. 129, 136; Picts' Wall, V. 4.

Stobow, Adam, *d. c.* 1679, Covenanting preacher of Fife: and Creichton, V. 131.

Stocker, A. F.: acknowledgement, XIV. vii.

Stocks (financial speculation): *see* MONEYED INTEREST.

Stoics: Christians superior, IX. 113–14; and Cicero, IV. 44; 'cutting off our feet', I. 244; and Seneca, IV. 44; Zeno and his followers, IX. 247, 250.

Stones, precious: and avarice, XI. 260–1.

Stopford, James, *c.* 1697–1759, vicar of Finglas and (later) Bishop of Cloyne: and Carteret, XII. xxix, 164; character, XII. 164; JS's bequest to, XIII. 154–5; JS's executor, XIII. 157, 200.

Story of the Injured Lady

(written *c.* 1707), by JS: **IX. 1-12**; *Answer to the Injured Lady,* IX. 10–12; background, IX. ix–xi; composition, IX. x; date, IX. x, *n.* 1; theme summarized, VIII. 50; textual notes, IX. 369; title-page facsimile, IX. 1.

Stoyte, Francis (B.A., Trinity College, Dublin, 1715; *d.* 1733), Recorder of Dublin: and recordership, XIII. xxiv; 'worthy gentleman', XIII. 69.

Strabo, *c.* 64 B.C.–A.D. 19, geographer: pun upon name, IV. 236.

Strafford, Thomas Wentworth, 1st Earl of, 1593–1641, statesman: 'chief minister', IX. 222; Clarendon and JS on, V. 297–9; envy caused fall, VIII. 138; and laws *ex post facto,* VIII. 34; praised, XII. 39; trial, V. 84.

Strafford, Thomas Wentworth, 3rd Lord Raby and 3rd Earl of, 1672–1739, diplomat: Bolingbroke's letters to, VII. 205–12; correspondence surrendered (1714), VIII. xxxi; created earl (1711), VII. 52; returns to England (1711), VII. 52; — (1712), VII. 126, 155; and Eugene (1712), VII. 140; at The Hague (1711), VII. 110, 111, 163; and Heinsius, VII. 38; goes to Holland, (The Hague, 1711), VI. viii; VII. 52; Macky and JS on, V. 261; and Marlborough, VII. 38–9; and Mesnager, VII. 159; message to Ormonde (1712), VII. 139; and Townshend, VII. 38–9; at Utrecht (1712–13), VII. 139; — ambassador extraordinary, VII. 162, 165,

198; — French quarrel with Dutch, VII. 158, 159, 163; — separate peace, VII. 163; and Treaty of Utrecht, VII. 13, 153, 155-7, 158, 165; and Whigs, VIII. 166.

Strasbourg: VII. 113.

Stratford, William, *d.* 1729, Archdeacon of Richmond, canon of Christ Church, Oxford: on *Gulliver's Travels*, XI. xxiii.

Straw: stumbling at, IV. 246.

Strawberry Hill, near Richmond, Surrey: home of Horace Walpole, XIII. 207.

Streighton, Captain: V. 161.

Strephon and Chloe, poem by JS: composition, XII. xxxiii.

Struldbruggs (the immortals of Luggnagg, in *Gulliver's Travels*, Part III): XI. 207-15.

'Strut, Captain': character in *Polite Conversation*, IV. 151-2.

Stuart (or Stewart), Francis, of Coldingham, *d.* 1685, grandson of Earl of Bothwell, captain of dragoons: V. 135, 138, 140, 141, 145, 159.

Stuart, Sir Robert: *see* STEWART.

Stubbs, John, *c.* 1543-91, Puritan zealot: *The Discoverie of a Gaping Gulf Whereinto England Is Like to Be Swallowed*, VIII. 189-90.

Sturmy, Samuel, *b.* 1633: *Mariner's Magazine* (1669) and *Gulliver's Travels* — paragraph borrowed, XI. 84.

Style, literary: acknowledgements, I. 115; aposiopesis, VI. 155; best in 17th century, II. xxxiv; Burnet's style censured, IV. 69-70, 82-3; V. 266-94; — low expressions listed, V. 184;

Dryden's style ridiculed, I. 3-4, 42; epistolary form, I. 171-2; flat epithets, IX. 68; common faults, IX. 68; Fleetwood's style ridiculed, VI. 153-5; hard words, IX. 65; pretense of haste, I. 172; L'Estrange's style ridiculed, I. 3-4; modern style censured, II. 173-7; old phrases, IX. 68; prefaces and introductions, I. 81-2, 115; repetition, VI. 153; VIII. 10-11; similes, VIII. 43-4; simplicity praised, IV. xxxi; IX. 66, 68; XI. 137; JS's views summarized, IX. xxiv; Temple's style, I. 258, 268-70; titles, I. 43; verbose poetry, IX. 338. *See also* STEELE, *style*.

Suarez, Francisco, 1548-1617, Jesuit theologian and casuist: and Aristotle, II. 81; and government by consent, IX. 19.

Subordination, social: *see* SOCIAL LEVELS AND CLASSES.

Subscribers to the Bank Plac'd According to Their Order and Quality with Notes and Queries (1721), probably by JS: **IX. 288-90;** 'Answer', IX. 317-18; background, IX. xvi-xvii, xix-xxi; publication, IX. xix-xx; textual notes, IX. 378.

Subscription, publication by: JS's views, VIII. 32-3; XIV. 3, 42.

Substance of What Was Said by the Dean (1730), by JS: **XII. 145-8;** background, XII. xxiv-xxvii; and Gulliver, XII. xxvi; textual notes, XII. 337.

Succession to the British throne: and Bodin, V. 246-7; general discussion, II. 18-23; V. 47; Roman Catholic opposed, IX.

31. *See also* HANOVERIAN SUC-
CESSION.

'Such': VI. 153.

Suckling, Sir John, 1609–42,
poet: pun upon name, IV. 273.

Suetonius, *c.* A.D. 70–*c.* 160,
Roman historian: JS's marginalia, V. xxxi–xxxii and *n.* 1;
allusion to *De vita Caesarum* 1.
xix: I. 302 ('Cato's opinion').

Suffering and patience: V. 208.

Suffolk, Charles Howard, 9th Earl
of, 1675–1733: 'husband', V.
213, 215.

Suffolk, Edmund de la Pole, Earl
of, *c.* 1471–1513: executed, V.
247.

Suffolk, Henrietta Howard (*née*
Hobart), Countess of, *c.* 1688–
1767, wife of 9th Earl, mistress of
George II: and Queen Caroline,
V. xxvii–xxviii, 213; **JS's character of** (1727), V. 213–15; *Letters
to and from Henrietta, Countess of
Suffolk* (1824), V. xxvii, *n.* 3;
religion, V. 214; **and JS** —
correspondence, V. xv, xxviii;
XII. xxxv; — his false friend, V.
xxviii; — Irish plaid, V. xxvii;
— crown of Lilliput, V. xxvii; —
meetings (1726–27), V. xxvii; —
preferment in England (1727),
V. xxviii; — *Verses on the Death
of Dr. Swift*, V. xxviii; and
Walpole, V. xv, 213. *See also*
CHARACTER OF MRS. HOWARD.

Suffolk, John de la Pole, 2nd
Duke of, 1442–*c.* 1492: son
executed, V. 247.

Suidas, tenth-century Byzantine
lexicographer: meaning of *crisis*,
VIII. 34; and English language,
IV. 238.

Sulla (or Sylla), Lucius Cornelius,
138–78 B.C., Roman statesman:
corrupter of common people,
VI. 80; and Gracchi, I. 219; and
Pompey, I. 220; becomes tyrant,
I. 219.

Sumatra: and map of Lilliput,
XI. 18.

Summa imperii: unlimited power,
I. 227.

Summum bonum: I. 174.

Sun: Laputan fears, XI. 164–5.

Sunderland, Charles Spencer, 3rd
Earl of, *c.* 1674–1722, Secretary
of State, member of Whig Junto:
and Addison, II. xxvi; and
Queen Anne — will not forgive
her, VII. 9; — 'others', III. 80;
— rude to her, 'some persons',
VII. 6, 9; VIII. 112, 118; **JS's
character of**, VII. 9; 'Cinna',
III. 77; and Dartmouth, III. 80;
dismissed ('two persons'), III.
20, 25 and *n.*†, 64; VIII. 102,
118; and Irish preferment, X. 121
and *n.**; library ridiculed, VII.
9; — 'another Lord's', III.
197; Macky and JS on, V. 259;
will not forgive Oxford, VII. 9;
and JS — 'great man' ignores
JS, III. 80; — 'old acquaintance',
VIII. 119; — praised as 'learned
and excellent Lord', I. xxxvi, 268;
Charles Trimnell his tutor, VII. 9.

Sunderland, Robert Spencer, 2nd
Earl of, 1641–1702, statesman:
falls from power (1698), I. xviii;
frank manner, VIII. 137; becomes Roman Catholic, V. 86;
and son's atheism ('divinity'),
VII. 9; and JS's preferment,
IX. xviii; and Sir William
Temple, I. 268.

Sundon, Lady: *see* CLAYTON.

Superstition: in Laputa, XI. 164–5; Roman Catholics', I. 2.

Supremacy, Act of, in Scotland: V. 274.

Surat, Bombay, India: Gulliver's destination, XI. 80, 83.

'Surrendry' (i.e., surrender): VII. 140, 243.

Surrey: Temple's house in, I. x.

Suspense: life of a spider, I. 244.

Sussex, Thomas Lennard, Lord Dacre, Earl of, 1654–1715: and Erasmus Lewis, VI. 173–4, 176, 177.

Sutherland, John Gordon (or Sutherland), 16th Earl of, 1661–1733, statesman: Macky and JS on, V. 262.

Sutton, Robert: *see* LEXINGTON.

'Swallow': Gulliver's ship, XI. 19.

Swan, Mr., famous for puns in the reign of William III (*Spectator*, no. 61): and Tindal, II. 92; verses attributed to, XII. 230–1.

Swandlingbar (now Swanlinbar), co. Cavan, Ireland: IV. 282.

Swans: XI. 118.

Swearers Bank (1721, probably not by Swift): IX. 294–8; authorship, IX. xix; background, IX. xvi–xvii, xix–xxi; textual notes, IX. 378.

Swearing: act of Parliament against, IX. 295; fines discourage, IX. 297; medicinal use, IX. 297; revenues for charity, IX. 297; theatre encourages, IX. 343. *See also* OATHS, PROFANITY.

Sweden: British guarantees to, 'princes of the north': VI. 82–4; VII. 148; church of 'Suevia' and papacy, XIV. 28; compared to

England, V. 244; and English language, IV. 12; invaded by Scots, II. 134–5; King of: *see* CHARLES XII; liberty of conscience, IX. 263. *See also* NORTHERN WAR.

Sweeny, Counsellor (probably William Sweeny, *fl.* 1700–20, Dublin lawyer): mare stolen, IX. 366.

Sweet-Singers (Scottish fanatics): and free-thinkers, IV. 31; and public offices, III. 144.

Sweet Singers of Israel: antinomian sect, I. 188.

Sweethearts, a kind of sugar-cake: XII. 219 and *n*.*.

Swegn (or Sweyn, Swein, or Svein) Forkbeard, King of England and Denmark, *d.* 1014: conquers England, V. 5.

Swift and Company, Dublin bankers: and fire insurance, XIII. 175.

Swift, Abigail (*née* Erick), 1640–1710, JS's mother: daughter of Rev. James Ericke, vicar of Thornton, Leicestershire, probably born in Dublin: V. 192, 193; character, V. xxiii, 196; death, V. xxiii; — **JS's account of, V. 196**; — — errata, XIV. 53; family, V. 191; JS visits (1707), II. ix.

Swift, Adam, 1642–1704, JS's uncle, 6th son of Rev. Thomas Swift: V. 191; father of Mrs. Whiteway, VII. xxv, *n*. 3.

Swift, 'Cavaliero': *see* CARLINGFORD.

Swift, Deane, 1706–83, biographer and editor of JS; son of JS's cousin: *An Essay upon the*

Life, Writings and Character, of Dr. Jonathan Swift (1755), IX. x, *n.* 1, 98, *n.* 4; JS's *Answer of Pulteney . . . to . . . Walpole*, V. xvi; JS's bequest to, XIII. 156; and manuscript of JS's *Directions to Servants*, XIII. xxi; editions of JS's posthumous works, etc. (1765), V. ix; VII. xii, *n.* 6, xiii, *n.* 2; — editorial method, V. xxii–xxiii; and JS's *Enquiry into the Behaviour of the Queen's Last Ministry*, VIII. xxxviii; and JS's *Family of Swift*, V. xxii–xxiii; on composition of *Gulliver's Travels*, XI. xvii; on the text of *Gulliver's Travels*, XI. xxvi, *n.* 3; and JS's *Hints on Good Manners*, IV. xxxvi; and JS's *History of the Second Solomon*, V. xxx; and JS's character of Mrs. Johnson, V. xxvi; and JS's *A Letter to the Writer of the Occasional Paper* (1765), V. xii, xiii; and JS's manuscripts, II. xii; prints JS's *Of the Education of Ladies*, IV. xxxvii; and JS's sermons, IX. 98; and JS's *The Story of the Injured Lady*, IX. x, *n.* 1; on composition of JS's *Tale of a Tub*, I. ix; and Rev. Thomas Swift's estate ('the landlord'), V. 188; and William Swift's estate ('a great-great-grandson'), V. 188; wife: *see* HARRISON, MARY.

Swift, Dryden, *b.* 1629, JS's uncle, 2nd son of Rev. Thomas Swift: V. 191.

Swift, Sir Edward: V. 187.

Swift, Godwin, 1624–95, JS's uncle, eldest son of Rev. Thomas Swift: V. 190–1; — picture and seal of Thomas Swift, V. 188;

his family, V. xxii–xxiii; and Swandlingbar, IV. 282.

Swift, Godwin, *d. c.* 1740, son of JS's uncle Godwin: and William Swift's portrait, V. 188.

Swift, Hannah (or Anne, *née* Deane), 3rd wife of JS's uncle Godwin (married 1673): V. 191.

Swift, Jane: *see* FENTON.

Swift, Jonathan, 1640–67, JS's father, 5th son of Rev. Thomas Swift: V. 191.

Swift, Jonathan, 1667–1745, vicar of Laracor and Dean of St. Patrick's Cathedral: [For JS's works and related facts, see under the separate titles; for collected works, see under editors' names; for JS's relations with other persons, see under their names; for JS's opinions, see under the separate topics. This article is limited to aspects of JS as an individual, autobiographical details mentioned in the introductions, etc.]

Ambitions: (1708–11) in *Miscellanies*, II. xix–xx; (1699) to be secretary to the Earl of Berkeley, V. 195; (1711–14) to be Historiographer Royal, VIII. xxxi, xxxix, 109–10, 200; — **memorial, VIII. 200**; — — textual note, VIII. 232; — claims he refused post, IX. 26; (1713) for retirement, 'weary of courts and ministers', VII. 181;

Biography (exclusive of church career, literary career, travels): (1667–1700) V. 192–5; birth — 'I am a Teague, or an Irishman', XIII. 112; (1668–70) nurse, I. ix; — nurse kidnaps him, V.

192; (1670) could read Bible at three, I. ix; V. 192; (c. 1673–82) Kilkenny School, V. 192; (1682–89) at Trinity College, Dublin, I. x; V. 192; — dissatisfied, I. ix; — (1686) B. A. *speciali gratia*, I. ix; V. 192; — (1688) Tripos, I. ix–x; (1692) Oxford M.A., I. xii; (1701–11), VIII. 119–25; (1701), V. 227–8; (1703–19), V. 11–12; (1714–20), IX. 25–31; (1714) licence of absence, VIII. xxviii; (1724–45) last decades, XIII. 201–207; (27 May 1730), freeman of Dublin, XII. xxiv, xxv–xxvii, 141, 145–8; (1734) death rumoured, XIII. xxix; (1737) seventieth birthday celebrations, XIII. xl; (1737) old age, VII. xv; (1741) old age, VII. xvi–xvii; (1745) death and burial, XIII. 149;

Character: attacked (1721) for opposing bank scheme, IX. 317–18; attacked (1712) by *Protestant Post-Boy*, VI. x; common sense in theology, IX. 108; 'conjured spirit', I. xi; disinterestedness (1710–14), VII. xxxv; humanitarianism, IX. 130; Charles Lucas on, VII. 172, 175; not precocious, I. ix; in sermons, IX. 102; 'celebrated wit', IX. 274–5;

Church career: beliefs reflected in sermons, IX. 101; 'no bigot', II. 2; champions Church of England, II. ix–x, xv–xxi; clergyman's duties, IX. 262; controversies of doctrine, IX. 107–8; a moderate (1708), II. xv; and politics, XII. x; preaching and politics, IX. 98; (1694) ordina-tion, I. xv; (1695) Kilroot, I. xv; V. 194; — (January 1698) resigns, I. xviii; V. 194; (1699) hopes to be prebendary of Canterbury Cathedral or Westminster Abbey, V. 195; (1699) chaplain to Berkeley, I. xix; V. 195; (1700) hopes to be Dean of Derry, V. 195; (1700) vicar of Laracor, V. 195; (1707–09) preferment missed, II. ix; — Whigs responsible, II. xxi; (1708) Partridge attacked as anti-clerical, II. x–xiv; (1708) Wharton's chaplaincy, II. xxi, xxiii–xxiv; — 'the other Divine', II. 284; (1708) and *Letter . . . Concerning the Sacramental Test*, II. xxxix; (1710) First Fruits mission, II. xxxiii; (1713) Dean of St. Patrick's, VII. xi; (1713–14) Dean of St. Patrick's, VII. xxxiii; IX. 117; — (1713) oaths to be taken, VIII. xxviii; — (1713) early discontent, VIII. ix; — (1716) contempt for deanship, VIII. xxxiii; (1727) English preferment, V. xiii, xxviii;

dreams, V. xxv, 203, 205–6; family, V. 187–92;

Health: loves fruit, I. x; V. 193; (c. 1688) vertigo begins (i.e., Ménière's syndrome, or labyrinthine vertigo), 'before twenty' here, but elsewhere after move to England, I. x; — 'giddyness', V. 193; (1712) painful case of shingles, VI. xvi; (1720) illness, IX. xxv; (1724) deafness, X. xix; (1727) vertigo and deafness, V. 205; XII. ix; (1728) illness, XII. x; (1729) feels well, XII. xviii;

Literary career: [For JS's works and all related facts, see under separate titles; for collected works, see under editors' names; for his opinions on literary subjects, see under particular topics]: anonymity, XIII. 181; — (1721), IX. 318; false attributions, IX. 28; beginnings at Trinity College, I. ix–x; canon of works, I. vi; and dunces' reputations, V. 201; 'Hiereus' as pseudonym, II. 262;

historian, VII. 171–7; — role of conjecture, VIII. 80; — 'well versed in English history', V. 194, — function, VII. xxxiv; VIII. 56–7, 110, 141; — value of journal, VIII. 107–8; — scholarship, V. xxxvii–xxxviii; VII. 181–218; inventiveness slight, I. xxix;

journalism — background of career, VIII. xxxi; — integrity defended, VI. 96; — no reformer, III. xvii; — (1704–06) pause in production, I. xxxiv; — (1709) Mary Astell attacks, II. xxxi, *n.* 1; — (1710–14) unpaid, III. 31, 78, 145; — (1710–13) aids Oxford ministry, VII. 104–5; — (1710–12) attacks upon him, VIII. 136; — (1710) Harley enlists him, VIII. 122–3; — (1710) attacks upon him, III. 14–15, 18, 29–30, 32–3, 35–40; — (1710) subjects 'things, not persons', III. 24–5; — (1710) success, III. 30, 171–3; — (1712) confidential information, VI. 74; — (1712) pamphlet unidentified, VI. xx; — (1712) venality alleged, VI. xv; — (1712) gap in production (Mar.–Apr.), VI. xvi; — (1713) disheartened, VIII. ix; — (1713) defends Oxford ministry, IV. xvi, xx; — (1714–20) reviewed in *Letter to Pope,* IX. xiv, 25–34; — (1714) danger resented, VIII. xxii; — (1720) Irish pamphlets, VIII. xxxvi; — *see also* EXAMINER;

late in starting, I. ix; originality, XIII. 184;

poetry — (1691–93) Pindaric odes, I. xi–xiv; — (1691–92) Temple encourages him, I. xii–xiii; — (1691) begins writing, I. xi–xii; — (1692) self-admiration, I. xii; — (1693) odes in couplets, I. xv; — (1694–*c.* 1698) stops writing, I. xv; — (1731) fully engaged in, XII. xxxiii;

prose — (1695) writes 'clear direct' prose, I. xv; — (1730) 'have left off writing', V. xvi; reputation — (1727), XII. ix; today, XI. ix; revisions, I. v; rewards, I. xix; III. 78; satire — use of *reductio ad absurdum,* IV. xix–xx; — *Tale of a Tub* unrestrained, I. xxvi–xxviii; — Temple disapproves, I. xiv; self-doubt (1731), XII. xxiv, xxxiii; writing habits, XII. xviii;

Politics: [For JS's opinions and principles, see under particular topics and parties]: church as chief concern, VIII. 174; and First Fruits, IX. ix; integrity defended, IX. 34; alleged Jacobitism, V. xxiv; VI. xv; IX. 117; *Memoirs* review career, VIII. xxiv; (1708) nonpartisanship, II. xv–xvii; (1710) both parties IX. 101; (*c.* 1698) anti-Tory, I.

111; (1701) career begins, VIII. 119; (1701) defends Whigs against impeachment, IV. xxiv; (1708) independence, II. xxii-xxiv; (1708) nonpartisanship, II. xv–xvii; (1710) both parties approach him, II. xxxiii; (1710) change of parties, III. x–xii; XII. xl; (1711) non-partisanship, III. xii–xiii, 145; (1712) views indicated in *Proposal for Correcting . . . the English Tongue*, IV. xii–xiii; (1713) 'weary of courts and ministers', VIII. x; (1714–45) in Ireland, IX. ix; (1714–20) alleged withdrawal, IX. 26; (1714–20) attacked, IX. 30; (1714) withdrawal, VIII. xxv; (1715–33) Irish reputation, V. xxiv; (1715) correspondence intercepted, VIII. xxxii; (1720) misunderstood, IX. 33; (1721) attacked, IX. 317–18; (1727) and church career, XII. x;

portraits, I. vi; — by Barber, facing IX. iii; — by Bindon, facing X. iii; — mezzotint after Bindon, facing XIII. iii; — Briscoe portrait, facing II. iii; — — not authentic, XIV. 50; — as Drapier, facing X. 1; — as Drapier (engraved by Vertue), facing XII. iii; — by Jervas (in Bodleian Library), facing I. iii; — — (in National Portrait Gallery), facing III. iii; — bust by Roubillac, facing V. iii; — Vertue's engravings, XIV. 43;

proclamations against — (1714, £300) VII. xxxiv; VIII. xxi-xxii, facing p. xxii, 198–9; — (1724, £300) X. xix–xxi, xxvi, 69, 71, 81, 87, 90, 101, 106, 111, 123, 127, 173, 205; puns upon his name, IV. 261;

Reading: [i.e., works which JS is known to have read and which are mentioned in his prose works or by the editors of this edition; for complete details of each, refer to the general index. I give usually the author's surname and one reference to Swift's acquaintance with the work. I omit most contemporary journalism, works answered by Swift, and the following: Addison, Aristotle, Bible, Cicero, Congreve, Dryden, Homer, Horace, Livy, Lucian, Lucretius, Milton, Ovid, Plato, Plautus, Plutarch, Rabelais, Seneca, Steele, Tacitus, Temple, Virgil.]

Aesop, I, *passim*; Atterbury, IV. 43–4; Bacon, *Essays*, X. 55; Baker, V. x; Baronius, V. xxxvii; Bentley, I, *passim*; Bernier, I. 178; Blackmore, I. 116; Boccalini, I. 17; Bodin, V. 244; R. Boyle, I. 239; T. Brown, IV. 118; John Browne, V. 256; Buckingham (2nd Duke), I. 7; Burnet, IV. ix–x, 57–84; V. 266; Callières, I. xxix; Cervantes, I. 17, 124; Clarendon, V. 295; Coke, X. 9–10; A. Collins, IV. x, 25; Commines, X. 171; Cowley, I. xv; Ctesias, I. xxv; Cyrano de Bergerac, XI. xv; Dampier, XI. xiv; Daniel, V. x; Descartes, I. 105; XI. 197; Diodorus Siculus, I. 61; Dionysius of Halicarnassus, XI. 133; Eachard, I. 4; Filmer, X. 94; Fontenelle, I. 157; Gay, XII. 32; Glanvill, I. xxxiv; Grammont

('Lati'), X. 110; Grynaeus, XI. xiv; Hakluyt, XI. xiv; Edward, Lord Herbert, V. 247; T. Herbert, V. xxxii; Herodotus, I. xxv; V. 243; P. Heylyn, V. 255; history, V. x; Hobbes, I. 24, 146, 152, 181; Holinshed, V. x; W. Howells, V. 262; Irenaeus, I. xxxix; Josephus, IV. 45; La Bruyère, I. 17; C. Leslie, IV. 84; L'Estrange, I. 3; La Rochefoucauld, I. xxxv; Locke, X. 86; Lucan, I. 158; J. Macky, V. 257; Marvell, I. 5; W. Molyneux, X. xviii; H. More, I. 79, *n.*†; Orrery (4th Earl), I, *passim*; R. Parsons, V. 241; Pausanias, I. xxv; Polybius, I. 199; Purchas, XI. xiv; Ray's *Collection of English Proverbs*, IV. xxxiii; H. Savile, V. x; A. Sidney, *Discourse concerning Government*, X. 86; R. South, IV. 34; Suetonius, V. xxxi–xxxii; J. Taylor, IV. 34; *Théâtre italien*, XII. 32; Thucydides, I. 198; Tillotson, IV. 34; Tindal, II. xviii; travel books, XI. xiv–xv, 233, 291–3; — evaluated, XI. 147; T. Twysden, V. x; T. Vaughan, I. 119, *n.**; P. Virgil, I. 152; H. Wharton, IV. 60; W. Wotton, I, *passim*;

servants: V. 206–7, 221; XIII. 161–2; — *see also* WAT;

Travels and residences: (*c.* 1668) taken to England, V. 192; (*c.* 1671) returned to Ireland, V. 192; (*c.* 1688–89) leaves Ireland, visits mother in Leicester, goes to live with Sir William Temple, I. x; V. 193; (*c.* 1689–90) at Moor Park, I. x; — (*c.* 1689–99), V. 193–4; (1690) returns to

Ireland for health, I. x; V. 193; (1691–99) at Moor Park, I. x–xi; (1691) goes to England, I. x; V. 193; (1694) returns to Ireland, I. xv; V. 194; (1696) goes to England, I. xvi; V. 194; (1699) returns to Ireland, I. xix; V. 195; — danger of crossing, I. xix; (Apr. 1701) goes to England, I. xix–xx; VIII. 119; (1701) returns to Ireland, I. xxi; VIII. 119; (1702) goes to England, I. xxi; VIII. 119; (1702) returns to Ireland, I. xxi; (Nov. 1703) goes to England, I. xxi; (June 1704) returns to Ireland, I. xxxiv; (Nov. 1707) goes to England, II. ix; IV. xxix; IX. ix; (Dec. 1707–Jan. 1708) with Fountaine in Leicester Fields, IV. xxix; V. xxiii; (1709) possibly visits York, II. xxix and *n.* 2; (May–June 1709) leaves London and visits Leicester, II. xxv, xxviii–xxix; (June 1709) returns to Ireland, II. ix, xxix; VIII. 121; (1710) goes to England, II. xxv, *n.* 1, xxxii, xxxiii; (1713) within England, IV. xx; (June 1713) returns to Ireland, VII. xxiii; 181; (summer 1713) visits Laracor, VIII. ix; (Aug.–Sept. 1713) goes to England, IV. xx; VII. 181; VIII. x; (June–Aug. 1714) at Letcombe Bassett, Berks., VII. xii, xxxvi, 181; VIII. 132; (Aug. 1714) returns to Ireland, VII. xii, xxxvi, 181; VIII. 132; IX. 117; (1714–26) in Ireland, VII. xxxvi; (1715) in Dublin, VIII. xxxi; (1715) Irish visits VIII. xxxi; (Feb. 1716) goes to Laracor, VIII. xxxiii; (1723) Cork,

X. 140; (summer 1725) Quilca, V. xxix; (1726) visits England XIII. 201–2; (1727) visits England, V. xii, xxvii; VII. xii; XII. ix; XIII. 202; — 'used like an emperor', V. 205; (summer 1727) visits Wimpole, VII. xiv, *n.* 1; (1727) French trip cancelled, V. xiii; (1727) returns to Ireland, V. xiii, xxiv–xxv, xxvii; (1728) tours south-east Ireland, V. xxix; (1728–29) at Market Hill (Acheson), VII. xii; VIII. xxxvi; (summer 1729) at Market Hill, V. xvii, xviii, 120; XII. xvii, xviii, xix; (1729) returns to Dublin, XII. xix; (summer 1730) at Market Hill, V. xviii, 120; works: see headnote to this article; writing paper, watermark, XIII. xii, xxi.

Swift, Theophilus, 1746–1815, son of Deane Swift: XI. xxvi, *n.* 3; and manuscript of *Directions to Servants*, XIII. xxi.

Swift (or Swyfte), Thomas, 1535–92, rector of St. Andrew's, Canterbury; ancestor of JS: in *Family of Swift*, by JS, V. xxii–xxiii.

Swift, Thomas, 1595–1658, JS's grandfather, vicar of Goodrich, Herefordshire: account of, V. 188–91; and Charles I, V. 188–9; disinherited, V. 187–8; and Sir Edward Harley, V. 190; house, V. 188; picture, V. 188; uses *Prayer Book* during Commonwealth, II. 121; seal, V. 188; tomb, V. 334.

Swift, Thomas, 1633–c. 1670, JS's uncle, rector of St. Edmund's, Lombard Street, London: V. 191.

Swift, Thomas, 1665–1752, JS's cousin, son of Thomas Swift, grandson of William Davenant, and rector of Puttenham, Surrey: V. 191; and *Battle of the Books*, I. 279, *n.**; and JS — correspondence, I. xii; — cousins, I. xxx, 281; Davenant's grandson, I. xxx, 281; and *Mechanical Operation of the Spirit*, I. 280–1; and *Tale of a Tub*, I. xxx–xxxii, 280–1; — annotated copy, I. xxxii, *n.**; and Sir W. Temple, I. xxx, 280, 281; and B. Tooke, I. xxx–xxxi.

Swift, William, 1566–1624, rector of St. Andrew's, Canterbury; great-grandfather of JS: account of, V. 187–8; in *Family of Swift*, by JS: V. xxii–xxiii; portrait mentioned, V. 188.

Swift, William, 1637–1706, JS's uncle, 4th son of Rev. Thomas Swift: V. 191.

Swine: as ploughs, XI. 180.

'Swinged off': III. 35.

Switzerland: loans to France (1710), VII. 72; and republican government, XII. 278; 'Rhætia', home of Paracelsus, I. 152.

Swords, co. Dublin, Ireland: and Molesworth, X. 79, 81.

Swyn canal: *see* ZWIN.

Syam, Voyage de: XI. xiv.

Sybarites: and Charondas, I. 233.

Sylla: *see* SULLA.

'Sylva Caledonia': Presbyterian preaching, I. 35.

Sylverius: *see* SILVERIUS.

'Sylvia', correspondent in Harrison's *Tatler*, No. 28: II. 260–63.

Symmachus, Pope (in office 498–514): and Theodoric, XIV. 26.

Symnele: *see* SIMNEL.

'Sympson, Richard' (fictitious cousin of Gulliver and 'publisher' of *Gulliver's Travels*): XI. xxi–xxii, xxiv, xxvii and *n*. 1, 3–10; letter from Gulliver to: *see* GULLIVER'S TRAVELS.

Synesius, *c*. 370–*c*. 414, Bishop of Ptolemais: 'free-thinker', IV. 46.

Synge family: library, XIV. xi.

Synge, Edward, 1659–1741, Archbishop of Tuam: member of Privy Council of Ireland, X. 182.

Synge, Edward, *c*. 1691–1762, Bishop of Elphin: and book owned by JS, XIV. xi.

Syphilis: XI. 253, 256.

Syracuse: petalism, I. 225.

Syriac language: and Hebrew alphabet, V. 331.

Sysamnes: Persian judge flayed by Cambyses, X. 92.

T

'Tables are turned': a gambling term, V. 283.

Tabula rasa: I. 250.

Tacitus: on Germany, I. 200; and linguistic change, IV. 14; on too much merit, III. 19; and Wharton, III. 26;

quotations and allusions: *Agricola* IX: III. 149; — XXIV: IV. 280; *Annales* I. ii. 2: X. 157; — I. lxxiii: II. 29; IV. 27, 50; IX. 151; — II. VIII. 80; — III. lxv ('a maxim'): VIII. 141; — VI. xxxix or XVI. xviii: I. 111 and *n*.*; *Germania* XI. xi: II. 82–3; — textual note, II. 280.

'Tacking': defined, VII. 102; discussed, VII. 102–3.

Tailor: 'mad with pride', I. 113; and Gulliver, XI. 63–4, 162, 288; worship of, I. 46–55.

Talapoin, the title of a Buddhist monk: IV. 32, 33.

Tale of a Tub (1704) by JS: **I. xxxix-135;** *Abstract* of supposed additions (1720), not by JS, I. 275–95; — reprinted by various editors, I. xxxii; Aeolists, I. xxvii, 95–101; aims, I. xv, xxii, 1–6; analysis, I. xxi–xxviii; annotated copies, I. xxxi–xxxii and *n*.*; anonymity, VI. x; **'Apology'** by JS, **I. 1–11;** — composition, I. xvi, 296; — date, I. 11; II. xxxvii; — discussion of, I. xiv–xvi, xxiv, xxvii–xxviii, xxxi; quoted, II. ix; — and Tooke, I. xxxi; Atterbury on, I. xxviii; authorship, I. xxii–xxiii, xxx–xxxii, 12, 296; II. xii and *n*. 4; — confessed to Faulkner, XIII. 203; — JS denies, I. 279; — Thomas Swift, I. 280–81; — attributed to Temple, I. 279; background, I. xvi, xviii, xxiv–xxv, xxvii; 'Bookseller to the Reader', by JS, I. 17; — composition, I. xxii, *n*.*; 'Booksellers Advertisement' (1720) not by JS, I. 277–81; and Church of England, I. xvi, 2; *Complete Key*: *see* COMPLETE KEY; composition, I. ix, xiv–xvi, xviii, xix, xxi, xxxiv, 1–2, 17, 279; XI. x; and *Conduct of the Allies*, VI. x; and JS's *Contests and Dissensions*, I. xx; date, I. 1, 17; dedication to Lord Somers, by JS, I. 13–16; — composition, I. xxii and *n*.*; and Defoe, I. xxvi, *n*.‖ ; deletions, I. 12, 17, 37, *n*.†; 'Digression on

Madness', by JS, I. 102–14; — analysis, I. xxvi–xxviii; 'A Digression on the Nature . . . of Wars', not by JS, I. 289–90; — authorship, I. xxxii; digressions, I. xxii–xxv; — date, I. xvi; editions, I. 296; — 4th ed. (1705), I. xxviii; — 5th ed. (1710), I. xvi, xxx–xxxii, xxxix; II. xxxvii; — of 1720, I. xxxii, 275–95; — Dublin, XIII. xliv; — by Guthkelch and Nichol Smith: *see* GUTHKELCH; 'Epistle Dedicatory, to . . . Prince Posterity', by JS, I. 18–23; — date, I. 23; — 'large', I. 13; errata and corrigenda, XIV. 49–50; and Bishop Fleetwood, VI. xix; frontispiece facsimile, I. xxxix; *Gulliver's Travels* compared to, XI. ix–xi; hiatuses, I. 37, *n*. †; 'History of Martin' (1720), not by JS, I. xxxii, 286–9; illustrations, II. ix, *n*. 2; 'Introduction', by JS, I. 33–43; — machines, I. 4; Johnson on, I. xxii–xxiii; W. King on, I. xxviii; manuscript, I. ix, xix, xxi, xxxi, 9, 17; and JS's *Meditation upon a Broom Stick*, I. xxxiv; and JS's odes, I. xiii–xiv, xvi, and *n*. †; alleged plagiarism, I. xxviii, 6–8, 12; oaths, I. 10; on preaching, IX. 132; 'Preface' by JS, I. 24–32; — date, I. 26; 'A Project for the Universal Benefit of Mankind' (1720), not by JS, I. 293–4; authorship, I. xxxii; publication, I. xviii, xix, xxi, xxii, xxxix, 9, 12, 17, 296; — and Temple, I. xviii; Quintana on, I. xxviii, *n*. †; reception, I. xxvi–xxviii, 1–2; — allegedly Whig, VI. x; religious allegory ('tale of a tub'), I. xxiii, xxix, 1, 7; sources, I. xiv, xxix, 7; style, I. xv, xvi, xxii–xxv, xxvii; and Thomas Swift, I. xxxi–xxxii; 'A Table, or Index, or Key, to the Tale of a Tub' (1720), unauthorized addition, I. 282–295; text — revision of scandalous language, I. x; — — 'God', I. 296; — — 'genitals', I. 297; — — 'cunnus', I. 297; — — 'Providence', I. 298; — — 'cloven tongues', I. 298; text — JS on, I. 9; textual notes, I. 296–8; and JS's *Thoughts on Various Subjects*, I. xxxv; title-page facsimiles, I. xxxix, 275; French translation, I. xxxii; list of imaginary 'treatises', I. xl; 'tub', meaning, I. 24–5; Wotton on, I. xxviii.

Tale of a Tub, Revers'd (1705): 'many others', I. 1.

Talents: charity increases, IX. 148; good men's, IX. 147–8; must be used, IX. 149.

'Talkall, Mrs.': character in *Polite Conversation*, IV. 162.

'Talkham, Countess of': character in *Polite Conversation*, IV. 194.

Tallard, Camille d'Hostun, comte de, 1652–1728, French general and diplomat: and author of *Answer to Bickerstaff*, II. 199; and Gaultier ('foreign ministers'), VII. 34; house and garden, V. 204.

Tallies: VII. 70–72.

Talmudists: and Isaac, IV. 239.

Tankerville, Ford Grey (Lord Grey of Warke), Earl of, 1655–1701: Macky and JS on, V. 260.

Tankerville, William de, *d*. 1129,

chamberlain of England and Normandy: defeats enemies of Henry I, V. 41.

Tanning: XII. 19.

'Tantivyes': XII. 169.

Targum: and English language, IV. 239.

Tariff of 1664 (i.e., duty on Dutch goods imported into France, as settled in 1664): French promise Dutch (1697), VI. 12; granted Dutch (1713), VII. 55, 113–4; — goods excepted, VII. 153, 154, 156, 160–1.

Tariffs: *see also* TAXES.

Tarquin the Proud (Tarquinius Superbus, half-legendary last king of Rome), 6th century B.C.: expelled, II. 23; parallel to James II, I. 213; tyrant, I. 213.

Tarquinius Priscus (half-legendary king of Rome): parallel to Charles I's creation of peers, I. 213; elected, I. 212–13.

Tartars: and Chinese language, IV. 9; ate no corn, XII. 19; and Irish, I. 178; code for Scots, III. 40.

Tartary (i.e., Siberia together with some other parts of Asia): XI. 111; and Gulliver, XI. 84, 111.

Tasmania (or Van Diemen's Land): and Gulliver, XI. 18, 20, 78.

Tasso, Torquato, 1544–95, Italian poet: pretends to lead the Moderns, I. 152.

Tate, Nahum, 1652–1715, poet and playwright: ridiculed in *Tale of a Tub*, I. xxiv, 22.

Tatler: and Addison, II. xxv–xxvi; authorship, II. xxv–xxxv, 141, *n.**, 172, 173, *n.**; in *Exam-*

iner, XIV. 11; frontispiece facsimile, facing II. 171; compared to *Spectator*, II. xxxvi;

no. 1 (12 Apr. 1709) and *Vindication of Isaac Bickerstaff Esq.*, II. xxvi; no. 183 (on bad taste), III. 35; no. 220 (5, not 4 Sept. 1710), and *Proposal Humbly Offered . . . for . . . Preventing the Further Growth of Popery*, XII. xxxii. *See also* STEELE; ADDISON.

JS's contributions, II. xxv–xxxvii, 141, *n.**; — no. 4 (Italian opera), II. xxvii; — no. 7 (Bickerstaff's will), II. xxviii; — no. 10 (Jenny Distaff), not by JS, II. xxviii; — no. 21 (advertisements), II. 235–7; — — authorship, II. xxix; — no. 31 (conversation), II. 237–8; — — authorship, II. xxix; — no. 32 (ladies' monastery) not by JS, II. xxix–xxxi and *n.* 1; — no. 67 ('Tables of Fame'), II. 238–40; — — authorship, II. xxxi, 173, *n.**; — no. 68 ('Tables of Fame'), II. 240–2; — — authorship, II. xxxi, 173, *n.**; — no. 74 not by JS, II. xxxi–xxxii; — no. 81 ('Tables of Fame'), not by JS, II. xxxi–xxxii, 173, *n.* *;— **no. 230** (28 Sept. 1710, on language), by JS, **II. 173-7**; — analysis, II. xxxiii; IV. xi, xxxi; — — background, III. x; — — textual notes, II. 289; — no. 236, II. xxxiv, *n.* 3; — no. 249 ('Adventures of a Shilling'), II. 243–6; — — authorship, II. xxxii, xxxv, 173, *n.**; — no. 258 (2 Dec. 1710, on 'North Britain'), II. 247.

Tatler (continued by William Har-

rison and others): authorship, II. xxxv–xxxvi; JS's contributions — no. 1, II. 249–51; — — authorship, II. xxxv; — no. 2, II. 252–6; — — authorship, II. xxxv; — **no. 5** (lion and virgins), by JS, **II. 178-83**; — — authorship, II. xxxv; — — textual notes, II. 289; — no. 8 (15 Mar. 1711), II. 257–9; — — authorship, II. xxxv; — — erratum, XIV. 51; — **no. 20** (6 Mar. 1710 on good manners), by JS, **II. 184-7**; — — authorship, II. xxxv; — — textual notes, II. 290; — no. 28 or 306 (24 Mar. 1711, Bickerstaff's incarnations), II. 260–3; — — authorship, II. xxxvi.

Tatler (unauthorized continuation published by John Morphew, from no. 272 to 285, or 6 Jan. to 3 Feb. 1711, when it was merged with Harrison's *Tatler*): called 'idle paper', II. 249.

Taverner, William, *fl.* 1728–75, vicar choral of St. Patrick's Cathedral: XIII. 197.

Taverns: hours, II. 60; signs on, XII. 222–6.

Taxes: and balance of power, V. 245; and bishops, XII. xxxix–xl; high tariffs, XII. 21, 125; Irish and English compared, XII. 21; and Irish national debt, XII. 205–12; and maxims of state, XII. 136; and posterity, I. 243; and tithes (tax on luxuries), XII. 136, 309; on 'unwholesome' luxuries, XII. 20; on virtues and vices, XI. 189–90; on wine, XII. 20, 124–6; — and Irish national debt, XII. 124–6.

Taylor, Jeremy, 1613–67, Bishop of Down and Connor: and religion, IV. 34; on the Trinity, IV. 34; 'unwholesome', XII. 20.

Teerink, Herman: *Bibliography of . . . Swift* (1937) — on *Gulliver's Travels*, XI. 301.

Telemachus: and Homer, I. 244.

Temperance: in ancient philosophy, IX. 249.

Temple family: and JS, I. xxxvi.

Temple, Henry: *see* PALMERSTON.

Temple, Sir John, 1600–77, Master of the Rolls in Ireland, father of Sir William: V. 193; and JS's family, I. x.

Temple, John, 1655–89, son of Sir William Temple: father's letter to, I. 269.

Temple, John, *c.* 1680–1752, nephew of Sir William Temple: correspondence with JS, II. xxxiv, *n.* 3.

Temple, Sir William, Bart., 1628–99, statesman, patron of JS: leads Ancients, I. 147, 152–65; aided by Athene and Apollo, I. 162–3; and Athenian Society, I. xii; and Bentley, 'unmannerly pedant', I. xviii; on 'Boyle's' *Examination*, I. xviii; Burnet and JS on, V. 276; career as writer and diplomat, I. 257–9, 262–3, 266, 268–71; *Essay upon the Ancient and Modern Learning* (1690), and *Tale of a Tub*, I. xvi; *Essay upon the Original . . . of Government*, par. 9 quoted, I. 211; and Earl of Godolphin, I. 268; on humour, XII. 32; *Introduction to the History of England*, and JS's *Abstract*, V. ix; on valiant kings, V. 251; *Letters to the King . . . and other Persons*

(1703), edited by JS, I. 265–6, 304; XIV. 45; — **inscription** by JS, **I. 304**; — 'The Preface', by JS, **I. 266**, 304; — publication, I. xxi, 266; — title-page facsimile, I. 265; *Letters Written by Sir W. Temple* (1700), edited by JS — (mistitled *Works*, 1702) date, V. ix; — **dedication** by JS, **I. 256**; — publication, I. xix; — 'The Publisher's Epistle to the Reader', by JS, **I. 257-9**; — — date, XI. x, *n.* 1; — and JS's *Contests and Dissensions*, I. xx; — title-page facsimile, I. 255; *Memoirs — Part I* destroyed, I. 270; *Memoirs. Part III* (1709), edited by JS — and Lady Giffard, I. xxxvi; — and Godolphin, II. xxxix; — **inscription** by JS, **I. 304**; — 'The Preface', by JS, **I. 268-71**; — Temple's 'Preface' quoted, I. 269; — publication, I. xxxvi, 268; — style, I. 268–70; — JS's edition, II. xxvi; — title, I. 269–70; — title-page facsimile, I. 267; on Lord Middleton, V. 262; *Miscellanea. The Third Part* (1701), edited by JS — note by JS, **I. 263**; — publication, I. xx, 262; — 'The Publisher to the Reader', by JS, **I. 262**; — — date, XI. x, *n.* 1; — title-page facsimile, I. 261; seat at Moor Park: *see* MOOR PARK; and Peace of Nimwegen (1678), V. 193; *Of Health and Long-Life*, essay in *Miscellanea III*, I. 261–2; *Of Popular Discontents*, essay in *Miscellanea III*, I. 261–2; letter to 1st Duke of Ormonde — **JS's note, XIV. 1**; — — publica-

tion, XIV. xi; — — textual note, XIV. 45; *Poems*, 1679, I. 262; and Porsenna, I. 6; and Earl of Rochester, I. 268; disapproves of satire, I. xiv; *Some Thoughts upon Reviewing the Essay of Antient and Modern Learning*, essay in *Miscellanea III*, I. 261–2; — **JS's note, I. 263**; ('a person') and Stella, V. 228; style, I. xxxvi, 268–70; and Charles, Earl of Sunderland, I. 268; and Robert, Earl of Sunderland, I. 268;

and JS: I. x–xix; V. 193–4; bitterness toward Temple, I. xxxvi; — certificate supplied (1694), V. xxvii; his confidence in JS, I. x; death of Temple (1699) and JS's career, I. xviii; JS at Moor Park, I. x–xix; V. 193–4; poems on Temple, I. xiii, xv; poetry encouraged, I. xii; post offered to JS (*c.* 1694), V. 194; JS his secretary, I. 280, 281; XI. ix; and authorship of *Tale of a Tub*, I. 279; recommendation to William III, I. xi; writings admired by JS, I. xii–xiii;

Thomas Swift employed by him, I. xxx, 279–80; 'Time's' friend, I. 22; and Tyrconnel, V. 291; *Upon the Gardens of Epicurus* (1685, essay in *Miscellanea II*), IX. 113 and *n.* 1; 'a man of virtue', V. 276; and William III, I. xi; V. 193; Wotton attacks, I. xxxvi, 5–6, 22; — *see also* WOTTON.

Temptation to evil: resistance, IX. 351; and resolutions, IX. 353; and wealth, IX. 196.

Tenerchebray: *see* TINCHEBRAY.

Tenerife (or Tenariff), one of the Canary Islands: and Gulliver, XI. 221.

Tenison, Edward, 1673–1735, Bishop of Ossory: and Irish clergy, XII. xxxv.

Tenison, Thomas, 1636–1715, Archbishop of Canterbury: III. 49–50; Burnet and JS on, V. 271; and *Dialogue between the Archbishop of Canterbury and Mr. Higgins*, II. 282; and discretion, XII. 40; Macky and JS on, V. 260; and JS, II. ix.

Terence, Roman playwright, *c.* 195–159 B.C.: prologues and the *malevoli*, I. 62.

Termonde: *see* DENDERMONDE.

Terra Australis Incognita: imaginary treatise by native of, I. xl. *See also* WEST INDIES.

Tertullian, 2nd–3rd century A.D., church father: *Apologeticus ad gentes* 50, *ad finem* ('semen est sanguis'): III. 56.

Tessé, René de Froulai, comte de, 1651–1725, French marshal: and Toulon, VI. 35.

Test Act, English (Sacramental Test, enacted 1673): Dissenters oppose, II. 110–125; free-thinkers attack, II. 26–39; injustice alleged, VII. 96; Lambert opposes repeal, II. 284; and liberty of conscience, II. 5–8; 'reasonable', V. 280; repeal — and abolition of Christianity, II. 26–39; — and comprehension of Dissenters, IX. 119; — Tories oppose, VI. 130; — Whigs attempt, III. 54–5; and Stillingfleet, II. 79 and *n.**; and JS —

repeal opposed, II. xix; — he supports, II. xvi; and Tindal, II. 86–90, 92–3, 102–3; Whigs oppose, II. xvi, 3; III. 71.

Test Act, Irish (Sacramental Test, enacted 1704): and army officers, II. 123–4; clergy supports, II. 119; consequences of, II. 111; and Dorset, XII. xl; oath as alternative, II. 123; XII. 277–8; and British Parliament, II. 113–14; and S. Powell, XII. xxxii; **repeal** — attempted, II. ix; — and clergy, XII. xl–xlvii; — consequences, II. 116–18; — defeated (1733), XIII. xxx, 97, 103; — Dissenters attempt, II. 112–13; — impossible, II. 118; —opposed, II. 120–3; — and Presbyterians, XII. 263–79; — and Quakers, XII. 299; — and Roman Catholics, XII. 283–95; — and Speaker of the Irish House of Commons, II. xxxii–xxxiii, 131, 132–3; and JS — letter to William Lloyd, II. xxxix–xl and *n.* 1; — opposes repeal, XII. xl–xlvii; — he supports, II. xxii, 134; — and Whigs, XII. xl; Whigs censured, II. xiv–xv; Whigs urge repeal, II. 131. *See also* JS's QUERIES RELATING TO THE SACRAMENTAL TEST; JS's ADVANTAGES PROPOSED BY REPEALING THE SACRAMENTAL TEST.

'Testimonial of the Death of Mr. Partridge': II. 231.

Testimony of Conscience, sermon by JS: **IX. 150-8**; analysis, IX. 102, 106, 111, 114–16; composition, IX. 133, 137; textual

notes, IX. 375–6; title-page facsimile, IX. 139.

Teviot, Thomas Livingstone (or Levingston), 1st Viscount, *c.* 1652–1711, lieutenant general: and Creichton, V. 167, 169–71; imprisoned (1689), V. 171; Macky and JS on, V. 261.

Tew, David, *d.* 1744, Lord Mayor of Dublin (1743): on Dublin grand jury (1724), X. 76.

Text of this edition, principles for establishing: V. xxi–xxii.

Thales of Miletus, 6th century B.C. Greek philosopher: and morality, IX. 246; 'that philosopher', I. 190.

'Thalestris': pseudonym of female mason, V. 333.

Thames River: and Brobdingnag's rivers, XI. 99; twice frozen, II. 165, 168; and *Polite Conversation*, IV. 146, *n.**.

Thanet, Thomas Tufton, 6th Earl of, 1644–1729: Macky and JS on, V. 259.

Thatch'd House Tavern, Avemary Lane, London: VI. 175.

Théâtre Italien: see GHERARDI, EVARISTE.

Theatres: see STAGE.

Thebes, Bœotia, Greece: and Alexander the Great, I. 209; and balance of power, II. 16; and Greece, I. 202, 208.

Themistocles, *c.* 525–*c.* 460 B.C., Athenian statesman and general: and literary critics, I. 62; fall from power, I. 207, 210; — caused by envy, VIII. 138; 'Themistocles', pseudonym for Lord Orford: I. xx, 207, 210.

Theobald IV, Count of Blois,

1093–1152, elder brother of King Stephen: V. 47–8; Henry I his uncle, V. 38; Louis VI attacks, VI. 38; desires Normandy, V. 51; Stephen pensions him, V. 51.

Theobald of Bec, Archbishop of Canterbury, *d.* 1161: and Stephen, V. 67–70.

Theobald, Lewis, 1688–1744, lawyer, writer, editor: 'Tibbalds', IV. xxxii; 'quoted', IV. 121; and Wagstaff, IV. 123.

Theodoric, King of the East Goths, *c.* 454–526: pope subordinate to, XIV. 31; and Pope John I, XIV. 29; and Symmachus, XIV. 20.

Theodosius II, Emperor of the East, 401–450: Baronius and JS on, XIV. 21; and 'Robber' Council of Ephesus, XIV. 22; JS denounces, XIV. 20.

Theological controversy: IX. 107–8.

Theophilus, Archbishop of Alexandria: and Innocent I, XIV. 18.

Theophrastus: see PARACELSUS.

Theseus, legendary Athenian hero: established Athens, I. 204; divinity, I. 57.

Thesse: see TESSÉ.

Thierry, Count of Alsace and Flanders, *d.* 1168: and William the Clito, V. 43–44.

Thistle, Order of: and James I, I. 29; ridiculed ('green'), XI. 39.

Thomas, William, *d.* 1554, Italian scholar and clerk of the Council to Edward VI: V. 251.

Thompson, Edward, *d.* 1742, M.P. for York, Commissioner of Revenue in Ireland: and excise, XIII. 83.

Thompson, Paul V.: on JS and *Tatler*, II. xxxiv, *n.* 3.

Thomson, James, 1700–48, poet: quoted, XIII. xxxi.

Thoughts on Religion, by JS: IX. **261-3**; textual note, IX. 377.

Thoughts on Various Subjects (written *c.* 1696–1706), by JS: I. **241-5**; authorship, I. xxxv, 303; composition and date, I. xxxiv–xxxv; date, XIV. 49; and La Rochefoucauld, I. xxxv; and *Tale of a Tub*, I. xxxv.

Thoughts on Various Subjects (1727 and 1745), by JS: IV. **243-54**; authorship, IV. 300; publication, IV. xxxix; textual notes, IV. 300-1.

Thrasybulus, *d.* 388 B.C., Athenian general: and Athenian government, I. 208.

Three (number): in *Tale of a Tub*, I. xl, 4, 34-5; imaginary treatise on, I. xl.

Three Sermons (1744), by JS: IX. 139–68; textual notes, IX. 375–6; title-page facsimile, IX. 139.

Thucydides: allusions — I. ii: I. 204; — VIII. lvii–lviii, lxxxii, xcii–xcv, xcvii: I. 198; correct text, IV. 33.

Thurstan, Archbishop of York, *d.* 1140: and War of the Standard, V. 53-4.

Tibbalds: *see* THEOBALD.

Tiberius (Claudius Nero) Caesar, 42 B.C.–A.D. 37, Roman emperor: on blasphemy, II. 29; IV, 50; IX. 151; and fall of Rome, I. 222; politician, VIII. 77.

Tibullus, Albius, *c.* 50–*c.* 19 B.C., Roman poet: imitated by Temple, I. 262.

Tickell, Thomas, 1686–1740, poet, statesman: Carteret's secretary, V. xxix; pun on name, IV. 275; and JS's illness (1724), X. xix; JS recommends Sheridan, V. xxix; on *Tatler*, II. xxvi, *n.* 1.

Tidcomb, John, 1642–1713, general: XII. 192.

Tigellius (mentioned in Horace *Satires* I. x. 90): I. 57.

Tighe, Sir Richard, *c.* 1678–1736, Irish M.P. and Privy Councillor: and *Intelligencer* no. 8, XII. xxviii–xxix; 'one person', XII. 163; 'Pistorides', XII. xxvii, xxix, 155, 156-7, 160; and Sheridan, XII. xxviii; JS attacks, XII. xxvii–xxix; threatens JS, XIII. xxix.

Tighe, Stearne, *d.* 1761, M.P. for Kildare: on Dublin grand jury, X. 76.

Tillotson, John, 1630–94, Archbishop of Canterbury: and Burnet, IV. 60–61; and freethinkers, IV. 47; on Hell, IV. 34, 35; and Archbishop King, II. 282; elaborate sermons, IX. 67.

'Tim': defined by JS, V. 336.

'Time', guardian of posterity: I. 19 ff.

Tinchebray ('Tenerchebray'), Orne, France: battle (1106), V. 32-3.

Tindal, Matthew, 1657–1733, deist, controversialist: atheist, III. 142; and Burnet, IV. xxv; attacks Christianity, II. 36; and Collins, IV. xvii; and freethinking, IV. 37, 41, 45; and Middlesex grand jury, II. xviii, 191-2; and public offices, III. 71;

quotation, II. 115; *The Rights of the Christian Church Asserted* — JS's copy, II. 280; — Part I, reviewed by JS, II. 67–107; — Part II mentioned, II. 71, 99, 107; Roman Catholic convert, II. 37, 104; style censured, II. 80, 99; and JS, II. xvii–xviii; — JS attacks, II. xix, 29; and the Test Act, III. 54, 55; and the universities, III. 37; and Whigs, III. 39.

Tinmouth: *see* TYNEMOUTH.

Tirel (or Tyrrell), Walter, *fl.* 1100, reputed slayer of William II: V. 24.

Tisdall, William, 1669–1735, Irish clergyman and controversialist, early friend of Swift: author of the *Correspondent*, XII. xlii; on Prebyterians, XII. 276 and *n.* *, 277; *Tom-Punsibi Metamorphosed* (1724), IX. xvii, *n.* 1.

Tissaphenes, *d. c.* 395 B.C., Persian satrap of Sardis: 'lieutenant', I. 208.

Tithes: human or divine institution, IX. 59–60; and religious freedom, II. 102; Tindal on, II. 89–90, 95; of the Church of Ireland — collection difficult, XIII. 98; — depreciation, IX. 57; XIII. 98, 107; — and emigration from Ireland, XII. 76, 78; — and landlords, XIII. 205; most tithes parochial, V. 90.

Titus, Silius, 1622–1704, F.R.S., politician and colonel: Burnet and JS on, V. 266; and James II, III. 118.

'Toandagain, Miss': character in *Polite Conversation*, IV. 156.

Tobacco: disapproved, II. 52; to stop Gulliver's nose, XI. 288, 295.

Tobit: and his dog, I. 53, *n.**, 244. *See also under* BIBLE.

'Toby', nephew of Abel Roper (pseudonym of author of *Character of Richard Steele*): VIII. xiv, 67.

Tofts, Catherine or Katherine, *c.* 1680–1756, singer: II. 32.

Tokyo, Japan: Gulliver in 'Yedo', XI. 216–17.

Toland, John, 1670–1722, deist, controversialist: atheist, III. 142; and Bickerstaff, II. xxiv, *n.* 1; and Burnet, IV. xxv, 70; *Christianity Not Mysterious* (1696), IX. 108; attacks Christianity, II. 36, 72; and clergy, IV. 37; malice against clergy, IX. 56; and Collins, IV. xvii; and explicit faith, IX. 111; and free-thinking, IV. 41; and Molesworth, IV. xxvi, xxvii, xxviii; Roman Catholic, II. 37; conversion to Roman Catholicism satirized, II. xxiv, *n.* 1; and Somers (implied as 'conversed with'), III. 79; JS attacks, II. xix, 29; attacks JS's academy project, IV. xiv; and Test Act, III. 55, 71.

Toleration Act (1689): against Roman Catholics, II. 120.

Toleration, religious (liberty of conscience, religious freedom): King of Brobdingnag on, XI. 131; and Dissenters, XIV. 11; hackneyed subject, I. 42; Nonconformists lack, IX. 151; private opinion, IX. 261; JS would limit, IX. 118–19; and traditional faith, XII. 290.

'Tolgo Phonac' (Lilliputian phrase of command): XI. 22.

To Mr. Congreve, poem by JS: composition, I. xv; parallels with *Tale of a Tub*, I. xvi, *n.**.

To Mr. Delany (1718), poem by JS: on Sheridan, V. xxviii–xxix.

To Mr. Gay, poem by JS: composition, XII. xxxiii.

To My Lord High Admirall: *see* HUMBLE PETITION OF THE DOCTOR.

To Quilca, a Country House (composed 1725), poem by JS: composition, V. xxix.

'To rights': XI. 144.

To the Honourable the Society . . . for the New Plantation in Ulster, by JS: *see* DUNKIN.

To the Provost . . . of Trinity College, by JS: *see* DUNKIN.

To the Right Worshipful the Mayor . . . of the City of Corke, by JS: *see* CORK.

Tom (i.e. Great Tom), bell in tower of Christ Church College, Oxford: XII. 41.

Tom Thumb: I. 41.

Tommy Potts: *see* LOVERS QUARREL.

Tom's Coffee House (probably in Devereux Court), London: IV. 28.

Tonbridge, Kent: Irish absentees in, XII. 71; William II takes, V. 14.

Tonkin (or Tonquin), Vietnam: and Gulliver: XI. 148, 154.

Tonson, Jacob, *c.* 1656–1736, publisher: copyrights, XIII. 206; publishes Temple's *Letters*, I. 255.

Tooke, Benjamin, *c.* 1642–1716, bookseller and printer: printer of the *London Gazette* (1711), VI. xxiii; **and JS** — correspondence (1710), I. xxx–xxxi; — publishes *Miscellanies* (1711), I. xxxiii; II. xxxvii–xxxviii, 275; XIV. xi; — publishes *Project for the Advancement of Religion* (1709), II. 41; — publishes *Proposal for Correcting . . . the English Tongue*, IV. 3; — publishes *Tale of a Tub* (5th ed., 1710), I. xxx; and Thomas Swift, I. xxxi; publishes Temple's *Letters to the King . . .*, I. 265; publishes Temple's *Memoirs*, I. 267; publishes Temple's *Miscellanea III*, I. 261.

Topham, Andrew: funeral of bank, IX. 309.

Topinambou (or Tobinambou), Brazil, proverbial stronghold of wildest savagery: Ireland compared with, XII. 116; literati of, I. 172.

Torcy, Jean Baptiste Colbert, marquis de, 1665–1746, French statesman: his brother: *see* CROISSY; English sympathies, VII. 46, 147; and Gaultier, VII. 34–5, 37; at The Hague (1709), VII. 32–3; secretary to Louis XIV, VII. 160; called 'Monsieur de la Bastide', III. 210–17; and the 'spirit of negotiating', VIII. 78; and peace terms of 1709, VII. 32–3; desires peace (1711), VII. 46, 160; and peace overtures (1711), VII. 36–7; and peace preliminaries, III. 210–18; VII. 154; answer to peace preliminaries (1711), VII. 184–95; agrees to general peace (1713), VII. 164–5; and Petkum, VII. 40–41; and Philip V's renunciation,

VII. 120, 124–5; and Prior,
III. 210–18, VII. 154; and
Shrewsbury, VII. 160, 164–5;
JS praises him, VII. 160; his
uncle: *see* COLBERT, JEAN-
BAPTISTE, MARQUIS DE SEIGNE-
LAY; and Villars, VII. 126.
Tories: Addison and JS on, V.
253: and Queen Anne, I. xxi;
VIII. 146, 148; — she favours
them (1713), VIII. 154–5; and
Burnet, IV. 62–3, 64, 68; character, III. 126; and Church of
England, I. xxi; VI. 130; VIII.
164; — funds for new churches,
VII. 3; and Treaty of Commerce (1713), VIII. 21, 22; dis-
agreements tolerated, VI. 130;
condemn Dissent, II. 3–4; and
divine right of kings, VI. 161;
in *Examiner*, XIV. 11–12; and
Flying-Post, VIII. 14; and France,
VII. 28; — and Dunkirk, VI.
190; and free-thinkers, IV. 63;
and George I, V. 99–100; VIII.
94–5; — Elector rejects them,
VII. 145; — 'his majesty' rejects them, XI. 48; Godolphin
in 'church interest' (1701), VI.
11; and Godolphin ministry, III.
68; VI. 42, 130–1; and Hanoverian Succession, VIII. 48, 92;
— limited support, VIII. xvii; —
support it, VIII. xviii, 40; 'high-
heels' in *Gulliver's Travels*, XI.
48; in House of Commons —
majority overwhelming (1710),
III. 26; — majority unwieldy
(1710–12), VIII. 126, 143; —
majority very large (1714), VIII.
48; in House of Lords — no
bribery' VI. 126; — 'crazy
majority' (1711), VII. 13, 15; and

Indian Kings, II. 265; in Ireland:
see TORIES, IRISH; and Jacobites,
V. 251; VI. 145–6; and James
II, V. 255; — no correspondence, VI. 145; and landed
interest, VI. 126; VIII. 48;
majority in Commons (1712),
VI. 126; Marlborough's early
leanings, VII. 7; and Marlborough's grant, VI. 130; and
moderation, II. 13; VI. 77; and
Naturalization Bill, VII. 130; and
Nottingham — he defects, VII.
11; — would lead them, VII.
11–12; — threat from 'same
quarter' (1712), VI. 77; and
Occasional Conformity Bill
(1703–4), I. xxi; and October
Club: *see* OCTOBER CLUB; origins,
V. 99; and Oxford — 'on whom
we so much depend', VI. 72;
and Oxford ministry — fear
comprehension, VIII. 86; —
alleged differences, VI. 73; —
disaffection in 'same quarter',
VI. 77; — majority dependent
on, VI. 80; — preferments delayed, VI. 73; VIII. 143–4; —
secrecy, VI. 74, 75; pamphlets —
and Hanoverian Succession,
VIII.168–9;—interrupted(1711),
VI. 71; — prosecuted (1712),
VII. 19; — allegedly suppressed
(to 1710), III. 188; not a party,
III. 104–5; peace lovers, VII. 3;
and vote against 'peace without
Spain' ('an incident', 1711), VI.
71; and creation of twelve peers
(1712), VII. 20, 31; on Philip V
(1701), VI. 11; in power (*c.* 1702),
VI. 42; and royal prerogative,
VI. 130; and Pretender, III. 131;
V. 104–5; VII. 28; VIII. 71–2,

163–80; and public welfare, VI. 133–4; and rebellion of 1715, V. 99–100, 104–5; — 'civil war', VIII. 218; and Revolution of 1688, VIII. 92; 'Rigides', III. 209; and Roman Catholicism, IV. 75–6; — Addison and JS on, V. 255; and Sacheverell, VI. 130; — 'one of their members' defends him, VII. 3; JS satirizes them (*c.* 1698), I. 111; JS counts himself as one (1712), VI. 71–80; and tacking, VII. 100; Test Act supported, VI. 130; and toleration, VI. 127; Trimmers, II. 32; on Union (1713), VIII. 50; and Wagstaff, IV. 121; and Walpole, V. 101; — excludes them through corruption (1727), V. xv; oppose War of Spanish Succession, VI. 11; and Whigs — history of parties, III. 162–7; — Tories ('high-heels') more numerous, XI. 48; — principles compared, II. 1–25; III. 121–6; VI. 127–31; — public manners, III. 102; — similarities, II. 13–14; — theatre audiences divided, III. 102; — Tories less vindictive, VI. 77–8; 'Whimsicals', VIII. 82–3. *See also* HIGH CHURCH; PARTIES.

Tories, Irish: Carteret's preferments, XII. 155–69; chimney sweeps spy for, XII. 222; and Church of Ireland, IX. 56; dogs become Whigs, XII. 222; and dustmen's cry, XII. 219–20; their principles, II. 118; IX. 56–7; public offices, XII. xxvii–xxviii, xxix; Sheridan alienates them, V. xxx; and Wood's coins, X. xxiv, xxv.

Toulon, French seaport: Oxford ministry would accept, VI. 191; surprise attack fails (1707) — Austria blamed, VI. 34–5; — Godolphin ministry blamed, III. 149; — Oxford blamed, VI. 97; — prediction, II. 143, 203, 206.

Toupees: defined, XII. 219 and *n.* †; and footmen, XII. 235–6; JS censures, XII. xxxiii–xxxiv.

Tournai, Hainaut, Belgium: and Barrier Treaty, VI. 109; and English merchants, VI. 116; blocks English troops, VII. 141; and Treaty of Utrecht, VII. 113, 152–5, 159.

Tower of London: seven bishops sent to, VII. 5; allegedly built by William II, V. 27.

Townshend, Charles Townshend, 2nd Viscount, 1675–1738, statesman: and Barrier Treaty, VI. 85, 116; VII. 78, 79; — 'ambassador' ignores instructions, VII. 91; — given full authority, VI. 98; — acts without authority, VII. 93; censured by Commons (1712), VII. 79, 93; — fears Commons (1710), VII. 23; — signs it, VI. 29, 106, 108, 109; Godolphin ministry favours, VI. 29; and Gregg, III. xxix, 185–205, 243–58; and Harley's alleged treason, III. xxix; letters, VI. xv–xvi; Macky and JS on, V. 259; hinders Strafford (Raby) in 1709, VII. 38–9; titles, VI. 98; removed as Captain of Her Majesty's Guard of Yeomen, III. 204.

Trade, English: with Antwerp, VI. 51; and Assiento: *see* ASSIENTO; and Austria,

VI. 51; and Austria's ambitions (1714), VIII. 60; and Barrier Treaty, VI. 51, 85, 116–17; VII. 90–2; beef, VI. 116; and Bruges, VI. 85, 116–17; and House of Burgundy, VII. 92; butter, VI. 116; at Cadiz, VI. 22; and constitution of England, III. 48–9; domestic commerce and Dunkirk, VII. 132; and Dunkirk, VI. 112; with Dutch VII. 123; — contraband, VI. 116–17; and Dutch Barrier, VI. 55, 116–17; VII. 91; Dutch rivalry, VI. 20–1; VII. 119, 121; — in Flanders, VI. 28–9, 38, 91–3; VII. 61–2; with France, VII. 114; — privileges to be granted, VII. 48–9, 131; and French ambitions (1714), VIII. 60; and French privateers, VI. 60, 112; and Grand Alliance, VII. 92; Gulliver's account of, XI. 251–3; herrings, VI. 117; hides, VI. 116; and Ireland — boycott proposed, IX. xv; and luxury, XI. 251–2; Mediterranean, VII. 132; and Naples, VI. 111; necessities exported, XI. 252; and North America, VII. 132; and Northern War, VI. 63; and peace negotiations (1709–10), VI. 50–1; with Peru, VI. 22; and Plata (or Plate) River, Argentina, VII. 49, 115; with Portugal, VIII. 61; — duties VI. 39; rape oil, VI. 117; in 'Representation of the British Merchants at Bruges', VI. 85, 91, 116–17; salmon, VI. 116; salt, VI. 117; and Sicily, VI. 111; with Spain — and 'Charles III', VI. 51; — privileges to be granted, VII. 115; and union of Spain and France, VI. 17; with Spanish empire, VI. 28–9; VII. 37, 77; — and Barrier Treaty, VII. 92–3; — Dutch to share (1709), VI. 92; — parity with France, (1701), VI. 47; — in peace overtures (1711), VII. 37; — privileges to be granted (1709), VI. 104; —— (1711) VII. 43, 48–9, 92, 132; — *see also* As-SIENTO; and Spanish Netherlands (i.e., Belgium), VI. 28–9, 85, 116–17; VII. 91–2; — and Barrier Treaty, VI. 90, 104, 113; VII. 61–2, 90–4, 114; — Dutch discourage, VI. 91–2; — duties, VI. 91, 116–17; VII. 91–2; — and Treaty of Münster, VII. 61; — and Treaty of Utrecht, VII. 61–2; with Spanish West Indies — and Lille, VI. 117; — and War of Spanish Succession, VI. 50, 97; spirits, VI. 117; tallow, VI. 116; and Treaty of Utrecht, VII. 43, 45; — balance sought, VII. 46; — 'concessions' at Utrecht, VII. 122; and War of Spanish Succession, VII. 61–2, 90; — benefits proposed, VI. 15; VII. 81–2; and West Indies, III. 198, whale oil, VI. 117; Whig motto, VIII. 164; wool — carried by Dutch, VI. 28; — Flanders threatens, VI. 28; — and Gulliver's sheep, XI. 80; woollen manufacture supreme, IX. 269. *See also* SOUTH SEA COMPANY; UTRECHT, TREATY OF, *Treaty of Commerce.*

Trade, Irish: and armies abroad, XII. 174–5; balance of, XII. 9–10, 20; XIII. 167; — important, IX. 129; and bank scheme, IX. xvi; beef, XII. 18–19; John

Browne and JS on, V. 256–7; butter, XII. 10; cattle, XII. 174; cloth, XIII. xxvi–xxvii; and national debt, XII. 207; declining, XIII. 176; difficulties, IX. 200; dishonesty against self-interest, IX. 237; XIII. 176; with England, boycott proposed, IX. 15–22; England's restrictions, IX. 6, 200; XII. xi–xii, xix, xxi, xxii, 5–12, 55, 66–7, 76–8, 86, 89, 118, 121–5, 131–2, 173; — and interest rate, XII. 133–4; — recommended (ironically), XII. 175–8; — unfair, V. 256–7; XII. 173; exports, V. 256; fish, XIII. 111–13; foreign goods denounced, IX. 128–9; X. 135; XII. 173; with France, IX. 16; XII. 125; freedom proposed, IX. 11; linen, XII. 10; XIII. xxix, 104, 113, 176; and Navigation Act, XII. 8, 66, 132; proposals to improve, XII. xvii, 79–80; public concern lacking, IX. 236; sheep, XII. 18–19; in JS's sermons, IX. 102; woollen: *see* WOOLLEN TRADE, IRISH. *See also* MANUFACTURES; MERCHANTS, IRISH; SHOPKEEPERS, IRISH.

Trajan (Marcus Ulpius Trajanus), *c.* 53–117, Roman Emperor: his critics, X. 159–60; and linguistic change, IV. 16.

Traldraggdubb, or Trildrogdrib, capital of Luggnagg: XI. 204.

'Tramecksan' (name of Lilliputian high-heel party; i.e., the Tories): XI. 48.

Transubstantiation: ridiculed, I. 72–4; XI. 246.

Traquair, John Stewart, 1st Earl of, *c.* 1600–1659: Burnet and JS on, V. 266.

Trarbach, Germany, on the Moselle between Treves and Coblenz: VIII. 59.

Traulus (from Greek *traulos*, stammering), pseudonym for Joshua, Viscount Allen, possibly punning on 'trowell': XII. xxvii, xxix, 157–8.

Traulus (1730), poem by JS: XII. xxvii.

Travel books: Gulliver criticizes, XI. 147, 233; and Gulliver's literary aims, XI. 291–3; JS's reading of, XI. xiv–xvi and notes.

Travels Into Several Remote Nations of the World: *see* GULLIVER'S TRAVELS.

Travendal (*i.e.*, Traventhal, near Lübeck, Germany), Treaty of (1700): VI. 62.

Treason: and God's mercy, IX. 239; ingratitude, IX. 239; terrible sin, IX. 239; unpardonable by nation, IX. 238; witness essential, IX. 188.

Treasurer, Lord: *see* GODOLPHIN; OXFORD, 1ST EARL OF.

Treasury Commissioners, English: and Newton's assay, X. 187–8.

Treatise on Good-Manners and Good-Breeding (published 1754), by JS: **IV. 213-8**; background, IV. xxxvi–xxxvii; publication, IV. xxxvi, 299; textual notes, IV. 299.

Trebatius Testa, Gaius, 1st century B.C., Roman jurist, friend of Cicero: I. 106 and *n.**.

Trent, Council of, 1545–63: not cautious, XIV. 33.

Trevelyan, George Macaulay, 1876–1962: *England under Queen Anne* (1930–34), III. xiii, *n.* 2, xxix, *n.* 4.

Trevor, Sir John, 1637–1717, judge and Speaker of the House of Commons: his education, XII. 47; and Irish national debt, XII. xxii.

Trevor, Thomas, Lord, 1658–1730, Chief Justice of the Common Pleas: and Oxford, VIII. 156; and Oxford's quarrel with Bolingbroke, VIII. 158.

Trezenii (*i.e.*, people of Troezen, Argolis, Greece): 'polite nation in Greece', I. 134.

'Tribnia' (anagram of 'Britain'): XI. 191.

Triennial Act (1641): and Charles I's ruin, V. 193–4.

Triennial Act (1693–4): and William III, V. 193–4.

'Trimmers': II. 32.

Trimnell, Charles, 1663–1723, tutor of 3rd Earl of Sunderland, later Bishop of Norwich, then of Winchester: VII. 9 and *n.**.

Tringham, Walter or William, vicar of Marden, Herefordshire: possibly 'a fanatical saint', V. 190.

Trinitarians: *see* CHRISTIANITY.

Trinity College, Cambridge: and Bentley, I. xxii, *n.**.

Trinity College, Dublin (T.C.D., University of Dublin): and Delany, XII. xxviii; and Dunkin, XIII. 188–9; folly and vice at, XII. 29; and Edward Forbes, II. 112; and repeal of Limitation Act, IX. 55; provostship (1710), III. 183–4; JS at, I. x; V. 192; JS's B.A. *speciali gratia*, V. 192; JS denied a fellowship, I. xi; — his fellowship project, XIII. 198; and *Tale of a Tub*, I. ix, xvi; and Wharton, III. 183–4.

Trinity, mystery of: adversaries wrong, IX. 167; belief required, IX. 162; Collins' attack ridiculed, IV. 34, 35; not conceivable, IX. 161; controversial, IX. 159; and deism, IX. 108–11; divine authority, IX. 110; doctrine fundamental, IV. 34, 35; doctrine stated, IX. 160; doctrine summarized, IX. 168; and freethinkers, IV. 48; 'an invention of statesmen and politicians', IV. 43; nominal Trinitarians, II. 27; origin, IX. 160; above reason, IX. 165; Stillingfleet on, IX. 79, *n.**; in *Tale of a Tub*, I. 4; and Tindal, II. 91; understanding, IV. 34.

Trinity, sermon on, by JS: **IX. 159-68**; analysis, IX. 102, 106, 107–11; composition, IX. 133–4, 137; textual notes, IX. 375–6; title-page facsimile, IX. 139.

Triple Alliance (1668) of England, Sweden and United Provinces: and Temple, I. 257, 259, 270.

Tripos of Terrae Filius at Trinity College, Dublin: *see* JONES, JOHN.

Tritical Essay upon the Faculties of the Mind (written *c.* 1707), by JS: **I. 246-51**; background, I. xxxv; date of composition, I. xxxv, 303; XIV. 49; dedication (possibly to Sir Andrew Fountaine), I. 246; textual notes, I. 303.

Tritons: pun upon, IV. 235.

Trojans: and palladium, IX. 269.

Troy: and Astyanax, IV. 234; and Homer, I. 211; IV. 232–3; and Ucalegon, IV. 234–5.

'Trueman, Andrew', pseudonym for a writer of *Letter from Some Farmers . . . Removing to the British Plantations*: one of the 'gentlemen', XII. 75–81; JS answers, XII. 85–90.

Truth and falsehood: and civil war, V. 63; Gulliver and Houyhnhnms, XI. 258; Houyhnhnms ignorant of lying, XI. 235, 240, 287; and law, XI. 248–51; lies useless in afterlife, XI. 195; political lies, III. 8–13; and reason, IX. 166; zeal untrustworthy, IX. 261.

Tuam, Archbishop of: *see* EDWARD SYNGE.

Tudor, Owen, *d.* 1461: tomb, V. 202.

Tugghe, Monsieur, French deputy of the magistrates of Dunkirk: his memorial to Queen Anne, VIII. 4, 18, 67; — answered by Steele, VIII. 8–12.

Tullus Hostilius, legendary King of Rome: I. 212.

Tully: *see* CICERO.

Tunbridge: *see* TONBRIDGE.

Turin, Battle of (1706): Emperor's negligence, VIII. 58.

Turk, Great: Jack drives off, I. 126.

Turkeys: XI. 106.

Turks: and Austria — war, III. 129; — war threat alleged (1711), VII. 59; and Collins, IV. 28; and the Crusades, V. 21; destruction, IX. 224–5; and divine law, XII. 244; English alliance with, II. 38; and free-thinkers, IV. 33; government longlived, VIII. 180; and Henry IV of France, I. 103; and Ireland — invasion absurd, XII. 260; religion of, IV. 32; and religious freedom, II. 89, 115; IV. 39; cruelty of Grand Signior, III. 205; slaves, IV. xxxiv, 209.

'Turn in': 'go to bed', XI. 144.

Turner, Francis, *c.* 1638–1700, Bishop of Ely: and JS, I. xiii; attacks Tindal, II. xviii, *n.* 2.

'Turpis': mock-etymology, IV. 232.

Tuscany: Austria to have, VII. 133; cardinal from, to be pope (hoax), II. 148.

Tutchin, John, *c.* 1661–1707, Whig pamphleteer: 'Observator' on Drogheda affair, II. 282; 'Observator' a liar, II. 113. *See also* OBSERVATOR.

'Tutoress': directions to, XIII. 65.

Tweed River, between Scotland and England: royal army crosses (1688), V. 161; satire imported from Scotland, I. 29; and true Scots, XII. 275.

Twelve Tables (ancient Roman legal code): I. 215.

Twickenham, Middlesex, near London: Pope's house, XIII. 201.

Twysden, Sir Roger, 2nd Bart., 1597–1672: *Historiae anglicanae scriptores decem*, and JS's history, V.x.

Tyburn, London: and execution of state criminals, IV. 283; VIII. 190.

Tynemouth, Northumberland: William II captures, V. 21.

Tyranny: I. 197–236; Caesars and successors, IX. 33; natural in kings, IV. 244; one tyrant better than many, I. 250; unjustifiable, IX. 229; and Wood's coins, X. 86–7, 104–5, 126–7, and *passim*.

Tyrawley, Charles O'Hara, 1st Lord, *c.* 1640–1724, general: Macky and JS on, V. 261.

Tyrconnel, Richard Talbot, Earl and titular Duke of, 1630–91: and Temple, V. 291.

Tyrone, county of Ireland: Creichton settles there, V. 180.

Tyrone, Hugh O'Neill, 2nd Earl of, *c.* 1550–1616: his rebellion, X. 10, 38, 40.

Tyrrell, Walter: *see* TIREL.

Tyson, Edward, 1650–1708, physician: possibly, 'a virtuoso', II. 76.

U

Ucalegon, Trojan leader, character in *Aeneid*: pun on name, IV. 234–5.

Ulm, Germany, on the Danube: 'conquered' by Britain, VI. 38.

Ulster, province of Ireland: New Plantation: *see* DUNKIN; Scottish Presbyterian settlers, V. 271; XII. 78; — 'encroachments', IX. 10; tithes in, XII. 78.

Ulysses: and Polyphemus, I. 249.

Union, Act of: *see* SCOTLAND.

Unitarians: *see* HERESIES.

United Provinces: *see* DUTCH.

'Universal pickle': holy water, I. 67–8.

Universities: bill for encouragement of learning (1710), III. 37;

Burnet and JS on, V. 286; conversation about, IV. 89; discipline wanting, II. 51–2; education defended, IX. 78–9; XII. 49, 51–2; and English language, IV. 12–13; and Ned Fashion, II. 186–7; and George I, V. 286; and holy orders, III. 37; VI. 130; and the Irish, X. 128; and Irish economy, XII. 9; language in, II. 176–7; and young nobility, II. 52; III. 150–1; VI. 125; VIII. 38; Oxford University's decree of 1683, III. 144; praised, IV. 227–8; Steele on, VIII. 37–8; and Tindal, II. 103; Whigs revile, III. 150–1.

'Untah' (Laputan word for 'governor'): XI. 162.

Upon Giving Badges to the Poor (written 1726), by JS: **XIII. 172–3**; background, XIII. xxxviii–xxxix; textual notes, XIII. 224. *See also* PROPOSAL FOR GIVING BADGES TO THE BEGGARS.

Upton, Anthony, *d.* 1718 (suicide), Justice of the Common Pleas of Ireland (1702–14): and Whitshed, X. 164.

Urban II, Pope, *c.* 1042–1099: and the Crusades, V. 21.

Uriel, character in *Paradise Lost*: and hypocrisy, V. xvii.

Urry (or Hurry), Sir John, *d.* 1650, Scottish royalist soldier: 'a miracle', V. 303.

Ursa Major: tavern sign, XII. 224.

Utica: *see* CATO.

Utopia: and enthusiasm, I. 174; and Houyhnhnmland, XI. 8; and truth, I. 248.

Utrecht, city of Netherlands:

professor on Bickerstaff, II. 161.

Utrecht, province of United Provinces of the Netherlands: accepts new Barrier Treaty (1712), VII. 157; declares for peace, VI. 167.

Utrecht, Treaty or Peace of (1713), ending War of the Spanish Succession (involving, as the main participants, Britain, the United Provinces, Austria, France, Spain): allegory (fire extinguished), XI. 56; Allies' last meeting (1713), VII. 162–3; Anne's speech(1712), VII. 130–4; Austria — barrier for, VII. 50; — British coercion (1711), VII. 54–6; — bypassed (1713), VII. 164; — false compliance, VII. 157; — peace obstructed, VII. 119, 136–7; — among late signatories, VII. 158, 163, 165–7; and Barrier Treaty: *see* BARRIER TREATY; Bavaria — and Duke of Savoy, VII. 60, 148; Britain's leadership, VI. 57; letter to Buys (1711), VII. 56, 203–5; Catalonia, VII. 40; VIII. 61–3; cessation of arms (1712), VII. 148; colonies, VII. 43, 48–9; Treaty of Commerce (with France), VII. 160, 165; — begun (1712), VII. 131; — defeated, VII. xi; — opposed by Allies, VII. 157; — projected, VII. 43, 48, 114; — ratified, VII. 167; Commons informed, VII. 31; conference (or congress) — to be called (1711), VII. 37; — announced, VII. 60; — begun, VII. 117; consequences, V. 113; closing date, VII. 112; initial demands, VII. 112–13; demands

of Allies (1711), VI. 88; VII. 42–4, 183–4; — French reply, VII. 44–9, 184–7; doubts concerning, VIII. 71; and Dunkirk, VI. 88; VII. 43, 48–9, 55, 114, 125, 132, 137, 139–43;

Dutch — alliance proposed (1711), VII. 56; — Assiento, VII. 117, 123; VIII. 170–1; — and Austria, VII. 118, 124; — barrier: *see* BARRIER, DUTCH; — and Cambrai, VII. 135; — compliance, VII. 57–8, 60, 160–1; — and Condé, VII. 161; — deceitful, VII. 38, 63, 157; — delays, VI. 167; VII. 34, 59–60, 118, 121–2, 124, 154, 156, 163–6; — demands, VII. 120, 153; — John Drummond ('a gentleman') on, VIII. 171; — French and British suspected, VII. 38, 39, 41, 42, 54, 56–7, 108–9, 121–2; — French distrust them, VII. 35–6; — good faith toward (1711), VII. 52–3, 54, 116, 122; — humble letter (1713), VII. 160–1; — informed of plans, VII. 111–12; — and Lorraine, VII. 42; — opposition to peace, VI. 166–8; VII. 23, 39–40, 145, 166; — pressed to negotiate (1711), VII. 59, 119, 120; — separate peace sought with France, VI. 47, 57; VII. 36, 38–42, 46, 118, 121, 124, 143, 152–3, 157, 159; — sign, VII. 166; — and Tournai, VII. 153–5;

England's leadership, VII. 35–8, 41, 44–5, 54, 56–7, 61, 124, 145, 153, 166; — Dutch resentment, VII. 23–4, 40–2, 52–3, 56, 57, 118, 124, 126, 157; Flemish towns occupied, VII. 142;

France — accepts terms (1713), VII. 162; — Assiento (1711), VII. 43, 48, 115, 132; — difficulties with Dutch, VI. 12; VII. 36, 39, 154, 158–9, 165; — and English politics, VII. 154; — final pressure on, VII. 161–3; — first proposals (1711, confused with 'those proposals' of 1709–10), VII. 36–7, 41; — first proposals and Dutch queries, VII. 2–3, 37–9, 41, 52, 55–7; — negotiations with England begin (1711), VII. 12–13; — overtures (1710), VII. 35–6; VIII. 163; — passports, VII. 60; — plenipotentiaries (1711), VII. 60; — preliminary articles (1711), VI. 166–7; VII. 49–52; — war party, VII. 46;

Gertruydenburg ('two years ago') contrasted, VI. 59; Gibraltar, VII. 43, 45, 48, 115, 119, 132; and Hanoverian Succession, VIII. 169–71; Hudson's Bay, VII. 43, 49, 114, 132; Kehl, VII. 113, 132; Louis XIV favours, VII. 44, 45; and Marlborough, VII. 38; Ménager, VII 46–8, 52, 117, 143, 154, 158–9; ministers (plenipotentiaries), VII. 60, 112, 162, 165, 198; — appointed, VII. 63; — instructions, VII. 111–15, 155–6, 212–18; Minorca, VII. 115, 132; Newfoundland, VII. 43, 49, 114, 132; Nova Scotia, VII. 115, 132; Port-Mahon, VII. 43, 48, 119–20, 132; Portugal: *see* PORTUGAL; and Pretender, VII. 114, 158, 165; VIII. 169–70; Prior: *see* PRIOR; proclaimed, VII. 167; ratified, VI. 127; VII. 167;

recess (1712), VII. 149; Rhine fortresses, VII. 132; St. Christopher, VII. 131–2; secretary, VII. 118;

separate peace (between France and England), III. xxxii; VI. 57; VII. 12–13, 15, 43–4, 117, 119, 120, 125–9, 132, 138, 145, 154, 156, 158, 160–3; — Anne resents charge, VII. 53; — and Buys, VII. 57; — denied, VII. 31, 41, 47, 52–3, 54, 111–12, 116; — Dutch concern, VI. viii; VII. 2–3, 37, 49, 52–6, 63; — opposed, VI. x; — prohibited, VI. 47; — reasons, VII. 35–8, 49, 51, 53, 56, 127–9; — secrecy needed, VII. 51; — suspension of arms reveals, VII. 126–7; — *see also* WAR OF THE SPANISH SUCCESSION, *Ormonde's 'restraining orders'*;

signing of, VII. 162–6; — late signatories, VII. 158, 163–6; site, VII. 52, 54, 60; Somers opposes, VII. 6; Somerset opposes, VII. 15; Spain — Treaty of Commerce, VI. 117; Strafford — dinner, VII. 166; — instructions, VII. 52–5, 116, 198–203; and JS, IV. xvi, xx; and JS's *History of the Four Last Years*, VII. xi, xv; and Tariff of 1664: *see* TARIFF OF 1664; Torcy, VII. 45–6; Tournai, VI. 31, 101, 109; VII. 136, 153–5, 159; Trarbach, VIII. 59; and Whigs: *see* WHIGS.

Uxbridge, Middlesex: and Glorious Revolution, V. 163.

Uxelles (or Huxelles), Nicolas du Blé, marquis d', 1652–1730, French marshal: and Treaty of

Utrecht, VII. 60; — 'his col-league' (i.e., Uxelles) delays, VII. 165; — favours Dutch, VII. 143; — and Ménager, VII. 159.

V

Vails (or vales): for chambermaid, XIII. 52; face guest, XIII. 24–5; few for footman, XIII. 33; line up to get, XIII. 12–13; stranger's servants assisted, XIII. 49.

Vairasse d'Allais, Denis, *L'Histoire des Sévarambes* (1677–9), XI. xv.

Valencia, Spain: and Lord Galway, VI. 37.

Valenciennes, Nord, France: and Dutch Barrier, VI. 101, 109; VII. 113.

Valengin (*i.e.*, Valangin), Neuchâtel, Switzerland: Prussia secures, VII. 113.

Valentia: *see* VALENZA.

Valentines: III. 77.

Valentini, an Italian singer (male contralto, London career, 1707–15): and trimmers, II. 32.

Valenza (Valentia), Italy: and Duke of Savoy: VI. 13.

Valet, duties of: beds, XIII. 164–5; boots, XIII. 165; cooking, XIII. 164; at inns, XIII. 163–5; packing, XIII. 164.

Vandals: destroy civilization, IX. 50; invade Rome, IV. 8; V. 3.

Vanderdussen, Bruno, 1660–1741, Dutch plenipotentiary: and Petkum, VII. 40; and separate peace of French and Dutch, VII. 40–1.

Van Diemen's Land (Tasmania):

and Gulliver's voyages, XI. 20, 78; on map, XI. 18.

Van Dyck, Sir Anthony, 1599–1641, painter: picture of Charles I, XIII. 155.

Vane, Sir Henry, 1613–62, statesman: Burnet and JS on, V. 270.

Vanessa: *see* VANHOMRIGH, ESTHER.

Van Gheel, Cornelius, Lord of Spanbrock Bulkesteyn, Dutch plenipotentiary: and Barrier Treaty, VI. 99.

'Vangrult, Theodorus' (ship's captain in *Gulliver's Travels*): XI. 217.

Vanhomrigh, Ginkell, *c.* 1694–1710, brother of Vanessa: and JS's treaty with Anne Long, V. xxiv, 197–8.

Vanhomrigh, Esther (or Hester), 1688–1723, JS's friend 'Vanessa': sees *Gulliver's Travels* (1722), XI. xvii; and JS's *History of the Four Last Years*, VII. xi–xii; letter to (July 1713), VIII. ix; — (July 1722), V. xxxii; Anne Long and 'Hessy', V. 197–8.

Vanhomrigh, Hester (*née* Stone), *d.* 1714, Vanessa's mother: V. 197–8.

Vanini, Giulio Cesare, *c.* 1585–1619: *De admirandis naturae reginae deaeque mortaliim arcanis* (1616), IV. 267.

'Vapours': I. 102–14. *See also* SPLEEN.

'Vardi': verdict, XIII. 136.

Various Thoughts, Moral and Diverting: *see* THOUGHTS ON VARIOUS SUBJECTS (1711).

Varro, Marcus Terentius, 116–27

B.C., erudite Roman author: and free-thinking, IV. 43.

Vaughan, Sir John, 1603–74, Chief Justice of the Common Pleas: on juries, X. 161.

Vaughan, Thomas (pseudonym, Eugenius Philalethes), 1622–66, alchemist and poet: *Anima magica abscondita*, I. 119 and *n.**; *Anthroposophia theomagica*, I. 79 and *n.* †, 119 and *n.**.

Venereal disease: almanac remedies, II. 143; and nobility, XI. 256; and prostitutes, XI. 253; and sailors, XI. 244.

Veneti, Roman faction: II. 32.

Venice, Italy: aristocracy, II. 14; government, III. 122; XI. 138; mercenary soldiers, III. 41.

Venlo, Limburg, Netherlands: and Barrier Treaty, VI. 115.

Venner, Thomas, *d.* 1661, Fifth Monarchist: Burnet on, V. 269.

Venus: mourns for Cowley, I. 159; and Diomedes, IV. 233; and Ixion, V. 323; and Juno, IV. 247; and Mars, IV. 165; 'Venus', a mistress, I. 32 and *n.**.

Vere, family of: VIII. 135.

Vereilles, John: X. 76.

Vergil, Polydore: *see* VIRGIL.

Vernon, Mrs. (probably the wife of James): and Erasmus Lewis, VI. 173.

Vernon, Edward, 1684–1757, admiral: *Considerations upon the White Herring and Cod Fisheries* (1749), XIII. xxxii.

Vernon, James, 1646–1727, Secretary of State (1697–1700): his education, XII. 47.

Verres, Gaius, *d.* 43 B.C., governor of Sicily: name a pseudonym for Wharton, III. xix, 26–9.

Versailles, France: Bassin de Neptune, XI. 120; magnificence, III. 213–14; Matthew Prior received (1711), III. 214–17; VII. 44.

Verses Made for Women Who Cry Apples, by JS: XII. xxxiv.

Verses on the Death of Dr. Swift (written 1731, published 1739), by JS: and Queen Caroline, XII. xxxv; composition, XII. xxxiii; Lady Suffolk, V. xxviii.

Verstegen (or Vorstigan), pseudonym for Richard Rowlands, *fl.* 1565–1620, antiquary: on English language, IV. 231.

Vesey, John, 1638–1716, Archbishop of Tuam: on Irish trade ('Burn everything English'), IX. 17, 269–70.

Vespasian (Titus Flavius Vespasianus), A.D. 9–79, Roman emperor: compared to Henry VII, IX. 49–50.

Vestments, liturgical: XI. 246.

Veturia, 5th Century B.C., mother of Coriolanus: V. 86.

Vicars choral of St. Patrick's Cathedral, **JS's letter to** (1742): **XIII. 196–7**; background, XIII. xliii–xliv; textual note, XIII. 225.

Vice: and atheism, II. 37–8, 70; IX. 165; and heresy, IX. 171; honour does not check, IX. 153; brotherly love opposes, IX. 174; mortality does not check, IX. 152; religion opposes, IX. 157; and success, IX. 155. *See also* SIN.

Victor I, St., Pope, *d.* A.D. 199: and Scotland, XIV. 20.

Victor Amadeus II, Duke of Savoy Piedmont, 1666–1732: Anne favours him, VII. 59, 133, 148; and Austria, VI. 52–3; VII. 164; — dispute over campaigns (1704–5), VI. 35–6; — treaty (1703), VI. 35; barrier, VII. 133; VIII. 63; his duchess: *see* ANNA MARIA; and Dublin street cries, XII. 227–8; Dutch asked to support, VII. 156; and English crown, VIII. 54–5; joins Grand Alliance, VI. 13; greatest power in Italy, VIII. 64; Louis XIV alleged to favour, VIII. 63–4; and Louis XIV allied by marriage, VI. 52; gains Sicily (1713), VII. 155; VIII. 54; removes to Sicily (1714), VIII. 64; and attack on Toulon, VI. 35; and Treaty of Utrecht, VI. 167; VII. 43, 45, 59, 60, 156; — delays peace (1711), VII. 59–60; — gains in, VIII. 63; and War of Spanish Succession — interests in, VI. 13; VII. 114; — campaign in Italy (1711), VI. 35–6; — risk slight, VI. 13.

Victoria, Queen of England, 1819–1901: manuscript of JS's *History of the Four Last Years,* VII. xxiii.

Victoria and Albert Museum: *see* FORSTER COLLECTION.

Victorinus Afer, Fabius Marius, 4th century A.D., Christian grammarian: edition of Cicero, IV. 267; and free-thinking, IV. 38.

Victualling Office: accounts (1712), VII. 77.

Vienna, Austria: letters from (1712), VII. 124; ministers of

court at, VI. 23, 113; VII. 55; Peterborough at, VI. 35; plague at, VIII. 61; JS may take a post there (1708), II. xxi; and Whigs, III. 226; Whitworth at, VI. 36.

Vigevenasco, region around Vigevano, Pavia, northern Italy: Savoy to secure, VI. 13.

Vigilius, Pope, *d.* 555: and 2nd Council of Constantinople, XIV. 34; election irregular, XIV. 32.

Vigo, Spanish seaport: and Ormonde, VIII. 133; — possible allusion to (in capture of fleet of Blefuscu), XI. 52; Portugal to secure, VI. 25.

Villars, Claude, duc de, 1653–1734, Marshal of France: captures Albemarle, VII. 146–7; letter to Ormonde, VII. 152; and Ormonde's 'restraining orders', VII. 126, 135, 138; and Dunkirk, VII. 137, 143.

Villeinage ('villanage'): abolished, I. 230.

Vindication of His Excellency the Lord Carteret (1730), by JS: **XII. 150-69**; background, XII. xxiv–xxix; composition, XII. 153, 168; errata, XIV. 57; textual notes, XII. 337–9; XIV. 57; title-page facsimiles, XII. 150–1.

Vindication of Isaac Bickerstaff (1709), by JS: **II. 157-64**; background, II. xxiv, 225; erratum, XIV. 51; publication, II. 286–7; reception foreseen, II. 162; and *Tatler* no. 1, II. xxvi; textual notes, II. 287–8; title-page facsimile, II. 157.

A Vindication of the Protestant Dissenters from the Aspersions

Cast upon Them in . . . the Presby-terians Plea of Merit (not by JS): XII. xliv–xlv.

Viner, Charles, 1678–1756, jurist: *Abridgement of Law and Equity* (1742–53) printed in his house, XIII. 207; Vinerian Professor-ship (Oxford), XIII. 207.

Vineyard, JS's: *see* NABOTH'S VINEYARD.

Violante, Madam, Italian rope-dancer: XII. 156 and *n*.*.

Virgil: and Corusodes, XII. 41–2; Cotton's travesty, IV. 274; and Dryden — and Wither, I. 146; Dryden's translation — armour exchanged, I. 157–8; — dedica-tions, I. 43; — and fashion, I. 22; enemies immortalized, V. 201; great figure, V. xi, 84; immor-tality, I. 242; JS translates, I. xii; JS wiser, V. xxv, 201; and authorship of *Tatler*, II. xxvi, *n*. 1; Temple's translations, I. 262; correct text, IV. 33; theatre audience venerates, V. 84; and *Tobit*, I. 244; works personified, I. 139.

Quotations and allusions: *Aeneid* I. 48–9 ('Who then'): I. 154; — I. 135: III. 149; — I. 148–53: VIII. 43–4; — I. 204–5: II. 243; — I. 341–2: III. 3; — I. 412 ('vanished in a mist'): I. 155; — I. 461–2: III. 116; — I. 567–8: IX. 29; — I. 460: IV. 249; — II. 49: VI. 189; — II. 79–80: XI. 292; — II. 98–9: IV. 53–5; — II. 297: I. 98; — II. 521–2: III. 35; — II. 729 (misquoted ironically): VII. 29; — IV. 176: VI. 173; — IV. 178–9 ('last offspring'): III. 9;

— V. 194–5: X. 77; — V. 525–8 (not Evander but Acestes): I. 152; — VI. 128–9: I. 33; — VI. 648–9: III. 152; — VI. 893–6: IV. 252; —VII. 641–8 ('Say, Goddess'): I. 156; — IX. 340–1: II. 178; — IX. 446–9 ('loving pair'): I. 165; — X. 63: I. 51; — XI. 794–5 ('scattered in the air'): I. 163; — XI. 848–9: III. 110; — XI. 849–51 (tomb): I. 161; — XII. 899–900: I. 159; *Apud Donati vitam* 17: XII. 54; *Eclogues* IV. 34–5: II. 148; — VIII. 80: XII. 225; — IX. 2–4: II. 257; — IX. 30: III. 36; *Georgics* I. 123: IV. 245; — I. 505–6: III. 29; — III. 226–7: X. 119; — III. 463 (misquoted): XII. 178; — IV. 87: I. 69; — IV. 440–2 ('thou-sand forms'): I. 150; — IV. 549–56: V. 327–8.

Virgil, Polydore, 1470–1555, historian: leads infantry of Moderns, I. 152; on nobility ('nec vir fortis, etc.'), XI. 198; 'one author' on origins of Parliament ('consilium principum'), V. 36.

Virginia, U.S.A.: emigration to, XII. 76.

Virginia, legendary Roman maiden, killed by her father to save her chastity: 'lady of great virtue', I. 198.

Virginity: real and professed, II. 180–3.

Virtue: advancement of, II. 43–63; in antiquity, IX. 155; and King of Brobdingnag, XI. 135; and conscience, IX. 155, 158; disinterested virtue impossible, IX. 113; and happiness, IX. 155; and honour, IX. 116, 153;

nature of Houyhnhnms, XI. 267; idleness destroys, IX. 196; philosophers disagree, IX. 244; poetry ignores, IX. 329; and reason, IX. 154; its own reward, IX. 244; JS's proposal for, XIV. 14–15; wealth unnecessary, IX. 194–5.

Virtues of Sid Hamet the Magician's Rod (1710), poem by JS: and Godolphin, II. xxxix; III. x, xvi.

Vitalian, *d.* 519, rebellious Gothic chief: Justin kills, XIV. 29.

'Volpone': Sacheverell's pseudonym for Godolphin, VII. 9.

Voltaire: *An Essay upon the Civil Wars of France* (Dublin 1728), JS's preface, V. 109; — textual note, V. 351; title-page facsimile, facing V. 108; JS's account of, V. 109; JS meets (1727), XII. ix.

Voraginus, Jacobus (Iacopo da Varazze), *c.* 1228–98, Italian hagiographer, author of *Golden Legend*: IX. 283.

Vorstigan: *see* VERSTEGEN.

Vortigern, *fl.* 450, the prince of south-east Britain: made king, V. 4.

Vossius, Gerard John, 1577–1649, Dutch scholar and theologian: fights for the Ancients, I. 152.

'Vox populi, vox dei': I. 225.

Voyage de Maroc: XI. xiv.

Voyage de Syam: XI. xiv.

Voyage into England, by a Person of Quality in Terra Australis Incognita, Translated from the Original: imaginary treatise by the author of *Tale of a Tub*: I. xl.

Voyages and Discoveries in South America: XI. xiv.

W

Waas, Pays de (north-east corner of Flanders): Dutch to control, VI. 28.

Wadlington, Mrs.: sees comets, IV. 207.

Wafer, Lionel, *c.* 1660–*c.* 1705, buccaneer: *New Voyage and Description of the Isthmus of America*, XI. xiv.

'Wagstaff, Humphry', a character in Harrison's *Tatler*, No. 1: II. 251.

'Wagstaff, Simon', pseudonym for JS in *Polite Conversation*: IV. 97–124; significance of name, IV. xxix–xxx; deserves reward, IV. 119–22; table book, IV. xxxiii.

Wagstaffe, William, 1685–1725, physician: and *The Character of Richard St——le*, VIII. xiv–xv.

'Waiting maid' (in *Directions to Servants*): XIII. 56–60; assignations, XIII. 59; and chaplain, XIII. 57; and footman, XIII. 59; her lady's lovers, XIII. 58–60; and her master, XIII. 57; perquisites, XIII. 56; and eldest son, XIII. 58; and tea, XIII. 56–7; and valet, XIII. 57.

Wake, William, 1657–1737, Archbishop of Canterbury: letter from Bishop Evans, XIV. xiv; letter from Bishop Nicolson, X. xxx–xxxi and *n.* 1.

Waleff ('Wales'), Blaise-Henri de Corte, baron de, 1652–1734, Belgian poet and general; colonel of regiment of dragoons of Liège: follows Ormonde, VII. 140–1.

Wales: and education, IV. 228;

Henry I puts down rebellion, V.
34–5; and justice, X. 82; early
kings, V. 5; Prince of, as title,
V. 40; JS in Holyhead, V. 201–8;
William II, V. 19–20, 23.

Wales, Count: *see* WALEFF.

Walker, George, 1618–90, governor of Londonderry: V. 290.

Walker, John, 1674–1747, ecclesiastical historian: *An Attempt
towards Recovering an Account of
the Numbers and Sufferings of the
Clergy of the Church of England*
(1714), 'another in folio', V.
188–9.

Walker, Richard: Dublin grand
jury (1724), X. 76.

Waller, Edmund, 1606–87, poet:
pun upon his name, IV. 274.

Wallis, John, 1616–1703, mathematician: deciphering skill and
free-thinking, IV. 34.

Walls, Thomas, *c.* 1672–1750,
Archdeacon of Achonry, master
of St. Patrick's School, friend of
JS: letters from JS — (Nov.
1708), II. xxi; — (Oct. 1713),
VII. 181; — (Feb. 1714), VIII.
xvi; — (Mar. 1714), VIII.
xxiii.

Walpole, Horace or Horatio, 1st
Lord Walpole of Wolterton,
1678–1757, diplomat, brother
of Sir Robert Walpole: ambassador to France, XII. 48; 'secretary to the embassy' at Gertruydenburg, VI. 50; VII. 33; secretary to Lord Lieutenant of
Ireland, thanks grand jury, XII.
122.

Walpole, Horace, 1717–97 (became 4th Earl of Orford in 1791),
author: his *Catalogue of Royal*

and Noble Authors printed at his
own press (1758), XIII. 207.

Walpole, Sir Robert, 1st Earl of
Orford, 1676–1745, Secretary at
War (1708–10), Chancellor of
the Exchequer, Prime Minister:
to 'blush' for his party's errors,
III. 86, 222; and Bolingbroke's
Occasional Letters, V. xii; the
Brazen Head his sign, V. 97;
St. John Brodrick and Wood's
coins, X. 99; Burnet and JS on,
V. 294; character, V. xiv–xv; —
('a private person'), V. 97;
JS's character of, V. 101–2;
VII. 65; bribes House of Com-
mons, V. 105; expelled from
Commons (1712), VII. 65;
Compton (Lord Wilmington)
hates him, V. 103; corruption,
V. xiv–xv, 102, 111–12; VII. 65;
defends corruption, V. 105–7;
debts of '13' (possible allusion),
VI. 145; and *Drapier's Letters*,
X. xviii–xix; his education, XII.
47–8; management of elections,
V. 103, 105–6, 107; Flimnap, in
Gulliver's Travels, partly modelled
on, XI. xix, 38–72; and John
Gay, XII. 34 and *n.**, 35; and
George I, V. 101; — 'corrupted
ministry' (possible allusion), XI.
130; — governs George I
('favourite'), XI. 66; and George
II. V. 103–7; — George II re-
lieved of duties, V. 106; his
informers, V. xii, 95; XI. 65;
his journalists, V. 94–6, 111,
112–13, 117–18; and Duchess of
Kendal, XI. xix; — 'cushion',
XI. 39; 'Lelop-Aw' as pseudonym, V. 97–107; *A Letter
from the Right Honourable Sir*

R. *W. to the Right Honourable W. P. Esq.* — authorship, V. 111; ostentation, V. 101; Oxford contrasted with, V. 113; political dexterity ('Flimnap'), XI. 38–9; attacked as prime minister, V. xvii; and Pulteney — *The Answer of . . . Pulteney to . . . Walpole* (probably by JS), V. xv–xvi, 111–19; moves 'no peace without Spain' (Dec. 1711), VII. 18; probably 'Stentor of the Chappell', III. 223; and Lady Suffolk, V. 213; **and JS** — attacked by JS in *Account of Japan*, V. xiv; — speaks against JS, X. 102; — JS 'never offended' him, V. xv; — preferment in England, V. xiii; and Tories — their enemy, V. 101; — ignores their criticism, V. 117; sent to the Tower, VII. 65; breach of trust (1712), V. 101; VII. 65; Whig ties, VII. 65; Wood claims his support, X. 67–8; and Wood's coins — will force them on Ireland, X. xvii, 67–8; patent supposedly withdrawn, X. 63; — Walpole's responsibility, X. 102–3.

Walsh, William, 1663–1708, poet and critic: praised, I. 249.

Walter (or Walters), Sir John, Bart., *c.* 1673–1722, M.P. for Oxford: coat of 'J. W.', I. 52.

Walter, Lady, wife of Sir John Walter, Bart.: and Erasmus Lewis, VI. 173.

Walter (or Walters), Peter, *c.* 1664–1746, dishonest attorney and land steward: XII. 306; Walpole compared to, V. 117.

Walters, Mr.: and juries, X. 161.

Wapping, Thameside suburb of London: Gulliver moves to, XI. 20.

War: causes of a just war, VI. 7–8; causes satirized, I. 102–4, 141–2; confederate war analysed, VI. 8–9; endurance and victory, VI. 61; horrors described, XI. 245–8; inevitable consequence of human nature, VI. 55; past and present, I. 241; peace as aim, III. 61–2; and providence, III. 140–1; and public revenues, XII. 6; religious wars absurd, XI. 49–50, 246; and royal prerogative, VI. 165; X. 33; and trade, XII. 6, 8; satirized in Yahoos, XI. 260–1.

War of the League of Ausgburg, 1689–97 (the main parties, England, Spain, Austria, and the United Provinces, against France and her allies): and Bavaria, VI. 14; causes, VI. 10–11; and Cologne, VI. 14; Convention Parliament opposes, VII. 68; cost excessive, VI. 11; origin of national debt, VI. 10; VII. 68; England's part, VI. 10–11; French success doubtful, VI. 61; length unexpected, VII. 68; results negligible, VI. 11, 16; and Spain, VI. 14; success doubtful, VI. 14; William III's responsibility, VI. 11.

War of the Spanish Succession, 1701–13 (the main parties, England, Austria, and the United Provinces against France and Spain): Allies desert (1712), VII. 127, 135–40, 146–7; VIII. 57; armistice declared (1712), VII. 141; — Dutch accept, VII.

152–4, 157; — Dutch oppose, VII. 135–7, 140, 143, 146–9, 152; — foreseen, VII. 137; — promised, VII. 125; — proposed, VII. 135–7;

Austria: would continue war (1711–13), VI. 36; VII. 25, 136–7, 156–7, 164; VIII. 57–8; effort to slacken (1711), VI. 56–7; increased effort asked, VII. 89–90; deserts England (1712), VII. 127; England helps, VI. 38, 87; gains from war, VI. 38, 50, 57; VII. 89; German princes fail to support, VI. 14, 62; interests in Italy, VI. 33–4; Marlborough defends, VII. 163; Marlborough rewarded by, VI. 34; seizes Naples (1707), VI. 34–5; selfishness, VI. 34–5; and crown of Spain, VII. 86; subsidies, VI. 33; and Toulon, VI. 34–5; treachery, VII. 137, 163;

campaign (1712), VII. 31; — funds voted, VII. 25; — money lacking, VI. 54–56, 64, 124; Castile (1706), VII. 85; casualties, XI. 245, 247; and Collins, IV. 28; cost, VI. 18–19, 31–3, 37–9, 54–9; VII. 82–90; and national debt, III. 135; VI. 53–9; VII. 3, 22, 71–8; declaration of war (1702), VI. 12–13, 16–17, 45–6;

Dutch: oppose armistice, VII. 135–7, 146–9, 152; — accept armistice, VII. 153–4, 157; burden second to England's, VI. 95; would continue war, VI. 49, 89; VII. 23, 36, 166; VIII. 57; declaration of war (1702), VI. 12, 45–6; increased effort asked (1712), VII. 89–90, 96; England

aided, III. 73; English troops requested (1701), VI. 17; turn against English army (1712), VII. 141; England renounced (1712), VII. 128–9; fight without England (1712), VII. 33, 152; restrain Eugene (1712), VIII. 57–8; finances, VII. 153; and Flanders, VI. 31, 38, 61, 94; VII. 84; French terms rejected (1709), VII. 32; French defeat them (1712), VII. 33; at mercy of French, VII. 149; gains from war, VI. 20–1, 57, 60–1; VII. 84, 89; interests in war, VI. 8–19, 49; VII. 81; and mercenaries, VII. 127, 138–9; and Ormonde, VII. 138–42; — oppose his troops, XIV. 13; peace efforts (1709), VII. 33; and Portugal, VI. 26; and Quebec expedition (1711), VI. 23–4; to slacken effort (1711), VI. 56–7; and campaigns in Spain, VI. 37, 94; VII. 85–7, 110; and Spanish Netherlands, VI. 38; subsidies not paid, VI. 32, 33, 37; VII. 87; tired of war (1711), VI. 57; VII. 153;

England — abused by Allies, VI. 5–65; — expense of war, XIV. 4; England's interests, VI. 8–19; — her quotas and her compensation, VI. 57; VII. 53–6, 61, 90, 109–110, 128–9, 131–4; England weakened by war, III. 7; VI. 53–9; financing of war, VII. 80, 82, 83, 86–8; — Genoese loan, VI. 32; — Marlborough's deduction, VII. 96; — no new taxes, VII. 71; Flanders — campaigns, VI. 20, 30, 60–2; VII. 141–2; — Marlborough's avarice ('Mesopotamia'), III.

83–5; — successes not exploited, III. 62;

France: defeats Allies (1712), VII. 33, 146–7, 152, 154; divides Allies, VII. 41–2; Dutch threatened (1700), VI. 12; alliance with England following peace, VIII. 169–71; seizes Milan (1701), VI. 12; moneyless (1711), VI. 23, 60–2; navy, VI. 60; VII. 83; eager for peace (1709–10), VI. 60; rallied by peace terms (1709), VII. 33; privateers, VI. 60; will recover easily, III. 7; and Duke of Savoy, VII. 43; seizes Spanish Netherlands (1701), VI. 12; and Spanish West Indies, VI. 60; war party, VII. 46, 160, 166; weakened by war (1714), VIII. 59;

and free-thinkers, IV. 31; Godolphin opposes war, VI. 11; historical parallel (Henry I and Louis VI), V. 32–3; honour lost, VI. 25, 29, 40; Hungarian troops, VII. 58–9; and Ireland, III. 177; Italy, VI. 29, 33–4; VII. 88–9; — diversion in Italy (1711), VI. 35–7; mercenary troops, VI. 14, 30, 32, 33, 39; VII. 65–6, 127, 135–9; money exported, III. 7; and moral reform, II. 57; navy neglected, VI. 22–3; VII. 84; and Northern War, VI. 62–4; Ormonde's 'restraining orders', VII. 122, 125–9, 135–9; — and armistice (JS's deliberate confusion), VIII. 57; — Dutch complain, VII. 127; — England denies, VII. 140; — Eugene marches (1712), VII. 140; — and Robinson, VII. 127–8; — Steele on, VIII. 15; and Partition Treaties: *see* PARTITION TREATY; peace negotiations: *see* GERTRUYDENBERG; HAGUE; UTRECHT, TREATY OF; Portugal: *see* PORTUGAL; and Pretender, VI. 12–13; and JS's *Proposal for Correcting . . . the English Tongue*, IV. 6; Prussia: *see* PRUSSIA; Quebec expedition (1711), VI. 23;

quotas, VI. 21–2, 29–30; VII. 12, 25–6, 78, 78–80, *et passim*; — Austria fails to fulfil, VI. 33, 34, 36, 37; VII. 25–6, 86, 89, 115, 137, 166; VIII. 58; — to be changed (1711), VII. 54–5; — Dutch fail to fulfil, VI. 26, 30, 32; VII. 57, 59, 78, 83–7, *et passim*; — in Flanders, VII. 85; naval, VI. 31–2; — in Portugal, VI. 37; VII. 85; — in Spain, VII. 85–6; — unfair, VII. 58–9, 78; religious causes satirized, XI. 49–50; and fear of Roman Catholicism, VII. 28; and Treaty of Ryswick: *see* RYSWICK; campaigns in Spain — (1704–5), VI. 21; VII. 85; — Austria neglects campaigns, VII. 25, 89; — England fights unaided, VI. 37–8; VII. 86–7, 110, 119; — expense, III. 198; — and terms of Grand Alliance, VII. 85; — 'no peace without Spain': *see* SPAIN; financial speculation, III. 6–7; subsidies to foreign princes, VI. 32–3, 37, 39; VII. 87; and Temple's letter to 1st Duke of Ormonde, XIV. xi; Toulon (1707), III. 149; wagers on, VI. 34; war party's motives, VI. 39–45; West Indies neglected, VI. 22, 24; Whigs would

continue, VI. 5, 126–7, 133, 166–8; Whigs prevent peace, VII. 13, 34; Whigs profit from, VI. 5–6, 17; VII. 89. *See also* GRAND ALLIANCE; *see also under* nations, towns, and generals involved.

War of the Standard: V. 53–4.

War party: *see* WHIGS.

Warburton, William, 1698–1779, Bishop of Gloucester: on conscience, IX. 114; on JS's *History of the Four Last Years*, VII. xii; and JS's sermons, IX. 100.

Waristoun, Lord: *see* JOHNSTON.

Warming pans: V. 287.

Ward, Edward, 1667–1731, comic writer: and JS, II. x; and Wagstaff, IV. 118.

Warner, T., London bookseller: and JS's *Vindication of Lord Carteret*, XII. 151.

Wars of the Roses: VI. 9.

Warwick, Edward Henry, 7th Earl, 1698–1721: and Pope's *Iliad*, IV. xxxv; pun on his name, IV. 208, 299.

Warwick Lane (site of Royal College of Physicians): author's thanks, in *Tale of a Tub*, I. 115; and madness, I. 113.

Washington, John: *Observations on the Ecclesiastical Jurisdiction of the Kings of England*, II. 82.

Wasp: and honey, IV. 248.

Watt, JS's servant: V. xxv, 202–7.

Waterford, Ireland: bishopric and JS, II. ix; coinage in, XII. 90; impropriations in, XII. 183.

Waters, Edward, *fl.* 1708–36, Dublin printer: JS's *History of Poetry*, IV. xxxvi; JS's *A Proposal for the Universal Use of Irish Manufacture*, IX. 13; — 'Journeyman Waters', IX. xvi; — prosecution, IX. xii, xvi, 26; X. 3, 109 and *n.**, 137; XII. 85, 121–2, 147 and *n.*†; JS's *Some Remarks upon a Pamphlet, Entitl'd, A Letter to the Seven Lords*, III. 278.

Waters, Peter: *see* WALTER.

Watford, Hertfordshire: James II's troops at: V. 163.

Watson, James, the younger, *d.* 1722, Edinburgh printer: *The Humble Representation of the Commons* (1711), VII. 235.

'Wayward, Mrs.': character in *Polite Conversation*, IV. 146.

Weavers, Irish: XII. 306; and employers, XIII. 90; methods of improving their condition, XII. 65–71; payment by merchants delayed, XIII. 171; and JS — his advice, XIII. 90–1; — he quiets mob (1734), XIII. xxix; — epilogue for benefit performance (1721), IX. xix; — *Proposal for the Universal Use of Irish Manufacture*, X. 3; XII. 121. *See also* LETTER TO THE ARCHBISHOP OF DUBLIN.

Weekly Journal or Saturday's Post, Dublin newspaper: and *The Present Miserable State of Ireland* (1721), XII. xv.

Weems, Earl of: *see* WEMYSS.

Welch, Mrs.: innkeeper in Holyhead, V. 202, 207.

'Welch, James' (character in *Gulliver's Travels*): XI. 222.

Welderen, Johann van, 1660–1724, deputy to the States-General: and Barrier Treaty, VI. 98, 106, 108.

Welsh language: spoken in early Britain, V. 5.

Wemyss (or Weems), David Wemyss, 3rd Earl of, 1678–1720, Vice-Admiral of Scotland: on fisheries, XIII. 111; Macky and JS on, V. 262.

Wenman, Richard Wenman, 5th Viscount, 1688–1729: lunacy of 'sober man', III. 78.

Wentworth, Thomas: see STRAFFORD.

Wesley, Samuel, 1662–1735, poet: Homer 'kills', I. 157.

West Indies: and Catalonia, VIII. 63; and clergy, II. 54–5; discovery, IX. 49; Gulliver recruits men, XI. 221–2; Gulliver travels to, XI. 20; and John Hill's expedition, III. 198; 'Terra Australis Incognita', and purgatory, I. 66; and War of Spanish Succession, VI. 22–4. *See also* SPAIN.

Westminster Abbey: JS desires prebend of, I. xv; V. 195.

Westminster Drolleries (1671, 1672): Grub Street product, I. 38.

Westminster Hall: X. 73; 'ancient temple' defiled, XI. 27–8; anecdote, X. 156; books sold there, I. 171; II. 174; and Brobdingnagian coach, XI. 112; English law and Whitshed, X. 159; English law and William Wood, X. 31; Jack walks there, I. 125; law and the Drapier, X. 81; law and royal prerogative, X. 108; lawyers' fare to, I. 112; II. 244; lawyers' resort, I. 112; lawyers thanked by author of *Tale of a Tub*, I. 115; William II builds, V. 27.

Westphalia, Peace of (1648), ending the Thirty Years' War: and Treaty of Utrecht, VII. 113, 133.

Wexford, town in Ireland: Governor Solomon (*sic*, correction of 'Jacob') Richards, XII. 270.

Whales: XI. 112.

Wharton, Henry, 1664–95, religious controversialist: Burnet attacks, IV. xxiii, 60–1; JS defends, against Burnet, IV. 84.

Wharton, Lucy (*née* Loftus), Countess of, *c*. 1670–1716, wife of Thomas, Earl of: adultery of 'his lady', III. 180; and Dr. Lloyd, III. 182–3.

Wharton, Philip Wharton, 4th Lord, 1613–96, father of Thomas: cowardice, V. 289; Presbyterian, VII. 10.

Wharton, Thomas Wharton, 1st Earl (1715, Marquess) of, 1648–1715, Lord Lieutenant of Ireland, Whig politician: and Addison, II. xiv, *n*. 2, xxii, *n*. 2; — his secretary, II. xxv–xxvi; IX. 30; Anne mortifies him, III. 183–4; and Anne's illness (1713), VIII. 154; and the arsenal, VII. 233–4; atheist, III. 179; VI. 155; VII. 10; and Thomas Brodrick, III. 182; character, III. xix; VI. 151–5; **JS's character of,** III. 27–9, 179–81; VII. 9–10; defiles a church, III. 28 and *n*.*, 68–9; attacked as 'Clodius', III. 77, 84; on dispensing power in monarch, IX. 20–1; electioneering, III. 27–8, 180; and Gregg, III. 185–205, 243–58; and Dr. Hall, III. 183–4; fears impeachment,

VII. 23; intriguer, III. 180; corrupt government of Ireland, III. 27–9, 177–84, 231–40; VII. 10; VIII. 121; on liberty in Ireland, X. 100; becomes Lord Lieutenant of Ireland ('great employments'), VI. 43; VIII. 113; removed as Lord Lieutenant of Ireland, III. 204; and Killigrew, IV. 249; and Lambert, II. 284; *Letter from*: see LETTER OF THANKS; liar, III. 179; and Dr. Lloyd, III. 182; lines on Anne Long (1703), V. 197 and *n*.*; and political lying, III. 8–13; Macky and JS on, V. 259; mistress in Ireland, III. 179, 182, *n*.*; hates Ormonde ('his patron'), III. 184; and Oxford's alleged treason (1711), III. xxix; foresees Oxford's ruin, VII. 18–19; and Benjamin Pratt, III. 183–4; Presbyterian, III. 179; VII. 10 and *n*.*; and Thomas Proby, III. 181–2; profligate, III. 179; reputation, VIII. 142; shameless, III. 178; and Shrewsbury, VIII. 118; and vote of 'no peace without Spain', VI. 43; JS attacks, III. xviii–xxi; V· xxiv; JS avoids, VIII. 121–2; JS and chaplainship, II. xxi, xxiii, 284; and JS's *Letter from the Pretender*, VI. xxii; JS parodies, VI. xix; relations with JS, III. xx, *n*. 3 and 4, 178; V. xxiv; — travel together, II. xxxii; and Test Act, XII. xl; and Trinity College, Dublin, III. 183–4; wealth, III. 27–8; and William III, III. 56–7.

What is it like?: children's game, IX. 336.

Wheldon, John: on the longitude, V. 206.

When I Come to Be Old (written 1699), by JS: I. xxxvii; background, I. xviii–xix; manuscript facsimile, facing I. xxxvii. 'Whiffler': III. 36.

'Whig': origin of term, IV. 282–3.

Whig Examiner, London weekly paper written by Addison in 1710: Addison's speech of Alcibiades, III. xix.

Whig-Lord, Letter to: see SOME REASONS TO PROVE; LETTER FROM THE PRETENDER.

'Whigarchy': VI. 166.

'Whig-borow': IV. 282, 283.

Whigs: and Anne: *see* ANNE; and Ashburnham, VI. xvii; and atheism, IV. 84; VII. 5; VIII. 10; and balance of power (1711), VII. 19–21; 'big with Whig', VI. 154; bishops corrupted by, III. 51; IV. 71; and Bothmar, VII. 25, 143, 144; lost cause (1711), III. 130; and Church of England — attack church, III. 199–200; — attack clergy, II. 8–9; — contempt for clergy, VIII. 120; — encourage heresies, III. 92; —attack high churchmen, II. 9; — weaken church, III. 89–90; VIII. 102; — *see also* CHURCH OF ENGLAND; BISHOPS; and Episcopal Church in Scotland, VII. 96–7; and A. Collins, IV. xviii; and constitution — would 'clip' it, VI. 45; — corrupting influence, VII. 19–20; — would ruin it, III. 91–3, 104; Country party origin, VI. 78; against court and country, VI. 78; Cowper subservient to, VII.

10; and Cromwell, III. 104; V.
255; to be crushed (1714), VII.
88–90; and national debt, VI.
154; VII. 69–70; Dissenters
drawn to, II. 3; III. 126–32;
Dissenters identified with, III.
145–6; V. 251; Dissenters supported by, III. 89–90; and
Dunkirk: *see* DUNKIRK; and the
Dutch: *see* DUTCH; BUYS; electioneering, III. 37, 72; and
Eugene: *see* EUGENE; in *Examiner*, XIV. 12; a faction, III.
128–9; fall (1710): *see* GODOL-
PHIN MINISTRY, *fall*; and First
Fruits, IX. ix; and France, VIII.
9–10; and free-thinkers, IV.
63;

   and George I, VIII. 93–4, 109,
132; — his bias foreseen, VII.
xxxiii; — Elector won over, V.
99–101; — — ('successor') won
over, VII. 143–5; VIII. 89; —
'his majesty' favours them, XI.
48; — he governs by them,
VIII. 218; — 'next successor'
their only hope, VI. 132; —
jealousies of 'next heir', VI. 130;
— and prerogative, VIII. 97;

   and Prince George of Denmark,
VIII. 112–13, 114; — his death,
VI. 43; and Godolphin — hate
him, VII. 9; — seduce him,
VIII. 56; and Godolphin minis-
try, VI. 42–3; — allied by war,
VIII. 148–9; — demand prefer-
ment, VI. 77; and William
Gregg: *see* GREGG; and Guis-
card, III. 148–9; and *The
Hereditary Right of the Crown of
England Asserted*, VIII. 64–5;
heterogeneous, III. xiii–xiv, 92,
111, 122; — 'monstrous and un-

natural' confederacy, VI. 76–7;
— unanimity disparaged, VI.
130; — unified by impotence and
evil, III. 96–7; — 'unnatural
league', III. 94; House of Commons — majority (1708–9), VIII.
114; House of Lords — majority, VI. 125–6; VII. 13, 29; —
creation of twelve peers weakens
them, VII. 20; VIII. 147–9;
'Husige' in Japan, V. 99–107'
impudence, XIV. 12; and Indian
Kings, II. 265; insolence, VIII;
9; Ireland supported by 'best.
Whigs, X. 63;

   in Ireland — Addison's opinion, IX. 30; — Carteret's preferments, XII. 169; enemies of
Church, IX. 56; — clergy are
Whigs, II. 119; — oppose
Dependency Act, IX. xi; — compared with English, IX. 30; —
preferments, XII. xxvii–xxviii,
xxix; — principles, II. 118; IX,
56; — support Test Act (1708),
II. 118–20; XII. xliv; — perse-
cute Tories, IX. 117; — and
Wood's coins, X. xxiv;

   Jacobitism, VI. xxii, 93, 145–6;
VIII. 10; XIV. 7, 10; — among
leaders, VIII. 39; and James II,
III. 127; — correspondence, III.
146;

   journalists, III. 75–78; —
'answer-jobbers', VI. 96–7; —
'bullies of the pen', III. 90–1;
— and change of ministry (1710)
III. 203; — and Church of
England, III. 189; — 'circulation
of dulness', III. 86–7; — freedom of press abused, III. 70–1;
— hardships ridiculed, III. 30–1;
— libels, III. 188–9, 202; — lies,

VIII. 59; — and Oxford, VIII. 136; — Oxford ministry indulges, III. 188; — paid well, VIII. 31; — 'perplex the world', VI. 129; — and politicians, III. 116–18; — like popish miracles, VIII. 34; — ridiculed, III. 35–40, 135–6, 152–7, 171–3; VI. 71; VII. 104; — 'rude invectives', III. 68; — seditious, VIII. 64; — and Walpole, V. 94–6, 111, 112–13, 117–18;—*see also* DEFOE; DUNTON; EXAMINER; RIDPATH; STEELE;

Junto: *see* JUNTO; opposed to landed gentry (1711), VI. 5; leaders, III. 77–80; VI. 127, 128–30; VII. 5–12; — their rewards, VI. 128, 131; — weak union, VI. 76–7; 'levelling principle', VIII. 24; likened to Louis XIV, VIII. 9–10; 'low-heels' in Lilliput, XI. 48; and Marlborough — oppose him to Anne, VII. 29 — joined by him, III. xii–xiii, 15, 135; VIII. 113–14; — seduce him, VII. 7; VIII. 56; — 'solemn league and covenant', VI. 42; ministers impeached (1700–01), I. xx; ministry (1702–10): *see* GODOLPHIN MINISTRY; ministry (1714 and following), republican, VII. xv; and Mohocks, VII. 27; and moneyed interests, III. 10; VI. 10, 42, 130; VII. 69–70; young nobility seduced, VIII. 38; and Nottingham, III. 38; VII. 13, 15, 16, 21, 29; — 'example of apostacy', VI. 129; and occasional conformity, VII. 16; and Occasional Conformity Bill (1703–04), I. xxi; — move Bill (1711), VII.

21; origins, III. 128, 162–7; V. 99; — origin of term 'Whig', IV. 282–3; and Oxford — 'bandbox' plot blamed on them, III. 199; — Guiscard's attack, III. 195, 197–8; — murder scheme, VII. 26–7;

and Oxford Ministry — acknowledge ministers' abilities, VIII. 82; — change in relations, VII. 4; — leniency of ministers, VI. 126; — leniency of ministers to end, VI. 130; — — (1712), VI. 75–6; moderates approve ministers, III. 119; — Whigs expect to return to power (1710), VII. 4; — attempts to ruin ministry ('secret instruments'), VI. 78–9, 130, 134–5; — — ('parade to tower'), VI. 135; — attempts to ruin ministry (1711), VII. 18–19, 22; — — (1712), VII. 124; — should support ministry, VI. 123–36; — Whigs seek vengeance, VI. 80; — *see also* OXFORD MINISTRY; SOME REASONS TO PROVE;

and passive obedience, III. 112–13; and Pope's *Iliad*, IV. xxxv; and Popish plot, VIII. 39; power — number increasing (1703–04), I. xxi; — increase strength (1711), VI. 72–3; — minority of nation, III. 105; VIII. 48; — gain power (1702 ff.), VI. 42; — greatest from 1688 to 1710, VIII. 148; — many in power (1711), VII. 2; — out of power (*c.* 1702), VI. 42; — 'ruined party' (1711), III. 64; — depend on war, VII. 78–9, 144; — weak (1712), VI. 76–7, 126–7, 139; VII. 144; and royal pre-

rogative, VI. 123, 127; VII. 20; VIII. 97, 164; and Presbyterians, V. 255; and the Pretender: *see* PRETENDER, OLD; principles — politics compared with religion, III. 39; Puritans identified with, III. 122, 126–32, 189; VI. 78; VII. 5; VIII. 42; — 'revolution principles', VI. 93; — 'Solemn League and Covenant', VI. 42; republicanism, VI. 152, 154; VII. 5; VIII. 9; and 'resistance', VIII. 40–1, 44–5; and bill for resumption of grants, VI. 134–5; VII. 100–1; their revolution principle, III. 147; VI. 93; and Revolution of 1688, VI. 10; and Roman Catholicism, IV. 75; and Thomas Sheridan, V. xxx; Somers their strategist, VII. 7; and Somerset, VII. 13–14, 29; and Duchess of Somerset ('a stratagem'), VI. 71; on union with Scotland, VIII. 50; and union of Spain and France, VIII. 59; and Steele: *see* STEELE; and the Succession, VI. 93;

and JS [*These references are mainly to editorial materials and not to JS's remarks.*] — (1701) *Contests and Dissensions* pleases them, I. xx; VIII. 119; XI. x; — (1701–3) they become his friends, XI. x; — (1702–4) early sympathies, VIII. 120–2; — (1704) calls himself one, I. xxi–xxii; — (1708) seeks preferment from them, II. xxi; — (*c.* 1708) censures them, II. xvii; — (*c.* 1708) appeals to them in *Argument against Abolishing Christianity*, II. xix; — (1708) warns them in *Letter . . . concerning the Sacramental Test*, II. xxii; — — *Letter* turns them against him, XIV. 2; — (1708–10) breaks with them, XII. xl; — (1710) shocked by their removal, III. x; — (1710) his alleged desertion, III. x, xii; V. xxiv; VI. x; — (1710–14) he protects Whig friends, VII. xxxv; IX. 28–9; XIII. 185; — (1711) he 'entirely subdues' them, III. 172; — (1712) denies he is one, VI. 93; — (1712) they attack *Proposal for Correcting . . . the English Tongue*, IV. xii–xiv; — (1712) agrees with 'reasonable sober Whigs', VI. 123; — (1712) feels mistreated by them, II. xxxvi; — (1714) they attack his *Publick Spirit of the Whigs*, IV. xxvii; VIII. xxi–xxii; — (1714 and later) his hatred, IX. ix; — (1715) fears new ministry, VIII. xxxi–xxxii; — (1720) his hatred, IX. xv; — (*c.* 1737) reproaches them for reflections on Oxford's ministry, VII. xxxv;

oppose Test Act, II. 3; III. 54–5; and Tories — compared, II. 13–14; III. 121–6; — some would join Tories, III. 132–6; — in society, III. 102; 'union' with Godolphin and Marlborough, VI. 42, 44; — *see also* TORIES; attack universities, II. 9; and Treaty of Utrecht — attack it, VIII. xix; — change opinion (1713), VII. 51–2; — dissuade Dutch (1713), VII. 163–4; — Dutch negotiations with French (1711), VII. 41; — opposition, VII. 13, 34, 166; venality, IV. 76; violence in an ill cause, VI. 78; and

Wagstaff, IV. 121; and Walpole — kept in power by corruption (1727), V. xv, 101–2; and War of Spanish Succession, VI. 42–3; — would continue war, III. 199; VI. 44; VII. 13, 22, 34, 98; XI. 53–4; — 'lovers of war', VII. 3; — 'no peace without Spain', VII. 41; — Ormonde's 'restraining orders', VII. 129; — vote against peace (1711–12), VII. 18–19; — 'pernicious designs', VI. 59; — unfair quotas, VII. 78–9; and William III, VI. 78; VII. 69–70; VIII. 148.

Whimsicals: *see* TORIES, *Whimsicals*.

Whiston, William, 1667–1752, theologian and mathematician: *Memoirs*, I. xxii, *n.**; Socinianism, IV. 31, 34, 36; 'Whistonism', IV. 207.

White, David, British merchant in Bruges: and Barrier Treaty, VI. 116.

White, William, gardener in Dublin: and JS's property, XIII. 156.

Whitechapel, district of London: and Jack, in *Tale of a Tub*, I. 126.

Whitefriars, district of London: coarse language, I. 10.

Whitehall, centre of government offices in Westminster: and free-thinking, IV. 109; and pride, I. 31.

Whitehaven, Cumberland: coal trade, IX. 19; and Creichton, V. 177; JS kidnapped as infant, V. 192.

White-rosalists (i.e., Jacobites): XII. 169.

White's Chocolate House (founded by Francis White), in St. James's Street, London: and free-thinking, IV. 28; and Henry Levi, VI. 175, 177; and Earl of Oxford, XII. 50; and *Tatler* no. 11, IV. xxix; — no. 32, II. xxix.

Whiteway, Ffolliott, second son of Martha Whiteway: JS's bequest, XIII. 153.

Whiteway, John, 1723–1798, surgeon, youngest son of Martha Whiteway: JS's bequest, XIII. 154, 199.

Whiteway, Martha, 1690–1768, cousin and dear friend of JS: and JS — his bequests, XIII. 153; — on his charity, XIII. xlii–xliii; — their cousinhood, VII. xxv, *n.* 3; — *Directions to Servants*, XIII. vii–viii; — *Enquiry into the Behaviour of the Queen's Last Ministry*, VIII. xxxvii; — *Family of Swift*, V. xxii; — friendship begins, VIII. xxxvii; — *History of the Four Last Years*, VII. xiv, xviii, xx, xxiii, xxv–xxvi; — *Some Free Thoughts*, VIII. xxiv–xxv; — his will, XIII. 198–9.

Whitshed, William, *c.* 1656–1727, Lord Chief Justice of the King's Bench in Ireland: and Lord Chancellorship of Ireland, X. xxiv; character, XII. 23–4; and Drapier, X, *passim*; — discovery of Drapier, X. 81; — proclamation against Drapier, X. 205; — Drapier to avoid prosecution, X. 111, 114; and 4th *Drapier's Letter*, X. 53; — his ghost, XII. 8; 'most iniquitous judge', XII. 147; discharge of grand jury, X. xxi, xxiii, xxvi, 73;

— 'some *late proceedings*', X. 122; letters attacking, X. xxv, 157–71; '*libertas et natale solum*' his motto, X. xxii–xxiii, 100–1; XII. 8; and Midleton, X. xxiv; printers prosecuted, XII. 85; **and JS,** IX. 25; — *Answer to a Paper Called a Memorial of the Poor . . . of Ireland*, XII. xiii; — JS's attacks defended, XII. xiii, 23–4; — Jacobitism alleged, IX. 27; — *A Proposal for the Universal Use of Irish Manufacture*, IX. xvi, 26–7; XII. 121; — *Short View of the State of Ireland*, XII. x–xi; prosecution of Waters, IX. xii–xiii; 26–7; X. 137; and Wharton, III. 237. *See also* LETTER FROM A FRIEND TO THE RIGHT HONOURABLE [CHIEF JUSTICE WHITSHED]; SECOND LETTER FROM A FRIEND TO THE RIGHT HONOURABLE [CHIEF JUSTICE WHITSHED].

Whittington and His Cat: see WHITTINGTON, RICHARD.

Whittington, Richard, *d.* 1423, Lord Mayor of London: legend of his cat, I. 41.

Whitworth, Charles, Lord Whitworth, 1675–1725, diplomat: sent to Russia, V. 85; sent to Vienna (July–Sept. 1711), VI. 36.

'Whnaholm Yahoo': Houyhnhnm expression possibly meaning a child's negligence, XI. 275.

Whole Duty of Man (1658): attributed to Richard Sterne, Archbishop of York, V. 282.

Whores: encourage criminals, IX. 39–41.

Wichers, Wicher, Dutch plenipotentiary, senator of the city of Gröningen: and Barrier Treaty, VI. 99, 106, 108.

Wicklow, county of Ireland: turf, IX. 19; Judge Upton at assizes, X. 164.

Wicklow Castle, Ireland: III. 237.

Wight, Isle of: and Charles I, XII. 265.

Wigs: hated by Henry I, V. 46.

'Wilcocks, Thomas' (ship's captain in *Gulliver's Travels*): rescues Gulliver, XI. 143–8.

Wilkins, John, 1614–72, Bishop of Chester and a founder of the Royal Society: leads engineers of Moderns, I. 152.

Will of JS (1740): **XIII. 147–58;** background, XII. xxi; XIII. xxxvi, xlii–xliii; manuscripts not mentioned in, VII. xix and *n.* 1; and St. Patrick's Hospital, XIII. 192–3; textual notes, XIII. 223–4. *See also* EXECUTORS.

Will of JS (*c.* 1737): executors, XIII. 200.

Will of JS (*c.* 1737), **codicil** (April 1737): **XIII. 198–200;** textual notes, XIII. 225.

Will of JS, **early draft: XIII. 198;** manuscript facsimile, facing XIII. 199; textual notes, XIII. 225.

William I ('the Conqueror'), King of England, 1027–87: great council, II. 82; death, V. 13; conquers England, V. 6–7; and English language, IV. 7–8; and Eric the Forester, V. 191; government and Whigs, III. 104; grievances against, V. 28; Henry I his son, V. 27; and

Malcolm's towns, V. 16; title to throne, VIII. 92.

William II ('Rufus'), King of England, 1056–1100: V. 11; avarice, V. 26; buildings, V. 27; and see of Canterbury, V. 15–17; character, V. 23–4; **JS's character of**, V. 25–7; dissolute courtiers, V. 28; death, V. 24–7; and Hélias de la Flèche, V. 23–4; Henry I contrasted with, V. 27–8, 46; his infamy, V. 15; and Lanfranc, V. 13–15; misogamy, V. 27; hunting in New Forest, V. 23–4; defeats Northumberland, V. 20–1; Parsons and JS on, V. 241; and Philip I of France, V. 15–16, 19–20; and Ralph, Bishop of Durham, V. 28; reign of, V. 13–27; religion, V. 16, 25–6; and Robert of Normandy, V. 14–16, 19–20; and Scotland, V. 16; recruiting of soldiers, III. 41; and the succession, V. 47; and JS's history, V. ix; taxation, V. 26; seizes throne, V. 13, 27; killed by Tirel (or Tyrrel), V. 24; trustworthy, V. 25; and the Welsh, V. 20, 24; and William I's treasure, V. 13, 27.

William III (William of Orange), King of England, 1650–1702: accession, V. 166; and Albemarle, V. 259; army to be paid from public revenue (1688), V. 264; plot to assassinate (1696) V. 264; Bill of Rights ('compositions and agreements'), V. 242; Burnet and JS on, V. 285–93; Calvinist, XII. 271; removes chimney tax, VII. 68; and Church of England, III. 5–6; VIII. 96; and Church of Scotland, V. 179–80; and Creichton, V. 120, 174; Creichton praises, V. 180; and Cromwell, II. 9; death, I. xxi; II. 76; — William Howell and JS on, V. 265; — predicted, II. 143; and national debt, III. 6; VI. 10; VII. 68–70; De Witt's murder, V. 275; anecdote of dog-keeper, VIII. 23–4; and Lord Dundee, V. 173; favours Dutch, VI. 11; management of elections, VIII. 148; invades England (1688), V. 161; IX. 31; adopts English customs, VIII. 95–6; English customs unfamiliar, VII. 102; Edward Forbes ('that person') insults memory, II. 112; — and Archbishop King, II. 282, *n.* 2; France recognizes (1697), VI. 11; and Godolphin — correspondence with Mary of Modena, VII. 8; — he resigns (1701), VI. 11; and Lord Granard, V. 165–6; bill to resume his grants (1711), VI. 134–5; VII. 100–2; denied Dutch guards, V. 85; 'vice' of homosexuality, V. 259, 285; honour lost, V. 277; Ireland — campaigns in, I. xi; II. 114–15; XII. 132; — grants of forfeited land ('conquered lands'), I. 218–19; VII. 102; — Whigs, II. 118; IX. 56; — wool trade limited, V. 256; and James II, II. 20; — oaths of allegiance to James, V. 165–6, 167–8; — orders James to leave London, V. 85; — title, III. 163; — withdrawal of James II, V. 163; ambition to be, king, V. 285, 288, 292; and Archbishop King, II. 282 and

n. 2; landed interest opposed to, VIII. 148; lords justices, VIII. 97; and prerogative of appointing ministers, III. 135; 'moderation', IX. 178; and moneyed interests, VI. 10; VII. 69–70; and Roger Moore, X. 41; neglects navy, VI. 11; 'new king from a Calvinistical commonwealth', VII. 5; and nonjuring clergy, V. 270; pun on 'orange' punch, XII. xxxiv, 225; loved by common people, I. 235; V. 242; and Presbyterians, V. 179–80; XII. 271; and Matthew Prior, III. 209; and Revolution of 1688, XI. 245; and Roman Catholicism, XII. 257; and Sancroft, II. xvii; and Scotland — Presbyterianism, V. 288, 290; — union with England, VIII. 48–9; Somers and 'late reign', I. 15; and Somerset, VII. 13; and the succession, VI. 95; **and JS**, V. 194; — audience, I. xx; II. 283; — his *Letter . . . concerning the Sacramental Test*, I. xx, *n.*‖; II. 283; — poem by JS, I. xi; — preferment, I. xi, xiv; IV. 195; — Temple's *Letters* (1700) dedicated to him, I. 256; and Sir William Temple, V. 193; — JS's preferment, V. 195; — Temple's *Letters to the King* (1703), I. 265; title, III. 163; — 'nephew', II. 21; — and nonjurors, III. 21–3; VIII. 168; and Triennial Act (1693–4), V. 193–4; and Treaty of Utrecht — possessions restored, VII. 113; vices ('pleasures'), V. 259; and Elizabeth Villiers (later Lady Orkney), V. 264, 285; and Wag-

staff, IV. 100; War of the League of Augsburg, VI. 14–15; — national debt, VII. 68; — Flanders, VI. 88–9; War of the Spanish Succession — Grand Alliance, VII. 81; — quotas, VII. 64; rumoured near Watford (1688), V. 163–4; and Wharton, III. 57; and Whigs, VIII. 148; — origin of 'new' Whigs, VI. 78; VII. 69–70.

William the Clito, Earl of Flanders, 1101–28, son of Robert of Normandy: death, V. 44; made Earl of Flanders, V. 43; and Louis VI, V. 38, 40; marries daughter of Geoffrey Plantagenet, Count of Anjou, V. 41–2; defeats Thierry of Alsace, V. 43–4.

William, Duke of Normandy, 1103–20, only son of Henry I: campaigns against Louis VI, V. 39–40; death, V. 40–2; marries Matilda, daughter of Fulk V, Count of Anjou, V. 42.

William, Earl of Boulogne, *c.* 1132–59, son of King Stephen: 'another son', V. 69; and Henry II, V. 69–71; — assassination plot, V. 70.

William of Corbeil, *d.* 1136, Archbishop of Canterbury: and Stephen's accession, V. 48.

William de Keynes (Kaynes, Cahaines), 1st half of 12th century: captures Stephen, V. 59.

William of Tankerville, *d.* 1129, Chamberlain of England and Normandy, Henry I's lieutenant in Normandy: V. 41.

William of Ypres, *d. c.* 1165, son of Philip, Count of Yypres

(erroneously styled Earl of Kent): and Henry II, V. 74; aids Stephen, V. 53, 60, 61.

Williamite War (Ireland, 1689–91): Dissenters' role in, II. 114–15.

Williams College, Williamstown, Massachusetts: copy of *Gulliver's Travels*, XI. 301.

Williams, Sir Harold, editor of JS's works: acknowledgements, I. vi; XI. 301; *Dean Swift's Library* (1932), II. 280; V. v; V. xxxi, *n.* 1; on letter concerning Bishop Evans, XIV. xiv, *n.* 1; edition of *Gulliver's Travels* (1926), XI. 301; 'Introduction' to *Gulliver's Travels*, XI. ix–xxviii, 301; on JS's *History of the Four Last Years*, VII. x; on JS's *Letter . . . concerning the Sacramental Test*, II. xl, *n.* 1; edition of JS's *Poems* (1937), I. ix, *n.*‖; II. xiv and *n.* 1; on *Tripos* attributed to JS, I. ix, *n.*‖.

Williams, John, 1582–1650, Archbishop of York: *Life of*, V. 202; JS visits tomb, V. 202.

'Williams, Peter': friend of Gulliver, XI. 79.

Williamson, David, a Covenanter: V. 130.

Williamson, Sir Joseph, 1633–1701, diplomat: treaty with Sweden, VI. 62.

Will's Coffee House, Covent Garden, London: conversation, IV. 90; 'seminary' of criticism, I. 154–5; dissipation, I. 45; and Eugenio, XII. 45; poets' meeting-place, I. 38 and *n.**; author's thanks, *Tale of a Tub*, I. 115; and *Tatler*, II. xxvii.

Wilmer, Mr.: and *ignoramus* jury, X. 165.

Wilmington, Spencer Compton, Earl of, *c.* 1673–1743, statesman: 'Nomptoc' in *Account of Japan*, V. 103; hates Walpole, V. 103.

Wilmot, John: *see* ROCHESTER.

Wilson, a Scots rebel captain: V. 144–5.

Wilson, Carroll: copy of *Gulliver's Travels*, XI. 301.

Wilson, Francis, *b. c.* 1695, prebendary of St. Patrick's Cathedral, JS's friend and executor of his will: and Anne Brent, XIII. 158; and theft of lead, XIII. 194; and JS's deanery tithes, XIII. 154; JS's executor, XIII. 157; witness to JS's signature, XIII. 197; and JS's will, XIII. 155.

Wilson, Frank Percy: acknowledgements, I. vi, xvii, *n.*†.

Wilson, James, Edinburgh printer: and *A Famous Prediction of Merlin*, by JS, II. 288.

Wilton, Wiltshire: pun upon, IV. 262; and King Stephen, V. 64.

Wiltshire: and the Ashe family, IV. 263, *n.**.

Wimpole, Cambridgeshire, seat of the 2nd Earl of Oxford: JS visits, VII. xiv, *n.* 1.

Wincam, Sir George: married Burnet's aunt, V. 268.

Winchester, Hampshire: Danes burn, V. 5; and Henry II, V. 73; and Queen Matilda (or Maude), V. 61; and Robert of Normandy, V. 29; Stephen meets Henry of Normandy, V. 69; and William II, V. 13; William II buried, V. 24.

Winchester College: acknowledgement, facing V. 243.

Winchilsea, Charles Finch, 4th Earl of, 1672–1712: Macky and JS on, V. 259.

'Wind': and enthusiasm, I. 95–101.

Winder, John, *d. c.* 1717, rector of Carnmoney; JS's successor at Kilroot: and JS's sermons, IX. 97, 99.

Windham: *see* WYNDHAM.

Windsor Castle: Cabinet council at (1711), VII. 14; maids of honour at, IV. 254; 'parliament' at (1126), V. 41; and composition of JS's *History of the Four Last Years*, VII. xxxiii; and William II, V. 27.

Windsor Castle, Royal Library: manuscript of JS's *History of the Four Last Years*, VII. vii, xxi–xxii, xxviii, 219.

Windsor Castle, St. George's Chapel: JS desires prebend of, I. xv.

Windsor Prophecy, poem by JS: composition, VI. xi.

Windybank: *see* ACCOUNT OF THE SHORT LIFE.

'Windybank, Michy': Irish bank scheme, IX. 308–10.

'Windybank, Sir Oliver' (pseudonym for Sir Oliver St. George): IX. 309–11.

Wine: necessary cordial in Ireland, XII. 124–6; use of, XI. 252.

Wing, Vincent, 1619–68, mathematician and almanac-maker: *Astronomia Britannica*, II. 163.

'Winter foraging': presents to military leaders, VI. 41–2.

Wise, T., bookseller: pirated edition of *Predictions for the Year* 1708, II. 286.

Wise Men of Goatham: and William Wotton, I. 41–2.

Wishart, Sir James, *d.* 1729, admiral: mission to Holland (Feb.-Apr. 1711), VI. 32.

Wishart, William, Scottish clergyman: Clarendon and JS on, V. 315.

Wit (literary genius, raillery, etc.): among *beaux esprits*, II. 257–9; Biblical sources, IX. 330; and Christianity, IX. 328; evacuation needed, IX. 341; modern wit ridiculed, I. 25–32, 132–3; offensive, IX. 341; and plagiarism, IX. 333; rare in preachers, IX. 213; 'with wits as with razors', I. 29; religion essential, IX. 329; self-inspired, IX. 333; and taste, I. 10; wit without knowledge like whipped cream, I. 140.

Witan: and parliaments, V. 35.

Witches: trial of, II. 235–7.

Wither, George, 1588–1667, poet: and Virgil, I. 146; pretends to lead Moderns, I. 152.

'Without': misused for 'unless', V. 262.

Witness, false: definition, IX. 181–4; malice, IX. 183; revenge, IX. 183; vexation, IX. 184. *See also* INFORMERS; TRUTH.

Witness, honest: characteristics, IX. 188; disinterest necessary, IX. 187.

Wolfenbüttel, near Braunschweig, Germany: and Louis XIV, VI. 12.

Wolley, Edward, *d.* 1684, Bishop of Clonfert: Burnet and JS on, V. 273.

Wolsey, Thomas, *c.* 1475–1530, cardinal and statesman: father 'no butcher', V. 263.

Women: bitches, II. 242; cleanliness, V. 338; IX. 87; clothes — extravagance, XI. 253; — fashion, IX. 87; mostly contemptible, IX. 90–1; conversation, IV. xxxi–xxxii, 107, 247; IX. 90; XII. 307; — and management of husbands, IX. 88; coquetry satirized, XI. 264; cowardice, IX. 93; cuckoldry, I. 244; diseases, XII. 68; education, IV. xxxvii–xxxviii; XII. 307–8; — conversation of men, IX. 91; — like men's, XI. 269; — neglected, IX. 85; — and respect, IX. 86, 90; and English language, IV. 13; and enthusiasm, I. 187–9; excuses, IV. 250–1; finances, IX. 94; flattery, IV. 246; choice of friends, IX. 88–9; gambling, II. 46; handwriting, XI. 57; and horses, IV. 253; and cowardly husbands, IV. 245; husbands to be esteemed, IX. 94; fondness for husbands, IX. 86; XI. 269, 274–5; hypocrisy with husbands, IX. 87; husband's judgement supreme, IX. 89; impertinence, IX. 88; inconstancy, XI. 165–6; insinuating, VIII. 167; and Irish imports, XII. 80; and Irish manufactures, XII. xix, xxi–xxii; luxury, XII. 116; and good manners, IV. 214; IX. 86; — wives without husbands, IX. 87; ideal marriage, XI. 268–9, 274–5; men compared with, IX. 92–3; men as foolish, XII. 307; occupations foolish, IX. 85, 90, 92; old age contemptible, IX. 92; patches ridiculed, II. 267; pedantry, IV. 90; reading aloud, IX. 92; ridiculed, XIII. 184; 'poisonous, devouring serpents', XII. 68; role in society, IV. 94–5; spelling, IX. 92; stubborn, VIII. 160; and JS — first advances, V. 197–8; in taverns, II. 60; tax on merits, XI. 190; vanity, IV. 244; V. 252; XII. 21, 135; — and Dublin, XII. 135; — and Irish manufactures, XII. 9, 67–8, 126–7; virginity, II. 180–3; — and Parliament, II. 75; visits, IX. 88; and waiting maids, IX. 89; whores encourage criminals, IX. 39–41; whores tolerated, II. 45–6; wit, IX. 93; manner of writing aslant, XI. 56; and Xenophon, I. 244. *See also* OF THE EDUCATION OF LADIES.

Wonder of All the Wonders, That Ever the World Wondered At (1721), probably by JS: **IX. 285–7**; authorship, IX. xvii and *n.* 1; background, IX. xvi–xxi; 'Key', IX. 311; publication, IX. xvii, xviii, 378; textual notes, IX. 378.

Wonderful Wonder of Wonders (*c.* 1721), probably by JS: **IX. 281–4**; authorship, IX. xvii; background, IX. xvi–xxi; and Irish bank scheme, IX. 378; 'Key', IX. 311; publication, IX. xvii, xviii, 378; textual notes, IX. 378.

Wood, William, 1671–1730, iron manufacturer, producer of 'Wood's halfpence': American coins, X. 44; and John Browne, XII. xiii; character, X. 28–9;

XIII. 187; mock execution, X. 145–9; father, X. 148; and House of Commons of Ireland, X. 5; allegedly jailed for debt, X. 89; and Maculla, XII. 94–5; 'projector', IX. 236; Drapier will shoot, X. 19–20.

Wood's coins (i.e., copper half-pence and farthings coined by William Wood for use in Ireland under a patent granted by George I about 1722): acceptance, X. 44–5; advantages deceptive, IX. 237–8; 'Advertisement' against, X. 23–4; 'black money', X. 10; and Commissioners of the Revenue, X. 44–5; compromise proposals, X. 17–20; counterfeits, X. 47; dangers, XII. 99; 'Declaration' against, X. 48–9; description, X. 188; and *Drapier's Letters*, X, *passim*; and 4th *Drapier's Letter*, XII. 122; and trade with Dutch, X. 7; and France, X. 8; and George I — his portrait, X. 137–8; Gulliver's allegory, XI. 309–10; and *Gulliver's Travels*, XI. xix; and Ireland — 'the great uniter', X. 61; not lawful, X. 8–11; and Maculla's coinage, XII. 96–7; not needed, X. 38; Newton's assay, IV. xxxviii; X. 187–90, 215; patent examined, X. 42–3; — precedents, X. 56; — surrendered, X. xxvii–xxxi; and *Polite Conversation*, IV. xxxi, 122; precedents, X. 41–2, 56; and royal prerogative, X. 28; promoters, IX. 134; retribution impossible, IX. 238–9; and Roman Catholics, X. 53–4, 61; and Scotland, X. 127; and JS,

XIII. xxxvi–xxxvii, 186–7; — Faulkner's edition of *Works*, XIII. 201; — joins with Archbishop King, V. xii; — motive for opposition, XIII. 112; — sermon on, IX. 127, 134–6, 232–40. *See also* DRAPIER'S LETTERS.

Woodstock, Oxfordshire: labyrinth, V. 77; and Marlborough, III. 21, 23.

Wool: burial in, IX. 16; — Irish act for (1734), XIII. xxix; Lilliputian sheep, XI. 80.

Woollen Act (English law of 1699, forbidding export of Irish woollen goods): singularity of law, XII. 8.

Woollen manufacturers, JS's *Observations*: *see* OBSERVATIONS OCCASIONED BY READING A PAPER.

Woollen trade, English: Ireland should ban goods, IX. 269; valuable, IX. 269.

Woollen trade, Irish: quality of cloth, XIII. 170; and Dutch, VI. 28; English monopoly, IX. 15; exports, IX. 269; and fashion, IX. 16–17; and foreign goods, XIII. 169; improvements, IX. 47; Irish interest, XIII. 168; merchants — advice to, XIII. 91–2; — avarice and ambition, XIII. 168; — dishonesty, XIII. xxviii, 90; — corrupt seal, XIII. 170; — undermine, XIII. 169; — weavers' pay delayed, XIII. 171; and William III, V. 256.

Woolley, David: acknowledgement, XIV. vii.

Woolly, Edward: *see* WOLLEY.

Wool-sack: emblem of power, IX. 269.

Wooly, agent for Dr. Sheridan at Quilca: XIV. 37.

Wooton: *see* WOTTON.

Worcester, England: and Odo of Bayeux, V. 14.

Worcester, Battle of (1651): V. 130, 154–5.

Worcester, bishopric of: II. 86.

Word machine, Academy of Lagado: XI. 182–4.

Words and things: II. 32, 75–6; XI. 185–6.

Workhouses (Dublin): XIII. xxxviii–xxxix; and increase of beggars, XIII. 132; finances, XIII. 177; mismanagement, XIII. 132; revenues, XIII. 132; JS omitted from commission, XIII. 131; unsuccessful, XIII. 176.

Worldliness: and church-going, IX. 216.

Worms: remedy for, I. 66, 127; writings on, II. 76.

Worrall, Mrs., wife of John: V. 196.

Worrall, John, *d.* 1751, dean's vicar of St. Patrick's Cathedral; vicar choral of St. Patrick's and Christ Church cathedrals: and 7th *Drapier's Letter*, X. xxvi–xxvii, xxviii; reading glass for, V. 334; JS's bequest, XIII. 156.

Worsley, Frances (*née* Thynne), Lady, *c.* 1673–1750, wife of Sir Robert, Bart.; mother of Lady Carteret: JS's desk, XIII. 153.

Wotton, Sir Henry, 1568–1639, diplomat and author: style censured, II. 177.

Wotton, William, 1666–1727, clergyman and scholar: and date of *Battle of Books*, I. xviii; occa-sion of *Battle of Books*, I. 280; as character in *Battle of Books* — expedition with Bentley, I. 159–65; — 'killed' by Boyle, I. 163–5; — Criticism visits, I. 155; — Helicon, I. 162; *The Case of the Present Convocation Consider'd*, III. xv, *n.* 2; — JS answers, III. 73–5; 'Computer', I. 92; *A Defense of the Reflections on Ancient and Modern Learning* — on author-ship of *Tale of a Tub*, I. 279; and Farnaby, I. xxix–xxx, 8; and Minellius, I. xxix–xxx, 8; *Obser-servations upon the Tale of a Tub* (in *Reflections*, 3rd ed., 1705) — JS answers, I. 5–9; — 'two or three treatises', I. xxviii, 1; *Reflections upon Ancient and Modern Learning* (1694) — JS ridicules, I. 80, 106, and *passim*; — and Temple's *Essay upon An-cient and Modern Learning*, I. xvi, 139, 279–80; — Temple an-swers, I. 261–2; — quotations and allusions, I. 1–165 and notes, *passim*; — (2nd ed., 1697), with Bentley's *Dissertation*, I. xvi–xvii; on snuffling, I. 183; and JS — 'no friend', I. 279; and date of *Tale of a Tub*, I. xviii; notes to *Tale of a Tub*, I. xxx, xxxix, 8, 18–131, *passim*; 'one of the heroes' of *Tale of a Tub*, I. 277; and Tindal, II. xviii and *n.* 2, 69; 'true critick', I. 57.

Wretched Condition of Ireland, sermon by JS: **IX. 199–209**; background, IX. 127–30, 136; composition, IX. 133, 136; pub-lication, IX. 376–7; textual notes, IX. 376–7.

Wright, Sir Nathan, 1654–1721,

judge: Macky and JS on, V. 258.

Wycherley, William, *c.* 1640–1716, playwright: pun on name, IV. 274; in JS's dream, V. 206.

Wyndham (or Windham), Sir William, Bart., 1687–1740, statesman: and Bolingbroke, VIII. 152.

Wynne, John, *d.* 1762, precenter and subdean of St. Patrick's Cathedral: and Lord Newtown's legacy, XIII. 158; appointed subdean, XIII. 195–6; witness to JS's will, XIII. 147, 157.

X

'Xamoschi', Japanese seaport (possibly fictitious): Gulliver at, XI. 215.

Xenophon: on kingdom of Media, V. 36; quotations and allusions — *Banquet* (or *Convivium*) IV. 6: I. 79; — *Cyropaedia*, I. 197; — *De re equestri*, I. 244; — *Hellenics* (*De rebus græcis*), I. 197–8; V. 36; — *Hellenics* (*De rebus græcis*) II. iii. 2–21: I. 198; — *Memorabilia* III. vi. 14: I. 199; — *Memorabilia* III. vii. 9: I. 225; — *On the Polity of the Athenians* (falsely attributed to Xenophon) II. 18: I. 31.

Xerxes, *c.* 519–465 B.C., Persian emperor: and death, I. 250; sea whipped by, I. 249.

Y

'Yahoo': Gulliver learns word, XI. 226–7.

Yahoos: first appearance, XI. 223–4; avarice, XI. 260–1; description, XI. 223–4, 229–30; diet, XI. 229, 230; diseases, XI. 262; drunkenness, XI. 262; Europeans compared with, XI. 259–60; to be exterminated, XI. 271–3; filth, XI. 263; Gulliver befouled, XI. 224; — sees himself as one, XI. 267, 278; — hides his likeness, XI. 236–7; — resists rape, XI. 266–7; mutual hatred, XI. 260; leaders, XI. 262–3; melancholy, XI. 263–4; men compared with, XI. 278–9; origin, XI. 271–2; — possibly English, XI. 322; pride, XI. 296; unteachable, XI. 6–7, 235, 266.

Yalden, Thomas, 1670–1736, poet: and *Squire Bickerstaff Detected*, II. xiv.

Yedo (i.e., Tokyo), Japan: Gulliver in, XI. 216–17.

Yeomen, English: and elections, XI. 201–2.

'Ylnhniamshy' (Houyhnhnms' word for 'aborigines'): XI. 271.

'Ynlhmnawihlma Yahoo' (Houyhnhnm expression for a period of bad weather): XI. 275.

'Ynholmhnmrohlnw Yahoo' (Houyhnhnm expression for an 'ill-contrived house'): XI. 275.

Yogis ('jauguis'): Indian saints, I. 178.

York, England: and King Stephen, V. 66; JS visits (1709), II. xxix and *n.* 2; and *Tatler* no. 21, II. 235; and War of the Standard, V. 53–4.

York, House of: Wars of the Roses, VI. 9.

York, Duchess of: *see* HYDE, ANNE.

York, Duke of: *see* JAMES II.

York Buildings, London: residence of Lord Oxford, XII. 227.

Yorkshire: drunkenness, XII. 293; Molesworth's estate in, X. 94; Philpot family, V. 187; school in, XII. 40.

'Yortes': anagram of Tories, V. 99–107.

Young, Charles and James, of co. Tyrone, Ireland: V. 129.

Young, Edward, 1683–1765, poet and clergyman: pun upon name, IV. 275; one of 'snarling brood', IV. xxxii, 118.

Young Man's Coffee-house, Charing Cross, London: and Whigs, VIII. 193.

Youth: education of, XI. 60–3, 128–9, 269–70; XII. 46–53; and *Modest Proposal*, XII. 109–18; relations with the old, I. xxxvii; studies neglected, IX. 67; temptations of, XII. 52; and admiration of women, XII. 126.

Ypres, Flanders: and Barrier Treaty, VI. 101, 102, 109; and Dutch Barrier, VII. 113, 125.

Ypres, William of: *see* WILLIAM OF YPRES.

Z

Zeal, religious: *see* ANALYTICAL DISCOURSE; DISSENTERS; ENTHUSIASM; FANATICISM.

Zeeland, province of Netherlands: VI. 99.

Zembla: *see* NOVOYA ZEMLYA.

Zend-Avesta ('Zundivastaw'): and Bible, IV. 32.

Zeno, *c.* 335–*c.* 264 B.C., Stoic philosopher: on crime, IX. 247; disciples disputatious, IX. 250.

Zibeta occidentalis (i.e., perfume of human excrement): I. 104.

Zincke, Christian, 1685–1767, painter: portrait of 1st Earl of Oxford, XIII. 154.

Zinzendorf (or Sinzendorf), Philip Louis, Count, 1671–1742, Austrian diplomat, Chancellor of the Holy Roman Empire: and Barrier Treaty, VI. 85, 113–15; Dutch distrust, VII. 153; seduces Dutch, VII. 136–7; letters from Gallas, VII. 58; memorial by Gallas, VII. 59; tries to borrow money, VII. 156–7; speeds negotiations, VII. 157; and peace conditions, VII. 166; would continue war (1712), VII. 146, 156–7.

Zoilus, *c.* 400–320 B.C., Greek grammarian: and Momus, I. 57.

Zosimus, 5th century A.D., Greek historian of Rome: JS praises, XIV. 17.

Zosimus, Pope (in office 417–18): condemns heretics: XIV. 19.

'Zundivastaw': *see* ZEND-AVESTA.

Zwin ('Swyn') canal (now silted up), Zeeland-Flanders, Netherlands: and Dutch Barrier, VI. 104; VII. 92.

DATE DUE

GAYLORD			PRINTED IN U.S.A.